Communications
in Computer and Information Science 188

T0074092

Vaclav Snasel   Jan Platos
Eyas El-Qawasmeh (Eds.)

Digital
Information Processing
and Communications

International Conference, ICDIPC 2011
Ostrava, Czech Republic, July 7-9, 2011
Proceedings, Part I

 Springer

Volume Editors

Vaclav Snasel
Jan Platos
VŠB-Technical University of Ostrava
Faculty of Electrical Engineering and Computer Science
17. listopadu 15, 708 33 Ostrava-Poruba, Czech Republic
E-mail: {vaclav.snasel, jan.platos}@vsb.cz

Eyas El-Qawasmeh
King Saud University
Information Systems Department
Riyadh 11543, Saudi Arabia
E-mail: eyasa@usa.net

ISSN 1865-0929   e-ISSN 1865-0937
ISBN 978-3-642-22388-4   e-ISBN 978-3-642-22389-1
DOI 10.1007/978-3-642-22389-1
Springer Heidelberg Dordrecht London New York

Library of Congress Control Number: 2011930951

CR Subject Classification (1998): I.2, H.4, H.3, C.2, D.2, H.5

Typesetting: Camera-ready by author, data conversion by Scientific Publishing Services, Chennai, India

Printed on acid-free paper

Springer is part of Springer Science+Business Media (www.springer.com)

Message from the Chairs

The International Conference on Digital Information Processing and Communications (ICDIPC 2011) co-sponsored by Springer was organized and hosted by the VSB Technical University of Ostrava, Czech Republic, during July 7–9, 2011, in association with the Society of Digital Information and Wireless Communications. ICDIPC a major event in the area of digital information and communications, and serves as a forum for scientists and engineers to meet and present their latest research results, ideas, and papers in the diverse areas of networking, data processing, digital information, computer science, and other related topics in this area.

ICDIPC 2011 included guest lectures and 94 research papers for presentation in the technical session. This meeting was a great opportunity for participants to exchange knowledge and experience. The attendees joined us from around the world to discuss new ideas in the areas of software requirements, development, testing, and other applications related to software engineering. We are grateful to the VSB Technical University of Ostrava, Czech Republic, for hosting this conference. We use this occasion to express our thanks to the Technical Committee and to all the external reviewers. We are grateful to Springer for co-sponsoring the event. Finally, we would like to thank all the participants and sponsors.

Vaclav Snasel
Yoshiro Imai
Jan Platos
Renata Wachowiak-Smolikova

Preface

On behalf of the ICDIPC 2011 conference, the Program Committee and the VSB Technical University of Ostrava, Czech Republic, we welcome you to the proceedings of The International Conference on Digital Information Processing and Communications (ICDIPC 2011) held at the VSB-Technical University of Ostrava.

The ICDIPC 2011 conference explored new advances in software engineering including software requirements, development, testing, computer systems, and digital information and data communications technologies. It brought together researchers from various areas of software engineering, information sciences, and data communications to address both theoretical and applied aspects of software engineering and computer systems. We hope that the discussions and exchange of ideas will contribute to advancements in the technology in the near future.

The conference received 235 papers, out of which 91 were accepted, resulting in an acceptance rate of 39%. The accepted papers are authored by researchers from 27 countries covering many significant areas of digital information and data communications. Each paper was evaluated by a minimum of two reviewers.

Finally, we believe that the proceedings document the best research in the studied areas. We express our thanks to the VSB Technical University of Ostrava, Czech Republic, Springer, the authors and the organizers of the conference.

Jan Martinovič

Organization

General Chairs

Vaclav Snasel   VSB Technical University of Ostrava,
                                   Czech Republic
Yoshiro Imai   Kagawa University, Japan

Program Chairs

Jan Platos   VSB Technical University of Ostrava,
                                   Czech Republic
Renata Wachowiak-Smolikova   Nipissing University, Canada

Program Co-chair

Noraziah Ahmad   Universiti Malaysia Pahang, Malaysia

Proceedings Chair

Jan Martinovič   VŠB TU Ostrava, Czech Republic

Publicity Chairs

Ezendu Ariwa   London Metropolitan University, UK
Eyas El-Qawasmeh   King Saud University, Saudi Arabia

Table of Contents – Part I

Neural Networks

Distributed and Parallel Processing

Biometrics Technologies

E-Learning

Information Ethics

Image Processing

Information and Data Management

Table of Contents – Part II

Software Engineering

Data Compression

Networks

Computer Security

Hardware and Systems

Multimedia

Ad Hoc Network

Artificial Intelligence

Signal Processing

Cloud Computing

Forensics

Security

Software and Systems

Mobile Networking

Miscellaneous Topics in Digital Information and Communications

Mobile Services Providing Devices Rating Based on Priority Settings in Wireless Communication Systems

Danielius Adomaitis[1], Violeta Bulbenkienė[2], Sergej Jakovlev[2],
Gintaras Pridotkas[3], and Arūnas Andziulis[2]

[1] Kaunas University of Technology, Department of Computer Networks,
Studentu str. 50-416, LT-51368, Kaunas, Lithuania
superlink.lt@gmail.com
[2] Klaipeda University, Department of Informatics Engineering, Bijunu str. 17-206,
LT-91225, Klaipeda, Lithuania
{bulbenkiene,s.jakovlev.86,arunas.iik.ku}@gmail.com
[3] Klaipeda University, Department of Mathematical Sciences, Herkaus Manto str. 84,
LT-92294, Klaipeda, Lithuania
gintaraspridotkas@gmail.com

Abstract. Industrial process control is becoming very important nowadays as more and more systems are integrated with most modern information technology based tools to achieve better process and its control performance results. Here the main problems arise during the execution operations due to poor coordination of the initial safety conditions and absence of services providing devices rating capability with further content error corrections in real time. The main solution would consist of secure middleware based software tools integration in the main service providing systems with devices rating based on the priority settings.

Keywords: safe middleware, network devices rating, service provider, priority setting, resources, successfully completed operations.

1 Introduction

With the rapid development of different mobile technologies, the number of different services provided by the intellectual agents in different information systems grew as well, raising the question of safe resource detection [1] and control mechanisms. Such services proved to be very effective in transport and logistics areas where precision and timeliness are very important. Complex systems are being designed to combine and control various portable devices in real time, where the application of functional protection algorithms help solve different security, privacy and authentication challenges. All general cryptographic algorithms used within the systems require a lot of system resources and in the end – increased service providing time and decreased information transfer and analysis speed. On the other hand, it makes the service providing process safer by controlling each separate devices confidence to each other device in the system. Nevertheless, the use of mobile services is directly linked to service [2] security assurance and in time error fix, which at this point is not very effective in practice.

V. Snasel, J. Platos, and E. El-Qawasmeh (Eds.): ICDIPC 2011, Part I, CCIS 188, pp. 1–8, 2011.
© Springer-Verlag Berlin Heidelberg 2011

Modern complex systems should include separate objects state control for a more effective resource and service management included in different models [3,4] based on the security assurance.

One of the most widely used IT proposals is such middleware, that enables connection of various programs, hardware computer systems, network devices and also information transfer control integration in one common system.

Despite all the advantages, there are still many flaws that need additional analysis and new adjusted models proposed that in the end is implemented in new software and hardware solutions enabling higher level security assurance of the services provided.

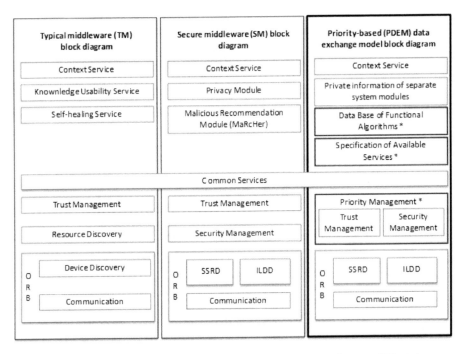

Fig. 1. Comparison of Middleware Structures (*Proposed new Structural Blocks)

Basically, all the middleware can be classified into two main groups (Fig. 1), with typical middleware [5] (TM) and Safe middleware (SM). Although, modern solutions require not only the main functionality described at the highest level, but also all new services such as device priority settings that would allow identification and use of each separate system devices trust/reliability with the network in a real time manner.

2 Description of the New Software Features for Mobile Service Management Systems

In this section, the main parameters which affect the service providing systems are presented. When they are respectively evaluated, it is possible to provide high level system reliability and sustain the highest level of confidence between separate system devices (services) that in turn allow fast and secure exchange of resources and others services.

2.1 The Main Criterions That Affect the Service Providing System

Network devices rating based on the priority settings needs to store information that describes the confidence levels (0 to 1.0) and is dependent upon the history of each devices negative or positive impact and the confidence level update rule. Information about this device resource/service group is also very important and such resource number varies from separate devices resources available R_e (from 0 to 1.0). Another important criterion is the information about the successfully accomplished service operations O_{sc} (from 0 to 1.0) that depends on the recommendations from other devices based upon successfully completed service providing operation number. Also, a function algorithm is introduced to store all the information about the data transfer events for further deeper separate device analysis.

Using the separate system modules, function algorithm database (DB) and the priority setting, similar or same trust value devices are combined into separate groups for faster and safer resource/service exchange. Using the priority setting control rules, devices get all the information needed for a safe disconnect from the system. Such could be the disconnect time range control resource/service provider disconnects only after a successfully implemented service, otherwise that device is introduced to the harmful devices list, gets lower trust level. That is how the systems reliability is assured, also providing the high level of confidence among all system devices. That in turn, enables more effective and reliable service providing functionality.

2.2 Formulation of Mean Trust Values for Wireless Networks

Confidence control determines the confidence values and confident/reliable links with other devices of the system (network). The basic confidence value calculations are performed based on the service providing devices and their customers provided initial parameters. Confidence values are constantly calculated and updated within the system (network) between the devices, based on the history of the device when it provides a service or becomes a customer.

After each new update all the newly calculated trust values for all of the devices are formed into a report and sent to the main security providing, control section. The mean trust value [6] can be calculated as (1) and presented in Table 1 for each provided service:

$$t(SP, A) = \left(\sum_{i=1}^{n} S_i \cdot T(SP_i, A, x) \right) \Big/ \sum_{i=1}^{n} S_i , \qquad (1)$$

here: SP – is the provider of the service, SP_i – is the (i) service of the provider device; $t(SP, A)$ – is the mean SP trust value for device A; S_i - i^{th} service security level ($1<=S_i<=10$); $T(SP_i, A, x)$ – is the A device trust value for service (i); $x(0.0 <= x <= 1.0)$ is the possible trust value that can be acquired; n – is the number of services that link SP with device A.

Based on the modelled devices locations in the system/network and the distances between them and the service provider (*SP*), a notion is made that the acquired trust values are decrease evenly (Fig. 2). In this case, *A* is the service provider and all others are the customers of the *A* device services. Devices *B*, *E* and *G* have the highest trust values among other devices. To them the additional services are provided as well.

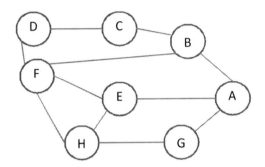

Fig. 2. Chosen network scheme with each device allocation

To determine the confidence level to each of the device of the system/network and to assign the services and their availability level, the primary conditions (device identification data) are introduced for each device, to which device *A* will provide its services (*SP*).

Table 1. Security assessment from each services trust values

Network Devices (Service Requesters)	Service 1	Service 2	Service 3	Service 4	Service 5	t (mean Trust value)
Device - B	0.7	0.8	0.8	0.8	0.6	0.84
Device - C	0.4	0.4	0.5	0.3	0.6	0.33
Device - D	0.2	0.3	0.4	0.3	0.2	0.20
Device - E	0.8	0.9	1.0	1.0	0.9	0.94
Device - F	0.6	0.5	0.7	0.5	0.6	0.53
Device - G	0.8	0.9	0.9	0.8	0.6	0.69
Device - H	0.6	0.5	0.4	0.4	0.5	0.46

To make the service providing system functionality more comfortable in use (device friendly), the main priorities need to be determined. The device with the highest priority could use all the services and provide their own without programmable selection function. For that purpose, (Fig. 3) presents 3 major service providing areas within the modelled network (devices *B, C, D, E, F, G, H* connected and sharing different services), based on the mean trust values, where the 1st area (highest 0.7 – 1.0), the 2nd area (middle 0.4 – 0.7) and the 3rd area (lowest 0.1 – 0.4) that have effect on the service providing functionality to all of the system service devices.

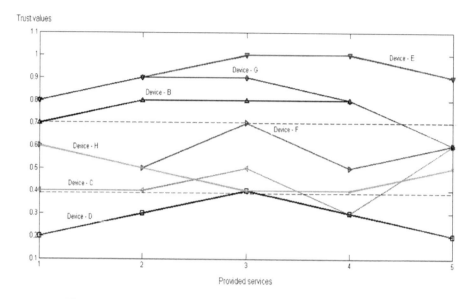

Fig. 3. Comparison of separate devices Trust values for provided services

2.3   Formulation of Mean Priority Values for Wireless Networks

All the mean priority values p are acquired by using the equation (2):

$$p(SP_m, X) = \left(\sum_{m=1}^{n} S_m \cdot \left(\frac{R_e}{O_{sc}} \right) \cdot t(SP_m, X) \right) \Big/ \sum_{m=1}^{n} S_m , \qquad (2)$$

here: R_e - are the used devices resources; O_{sc} - successful completed operation; n – number of services, between SP and $A,B,C,D,...X$; $p(SP_m, X)$ - mean SP priority values for device X; $t(SP_m, X)$ - mean SP trust value for device X; S_m - m service security value. Based on the system mean confidence values, it is possible to obtain the mean SP priority values for each separate device and to use them to form the service priority usage identification rule for each separate case and device, see initial conditions Table 2 and final calculations Table 3.

Based on the mean trust values the mean SP priority values are found (Fig. 4) for each separate device and thus each service use prerogative rule is defined. It is also advised to store all the needed data from the separate modules of the system for better priority control. Determining the mean priority values minimizes the reliable device search time and space this way providing continuous and safe data exchange.

Table 2. Initial conditions for the priority value (criteria) calculations for several services

Connected devices	Mean SP trust value for device X, t	Security values of Services, S_m	Succesful completed operation, O_{sc}	Used devices resources, R_e	Mean SP priority value for device X, $p(SP_m, X)$
B	0.6	$S_1=2; S_4=5;$ $S_6=6;$	0.4	0.6	0.90
C	0.4	$S_1=2; S_7=9;$	0.2	0.4	0.80
D	1.0	$S_1=2; S_2=10;$ $S_3=10; S_4=5;$ $S_5=8;$	1.0	1.0	1.00
E	0.6	$S_1=2; S_4=5;$ $S_6=6;$	0.5	0.6	0.72
F	0.8	$S_1=2; S_4=5;$ $S_5=8; S_7=9;$	0.7	0.8	0.91
G	0.6	$S_1=2; S_4=5;$ $S_5=8; S_7=9;$	0.5	0.6	0.72
H	0.7	$S_1=2; S_4=5;$ $S_7=9;$	0.6	0.7	0.82

Table 3. Calculated mean priority values based on the provided 7 services

Network Devices	1 Service	2 Service	3 Service	4 Service	5 Service	6 Service	7 Service	p
B	2	0	0	5	0	6	0	0.84
C	2	0	0	0	0	0	9	0.48
D	2	10	10	5	8	0	0	0.36
E	2	0	0	5	0	6	0	0.84
F	2	0	0	5	8	0	9	0.55
G	2	0	0	5	8	0	9	0.55
H	2	0	0	5	0	0	9	0.66

For the service providing system to have the highest level of reliability, all the newly connected devices get all the information needed for a safe disconnect from the system. When allocating network devices by priority levels, it is necessary to evaluate such aspects as resources and successfully performed operations (provided services). Substantial errors may occur when these aspect are overlooked (see Fig. 4), which may lead to false priorities distribution and as a result false resource sharing between

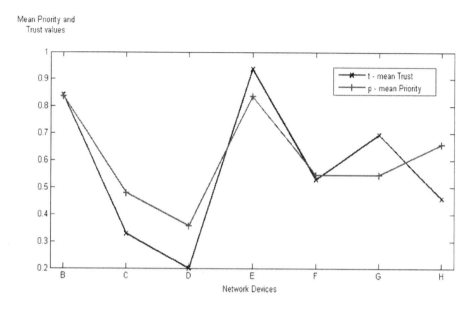

Fig. 4. Comparison of mean Priority and Trust values

devices with different priorities levels. Such allocation of devices in the network can lead to systemic unreliability and false services providing system functionality, that has direct impact on the security (users privacy) of the provided services. That is why the resource/service provider disconnects only after a succesfully implemented service, otherwise it is introduced to the harmful devices list and that in turn assures high level of systems reliability also provides high level of confidence among other system devices.

3 Conclusions

Simulation results suggest, that the devices with the same level of confidence in the system can exchange information without any additional verification, so making the system more effective with data transfer speed. This provides a higher security level to all system devices and minimizes all service or resource providing time.

In future work, this network devices rating model will be fully integrated in a real service providing system with additional parameters included.

Acknowledgement

The authors would like to thank project MOBAS „The development of information environment for mobile and wireless services" and Cross Border Cooperation Project LATLIT (LLII-061) for the support while writing and publishing the manuscript.

References

1. Sheikh, I.A., Moushumi, S.: A trust-based secure service discovery (TSSD) model for pervasive computing. Computer Communications 31(18), 4281–4293 (2008)
2. Sheikh, I.A., Haifeng, L., Nilothpal, T., Mehrab, M., Chowdhury, S.H.: Design and implementation of S-MARKS: A secure middleware for pervasive computing applications. Journal of Systems and Software 82(10), 1657–1677 (2009)
3. Sheikh, I.A., Munirul, M.H., Md. Endadul, H., Farzana, R., Nilothpal, T.: Design, analysis, and deployment of omnipresent Formal Trust Model (FTM) with trust bootstrapping for pervasive environments. Journal of Systems and Software 83(2), 253–270 (2010)
4. Adomaitis, D., Bulbenkiene, V., Andziulis, A.: Design and integration of software tools for control of services and resources in TI systems. In: 16th International Conference on Information and Software Technologies, Research Communications, pp. 29–32 (2010)
5. Sharmin, M., Ahmed, S., Ahamed, S.I.: MARKS (middleware adaptability for resource discovery, knowledge usability and self-healing) for mobile devices of pervasive computing environments. In: 3rd International Conference on Information Technology, New Generations, pp. 306–313 (2006)
6. Moushumi, S., Shameem, A., Sheikh, I.A.: An Adaptive Lightweight Trust Reliant Secure Resource Discovery for Pervasive Computing Environments. In: 4th IEEE International Conference on Pervasive Computing and Communications, pp. 258–263 (2006)

Symmetric Cryptography Protocol for Signing and Authenticating Digital Documents*

Juan C. Lopez Pimentel[1] and Raúl Monroy[2],
and Víctor Fernando Ramos Fon Bon[1]

[1] Universidad Politécnica de Chiapas
Calle Eduardo J. Selvas S/N y Avenida Manuel de
J. Cancino Col. Magisterial. C.P. 29082
jclopezpimentel@gmail.com, ramosfonbon@hotmail.com
[2] Computer Science Department
Tecnológico de Monterrey, Campus Estado de México
Carretera al lago de Guadalupe, Km 3.5, Atizapán, 52926, Mexico
raulm@itesm.mx

Abstract. The fast growth of technology and the demands of contemporary globalization have meant that most organizations use electronic means for communication and formalization of documents. One of the main problems faced by reviewers is recognizing counterfeit documents. The electronic signature of documents is a preliminary solution to the problem. In our research we are interested in developing a web service that allows to sign documents and verify their authenticity. To protect this web service against malicious activity there are aspects of computer security that must be considered such as steganography, cryptography and security protocols. In this article we introduce a security protocol using symmetric cryptography scheme in order to sign and authenticate digital documents. We have verified formally this protocol and found out that it provides the fourth level of authentication according to Lowe's hierarchy. In addition, we also address security aspects that must be taken into account to avoid attacks in these kinds of applications and some implementations we are developing.

Keywords: Security protocols, steganography, cryptography, fingerprinting and watermarking.

1 Introduction

The amount of printed documents currently generated in organizations overcomes the applicability of its review or management. In addition, its immoderate use causes massive destruction of forests and damage to the environment. One way to combat this type of problem is to use information technologies such as digital documents. Although digitization provides a considerable amount of advantages, there are also some disadvantages, particularly:

---

* The research reported here was supported by PROMEP UPCHS-PTC-035.

V. Snasel, J. Platos, and E. El-Qawasmeh (Eds.): ICDIPC 2011, Part I, CCIS 188, pp. 9–23, 2011.
© Springer-Verlag Berlin Heidelberg 2011

- Falsification: someone could at any given time using computational tools modify a document and fake it.
- Authentication: The previous problem generates another, *authenticity of documents*: how could we know the authenticity of a digital document? How do we know that a document was not forged?

Although these disadvantages are also presented in paper documents, researchers have focused in implementing redundant information in the content of a digital document applying steganography (the process of adding hidden extra information to a digital document, such as author, date, etc; which is so-called *watermarking*),[12,26].

Watermarking is used to hide proprietary information in digital media like photographs, digital music, digital video, documents [20]; the goal is to protect the interest of the content providers or proprietaries. Watermarking techniques are being used primarily for the following purposes: Copyright protection, Content archiving, Meta data Insertion, Tamper detection, Digital fingerprinting, Broadcast monitoring. We are focused on watermarking for tamper detection and meta-data insertion to ensure the authenticity of a digital document. Since digitalized data can be easily edited and reproduced, the protection and authentication of digital media have taken great importance in recent years,[4,13].

Every day the amount of digital images transmitted over non-secure channels such as the Internet has increased. The protection of images used as the base to make decisions is critical because if an image is manipulated the decision could be tampered; therefore, military, medical, legal, scholar records images must be protected against attempts to manipulate them, [10].

Our research goes beyond watermarking process. It consists in developing a web site where digital documents can be signed and also certified. In particular, we propose to carry out three main activities:

1. Providing copyright protection to a digital document (watermarking);
2. Verifying authenticity of a signed digital document (the process of retrieving information that includes the signature of the document, and that is used to provide evidence of originality), and;
3. Developing a web site able to do the first and second activities. This web site will reveal the authenticity of a document from any Internet access.

With the integration of the first two processes it would be possible to determine the authentication of a document and, thus, to know whether a document was forged or not. If for some reason the document is edited without authorization, the signature must be corrupt and its authenticity will be disproved.

While working on this research we have identified a lot of security aspects that we must take into account before implementation. In this paper we propose a cryptographic protocol, based on a symmetric key scheme, which provides the fourth level of authentication according to Lowe's hierarchy; we overview some implementations we are developing; and also we provide some recommendations of computer security in order to avoid attacks, or at least mitigate them.

The rest of the paper is organized as follows: Section 2 outlines our research project and describes the main related works; section 3 describes safety aspects to be taken into account to sign and verify digital signatures from the web service point of view; section 4 describes security aspects to be taken into account in the implementation of a web service to sign and check signatures; in both sections 3 and 4 we provide a description of our implementation. Section 5 shows our proposal, a symmetric cryptography protocol. Finally, section 6 describes our conclusions and future work.

2   Overview and Related Work

We aim at developing a Web Site able to sign digital documents and review its signature. To do that we must implement security mechanisms in order to make the Web Site secure. The next two subsections overview the general objective of our research and the main related works.

2.1   Overview

General Objective of our research:

To implement a secure Web Site that provides two main services: 1) to include a robust signature into a digital document, and 2) to certify the authenticity of a signed digital document.

Figure 1 and 2 illustrate the processes of signing and certifying, respectively; there S represents the agent acting like the Web Site and A represents the client agent. An arrow denotes the data flow and a double arrow the exchange of data between participants. Further, a double line arrow denotes a local process.

According to our general objective we have split the security mechanisms into two parts: a) Host and b)Network.

The host part involves the process of signing and verifying digital documents (process 2 :A in both figures, *signing()* and *revealing()*, respectively). Currently, the strategy used to provide authentication in digital documents is watermarking (derivative of steganography),[23]. However, if someone knows the steganography algorithm he could fake the information being used like a signature. So, cryptographic techniques must be implemented before steganography. More details of host part is can be found in section 3.

The network part involves three main process in order to sign and verify digital documents: i) authentication (between client and server), ii) sending and receiving data (SDD denotes Sending Digital Document) and iii) sending the result according to the process type being requested ($SADD$ denotes Sending Authenticated Digital Document and $SRADD$ Sending Result of Authenticated Digital Document). We must implement security mechanisms to protect the information travelling from the client to the server and vice-versa. If not, the website may have vulnerabilities and suffer from attacks from outside users. To ensure the data flow in a network, correct security protocols must be implemented (see, [16], for a survey on security protocols). We shall have more to say about the network part in section 4.

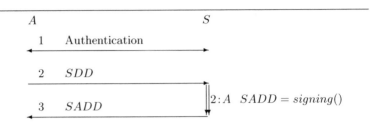

Fig. 1. Signing digital document process

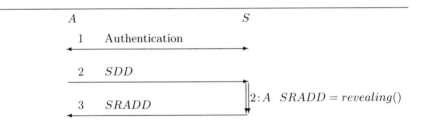

Fig. 2. Consulting the signature of an authenticated digital document

2.2   Related Work

Some works are closely related to the one we are developing. Here are a few.

Yusuke Lim, et.al. (2001), [15] propose a Web image authenticator, using invisible watermarks known as fragile. Any authorized user; i.e. one with valid access to the Web server, can generate an image with a watermark, or also can verify the authenticity of an image containing a watermark. They intend to use SSL (Secure Socket Layer) to ensure access to the server, but this is left as future work. Yusuke Lim's work is based on the work of Yeung and Nintzer, [26], which aims to verify the authenticity of an image and to detect when an image has been altered including a small image as watermark.

Most of these studies focus on detecting the watermark from a digital image even when the document has been changed. In our research, we believe that if a document is modified, their authenticity should be lost, since its integrity is being violated.

A number of watermarking protocols have been proposed to track down the distributors of illegal replicas. However, most of them ignore the fairness to the customers. These protocols have been designed to protect the seller's ownership of digital contents rather than the buyer's right. Without appropriate mechanisms to determine the actual distributor of a pirated copy, we arrive at the so-called the *Customer's Right Problem*, first identified by Qiao and Nahrstedt in [24].

Memon and Wong proposed a buyer-seller watermarking protocol [21] to deal with the customer's right problem and introduced in their solution a new issue: *the unbinding problem*. The unbinding problem consists of implementing security mechanisms to a digital content to avoid that the seller can transplant a watermark and to blame to the buyer for a piracy distribution. The proposed protocol is based on asymmetric cryptography. This requires having public key infrastructure available.

Chin-Laung Lei et.al [14] proposed a solution based on public key cryptography. Their solution was about to solve the customer's right problem and unbinding problem. Such a solution requires that buyers are provided with digital certificates issued by certification authorities. They proposed a protocol which fixes to Memon and Wong's scheme [21].

Franco Frattolillo et.al. [9], presented a watermark protocol to be adopted in a web context. The main idea is to ensure the copyright protection of digital content distributed on the Internet. This work is based on [14]. The protocol includes four agents: client, seller, watermark certification authority, and a server. These agents communicate using Secure Socket Layer (SSL). Recently, Franco Frattolillo [8], has improved its watermark protocol in such a way a client can be authenticated with the server although the first one is not provided with digital certificates.

While the protocols above try to deal with the customer's right problem and the unbinding problem, our research is not. In addition, these previous protocols are not verified formally. The idea we are focusing on is to do precisely such a step, because a lot of crimes have arisen for not considering it (see section 4 and 4.1 for more details about this.)

3 Security in Digital Signatures

To hide information the strategy is steganography. When it tries about including information in a document for authentication purposes, the literature refers to this concept as watermarking, [23]. Cryptographic techniques must be implemented if you want the signature to held confidentiality property[1]. The following sub-sections discuss these concepts.

3.1 Steganography and Watermarking

Steganography is the art of cover, data encapsulation or data hiding,[2]. Although steganography is different from cryptography, many authors categorize steganography as a form of cryptography because of their similarities, [11].

Steganography process generally involves two parts: the message you want to hide and the carrier[11]. The carrier, particularly in computing, is a file with a specific format (jpg, bmp, png, pdf, mp3, etc) where you want to hide a message.

---

[1] Cryptography: practice of encrypting and decrypting messages in a secret code to make it unreadable to everyone but who is to be the recipient of the message. Literature handles two types of encryption: symmetric key encryption and asymmetric. The use of each style depends on the application being developed.

Steganography provides important applications in the digital world, most notably digital watermarking. Watermarking is used primarily for document identification and involves embedding information in a carrier without changing it (at least that is not evident), it means, the carrier must be clearly distinguished. Some of the main applications of watermarking described by M. Vidyasagar Potdar, et. al. [23] is protection of copyright, content management, meta data insertion, broadcast monitoring, detection of documents' violation and fingerprint.

So far, we have implemented a steganography process using Least Significant Bit (LSB) with BMP format file. Our application has been implemented in a desktop application in Java, which it can be used to hide any information in text mode or hide information with fields previously established; using this second option, data are hidden in xml and it can be used for copyright protection. LSB technique is not so robust, however, our security strength is oriented to cryptography. We are working in implementing a robust watermarking technique that had already been developed.

It is noteworthy to say that only applying steganography in the signing process is risky, because we might be subject to a steganoanalysis process and retrieve information that is hidden. To reinforce this part is necessary to apply cryptographic techniques, which are described in the next sub-section.

3.2 Steganography with Cryptography

Cryptography is defined as the art of writing or solving codes[2]. Cryptography is also defined as the study of mathematical systems involving two types of security problems: privacy and authentication, [5].

Privacy prevents extraction of information transmitted over a public channel by unauthorized users. With this, the sender of the message is ensured that the message will be read only by the intended recipient. Therefore, we should implement encryption to the signature before the steganography process.

Authentication ensures to the recipient about the legitimacy of the message issuer. Authentication is usually related to two terms: message authentication and user authentication:

- Message authentication consists in verifying that a message was sent, who claims to be edited. In the case of a digital signature it must include information evidencing his creator.
- User authentication consists in verifying that an individual is who claims to be.

In general, cryptography has two main mechanisms: symmetric key cryptography and asymmetric key cryptography. With symmetric key we can encode and decode a message using the same key. On the other hand, in asymmetric one, we must have two keys: one to encode and another to decode (reciprocally). The best known algorithms in symmetric cryptography are Digital Encryption

---

[2] Concise Oxford Dictionary definition.

Standard (DES), [7] and the algorithm Advanced Encryption Standard (AES), [6]; and the most known algorithm in asymmetric key cryptography is RSA,[25]. Any of these algorithms, among others, could be considered to ensure digital signatures.

Now, let F be an e-document, K be a symmetric key (with implicit cyphering algorithm), al be a steganography algorithm and $\{dp\}$ be a personal data or information to hide. We apply the following formula to obtain a signed e-document using these data:

$$F' = signing(F, \{dp\}, al, K)$$

where F' denotes the new e-document and it provides the following: $F \neq F'$ and $F \overset{\odot}{\approx} F'$. Operator $\overset{\odot}{\approx}$ denotes that F is equal to F' according to the human view (in average).

Now, to know who has signed the previous e-document we use the following formula:

$$\{dp\} = revealing(F', al', K)$$

where al' is the inverse algorithm of al. Analyzing $\{dp\}$ we can know the signer.

So far, we have implemented the previous formalization in a desktop application using two different algorithms of symmetric cryptography: a) AES algorithm and b) based in password algorithm. The latter consists in applying a hash function into a password that is introduced by the user and after we apply it a XORing function.

4 Web Site Security

When we consult a website the information that travels could be seen by one or more Spies[3]. That means that any non-encrypted message transmitted on the network is considered unsafe. In the case of our web service, which will authenticate and sign digital documents, is essential to consider that active and passive attackers are always present on the network able to manipulate the transmitted messages. Therefore, it is necessary to implement encryption schemes: one option would be to implement *security protocols*; another option, but without providing authentication, is to implement secure tunneling, *virtual private network* (VPN).

A *security protocol* is a set of rules and conventions whereby one or more agents agree about each others' identity, usually ending up in the possession of one or more secrets [22]. These rules are usually encrypted under a scheme presented in the previous section.

Security protocols consist of only a few messages, but amazingly, they are very hard to get right. For example, the detection of a flaw in the 3-message Needham-Schroeder public key (NSPK) protocol took roughly 17 years [17]. Another example is, Andrew Secure RPC protocol, which we explain in the next sub-section. Thus, we could comment more examples, but they are documented in Clark-Jacob library[4] and AVISPA library[5].

---

[3] Sniffers are usually used to capture packets on a network.
[4] Clark-Jacob library is available in http://www.lsv.ens-cachan.fr/spore/index.html
[5] AVISPA library is available in http://www.avispa-project.org/

On the other hand, a virtual private network (VPN) encapsulates data transfers between two or more agents in a network; however the main problem is
to obtain authentication; so, the parts must authenticate before secure VPN
tunnels can be established.

Next two sub-sections provide evidence about how we are going to deal with
the process of authentication illustrated in figure 1 and 2 in order to a) sign
digital documents; and b) verify the sign of a document through a web site.

4.1 Security Protocol Using Symmetric Key in the Authentication Process

Only registered clients must be authenticated and to have the possibility of include a signature in a digital document. For that, we will need two agents, server
S, and client C. The last one requests secure connection to S. As a reference point,
we modified Andrew Secure RPC protocol,[6]. This protocol aims to distribute a
symmetric session key and to authenticate the participants so that later they
use a secure connection using the session key. The protocol that we present in
Alice-Bob notation is a modified version of the Lowe version, [18]. The protocol
is as follows:

$C : K_{CS}$
$S : \text{Key} , K_{CS} \in \text{Key}$

1. $\text{C} \to \text{S} : C; N_c$
2. $\text{S} \to \text{C} : \{N_c; K'_{CS}; S\}_{K_{CS}}$
3. $\text{C} \to \text{S} : \{N_c\}_{K'_{CS}}$

where $A : ik$ means the initial knowledge ik of A; Key denotes a set of shared
keys; $\text{C} \to \text{S} : M$ means that agent C sends a message M to S, which S receives;
symbol ";" denotes concatenation; K_{PQ} denotes a symmetric key which P and
Q share; $\{M\}_K$ denotes that M was ciphered under the key K.

Ideally, in step 1, C begins a run with S by sending him a plain-text containing
an identification so-called agent name[7] C and a nonce[8] N_c. Upon reception S
sends back a cyphered message, which only C could decrypt, containing the
received nonce N_c (like a challenge-response), a new session key K'_{CS} and his
agent name S like a proof of his identity. Having interpreted the message of step
2, C sends back (in step 3) a message cyphered under the new session key K'_{CS};
this message must be interpreted by S like a proof of authentication. C and S
are now ready to future communication using the distributed session key.

---

[6] Andrew Secure RPC protocol was found to have failures 2 years after its inception
and it was amended by Burrows, Abadi and Needham [3]; that version was also
flawed and Lowe suggested a new version, [18].

[7] Agent names are used to refer to the identity of a participant.

[8] A *nonce* is a random, unguessable number that has not been used before. This
newness is usually referred to as *freshness* in the literature.

We have verified this new protocol using The AVISPA Tool Web Interface[9]. We have proved that the protocol holds *agreement*, the fourth level of authentication according to the hierarchy of Lowe, [19]; in our proof agent C authenticates to S under nonce N_c and S authenticates agent C under session key K'_{CS}. However, considering the amount of plain-text encrypted in the last step of the protocol it could be subject of brute force attack. For that, we propose this new version:

$C : K_{CS}$
S : Key , $K_{CS} \in$ Key

1. C $\rightarrow$ S : $C; N_c$
2. S $\rightarrow$ C : $\{\!|N_c; K'_{CS}; S; N_s|\!\}_{K_{CS}}$
3. C $\rightarrow$ S : $\{\!|N_c; N_s|\!\}_{K'_{CS}}$

At the end of the protocol the secure connection between the participants will be established by means the codification of all transferred messages under the distributed session key, K'_{CS}.

We have also verified this new version of the protocol with The AVISPA Tool Web Interface and we found the same security guarantees than the first one. To implement this protocol we must consider that S will play the role of the web server, and C will be any client wanting to sign a digital document. It means that each C must have a different key, which it will be shared with S.

So far, we have introduced a security protocol in the authentication process. The cryptographic scheme used here will allow that only pre-registered users can sign and certify e-documents; which we have denominated *authorized users*. On the other hand, if we want to implement that *non-authorized users* can consult signatures, so, it would be implemented in plain-text; it means, susceptible to be attacked.

Implementing the consult process of the signature using symmetric cryptography we have 2 different alternatives, considering: a) authorized users; and b) non-authorized users.

Authorized users must have a shared key with the server and initiate an authentication process. The distributed session key would be used to send the file and receive its consulting result.

Non-authorized users can send a copyright e-document and the name of (apparently) the signer in a non secure channel; after the server has verified the signature (he can do it because he has all shared keys and signer usernames) he come backs the result of the copyright and the hash code of the document. The client can compare if the hash code corresponds to one sent by him and apparently trusts with the server result. This process could be subject to man in the middle attack because all the exchanged traffic goes in plain-text. In order to fix this weakness we introduce the next subsection.

---

[9] Available via http://www.avispa-project.org/

4.2 Security Protocol Using an Asymmetric Key in the Authentication Process

Consulting a digital signature consists in that any client submits a watermarked image to the server trough the web site. Once the image is uploaded, the server uses an inverse procedure of steganography to detect the signature and generate a result. While uploading the image an attack could exist; so we must implement security mechanisms to ensure the information transmitted (the e-document). In Figure 2 we schematize, as first action, an authentication process; moreover, in previous sub-section we proposed an authentication process using symmetric infrastructure. However, the problem we are tackling is to ensure the communication when any agent (maybe not having shared keys) wants to verify the signature of a digital document[10].

There is a protocol so-called Transport Layer Security (TLS) and its predecessor, Secure Socket Layer (SSL), which both work over the transport layer of TCP/IP. TLS protocol allows client/server agents to communicate across a hostile network; eventually, only the server is authenticated, it means that the client is not. Mutual authentication requires a public key infrastructure for clients[11].

Under our application, we consider that the identity of the client is not relevant while consulting digital signatures. In this case, the server should receive the correct data, maybe, in a secure tunneling. Because of that TLS protocol is suited for this process. In what follows an explanation of TLS protocol is described:

A TLS client and server negotiate a stateful connection by using a handshaking procedure, as follows:

1. $\mathsf{C} \to \mathsf{S} : \mathsf{C}; [L_c]$
2. $\mathsf{S} \to \mathsf{C} : f(L_c); \mathsf{S}; K_\mathsf{S}^+; \mathsf{S}_{CA}; \{\!|\mathsf{Hash}\ (\mathsf{S}; K_\mathsf{S}^+; \mathsf{S}_{CA})|\!\}_{K_\mathsf{S}^-}$
3. $\mathsf{C} \to \mathsf{S}_{CA} : Verification Process with CA$
4. $\mathsf{S}_{CA} \to \mathsf{C} : CA autenticates the identity of Server and tells it to client$
5. $\mathsf{C} \to \mathsf{S} : \{\!|\mathsf{C}; K_{cs};|\!\}_{K_\mathsf{S}^+}$

In words:

– First step:
  • A client connects to a TLS server requesting a secure connection and presents a list of supported CipherSuites (ciphers and hash functions), $[L_c]$.
– Second step:
  • From this list, the server picks the strongest cipher and hash function that it also supports and notifies the client of the decision.

---

[10] This is the case of a university wanting to give their students a digital diploma; the students can send their digital document with any employer; and this last one could verify its authenticity using a web site.

[11] TLS, the new version of SSL version 3.0, has become the predominant method and de-facto standard for securing information between web clients and web servers. SSL incorporates Diffie-Hellman Key Exchange algorithm, [5] which only the server can be authenticated; a review of this algorithm can be seen in [1].

- The server sends back its identity in the form of a digital certificate (plain-text). The certificate usually contains the server name, the trusted certificate authority (CA) and the server's public encryption key.
- Third and forth steps:
  - The client may contact the server that issued the certificate and confirm that the certificate is valid before proceeding.
- Fifth step:
  - In order to generate the session keys used for the secure connection, the client encrypts a random number (K_{CS}) with the server's public key and sends the result to the server. Only the server should be able to decrypt it, with its private key.
  - From the random number, both parties generate key material for encryption and decryption.

This protocol has become the standard one in e-commerce, a lot of commercial entities have used it. However, only the server is authenticated. Although we could implement additional mechanisms into TLS protocol to be used in the signing authentication process, we would need a public key infrastructure to implement it. Another alternative is to implement our own security protocol based on Diffie-Hellman protocol,[5]; but it is a future work.

5   Symmetric Cryptography Protocol Suggestion

In this section we give a suggestion that consists in a protocol using symmetric cryptography. Table 1 illustrates our general protocol, which consists on fourth stages: Initial Knowledge; Authentication; Signing and Secure Consulting process.

Initial Knowledge represents the knowledge that each agent owns at the beginning of the protocol. In this stage client must previously be registered with the server. It means that only authorized users will can sign and consult signatures. In such a register each client must also specify its steganography algorithm.

Authentication describes a run of the protocol where client, C, begins a run with server, S. The aims of the protocol is to obtain mutual authentication between participants and to obtain a session key, K'_{CS}, which will be used to encrypt later communications. After this stage, client is ready to sign or consult signatures.

Signing begins once the participants have been authenticated. In this stage, client uses session key K'_{CS} to encrypt the submitted e-document, F, and personal data $\{dp\}$. Server signs the e-document using formula $signing(F, \{dp\}, al, K_{CS})$, which it also uses its initial knowledge and makes a relation with the username, the steganography algorithm pre-selected by the client and its secret shared key.

Secure Consulting process begins after the stage II or III has been completed. An authenticated client can consult a signature of a signed e-document of

Table 1. Symmetric Cryptography Protocol for Signing and Authenticating Digital Documents

Stage	Process	Descriptions
I	Initial Knowledge $C : K_{CS}, un$ $S : \mathsf{Key}\ ,\ K_{CS} \in \mathsf{Key}\ ,\ \mathsf{AE}$	The Server must initially know all shared keys and all steganography algorithms previously chosen by the Client.
II	Authentication $1.\text{-}C \rightarrow S : C; N_c$ $2.\text{-}S \rightarrow C : \{\!\|N_c; K'_{CS}; S; N_s\|\!\}_{K_{CS}}$ $3.\text{-}C \rightarrow S : \{\!\|N_c; N_s\|\!\}_{K'_{CS}}$	The strenght of the protocol consists in that each client must keep in secret its shared key.
III	Signing $4.\text{-}C \rightarrow S : \{\!\|F; \{dp\}\|\!\}_{K'_{CS}}$ $\quad F' = signing(F, \{dp\}, al, K_{CS})$ $5.\text{-}S \rightarrow C : \{\!\|F'; \mathsf{Hash}\ (F)\|\!\}_{K'_{CS}}$	$F = File$ o denotes the digital document and $\{dp\}$ is a set o personal data. F' is a watermarked File under K_{CS} and using algorithm al, which is within AE .
IV	Secure Consulting process $4.\text{-}C \rightarrow S : \{\!\|F'; un\|\!\}_{K'_{CS}}$ $\quad \{dp\} = revealing(F', al', K_{CS})$ $5.\text{-}S \rightarrow C : \{\!\|\{dp\}; \mathsf{Hash}\ (F')\|\!\}_{K'_{CS}}$	The Server associates un (user name of any client) with its respective algorithm and key.

any authorized client. The server maps the username un with the corresponds algorithm al and shared key K_{CS} to use function $revealing(F', al', K_{CS})$ in order to reveal the personal data $\{dp\}$ that is included in the submitted e-document F'. The server sends back $\{dp\}$ and hashing evidence of the submitted e-document. All communications are encrypted using the session key.

In what follows, we abstract our implementation aspects. We have developed two kinds of applications: desktop and web site based application.

Our desktop application was done to implement host level: signing and consulting process. Our host level implement a steganography process using Least Significant Bit (LSB) with BMP format file. It has been implemented in Java, which can be used to hide any information in text mode or hide information with fields previously established; using this second option, data are hidden in xml and it can be used for copyright protection. With respects to cryptography, we have implemented two different algorithms of symmetric cryptography: a) AES-password algorithm and b) based in password algorithm. The former consists in generating a key and a password for each user. Each password is mapped with a key and so, AES algorithm is applied. The latter consists in applying a hash function into a password that is introduced by the user and after we apply it a XORing function.

Our Web Site application has been developed in an Intranet to implement network level. It uses JavaScript, JSP, PHP and MySQL technologies. To have our initial knowledge of the server we store a list of shared keys in a database. These keys are generated in the server side after client register its data and complete the step using an email-based registration. The authentication was

Table 2. Consulting Digital Documents without a Security Protocol

Stage	Process	Descriptions
I	Initial Knowledge $C : un$ S : Key , AE	The Server must initially know all shared keys and all steganography algorithms previously choosed by the Client.
II	There is not an authentication process	
III	No-Secure Consulting process 4.-C $\to$ S : $F'; un$ $\quad \{dp\} = revealing(F', al, K_{CS})$ 5.-S $\to$ C : $\{dp\}$; Hash (F')	$F' = File$ o digital document The server tries to reveal the signature iif F' was watermarked by un.

developed implementing in JavaScript an AES algorithm password-based, so, the client encode the information shared with the server. The same algorithm is implemented in the server. To do the signing and consulting process we re-used the same classes implemented in our desktop application.

Now, we have also implemented an option where clients can check signatures of any client (not authorized is necessary), however, it is susceptible to attacks because all information travels in plain-text. Table 2 illustrates such a mechanisms.

6 Conclusions and Further work

Implementing a secure web site where different agents will be participating in sending and receiving different kind of information is not easy, it is difficult because we need to take into account a lot of aspects; security in this kind of projects involves to consider host level and network level process as seen in previous sections. Network level involves authentication and all information that is used to sign and consult signatures. It's important to know that the ciphering process in the steganography phase depends of the kind of cryptography scheme used in the authentication process. In this paper we show a solution based on symmetric cryptography. The authentication part of the protocol here illustrated has been verified using The AVISPA Tool Web Interface. We have proved that the protocol holds *agreement*, the fourth level of authentication according to the hierarchy of Lowe, [19]; the rest of the protocol has not been verified because all messages depend on authentication process. So, it must be secure iif the key stays in safe. Another important aspect, although it is not tackled here, is implementation aspects; but, this will be left as future work.

Our research is ongoing, we have planned to implement strength security mechanisms in both host and network level. In the former we are searching for best security steganography algorithms. In the latter, we want to cover the issue where any user can sign and consult signatures; to do that, it is necessary to explore public key cryptography or Diffie-Hellman algorithms.

References

1. Carts, D.A.: A review of the diffie-hellman algorithm an its use in secure internet protocols. In: As part of the Information Security Reading Room, pp. 1–9. SANS Institute (2001)
2. Artz, D.: Digital steganography: Hiding data within data. IEEE Internet Computing 5, 75–80 (2001)
3. Burrows, M., Abadi, M., Needham, R.M.: A logic of authentication. Proceedings of the Royal Society of London 426(1), 233–271 (1989)
4. Cox, I.J., Miller, M., Bloom, J., Fridrich, J., Kalker, T.: Digital Watermarking and Steganography. Morgan Kaufmann, San Francisco (2007)
5. Diffie, W., Hellman, M.: New directions in cryptography. IEEE Transactions on Information Theory IT-22(6), 644–654 (1976)
6. 197 FIPS. Advanced encryption standard (aes). Technical report (2001)
7. 1977 FIPS 1977 FIPS. Data encryption standard. Technical Report Part 6 of Title 15 Code of Federal Regulations (1988)
8. Frattolillo, F.: Watermarking protocol for web context. IEEE Transactions on Information Forensics and Security 2(3-1), 350–363 (2007)
9. Frattolillo, F., D'Onofrio, S.: A web oriented watermarking protocol. In: IEC, Prague, pp. 91–96 (2005)
10. Haouzia, A., Noumeir, R.: Methods for image authentication: a survey. Multimedia Tools and Applications 39, 1–46 (2008) 10.1007/s11042-007-0154-3
11. Kessler, G.C., Ciphers, N.: An overview of steganography for the computer forensics examiner. Federal Bureau of Investigations, viewed 28 (2004)
12. Kostopoulos, I., Gilani, S.A.M., Skodras, A.N.: Colour image authentication based on a self-embedding technique. In: 14th International Conference on Digital Signal Processing DSP 2002, vol. 2(1), pp. 733–736 (2002)
13. Kundur, D., Lin, C.Y., Macq, B., Yu, H.: Special issue on enabling security technologies for digital rights management. In: Proceedings of the IEEE, pp. 879–882. IEEE, Los Alamitos (2004)
14. Lei, C.-L., Yu, P.-L., Tsai, P.-L., Chan, M.-H.: An efficient and anonymous buyer-seller watermarking protocol. IEEE Transactions on Image Processing, 13, 1618–1626 (2004)
15. Lim, Y., Xu, C., Feng, D.D.: Web based image authentication using invisible fragile watermark. In: Proceedings of the Pan-Sydney Area Workshop on Visual Information Processing VIP 2001, vol. 11, pp. 31–34. Australian Computer Society, Inc., Darlinghurst (2001)
16. López-Pimentel, J.C., Monroy, R.: Formal support to security protocol development: a survey. Journal Computacin y Sistemas, special volume celebrating 50 years of Computing in Mexico 12, 89–108 (2008)
17. Lowe, G.: An attack on the needham-schroeder public-key authentication protocol. Information Processing Letters 56(3), 131–133 (1995)
18. Lowe, G.: Some new attacks upon security protocols. In: Proceedings of the 9th IEEE Computer Security Foundations Workshop, CSFW 1996, pp. 162–169. IEEE Computer Society Press, Washington, DC, USA (1996)
19. Lowe, G.: A hierarchy of authentication specifications. In: Proceedings of the 10th IEEE Computer Security Foundations Workshop, CSFW 1997, pp. 31–44. IEEE Computer Society, Los Alamitos (1997)
20. Potdar, V.M., Han, E.C.S.: Survey of digital image watermarking techniques. In: 3rd International Conference on Industrial Informatics (INDIN 2005), pp. 709–716 (2005)

21. Memon, N., Wong, P.W.: A buyer-seller watermarking protocol. IEEE Trans. Image Processing 10, 643–649 (2001)
22. Paulson, L.C.: The inductive approach to verifying cryptographic protocols. Journal in Computer Security 6(1-2), 85–128 (1998)
23. Potdar, V.M., Han, S., Chang, E.: A survey of digital image watermarking techniques. In: 3rd IEEE International Conference on Industrial Informatics INDIN 2005, vol. 1(1), pp. 709–716 (2005)
24. Qiao, L., Nahrstedt, K.: Watermarking schemes and protocols for protecting rightful ownership and customer's rights. J. Vis. Commun. Image Representation 9, 194–210 (1999)
25. Rivest, R.L., Shamir, A., Adleman, L.: A method for obtaining digital signatures and public-key cryptosystems. Commun. ACM 21, 120–126 (1978)
26. Yeung, M.M., Mintzer, F.: An invisible watermarking technique for image verification. In: International Conference on Image Processing, vol. 2, p. 680 (1997)

Cooperative Black-Hole Attack: A Threat to the Future of Wireless Mesh Networking

Shree Om and Mohammad Talib

Department of Computer Science, University of Botswana
Gaborone, Botswana
shree.om@mopipi.ub.bw, talib@mopipi.ub.bw

Abstract. Wireless Mesh Network has come out to be the next generation wireless communication technology. It provides a good solution to cheap wireless networking. The Network Layer in WMN is responsible for routing packets delivery and intruders take a deep interest in sabotaging this layer. Black-hole attack is a type of Denial-of-Service (DoS) attack which when carried out can disrupt the services of this layer. When the malicious nodes collude, the attack is called Co-operative Black-hole attack and the result of this attack is far more severe. The aim of this paper is to reflect light on the drawbacks of the security mechanisms being used for the mitigation of this attack and propose an improved security schema.

Keywords: Wireless Mesh Network, Mobile ad- hoc network, Black-hole attack, Cooperative black-hole attack, Ad-hoc on demand distance vector, Internet Protocol, Merkle hash tree.

1 Introduction

One of the main advantages of Wireless Mesh Network (WMN) over the current 802.11 wireless technologies in use in most organizations is that it is cheaper and easier to implement and maintain. A WMN has this advantage because WMN constitutes an ad-hoc network i.e., nodes in the network automatically establish and maintain mesh-connectivity among themselves. A node can be a desktop, laptop, personal digital assistant (PDA) or a pocket PC (PPC) equipped with a wireless network interface card (NIC) which can be connected to a wireless mesh router.

The network layer of WMN defines how interconnected networks (inter-networks) function. The network layer is the one that is concerned with actually getting data from one computer to another even if it is on a remote network. Some of the most critical threats and attacks present at network layer are:

i) Black-hole attack: In this attack, the malicious node always replies positively to a route request from a source node although it may not have a valid route to the destination and will always be the first to reply to the route request message. Therefore, all the traffic from the source node will be directed toward the malicious node, which may drop all the packets, resulting in DoS [1].

V. Snasel, J. Platos, and E. El-Qawasmeh (Eds.): ICDIPC 2011, Part I, CCIS 188, pp. 24–32, 2011.
© Springer-Verlag Berlin Heidelberg 2011

ii) Wormhole attack: To launch this attack, an attacker connects two distant points in the network using a direct low latency communication link called the wormhole link. Once the wormhole-link is established, the attacker captures wireless transmission on one end, sends then through the wormhole link, and replays them at the other end [7]. Then the attacker starts dropping packets and cause network disruption. The attacker can also spy on the packets going through, use the information gained to launch new attacks, and thus compromise the security of the network.

iii) Sink-hole attack: In this attack, a malicious node can be made very attractive through the use of powerful transmitters and high-gain antennas to the surrounding nodes with respect to the routing algorithm [14].

iv) Sybil Attack: This attack is defined as a "malicious device illegitimately taking on multiple identities" [4]. This attack abuses the path diversity in the network used to increase the available bandwidth and reliability. The malicious node creates multiple identities in the network. The legitimate nodes, assuming these identities to be distinct network nodes, will add these identities in the list of distinct paths available to a particular destination thus including the malicious node on path of a data, which can affect packet transfer as well as drop them. But, Even if the malicious node does not launch any attack, the advantage of path diversity is diminished, resulting in degraded performance [14].

v) Byzantine attack: This is an internal attack in which a router or a few colluding routers disrupt the routing services by dropping, fabricating, modifying, or misrouting packets. Because these attacks are initiated by internal attackers, the network operation may seem to be normal and general to the other nodes. Therefore, detection of this attack is very difficult [10].

A solution is proposed by [2] to mitigate black-hole and cooperative black-hole attack in MANETs based on the principle of Merkle tree but has challenges. Our solution uses its fundamentals and makes modifications to address these challenges and helps mitigate Cooperative black-hole attack in hybrid WMNs. Before we get in to the description of the solution, we would like to give a brief background Co-operative black-hole attack and Merkle Tree.

2 Background

In this paper, we address operation of Co-operative black-hole attack by using AODV as an example protocol.

A. Co-operative Black Hole Attack
A complex form of black-hole attack, multiple malicious nodes collude together resulting in complete disruption of the routing and packet forwarding functionality of the network during a Co-operative black hole attack. For example, in fig 1, when multiple black hole nodes are acting in coordination with each other, the first black hole node H1 refers to one of its team-mates H2 as the next hop. According to the proposed methods in [3], the source node S sends a further request message to ask H2 if it has a routing to node H1 and a routing to destination node D. Because H2 is

cooperating with H1, its further reply is "yes" to answer both the questions. So source node S starts passing the date packets. Unfortunately, in reality, the packets are abstracted by node H1 and the security of the network is compromised [9].

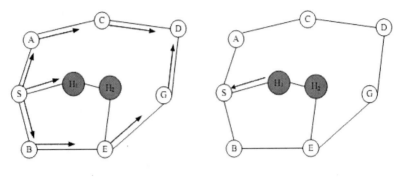

(a) Network Flooding of RREQ   (b) Propagation of RREP message

Fig. 1. Co-operative Black-hole attack [15]

B. Merkle Tree
Also called Merkle hash tree (MHT) is a binary tree relies on the properties of one way hash functions (OWHFs) [6]. A sample MHT is shown in fig. 2.

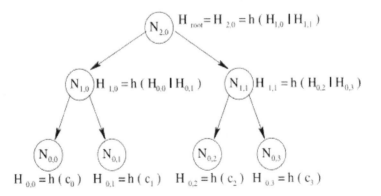

Fig. 2. A sample MHT [6]

- N_{ij} denotes the nodes within the MHT where i and j represent, respectively, the i-th level and the j-th node.
- H_{ij} denotes the cryptographic variable.
- h denotes a one way hash function e.g. the function SHA-1 [5].
- | is the concatenation operator.
- Nodes at level 0 are called "leaves".

- Each leaf carries a given value e.g. $h(C_0)$, $h(C_1)$, $h(C_2)$ and $h(C_3)$ in fig. 2.
- The value of an interior node (including the root) is a one-way hash function of the node's children values e.g. value of interior node $N_{1,0}$ is: $h(H_{0,0} | H_{0,1})$ which is the hashing result of the concatenation of values of children $N_{0,0}$ and $N_{0,1}$.

3 Related Works and Challenges

AODV does not incorporate any specific security mechanism, such as strong authentication. Therefore, there is no straightforward method to prevent mischievous behaviour of a node such as media access control (MAC) spoofing, IP spoofing, dropping packets, or altering the contents of the control packets.

Solutions have been proposed to mitigate black-hole nodes in [3, 9, 13]. However, the solutions, which are designed for MANETs, consider malicious nodes that work alone, i.e., each node is an attacker, and do not target attackers working in groups. For example, method proposed in [3] can help mitigate individual node attack because it requires the intermediate node to include information about the next hop to destination in the RREP packet. After the source node has received this packet, it sends a further route request (FREQ) to the next hop node asking if the node has route to the destination. In case this next hop node is been working together with the malicious node, then it will reply "yes" to the FREQ and the source node will transmit the packet to the malicious node that sent the first reply which is a black-hole node. A solution to defending cooperative black-hole attacks was proposed in [4] but no simulations or performance evaluations were done. The methodology used the concept of Data Routing Information (DRI) table and cross-checking further request (FREQ) and further reply (FREP). [12] used the algorithm proposed by [9] and modified it slightly to improve the accuracy of preventing the attack and efficiency of the process and simulated the new modified algorithm. The solution is proposed for MANETs which are usually mobile devices powered by battery. The maintenance of DRI increases overhead and cross-checking delays the communication process which leads to quicker drainage of battery life. [12] have compared their results with [3] and proved that their method is more efficient and accurate. Two authentication mechanisms for identifying multiple black hole nodes cooperating as a group in MANETs is proposed by [15]. The mechanism is based on the assumption that no other authentication mechanism such as a Public Key Infrastructure (PKI) is present which is not practical in MANETs. The source node checks the RREP messages to determine the data packets to pass with the authentication mechanisms proposed in [15]. However, the question that arises is, how will this authentication mechanism be protected from malicious nodes that might forge the reply if the hash key of any node is to be disclosed to all nodes. In [11], authors propose an enhancement of the basic AODV routing protocol to combat the cooperative black hole attack in MANET. They use a structure, which they call fidelity table wherein every participating node will be assigned a fidelity level that acts as a measure of reliability of that node. In case the level of any node drops to 0, it is considered to be a black hole node and is eliminated. In their approach, they assume that nodes are already authenticated which is a little strong assumption. [2] present a solution to avoid single node and co-operative Black-hole attacks in a MANET based on the principle of Merkle tree.

However, factors such as network density, nodes mobility and the number of black hole nodes which are determining factors in a solutions performance, in term of end to end delay and network load, were not considered.

4   Problem Statement

The state-of-the-art work is still insufficient for deploying sizeable WMNs because important aspects such as security still remain open problems. Cooperative black-hole attack is a severe DoS attack routing protocol threat, accomplished by dropping packets, which can be easily employed against routing in Wireless Mesh Networks, and has the effect of making the destination node unreachable or downgrade communications in the network. The black holes are invisible and can only be detected by monitoring lost traffic. The emergence of new applications of WMNs necessitates the need for strong privacy protection and security mechanisms of WMNs. The AODV, our case study protocol, does not have any security mechanisms and malicious nodes can perform many attacks by taking advantage of the loopholes in the protocol. The next section proposes a solution to prevent Cooperative black-hole attack in hybrid WMNs.

5   The Proposed Solution

The table 1 contains the notations used to describe the solution.

Table. 1. Notations

Notation	Significance
IDi	Identity of node i.
Si	Secret generated by node i.
H	OWHF
		Concatenation operator

In fig.3, we consider a piece of network made up of 4 nodes A, B, C and D. On this last, a Merkle tree is juxtaposed. We point out that our goal is to check that B and C conveys well, towards D, the traffic sent by A.

Node A is source node and has the value ψ (value of the root of the Merkle tree). Each node i holds the value $h(id_i / S_i)$. So as per method proposed by [2], if A has to send data to D through B and C, in order to make sure that B and C are not cooperating as black hole nodes D sends ω (value held by D) to C, then C sends λ and ω to B which in turn sends β, λ and ω to A. A then recalculates ψ from α, β, λ and ω, then compares the result with the value ψ of already held, if equality, the route (A,B,C,D) is secured, otherwise, the route contains a black hole node.

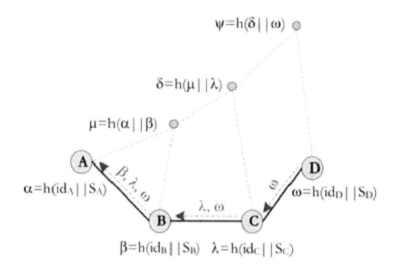

Fig. 3. Basic principle of the solution, Cooperative black-hole attack [2]

Nodes B and C can cooperate to conduct black hole attack, this is easy if D communicates to C its secret S_D based on trust and since C is cooperating with B, it will pass the secret S_D to B so that it can calculate ω. [2] have not addressed this problem as how to protect the secret S_i from being compromised. This could create problems in dense network. Our solution adds to [2]. When A requests for a route to D, B being an attacker replies with the highest sequence number to A. According to AODV, A would discard other RREPs. Our solution looks to modify AODV such that it records the second best RREP from the node claiming to have a route to D. We assume that this node is safe. We call this node X. Node X has the value θ which is equal to $h(id_x / S_x)$. Since B already has β, λ and ω, it forwards all these values to A without any further communication with C (assumption). We introduce change of secret on the source and destination node whenever there is a request for the hash value. This means that when D sends ω to node X, it is a completely different value from the value of B. But B did not even communicate with C or D. Similarly, A would hold a new ψ and new α. Now, when A recalculates ψ (call it $\psi1$) from new α, β, λ and ω, and compares the result with the new value of ψ already held, it would be different but when A recalculates ψ (call it $\psi2$) from new α, θ and new ω and compares the result with the new ψ already held, they will be same. This would mark node B to be a malicious node and it will be black listed from future communication. At the same time a update will be sent with the packet to D through node X informing it of the malicious behavior of B. D will black list node C because it never received any RREQ from it because B never communicated with C which should not have been the case if both nodes were trusted.

The steps below describe how the solution works assuming node D has already shared its secret with node C and node C has forwarded is secret to node B along with secret of node D.

Step 1:   Source node A sends RREQ for destination D.

Step 2:   Source node A updates its value of ψ and generates new secret for itself.

Step 3:   Intermediate node B sends RREP with highest sequence number.

Step 4:   Node A stores this information.

Step 5:   RREP from node X is received after RREP from node B.

Step6:   Instead of discarding this RREP, node A temporarily stores this information

Step 7:   In order to prove legitimacy, node B and node X have to send the hash values including that of destination D.

Step 8:   Node X requests for ω from node D.

Step 9:   Node D generates new secret, recalculates new ω and passes it to node X.

Step 10:   Node X passes θ and new ω to node A.

Step 11:   Node B passes β, λ and old ω (calculated on the basis of secret of D sent by node C).

Step 12:   Node A recalculates two values of ψ, ψ1 based on values from node B and ψ2 based on values from node X.

Step 13:   Node A compares ψ1 and ψ2 to the already held new value ψ.

Step 14:   Node A discovers ψ1 is not the same as new ψ.

Step 15:   Node A black lists node B.

Step 16:   Node A sends packet to node X to be delivered to node D with attached information about node B.

Step 17:   Node D receives packet.

Step 18:   Node D black lists node B.

Step 19:   Node D black lists node C based on assumption that node B was able to calculate ω because node C must have shared secret with node B, hence making node C an untrusted node.

Step 20:   Node D sends acknowledgement (ACK) packet to node A including information about untrustful behaviour of node C.

Step 21:   Node A updates its list of black listed nodes and adds node C to it.

Simulation works are currently under progress for the above mentioned solution. The method would successfully identify the colluding malicious nodes and when compared with other proposed methods would have

- Better packet delivery ratio (PDR) – the number of packets generated by the sources vs. the number of packets received at the destination.
- Reduced detection time - This is the time to detect the network, which has a black hole attack, measured by the attack detection time minus the traffic start time [12].
- Better average end-to-end delay - this is the average delay between the sending of the data packet by the source and its receipt at the corresponding receiver and includes all the delays caused during route acquisition, buffering and processing at intermediate nodes, retransmission delays at the MAC layer, etc [8]. It is measured in milliseconds.
- Reduced routing overhead – ratio of number of control packets generated to the data packets transmitted.

6 Future Work

In this paper we have described the Cooperative black hole attack that can be mounted against a WMN and proposed an improved solution for it in the AODV protocol. The solution can be applied to identify multiple black hole nodes cooperating with each other in a hybrid WMN. However, a lot of refinement still needs to be done to the solution. As future work, we intend to finalize an algorithm and simulation results which will include analysis of the performance of the proposed solution based on network density, nodes mobility and the number of black hole nodes.

References

1. Aad, I., Hubaux, P.J., Knightly, W.E.: Impact of Denial-of-Service Attacks on Ad-Hoc Networks. IEEE/ACM Trans. Network 16(4), 791–802 (2008)
2. Baddache, A., Belmehdi, A.: Avoiding Black Hole and Cooperative Black Hole Attacks in Wireless Ad Hoc Networks. International Journal of Computer Science and Information Security (IJCSIS) 7(1), 10–16 (2010)
3. Deng, H., Li, W., Agarwal, P.D.: Routing Security in Wireless Ad-hoc Networks. IEEE Communications Magazine 40(10), 70–75 (2002)
4. Imani, M., Rajabi, M.E., Taheri, M., Naderi, M.: Vulnerabilities in Network Layer at WMN. In: International Conference on Educational and Network Technology (ICENT 2010), Qinhuangdao, China, pp. 487–492 (2010)
5. Merkle, R.C.: A certified digital signature. In: Brassard, G. (ed.) CRYPTO 1989. LNCS, vol. 435, pp. 218–238. Springer, Heidelberg (1990)
6. Munoz, L.J., Forne, J., Esparaza, O., Soriano, M.: Certificate Revocation System Implementation Based on the Merkle Hash Tree. International Journal of Information Security 2(2), 110–124 (2004)
7. Nait-Abdesselam, F., Bensaou, B., Taleb, T.: Detecting and Avoiding Wormhole Attacks in Wireless Ad-Hoc Networks. IEEE Communication Magazine 46(4), 127–133 (2008)
8. Ramaswami, S.S., Upadhyaya, S.: Smart Handling of Colluding Black Hole Attacks in MANETs and Wireless Sensor Networks using Multipath Routing. In: IEEE Workshop on Information Assurance, New York, USA, pp. 253–260 (2006)
9. Ramaswamy, S., Fu, H., Sreekantaradhya, M., Dixon, J., Nygard, K.: Prevention of Cooperative Black Hole Attack in Wireless Ad Hoc Networks. In: International Conference on Wireless Networks (ICWN 2003), Las Vegas, Nevada, USA, pp. 570–575 (2003)
10. Siddiqui, S.M., Hong, S.C.: Security Issues in Wireless Mesh Networks. In: IEEE International Conference on Multimedia and Ubiquitous Engineering (MUE 2007), Seoul, South Korea, pp. 717–722 (2007)
11. Tamilselvan, L., Sankarnarayanan, V.: Prevention of Blackhole Attack in MANET. In: 2nd International Conference on Wireless Broadband and Ultraband Communications, Sydney, Australia, p. 21 (2007)
12. Weerasinghe, H., Fu, H.: Preventing Cooperative Black Hole Attacks in Mobile Ad Hoc Networks: Simulation Implementation and Evaluation. In: Future Generation Communication and Networking (FGCN), Jeju, South Korea, pp. 362–367 (2007)

13. Yin, J., Madria, S.: A Hierarchical Secure Routing Protocol against Black Hole. In: IEEE International Conference on Sensor Networks, Ubiquitous and Trustworthy Computing, Taichung, Taiwan, p. 8 (2006)
14. Zhang, V., Zheng, J., Hu, H.: Security in Wireless Mesh Networks. Auerbach Publications, Florida (2009)
15. Zhao, M., Zhou, J.: Cooperative Black Hole Attack Prevention for Mobile Ad Hoc Networks. In: International Symposium on Information Engineering and Electronic Commerce, Ternopil, Ukraine, p. 26 (2009)

Towards a Generic Cloud-Based Modeling Environment

Laszlo Juracz and Larry Howard

Institute for Software Integrated Systems, Vanderbilt University
Nashville, U.S.A.
{laszlo.juracz,larry.howard}@vanderbilt.edu

Abstract. This paper is aimed at presenting a concept of a flexible diagramming framework for building engineering and educational applications. The framework was designed to serve as a platform for online services and collaborative environments where users typically work on remotely stored, shared data through a browser-based user interface. The paper summarizes the common requirements towards such services, overviews related approaches and gives insights into some design challenges through the analysis of use-cases. The design problem is examined from a user-centered view: the key motivation of our research is to find innovative, possibly device-independent solutions that enable seamless user experiences. Finally a generic framework based on a HTML-JavaScript library is proposed, which could be employed for implementing wide range of software solutions from e-learning to cloud-based modeling environments.

Keywords: modeling, diagramming, e-learning, cloud-computing, web-applications, user-experience, collaborative, JavaScript.

1 Introduction

Diagrams have been used throughout history to visualize ideas and depict information. The earliest diagrammatic representations were land-maps and religious ideas, followed by graphical abstractions of mathematical concepts. The number of diagram types rapidly increased in the past century with the evolution of computer software and user interfaces (UI). It resulted in employing diagrams extensively across multiple disciplines [1].

Among these disciplines engineering relies on diagrams the most heavily. Hundreds of standardized notations are used from mechanical engineering to computer science to describe design concepts and to communicate and document technical specifications [2]. The few dozen most common types are node and connection-based, like flowcharts, mind maps and electric circuit diagrams. Others are less conventional-looking, such as the Nassi-Scheinderman diagram (NSD) [3] used in structured programming design or the House of Quality (HoQ) [4] employed in product design. Different aspects of the same design are depicted through specialized visual components; therefore, each diagramming application must support at least a couple of the most common diagram types.

In software engineering and model integrated computing [5] multi-aspect, domain-specific modeling languages (DSML) [6] are employed to build visual models, which

V. Snasel, J. Platos, and E. El-Qawasmeh (Eds.): ICDIPC 2011, Part I, CCIS 188, pp. 33–45, 2011.

represent the system being designed. These models are then used to generate program code to synthesize the application, to run simulations and analysis. DSML provides notation tailored towards the application domain, thus enabling ways to implement custom visualization is a key and fundamental feature of modeling tools.

Collaborative teamwork is also a crucial factor in design and development. For example, during brainstorming sessions, early concepts and ideas are visualized in the from of shared graphs and diagrams. In other cases, developers work simultaneously and individually on different parts of the same large-scale system model. Besides requiring convenient visual variety and flexibility for the construction task, there is a growing need for modeling and diagramming environments to support and promote the sharing, browsing and version-control of the content in a cloud-based environment.

Given the important role of diagrams in engineering, developing adequate and effective methods to teach diagrams and model-based techniques in higher education (and beyond) has been a focus of educators and researchers for decades. In blended learning environments, computer-based learning experiences are employed to complement classroom learning. Some of the experiences are delivered through adaptive, web-based systems. Since the available production tools were not suitable for building these systems, custom software components had to be designed and developed. The first generation of these applications was specifically built for a given visual language. Now there is an ongoing research to specify and design a framework that supports the authoring of not just diagram-based exercises, but also enables the easy creation of new visual libraries as well.

In our pursuit of a reusable, device-independent solution satisfying these needs, we conceptualized a flexible, generic web-application framework. This framework is designed to provide a basis for front ends of cloud-based diagramming and modeling applications, which support numerous visual languages and collaborative work. The focus in this paper is the visualization and the user-interaction layer (presentation tier) of the framework. We introduce an HTML-JavaScript cross-browser library, which is capable of handling custom authored visual languages.

2 Related Field

There is a well-developed market of free and commercial software products for authoring standard and commonly used types of diagrams (flowcharts, UML diagrams, mind-maps, wireframes etc.) and there are numerous tools supporting model-based development technologies.

Some of these offer solutions for custom visualization by creating new component libraries or defining new skins for diagram elements. The two most robust diagram-creator applications for the desktop are OmniGraffle [7] and Microsoft Visio[8]. The visual capabilities of these applications are very impressive. Users can create new templates and stencils (visual libraries) for authoring diagrams with custom shapes and elements. Shapes can be also interactive, their appearance and the layout of the diagram can be data-driven. The Generic Modeling Environment (GME) [9] introduces the concept of decorators for custom visualization.

Unfortunately all of these tools possess the limitations of classical desktop applications; they can import and export several file formats and can be extended through APIs but they do not provide built-in features for collaborative work, cloud-based storage and version control. The adaptation of their UI to different tasks and use-cases is unfeasible.

While it is hard to find any browser-based modeling tools, there are a few diagram editors implemented in Flash and HTML [10]. These applications are simple and quick to learn. The advanced ones have built in features for collaboration. Since the authored diagrams are stored in the cloud space, sharing them through a URL is easy and comes natural. Their visual libraries are also extensible. However, they do not offer as sophisticated and flexible solutions as the desktop applications mentioned above. They are not designed for integration into more complex systems.

However the available tools and approaches have built-in support for collaboration, none of them allow developers to work on separate instances of diagrams and models in parallel. Versioning of models gained attention in the recent years. Several research results were published in this field [11]. Although in this paper we do not discuss and detail any server-side solution, our framework is designed to support optimistic locking by logging operations and model changes [12][13].

We analyzed results of a research project working on collaborative, web-based diagramming environments [14] for learning. However some of the requirements and goals Tolosa et al. identified are similar to those we established for our project, they seem to be addressing them on different fronts. We are working in a lower-level solution that is suitable for not just diagramming, but modeling as well.

Some of our work is based on results and experiments with an earlier diagramming application developed and published by Roselli et al. in [15]

3 Design Challenges

The need of a generic diagramming framework arose several times in the past whenever we were conceptualizing web-based authoring. The actual functional requirements were gathered from two distinct fields of application: diagram-based e-learning and cloud-based modeling services.

3.1 A HTML-Based Diagramming Tool for Education

The Graphical Representations to Assess System Performance (GRASP) project examines new and innovative ways for using graphical assessments in engineering education. This research focuses on, but is not limited to, designing and implementing a set of software tools for web-based exercises and carrying out experiments with them. For simple construction-like GRASP exercises, there is a need for a browser-based diagramming system, which should be capable of handling an extensible set of visual languages.

The opening set of requirements toward this new diagramming tool was based on experiments with an earlier solution called the Free Body Diagram Assistant (FBDA) [15]. FBDA is an adaptive e-learning application employed to teach free body diagrams in biomedical engineering classes. Although the new system also could serve as a replacement for the FBDA, it is anticipated to have a much wider set of functionality and usability.

The pedagogical strategy, system architecture and the uses-cases of the new design are very similar to those of the predecessor's (see in Fig. 1.).

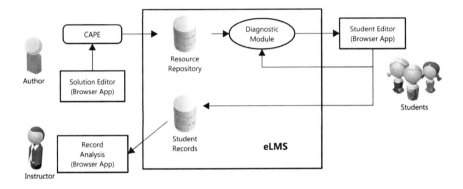

Fig. 1. Authors create new problems through the solution editor interface. Since the students' work is diagnosed through comparing the student diagram with an expert model, this step starts with choosing the visual library and building the expert diagram. When the expert diagram is ready, the author imports it with the Course Authoring Packaging Environment (CAPE) [16] and deploys it to the experimental Learning Management System (eLMS) [17] as a learning module. The instructors can create problem assignments and look up student records through the instructor interface. Students work on the solution in a browser-based student-editor; their work is evaluated and adaptive feedback is generated on the server-side.

Usability and User Experience. Most of the differences and improvements of the new system will emerge from a HTML-JavaScript diagramming component, which is going to replace both the old Microsoft Windows-executable solution editor and the browser-based student editor. These old applications were build in Adobe Flash. The new editor interface is not just going to provide a smoother user experience, but is desired to do it on a device- and visual language-independent way: it should work on desktop computers, hand-held devices and the same UI should be suitable for different kind of diagram-based assessments. The UI should be intuitive and easy to learn and understand without guidance: it should not cause interruptions for the user in accomplishing the given task; affordance and effectiveness are crucial factors [18]. Since the product needs to be optimized to serve the users without changing their behavior to accommodate the product, we based our development on user-centered design (UCD) [19].

The design process started with analyzing the old FBDA product based on preliminary identified usability and user experience goals. The outcome of this analysis and the newly established requirements yield a couple of different visual concepts. Several low-fidelity mockups were built during this phase of the development for testing and evaluation (see Fig.2.).

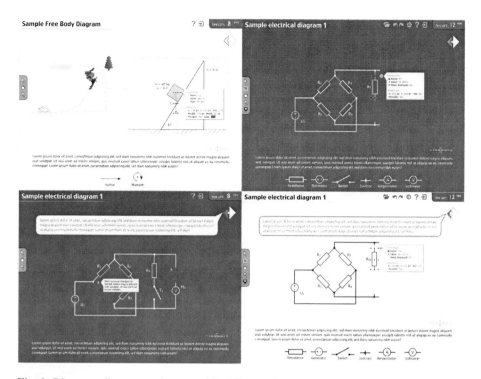

Fig. 2. Diagram editor screen layouts with different visual languages and modes: *(a)* Diagram editor in *author mode* with and FBD problem; *(b)* An electric circuit (EC) problem is being composed; *(c)* Feedback is sent back to the student during an EC solution exercise in *playback-mode*. Note the exclamation marks marking problematic elements; *(d)* Mockup depicting the UI in a very similar state to *(c)* with a different background color and an expanded property panel for the currently selected resistor component.

The requirement of providing a UI that is usable on touch-screen devices ruled out a few conventional UI elements, and called for designing custom interaction patterns. For example, tablet users do not get access to keyboard buttons during editing but can use gestures to trigger commands instead of shortcut keys.

Extendibility and Configurability. Easy-extendibility has to be a prime feature of the new application: there should be a descriptor language and a framework defined for implementing new visual libraries. This descriptor language should be robust enough to capture and model all of the common engineering diagram types; furthermore it should provide ways to specify how the users can interact with diagram instances of the given type in the described e-learning environment. Handling user permissions and privileges is also an important requirement. Although both authors and students interact essentially with the very same UI, they use the application in different modes. Diagram operations and visualization are different in author mode and edit mode. The UI should be adaptable to these modes and also, accessing the data behind the presentation should be controlled.

3.2 Browser-Based Modeling

Another system we have envisioned is a cloud-based collaboration environment for model integrated computing. However, the first generation of this system is not planned to implement a complete, web-based modeling toolkit to replace existing desktop applications, it is our intent to provide some modeling-related functions through the browser for better usability and accessibility. Also, in the scope of this project we are investigating fundamental challenges of an entirely browser- and cloud-based modeling environment.

One of the key examples of related functions is an HTML model-visualizer component for browsing available models in the model-repository. This component is conceptualized to be capable of visual rendering models created in standard notations or in any arbitrary DSML (with some limitations on visual representation). Such a model-visualizer also could be employed in the conflict resolution process of the version control services (see Fig. 3.).

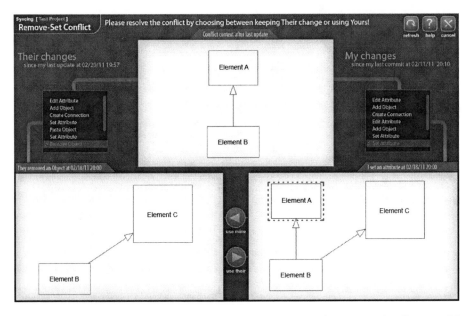

Fig. 3. Muckup of the HTML-JavaScript conflict-resolver. In this concept, the direct spatial context of the conflict would be visualized. The user would be able to navigate in the change log to better understand the intents of the other designer.

On the long term, this visualizer component could serve as the basis for an HTML-JavaScript UI of a future, browser-based modeling application. We have a vast experience with using GME [9] and other desktop-based modeling technologies. It is our interest to turn this valuable experience into needs and requirements towards a next-generation, entirely cloud-based modeling environment, where version control, conflict resolution, real-time sharing and collaborative authoring would be built-in features.

Usability versus Constraint Checking. Constraints enforce syntax and semantic rules, therefore both diagram construction and model building is guarded by constraints. Constraint-violating operations should be not allowed, aborted, or a warning message should be issued. It is desired that interactive components of the UI somehow inform the user of allowed edit operations that would not result in constraint violation.

A full-scale solution for this problem would rely on analyzing the current state of the model (or model components in the scope) and generating a set of the possible next states. This would involve constant constraint checking and running remote interpreters that could not be efficiently ported to the client-side JavaScript platform. Taking in consideration that just a single complete model validation itself is a heavyweight, time-consuming process, triggering such a robust mechanism after each user operation would cause a rather rough, paralyzing user experience.

Lightweight Constraints. A partial solution for the problems caused by constraint checking, is to make it possible for DSML designers to define *lightweight* constraints. Lightweight constraints form an optimal subset of all the constraints and rules, and are checked directly on the client side in JavaScript. The authoring environment enforces them construction-time, preferably in advance: it prevents constraint-validation by blocking the user from doing disallowed operations.

Complete model validation, including remote interpretation should be triggered less frequently or manually. If constraint violation occurs, context-aware, informative warning message has to be displayed; the author must be able to roll back to previous valid model states.

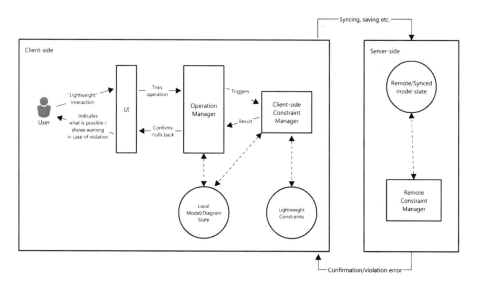

Fig. 4. Frequent, lightweight constraint checking mechanisms are run on the client-side. Remote, complete constraint checking is triggered less frequently, usually by saving operations.

4   Concept Overview

Our effort to overcome the design challenges we summarized above is embodied as a framework-concept that is built on a client-side HTML-JavaScript core. This core is responsible for essential visualization tasks and handling user interactions. Furthermore it also implements client-side functions for supporting version control, constraint management and other modeling concepts. Flexibility of the framework relies on a meta-language concept, which can be used to create new libraries, and an extendible object-oriented JavaScript code-base, which can be tailored for various applications. Further customization of functionality and visualization can be achieved through a plugin-architecture. The framework is designed to provide a server-side module for handling user-management, collaborative work, data storage, version control and remote extensions.

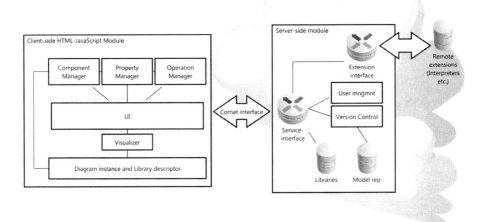

Fig. 5. High-level framework architecture

4.1   A Generic Meta-model for Visual Languages

Components and ComponentTypes. In our concept, language elements of a notation or DSML are called *ComponentTypes,* elements of diagram and model instances are called *Components.* The visual and interactive aspects of *Components* are referred to as *Skins.*

Properties and PropertyTypes. According to our terminology, the attributes of Components are called *Properties.* Properties are instances of *PropertyTypes,* which are defined for the corresponding ComponentType. PropertyTypes are derived from three basic types, depending on their role and behavior:

VariableType is the base type for atomic PropertyTypes specified with an arbitrary numeric or textual value and a *Quantity*. Variables with quantities can be primarily used to express physical properties and have a *symbol* and a set of *Units* attached. Furthermore, a *PropertyControl* (text field, drop-down list, etc.) and *ValidRanges* can be defined for VariableTypes.

The predefined valid ranges are taken in consideration by lightweight constraint checking mechanisms and can be used to display and enforce limitations on the possible values of the variable by the UI controls before value changing operations.

Variables can also be bound to skin attributes. For example, if the magnitude property of a vector component is bound to the width property of the vector skin (visualized as an arrow), the value of these properties are synchronized: if the user resizes the arrow on the canvas, the magnitude property gets changed as well. Similarly, when a new magnitude value is set through the properties panel, the width of the arrow reflects the value change accordingly.

ReferenceType is for expressing relations between components. The *targetType* attribute specifies which type the reference can point to, the *visaulizedAs* attribute tells the UI renderer how the reference instance should be visualized. The framework is going to be shipped with some essential visualization methods such as ports with wires and containment. Library developers will be able to build their own visualizers and deploy them as plugins.

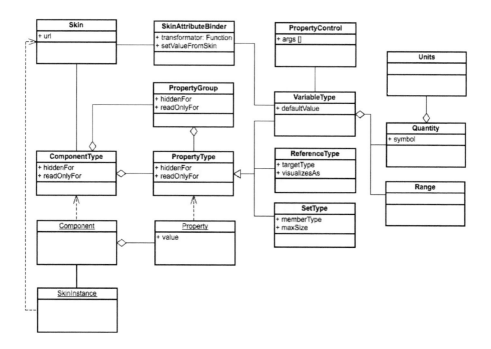

Fig. 6. Model elements for describing visual languages

SetType defines a collection of properties based on a member PropertType specified in the *memberType* attribute. The size of the set can be limited with the value of the *maxSize*, which is used by lightweight constraint checking.

Properties can be grouped through defining *PropertyGroup* structures. The UI renderer to visually organize property controls on automatically generated forms uses PropertyGroups.

Access Control and Visibility. Visibility and access is controlled by the *hiddenFor* and *readOnlyFor* attributes. These attributes can be set for ComponentTypes, PropertyTypes and PropertyGroups. The attribute values can be single user role identifiers or comma-separated lists. Users, and user roles are managed by the server-side module.

Libraries. *Libraries* refer to different diagram notations and DSMLs, and are implemented and deployed as *library packages*. Each library package has to contain an XML-based description of ComponentTypes, PropertyTypes and related artifacts (such as Quantities, Constraints, etc.) using the meta-language we introduced above. Skins are implemented in HTML-JavaScript and should be included in library packages as standalone HTML files. Custom CSS and JavaScript files containing plugin-codes and other assets (images etc.) should also be packaged together with the library descriptor.

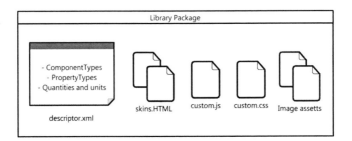

Fig. 7. Contents of the library package

4.2   Custom Visualization and UI Controls

The UI code of the framework is based on jQuery [20] and custom-built jQuery plugins for diagram drawing controls such as resize and rotate, and for visualizing references. For greater versatility, library developers will have the possibility to extend the basic visual functionality and to import their own UI control libraries.

4.3   Constraint Management

All the user operations affecting property values and altering component states are logged and managed by the *OperationManager* on the client side. A user-operation is basically a series of basic predefined actions and handled as a transaction: after each

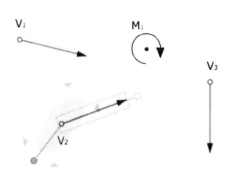

Fig. 8. A UI mockup showing built-in controls for rotating and resizing components

operation, lightweight constrain checking is triggered; if there is a constraint violation, a warning message is returned as response and the operation gets rolled back. Lightweight constraint checking can also be invoked under the hood before a possible value or state change.

Essential rules for lightweight constraint checking can be conveniently defined in the library descriptor (see description of PropertyTypes above). Custom rules and validation can be attached to properties as JavaScript code. Although, these snippets have access to the property- and component-registry, and can implement robust verification, developers should pay attention to the usability factors: massive, resource-intense validation, including remote mechanisms should rather be specified in the libraries *onVerification* event handler attribute than as lightweight constraints. Code placed in onVerification is called when the diagram or model is saved or synchronized with the storage.

4.4 Support for Version Control and Collaboration

Operations logged by the OperationManager are planned to be used as deltas by collaboration and version control facilities running on the server. The client side is intended to permit connection to the server module through a comet interface. This interface will allow the server to synchronize operations among multiple clients working on the same model or diagram continuously. For version control, the collected operations can be used as deltas.

5   Conclusions and Future Work

There is an increased need for cloud-based, collaborative diagramming and modeling environments in engineering and engineering education today. It is our goal to design and build a generic framework, which could provide a foundation for developing such environments.

Our preliminary design work discovered that usability, user experience, extendibility and flexibility are the key attributes of these applications. Among other design challenges, we found some of these attributes being in conflict with modeling concepts, such as constraint checking. To overcome the challenges we designed a browser-based modeling framework, introduced new concepts and implemented a generic meta-model for authoring visual languages.

The framework is currently under development. Implementation is carried out in two phases. In the first phase, the initial version of the HTML-JavaScript core is going to be implemented and evaluated; it will be integrated into the systems described in section 3. In parallel with this, the design of the server-side module is getting finalized, which will be implemented in phase 2.

Evaluations of experiments with working, high fidelity prototypes show positive results. Although some UI elements need to be fine-tuned for better touch screen usability, our general concept and approach appear to be feasible for building basic diagrams.

However, final requirements towards the server-side module and the design of the remote services are yet to be detailed, we are planning to use Python-based technologies for implementation.

Acknowledgements. This research was funded in part by the National Science Foundation (NSF) under award 817486.

References

1. Tsintsifas, A.: A Framework For The Computer Based 0A. ssessment Of Diagram-Based Coursework. Loughborough University (2002)
2. Lohse, G.L., Biolsi, K., Walker, N., Rueter, H.H.: A Classification Of Visual Representations. Commun. ACM 37, 36–49 (1994)
3. Nassi–Shneiderman Diagram, http://en.wikipedia.org/wiki/Nassi%E2%80%93Shneiderman_diagram
4. House Of Quality, http://en.wikipedia.org/wiki/House_of_Quality
5. Sztipanovits, J., Karsai, G.: Model-Integrated Computing. Computer 30, 110–111 (1997)
6. Van Deursen, A., Klint, P., Visser, J.: Domain-Specific Languages: An Annotated Bibliography. SIGPLAN Not. 35, 26–36 (2000)
7. Omnigraffle, http://www.omnigroup.com/products/omnigraffle
8. Microsoft Visio, http://office.microsoft.com/en-us/visio/
9. GME: Generic Modeling Environment, http://www.isis.vanderbilt.edu/Projects/gme/
10. Jay, A.: Five Best Online Diagramming Tools, http://www.smashingapps.com/2010/01/18/five-best-online-diagramming-tools.html
11. Altmanninger, K., Seidl, M., Wimmer, M.: A Survey On Model Versioning Approaches. IJWIS 5, 271–304 (2009)
12. Schneider, C., Zündorf, A.: Experiences In Using Optimisitic Locking In Fujaba. Softwaretechnik Trends 27 (2007)
13. Brosch, P., Langer, P., Seidl, M., Wimmer, M.: Towards End-User Adaptable Model Versioning: The By-Example Operation Recorder. In: Proceedings of the 2009 ICSE Workshop on Comparison and Versioning of Software Models, pp. 55–60. IEEE Computer Society, Washington, DC, USA (2009)

14. Tolosa, J.B., Gayo, J.E.L., Prieto, A.B.M., Núñez, S.M., Pablos, P.O.: Interactive Web Environment For Collaborative And Extensible Diagram Based Learning. Computers In Human Behavior 26, 210–217 (2010)
15. Roselli, R.J., Howard, L., Brophy, S.: A Computer-Based Free Body Diagram Assistant. Computer Applications In Engineering Education 14, 281–290 (2006)
16. Howard, L.: CAPE: A Visual Language For Courseware Authoring. In: Second Workshop On Domain-Specific Visual Languages (2002)
17. Howard, L.: The Elms Learning Platform, http://w3.isis.vanderbilt.edu/Projects/VaNTH/Index.htm
18. Bose, G.: Affordanc. In: Elearning, http://elearning.kern-comm.com/2006/09/affordance-in-elearning/
19. Tsintsifas, A.: A Framework For The Computer Based 0A. ssessment Of Diagram-Based Coursework. Loughborough University (2002)
20. Jquery: The Write Less, Do More, Javascript Library, http://jquery.com/

Tool for Sun Power Calculation
for Solar Systems

Michal Paluch, Radoslav Fasuga, and Martin Nemec

VSB–Technical University of Ostrava,
17.listopadu 15/2172, 708 33 Ostrava–Poruba, Czech Republic
{michal.paluch,radoslav.fasuga,martin.nemec}@vsb.cz

Abstract. This paper deals with the visualization of maps, spatial calculations of solar and photovoltaic systems. In particular, the issue of solar radiation and proper orientation and slope of photovoltaic panels in relation with the type and inclination of the landscape is discussed. The first part of the work focuses on the EU's interactive maps (Photovoltaic Geographical Information System) and describes the calculations and the input data used for developing the application; it is calculation of intensity of solar radiation data and SRTM DEM and ASTER GDEM data. The second part is devoted to the development of the custom applications. Applications use the Open Source control from the project GMaps.NET, Google maps and Silverlight Bing maps. In conclusion, results are compared to the EU model with own solutions.

Keywords: Visualization, Solar radiation, PVGIS, Photovoltaic, SRTM DEM, ASTER GDEM, AGDEM, Google maps, GMaps.NET, Bing, Silverlight, Web service.

1 Introduction

This article describes visualization of maps and problems of the photovoltaic systems (PVS). In particular, the issue of solar radiation and proper orientation and slope of photovoltaic panels in relation with to the type and inclination of the landscape is discussed. This paper contains description of formulas for calculating intensity of solar radiation, according to the given coordinates and season. The result of the project described in the article is implementation of the custom applications for calculation of solar radiation. This article is divided into two parts.

The first part deals with the EU's interactive maps and description of calculations and input data used for developing the applications. These parts are described in the second and third chapter of this article.

The second part is devoted to development of custom applications. This part is described in the rest of the article.

2 State of the Art

Electricity is one of the most important forms of energy for mankind; a great number of things commonly used today would not work without it. However,

V. Snasel, J. Platos, and E. El-Qawasmeh (Eds.): ICDIPC 2011, Part I, CCIS 188, pp. 46–60, 2011.
© Springer-Verlag Berlin Heidelberg 2011

most of the energy is produced from the fossil fuels, which are not inexhaustible. One of the alternatives to electricity generation from the fossil fuels is production of energy from solar radiation reaching the Earth and its conversion to electrical energy. For the conversion of solar energy into electricity, it is necessary to use an interface that carries out the conversion. Today, for such purposes photovoltaic modules (panels) are used. [1] [2].

EU's portal was created, which handles all the problems of obtaining electricity from the Sun. The portal also provides the interactive maps that are used for calculation the solar radiation.

2.1   EU's Interactive Maps for Calculation of Solar Radiation

Photovoltaic Geographical Information System – Interactive Map, (PVGIS) [3] [4] EU's web application for calculation of solar radiation (Fig. 1). Availability of the application is its main advantage. It is able to run on any computer having Internet connection and it is completely free.

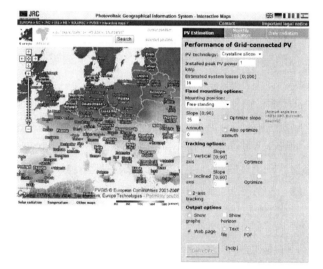

Fig. 1. EU's interactive maps application environment

Application environment. When you open the interactive maps website, the web application main user interface is appeared. Calculation of solar radiation is available both for Europe and Africa. The application environment can be divided into two parts: the first contains the interactive map; the second is designed to set the calculations. The following subsections describe environment of the both parts.

Interactive map. This section of the application contains both map and text field to entry the position for calculation. Interactive map uses Google maps and its own map data.

Using menu at the bottom of the map *Solar Radiation, Temperature, Other maps* different background maps can be set. In the menu *Solar Radiation* it can be solar radiation for horizontal, vertical or optimum angle of incidence of solar radiation, in the menu *Temperature* it can be, for example, map of average temperature for January and July, or an year.

Calculation settings. Calculation settings offers three calculation options:

1. estimated output of PV panel [5],
2. calculating the monthly global radiation,
3. calculating the daily global radiation.

Every option of calculation *Output options* enables to set, whether the output will contain graphs (*Show graphs*), height of the horizon (*Show horizon*), if the output appears on the website (*Web page*) or is to be saved into a text file (*Text file*), which will be offered for downloading, or into PDF file (*PDF*). Displaying the graphs in the calculation is not possible when output is the text file.

All calculation options contain the detailed help, which explains the different settings for calculation.

After the calculation completed, the requested data appear as the output on the web page. The outputs of the calculations are described separately for each possible output.

Performance of Grid-connected PV. In this part of the system the basic PVS parameters can be calculated, such as: average daily/monthly electricity production from the given system and average (daily) sum of global irradiation per square meter received by the modules of the given system.

Global irradiation data by month. In this part of the system the average monthly values of variables can be calculated, such as: irradiation on horizontal/optimally inclined plane, optimal inclination, Linke turbidity, ratio of diffuse to global irradiation and average daytime temperature.

Average daily solar irradiation. This section of the application enables to calculate the average daily values of solar radiation, such as: global irradiance / diffuse irradiance / global clear-sky on a fixed plane and global / diffuse irradiance on 2-axis tracking plane. In the settings you can choose how to calculate the average global solar radiation (real conditions of the average cloudiness for the given month), or the global radiation under condition of clear-sky (the value of radiation for cloudless sky). The output with average daily temperatures for the given month can be viewed, if the temperatures for the given geographical area are available.

3   Calculations and Input Data

The amount of solar energy that falls on the given area is affected by several factors. It might be geographical location, season, orientation and inclination of

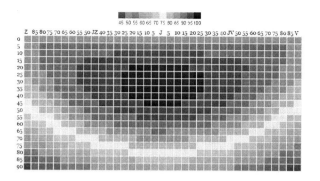

Fig. 2. Effect of PVS slope angle and orientation on their output

surface, and especially by clouds. Estimated intensity of solar radiation for the Czech Republic is 900 - 1500 kW/m^2 per year [6] [7].

The figure (Fig. 2) shows the effect of the solar panels' inclination and orientation on their performance. The figure shows that the most suitable orientation of photovoltaic panels in the Czech Republic is south with slope angle for approximately 35 degrees.

3.1   Calculating the Solar Radiation Intensity

The following calculations [8] enable to estimate the solar radiation that falls on the given area. Consistency of data for the calculation and the current conditions can never be guaranteed.

Beam radiation. The solar constant (I_0), is used for calculation, it represents the solar energy passing through the area of $1m^2$ in the middle distance of Earth from the Sun measured outside the Earth's atmosphere. The constant includes the entire spectrum of solar radiation, not just visible light, and its value is equal to $1367W.m^{-2}$. The distance from the Earth to the Sun changes over the year because of the Earth orbit eccentricity. Therefore, when calculating the extraterrestrial radiation $G_0[W.m^2]$ from the solar constant, the correction factor e for different distances is to be used:

$$G_0 = I_0 e \tag{1}$$

$$e = 1 + 0.03344 \cos(j' - 0.048869) \tag{2}$$

where j' is day angle in radians. Beam radiation of the normal solar radiation $B_{0c}[W.m^{-2}]$ is calculated as follows:

$$B_{0c} = G_0^{-0.08662 T_{LK} m d_R(m)} \tag{3}$$

The equation parameter $-0.08662 T_{LK} m d_R(m)$ is the air mass 2 Linke turbidity factor. Parameter m is the relative optical air mass as calculated by the equation:

$$m = \frac{p/p_0}{\sin(h_0^{ref}) + 0.50572(h_0^{ref} + 6.07995)^{-1.6364}} \quad (4)$$

h_0^{ref} is corrected height of the Sun h_0 (angle between the Sun and the horizon) in degrees of the atmosphere scattering Dh_0^{ref}:

Parameter $d_R(m)$ in equation (3) is Rayleigh optical thickness of the air mass m and is calculated according to the improved formula by Kasten (1996). Parameter p/p_0 in equation (4) is correction for the altitude z.

The beam irradiance on a horizontal surface $B_{hc}[W.m^{-2}]$ is calculated as:

$$B_{hc} = B_{0c}\sin(h_0) \quad (5)$$

where h_0 is the solar altitude angle.

The beam irradiance on an inclined surface $B_{ic}[W.m^{-2}]$ is then calculated as:

$$B_{ic} = B_{0c}\sin(d_{exp}) \quad (6)$$

where d_{exp} is the solar incidence angle between the Sun and an inclined surface.

Diffused radiation. Estimation of the diffused radiation on a horizontal surface $D_{hc}[W.m^{-2}]$ is the product of normal extraterrestrial radiation G_0, function T_n dependent on the Linke turbidity factor T_{LK} and the function of the Sun solar altitude F_d dependent on the height of the Sun h_0.

$$D_{hc} = G_0 T_n(T_{LK})F_d(h_0) \quad (7)$$

where $T_n(T_{LK})$:

$$T_n(T_{LK}) = -0.015843 + 0.030543T_{LK} + 0.0003797T_{LK}^2 \quad (8)$$

Radiation reflected from the ground. Radiation reflected from the ground $R_i[W.m^{-2}]$ is dependent on the global horizontal radiation G_{hc}, average ground reflectivity r_g and function $r_g(g_n)$, g_n is inclination angle:

$$R_i = G_{hc}r_g r_g(g_n) \quad (9)$$

$$r_g(g_n) = \frac{(1 - \cos(g_n))}{2} \quad (10)$$

Global radiation on horizontal surface $G_{hc}[W.m^{-2}]$ is calculated as a sum of beam and difussed components of radiation:

$$G_{hc} = B_{hc} + D_{hc} \quad (11)$$

The values from 0.15 to 2.0 are mostly used for reflectivity.

Calculation of the real-sky radiation. The real-sky radiation is calculated from the clear-sky radiation and parameter determining the clouds. The clear-sky values G_{hc} is multiplied by index k_c:

$$G_h = G_{hc}k_c \tag{12}$$

Index k_c expresses the ratio of global radiation on horizontal surface for cloudy-sky and clear-sky. It can be calculated from the measured global radiation G_{hs} and calculated values the clear-sky global radiation G_{hc}:

$$k_c = \frac{G_{hs}}{G_{hc}} \tag{13}$$

For the inclined surface it is calculated as follows:

$$D_h = D_{hc}k_c^d \tag{14}$$

$$B_h = B_{hc}k_c^b \tag{15}$$

Values for global radiation for horizontal surface G_{hs} and value for diffused radiation D_{hs} are derived from measurements or calculations of climatological data:

$$D_h = \frac{G_h D_{hs}}{G_{hs}} \tag{16}$$

$$B_h = G_h - D_h \tag{17}$$

$$k_c^d = \frac{D_h}{D_{hc}} \tag{18}$$

$$k_c^b = \frac{B_h}{B_{hc}} \tag{19}$$

3.2 Input Data

Applications use two types of input data for the altitude, which is the basis for the calculations. The altitude values are used both for calculating the intensity of solar radiation, and for calculating the terrain slope and orientation.

The first type is the Elevation model SRTM DEM [9], the second type is the Global elevation model ASTER GDEM [10] [11]. As is apparent from these data, ASTER GDEM data are more appropriate for the calculations in my application, they are more accurate, but also 9 times larger, and thereby more difficult for processing. Both types of data are available for free, the application supports both types of data, so it is up to the users, which type of input data they select.

SRTM DEM. The elevation model SRTM DEM (Shuttle Radar Topography Mission Digital Elevation Model) is international project of National Geospatial-Intelligence Agency (NGA) and National Aeronautics and Space Administration (NASA). Two variants of data are available:

1. **SRTM1** - data are available for the USA in a resolution of 1 arc second (approximately 30 meters on the equator),
2. **SRTM3** - data cover the Earth between 60° north latitude and 56° south latitude. Each area was scanned at least once, 95% of area was scanned twice.

Table 1. SRTM3 DEM basic parametres

Tile size	1200 x 1200 (1 x 1 grade angle)
Values range	3 arcsec (approximately 90 meters at the equator)
Coordinates	Latitude and longitude
DEM output format	16-bit GeoTIFF, Coordinate system WGS84/EGM96
Coverage	60° north latitude - 56° south latitude

ASTER GDEM. The global elevation model ASTER GDEM (ASTER Global Digital Elevation Map) arose from cooperation of Japanese Ministry of Economy, Trade and Industry (METI) and American National Aeronautics and Space Administration (NASA).

ASTER GDEM covers the Earth between 83° north latitude and 83° south latitude and consists of 22,600 tiles, and each tile represents one degree angle. GDEM ASTER data are provided in GeoTIFF format, where each pixel represents one elevation value. Tile size is 3601x3601 pixels (each tile overlaps with the next tile by one pixel). Version 1 contains the fixed elevation anomalies, which are located to the north from 60° north latitude, while the version 1 is not considered as mature and completed product, but it is intended to be further refined.

Table 2. ASTER GDEM basic parametres

Tile size	3601 x 3601 pixels (1 x 1 grade angle)
Values range	1 arcsec (approximately 30 meters at the equator)
Coordinates	Latitude and longitude
DEM output format	16-bit GeoTIFF, Coordinate system WGS84/EGM96
Coverage	83° north latitude - 83° south latitude

Fig. 3. Image derived from ASTER GDEM globe map data set [10]

4   Custom Applications

This chapter describes the applications that have been developed within range of the article.

All the applications developed have the following functions:

- searching the specified location on the map,
- entering the area or position for calculation of solar radiation for clear-sky,
- visualization of influence of inclination and orientation on the PVS output for the specified area on the map,
- detailed setting of calculations of solar radiation,
- calculation of solar radiation, including the following components of solar radiation (beam, diffused, reflected and global),
- determining the altitude and other information about the Sun,
- storing the graphs and the ability to process results of the calculations.

4.1   Desktop Application

This application was developed on .NET platform in programming language C# [12] and the Open Source control from project GMap.NET [13]. Installation of application is not needed, user just copies the files from the archive into the folder from which the application will run. .NET Framework at least version 3.5 is necessary for run of the application.

The application main window. After launching, the main application window (Fig. 4) appears. There is the map on the left, there are controls for controlling and setting map and calculations on the right.

After clicking on the map or on the marker the information about current position, altitude, altitude, obtained from a Web service, orientation and inclination appear in the first top text box at the bottom of the window. The second text box displays additional information about the resolution (distance between the separate altitude data) and the Sun for the current position and time.

Setting layer of efficiency. To adjust the calculation of solar radiation the *Layer of efficiency* panel is used. After clicking on the map the effectiveness of a given point is shown in the field *Efficiency*.

The following three options can be used to enter the area for calculation:

1. set the switch *Set size* and enter the area size using the drop-down lists X and Y,
2. set the switch *Capture area* and enter the corner points of area by clicking on the map,
3. set the area by and dragging the mouse and holding the Shift key.

After clicking the *View* button the calculation for a given area is processed, and the calculation result is displayed on the map. If the third option for entering

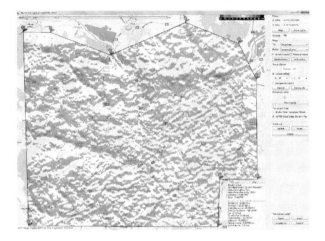

Fig. 4. The main window of the custom desktop application visualizes the influence of orientation and inclination of photovoltaic panels on their performance, with using the second option of entering the area

are is used, there is no need to click the *View* button, the calculation is done automatically when you release the hold mouse button.

Color-coding of areas corresponds with the color scale, which is located in the upper right corner of the map. The effect of orientation and inclination of photovoltaic panels on their performance is considered. Details of the scale are shown in the dialog box that appears after clicking on the scale. The areas that are north-oriented according to the calculations are white-colored. Transparency of all layers of the layer of efficiency can be changed by using the slider *Layer transparency*.

Setting the type of input data. The application supports both types of input data, which are described in chapter *Calculations and input data*. User can switch the type of input data using the switches in the panel *Input data type*.

Solar radiation calculation. The dialog box *Calculations* (Fig. 5), which appears in the main window after clicking on the *Calculations Window* button from the panel *Layer of efficiency*, enables to calculate solar radiation for a point or an area set on the map.

Description of separate tabs:

- *Day* - shows graph and table of the calculations of solar radiation results (beam, diffused, reflected and global) for a given day, including non-zero average, average and sum,
- *Month* - shows graph and table of the calculations of solar radiation results (beam, diffused, reflected and global) for the given days of the month, including the average and the sum,

- *Year* - shows graph and table of the calculations of solar radiation results (beam, diffused, reflected and global) for the given months of the year, including the average and the sum,
- *Sun* - shows the graph of the Sun altitude for a given day (only in the calculation for the point),
- *Hour* - contains the table of the detailed calculations and information for a given hour (only in the calculation for the point).

The greatest advantages of a desktop version are speed of processing and displaying the calculations results. It is not necessary to wait until the remote server will calculate and return the required output. Rendering objects in the map is also among the fastest ones. Possibility to work offline and not to download the documents from the Internet is other advantage. Saving the map view as a picture into a file is very convenient option also.

The disadvantages include the necessity to have stored the input data, which are used in the calculations, they take up considerable capacity of hard disk. These data are used for determining altitudes, where size of one tile data (1 x 1 degree angle) ASTER GDEM has 24.7 MB and SRTM DEM has a size of 2.75 MB. 21 tiles are needed to cover the entire Czech Republic area. So, the total estimated size for ASTER GDEM data is 519 MB and for SRTM DEM data is 57.7 MB. If the data for the position are unavailable, they are automatically

Table 3. Explanation of the calculation settings

Parameter	Explanation
Setting	
Date	Date setting
The Linke atmospheric turbidity factor	The Linke atmospheric turbidity factor indicates how much the sunlight is dimmed by aerosols. It illustrates the optical density of hazy and humid atmosphere to clean and dry atmosphere. (1-7)
Albedo	Surface reflectance
Slope	Slope to be used, if the field *Apply the slope specified* is marked
Apply the slope specified	The slope specified in the field *Slope* will be applied for calculation point/area
Time settings	The settings are used for calculation for Day and Hour
Start	Time to start the calculation of solar radiation
Finish	Time to finish the calculation of solar radiation
Step	Time step (1 - calculation for an hour is performed 1 time; 0.5 - calculation for an hour is performed 2 times)
Hour	Hour for which calculation and displaying of results in output *Hour* will be processed
Calculation	
Point	Calculation is performed for a given point on the map, area 1 m^2
Area	Calculation is performed for a given area on the map, the results are averages for an area 1 m^2

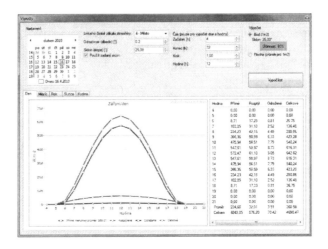

Fig. 5. Dialog window Calculations of desktop application with example of output

downloaded from the Internet. Therefore, it is not necessary to have all the data
stored on disk, but only those that are currently used.

5   JavaScript Application

It is Internet application, which uses Google maps [14] and displays information
on the map using JavaScript, and via the script communicates with web service,
which has been created in the range of the article. The application has been
developed on .NET platform using the technology ASP.NET version 4.0 [15] for
websites development and programming language C# for communication with
web service. JavaScript library jQuery [16] is used in application.

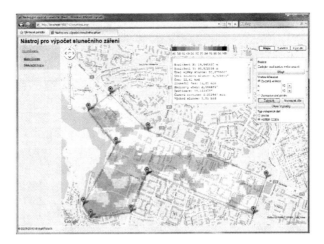

Fig. 6. Example of visualization of inclinations in the JavaScript version of application

The application (Fig. 6) provides the same options of the calculation as the desktop application.

Independence on the platform and operating system used can be considered as the advantages of JavaScript version. Maps are displayed in the most of web browsers used today. Processing of calculations by server and non-loading the local stations with complex calculations are other advantages.

The biggest disadvantage is speed of rendering, which is affected by the a web browser speed.

6   Silverlight Application

This application is developed using Silverlight technology on .NET platform version 4.0 with programming language C#. Bing maps by Microsoft [17] are used to view the maps. Data obtained from the Web service are used to display information on the map. The browser add-in need to be installed which enables to display the application.

The application (Fig. 7), as JavaScript application, provides the same number of the calculation as the desktop application.

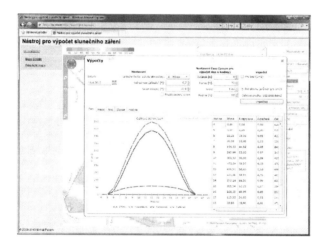

Fig. 7. Silverlight application with example of calculation results

The advantage of Silverlight version is the rendering speed, which was comparable with the desktop version. The same advantage as in the JavaScript version is transferring of the complex calculations load from local stations to server. Possibility of maximizing the window for using the entire screen area and 'installation' of the application are also the positive features.

The disadvantages are the worse maps and the need to install a browser add-on.

7   Testing the Application

All three of the developed applications use a similar user interface that is customized for each specific application. The uniform user interface allows the use of any version of the application and easy orientation in the application environment, when moves between the applications of different technologies.

Functionality of all the custom applications has been properly tested and found to be fully operational for the two personal computers: AMD Athlon™ 64 X2 5000+ 2.6 GHz, 4GB RAM, Windows 7 x64 and Intel Atom 1.6 GHz, 1GB RAM, Windows XP. Web applications were tested on the following versions of Internet browsers: Internet Explorer 8.0, Mozilla Firefox 3.6, Opera 10.5 and Google Chrome 10.0.

Calculations of custom applications were compared with the results of calculations of the EU's Interactive maps. Example of the comparison was processed for the following geographic coordinates: 49.830N, 18.164E. The following table shows the calculated values of solar radiation for each month of the year, some differences are obvious form the table. Setting the rates for beam and reflected radiation influences a lot on calculation of the actual radiation. For the applications described in this article, those rates are set for annual averages, so, the results in some months are more or less different. (Results of the custom applications had to be divided by the number of days per month or the number of days per year.)

Table 4. Comparison of calculations of EU's interactive maps and custom applications

	EU's Interactive maps $[W.m^{-2}]$		Custom application $[W.m^{-2}]$	
Month	Slope 0°	Slope 35°	Slope 0°	Slope 35°
January	791	1280	845	1206
February	1440	2100	1529	1949
March	2390	2970	2630	2982
April	3560	3940	3865	4010
May	4710	4780	4821	4694
June	4810	4670	5243	4959
Jule	5050	5020	5023	4816
August	4220	4530	4219	4260
September	2800	3350	3073	3350
October	1940	2790	1891	2296
November	889	1340	1022	1406
December	592	942	672	1007
Year average	2780	3150	2903	3078

8   Conclusion

The result of the project described in this article are three applications that further expand and add new possibilities of the existing EU's interactive maps:

- visualization inclination of landscape,
- several options for entering the area and the inclusion of larger areas in the calculation,
- detailed calculation options to set the solar radiation,
- simple export of output graphs and tables,
- determining the altitude and other information about the Sun.

The developed applications can be extended. It may be, for example, counting with the cloudiness in relation to the average cloudiness, which would precise the calculations; or design of the PVS effective deployment into the specified area or the roof with 3D visualization of the deployment, including consideration of shading of the area caused by buildings, forests, elevations. Another possible enhancement is analysis of the photographs from which the trees, not included into the maps, would be added into analysis of the deployment of the solar panels. Furthermore, the WPF [18] technology can be used for the application development, it allows to create rich user interface and supports the hardware graphics acceleration using the graphics card, thereby would further accelerate rendering the objects on the maps for the desktop version.

Work is partially supported by Grant of GACR No. P202/10/0573.

References

1. Suri, M., Huld, T.A., Dunlop, E.D., Ossenbrink, H.: Potential of Solar Electricity Generation in the European Union Member States and Candidate Countries. Solar energy 81(10), 1295–1305 (2007)
2. Huld, T., Suri, M., Dunlop, E.D.: Comparison of Potential Solar Electricity Output From Fixed-inclined and Two-axis Tracking Photovoltaic Modules in Europe. Progresss in photovoltaics 16(1), 47–59 (2008)
3. Photovoltaic Geographical Information System - Interactive Maps, http://re.jrc.ec.europa.eu/pvgis/apps3/pvest.php
4. Suri, M., Huld, T., Cebecauer, T., Dunlop, E.D.: Geographic Aspects of Photovoltaics in Europe: Contribution of the PVGIS Website. IEEE Journal of Selected Topics in Applied Earth Observations and Remote Sensing 1(1), 34–41 (2008)
5. Calleja, H., Jimenez, H.: Performance of a Grid Connected PV System Used as Active Filter. Energy Conversion and Management 45(15-16), 2417–2428 (2004)
6. Deutsche Gesellschaft für Sonnenenergie. Planning and Installing Photovoltaic Systems: A Guide for Installers, Architects, and Engineers. Earthscan (2005)
7. Murtinger, K., Beranovsky, J., Tomes, M.: Fotovoltaika: Elektrina ze Slunce. In: ERA (2008)
8. Solar Radiation and GIS, http://re.jrc.ec.europa.eu/pvgis/solres/solmod3.htm
9. Shuttle Radar Topography Mission, http://www2.jpl.nasa.gov/srtm/index.html
10. ASTER Global Digital Elevation Map, http://asterweb.jpl.nasa.gov/gdem.asp
11. Reuter, H.I., Nelson, A., Strobl, P., Mehl, W., Jarvis, A.: A First Assessment of ASTER GDEM Tiles for Absolute Accuracy, Relative Accuracy and Terrain Parameters. In: IEEE International Geoscience and Remote Sensing Symposium, IGARSS. LNCS, vol. 1-5, pp. 3665–3668 (2009)
12. Behalek, M.: Programovaci jazyk C#. VSB –TU Ostrava

13. GMap.NET - Great Maps for Windows Forms & Presentation, http://greatmaps.codeplex.com/
14. Google Maps, API – Google Code, http://code.google.com/intl/cs-CZ/apis/maps/documentation/javascript/tutorial.html
15. Professional ASP. NET 3.5: In C# and VB. Wiley Publishing, Inc., (2008)
16. jQuery: The Write Less, Do More, JavaScript Library, http://jquery.com/
17. Bing Maps Platform - Integrated Mapping, Imaging, Search and Location Web Service, http://www.microsoft.com/maps/
18. Windows Presentation Foundation, http://msdn.microsoft.com/en-us/library/ms754130

FWebQ – A Framework for Websites Quality Evaluation

Álvaro Rocha

University Fernando Pessoa, Praça 9 de Abril, 349, 4249-004 Porto, Portugal
amrocha@ufp.edu.pt

Abstract. Websites quality is strategically important for organizations and for the satisfaction of their clients. In this paper we propose a high-level structure for a global quality evaluation of a website. This structure is based in three main dimensions (contents, services, technical), characteristics, sub-characteristics and attributes, that will substantiate the development of broad websites quality evaluation, comparison and improvement methodologies, according to particular sectors of activity.

Keywords: Websites Evaluation, Contents Quality, Services Quality, Technical Quality.

1 Introduction

With the increasing number of websites and websites investments, the websites quality evaluation has become an important activity [23]. Organizations invest time and money to develop and maintain their website's quality. These websites should establish an effective information and communication channel between organizations and their clients. In some cases, they are part of the offered product, since they make useful services available to clients [7].

A website should clearly reflect the quality efforts set in place by the organization, because it establishes an important connection with clients. Modern websites show a significant range of aspects, complexity of structure and diversity of offered services [17]. Like in all information systems, websites evaluation is an important development and operational factor that may lead to the improvement of their user's satisfaction [7] and to the optimization of invested resources [6].

In this research we want to propose a high-level structure for a global quality evaluation of a website. That structure can become a platform for the development of specific websites quality evaluation, comparison and improvement methodologies, according to different sectors of activity. We will thus introduce in the following sections the concept of quality, propose three main dimensions for websites quality and indentify methods for the quality evaluation in each of these dimensions, we will propose the structure for a global quality evaluation of a website and, finally, we will offer some conclusions.

2 Software Quality

People look for quality in each object they create, and software is not an exception. Software is one of the strategic assets in the Information Society. With the Internet

V. Snasel, J. Platos, and E. El-Qawasmeh (Eds.): ICDIPC 2011, Part I, CCIS 188, pp. 61–71, 2011.
© Springer-Verlag Berlin Heidelberg 2011

boom, and the following exponential increase in contents and services made available through websites, a quality revolution quickly spread throughout the whole world [23].

Aspects related to the quality of websites have, therefore, become relevant to many sectors of activity. Several contributions to the field of websites quality and different schools of thought have primarily focused in the definition of quality, in its structure and in the way it can be measured [e.g., 11, 21].

In this paper we adopt the definition of quality published in the most recent ISO (International Organization for Standardization) standard for software quality, because it agrees with our purposes, because of its broadness and completeness and because of the prestige of the mentioned organization. We, therefore, understand quality as the "*capability of a software product to satisfy stated and implied needs when used under specified conditions*" [16].

3   Dimensions of Websites Quality

The content and services are the reasons for the existence of a Web site. Thus, considering the results of some studies conducted and/or oriented by the author [30], as well as the systematization of the knowledge available in several bibliographies, we can group websites quality in three main dimensions (*Figure 1*): Content quality; Service quality; and Technical quality.

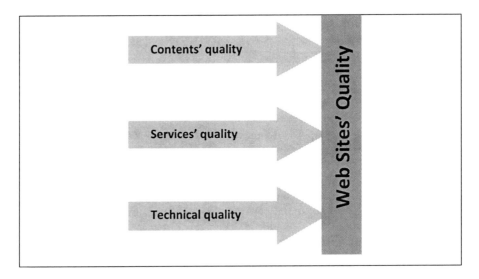

Fig. 1. Main Dimensions for Websites Quality

In the first dimension, the main concerns focus in contents quality and not in its existence, this should be a technical quality concern. In contents quality, attributes like accuracy/precision, completeness, relevance, opportunity, consistence, coherence, update, orthography and syntax are evaluated.

In the second dimension, concerns are focused in the quality of services offered in websites. In services quality, attributes like security, reliability, privacy, performance, efficiency, accuracy, opportunity, availability, response time, time saving, empathy, reputation and personalization are evaluated.

Finally, in the third dimension, concerns are focused on the technical quality of websites, i.e., on quality attributes that are usually in quality standards for software, such as ISO/IEC 9126 [14] and its successor ISO/IEC 25010 [12]. Thus, attributes like navigation map, path, search engine, download time of pages, browser compatibility, broken links and accessibility are evaluated.

Through bibliography and through our experience we have observed that there is no evaluation methodology that focuses in these three main websites quality dimensions, in a broad, integrated and transversal sense.

4 Contents Quality Evaluation

Content quality evaluation primarily employs methodologies based in the Likert scale, which evaluates the quality of these contents amongst respondents (users, linguists and experts in the contents presented in websites). Some studies related to this dimension are worth mentioning, such as: Bernstam et al. [3], Caro et al. [4] Hargrave et al. [9], Moraga et al. [22], Parker et al. [26] and Richard et al. [29].

A possible structure for a contents quality measuring instrument can have a similar format to the one presented by Moraga et al. [22] (Table 1), already consistent with the ISO 25012 standard [13], which is the most relevant contribution that we found in the literature for this dimension.

To classify each attribute, the analyzers should carefully read and analyze either every webpage content of the website or every webpage content until a certain predefined level of depth is reached.

Analyzers can classify webpage content quality in a five point Likert scale (1- Bad, 2 – Mediocre, 3 – Reasonable, 4 – Good, 5 – Very Good).

5 Services Quality Evaluation

Online services quality evaluation, which includes, for instance, in the health area, healthcare acts scheduling, prescriptions renewal or drug acquisition, usually employs evaluation methodologies for back-office procedures and/or users' satisfaction towards services available in websites. Some studies related to this dimension are worth mentioning, such as: Al-Momani and Noor [1], Arshad et al. [2], Cernea et al. [5], Hamadi [8], Li and Suomi [18], Li and Suomi [19], Parasuraman et al. [27] and Zhao [31].

A possible structure for a services quality measurement instrument can have the format presented in Table 2, based in Parasuraman's services quality scale [27], which is the most relevant contribution that we found in the literature for this dimension. The variables (2nd column) are grouped by characteristics (1st column).

Analyzers can classify websites services quality in a 5 point Likert scale (1 – Completely disagree; 2 – Disagree; 3 – Don't agree or disagree; 4 – Agree; 5 – Completely agree).

Table 1. Structure for contents quality measurement [Moraga et al. 22]

Point of view	Category	Characteristic	Subcharacteristic
Inherent	**Intrinsic**: *It denote that data have quality in their own right*	Accuracy	
		Credibility:	Objectivity
			Reputation
		Traceability	
		Currentness	
		Expiration	
		Completeness	
		Consistency	
		Accessibility	
		Compliance	
		Confidentiality	
		Efficiency	
		Precision	
		Understandability	
System Dependent	**Operational**: *It emphasized the importance of the role of Systems; that is, the system must be accessible but secure*	Availability	
		Accessibility	Interactive
			Ease of operation
			Customer Support
		Verifiability	
		Confidentiality	
		Portability	
		Recoverability	
	Contextual: *It highlights the requirement which states that data quality must be considered within the context of the task in hand*	Validity	Reliability
			Scope
		Value-added	Applicability
			Flexibility
			Novelty
		Relevancy	Novelty
			Timeliness
		Specialization	
		Usefulness	
		Efficiency	
		Effectiveness	
		Traceability	
		Compliance	
		Precision	
	Representational: *It denotes that the system must present data in such a way that they are interpretable, easy to understand, and concisely and consistently represented*	Concise Representation	
		Consistent Representation	
		Understandability	Interpretability
			Amount of data
			Documentation
			Organization
		Attractiveness	
		Readability	

Table 2. Services Quality Measurement Structure [27]

Characteristic	Attribute	1	2	3	4	5
Efficiency: *The ease and speed of* *accessing and using the site*	This site makes it easy to find what I need					
	It makes it easy to get anywhere on the site					
	It enables me to complete a transaction quickly					
	Information at this site is well organized					
	It loads its pages fast					
	This site is simple to use					
	This site enables me to get on to it quickly					
	This site is well organized					
Fulfillment: *The extent to which the site's* *promises* *about order delivery and* *item availability* *are fulfilled*	It delivers orders when promised					
	This site makes items available for delivery within a suitable time frame					
	It quickly delivers what I order					
	It sends out the items ordered					
	It has in stock the items the company claims to have					
	It is truthful about its offerings					
	It makes accurate promises about delivery of products					
System availability: *The correct technical* *functioning of the site*	This site is always available for business					
	This site launches and runs right away					
	This site does not crash					
	Pages at this site do not freeze after I enter my order information					
Privacy: *The degree to which the site* *is safe and* *Protects customer* *information*	It protects information about my Web-shopping behavior					
	It does not share my personal information with other sites					
	This site protects information about my credit card					
Responsiveness. *Effective handling of* *problems and returns* *through the site*	It provides me with convenient options for returning items					
	This site handles product returns well					
	This site offers a meaningful guarantee					
	It tells me what to do if my transaction is not processed					
	It takes care of problems promptly					

Table 2. (*Continued*)

Characteristic	Attribute	1	2	3	4	5
Compensation: *The degree to which the site compensates customers for problems*	This site compensates me for problems it creates					
	It compensates me when what I ordered doesn't arrive on time					
	It picks up items I want to return from my home or business					
Contact: *The availability of assistance through telephone or online representatives*	This site provides a telephone number to reach the company					
	This site has customer service representatives available online					
	It offers the ability to speak to a live person if there is a problem					

6   Technical Quality Evaluation

The technical dimension is related to how the content and services are assembled and made available on a Web site.

Technical quality evaluation is based in software quality models or standards and in methods focused in usability, methods developed through studies in the area of Human-Computer Interaction (HCI). The first group methodologies include, amongst others, ISO/IEC 9126 [14] and ISO/IEC 25010 [12] standards. The second group includes an approach that emerged with the hypermedia nature of the Internet and the relevance of interface conception to speed access to information and globally improve human-computer interaction, and includes standards like ISO/IEC 9241 [15]. This approach defines quality according to usability, considering the users' point of view [e.g., 10, 24].

Technical quality is, amongst the three main dimensions, the one that has received a higher degree of attention from researchers, and several methodologies have been proposed for its evaluation. Amongst those, we consider the work developed by Olsina [25] and other works that followed this line [e.g.: 20, 28] the most relevant, since they base their methodologies in ISO 9126 [14] and its high level quality characteristics that interest websites users (usability, functionality, reliability, efficiency). Figure 2 shows part of the structure adopted by Reis [28] to evaluate technical quality.

Technical quality measurement can also be classified in a three or five point Likert scale.

7   Structure for a Global Quality Evaluation of a Website

Bearing in mind the three main dimensions for websites quality defined in this paper, resulting of literature systematization and based in our experience as websites users and websites engineering researchers, we now propose a high-level structure to evaluate global quality of a website in a broad, transversal and detailed form.

```
1.    Usability
1.1   Global schema of the site
1.1.1 Global organization scheme
1.1.1.1    Site map
1.1.1.2    Table of contents
1.1.1.3    Alphabetic index
1.1.1.4    Localizer on map
1.1.2 Navigation tasks
1.1.2.1    Navigation
1.1.2.1.1        Guidance
1.1.2.1.1.1      Path indicator
1.1.2.1.1.2      Bookmark of current position
1.1.2.2    Objects of navigation control
1.1.2.2.1        Presentation of contextual controls
1.1.2.2.1.1      Permanence of the controls
1.1.2.2.1.2      Intuitiveness of the controls
1.1.2.2.2        Scroll mechanisms
1.1.2.2.2.1      Vertical
1.1.2.2.2.2      Horizontal
1.1.2.3    Navigation intuitiveness
1.1.2.3.1        Link title
1.1.2.3.2        Link phrase quality
1.1.3 Guided tour for students
1.1.4 Map of images
1.2   User help
1.2.1 Help quality
1.2.1.1    General help directed to the student
1.2.1.2    Help for search
1.2.2 Indicator of update
1.2.2.1    Global
1.2.2.2    Per subsite or page
1.2.3 Access to addresses
1.2.3.1    Access to addresses
1.2.3.2    Phone/Fax
1.2.3.3    Internal extensions
1.2.3.4    Addresses for correspondence
1.2.4 FAQ
1.2.5 Feedback form
1.2.5.1    Questionnaires
1.2.5.2    Guestbooks
1.2.5.3    Comments
```

Fig. 2. Part of the technical quality evaluation structure [28]

This structure is organized according to the three main website quality dimensions, comprised by characteristics which, in their turn, are comprised by attributes, as shown in Figure 3. Characteristics can sometimes be comprised by more than one level of sub-characteristics.

Websites quality evaluation, comparison and improvement methodologies developed through the proposed structure should be designed to incorporate adjustments to the activity sector in which they are applied, since the suitable structure for quality sub-characteristics and attributes generally differs between activity sectors. Simultaneously, they must be configured without the existence of overlap between the characteristics, sub-characteristics and attributes of the three dimensions.

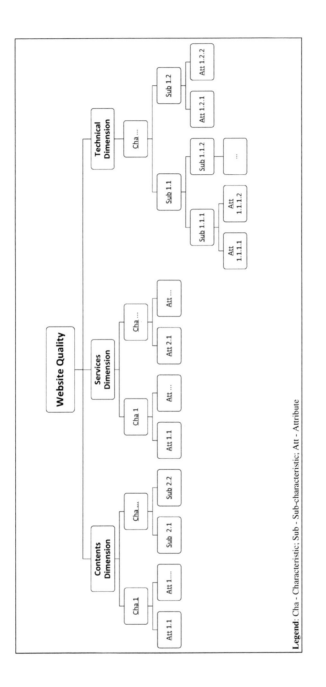

Fig. 3. Part of the high-level structure for a global quality evaluation of a website

Legend: Cha - Characteristic; Sub - Sub-characteristic; Att - Attribute

8 Conclusion

In this paper we intend to propose a high-level structure for a global quality evaluation of a website. We can highlight a few aspects as a conclusion:

a) Websites quality is strategically important for organizations and for the satisfaction of their clients;
b) Websites quality should be based in the quality measurement the three main dimensions: content, services, and technical;
c) A structure based in these three dimensions, characteristics, sub-characteristics and attributes will substantiate a broad, integrated, transversal and detailed quality evaluation of a website;
d) A good evaluation, comparison and improvement methodology for websites quality should properly comprise the three mentioned quality dimensions and allow the adjustment to a specific activity sector.

The next step in our study will be the development of an evaluation, comparison and improvement methodology for the quality of institutional and hospital websites, based in the high-level structure proposed in this paper and will be built and validated with help of Web engineering experts and hospital websites' users. The need for this methodology is justified by the fact that we do not know any that provides a broad and detailed assessment, integrating the three main quality dimensions of a website: content, services and technical.

References

1. Al-Momani1, K., Noor, N.: E- Service Quality, Ease of Use, Usability and Enjoyment as Antecedents of E-CRM Performance: An Empirical Investigation in Jordan Mobile Phone Services. The Asian Journal of Technology Management 2(2), 11–25 (2009)
2. Arshad, N., Ahmad, F., Janom, N.: Empirical Study on Electronic Service Quality. Public Sector ICT Management Review 2(1), 29–37 (2007)
3. Bernstam, E.V., Shelton, D., Walji, M., Meric-Bernstam, F.: Instruments to assess the quality of health information on the World Wide Web: What can our patients actually use? International Journal of Medical Informatics 74, 13–19 (2005)
4. Caro, A., Calero, C., Caballero, I., Piattini, M.: A proposal for a set of attributes relevant for Web portal data quality. Software Quality Journal 16, 513–542 (2008)
5. Cernea, S.O., Sîrbu, J., Mărginean, N.: Determination of Users Satisfaction Level Regarding the Quality of E-Services Provided by Bogdan-Voda University. Annales Universitatis Apulensis Series Oeconomica 11(2), 652–661 (2009)
6. Cheung, C., Lee, M.: The Structure of Web-Based Information Systems Satisfaction: Testing of Competing Models. Journal of the American Society for Information Science and Technology 59(10), 1617–1630 (2008)
7. Grigoroudis, E., Litos, C., Moustakis, V., Politis, Y., Tsironis, L.: The assessment of user-perceived web quality: Application of a satisfaction benchmarking approach. European Journal of Operational Research 187(3), 1346–1357 (2008)
8. Hamadi, C.: The Impact of Quality of Online Banking on Customer Commitment. Communications of the IBIMA, 1–8 (2010)

9. Hargrave, D.R., Hargrave, U.A., Bouffet, E.: Quality of health information on the Internet. Neuro-Oncology 8, 175–182 (2006)
10. Hinchliffe, A., Mummery, W.K.: Applying usability testing techniques to improve a health promotion website. Health Promotion Journal of Australia 19(1), 29–35 (2008)
11. Ho-Won, J., Seung-Gweon, K., Chung, C.-S.: Measuring Software Product Quality: A Survey of ISO/IEC 9126. IEEE Software 21(5), 88–92 (2004)
12. ISO. ISO/IEC 25010:2011, Systems and software engineering – Systems and software Quality Requirements and Evaluation (SQuaRE) – System and software quality models, International Organization for Standardization (2011)
13. ISO/IEC. ISO/IEC 25012:2008, Software engineering – Software product Quality Requirements and Evaluation (SQuaRE) – Data quality model, International Organization for Standardization (2008)
14. ISO/IEC. ISO 9126-1:2001, Software engineering – Product quality – Part 1: Quality model, International Organization for Standardization (2001)
15. ISO/IEC, ISO 9241-11:1998 - Ergonomic requirements for office work with visual display terminals (VDTs) – Part 11: Guidance on usability, International Organization for Standardization (1998)
16. ISO/IEC, ISO/IEC 25000: Software Engineering – Software product Quality Requirements and Evaluation (SQuaRE) – Guide to SQuaRE. International Organization for Standardization (2005)
17. Kappel, G., Proll, B., Reich, S., Retschitzegger, W.: Web Engineering: The Discipline of Systematic Development of Web Applications. Wiley, Chichester (2006)
18. Li, H., Suomi, R.: Evaluating Electronic Service Quality: A Transaction Process Based Evaluation Model. In: Proceedings of ECIME 2007: The European Conference on Information Management and Evaluation, Montpellier, France, pp. 331–340 (September 20-21, 2007)
19. Li, H., Suomi, R.: A Proposed Scale for Measuring E-service Quality. International Journal of u- and e-Service, Science and Technology 2(1), 1–10 (2009)
20. Machado, R., e Rocha, A.: Avaliação da Qualidade de Sítios Web Institucionais: Aplicação de Métrica às Faculdades de Medicina do Espaço Ibérico. Revista da Faculdade de Ciência e Tecnologia da Universidade Fernando Pessoa 3, 76–87 (2008)
21. Mich, L., Franch, M., Gaio, L.: Evaluating and Designing Web Site Quality. IEEE Multimedia 10(1), 34–43 (2003)
22. Moraga, C., Moraga, M.A., Caro, A.: SQuaRE-Aligned Data Quality Model for Web Portals. In: Proceedings of 2009 Ninth International Conference on Quality Software, Jeju, Korea, pp. 117–122 (August 24-25, 2009)
23. Naik, K., Tripathy, P.: Software Testing and Quality Assurance. Wiley, Chichester (2008)
24. Obeso, M.: Metodología de Medición y Evaluación de la Usabilidad en Sitios Web Educativos. Tesis Doctoral, Universidad de Oviedo (2004)
25. Olsina, L.: Metodología Cuantitativa para la Evaluación y Comparación de la Calidad de Sitios Web. Tesis Doctoral. Universidad Nacional de La Plata, Argentina (2000)
26. Parker, M.B., Moleshe, V., De la Harpe, R., Wills, G.B.: An evaluation of Information quality frameworks for the World Wide Web. In: 8th Annual Conference on WWW Applications, Bloemfontein, Free State Province, South Africa (September 6-8, 2006)
27. Parasuraman, A., Zeithaml, V.A., Malhotra, A.: E-S-QUAL a multiple-item scale for assessing electronic service quality. Journal of Service Research 7, 213–233 (2005)

28. Reis, T.: REQE - Uma Metodologia para Medição de Qualidade de Aplicações Web na Fase de Requisitos. Dissertação de Mestrado, Universidade de Pernambuco, Brasil (2004)
29. Richard, J.L., Schuldiner, S., Jourdan, N., Daurès, J.P., Vannerau, D., Rodier, M., Lavit, P.: The Internet and the diabetic foot: quality of online information in French language. Diabetes & Metabolism 33(3), 197–204 (2007)
30. Rocha, A., Victor, A.: Quality of Hotel Websites - Proposal for Development of an Assessment Methodology. TOURISMOS - An International Multidisciplinary Journal of Tourism 5(1), 173–178 (2010)
31. Zhao, P.: Relationship between Online Service Quality and Customer Satisfaction: A Study in Internet Banking, Master Thesis, Luleå University of Technology, Sweden (2005)

A JRuby Infrastructure for Converged Web and SIP Applications

Edin Pjanić and Amer Hasanović

University of Tuzla, Faculty of Electrical Engineering
Franjevačka 2, 75000 Tuzla, Bosnia and Herzegovina
{edin.pjanic,amer.hasanovic}@untz.ba
http://ictlab.com.ba

Abstract. In this paper we present a Ruby infrastructure that can be used for rapid development of Web applications with SIP signaling capabilities. We construct this infrastructure by combining the Java based Cipango SIP/HTTP Servlet Application Server with the Ruby on Rails Web development framework. We provide detailed explanations of the steps required to build this infrastructure and produce a SIP registrar example application with a simple Web interface. The described infrastructure allows Ruby applications to utilize the entire functionality provided by the SIP Servlet API and can be used as a good starting point for the development of Ruby-based domain specific languages for the SIP protocol. We also compare the proposed infrastructure with the existing Ruby frameworks for SIP application development.

Keywords: software infrastructure, SIP, converged applications, dynamic languages, interoperability, Ruby, JRuby, Cipango, Jetty.

1 Introduction

In the nineties, software development was mostly focused on desktop applications utilizing tools, libraries and paradigms built around Java and C++, the two most dominant programming languages of that time. During the last decade, this focus started shifting towards Web applications, agile practices and dynamic programming languages [1][2][3].

The Ruby programming language [4] received a lot of attention in the software industry, primarily because of the flexible Web frameworks, such as Ruby on Rails [5] and Sinatra [6], as well as Ruby's support for the development of domain specific languages (DSL) [7][8].

With the recent rise of social Web applications, there is an increased interest to bring other services to the Web domain, real-time voice and video in particular. Based on the HTTP model, the Session Initiation Protocol (SIP) [9] was developed to support these services. The telecommunications industry has accepted the SIP protocol, which is now widely implemented and used in telecom application servers.

While Ruby has excellent support for HTTP, due to the Web frameworks, it lacks the adequate support for SIP. On the other hand, Java has well developed

V. Snasel, J. Platos, and E. El-Qawasmeh (Eds.): ICDIPC 2011, Part I, CCIS 188, pp. 72–84, 2011.

APIs, libraries and tools for the SIP protocol, such as the SIP Servlets [10] and JAIN SLEE [11]. Therefore, it would be beneficial to combine Ruby's proven agility [3] and Java robustness in a single infrastructure for rapid development of SIP applications. The main concepts of this integration were discussed in [12].

In this paper, we demonstrate the steps required to build the infrastructure which allows hosting of Web applications with real-time VoIP capabilities entirely in Ruby. We reuse well-known and tested open-source components as the basis for this infrastructure. More specifically, we glue together the code provided by the Ruby on Rails Web framework and a Java based Cipango SIP/HTTP Servlet Application Server [13]. We realize this concept with JRuby [14], a Java implementation of the Ruby language. We also provide a detailed explanation of the techniques we use for interoperation between JRuby and Java. Finally, we compare our approach with similar Ruby infrastructures for SIP application development.

The paper is organized as follows. In Sec. 2 we shortly outline the related infrastructures and compare them with our approach. In Sect. 3 we focus on interoperability between JRuby and Java, which is essential for utilizing Java libraries from within the Ruby code. In Sect. 4 we discuss the Cipango SIP/HTTP application server architecture and identify the key classes that can be used to embed the server engine inside a Ruby application. We provide an in-depth procedure to construct the proposed infrastructure by building an example Web application with SIP capabilities in Sect. 5. Finally, in Sect. 6 we provide a conclusion and map a course for the future work.

2 Related Work

At the time of writing this paper, we are aware of the two Ruby infrastructures for SIP application development. In this section we give a brief overview of these frameworks and compare them to our approach.

2.1 TorqueBox

TorqueBox [15] is a Ruby application platform that integrates JRuby Web applications based on Rack [16] frameworks, such as Ruby on Rails, with the JBoss Application Server [17], utilizing the features provided by JBoss. Currently, TorqueBox provides the SIP support in the beta versions.

Building converged applications with TorqueBox is similar to our approach. The main differences are in the application deployment and integration with the SIP application server. This is a direct result of the fact that the TorqueBox uses the JBoss while in our approach we utilize the Cipango application server. Additionally, the TorqueBox application deployer does not support all the features provided by the SIP servlet API from within Ruby code. For instance, listener objects are created and added to the SIP application context during the deployment of the application. The classes for these objects are defined in the `sip.xml` deployment descriptor file and cannot be Ruby classes.

Application deployment in our approach is completely different. Instead of deploying an application to the server, we incorporate the server inside the Ruby application. This means that we can utilize the full stack of the SIP Servlet API and control all the features provided by the Cipango application server, including the creation and specification of listener objects, as shown in the demo application. Furthermore, this gives us a possibility to develop and integrate Ruby DSLs in order to speed up and simplify VoIP applications development.

Moreover, the lightweight infrastructure of the Cipango engine allows faster application startup times, which is very important in short development iteration cycles.

2.2   Sipatra

Sipatra [18] is a Ruby DSL for SIP Servlets and targets SIP Servlet 1.1 compatible application servers. Its syntax is much like the syntax used in Sinatra Web DSL, but adapted to support the specific features of the SIP protocol.

Sipatra SIP message handlers are defined as blocks of code that are called when certain conditions are satisfied. The conditions are specified as regular expressions that must match the message's SIP request method, response code, URI or headers in order for the handler to be invoked. There can be more than one handler for the same SIP message type. The handlers are evaluated in the order they appear in the code and the first handler that matches the condition is executed. An example of the syntax is shown in the following listing that is self explanatory:

```
invite /sip:.*@sipatra.org/ do
   ...
end

invite /sip:.*@otherdomain.org/ do
   ...
end

invite do
   ...
end

response :INVITE, 200 do
   ...
end
```

Similar to our approach, Sipatra uses the Cipango application server. However, the application deployment procedure is similar to the one used in the TorqueBox project. Hence, it suffers from the same limitations discussed in Section 2.1.

3   JRuby and Java Interoperability

Matz's Ruby Interpreter or Ruby MRI is the reference implementation of Ruby, written in C by Yukihiro Matsumoto. However, this is not the only implementation of Ruby. One especially successful open source implementation, called JRuby, is written for the Java Virtual Machine. While being fully compatible with Ruby MRI, it offers certain advantages. First, since it is implemented on top of the Java Virtual Machine (JVM), JRuby threads are mapped to the kernel threads, and Unicode strings are automatically supported in JRuby. Second, JRuby can seamlessly interoperate with Java. Meaning, that we can use Java objects as normal Ruby objects, and vice versa. Hence, we can exploit the wealth of Java libraries, using the power of Ruby's flexible syntax. To demonstrate the interoperability between JRuby and Java, we use the following Java listing in which we define the Foo Java class.

```
package org.test;
public class Foo {
  private int var = 0;
  public void setVar(int v) {
    var = v;
  }
  public int getVar() {
    return var;
  }
  public void method1() {
    System.out.println("In Java "+var);
  }
  public static void method2(Foo obj) {
    obj.method1();
  }
}
```

We compile the class and put it in the example.jar library. Now, we can use the Foo class in JRuby. To demonstrate this, we write the Ruby program 'test_program.rb', shown in Fig. 1.

```
[ 1]  require 'java'
[ 2]  require 'example.jar'
[ 3]  include_class 'org.test.Foo'
[ 4]  class Bar < Foo
[ 5]    def method1
[ 6]      puts "In Ruby "+var.to_s
[ 7]    end
[ 8]  end
[ 9]  java_object = Foo.new
[10]  ruby_object = Bar.new
[11]  ruby_object.var = 10
[12]  Foo::method2 java_object
[13]  Foo::method2 ruby_object
```

Fig. 1. The code of the 'test_program.rb' script

Since the native Java classes in JRuby are wrapped inside the java module, we include this module in the first line of the script. To access the Foo class, we require example.jar as a Ruby module, and include the class from it's package in lines 2 and 3. Next, we define a Ruby class, called Bar, by subclassing the Foo class. In the Bar class code, we override method1 to print a Ruby message.

We create the two Ruby objects, named java_object and ruby_object, in lines 9 and 10. In line 11, it looks like we are directly setting the var field of ruby_object. This however is not allowed, since we don't have access to the private fields of the base class. JRuby instead, calls the provided Java setter method `setVar`, inherited from `Foo`, and passes value 10 to the method. Similarly, JRuby calls the getter method `getVar` when we try to read from `var` in line 6. Finally, we send the two objects to the static Java method of the `Foo` class, in lines 12 and 13. When we execute the program, it prints the following output:

```
$ jruby test_program.rb
In Java 0
In Ruby 10
```

We can see that during the second call, when we send `ruby_object` to the Java world, the Ruby version of `method1` gets called inside the code of the Java class.

We use the described interoperability features extensively to embed, configure and manipulate a Java SIP application server inside the code of a converged Web and SIP JRuby application.

4 Cipango SIP Application Server

In the telecom Next Generation Networks paradigm, SIP is one of the core protocols used in the Service Delivery Platforms. These platforms can be built around Java Enterprise Edition (EE) [19] servers, extended to support SIP Servlet specification [10]. Using these extensions, applications that support SIP services can be built in Java with SIP servlets, in a similar way Web applications are built with HTTP servlets. Applications are deployed to Java EE servers in the `war` archives. The server unpacks the archive, initializes the application and invokes it when an appropriate HTTP or SIP message is received, or when a certain event occurs. Technique similar to this is used in the open source TorqueBox project [15] to deploy JRuby applications to the Mobicents SIP application server [20]. However, with this approach it can be difficult to access from JRuby some features provided by the application server. For instance, creating and controlling the SIP servlet timers.

In this paper, we use another approach. The open source Cipango SIP/HTTP Servlet Application Server, built on top of the Jetty Web Server [21], supports an interesting option of embedding. Using this option, instead of deploying an application to the server, we incorporate the server engine in our application and control it completely.

The Cipango engine consists of the core classes that are shown in Fig. 2. To embed the engine, we need to create the following Java objects in a JRuby application:

- one `Server` instance,
- a number of connector instances that specify the sockets used for communication,
- at least one `SipAppContext` that represents a context in which we add SIP and HTTP servlets, and finally,
- a number of `SipServlet` and `HttpServlet` instances that we use inside the context to handle the specific HTTP and SIP requests and/or responses.

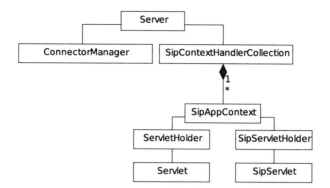

Fig. 2. Core Cipango classes

5   The Demo Application

When a SIP VoIP client starts up, it sends a SIP REGISTER request to the
SIP registrar server. The request has a dual purpose. It is used to authenti-
cate the user, and provide the server with the current IP location of the user.
Here, we build a simple registrar server with JRuby. Besides processing the SIP
REGISTER messages, the application provides a simple Web interface for ad-
ministration purposes.

We first prepare the Web interface, by using the Rails framework. Then, we
create the application in which we embed the Cipango SIP engine. Inside the
application code, we configure the Cipango engine to host the Rails generated
Web interface, and to handle the SIP REGISTER messages using the SIP servlet
defined in the application.

5.1   Building the Database and Web Interface

We start building the application by downloading the latest JRuby distribution
archive from the JRuby Web site [22]. After uncompressing the archive, we add
the **bin** directory of the JRuby distribution to the system path, since we use the
command line interface to build the application.

Next, using the **gem** infrastructure, we install the Rails framework and the
SQLite3 database adapter.

```
$ jruby -S gem install rails \
    activerecord-jdbcsqlite3-adapter --no-ri --no-rdoc
```

The previous command installed the latest Rails framework to the JRuby
distribution, but without the default documentation.

To build the Web interface from scratch we use the Rails code generators,
which we invoke from the command line. For the deeper understanding of these
commands, we direct the reader to [23] and [24].

We first build the skeleton Rails project called **registrar** by issuing the
following command:

```
$ jruby -S rails new registrar --template http://jruby.org
```

Based on the template for JRuby Rails applications, this created the `registrar` project directory, together with the subdirectories that hold the default Rails project infrastructure.

Next, in the project's directory, in order to construct the Web interface for user administration, we execute the `generate scaffold` command:

```
$ jruby -S rails generate scaffold sip_user \
    user_name:string first_name:string last_name:string
```

As described in [23], Rails is based on the MVC design pattern. The previous command created the model, view and controller classes for the `sip_user` resource with the following three fields of the string type: `user_name`, `first_name` and `last_name`. Before we can access this resource through the Web interface for CRUD (create, read, update and delete) operations, we need to build the database to hold the resource data. The previous command has also generated the migration script, which we use to create the SQLite database with the appropriate schema that describes the resource. To start the migration process and generate the production database, we execute the following Rake `db:migrate` command.

```
$ jruby -S rake db:migrate RAILS_ENV=production
```

We are done building the database and Web interface, which is shown in Fig. 3. Now, we need to add the required Java libraries to the registrar project in order to provide the SIP protocol support for our application.

Fig. 3. Rails generated Web interface

5.2 Adding the Java Libraries

We download the Cipango application server distribution, version 1.0.0, from its Web site [13]. After we uncompress the Cipango distribution, from the distribution's `lib` directory, we need the following jar files: `cipango`, `jetty`, `jetty-util`, `servlet-api`, `sip-api`, and also `cipango-dar` from the `lib/ext` folder. In the

Rails `registrar` project directory, we create the `jars` folder. This is where we copy the required jar files from the Cipango distribution.

To host the Rails generated Web interface, we also need the JRuby-Rack library [25]. This library was developed specifically to enable the hosting of JRuby Web applications, inside Java EE-compliant servers. We use the JRuby-Rack library to connect the Rails generated code with the embedded Cipango server. The library is provided in a single jar file, which we obtain from its Web site [25]. We copy the downloaded JRuby-Rack jar file to the `jars` directory of the `registrar` project.

5.3   Creating the Converged Application

To glue the entire project together, we create the JRuby application in a file called 'application.rb', which we save in the top level directory of the Rails `registrar` project. The application code is shown in Fig. 4.

In line 2 of the Fig. 4 listing, in order to gain access to the Java classes, we require all the jar files stored in the `jars` directory relative to the current path. We include the Java classes from their packages in lines 5-19, which are omitted from the listing for simplicity. We later explain the purpose and content of 'my_factories.rb' and 'my_sip_servlet.rb', the files we require in lines 3 and 4.

```
[ 1] require 'java'
[ 2] Dir["jars/*.jar"].each { |jar| require jar }
[ 3] require 'my_factories'
[ 4] require 'my_sip_servlet'
[ 5]
... < include the necessary Java classes > ...
[19]
[20] cipango = Server.new
[21] context_collection = SipContextHandlerCollection.new
[22] cipango.handler = context_collection
[23]
... < setup TCP and UDP connectors > ...
[29]
[30] context = SipAppContext.new
[31] context.resource_base = "."
[32] context.context_path = "/"
[33] context.add_servlet( ServletHolder.new( DefaultServlet.new), "/*" )
[34] context.init_params = HashMap.new(
[35]    'org.mortbay.jetty.servlet.Default.relativeResourceBase' => '/public',
[36]    'rackup' => File.read('config.ru'),
[37]    'jruby.max.runtimes' => '1'
[38] )
[39] context.add_filter("org.jruby.rack.RackFilter", "/*", Handler::DEFAULT)
[40] context.add_event_listener( MyListener.new )
[41] my_sip_servlet = MySipServlet.new
[42] context.add_event_listener( my_sip_servlet )
[43] context.add_sip_servlet( SipServletHolder.new(my_sip_servlet) )
[44] context_collection.add_handler(context)
[45] cipango.start
[46] cipango.join
```

Fig. 4. Ruby application which embeds the Cipango server

In lines 20-22, we start embedding the Cipango engine by creating the `Server` instance and assigning a handler to the server. The handler processes the SIP and HTTP messages received by the server. Next, we define and configure the two server connectors, the UDP connector for the SIP traffic and the TCP connector for the HTTP traffic, with the corresponding ports 5060 and 3000. For simplicity, we omitted the code of the connectors setup from the listing.

We create the converged application context in line 30, and configure it in lines 31-38. More specifically, in lines 31-32, we set the current directory as the resource base for the converged application, and map the application to the root URL of the server. Next, in line 33 we add the default Jetty servlet to the application context. We use it to handle the requests for static content of our Web interface. Therefore, in line 35, we initialize the Jetty servlet resource base to the `public` directory of the `registrar` project, where we store the static content of the Rails application. We incorporate the entire Web interface, generated with Rails, by adding the servlet filter to the converged context in line 39. We use the servlet filter class called `RackFilter`, which is provided by the JRuby-Rack library. This servlet filter detects if an HTTP request matches a dynamic URL handled by the Rails generated interface. If the request is matched, the filter uses the Rails framework to process the request. Otherwise, it just passes the request to the other servlets in the converged context. Therefore, if the request is for static content, such as images, css and javascript files, the filter passes the request to the default Jetty servlet, which we previously added to the context.

We now need to modify the default behaviour of the JRuby-Rack library. The library usually operates in the mode where a Rails application is deployed to a Java EE server in a single `war` archive, together with the complete Ruby on Rails and JRuby distributions. Since there is no JRuby runtime in the server's JVM, JRuby-Rack creates the runtime and initializes it with the Rails environment. The library then starts the servlet filter operations and connects the created runtime with the Java server using the `RackFilter` object. Since we are running the Cipango server embedded in a JRuby application, we override the default behaviour and force JRuby-Rack to use the application's JRuby runtime, instead of creating a new one. We do this in line 40, by providing the converged application context with a custom listener object of the `MyListener` class. `MyListener` class is defined in the 'my_factories.rb' file shown in Fig. 5.

We can see that inside the `MyListener` class we override the `newApplicationFactory` method, inherited from the `RackServletContextListener` Java class. We implement this method to return a custom factory object, which is used for JRuby runtime creation when the converged application context is initialized. The custom factory object is of the `MyFactory` class. We define this class inside the same file. In this class we only override the inherited `newRuntime` method. We change the method so that, instead of creating and returning a brand new JRuby runtime, it returns the current runtime in which the application is already running. Furthermore, we perform the necessary initialization of the application's runtime to prepare it for the `RackFilter` operations.

```
['org.jruby.rack.DefaultRackApplicationFactory',
 'org.jruby.rack.SharedRackApplicationFactory',
 'org.jruby.rack.RackServletContextListener',
 'org.jruby.Ruby'
].each {|c| include_class c }

class MyFactory < DefaultRackApplicationFactory
  field_accessor :rackContext
  def newRuntime
    runtime = Ruby.get_global_runtime
    $servlet_context=rackContext
    require 'rack/handler/servlet'
    return runtime
  end
end
class MyListener < RackServletContextListener
  field_reader :factory
  def newApplicationFactory(context)
    if factory
      return factory
    else
      return (
        SharedRackApplicationFactory.new(MyFactory.new)
      )
    end
  end
end
```

Fig. 5. The code of the 'my_factories.rb' file

In line 36, we configure the JRuby-Rack library to load 'config.ru', a Web application configuration file generated by Rails in the top level directory of the project.

To handle the SIP traffic, we create and add a sip servlet object to the converged application context, in lines 41-43 of the Fig. 4 listing. This object is an instance of the MySipServlet class, which we define in 'my_sip_servlet.rb' file. We implement the MySipServlet class with the following code:

```
include_class 'javax.servlet.sip.SipServlet'
include_class 'javax.servlet.sip.SipSessionListener'
class MySipServlet < SipServlet
  include SipSessionListener
  def doRegister(request)
    user_name=request.get_from.get_uri.get_user
    user=SipUser.find_by_user_name(user_name)
    if user
      request.create_response(200).send
    else
      request.create_response(404).send
    end
  end

  def sessionCreated(event)
    ... < handle the event > ...
  end
end
```

By defining the doRegister method of the SIP servlet, we only process the SIP REGISTER requests. Inside the method, from the received SIP request, we first extract the user name. Then, using the Rails generated model class SipUser, we query the system database for a valid user with the extracted user name. If we find the user in the database, we return the 200 'OK' response, meaning that the current user has successfully registered. Otherwise, we send the 404 'Not fould' (User not found) response. For simplicity, we omit the operations a normal registrar server would perform, such as user authentication and keeping track of the user's IP number.

Finally, in line 44 of the Fig. 4 listing, we add the application context to `context_collection` of the server, and start the server in line 45.

We execute the application using the command:

```
$ jruby application.rb
```

Once the application is fully initialized and running, we can create, update and delete the users of the registrar server through the Web interface on port 3000, and the URL shown in Fig. 3.

Furthermore, we can configure a SIP VoIP client to register with our application by providing: a valid user name, port 5060, and the IP address of our application, or a fully qualified host name. Figure 6 shows a successful registration of the Linphone Linux SIP client with the registrar application.

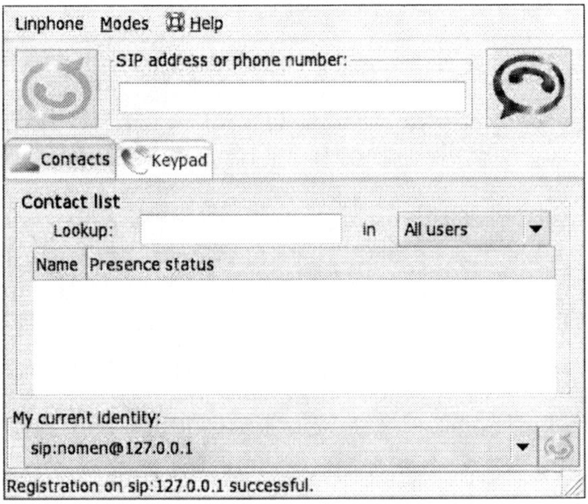

Fig. 6. Successful registration of a SIP VoIP client

By utilizing the approach presented in this paper, Ruby objects can also be registered as handlers to specific events generated by the server. To demonstrate this feature, as an example, `MySipServlet` class implements the SIP Servlet API interface `SipSessionListener`. The Ruby servlet object is registered with the application to receive events in line 42 of the Fig. 4 listing. When session creation event is generated by the server, the application invokes the `sessionCreated` method on the servlet object. Other events can be processed in a similar manner.

6   Conclusion

In this paper, we have presented an infrastructure that supports development of full featured converged Web and SIP applications entirely in Ruby. The infrastructure is based on an embedded Cipango SIP/HTTP Servlet Application Server, a lightweight SIP/HTTP server based on the Jetty Web Server. We have presented a simple demo application only as an example on how to use this infrastructure. By adding handcrafted Rails code, and redefining inherited servlet methods of the `MySipServlet` class, we could extend our application further. For instance, we could easily provide a Web page where a user could examine the currently registered users, and start a voice communication, by clicking on the appropriate links.

The Ruby application shown in Fig. 4 is flexible enough so that we could use it to serve a different Rails application, without any modifications of the code. Furthermore, by changing the 'config.ru' file loaded in line 36 of Fig. 4, we could incorporate a Web interface developed with another Rack-compatible Web framework, such as the Sinatra.

To handle the SIP signaling in JRuby, we relied on the Java SIP servlet API, as implemented by the Cipango engine. This is adequate for a simple application. However, for the more complex SIP call flows, it would be beneficial to develop, on top of the described infrastructure, a custom Ruby DSL for SIP handling. This DSL could provide the Ruby language a flexible SIP service support similar to the one the Rails framework provides for Web services. This infrastructure can be used as a good starting base for development of DSLs and other facilities for VoIP application development utilizing the full potential of SIP Servlet API and Ruby programming language.

References

1. Tratt, L.: Dynamically Typed Languages. Advances in Computers 77, 149–184 (2009)
2. Paulson, L.D.: Developers Shift to Dynamic Programming Languages. Computer 40, 12–15 (2007)
3. Tate, B.: Beyond Java. Reilly Media (2005)
4. Flanagan, D., Matsumoto, Y.: The Ruby Programming Language, 1st edn. OReilly Media, Sebastopol (2008)
5. Bachle, M., Kirchberg, P.: Ruby on Rails. IEEE Software 24, 105–108 (2007)
6. Mizerany, B.: Sinatra, http://www.sinatrarb.com
7. Ghosh, D.: DSLs in Action, 1st edn. Manning Publications (2010)
8. Gunther, S.: Multi-DSL Applications with Ruby. IEEE Software 27, 25–30 (2010)
9. Rosenberg, J., Schulzrinne, H., Camarillo, G., Johnston, A., Peterson, J., Sparks, R., Handley, M., Schooler, E.: SIP: Session Initiation Protocol. RFC 3261 (Proposed Standard) (2002), updated by RFCs 3265, 3853, 4320, 4916, 5393, 5621, http://www.ietf.org/rfc/rfc3261.txt
10. Cosmadopoulos, Y., Kulkarni, M.: SIP Servlet v1.1. JSR 289 (2008), http://jcp.org/en/jsr/detail?id=289

11. Ferry, D.: JAIN SLEE (JSLEE) v1.1. JSR 240 (2008),
    http://jcp.org/en/jsr/detail?id=240
12. Hasanovic, A., Suljanovic, N., Mujcic, A., Sernec, R.: Dynamic Languages Integration Path for Telecom Applications. In: The Fourth International Conference on Digital Telecommunications, Colmar, France, pp. 133–137 (2009)
13. Cipango - SIP/HTTP Servlets Application Server, http://cipango.org
14. Nutter, C.O., Enebo, T., Sieger, N., Bini, O., Dees, I.: Using JRuby: Bringing Ruby to Java, 1st edn. Pragmatic Bookshelf (2011)
15. TorqueBox, http://torquebox.org
16. Rack: a Ruby Webserver Interface, http://rack.rubyforge.org/
17. JBoss, http://jboss.org
18. Broeglin, D.: Sipatra, http://confluence.cipango.org/display/DOC/Sipatra
19. Java Platform, Enterprise Edition (Java EE) Technical Documentation, http://download.oracle.com/javaee/
20. Mobicents, http://www.mobicents.org
21. Jetty - Servlet Engine and HTTP Server, http://www.eclipse.org/jetty/
22. JRuby, http://jruby.org
23. Viswanathan, V.: Rapid Web Application Development: A Ruby on Rails Tutorial. IEEE Software 25(6), 98–106 (2008)
24. Ruby on Rails Guides, http://guides.rubyonrails.org
25. Sieger, N.: JRuby-Rack, https://github.com/nicksieger/jruby-rack

XML Documents – Publishing from Relational Databases

Mihai Stancu

Faculty of Mathematics and Computer Science,
Department of Computer Science,
University of Craiova, Romania
`mihai.stancu@yahoo.com`

Abstract. XML language tends to become a standard for data exchanges between various Web applications. However, despite the big extent of the XML language, most of this applications store their information in relational databases. This fact is unlikely to be changed considering many advantages of the relational database systems like: fiability, scalability, performance and working tools. Thus, while XML language is under development, the necessity of some mechanism to publish XML documents from relational databases is obvious.

Keywords: XML, databases, publishing.

1 Introduction

Currently, the main research issues related to XML documents are: XML documents publishing, validity and typechecking of published XML documents and storing the XML documents. In this paper we will consider the issue of publishing XML documents.

The process of publishing relational data in XML documents needs two requirements to be accomplished. First requirement is a language that can specify the conversion beetwen relational data and XML documents. The second requirement refers to an efficient implementation of the conversion mechanism. The language specification describe the way that the records from one or more tables are structured and tagged to the hierarchical XML document. Considering a conversion language of this kind, an efficient implementation of the conversion mechanism raises many problems: the relational information is flat, while XML documents are hierarchical and tagged. In this paper we will analyze different variants of implementations for publishing XML documents.

The rest of this paper is organized as follows. Section 2 provides a short overview of XML language and defines a transformation language specification. Section 3 presents the space of alternatives for XML publishing and a comparison of these alternatives. The section 4 describes node outer union approach. Section 5 analyzes some potential problems that can arrive when implementing node outer union approach and provides a usefull way to avoid them. Section 6 presents some conclusions and future work directions.

V. Snasel, J. Platos, and E. El-Qawasmeh (Eds.): ICDIPC 2011, Part I, CCIS 188, pp. 85–96, 2011.

2   An Generic Transformation Language Specification

Extensible Markup Language (XML) [8] is a hierarchical data representation standard for information exchange in Web. Many industry proposals [11] standardize document type descriptors (DTDs) [8], which are basically schemas for XML documents. These DTDs are being developed for domains as diverse as Business Solutions, Outsourcing [10] and Manufacturing [12]. Other alternative to DTDs is XMLSchema [13] that provides a detailed way to define data constraints. An XML document is a structure of nested elements, starting from one root element. Each element has an associated tag and can have attributes with associated values and/or nested elements. Figure 1 represents an XML document that store information for a web application in a version management tool.

```
<application id="C1">
        <name> Case Management </name>
        <versions>
                <version id="CN1"> 1 </version>
                <version id="CN2"> 2 </version>
        </versions>
        < modules >
                < module id="CE1" vers="CN2">
                        <date> 1 January 2006 </date>
                        <controllers>
                                <controller id="I1"> Dispatcher controller </controller>
                                <controller id="I2"> Download controller </controller>
                        </controllers>
                        <views>
                                <view id="P1"> /pages/login.jspx </ view>
                                <view id="P2"> /pages/home.jspx </ view>
                                <view id="P3"> /pages/download.jspx </view>
                        </views>
                </ module>
                < module id="CE2" vers="CN1">
                        ....
                </ module>
        </ modules>
</ application>
```

Fig. 1. An XML document that describes an application

The application is represented by <application> element that is the document's root. The application has an id attribute with C1 value. The id attribute is a special one that has the role to uniqely identify another element from the XML document. Each application has a name denote by <name> subelement of the application element. Also, application element has subelements for his versions and modules. More details on XML can be found in [7].

We need a generic transformation language to define the conversion from relational data to XML documents. We will consider a SQL-based language in witch nested SQL clauses are used to model the imbrication and SQL functions are used for XML element construction [4].

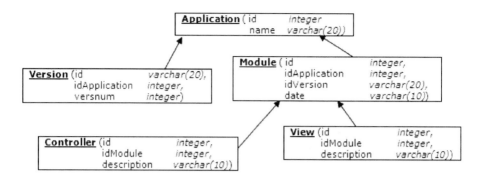

Fig. 2. Application relational schema

We should consider the relational schema in Figure 2 that models the application information in Figure 1 in a relational form. The tables considered are: Application, Version, Module, Controller and View. Each table contains an id field that is a primary key and the relations between the tables are accomplished by foreign keys identifiable by arrows. In order to convert data in this relational schema to the XML document in Figure 1, we can write an SQL query which follows the nested structure of the document, as there can be seen in Figure 3.

```
01. Select app.name APP(app.id, app.name
02.                 ( Select XMLAGG(VERS(vers.id, vers.versnum))
03.                     From Version vers
04.                     Where vers.idApplication = app.id),
05.                 ( Select XMLAGG(MODL(modl.id, modl.idVersion, modl.date,
06.                             ( Select XMLAGG(CONTROLLER(controller.id, controller.description))
07.                                 From Controller controller
08.                                 Where controller.idModule = modl.id),
09.                             ( Select XMLAGG(VIEW(view.id, view.description))
10.                                 From View view
11.                                 Where view.idModule = modl.id)))
12.                     group order by modl.date
13.                     From Module modl
14.                     Where modl.idApplication = app.id))
15. From Application app
```

Fig. 3. SQL query to construct XML documents from relational data

The query in Figure 3 produces both SQL and XML data. Each resulted tuple contains the name of the application together with the XML representation of the application. The entire query consists of a number of correlated sub-queries. Analysing the query from top to bottom we can see that on the first level, the highest one, there is the query that elicits each application from the Application table. For each application, there are used correlated sub-queries in order to retrieve the application's versions (lines 02-04), respectively the modules (lines 05-14).

The definition of XML APP constructor can be seen in Figure 4. Conceptually, it is perceived as a scalar function that returns an XML. For each tuple, it tags the specific columns producing thus an XML fragment.

```
create function APP (idApplication: integer, nameApplication: varchar(20), listVersions: xml, listModules: xml)
returns xml language xml return
<application id={idApplication} >
<name> {nameApplication} </name>
<versions> {listVersions} </versions>
<modules> {listModules} </modules>
</application>
```

Fig. 4. An XML constructor definition

The other correlated sub-queries can be similarly interpreted with the VERS, MODL, CONTROLLER and VIEW constructors, analogous to APP. This way each nested query returns an XML fragment. The XMLAGG aggregate function is used to concatenate these XML fragments produced by the constructors.

To order XML fragments, the XMLAGG aggregate function must get ordered inputs. For example, to order the modules achieved by a application chronologically we must make sure that the XMLAGG function from line 05 of Figure 3 concatenates the modules in this exact order. Because the ordered inputs for aggregation functions are not born by the SQL standard, extensions of the SQL language that tolerate this facility can be used. Such an extension can be the introduction of the group order by clause as there can be seen in Figure 3 line 12, to chronologically order a application's modules before they are introduces in the aggregate XMLAGG function.

3   Variants of Implementation

To be able to analyse the alternatives for publishing relational data as XML documents we have to take into account the main difference between the relational tables and the XML documents which means that XML documents, unlike the relational tables, have tags and nested structure. Therefore, somewhere along the process of converting relational tables to XML documents, the tags and the structure must be added. We can thus distinguish several possibilities of approaching and that is the adding of tags during the final step of the query processing (late-tagging) or by doing this at the beginning of the process (early-tagging). Similarly, the structure

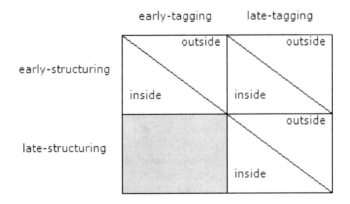

Fig. 5. Space of alternatives for XML documents publishing [4]

adding can be done as the final step of processing (late-structuring) or it can be done earlier (early-structuring) [4]. These two dimensions of tagging and structuring gave rise to a space of processing alternatives represented in Figure 5.

All these alternatives have variants that depend on accomplishing these operations inside or outside the SGBD. We should see that inside refers to the fact that tagging and structuring are completely accomplished inside the relational engine, while outside, the fact that these operations are done totally outside the relational engine. There can also be observed that early-tagging and late-structuring is not a viable variant because the tagging of an XML document cannot be done without already having its structure.

Comparative studies of these alternatives [4] show the advantages and disadvantages for each one and when it is useful to choose one or another alternative. The main characteristics have been summarized in Figure 6.

The qualitative assessments indicate that every alternative has some potential disadvantage. Taking into account the various implementations of the presented approaches, we can draw the following conclusions:

Clasification		Approach	Description	Potential problems
Early-structuring Early-tagging	Outside	Stored procedure	Perform separate queries conform to document's structure by doing iterative nested joins outside the relational engine.	1) Many SQL queries. 2) Fixed join strategy (iterative nested joins).
	Inside	correlated CLOB	Internal variant of the stored procedure approach. Use CLOB fields to construct intermediate XML fragments.	1) Fixed join strategy (iterative nested joins). 2) Many intermediate CLOB fields created during query processing.
	Inside	De-correlated CLOB	De-correlated version of the corelattes CLOB approach. Use also intermediate CLOB fields.	1) Many intermediate CLOB fields created during query processing.
Late-structuring Late-tagging	Inside or outside	Redundant relation	Create a relation with redundancy because each child of a parent is repeated many times.	1) Data redundancy. 2) Memory overflow in the hash-based tagging mechanism.
	Inside or outside	Unsorted path outer union	Create outer union of the leaf elements to avoid redundancy. Use a hash-based tagging mechanism.	1) Data redundancy (on a smaller scale). 2) Memory overflow in the hash-based tagging mechanism. 3) Wide tuples.
	Inside or outside	Unsorted node outer union	Similar to unsorted path outer union, but include also tuples for non-leaf elements in outer union.	1) Memory overflow in the hash-based tagging mechanism. 2) Wide tuples.
Early-structuring Late-tagging	Inside or outside	Sorted path uuter union	Structure the results of unsorted path outer union by sorting these results in document order.	1) Data redundancy (on a smaller scale). 2) Wide tuples. 3) Require total order of Relational result.
	Inside or outside	Sorted node outer union	Structure the results of unsorted node outer union by sorting these results in document order.	1) Wide tuples. 2) Require total order of Relational result.

Fig. 6. Approaches for publishing XML documents

1. Building XML documents inside the relational system is more efficient than outside it
2. When processing can be done only by using the main memory, the unsorted outer union approach is stable always among the best (inside or outside)
3. When processing cannot be done just by using the main memory, the sorted outer union approach (inside or outside) is the choice. This is due to the fact that the relational sorting operator scales very easily.

Performance evaluation of the alternatives was done [4] in order to determine which ones are likely to win in practice (and in what situations). Seen as a whole, the main disadvantages of the outer union approaches are not significant. They refer to the fact that tuples of large sizes are created but with many null values. The efficient methods of compressing null values can considerably reduce the size of the tuples appeared as a result of outer union.

4 Early-Structuring, Late-Tagging

These alternatives try to diminuate the disadvantages from the late tagging and late structuring approaches that is the hash-based tagger that needs to perform complex memory management when memory is insufficient. To eliminate this problem, the relational engine can be used to produce "structured relational content", which can then be tagged by using a constant space tagger.

4.1 Sorted Node Outer Union Approach

The key to structuring relational content is to order it the same way that it needs to appear in the result XML document. This can be achieved by ensuring that:
1. The information of any parent node appear before or along with any of his descendant's information.
2. All the information of a parent node and his descendants appear successively in the sequence of tuples.
3. The information of a node of a certain type appear before the information of any of his seablings of other type.
4. The tuples order respect any other criteria defined by the user.

In order to ensure the following of the four conditions, we only need to sort the results of the node outer union approach on the id field and follow the criteria the user has defined [4], so that:

- the id field of a parent node comes before the id fields of his children
- the id field of a brother node comes in the reversed order of the brother nodes sorting in XML document;
- the sorting fields of a node defined by the user come right before the id node of that particular node.

Thus, in our example, sorting the result on the node outer union method will be done on the sequence: (*AppId, VersId, POId, ControllerId, ViewId*). This way the results will be sorted in document order.

The query execution plan and the corresponding SQL query are shown in Figures 7, 8 and 9.

For the operations to be done correctly the user-defined sorting fields must be propagated from a parent node to the descending nodes before outer union as shown in Figure 9. We must also make sure that tuples having null values in the sort fields occur before tuples having non-null values for these fields (null-low sort). This is necessary for us to be sure that parents and brothers come in right order.

The sorted outer union approach has the advantage of scaling large data volumes because relational database sorting is disk-friendly. The approach can also ensure user-specified orderings with little additional cost. However, it does do more work than necessary, since a total order is produced when only a partial order is needed.

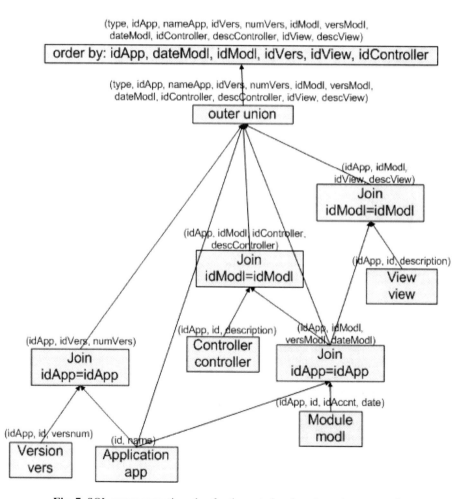

Fig. 7. SQL query execution plan for the sorted node outer union approach

```
-- We compute all paths from root to leafs
01. with app (idApp integer, nameApp varchar(20)) as (
02.     select app.id, app.name
03.     from Application app
04. ),
05. versApp (idApp integer, idVers integer, numVers integer) as (
02.     select app.id, vers.id, vers.versnum
03.     from Version vers, app
04.     where vers.idApplication = app.id
05. ),
06. modlApp (idApp integer, idModl integer, versionModl varchar(20), dateModl varchar(10)) as (
07.     select app.id, modl.id, modl.idVersion, modl.date
08.     from app, Module modl
09.     where app.id = modl.idApplication
10. ),
11. controllerModlApp (idApp integer, idModl integer, idController integer, descController varchar(20)) as (
12.     select modlapp.idApp, modlapp.idModl, controller.id, controller.description
13.     from Controller controller, modlApp modlapp
14.     where controller.idModule = modlapp.idModl
15. ),
16. viewModlApp (idApp integer, idModl integer, idView integer, descView varchar(20)) as (
17.     select modlapp.idApp, modlapp.idModl, view.id, view.description
18.     from modlApp modlapp, View view
19.     where modlapp.idModl = view.idModule
20. ),
21. -- Main query that make node outer union
22. select 0, idApp, nameApp, null, null, null, null, null, null, null, null, null
23. from app
24.     union all
25. select 1, idApp, null, idVers, numVers, null, null, null, null, null, null, null
26. from versApp
27.     union all
28. select 2, idApp, null, null, null, idModl, versionModl, dateModl, null, null, null, null
29. from modlApp
30.     union all
31. select 3, idApp, null, null, null, idModl, null, null, idController, descController, null, null
32. from controllerModlApp
33.     union all
34. select 4, idApp, null, null, null, idModl, null, null, null, null, idView, descView
35. from viewModlApp
```

Fig. 8. SQL query for the unsorted node outer union approach

```
-- The lines 1-38 compute node outer union  same like in figure 8
01.
... //compute node outer union into "NOU" temporary table
38. ),
39. - Main query that sort the results of outer union
40. select type, idApp, nameApp, idVers, numVers, idModl, versionModl, dateModl, idController, descController,
idView, descView
40. from outerUnion
41. order by idApp, dateModl, idModl, idVers, idView, idController
```

Fig. 9. SQL query for the sorted node outer union approach

4.2 Constant Space Tagger

Once structured content is created, the last step is to tag and construct the result XML document. Since tuples arrive in document order, they can be immediately tagged and written out. The tagger only requires memory to remember the *id* field of the last parent. These ids are used to detect when all the children of a particular parent node have been seen so that the closing tag associated with the parent can be written out. For example, after all the controllers and views of a module have been seen, the closing tag for module (</module>) has to be written out. To detect this, the tagger stores the id of the current module and compares it with that of the next tuple. The storage space required by the constant space tagger is proportional only to the level of nesting and is independent of the size of the XML document.

5 Sample Implementation and Fine-Tuning

Considering the conclusions from previouse section, we will try to implement XML documents publishing using node outer union approach. Choosing the sorted or unsorted variant depends by the size of the data volume that need's to be processed. Despite that memory allocation problems are permanently supported by hardware evolution, the high data volume needed by applications is growing in time so that the maintenance process of these applications can be problematic. In these conditions, the sorted node outer union approach can be a viable option.

```
CREATE OR REPLACE VIEW "public"."app" (idapp, nameapp) AS SELECT "Application".id AS idapp,
"Application".name AS nameapp FROM "Application";

CREATE OR REPLACE VIEW "public"."versApp" (idapp, idvers, numvers) AS SELECT app.idapp, "Version".id AS
idvers, "Version".versnum AS numvers FROM "Version", app WHERE ("Version"."idApplication" = app.idapp);

CREATE OR REPLACE VIEW "public"."modlapp" (idapp, idmodl, accountmodl, datemodl) AS SELECT app.idapp,
"Module".id AS idmodl, "Module"."idVersion" AS versionmodl, "Module".date AS datemodl FROM app, "Module"
WHERE (app.idapp = "Module"."idApplication");

CREATE OR REPLACE VIEW "public"."controllermodlapp" (idapp, idmodl, datemodl, idcontroller, desccontroller)
AS SELECT modlapp.idapp, modlapp.idmodl, modlapp.datemodl, "Controller".id AS idcontroller,
"Controller".description AS desccontroller FROM "Controller", modlapp WHERE ("Controller"."idModule" =
modlapp.idmodl);

CREATE OR REPLACE VIEW "public"."viewmodlapp" (idapp, idmodl, datemodl, idview, descview) AS SELECT
modlapp.idapp, modlapp.idmodl, modlapp.datemodl, "View".id AS idview, "View".description AS descview
FROM modlapp, "View" WHERE (modlapp.idmodl = "View"."idModule");

CREATE OR REPLACE VIEW "public"."nou" (type, idapp, nameapp, idvers, numvers, idmodl, versionmodl,
datemodl, idcontroller, desccontroller, idview, descview) AS ((( SELECT 0 AS type, app.idapp, app.nameapp,
NULL::"unknown" AS idvers, NULL::"unknown" AS numvers, NULL::integer AS idmodl, NULL::"unknown" AS
versionmodl, NULL::date AS datemodl, NULL::integer AS idcontroller, NULL::"unknown" AS desccontroller,
NULL::integer AS idview, NULL::"unknown" AS descview FROM app

UNION ALL
SELECT 1 AS type, "versApp".idapp, NULL::"unknown" AS nameapp, "versApp".idvers, "versApp".numvers,
    NULL::integer AS idmodl, NULL::"unknown" AS versionmodl, NULL::date AS datemodl, NULL::integer AS
    idcontroller, NULL::"unknown" AS desccontroller, NULL::integer AS idview, NULL::"unknown" AS descview
FROM "versApp")

UNION ALL
SELECT 2 AS type, modlapp.idapp, NULL::"unknown" AS nameapp, NULL::"unknown" AS idvers,
    NULL::"unknown" AS numvers, modlapp.idmodl, modlapp.versionmodl, modlapp.datemodl, NULL::integer
    AS idcontroller, NULL::"unknown" AS desccontroller, NULL::integer AS idview, NULL::"unknown" AS
descview
FROM modlapp)

UNION ALL
SELECT 3 AS type, controllermodlapp.idapp, NULL::"unknown" AS nameapp, NULL::"unknown" AS idvers,
    NULL::"unknown" AS numvers, controllermodlapp.idmodl, NULL::"unknown" AS versionmodl,
temmodlapp.datemodl,
    controllermodlapp.idcontroller, controllermodlapp.desccontroller, NULL::integer AS idview, NULL::"unknown"
AS descview
FROM controllermodlapp)

UNION ALL
SELECT 4 AS type, viewmodlapp.idapp, NULL::"unknown" AS nameapp, NULL::"unknown" AS idvers,
    NULL::"unknown" AS numvers, viewmodlapp.idmodl, NULL::"unknown" AS versionmodl,
viewmodlapp.datemodl,
    NULL::"unknown" AS idcontroller, NULL::"unknown" AS desccontroller, viewmodlapp.idview,
viewmodlapp.descview
FROM viewmodlapp;
```

Fig. 10. PostgreSQL VIEWS

In this sample implementation we use PostgreSQL 8.0 [9] as the relational engine and coding was done in Java (JDK 1.4.2_05) [14]. The database connection was made through JDBC driver postgresql-8.0.309.jdbc3.jar.

Considering Postgres specific SQL syntax, the implementation of the functions *app, versApp, modlApp, controllerModlApp, viewModlApp* and *NOU* from Figure 9, was done using VIEW elements (Figure 10).

One problem met when using PostgreSQL relational database engine is that the *null* values are sortes high (null-high sort). For this publishing approach, this fact is a drawback and it was avoided by adding an additional sorting criteria for each original sorting criteria. For instance, in *order by* clause, instead of *idVers asc*, we can use *idVers not null, idVers asc*. Thus, first sorting criteria will assure us that *null* values of the sorted column will appear first in the results and the second sorting criteria will assure us the effective order of the column.

The constant space tagger was implemented in Java. The document's generation is relatively simple, done by looping through the sorting results. Additional attention is needed when closing the elements tags for parents nodes. This thing was done using a stack data structure. After we run the constant space tagger, the generated applications.xml file is obtained and can be seen in Figure 13.

The main query that sort the results of the node outer union is shown in figure 11 and the obtained results in Figure 12.

```
Select
    type, idapp, nameapp, idvers, numvers,
    idmodl, versionmodl, datemodl, idcontroller, desccontroller, idview, descview
from NOU
order by
    idapp is not null, idapp asc,
    datemodl is not null, datemodl asc, idmodl is not null, idmodl asc,
    idvers is not null, idvers asc,
    idview is not null, idview asc,
    idcontroller is not null, idcontroller asc
```

Fig. 11. Main SQL query

type	idapp	nameapp	idvers	numvers	idmodl	versionmodl	datemodl	idcontroller	desccontroller	idview	descview
0	1	Case Management	Null	Null	Null	Null	Null	Null	Null	Null	Null
1	1	Null	CN1	1	Null	Null	Null	Null	Null	Null	Null
1	1	Null	CN2	2	Null	Null	Null	Null	Null	Null	Null
2	1	Null	Null	Null	CE1	CN2	1/1/2006	Null	Null	Null	Null
3	1	Null	Null	Null	CE1	Null	1/1/2006	I1	Dispatcher controller	Null	Null
3	1	Null	Null	Null	CE1	Null	1/1/2006	I2	Download controller	Null	Null
4	1	Null	Null	Null	CE1	Null	1/1/2006	Null	Null	P1	/pages/login.jspx
4	1	Null	Null	Null	CE1	Null	1/1/2006	Null	Null	P2	/pages/home.jspx
4	1	Null	Null	Null	CE1	Null	1/1/2006	Null	Null	P3	/pages/download.jspx
2	1	Null	Null	Null	CE2	CN1	1/15/2006	Null	Null	Null	Null
3	1	Null	Null	Null	CE2	Null	1/15/2006	I3	Reports controller	Null	Null
0	2	Contracts Management	Null	Null	Null	Null	Null	Null	Null	Null	Null
1	2	Null	CN3	1	Null	Null	Null	Null	Null	Null	Null

Fig. 12. Results of the main SQL query

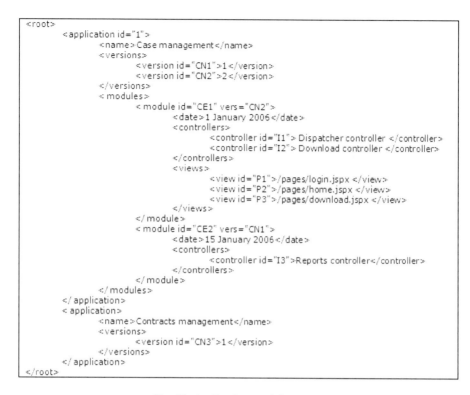

```
<root>
    <application id="1">
        <name>Case management</name>
        <versions>
            <version id="CN1">1</version>
            <version id="CN2">2</version>
        </versions>
        <modules>
            <module id="CE1" vers="CN2">
                <date>1 January 2006</date>
                <controllers>
                    <controller id="I1"> Dispatcher controller </controller>
                    <controller id="I2"> Download controller </controller>
                </controllers>
                <views>
                    <view id="P1">/pages/login.jspx </view>
                    <view id="P2">/pages/home.jspx </view>
                    <view id="P3">/pages/download.jspx </view>
                </views>
            </module>
            <module id="CE2" vers="CN1">
                <date>15 January 2006</date>
                <controllers>
                    <controller id="I3">Reports controller</controller>
                </controllers>
            </module>
        </modules>
    </application>
    <application>
        <name>Contracts management</name>
        <versions>
            <version id="CN3">1</version>
        </versions>
    </application>
</root>
```

Fig. 13. Applications.xml document

6   Conclusions and Future Work

In this paper we have presented various alternatives for XML publishing from relational database systems and we focus on a specific alternative. We analyzed potential problems that can rise for node outer union implementation and we found some way to avoid them.

The future work can include various possibilities as the impact of parallelism, the addition of new operators inside the relational database engine to increase the performance of the outer union execution, and the design of efficient memory management techniques for unsorted outer union approach.

References

1. Suciu, D.: On Database Theory and XML. SIGMOD Record 30(3) (2001)
2. Fernandez, M., Kadiyska, Y., Suciu, D., Morishima, A., Tan, W.: SilkRoute: A Framework for Publishing Relational Data in XML. ACM Transactions on Database Systems 27(4), 438–493 (2002)

3. Carey, M., Florescu, D., Ives, Z., Lu, Y., Shanmugasundaram, J., Shekita, E., Subramanian, S.: XPERANTO: Publishing Object-Relational Data as XML. In: International Workshop on the Web and Databases (2000)
4. Jayavel, S., Eugene, S., Rimon, B., Michael, C., Bruce, L., Hamid, P., Berthold, R.: Effciently publishing relational data as XML documents. The VLDB Journal (2001)
5. Seshadri, P., Pirahesh, H., Leung, T.Y.C.: Complex Query Decorrelation. In: Proc. International Conference on Data Engineering (ICDE), La, USA (1996)
6. Fagin, R.: Multi-valued Dependencies and a New Normal Form for Relational Databases. ACM Transactions on Database Systems 2(3) (1977)
7. Rusty, H., Scott Means, W.: Xml in a Nutshell. O'Reilly & Associates, Inc., Sebastopol (2004)
8. W3C - World Wide Web Consortium, Extensible Markup Language (XML) 1.1 (2nd edn), W3C Recommendation (2006), http://www.w3.org/TR/xml11/
9. PostgreSQL, PostgreSQL - Documentation, http://www.postgresql.org/docs/
10. LionBridge, http://en-us.lionbridge.com/Default.aspx?LangType=1033
11. Cover R., The XML Cover Pages, http://www.xml.coverpages.org/
12. PLUS Vision Corp., http://www.plus-vision.com/
13. W3C - World Wide Web Consortium, XML Schema, W3C Candidate Recommendation (2004), http://www.w3.org/TR/xmlschema-2/
14. Oracle, Java Platform - Standard Edition, http://www.oracle.com/technetwork/java/javase/overview/index.html

Simple Rules for Syllabification of Arabic Texts

Hussein Soori, Jan Platos, Vaclav Snasel, and Hussam Abdulla

Department of Computer Science, Faculty of Electrical Engineering and Computer Science,
VSB-Technical University of Ostrava, 17. listopadu 15,
70833 Ostrava, Czech Republic
{sen.soori,jan.platos,vaclav.snasel,hussam.dahwa}@vsb.cz

Abstract. The Arabic language is the sixth most used language in the world today. It is also used by United Nation. Moreover, the Arabic alphabet is the second most widely used alphabet around the world. Therefore, the computer processing of Arabic language or Arabic alphabet is more and more important task. In the past, several books about analyzing of the Arabic language were published. But the language analysis is only one step in the language processing. Several approaches to the text compression were developed in the field of text compression. The first and most intuitive is character based compression which is suitable for small files. Another approach called word-based compression become very suitable for very long files. The third approach is called syllable-based, it use syllable as basic element. Algorithms for the syllabification of the English, German or other European language are well known, but syllabification algorithms for Arabic and their usage in text compression has not been deeply investigated. This paper describes a new and very simple algorithm for syllabification of Arabic and its usage in text compression.

Keywords: Arabic, syllables, syllabification, text compression.

1 Introduction

The importance of conducting research in the area of syllabification of Arabic is called for two main reasons: the rapidly growing number of computer and internet users in the Arab world and the fact that the Arabic language is the sixth most used language in the world today. It is also one of the six languages used in the United Nations (www.un.org). Another important factor is, after the Latin alphabet (Latin alphabet), Arabic alphabet is the second-most widely used alphabet around the world. Arabic script has been used and adapted to such diverse languages as the Slavic tongues (also known as Slavic languages), Spanish, Persian, Urdu, Turkish, Hebrew, Amazigh (Berber), Swahili, Malay (Jawi in Malaysi and Indonesia), Hausa, and Mandinka (in West Africa), Swahili (in East Africa), Sudanese, and some other languages [10].

1.1 Some Possible Challenges to Be Considered When Working with Arabic Texts

One of challenges faced by researchers in this area has to do with the special nature of Arabic script in Arabic. Arabic is written horizontally from right to left. The shape of

V. Snasel, J. Platos, and E. El-Qawasmeh (Eds.): ICDIPC 2011, Part I, CCIS 188, pp. 97–105, 2011.

each letter depends on its position in a word—initial, medial, and final. There is a fourth form of the letter when written alone. The letters *alif*, *waw*, and *ya* (standing for glottal stop, w, and y, respectively) are used to represent the long vowels a, u, and i. This is very much different from Roman alphabet which is naturally not linked. Other orthographic challenges can be the the persistent and widespread variation in the spelling of letters such as *hamza* (ء) and *ta' marbuTa* (ة), as well as, the increasing lack of differentiation between word-final *ya* (ي) and *alif maqSura* (ى). Another problem that may appear is that typists often neglect to insert a space after words that end with a non-connector letter such as, "ز, ر, ذ" [3]. In addition to that, Arabic has eight short vowles and diacritics (ٰ , ٖ , ٗ , ٘ , ٙ , ٚ , ٛ , ٜ). Typists normally ignore putting them in a text, but in case of texts where they exist, they are pre-normalized –in value- to avoid any mismatching with the dictionary or corpus in light stemming. As a result, the letters in the decompressed text, appear without these special diacritics.

Diacritization has always been a problem for researches. According to Habash [12], since diacritical problems in Arabic occur so infrequently, they are removed from the text by most researchers. Other text recognition studies in Arabic include, Andrew Gillies et. al. [11], John Trenkle et al. [30] and Maamouri et al. [20].

2 Text Compression

The key to data compression is the ability to model data to improve the efficiency of prediction [25]. The modeling of the data consists of modeling the context [1]. Modeling textual data means the modeling of the language. The most analyzed language is English. The first analysis of English was made by Shannon, who computed its entropy [26]. The latter analysis of English was closely related to the PPM compression method. Bell et al., in an excellent survey in [1], describe the state of the modeling of data at the end of the year 1989. They describe the principles of data modeling for context models (such as the PPM compression method). Moreover, the paper describes the principles of other possible models - finite state models like Dynamic Markov Compression [6, 13] and grammar or syntactic models [4, 15]. PPM-based compression usually uses contexts with a limited length. For English, a context with a maximal length of 6 symbols is standard [1]. Cleary et al. [5] and Bloom [2] inspect the possibility of unlimited context length. Skibinski and Grabowski [28] summarize both the previous methods and describe their own improvements based on variable-length context. The problem of the memory requirements of the PPM model is discussed by Drinic et al. in [7]. In [27] Shkarin describes the practical implementation of the PPM method using instruction sets of modern processors and Lelewer and Hirschberg [19] suggest a variation of PPM optimized for speed.

Compression based on a combination of several models using neural networks was presented by Mahoney [21].This concept is called context mixing. Algorithms based on this principle are the most efficient in several independent compression benchmarks.

Another research study in the field of text compression focuses on analyzing context information in files of various sizes. The main advantage of this approach is that the compression algorithms may be used without any modification. The efficiency (scalability) of the compression methods used for text compression may be related with the selection of the basic elements.

The first approaches focused on the compression of large text files. For large files, words were used as the basic elements. This approach is called word-based compression [14, 8, 31]. All the basic compression methods were adapted to this type of compression. The first modification was a modification of Huffman encoding called Huffword [31]. Later, other methods followed: WLZW as a modification of the LZW method [14, 8], and WBW as a modification of the Burrows-Wheeler transformation-based compression [9, 22]. PPM has its modification for word-based compression[31], too. The last modification for word-based compression was made for LZ77 compression [23]. As written above, all these modifications left the main compression unchanged. The only change is made in the first part of the algorithms, where the input symbols are read. The input file is read as a character sequence. From this sequence several types of elements are decomposed. Usually, two basic element types are recognized - words, which are represented as sequences of letters, and non-words, which are represented as sequences of white spaces, numbers, and other symbols. Algorithms must solve problems with capital letters, special types of words, hapax-legomenons (words which are present only once in the file), etc. A third type of element is sometimes also defined. The most commonly used one is a tag, which is used for structured documents such as XML, HTML, SGML, and others. A very interesting survey of dictionary-based text compression and transformation presented by Skibinski et al. [29].

The second approach evolved by Lansky [18, 17] is syllable-based compression. Lansky made experiments with LZW, Huffman encoding, and Burrows-Wheeler transformation based compression methods adapted for using syllables as basic elements[18, 17]. The main problem of this approach is the process of separation of the syllables, also called hyphenation algorithms. This algorithm is specific to any language. The rules for word hyphenation may be heuristic, linguistically based, or other. The first two approaches were described for the Czech, English, and German languages in [18, 17]. A soft computing approach to hyphenation is described in [16], where a genetic algorithm is used for preparing the optimal set of syllables for achieving optimum compression using Huffman encoding.

Three different approaches to text compression, based on the selection of input symbols, were defined - character-based, syllable-based, and word-based. The question is what type is the most suitable for defined texts. In [17], authors compare the single file parsing methods used on input text files of a size 1KB-5MB by means of the Burrows-Wheeler Transform for different languages (English, Czech, and German). They consider these input symbol types: letters, syllables, words, 3-grams, and 5-grams. Comparing letter-based, syllable-based, and word-based compression, they came to the conclusion that character-based compression is the most suitable for small files (up to 200KB) and that syllable-based compression is the best for files of a size 200KB-5MB. The compression type which uses natural text units such as words or syllables is 10-30% better than the compression with 5-grams and 3-grams. For larger files, word-based compression methods are the most efficient.

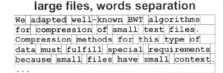

large files, words separation

```
We adapted well-known BWT algorithms
for compression of small text files.
Compression methods for this type of
data must fulfill special requirements
because small files have small context.
. . .
```

(a)

medium files, sylables separation

```
We adapted well-known BWT algorithms
for compression of small text files.
Compression methods for this type of
data must fulfill special requirements
because small files have small context.
. . .
```

(b)

small files, character separation

```
We adapted well-known BWT algorithms
for compression of small text files.
Compression methods for this type of
data must fulfill special requirements
because small files have small context.
. . .
```

(c)

Fig. 1. Context information in text files of various sizes

These findings correspond to the amount of contextual information stored in files. Contextual information in large text files (larger than 5 MB) is very big and therefore it is sufficient to process them using word-based compression (see Figure 1a). Medium-sized text files (200KB-5MB) have less contextual information than large text files, and, therefore, it is insufficient to take the word as a base unit; however, we can take a smaller grammatical part and use syllable-based compression (see Figure 1b). Contextual information in small files (10KB - 200KB) is difficult to obtain. In small files, the contextual information is sufficient only when we process them by characters (see Figure 1c).

The efficiency of the text compression when multiple documents are compressed may be improved with simple modification. In, cluster [24]analysis is used for improving the efficiency of the compression methods. All the main compression methods adapted for word-based compression are tested and the compression ratio is improved by up to 4 percent.

3   Rule Set

The rules for syllable separation are well defined for English, German, Czech and many other European languages. However, as far as Arabic is concerned, research in this area is still young. Arabic script is different than languages using Roman characters in many aspects, for example: text direction (right to left) and connection of letters in a word.

In this study, we define several rules for decomposition of Arabic words into syllables. These rules are based on splitting the text according to some linguistic criteria called here, split markers. The basic criterion for splitting the text is tracing the vowel letter in a text.

Basically, in this study, the term Arabic vowels include the following: vowels, long vowels and diphthongs:

(ا ,أ ,و ,ي ,ى ,ؤ ,ء ,ئ ,آ ,لآ ,لا)

It is to be mentioned here that the letters (لآ, لا) are dual letters, i.e., they both contain two letters of which the first is a consonant letter and the second is a vowel.

It is also worth mentioning here that, interestingly enough, the Unicode value of the dual letters is not always equal to the total value of two letters if taken separately. While the total Unicode value of the letters in (لآ, لا) are the same if taken separately, dual letter characters such as (ؤ, ئ) carry a new Unicode value.

Split markers include also some other kinds of vowels which are indicated by diacritical marks called, short vowels. These are placed above or below the letter, such as, (ˇ , ´ , ˎ). Another diacritical marks that are included among the split markers in this study are nunations such as (´ , ˝ , ˌ) In written Arabic, nunation is indicated by doubling the vowel diacritic at the end of the word. These diacritical marks mentioned above are used in fully vocalized texts in Arabic.

Fig. 2. Example of the syllabification

4 Algorithm

The rule set defined in the previous section leads to an algorithm which may be
defined as follows:

1. Read the input file and process all words by the following steps.
2. When the length of the word is less than 3 characters, ignore it.
3. When the second and third letters are vowels, make a split between second
    and third letter.
4. Otherwise, make a split after the third letter.

As may be seen, the algorithm is quiet simple. The example of the syllabification using
this algorithm may be seen in the Figure 2. The hyphens are used as splitting marks.

5 Processing of Text Files

For testing purposes, we test several text files written in Arabic language. The first
group is short texts from Arabic newspapers. The second group contains several
larger files. The statistics of the used files is shown in Table 1. For each file we test
decomposition into 2-grams, 3-grams, characters, syllables using described algorithm
and decomposition into words. The whitespaces are handled as a one syllable/word in
syllable and word decomposition. The size of the alphabet extracted from the testing
files using mentioned methods are also depicted in Table 1.

The testing files are selected from two sources. The first source is four short texts
taken from the web-pages of Arabic international news channels, and the long text is
taken from shareware Arabic books from the web. All texts are encoded using
CodePage 1256 - Arabic Script.

Table 1. Statistics of Testing Files

File:	Short1	Short2	Short3	Short4	Long1	Long2
File size (B)	1922	7926	2910	12278	1547552	845431
Unique Chars	45	64	51	71	95	60
Unique Syllables	320	898	490	1117	9342	6521
Unique Words	232	837	391	1187	55006	28336
Unique 2-grams	301	623	425	712	2208	1251
Unique 3-grams	429	1397	680	1843	19377	11113

As may be seen from Table 1 that the number of the extracted unique syllables is
rather high, but it is always less than the number of 3-grams. And for the files bigger
than 10kB, it is also lower than the number of words.

6 Compression Experiments

In this section, experiments using two different compression algorithms will be
performed. The first algorithm is based on Burrows-Wheeler transformation with

combination Huffman encoding and Move-To-Front and RLE transformation. This algorithm is chosen because its efficiency is based on the relationships between sibling symbols. The second algorithm is LZW compression algorithm which gains its efficiency from repetitions of symbols.

During experiments we use large enough dictionary for LZW algorithm and large enough block size for BWT based algorithm to avoid clearing of dictionary and splitting input into several blocks.

The results of the experiment are shown in Table 2. For comparison purposes, is necessary to compare sizes of the compressed texts together with the size of the used dictionary.

Table 2. Experimental Results (all sizes are in bytes)

File:	Short1	Short2	Short3	Short4	Long1	Long2
File size (B)	1922	7926	2910	12278	1547552	845431
Chars Dict.	90	128	102	142	190	120
Chars BWT	961	3837	1554	5666	616079	307654
Chars LZW	1119	4484	1801	6696	727257	362236
Syllables Dict.	1110	3311	1764	4124	48115	27950
Syllables	814	3549	1358	5430	608502	308506
Syllables	904	3947	1511	6032	734357	359564
Words Dict.	1433	5049	2357	7566	369092	186962
Words BWT	438	2190	765	3318	533775	265799
Words LZW	602	2801	1048	4236	644161	307962
2-grams Dict.	903	1869	1275	2136	6624	3752
2-grams BWT	900	3849	1485	5764	634955	303076
2-grams LZW	987	4325	1648	6595	768174	374316
3-grams Dict	1715	5588	2720	7371	77507	44450
3-grams BWT	687	3216	1133	5078	649286	311581
3-grams LZW	751	3527	1246	5610	812509	389112

As may be seen from the results, the most efficient compression algorithm for small files (Short1-Short4) is character based compression. All other approaches achieved worst results. This corresponds with information mentioned in Section 2. The best results for larger files (Long1 and Long2) were achieved by 2-grams approach, but the character and syllable approach have almost same efficiency. These experiments show that our syllabification algorithm needs to be improved and also more experiments must be performed.

7   Conclusion

This paper describes a new simple set of rules for syllabification of Arabic language. The algorithm uses only two basic rules, but it achieves very good results in the identifying of syllables. We used this algorithm in text compression for 2 types of input files. The short files contain up to 12,000 characters. The long files are more than 800,000 characters. We compare efficiency of the compression using the syllable approach with characters, words, 2-grams and 3-grams approaches on these two groups of files. The best result for short files were achieved by character based approach, as was expected. For long files, the best results were achieved by 2-grams approach, but character approach and syllable approach were also very efficient.

In the future, a correction must be done especially in non-word and non-syllable handling and more sophisticated syllabification algorithm must be tested.

Acknowledgments. This work was supported by the Grant Agency of the Czech Republic, under the grant no. P202/11/P142.

References

[1] Bell, T., Witten, I.H., Cleary, J.G.: Modeling for text compression. ACM Comput. Surv. 21(4), 557–591 (1989)

[2] Bloom, C.: Solving the problems of context modeling (March 1998), http://www.cbloom.com/papers/index.html

[3] Buckwalter, T.: Issues in arabic morphological analysis. In: Ide, N., Veronis, J., Soudi, A., Bosch, A.v.d., Neumann, G. (eds.) Arabic Computational Morphology, Text, Speech and Language Technology, vol. 38, pp. 23–41. Springer, Netherlands (2007), http://dx.doi.org/10.1007/978-1-4020-6046-5_3, doi:10.1007/978-1-4020-6046-5_3

[4] Cameron, R.: Source encoding using syntactic information source models. IEEE Transactions on Information Theory 34(4), 843–850 (1988)

[5] Cleary, J.G., Teahan, W.J., Witten, I.H.: Unbounded length contexts for ppm. In: DCC 1995: Proceedings of the Conference on Data Compression, p. 52. IEEE Computer Society, Washington, DC, USA (1995)

[6] Cormack, G.V., Horspool, R.N.S.: Data compression using dynamic markov modelling. Comput. J. 30(6), 541–550 (1987)

[7] Drinic, M., Kirovski, D., Potkonjak, M.: Ppm model cleaning. In: Proceedings of Data Compression Conference DCC 2003, pp. 163–172 (March 2003)

[8] Dvorsky, J., Pokorny, J., Snasel, V.: Word-based compression methods and indexing for text retrieval systems. In: Eder, J., Rozman, I., Welzer, T. (eds.) ADBIS 1999. LNCS, vol. 1691, pp. 75–84. Springer, Heidelberg (1999)

[9] Dvorsky, J., Snasel, V.: Modifications in burrows-wheeler compression algorithm. In: Proceedings of ISM 2001 (2001)

[10] Encyclopaedia Britannica Online: Alphabet. (February 2011), http://www.britannica.com/EBchecked/topic/17212/alphabet

[11] Gillies, A., Erl, E., Trenkle, J., Schlosser, S.: Arabic text recognition system. In: Proceedings of the Symposium on Document Image Understanding Technology (1999)

[12] Habash, N.Y.: Introduction to arabic natural language processing. Synthesis Lectures on Human Language Technologies 3(1), 1–187 (2010), http://www.morganclaypool.com/doi/abs/10.2200/S00277ED1V01Y201008HLT010

[13] Horspool, R.N.S., Cormack, G.V.: Dynamic markov modeling - a prediction technique, pp. 700–707 (1986)

[14] Horspool, R.N.: Constructing word-based text compression algorithms. In: Proc. IEEE Data Compression Conference, pp. 62–81. IEEE Computer Society Press, Los Alamitos (1992)

[15] Katajainen, J., Penttonen, M., Teuhola, J.: Syntax-directed compression of program files. Softw. Pract. Exper. 16(3), 269–276 (1986)
[16] Kuthan, T., Lansky, J.: Genetic algorithms in syllable-based text compression. In: DATESO (2007)
[17] Lansky, J., Chernik, K., Vlickova, Z.: Comparison of text models for bwt. In: DCC 2007: Proceedings of the 2007 Data Compression Conference, p. 389. IEEE Computer Society, Washington, DC, USA (2007)
[18] Lansky, J., Zemlicka, M.: Compression of small text files using syllables. In: DCC 2006: Proceedings of the Data Compression Conference, p. 458. IEEE Computer Society, Washington, DC, USA (2006)
[19] Lelewer, D., Hirschberg, D.: Streamlining context models for data compression. In: Data Compression Conference, DCC 1991, pp. 313–322 (April 1991)
[20] Maamouri, M., Bies, A., Kulick, S.: Diacritization: A challenge to arabic treebank annotation and parsing. In: Proceedings Of The British Computer Society Arabic Nlp/Mt Conference (2006)
[21] Mahoney, M.V.: Fast text compression with neural networks. In: Proceedings of the Thirteenth International Florida Artificial Intelligence Research Society Conference, pp. 230–234. AAAI Press, Menlo Park (2000)
[22] Moffat, A., Isal, R.Y.K.: Word-based text compression using the burrows-wheeler transform. Inf. Process. Manage 41(5), 1175–1192 (2005)
[23] Platos, J., Dvorsky, J.: Word-based text compression. CoRR abs/0804.3680, 7 (2008)
[24] Platos, J., Dvorsky, J., Martinovic, J.: Using Clustering to Improve WLZ77 Compression. In: First International Conference on the Applications of Digital Information and Web Technologies, Ostrava, CZECH REPUBLIC, August 04-06, vol. 1&2, pp. 315–320. IEEE Commun Soc., IEEE, New York (2008)
[25] Rissanen, J., Langdon, G.J.: Universal modeling and coding. IEEE Transactions on Information Theory 27(1), 12–23 (1981)
[26] Shannon, C.E.: Prediction and Entropy of Printed English. Bell System Technical Journal 30, 50–64 (1951)
[27] Shkarin, D.: Ppm: one step to practicality. In: Proceedings of Data Compression Conference, DCC 2002, pp. 202–211 (2002)
[28] Skibinski, P., Grabowski, S.: Variable-length contexts for ppm. Data Compression Conference, 409 (2004)
[29] Skibinski, P., Grabowski, S., Deorowicz, S.: Revisiting dictionary-based compression: Research articles. Softw. Pract. Exper. 35(15), 1455–1476 (2005)
[30] Trenkle, J., Gilles, A., Eriandson, E., Schlosser, S., Cavin, S.: Advances in arabic text recognition. In: Symposium on Document Image Understanding Technology, pp. 159–168 (April 2001)
[31] Witten, I.H., Moffat, A., Bell, T.C.: Managing Gigabytes: Compressing and Indexing Documents and Images, 2nd edn. Morgan Kaufmann, San Francisco (1999)

Automatic Classification of Sleep/Wake Stages Using Two-Step System

Lukáš Zoubek[1] and Florian Chapotot[2]

[1] Department of Information and Communication Technologies, University of Ostrava,
Českobratrská 16, 701 03 Ostrava, Czech Republic
lukas.zoubek@osu.cz
[2] Department of Medicine, The University of Chicago, 5841 South Maryland Avenue,
Chicago, IL 60637 - USA
fchapotot@uchicago.edu

Abstract. This paper presents application of an automatic classification system on 53 animal polysomnographic recordings. A two-step automatic system is used to score the recordings into three traditional stages: wake, NREM sleep and REM sleep. In the first step of the analysis, monitored signals are analyzed using artifact identification strategy and artifact-free signals are selected. Then, 30sec epochs are classified according to relevant features extracted from available signals using artificial neural networks. The overall classification accuracy reached by the presented classification system exceeded 95%, when analyzed 53 polysomnographic recordings.

Keywords: decision making, diagnosis, medical applications, pattern recognition, signal processing.

1 Introduction

Polysomnography represents a diagnostic method used to analyze sleep and sleep disorders. Classification of the polysomnographic recordings into sleep/wake stages is a fundamental part of sleep research. The method consists in simultaneous monitoring of several physiological parameters. For the analysis of animal sleep, electroencephalogram (EEG) and electromyogram (EMG) are typically used. In the animal sleep research, rats are frequently used.

The aim of the sleep analysis is to classify the polysomnographic recording into succession of predefined sleep/wake stages. For the need of the sleep/wake stage classification, the recording is typically split into equidistant intervals – epochs. Traditional epoch length is 20sec or 30sec, but in the animal sleep/wake stage analysis, shorter epochs are also frequently used.

The manual classification of polysomnographic recording is performed by an expert and consists in visual analysis of monitored signals and assignment of appropriate sleep/wake stage to the epochs. In the case of rat sleep analysis, the classification is done into one of three stages: Wake, NREM (non-rapid-eye-movement) sleep and REM (rapid-eye-movement) sleep. The stages are distinguished by the expert according to the typical manifestations, activities and powers in the

V. Snasel, J. Platos, and E. El-Qawasmeh (Eds.): ICDIPC 2011, Part I, CCIS 188, pp. 106–117, 2011.
© Springer-Verlag Berlin Heidelberg 2011

EEG and EMG signals. Traditional manual classification performed by an expert is also strongly influenced by his/her experience, which can in the consequence lead to high heterogeneity of the classifications.

In order to automate, simplify and unify the sleep classifications, a huge effort to develop automated sleep/wake stagers has been made in the last decades [1], [2], [3], [4]. In general, the research is mainly focused on three main tasks in automated sleep analysis: choice of adequate type and structure of an automatic classifier, implementation of algorithms for artifact identification and minimization, and extraction of relevant features representing the epochs of the polysomnographic signals.

This paper presents application of a two-step classification system on a database of rat polysomnographic recordings. The automatic system used takes into account presence of possible artifacts and performs classification using features extracted from available artifact-free signals. The main idea of the classification is to use a different classifier for each epoch to be classified, depending on the quality of the monitored signals.

The outline of the paper is the following. The automatic system proposed is presented in the second section. The whole polysomnographic database is presented in the third section. Then, final results are presented and discussed in the section number four. At the end of the paper, short conclusions are presented.

2   System for Automatic Classification

The process of automatic sleep staging typically consists in several successive steps – artifact processing, extraction of significant features from epochs of the polysomnographic recordings, and application of the features as inputs to the classifier. In this project, a complex two-step automatic system was used to process the polysomnographic recordings. The two-step classification system has been already presented and evaluated on human polysomnographic recordings [5]. In the next part of the paper, principle of the two-step classification system will be described briefly.

2.1   Description of the Two-Step System

The two-step automatic system performs artifact identification procedure separately from the classification. Thus, it can combine the results of an artifact identification procedure with an adequate automatic classification using relevant features extracted from the available artifact-free signals.

Artifact Detection
The first step consists in artifact analysis of the signals to be tested (EEG and EMG in this research). The aim is to determine if any artifact is present in the epoch to be classified. In order to allow effective identification of short artifacts which are rather common in polysomnographic recordings, the original time resolution has been changed from 30sec epoch to 2sec segments. In the concrete, each 30sec epoch has been split into succession of fifteen 2sec segments. Detection algorithm dealing with shorter segments can be more precise in localization of the artifacts and also thriftier of the data. If no artifact is present in a signal or only a small part of a signal in the

30sec epoch is artifacted (less than four 2sec segments), the epoch is marked as "artifact-free" and features are computed from the parts of the signal which are not artifacted. The artifacted segments of a signal are removed from the processing. If too large part of a signal in the epoch is artifacted (more than three 2-sec segments), the epoch is marked as "artifacted" and is completely removed from the classification. This strategy ensures that only the signals that can be used to classify the current epoch are selected.

Artifact identification procedure has been performed using a specialized PRANA Software which is equipped with a universal automatic artifact detection algorithm, inspired by the work of Bruner [6]. The algorithm can use either fixed or adaptive thresholds for identification. The algorithm was tuned so as to identify the artifacts most frequently present in the polysomnographic signals, using physiological knowledge. For the need of the actual research, eight different artifacts were automatically detected, six of them (overflow, electrode detachment, power line artifact, ECG artifact, high-frequency artifact, flat-line) being detected using a priori fixed thresholds and two (low-frequency artifact, muscular activity) using adaptive thresholds. Since the polysomnographic database did not contain artifact analysis performed visually by an expert, the tuning and performances of the artifact detectors have not been properly validated. For more details about artifact identification strategy used in the analysis see [5], [7].

Classification

The second step of the analysis represents the automatic classification. The signals selected in the previous step as artifact-free are used in the decision system: the relevant features are extracted and used in an appropriate automatic classifier. The decision system is formed by a bank of different classifiers: one classifier for each combination of monitored signals. Then, the proper classifier is selected from the bank of classifiers, using the results of the artifact identification procedure performed on the signals. In the actual research, the bank of classifiers contains only two classifiers corresponding to the two possible combinations of signals: EEG only and EEG and EMG. The EEG signal is considered to be indispensable for the automatic sleep/wake stage classification, so if the EEG signal is artifacted, the epoch cannot be classified by the system.

The principle of the automatic classification is the following: at first, relevant features are extracted from the polysomnographic signals recorded during an epoch using signal processing techniques and form so called feature vector. This first step transforms the raw signals into a set of characteristics describing the signals shape during one epoch. In a second step, the feature vector is used as an input for a automatic classifier.

Artificial neural networks have been selected as automatic classifiers used in this research. This selection is based on previous research studies [4], [5], [7]. In the concrete, two different architectures of supervised artificial neural networks have been used:

-   feedforward neural networks with three layers. For the first layer, number of neurons is defined by actual number of input features extracted from the epoch to be processed. Hyperbolic tangent transfer function is used for the neurons of

first layer. The second layer of the network contains 6 neurons; the transfer function is a logarithmic sigmoid function. The output layer of the network consists of 5 neurons each corresponding to one sleep/wake stage; the transfer function of each neuron is a hyperbolic tangent.
- radial basis neural networks with two layers. Spread of radial basis functions in the hidden layer has been set to value 0.5.

2.2 Features

For both the possible combinations of signals (EEG only, and EEG and EMG) have been selected the most relevant features out of a set of 22 features extracted from the polysomnographic recordings. 13 features have been extracted from the EEG signal and 9 features have been extracted from the EMG signal.

Features Computed from EEG Signal Only

- A set of five features is used to describe the spectral activity of EEG signal in traditional frequency bands: δ delta [0.5 ; 4.5] Hz, θ theta [4.5 ; 8.5] Hz, α alpha [8.5 ; 11.5] Hz, σ sigma [11.5 ; 15.5] Hz and β beta [15.5 ; 32.5] Hz. Welch's periodogram Fourier transformation computed on 2 sec periods has been used The features represent relative powers, *Prel*, in the five frequency bands.

Features Computed from EMG Signal Only

- The relative power of EMG in the high frequency band [12.5 ; 32] Hz was calculated. The total frequency band was defined as [8 ; 32] Hz.

Features Computed from EEG and EMG

- The spectral edge frequency 95 (*SEF95*) indicates the highest frequency below which 95% of the total signal power is located [8].
- The entropy (*entr*) of the signal measures the signal variability, from the distribution of its amplitude values [9].
- A set of three quantitative parameters defined by Hjorth [10] : activity (*act*), mobility (*mob*) and complexity (*comp*).
- The standard deviation (*std*) of a random variable.
- The skewness (*skew*) and the kurtosis (*kurt*) characterizes the probability distribution function of a signal.

All the features have been extracted from the polysomnographic recordings contained in the database. For each recording, each feature was transformed and normalized in order to reduce the extreme and outlying values. This transformation strategy has been inspired by [7].

To select the most relevant features, Sequential Forward Selection (SFS) strategy has been applied for both the possible combinations of signals (EEG, and EEG+EMG). Sequential Forward Selection is an iterative method which at each step selects the optimal set of features by increasing the number of features selected so as to maximize the classification criterion (function of the percentage of epochs correctly classified by a classifier).

3 Data

3.1 Database of Polysomnographic Recordings

A large database of conventional animal polysomnographic recordings has been used in this research. The full database contains the 24-hour recordings of a total of 60 adult Sprague-Dawley rats. The recordings included 2 channels per animal, with one EEG (electroencephalogram) and one EMG (electromyogram) signals, and were performed continuously while the animals were housed in individual cages placed in sound-attenuated chambers at an ambient temperature of 21°C with a 12:12-hour light-dark cycle and unlimited access to food and water. To achieve the recordings, animals were anesthetized, placed in a stereotaxic frame and surgically equipped with electroencephalographic (EEG) and electromyographic (EMG). Two miniature stainless steel screws served as EEG electrodes and were inserted into the animal skull through small trepanation holes drilled at the level of the right central and midsaggital cortex. Two stainless steel wire electrodes were inserted beneath the neck muscles to record the electromyogram (EMG). All electrode wires were soldered to a mini-connector anchored to the skull with acrylic dental cement. A period of one week was allowed for recovery from the surgical procedure. The animals were then acclimated to the recording conditions. To allow the rat to move freely, a light cable and a rotating commuter were used to connect the electrodes and the recording unit. Recordings began 7 to 10 days later, and one day of stable baseline data were obtained for the purpose of this study. The EEG and EMG signals were both collected in a bipolar montage by connecting each pair of electrodes to the positive and negative inputs of the recording unit amplifiers. The signals were digitalized and stored at a sampling frequency of 100 Hz using a quantization range of -/+ 500 uV and a 16-bit analog-to-digital converter. Four rats were recorded simultaneously on a 500 Mbytes Flash card using an Embla battery-powered recording unit and the Somnologica acquisition software (Resmed, Saint-Priest, France). A common ground was used for the four animals of each recording batch by connecting the cage hosting the animals directly to the recording equipment.

After data collection, the PSG recordings were scored a first time for sleep/wake stages by one sleep expert using the Somnologica software. Recordings were then converted into EDF recording files, transferred to another computer, and re-scored by an independent expert using the PRANA reviewing and analysis software (PhiTools, Strasbourg, France). The PSG recordings were scored visually by 30sec epochs into 3 sleep/wake stages according to conventional criteria. The sleep-wake states were identified as follows: Wake (desynchronized EEG, low EEG amplitude, high to medium EMG levels); NREM sleep (synchronized EEG with low to high-amplitude synchronized EEG and low EMG levels); and REM sleep (desynchronized EEG with predominant theta rhythm of 6-9 Hz, low to medium EEG amplitude, and very low EMG levels). The experts could also score an epoch as a movement or leave the epoch undefined. These two categories were used only rarely, so they have not been included into the analysis. Seven recordings have been removed from the research because of missing expert classification. So, 53 polysomnographic recordings left for the analysis. The total database contains 153,020 epochs scored by two experts. In order to reduce the uncertainty in the data, only the epochs with relevant classification (Wake, NREM sleep and REM sleep) and concordant visual scoring of both experts have been included in the study. Thus, out of the 153,020 epochs, 17,749 epochs have been removed. The inter-expert agreement reached about 88%. So, 135,271 epochs has left for the analysis. Three recordings are characterized by markedly high number of undefined of movement epochs by one of the experts.

4   Results

The results achieved can be split into three main parts: artifact identification, creation of classifiers, and evaluation of the two-step system.

4.1   Artifact Identification

Artifact processing strategy has been characterized in the second section. Both the analyzed signals, EEG and EMG, have been processed separately. Results of artifact identification performed on the 53 polysomnographic recordings are summarized in Table 1. Out of the 135,271 epochs contained in the final database 134,625 epochs have EEG signal artifact-free and 77,009 epochs have EMG signal artifact-free. Only 76,845 epochs have both signals (EEG and EMG) artifact-free.

Table 1. Description of the polysomnographic database summarizing artifact identification

	Final database	EEG Artifact-free	EMG Artifact-free	EEG+EMG Artifact-free
Total	135,271	134,625	77,009	76,845
Wake	61,379	60,904	33,368	33,263
NREM	62,600	62,498	36,780	36,732
REM	11,292	11,223	6,861	6,850

Automatic classification strongly depends on quality and relevancy of the input data – features. To ensure the quality of the data used during phase of learning the classifiers, only recordings containing at least 80% of artifact-free epochs (EEG+EMG) have been used. Only 23 polysomnographic recordings have met this criterion. These recordings forming reduced database are characterized in Table 2.

Table 2. Description of the reduced database used for learning of classifiers

Reduced database	EEG Artifact-free	EMG Artifact-free	EEG+EMG Artifact-free	EEG+EMG Artifact-free Wake	EEG+EMG Artifact-free NREM	EEG+EMG Artifact-free REM
61,979	61,837	60,008	59,897	26,484	28,171	5,242

4.2 Creation of Classifiers

An automatic classifier represents a decision system that makes its decision on the basis of a predefined set of features. In the actual research, two decision systems based on artificial neural networks theory have been evaluated - feedforward neural networks and radial basis neural networks.

As could be seen in Table 1 and Table 2, distribution of the epochs in the sleep/wake stages analyzed is not the same for every stage which corresponds to the general sleep structure. In order to avoid errors in the classification results that could be caused by the difference in classes representation, a small test database containing 6,000 epochs in which all analyzed stages (Wake, NREM and REM) are represented by about the same number of epochs has been created out of the epochs with EEG and EMG detected as artifact-free. The epochs have been selected randomly from the reduced database. The test database has been then split into ten test subsets S = {S1, S2,..., S10}, each subset Sk containing 600 epochs, evenly distributed in the stages (see Table 3).

Table 3. Description of the test database – stages represented by about the same number of epochs

	Wake	NREM	REM
Test database	2,050	2,050	1,900
Test subset	205	205	190

The test subsets have been then used for feature selection and process of learning of automatic classifiers. Feature selection (Sequential Forward Selection – SFS) has been performed for both possible combinations of signals (EEG, and EEG+EMG) and for both types of neural networks used.

At each step of the feature selection, a circular permutation is performed on the 10 test subsets Sk. The classifier is trained 10 times. Each time a classifier is trained on one subset Sk and validated on the dataset $\bar{S}_k$ containing data from the other 9 subsets $S_{\bar{k}}$, $S_{\bar{k}} \in \bar{S}_k$ with $\bar{S}_k = S - S_k$. Each time an accuracy function is calculated so as to determine percentage of correctly classified epochs from the set $\bar{S}_k$. Then, the criterion J used to select the features is computed as a mean value over the 10 $Acc(k, \bar{k})$ values.

As presented in the second section, 22 features have been extracted from the polysomnographic recordings. The initial set of features for the feature selection process depends on the available physiological signals used. The features selection was achieved for two combinations of signals: EEG, and EEG + EMG. The initial pool of features contained 13 features when only EEG has been available, and 22 features for EEG + EMG combination of signals. The optimal feature sets selected by SFS are presented below. For each feature selection is indicated also the value of criterion J computed on the test subsets.

Feedforward Neural Networks

- EEG. Relevant set of features: *entrEEG*, *Prelδ*, *Prelθ*, *skewEEG* and *compEEG*. *J* = 95.78%.
- EEG + EMG. Relevant set of features: *entrEEG*, *Prelδ*, *entrEMG* and *Prelθ*. *J* = 96.67%.

Radial Basis Neural Networks

- EEG. Relevant set of features: *entrEEG*, *Prelδ*, *Prelθ*, *skewEEG* and *compEEG*. *J* = 95.82%.
- EEG + EMG. Relevant set of features: *entrEEG*, *Prelδ*, *entrEMG* and *Prelθ*. *J* = 96.74%.

As could be seen, the same feature sets have been selected by both neural network types used in the research Results of the selection process correspond to the presumption that the EEG signal represents the indispensable information for sleep staging. However, automatic classification using relevant information extracted from both EEG and EMG signals can typically lead to higher classification accuracy achieved with smaller number of parameters.

When the relevant features have been selected, a two-step classification system can be implemented. For the final implementation of the two-step classification system, only one of the ten neural network classifiers trained has been selected for each combination of monitored physiological signals and for each type of neural network. In the concrete, the neural network classifier characterized with the highest classification accuracy computed on the corresponding dataset $\bar{S}_k$ has been chosen and stored in the bank of classifiers (EEG only, and EEG+EMG). This selection ensures that only 600 epochs were used to train the classifiers. The proposed system is then ready to be used to analyze and score the whole night polysomnographic recordings contained in the database.

4.3 Evaluation on PSG Recordings

As presented above, the original database contains 53 recordings visually scored on 30sec epochs. The database is characterized in Table 1. As could be seen, due to the artifacts, only 76,845 epochs out of the total set of 135,271 epochs have EEG and EMG signal artifact-free. Thus, traditional classification system requiring presence of both the signals would be able to process only about 57% of the database. This fact strongly limits application of such traditional automatic classification systems.

The two-step structure combined with a bank of classifiers is able to classify also epochs, in which EMG signal is not available due to artifacts. Such a system can score almost all the epochs from the original database (99.5% of the epochs).

Analysis of the 53 polysomnographic recordings performed by the two-step automatic system is summarized in Table 4. For both types of neural networks, the global classification accuracy achieved by the two-step system is over 95% (column Totally classified). During the classification process, both classifiers have been used – EEG only, and EEG+EMG. 57,780 epochs have been scored by classifier using only EEG features, with classification accuracy 93.55%. All the remaining epochs (76,845 epochs) have been scored by classifier combining features from EEG and EMG signals with classification accuracy 96.65%.

Classification accuracy achieved for the traditional classifier which corresponds to the combination EEG+EMG (last column of the Table 4) is only about 1% higher than the accuracy achieved for the two-step system. The main difference between traditional classifier and the two-step system with bank of classifiers is thus in the number of epochs actually scored. This criterion proves advantage of the proposed system. As could be seen, the proposed structure using bank of classifiers allows classifying of 134,625 epochs out of the total sum of 135,271 epochs contained in the database analyzed. On the contrary, the traditional automatic classifier requiring both EEG and EMG could classify only 76,845 epochs which represents about 57% of the database.

Table 4. Results of classification using system based of bank of classifiers

	Totally classified	EEG only classifier	EEG+EMG classifier
Number of epochs scored	134,625	57,780	76,845
Classification accuracy (feedforward)	95.32%	93.55%	96.65%
Classification accuracy (radial basis)	95.55%	94.34%	96.45%

To provide more detail information about the automatic classification, confusion matrix presenting classification of individual stages has been also prepared. The columns of the confusion matrix represent the stages determined by the automatic classifier and the rows represent the stages determined by the experts. Each case (i,j) corresponds to the number of examples classified as i by the experts and j by the classifier, expressed as a percentage of the examples classified as i by the experts.

Table 5. Confusion matrix summarizing classification of the whole database – feedforward neural networks

		automatic classifier		
		Wake	NREM	REM
expert	Wake	93.20	4.51	2.29
	NREM	2.07	97.22	0.71
	REM	2.76	1.04	96.20

Table 6. Confusion matrix summarizing classification of the whole database – radial basis neural networks

		automatic classifier		
		Wake	NREM	REM
expert	Wake	93.56	4. 12	2.32
	NREM	1.88	97.25	0.87
	REM	2.74	0. 47	96.79

As could be seen in Table 5 and Table 6, classification accuracies reached for all the stages determined significantly exceeded 90%. The highest classification accuracy has been achieved for NREM sleep (over 97%) and REM sleep (over 96%). Accuracy achieved for stage Wake is slightly lower and exceeded 93%. This indicates that the individual stages have been well discerned by the features determined during feature selection process.

5 Conclusions

This paper presents performance of a two-step classification system on a database of animal polysomnographic recordings. The presented decision system performs identification of possible artifacts separately from the classification process. Moreover, since each of the monitored signals is analyzed for the presence of artifacts independently to the other signals, parameters characterizing only the manifestations referred to the sleep are extracted from the available artifact-free signals and then used during automatic classification. For the phase of classification, structure based on a bank of classifiers differing in origin of their input features (EEG only, or EEG+EMG) is used.

Phase of artifact identification is implemented in order to ensure quality and relevance of the analyzed signals and extracted features. Careful artifact identification can play crucial role in the whole process of automatic sleep staging. If no artifact identification is performed, or artifact identification is of insufficient quality, automatic classification based on the features extracted from the analyzed signal does not reflects the physiological mechanisms of sleeping animal. In such case, relevant information and knowledge cannot be mined from the data, even thought the global classification accuracy can be sometimes higher when artifacts are not processed and removed from the recordings. In the phase of research and system development, the knowledge gained and problem understanding should outweigh the pure classification accuracy value achieved. In the actual project, eight typical artifact types have been identified. As a result of the artifact identification performed on the polysomnographic database, EMG signal has been much more confused by artifacts than the EEG signal. This fact confirms the need to handle possible missing attributes in the case of traditional automatic classifiers.

The approach based on application of a bank of classifiers is used to allow classification of epochs characterized by incomplete set of recordings after the artifact identification phase. The results show, that large amount of data may be not classified because of missing values using a traditional automatic classifier.

To improve performance of the system, effort should be specially paid on two crucial activities. Optimization of artifact identification algorithms is necessary to prepare segments of signals containing only the information related to the sleep manifestations. It is evident that presence of artifacts can mask the original activity of the body. Nevertheless, the artifact identification algorithms should also avoid false positive detections which could lead to loss of available data to be successfully scored. The second critical point corresponds to extraction and selection of relevant features used during classification. Features representing information important for the automatic classification must be extracted from the artifact-free signals in order to simulate expert decision as well as to propose automatic classification system independent to the measuring system.

Acknowledgments

Authors are grateful to Dr. Raymond Cespuglio, INSERM U480 for providing the database of polysomnographic recordings.

The first author would like to thank to the self-government of the Moravian-Silesian Region, Czech Republic for financial support of his research internship at University of Chicago.

This publication is supported by the ESF project OP VK CZ.1.07/2.2.00/07.0339 title Personalization of teaching through E-learning.

References

1. Robert, C., Guilpin, C., Limoge, A.: Review of neural network applications in sleep research. Journal of Neuroscience Methods 79, 187–193 (1998)
2. Schaltenbrand, N., Lengelle, R., Macher, J.P.: Neural network model: application to automatic analysis of human sleep. Computers and Biomedical Research 26, 157–171 (1993)
3. Robert, C., Karasinski, P., Natowicz, R., Limoge, A.: Adult rat vigilance state discrimination by artificial neural network using a single EEG channel. Physiol and Behav. 59(6), 1051–1060 (1996)
4. Becq, G., Charbonnier, S., Chapotot, F., Buguet, A., Bourdon, L., Baconnier, P.: Comparison between five classifiers for automatic scoring of human sleep recordings. In: Halgamuge, S.K., Wang, L. (eds.) Studies in Computational Intelligence (SCI). Classification and clustering for knowledge discovery, vol. 4, pp. 113–127. Springer, Heidelberg (2005)
5. Zoubek, L., Carbonnier, S., Lesecq, S., Buguet, A., Chapotot, F.: A Two-steps Sleep/wake Stages Classifier Taking into Account Artefacts in The Polysomnographic Signals. In: Proceedings of the 17th IFAC World Congress (2008) ISBN 978-3-902661-00-5
6. Brunner, D., Vasko, R., Detka, C., Monahan, J., Reynolds, C., Kupfer, D.: Muscle artifacts in the sleep EEG: Automated detection and effect on all-night EEG power spectra. Journal of Sleep Research 5, 155–164 (1996)
7. Zoubek, L., Charbonnier, S., Lesecq, S., Buguet, A., Chapotot, F.: Feature selection for sleep/wake stages classification using data driven methods. Biomedical Signal Processing and Control 2(3), 171–179 (2007)

8. Rampil, I.J., Sasse, F.J., Smith, N.T., Hoff, B.H., Fleming, D.C.: Spectral edge frequency-a new correlate of anesthetic depth. Anesthesiology 53, 512–517 (1980)
9. Moddemeijer, R.: On Estimation of Entropy and Mutual Information of Continuous Distributions. Signal Processing 16, 233–246 (1989)
10. Hjorth, B.: EEG analysis based on time domain properties. Electroencephalography and Clinical Neurophysiology 29, 306–310 (1970)

T-SPPA: Trended Statistical PreProcessing Algorithm

Tiago Silva and Inês Dutra

CRACS - INESC Porto LA, Dep. Ciência de Computadores - Faculdade de Ciências da
Universidade do Porto, Porto, Portugal
`tiagosilva@inbox.com, ines@dcc.fc.up.pt`

Abstract. Traditional machine learning systems learn from non-relational data
but in fact most of the real world data is relational. Normally the learning task is
done using a single flat file, which prevents the discovery of effective relations
among records. Inductive logic programming and statistical relational learning
partially solve this problem. In this work, we resource to another method to overcome this problem and propose the T-SPPA: Trended Statistical PreProcessing
Algorithm, a preprocessing method that translates related records to one single
record before learning. Using different kinds of data, we compare our results
when learning with the transformed data with results produced when learning
from the original data to demonstrate the efficacy of our method.

Keywords: Machine Learning, Preprocessing, Aggregation, Relational
Learning, Statistics.

1 Introduction

Most machine learning techniques learn from one single dataset containing unrelated
records where each record represents an independent instance of one object that doesn't
explicitly relates to other record on the dataset. Data collected on real world environments is normally relational. By relational we do not mean, data spread out in multiple
tables, but records in the same table that have some kind of temporal correlation. For
example, multiple exams of a same patient, multiple weather observations on a same
location, stock exchange observations or costumer preferences, are all relational data.
However, it is not possible to simply relate records on a single dataset and then feed it
to a machine learning algorithm.

Inductive logic programming (ILP) [7] and statistical relational learning (SRL) [4]
can partially overcome this problem, but in both cases, additional knowledge must be
manually added to force relations between records. Also, these methods are somehow
complex to handle and to retrieve results compared to traditional machine learning systems. Another possible approach is to manually group all related records in the same
fold when using cross-validation, but again, this is a complex task that requires manual
operation on data.

In this paper we present T-SPPA: Trended Statistical PreProcessing Algorithm, a preprocessing algorithm that aggregates related records on a single instance before learning. We show that aggregating related data before learning has a better cost-benefit than
using all records. With T-SPPA we propose a generic algorithm capable to preprocess

V. Snasel, J. Platos, and E. El-Qawasmeh (Eds.): ICDIPC 2011, Part I, CCIS 188, pp. 118–131, 2011.

all kinds of related data before learning. We apply T-SPPA to three distinct datasets of different domains, one containing voice analysis data, another containing weather observation data and the third containing biological data. We tested the performance of our method using the WEKA Machine Learning algorithms [5] comparing the classifiers learned from the original dataset with the classifiers learned from our T-SPPA preprocessed datasets. Our results demonstrate that applying T-SPPA to the original correlated data, before the learning task, can produce classifiers that are better than the ones trained using the original datasets with all records.

This paper is organized as follows. Section 2 reviews the main works in the literature related to classification of multiple records. In Section 3 we formally define the problem to be solved. In Section 4, we describe the transformation approach used in this work. In Section 5, we discuss the methodology used to run our experiments and present the datasets. In Section 6, we present our results. Finally, in Section 7, we draw our conclusions and future work.

2 Relational Data

Machine learning methods normally takes data represented in just one single table to execute their learning tasks. Systems like WEKA [5], RapidMiner [9] or KNIME [1] read the input from one table (e.g. CSV or ARFF files). This kind of encoding, where all the data is expressed as a single table, prevents the machine learning methods of capturing important information if records have some correlation. This problem occurs because we are working with flat files or denormalized data as described in [13].

If we have a dataset containing multiple time-series data for different objects, there is no effective way to create relations among the time-series of each object and learn from these relations. A good example that illustrates this kind of problem is the one described by K. Theja and Vanajakshi [10] where the traffic stream observed on a bridge was represented as a vector containing five one-minute observations. This kind of data representation does not create relations between observations beyond those 5 minutes represented on a vector. Besides, if the number of time frames is too big, the number of attributes in the vector can be impractical.

Inductive logic programming (ILP) systems, like ALEPH, partially solve this kind of problem using first order logic to establish relations between records [12]. However these relations must be explicitly described by the user in the background knowledge. One further issue is that ILP systems can work only with 2-valued class variables pushing away all other kinds of classification, clustering or regression tasks.

Another related approach to solve this problem has been tried by Knobbe et al. [6], where the focus is on aggregating correlated data distributed over multiple tables using denormalization techniques to form a new table containing the summary of the existing data over the different tables. Our work aggregates implicit correlated data contained on a single table which is somehow different from this technique that solves the problem of aggregating distributed data over several tables. However, some basic ideas about data aggregation functions are shared in the two techniques.

The most well known generic preprocessing methods are concerned with data filtering tasks like instance and feature selection, missing values or noise data cleansing.

None of them focus on grouping related records in such way that they can be correctly handled by machine learning techniques. A summary of the most popular preprocessing techniques and their practical results can be found in [11].

To the best of our knowledge, our work is the first that tries to formalise and solve the problem of learning from correlated data in the sense defined here: learn from subgroups of records that have some temporal relation, while learning from the whole dataset.

3   Definition of Correlated Data

Let D be a dataset of n observations, each one with a number of attributes (A), where one of the attributes is a class variable (attribute c). We define correlated data as a subgroup of s instances ($s < n$), whose attribute $a \in A$, categorized as a primary key, $a \neq c$ has the same value for all of the s instances. The n observations can have several subgroups characterized as such. The problem we are interested in solving is how to classify any subset of s_1, s_2,...,s_n/k, $k > 0$, instances, without missing the classification of the n observations. This problem is particularly tricky when using cross-validation, since we do not want to place elements of any of the s_i instances in different folds. The simplest approach to solve this problem is to aggregate the instances in each of the s_i subsets, therefore transforming the data to a new set that contains one row for each summary of a subgroup. This is the approach followed in this work. However, we need to decide which kind of aggregation is going to be performed for each kind of attribute, specially to the class variable and how to use the attribute values of each subgroup, in order not to loose too much information and keep the most relevant record values. In the next Section, we discuss ways of reaching this goal.

4   An Approach to Classify Multiple Correlated Data

There are several ways of aggregating data and the most usual ones are to use summaries like averages, maximum and minimum values. We also use these aggregates, but add other attributes that we find important and that can represent a trend on the data.

T-SPPA is a two-step algorithm that captures the hierarchical aspect of learning from a dataset with multiple implicitly correlated records. The first step is to separate and consolidate records that belong to the same entity, which might be a patient, a location or a time interval, depending on the kind of data we are using. We use a transformation that maps several records into just one record along with a transformation on the original attributes. The user needs to provide the name of the attribute that will be used as pivot to perform this separation (e.g. attribute Id) and the name of the class attribute. The user must also provide the aggregation attributes to be used on the transformed dataset and the number of instances per entity to aggregate (argument N), if an aggregation group has a total number of records greater than the maximum N given by the user, the older records are discarded. We assume that the data is chronologically sorted in the case of using time-related data. Therefore, each entity must be a number of records equal or greater than N to be represented in the transformed dataset.

Our method begins by reading all the original dataset's attributes and returns different outputs depending on attribute types. Attributes of type String remain as the original attribute, as well as the attribute Id and the class attribute, regardless their data types. Attributes of type Numeric generate the following new attributes: *max, min, avg, last, ltrend* and *btrend*. The first three attributes represent the maximum, the minimum and the simple average of the grouped instances for a given Id, the attribute *last* is the last found value for the group. The *ltrend* represents the linear trend prediction for a hypothetical next record on the group using the least squares equation [2] and the *btrend* is a binary value which assumes 0 if the *ltrend* value is smaller or equal than the *last* value or 1 otherwise. The user can choose among these attributes those that are going to be considered for the preprocessed dataset. Attributes of type Nominal are unfolded in the multiple possible values, one attribute per value, representing the relative frequency in which each value appears on the group plus the last observed value. The user must choose if the last observed value for nominal attributes should be included in the preprocessed dataset. The attribute conversions using T-SPPA can be found on Table 1.

Table 1. T-SPPA attribute conversion

Input attribute	Output
Attribute Id	Attribute Id
Attribute Class	Attribute Class
String	String
Numeric	Attributes min, max, avg, last, ltrend and bintrend
Nominal	Frequency attributes for each value and last value

The total number of attributes on the transformed dataset is given by the equation

$$A = 1 + s + n \times a + \sum_{i=1}^{w} (V(w_i)) \tag{1}$$

where s is the number of type String attributes on the original dataset, n is the number of numeric attributes on the original dataset, a is the number of chosen attributes for numeric attributes among those described above, w is the number of nominal attributes and the function $V(w)$ is the number of values of the nominal attribute w, for all non-class attributes plus one if the attribute *last* for nominal attributes is set by the user. The number of records on the transformed dataset is equal to the number of different unique *ids* on the original datasets with at least the minimum of related records set by the user. The second step is to feed the preprocessed dataset to a machine learning algorithm.

This basic version of the algorithm maps groups of records of each observation to just one record by computing aggregates for the values of the attributes. In the case of values of type String, we keep the last value. But what to do with the class variable? In this algorithm, the user can choose what to do with it, either keeping the last class value of the group (i.e., the most recent observation) or the most dominant class value among the group's instances (i.e., the most frequent class). Choosing one or another reflects the kind of data that we are dealing with. For example, when dealing with several exams of the same kind for the same patient, choosing the last class value for that patient corresponds to the end of a patient evolution, while when dealing with weather observations records, choosing the dominant class value could correspond to choose the most frequent weather condition for a given time interval.

The records with no relation (e.g. an Id with a unique record) are discarded, as all the related records below the number of records per group chosen by the user. An example of a transformation performed by TSPPA is given in Figures 1 and 2, where the algorithm generates all the aggregation attributes (min, max, avg, ltrend and btrend). The algorithm also considers that the number of records to be aggregated per group is 3. The chosen class value is the last value of the class variable for each group of 3 records in the original dataset.

In the illustrated example, the original dataset represented in Figure 1 is a group of 7 generic records with 4 attributes each. The first of type String is the Id and it will act as the pivot attribute during the preprocessing task. The second attribute is of type Numeric, the third is of type Nominal with 3 possible values and the last one is our class type Nominal with 2 values. We fed this dataset to our T-SPPA algorithm and the output is the dataset illustrated in Figure 2. We enabled all the available aggregation attributes and set the number of records per aggregation to 3. The preprocessed dataset contains only 2 records while the attributes raised to 12. The first attribute is the Id, the next 4 attributes are numeric values corresponding to the maximum, minimum, average and last values of the *A1* attribute. The next attribute, *Trend*, is a numeric value corresponding to the prediction of the next hypothetical value using the least squares method with all values present in the group. The attribute *BinaryTrend* is a simple comparison between the *Last* value and the *Trend* value, the value of this attribute is 0 if *Last* is greater than *Trend* or 1 if not. The following 3 numeric values correspond to the relative frequencies of each nominal value of the attribute *A2*. The following attribute is a nominal value representing the last observed value for the *A2* attribute. The last attribute is the last value of the class attribute for the group.

The first record of the original dataset is discarded because we set the number of records per aggregation to 3 and the *id1*-related records are 4, only the 3 last records are considered to aggregate.

```
@ATTRIBUTE Id String
@ATTRIBUTE A1 Numeric
@ATTRIBUTE A2 {v1, v2, v3}
@ATTRIBUTE Class {0, 1}
@DATA
id1,23,v3,1
id1,20,v1,0
id1,22,v1,0
id1,18,v2,0
id2,5,v3,1
id2,6,v2,0
id2,7,v3,1
```

Fig. 1. Original dataset

Data:
Dataset, // original dataset
Input:
Iterations, // number of records per group
Input:
Attributes, // attributes chosen
Result:
Out, // original dataset transformed

Initialize a new empty dataset Out;
Read $Dataset$;
foreach *Attribute a in Dataset* **do**
    if *a has type Numeric* **then**
        create Attributes present on $Attributes$ from the possible a-Maximum,
        a-Minimum, a-Average, a-Last, a-LTrend and a-BTrend on Out;
    end
    else if *a is Nominal* **then**
        create Attributes a-Frequency for each nominal value and a-Last on Out;
    end
    else
        copy a to Out;
    end
end
Group records of the same id sorting them according to date up to $Iterations$ number of records;
foreach *Group i* **do**
    read each individual attribute value A;
    if *A has type String or is the ID* **then**
        copy A to Out;
    end
    if *A has type numeric* **then**
        calculate Maximum, Minimum, Average, Last, Linear Trend and Binary Trend
        values among all values of A according to $Attributes$ for group i;
        copy them to Out;
    end
    if *A is nominal* **then**
        copy frequency and the last value of A in group i to Out;
    end
    Take the value of the class variable of last instance or the most dominant value of
    Group i;
    Copy it to Out to complete the record
end

Algorithm 1. Transformation algorithm

```
@ATTRIBUTE Id STRING
@ATTRIBUTE A1_MAX NUMERIC
@ATTRIBUTE A1_MIN NUMERIC
@ATTRIBUTE A1_AVG NUMERIC
@ATTRIBUTE A1_LAST NUMERIC
@ATTRIBUTE A1_TREND NUMERIC
@ATTRIBUTE A1_BINARYTREND {0, 1}
@ATTRIBUTE A2_v1_PERC NUMERIC
@ATTRIBUTE A2_v2_PERC NUMERIC
@ATTRIBUTE A2_v3_PERC NUMERIC
@ATTRIBUTE A2_LAST {v1, v2, v3}
@ATTRIBUTE Class {0, 1}
@DATA
id1,22,18,20,18,18,0,66.66,33.33,0,v2,0
id2,7,5,6,7,8,1,0,33.33,66.66,v3,1
```

Fig. 2. Preprocessed dataset

This method is applicable to all kinds of data as long as it exists at least two correlated records on the original dataset to aggregate. The time complexity of our algorithm in the worst case scenario is given by the expression

$$O(A \times g) \tag{2}$$

where A is the total number of attributes on the transformed dataset and expressed in the equation 1 and g is the number of generated instances which is also the number of different aggregation groups found by our algorithm.

5   Methodology and Applications

We applied our method to three different datasets with different kinds of data. The first dataset is the well known UCI's Parkinsons dataset [8], a representation of multiple biomedical voice measurements of several individuals with and without Parkinson's disease. There are multiple individual exams for the same patient and to various patients present on this dataset. The second dataset is the Aljezur dataset which contains 4 daily weather and sea condition observations for 48 consecutive days. Each record classify the conditions to practice surf. The third dataset is the Mutagenesis dataset [3] that has the description of chemical mutagenic compounds.

After applying our algorithm to the datasets, we performed learning experiments using the WEKA v3.6.4 tool, developed at Waikato University, New Zealand. The experiments were performed using the WEKA's Experimenter module, where we set several parameters, including the statistical significance test and confidence interval, and the algorithms we wanted to use (OneR, ZeroR, PART, J48, SimpleCart, DecisionStump, Random Forests, SMO, Naive Bayes, BayesNet with TAN and K2, NBTree and

DTNB). The WEKA experimenter produces a table with the performance metrics of all algorithms with an indication of statistical differences, using one of the algorithms as a reference. The significance tests were performed using standard corrected t-test with a significance level of 0.01. The parameters used for the learning algorithms are the WEKA defaults. For all experiments we used 10-fold stratified cross-validation and report results for the test sets.

We varied the parameters of our pre-processing algorithm for each dataset trying to achieve the configuration that maximizes our results. The parameters we mixed were the number of iterations (or the number of records per aggregation group) and the available attributes for the preprocessed dataset. Here we show only the configurations that produced the best results.

Our goal is to show that our preprocessing method performs better than original datasets for most classification algorithms available for all considered metrics without any kind of parameter tuning on the selected algorithms or data selection.

5.1 Voice Data – Parkinsons Dataset

The Parkinsons dataset contains multiple voice analysis of 32 individuals in a total of 195 instances. Each instance has a unique Id, represented by the first attribute of type String, that identifies the patient and the exam. All the other 23 attributes are numeric, except the last one, the class attribute, of type Nominal with two possible values, 0 and 1, representing the patient status on Parkinson's disease. The class distribution is 25% for class 0 and 75% for class 1.

As this dataset contains between 6 and 7 voice analysis for 32 individuals, each one represented on a different record, there is an implicit relation between these records that is not represented on the original dataset. Therefore, this dataset is a good example to be preprocessed before the learning task, because we can change the learning focus from the exam to the patient and still learn from the exam.

5.2 Weather Data – Aljezur Dataset

The Aljezur dataset contains four daily observations of wind and sea conditions taken from the Aljezur beach, Portugal, between November 18th 2010 and January 6th 2011, in the total of 192 instances. The 10 attributes are: date, hour, total sea height, wave height, wave direction, wind wave height, wind speed, wind direction, water temperature and wave set quality to practice surf. This last attribute is our class which can have 2 different values: 0 and 1, where 0 means that the weather and sea conditions are not good for surf practice, and 1 means that there are good conditions to surf. A detailed description of this dataset can be seen on Table 2. The class distribution is 25% for class 0 and 75% for class 1.

The main motivation for using T-SPPA on this particular dataset is because the data is highly relational and all the instances represent a sequence of events on the same location, where one event influences all the next events and is influenced by all before it. Ordinary machine learning techniques can't reflect this property in the learning task.

Table 2. Original Aljezur dataset attributes

Attribute	Type	Values
Date	String	
Hour	Nominal	0, 6, 12, 18
Wave Total	Numeric	
Wave	Numeric	
Wave Direction	Nominal	N, NE, E, SE, S, SW, W, NW
Vaga	Numeric	
Wind Speed	Numeric	
Wind Direction	Nominal	N, NE, E, SE, S, SW, W, NW
Water Temperature	Numeric	
Sets	Nominal (Class)	0,1

5.3 Biological Data – Mutagenesis Dataset

The Mutagenesis dataset has 10486 instances and 9 attributes describing the mutagenic activity and the molecular structure of over 200 compounds. Each instance is classified with 1 if the compound is mutagenic or 0 if not. This dataset is generally made available as a simple classification problem, however, under a certain point of view, this data can be seen as a time-series problem as there is a sequence of mutation for each compound. The data is also strongly relational, each compound appears several times under different configurations, a typical 1-to-N relation.

The original dataset has a class distribution of 2696 instances for class 0 and 7790 for class 1. The relative distribution is 26% for class 0 and 74% for class 1.

We tried multiple configurations on T-SPPA algorithm to perform the preprocessing before the learning task.

6 Results

We compared our results obtained in WEKA using our preprocessing method T-SPPA with the results obtained using the original datasets. We show our best results for Percentage of Correctly Classified Instances (CCI), Precision (Precis.) and Recall. The significance tests were performed using standard corrected t-test with a significance level of 0.01. The parameters used for the learning algorithms are the WEKA defaults. For all experiments we used 10-fold stratified cross-validation and report results for the test sets.

We applied our method to the three datasets described above with various configurations (multiple available attribute combinations and number of instances per aggregation group), however here we show only our best results.

6.1 Parkinsons Dataset Results

The original dataset contains 195 records for 32 different patients. We sorted all the instances per patient Id and then preprocessed multiple times using different combinations of options. The best results were obtained with 3 instances per aggregation group (the 3 last exams) and using only the attributes average and binary trend for the numeric values. We also choose the last observed class instead of the dominant class for each aggregated group of records. Since there is no variation of class between records of the same patient, using the last or the most frequent class is irrelevant in this example.

Using the T-SPPA configuration described above, the preprocessed dataset has 32 instances, one for each unique patient Id. The number of attributes is variable depending on the user's options, but with this configuration, the number of attributes is 45. For this experiment we performed multiple combinations of attributes and number of records per aggregation group. The class distribution remains 25% for class 0 and 75% for class 1.

The results we obtained for class 1 using this T-SPPA configuration on WEKA and the comparison with the original dataset can be seen on Table 3. The results using T-SPPA were better than the original dataset for correctly classified instances using Naive Bayes, DTNB, OneR, PART, Decision Table and J48 where the gains rounded 3%. There were also some gains when looking for precision and recall metrics.

We also obtained good results using all available attributes with 2 records per aggregation, being the CCI for Bayes Net and Naive Bayes better in our preprocessed dataset. This is also true for the same configuration but using 4 records per aggregation.

Table 3. Transformed Parkinsons results for class 1

	Original Dataset			T-SPPA dataset		
	CCI%	Precis.	Recall	CCI%	Precis.	Recall
Bayes Net (K2)	79.43	0.92	0.80	72.58	0.86	0.76
Bayes Net (TAN)	86.17	0.90	0.92	81.92	0.88	0.89
Naive Bayes	68.85	0.97	0.61	71.92	0.87	0.67
SMO	86.95	0.86	0.99	84.00	0.85	0.99
DTNB	83.32	0.89	0.89	85.75	0.92	0.91
OneR	87.70	0.88	0.97	89.67	0.92	0.95
ZeroR	75.39	0.75	1.00	75.00	0.75	1.00
PART	84.94	0.90	0.90	88.17	0.91	0.93
Decision Table	83.12	0.86	0.93	86.92	0.90	0.95
Decision Stump	84.21	0.89	0.91	83.00	0.88	0.86
J48	84.74	0.91	0.89	88.17	0.91	0.93
NB Tree	88.18	0.93	0.92	72.58	0.86	0.76
Random Forest	90.53	0.91	0.97	77.42	0.82	0.90
Simple CART	86.33	0.90	0.93	85.17	0.88	0.95

6.2 Aljezur Dataset Results

In this example, our transformation considers the original attribute *date* as the *Id* to preprocess the dataset. Our best results were obtained using 2 instances per aggregation group and the attributes average and binary trend for the grouped numeric attributes. We also choose to classify the preprocessed dataset with the dominant class, i.e., the most frequent class on the aggregation group, in our case the most prominent weather and sea conditions during a given day.

The preprocessed dataset using T-SPPA method with configuration described above has 48 instances, one for each observed day, the number of attributes vary with the user's options but with this configuration is 30. The class distribution is now 17% for class 0 and 83% for class 1. The results we obtained for class 1 on WEKA and the comparison with the original dataset can be seen on Table 4.

Table 4. Transformed Aljezur results for class 1

	Original Dataset			T-SPPA dataset		
	CCI%	Precis.	Recall	CCI%	Precis.	Recall
Bayes Net (K2)	74.00	0.75	0.98	84.00	0.84	1.00
Bayes Net (TAN)	73.07	0.75	0.96	83.20	0.84	0.99
Naive Bayes	63.52	0.77	0.74	71.50	0.85	0.81
SMO	75.53	0.76	1.00	84.00	0.84	1.00
DTNB	73.54	0.75	0.97	82.05	0.83	0.98
One R	74.32	0.77	0.95	81.65	0.84	0.97
Zero R	75.53	0.76	1.00	84.00	0.84	1.00
PART	67.52	0.77	0.82	75.20	0.82	0.90
Decision Table	73.59	0.75	0.97	84.00	0.84	1.00
Decision Stump	75.16	0.76	0.98	81.65	0.84	0.97
J48	74.37	0.76	0.97	79.95	0.83	0.95
NB Tree	74.32	0.76	0.96	84.00	0.84	1.00
Random Forest	72.55	0.81	0.84	74.60	0.82	0.89
Simple CART	74.63	0.76	0.98	84.21	0.84	1.00

When looking for correctly classified instances percentage, our gains rounded 10% in certain algorithms like Bayes Net, Decision Table, NB Tree, Random Forest and Simple CART. Precision and Recall metrics had a remarkable gain in the majority of the tested algorithms.

We obtained good results using other configurations as well. For example we got better CCI percentage than the original for almost every classification algorithms using only the Binary Trend attribute for numeric attributes aggregation. We also obtained better results than the original datasets using 4 records per aggregation and for classifiers for the class 0. In general, our best results among all experiments we performed with this dataset, were with preprocessed datasets using the dominant class and with 2 records for each aggregation group.

6.3 Mutagenesis Dataset Results

The main concern with this dataset was to find an optimal number of instances per aggregation (argument N) in order to keep the class distribution and a satisfactory number of records on the preprocessed dataset to feed the machine learning algorithms. After some tests, we found that this number was between 35 and 45. Table 5 shows the number of instances and class distribution for our dataset preprocessing task with different values for the argument N in comparison with the original Mutagenesis dataset represented on the first row.

Table 5. Mutagenesis class distribution for multiple minimum number of instances

Dataset	Number of Instances	Class			
		Class = 0	Class = 1	Class = 0 Freq.	Class = 1 Freq.
Original	10486	2696	7790	26%	74%
N = 2	188	63	125	34%	66%
N = 10	188	63	125	34%	66%
N = 20	188	63	125	34%	66%
N = 35	172	51	121	30%	70%
N = 40	159	40	119	25%	75%
N = 45	139	23	116	17%	83%
N = 50	129	18	111	14%	86%
N = 60	81	4	77	5%	95%
N = 41	150	33	117	22%	78%

Table 6. Transformed Mutagenesis results for class 1

	Original Dataset			T-SPPA dataset		
	CCI%	Precis.	Recall	CCI%	Precis.	Recall
Bayes Net (K2)	84.59	0.91	0.88	76.73	0.89	0.80
Bayes Net (TAN)	86.74	0.89	0.93	83.53	0.88	0.93
Naive Bayes	67.48	0.76	0.83	70.47	0.89	0.72
SMO	74.48	0.75	1.00	81.33	0.84	0.94
DTNB	86.33	0.91	0.91	83.87	0.91	0.89
One R	86.10	0.89	0.93	77.53	0.83	0.90
Zero R	74.29	0.74	1.00	78.00	0.78	1.00
PART	85.97	0.89	0.93	85.73	0.91	0.92
Decision Table	86.32	0.89	0.93	84.00	0.88	0.94
Decision Stump	74.29	0.74	1.00	78.00	0.78	1.00
J48	86.97	0.90	0.93	87.60	0.83	0.92
NB Tree	84.80	0.90	0.89	85.27	0.91	0.90
Random Forest	88.71	0.91	0.94	87.27	0.91	0.93
Simple CART	87.66	0.90	0.93	87.47	0.92	0.93

On the multiple tests we've done with numerous configurations, the WEKA's algorithms correctly classified instances results were getting better as the argument N was getting bigger, however, the class distribution didn't reflect the class distribution present on the original dataset. We choose a number of 41 instances per aggregation group and the attributes *minimum, maximum, average, last* and *binary trend* for numeric attributes. We choose also to get the dominant class instead of the last observed class. The results obtained with this configuration and the comparison with the results obtained with the original dataset can be seen on Table 6.

Several gains were achieved in the tested algorithms with the preprocessed dataset compared with the original dataset, namely on Naive Bayes, SMO, ZeroR, Decision Stump, J48, NB Tree and Simple CART, when looking for correctly classified instances, precision and recall. The most impressive gain was when using support vector machine's SMO algorithm, the correctly classified instances percentage has raised almost 7% in comparison with the original dataset.

7 Conclusions and Future Work

Handling relational data for machine learning tasks has always been a complex problem. Many approaches have been tried to overcome this obstacle, mainly using methods based on first order logic. T-SPPA has a different approach to the problem, it learns from a subgroup of records while still learning from all dataset. All correlated records are grouped in one single record and their values are transformed into a statistical representation of all values.

In this paper we have shown that T-SPPA is applicable to different kinds of data from biological data to weather data, being generic enough to handle other kinds of data. T-SPPA is also very flexible, giving to the user multiple options to adjust the preprocessing method in order to achieve more accurate results.

In our examples the performance gain with T-SPPA is clearly visible on the Aljezur dataset on almost every analyzed metric. The gain is still visible on the Parkinsons dataset, however the number of records is the main factor to achieve a better preprocessed dataset and the Parkinsons dataset has less instances than Aljezur dataset.

Using T-SPPA also reduces the data complexity. Normally the number of instances is largely reduced and with a careful choice of aggregation method's parameters the number of attributes may remain the same. However, the granularity of the problem is generally increased, for instance, in the Parkinsons dataset, before preprocessing, each instance corresponds to an exam of a patient. After preprocessing, each instance corresponds to a sets of exams (or a summary of exams of a single patient).

T-SPPA is still a work in progress in spite of its good results. We believe that some improvements like automatic attribute selection can bring better overall performance to the algorithm. Other task to do in the future is the development of a method to automatically calculate the optimal number of minimum instances per aggregation group and keep the original class distribution. We also expect to test the method's performance on other kinds of data and with other tasks beyond classification like regression or clustering. In this paper we used only medical, biological and weather data for classification tasks, other kinds of data and tasks must be taken into account to reinforce our method's performance.

A beta version implemented in Java of T-SPPA and the Aljezur dataset are freely available at http://www.alunos.dcc.fc.up.pt/~c0316032/TSPPA

Acknowledgments

This work has been partially supported by the projects HORUS (PTDC/EIA-EIA/100897/2008) and Digiscope (PTDC/EIA-CCO/100844/2008) and by the Fundação para a Ciência e Tecnologia (FCT/Portugal). Tiago Silva has been supported by an FCT BI scholarship.

References

1. Berthold, M.R., Cebron, N., Dill, F., Gabriel, T.R., Kötter, T., Meinl, T., Ohl, P., Sieb, C., Thiel, K., Wiswedel, B.: KNIME: The Konstanz Information Miner. In: Studies in Classification, Data Analysis, and Knowledge Organization (GfKL 2007), Springer, Heidelberg (2007)
2. Helge Toutenberg, C., Rao, R.: Linear Models - Least Squares and Alternatives, 2nd edn. Springer, Heidelberg (1999)
3. Debnath, G., Shusterman, A., Hansch, C., Debnath, A.K, Lopez de Compadre, R.L.: Structure-activity relationship of mutagenic aromatic and heteroaromatic nitro compounds. correlation with molecular orbital energies and hydrophobicity. Journal of medicinal chemistry 34(2), 786–797 (1991)
4. Getoor, L., Taskar, B.: Introduction to Statistical Relational Learning. MIT Press, Cambridge (2007)
5. Hall, M., Frank, E., Holmes, G., Pfahringer, B., Reutemann, P., Witten, I.H.: The weka data mining software: an update. SIGKDD Explor. Newsl. 11 (November 2009)
6. Knobbe, A.J., de Haas, M., Siebes, A.: Propositionalisation and aggregates. In: De Raedt, L., Siebes, A. (eds.) PKDD 2001. LNCS (LNAI), vol. 2168, pp. 277–288. Springer, Heidelberg (2001)
7. Lavrac, N., Dzeroski, S.: Inductive Logic Programming: Techniques and Applications. chapter 11, Ellis Horwood, New York (1994)
8. Hunter, E.J., Ramig, L.O., Little, M.A., McSharry, P.: Suitability of dysphonia measurements for telemonitoring of parkinson's disease. IEEE Transactions on Biomedical Engineering (2008)
9. Mierswa, I., Wurst, M., Klinkenberg, R., Scholz, M., Euler, T.: Yale: Rapid prototyping for complex data mining tasks. In: Ungar, L., Craven, M., Gunopulos, D., Eliassi-Rad, T. (eds.) KDD 2006: Proceedings of the 12th ACM SIGKDD international conference on Knowledge discovery and data mining, pp. 935–940. ACM, New York (2006)
10. Theja, P.V.V.K., Vanajakshi, L.: Short term prediction of traffic parameters using support vector machines technique. In: 3rd International Conference on Emerging Trends in Engineering and Technology (ICETET) 2010, pp. 70–75 (2010)
11. Pintelas, P., Kotsiantis, S., Kanellopoulos, D.: Data preprocessing for supervised leaning. International Journal of Computer Science 1(2), 111–117 (2006)
12. Srinivasan, A.: The Aleph Manual (2001)
13. Witten, I.H., Frank, E.: Data Mining: Practical machine learning tools and techniques, 2nd edn. Morgan Kaufmann, San Francisco (2005)

Traffic Profiling in Mobile Networks Using Machine Learning Techniques

Henryk Maciejewski[1], Mateusz Sztukowski[2,3], and Bartlomiej Chowanski[2]

[1] Institute of Computer Engineering, Control and Robotics,
Wroclaw University of Technology,
Wybrzeze Wyspianskiego 27, 50-370 Wroclaw, Poland
henryk.maciejewski@pwr.wroc.pl
[2] Nokia Siemens Networks
Wroclaw, Poland
{mateusz.sztukowski,bartlomiej.chowanski}@nsn.com
[3] Academy of Management SWSPIZ, IT Institute
Sienkiewicza 9, 90-113 Lodz, Poland
m.sztukowski@swspiz.pl

Abstract. This paper tackles a problem of identifying characteristic usage profiles in the traffic related to packet services (PS) in mobile access networks. We demonstrate how this can be done through clustering of vast amounts of network monitoring data, and show how discovered clusters can be used to mathematically model the PS traffic. We also demonstrate accuracy of the models obtained using this methodology. This problem is important for accurate dimensioning of the infrastructure for mobile access network.

1 Introduction – Motivation of This Work

Packet services (PS) in mobile networks starts to be the most demanding resource consumer in 3G networks. The increased throughput of HSDPA and decreased delay under 50ms opened doors to the market previously reserved only for DSL operators. This service evolution and wide availability explains the rapid growth of mobile packet service share in total traffic varying from ca 30% to 99,5%. The growing trend is clearly visible and the share of packet services traffic can be regarded as the indication of maturity of packet services or deployment state in a particular mobile network. As a consequence, it is expected that in near future only the PS traffic will be considered in network dimensioning, especially interface dimensioning [1].

Estimation of offered traffic in dimensioning of the PS network is however a challenging task. Standard approaches are based on analysis of the Busy Hour (BH) traffic with a simplifying assumption that for the same service (i.e. HS-DPA) all areas and user groups have the same value of BH. This is schematically depicted in Fig. 1. Traffic in several areas (NodeB) with different BHs is aggregated at the RNC to yield the maximum observed traffic denoted B (Fig. 1, left). The required traffic estimated under the assumption of the same BH is denoted A

V. Snasel, J. Platos, and E. El-Qawasmeh (Eds.): ICDIPC 2011, Part I, CCIS 188, pp. 132–139, 2011.

(Fig. 1, right), and clearly A>B. In [1], we show that possible over-dimensioning of network interfaces can range up to 340%.

Hence, in order to more precisely estimate the required network capacity, complete 24-hour profiles of traffic should be considered. Once these profiles are mapped into specific groups of users or specific areas, this approach offers a new and powerful tool for precise estimation of offered traffic avoiding over-dimensioning of PS networks [1].

This work is focused on development of characteristic profiles of traffic generated by packet services. We show how these profiles can be obtained through clustering of vast amounts of PS network monitoring data and how the traffic can be modeled with these profiles. We also introduce measures of accuracy of the approximation and discuss how this model is translated into more realistic estimation of required capacity.

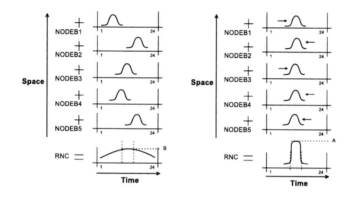

Fig. 1. Real maximum aggregated traffic at an RNC (denoted B, left) and the traffic estimated assuming the same BH (denoted A, right)

2 Characteristics of Performance Monitoring Data for Packet Services

The UMTS network consists of two main parts: the core network and the terrestrial radio access network (UTRAN). UTRAN connects NodeB and through its sectors (cells) UEs to the core network. The NodeBs in one region, called radio network subsystem (RNS) are connected to one RNC.

Our focus is the above-mentioned RNS. It is compound with Radio Network Controllers (RNC) that control the use and reliability of the radio resources and collect measurements from multiple NodeBs through IuB interface. The last level of this structure consists of cells (sectors of NodeB) which provide radio connection with User Equipment (UE). IDs of all these network elements uniquely identify every cell in the network.

Performance monitoring data measured at RNCs will be used for traffic profiling (clustering). Depending on the counter, RNCs aggregate data in 20-second intervals with additional updates when a connection is released or the active set is changed. Accordingly to the configuration, once per hour, 15 or 5 minutes data are gathered at the common Operation Support System (OSS) where data from the whole network are available.

In this research, we focus on the counter which measures the transferred volume. This counter records the amount of data transferred from the SRNC MAC-d to the IuB interface on a NodeB. The granularity of analyzed data is defined as the volume transferred in hourly intervals at a single cell in a NodeB. This is regarded as one of the most useful measures in offered traffic estimation.

Prior to traffic profiling described in the next section, we pre-summarize the monitoring data. For every cell of every NodeB, we calculate the average hourly traffic over two weeks (only working days) of monitoring data (based on the Cell Throughput counter). We thus obtain a 24-element feature vector (CellVolume(hour0),..,CellVolume(hour23)) per each cell. The set of such vectors indexed by (RCN_ID, NodeB_ID, Cell_ID) forms the database used for traffic profiling.

As shown in [1], PS traffic at different cells tends to have different BH (as shown in Fig. 1, left). To describe the distribution of BH in a collection of cells, we define the measure Load Distribution Factor (LDF):

$$LDF = \frac{\sum_1^n max\{CellVolume_i(hour0), ..., CellVolume_i(hour23)\}}{max\{\sum_1^n CellVolume_i(hour0), ..., \sum_1^n CellVolume_i(hour23)\}} \quad (1)$$

where n is the number of cells in the collection analyzed. Note that a collection of cells with the same BH realizes the $LDF = 1$. Similar measure can be also defined for a collection of NodeBs (then $LDF = A/B$, Fig. 1), or for a set of user groups or traffic profiles. LDF can be then interpreted as the measure of dispersion of BH within the set.

The value of LDF also indicates by how much the required capacity can be over-estimated if single BH per cell (or per NodeBs) is assumed. It can be shown [1] that for CS (circuit switch) traffic $LDF \approx 1$ (in this case the single BH assumption is well justified), while for typical PS traffic LDF is between $2 - 3$.

3   Clustering of the PS Traffic Monitoring Data

Through clustering of the aggregated traffic monitoring data described in the previous section, we attempt to identify groups of cells (clusters) with similar 24-hour traffic profiles.

The measure of similarity defined for the task of clustering should realize the goal of clustering, i.e. minimizing the within-cluster BH distribution. The Euclidean distance definition is not appropriate for this, because it would differentiate cells with different load instead of different load characteristics. For this reason, we propose to use the correlation distance defined as:

$$dist = \frac{1 - corr(v1, v2)}{2} \quad (2)$$

Traffic profiles of th clusters discovered will be then used to model (approximate) the traffic seen by the RNCs in the network. In this way, the required capacity for RNCs can be derived from the traffic profiles of clusters, eliminating the need for the simplifying assumption that all cells (or user related groups of cell) have the same BH.

For this approach to be feasible, we need to solve the challenging problem of choosing the right collection of clusters to form the model. This problem is challenging since results of clustering depend on the clustering algorithm (such as the linkage function), and determination of the right number of clusters in data is difficult [2]. We thus propose a criterion to estimate quality of a given set (denoted CLUS) of candidate clusters CLUS=$\{C_1,..,C_m\}$ from the perspective of the traffic model building:

$$LDF_{CLUS} = \sum_{i=l..m} w_i * LDF_{C_i} \qquad (3)$$

where the LDF_{Ci} is computed for cells in cluster C_i, and weights w_i represent the share of the total traffic comprised in cluster C_i. Minimizing this criterion we favour clusters which aggregate cells with similar BH. This characteristic of clusters is important from the perspective of traffic modeling.

The proposed approach to dimensioning can be summarized in the following steps:

- Based on the complete project data derive the set of clusters CLUS realizing the smallest value of LDF_{CLUS}. This should be done by applying proper distance definition and performing a comprehensive search over different parameters of clustering algorithms and different number of clusters in CLUS.
- Calculate the LDF improvement as $LDF_{IMP} = (LDF - LDF_{CLUS})/LDF$, where LDF is computed for all cells in the project (network). This measure indicates by how much dimensioning will improve by using the proposed approach as opposed to the constant BH-based approach.
- Taking into account that clusters will be mapped onto distinct user groups (further development), the final number of clusters should not exceed 10.
- If LDF is around 1, then capacity of RNCs in this network can be safely estimated using the standard approach (single BH).

This approach has been successfully verified on data collected from projects (networks) from 3 regions (Europe, Asia and Africa).

Here we illustrate the approach by a numerical example based on a network from Asia region.

Here is the summary of technical details pertaining to this example:

- The network comprised 2175 cells with data gathered over 2 weeks.
- Prior to clustering, 158 outlier cells were removed (cells not supporting the HSPDA service or cells with very low traffic load).
- The dimensionality of traffic profile vectors was reduced to include hours 8 through 23 (traffic in remaining hours was small and similar throughout all cells, thus was removed).

– We used hierarchical clustering algorithm with different linkage functions (ie., definitions of inter-cluster distance). We found that the Ward variance minimization linkage function outperformed other methods in terms on minimizing the LDF_{CLUS} criterion. We chose the final number of clusters to be 6 (as more clusters produce relative low growth of LDF_{IMP}).

The final set of 6 clusters derived through automated tuning of clustering parameters and used for traffic model building is depicted in Fig. 1 and summarized in Table 1. We observe from Table 1 that cluster 1 groups the biggest number of cells (552) with relatively least concentrated BH (as indicated by highest value of LDF). However, these cells (1/4 of the whole network) comprise only ca 10.8% total traffic in the network (as indicated by cluster weight). It means that we get high LDF but for group of cells with relatively low traffic (hence not important from dimensioning perspective). Clusters 2, 3, 4 and 6 group cells with more similar BH and account for 12-18% of traffic each.

Table 1. Characteristics of the 6 clusters selected for the traffic model. A and B measures are as in Fig.1.

Cluster ID	Cells	Percent of all cells	A	B	LDF
1	512	10.78	7 711 948 688	2 974 000 438	2.593
2	197	12.53	6 571 951 246	4 662 096 031	1.409
3	257	15.05	7 824 997 896	5 034 012 859	1.554
4	312	17.47	9 984 027 564	6 544 184 840	1.526
5	471	26.04	14 695 791 631	7 377 849 479	1.992
6	228	18.14	9 292 284 903	6 480 173 825	1.434

The overall LDF for the traffic model based on these clusters (calculated according to (2)) is given in Table 2. We compare this value with the LDF obtained from (1), ie. without the model, and conclude that the model leads to 43% improvement in LDF. This proves that the model based capacity estimation is much less influenced by the distribution of BH then the standard approach where single BH is (incorrectly) assumed for all cells (or NodeBs).

Table 2. LDF and LDF improvement

LDF per Project	LDF from model	Percent of LDF improvement
2.489	1.735	43.449

In Tables 3 and 4 more detailed analysis of accuracy of the model in terms of the LDF measure is summarized. Based on these results we conclude that application of the developed traffic model to individual RNCs leads to improved estimation of required capacity for the RNCs in the range from 25 to roughly 80%. This proves that the global traffic model (developed from the whole set of NodeBs and cells) holds locally for individual RNCs.

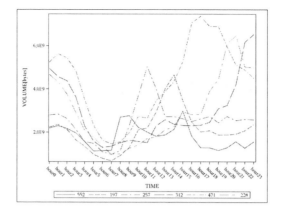

Fig. 2. Profiles of the final set of 6 clusters used for the traffic model

Table 3. Accuracy of the traffic model applied to individual RNCs measured in terms of *LDF* improvement

RNC_ID	Number of cells	% of all cells	LDF	LDF from model	% of LDF improvement
1	814	37.43	2.186	1.6	36.63
2	316	14.53	1.912	1.541	25.3
3	644	29.61	2.399	1.733	38.43
4	249	11.45	2.511	1.688	48.7
5	152	6.989	3.419	1.959	74.58

Table 4. Detailed traffic model for RNC=1. The table shows contribution of clusters in the RNC traffic. A and B measures are as in Fig.1.

Cluster ID	Number of cells	A	B	Percent of total traffic	LDF
1	196	2 126 634 603	950 947 073	10.78	2.236
2	85	2 830 259 690	2 074 350 170	12.53	1.364
3	103	3 032 840 254	2 198 728 783	15.05	1.379
4	112	4 085 100 502	3 153 388 183	17.47	1.295
5	166	5 411 722 662	2 758 477 235	26.04	1.962
6	88	3 936 242 987	2 937 017 189	18.14	1.34

Table 5. Accuracy of the traffic model for RNCs in the network

RNC_ID	Percent of model error
1	27.8
2	28
3	25.3
4	20.1
5	18.7

4   Accuracy of the Traffic Model

Although the most important measure to express the quality of the cluster based traffic model is based on the LDF improvement, we also directly compared the traffic model with the real traffic observed in different RNCs. The comparison (done for all RNCs in the project) is given in Fig. 3. In order to objectively compare the real and the model-based traffic, we introduce the measure

$$Error = \frac{\sum_{hour=0..23} |RT_h - MT_h|}{\sum_{hour=0..23} RT_h} * 100\% \tag{4}$$

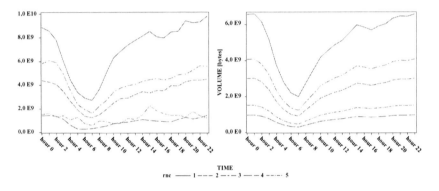

Fig. 3. Real traffic observed at different RNCs (left) and traffic for the same RNCs as predicted by the cluster based model (right)

where RT_h is the real and MT_h is the model-based traffic at hour h. This accuracy measure calculated for RNCs in the network is given in Table 3.

Table 5 presents inaccuracy for a sample day for the analyzed project. The first conclusion from this is that from varying LDF we get aproximately constant error calculated within 24-hours. In [1] detailed analysis of the error has been performed. By applying cross-validation for several projects we prove that this conclusion is valid also for various workdays of the week.

5   Conclusions

Based on inaccuracy of the model (approximately constant) the key conclusion of the work is that proposed machine learning techniques can significantly improve accuracy of dimensioning for mobile access networks. These are the two most important conclusions:

– Clustering cell trafic characteristics with the proper definition of distance between feature vectors leads to minimization of the effect of dispersion of BH on the estimated required capacity.

– Traffic model will be derived globally can be successfully applied on the RNC level.

For now, the results indicate that if we are able to identify the traffic profiles (clusters) and map them onto traffic model provided by operator, potential error in dimensioning of mobile access networks will be minimized.

Further research currenty undertaken consist in identification of these traffic profiles. Then this methodology will become a fully practical tool for telecom operators.

All data analyses were done with the SAS software. Clustering was done with hierarchical algorithm implemented in SAS/STAT.

References

1. Sztukowski, M., Maciejewski, H., Chowanski, B., Koonert, M.: Dimensioning of Packet Networks Based on Data-Driven Traffic Profile Modeling. In: Proc. of the First European Teletraffic Seminar (ETS 2011), Poznan (2011)
2. Han, J., Kamber, M.: Data Mining: Concepts and Techniques, 2nd edn.
3. Foster, I., Kesselman, C.: The Grid: Blueprint for a New Computing Infrastructure. Morgan Kaufmann, San Francisco (1999)
4. McGregor, A., Hall, M., Lorier, P., Brunskill, J.: Flow clustering using machine learning techniques. In: Barakat, C., Pratt, I. (eds.) PAM 2004. LNCS, vol. 3015, pp. 205–214. Springer, Heidelberg (2004)
5. Li X., Bigos W., Goerg C., Timm-Giel A., Klug A.: Dimensioning of the IP-based UMTS Radio Access Network with DiffServ QoS Support. In : Proc. of the 19th ITC Specialist Seminar on Network Usage and Traffic (ITC SS 19), at Technische Universität Berlin, and Deutsche TelekomLaboratories (2008)
6. Leung, K.K., Massey, W.A., Whitt, W.: Traffic Models for Wireless Communication Networks. IEEE Journal on Selected Areas in Communications 12(8) (1994)
7. 3GPP TS 25.401, Technical Specification Group Radio Access Network: UTRAN Overall Description

A Deterministic Approach to Association Rule Mining without Attribute Discretization[*]

Juan L. Domínguez-Olmedo, Jacinto Mata, Victoria Pachón, and Manuel J. Maña

Escuela Técnica Superior de Ingeniería, Universidad de Huelva,
Ctra. Palos de la Frontera SN, Huelva, Spain
{juan.dominguez,mata,vpachon,manuel.mana}@dti.uhu.es

Abstract. In association rule mining, when the attributes have numerical values the usual method employed in deterministic approaches is to discretize them defining proper intervals. But the type and parameters of the discretization can affect notably the quality of the rules generated. This work presents a method based on a deterministic exploration of the interval search space, with no use of a previous discretization but the dynamic generation of intervals. The algorithm also employs auxiliary data structures and certain optimizations to reduce the search and improve the quality of the rules extracted. Some experiments have been performed comparing it with the well known deterministic Apriori algorithm. Also, the algorithm has been used for the extraction of association rules from a dataset with information about Sub-Saharan African countries, obtaining a variety of good-quality rules.

Keywords: Data Mining, Association Rules, Attribute Discretization.

1 Introduction

In the field of data mining, association rules are a popular technique to find associations between several attributes in a dataset. Unlike classification, association rules are descriptive. Descriptive mining tasks characterize the general properties of the data [1].

Early studies on association rules focused on data with binary valued attributes, mainly applied to transactional format data, as for *market basket* datasets [2]. This name comes from the application to the problem of identifying new opportunities for cross-selling products to customers. Apart from market basket data, association rule mining is also applicable to other domains such as bioinformatics, medical diagnosis or scientific data analysis.

A variety of methods have been developed to treat this problem, mainly variations of the Apriori algorithm [3], [4]. In Apriori, the search for rules is based on the downward closure property, which states that a subset of a frequent itemset must also be frequent.

However, applying these methods to data containing numerical (quantitative) attributes, the common case in real-world applications, is usually approached by

---

[*] This work was partially funded by the Spanish Ministry of Science and Innovation, the Spanish Government Plan E and the European Union through ERDF (TIN2009-14057-C03-03).

V. Snasel, J. Platos, and E. El-Qawasmeh (Eds.): ICDIPC 2011, Part I, CCIS 188, pp. 140–150, 2011.

discretizing those attributes previously [5]. So, the rules are going to show associations between the values of some attributes, in the form of a numerical interval for each of them.

The generation of quantitative association rules is not trivial because of the computational complexity due to combinatorial explosion. Its computational complexity results to be NP-complete in the general case [6].

In this work, a deterministic method to generate association rules without the discretization of numerical variables is presented. The algorithm also employs auxiliary data structures and certain optimizations to reduce the search and improve the quality of the rules extracted.

The organization of this paper is as follows. The next section provides a preliminary on association rules and some quality measures. Section 3 describes the method employed. In section 4 the experimental results are shown. Finally, section 5 provides some conclusions.

2   Association Rules

An association rule is an expression of the form $A \Rightarrow C$, where A and C express conditions on attributes of the dataset, respectively, the *antecedent* and the *consequent* of the rule.

The basic measures of the quality of a rule are the *support* and the *confidence*. The support measures the number of instances (or the percentage) in which both the antecedent and the consequent of the rule hold (equation 1). The confidence is the quotient between the support of the rule and the number of instances in which the antecedent holds (equation 2).

$$support(A \Rightarrow C) = support(A \wedge C) . \tag{1}$$

$$confidence(A \Rightarrow C) = support(A \wedge C) / support(A) . \tag{2}$$

The usual parameters employed in the extraction of association rules are *minsup* and *minconf*, thresholds for the minimum support and minimum confidence of a rule to be considered interesting.

Another measure of the interestingness of a rule is the *lift* [7], which measures how many times more often the antecedent and consequent hold together in the dataset than would be expected if they were statistically independent. It can be computed by the quotient between the confidence of the rule and the probability of the consequent (equation 3).

$$lift(A \Rightarrow C) = confidence(A \Rightarrow C) / Probability(C) . \tag{3}$$

The classical approach to the treatment of numerical attributes in the generation of association rules is a previous discretization of them. But when discretization is applied to numerical attributes in association rule mining, is not possible to employ the usual methods of application in classification models, such as those based on the information theory [8], [9].

Instead, unsupervised discretization methods such as *equi-width* or *equi-frequency* have to be used [10]. In both of these methods, a parameter determines the number of bins, and each bin is associated with a distinct discrete value.

In equi-width, the continuous range is evenly divided into intervals that have an equal width and each interval represents a bin. In equi-frequency, an equal number of continuous values are placed in each bin.

3   Description of the Algorithm

This work presents a method based on a deterministic approach to treat the problem of generating association rules without a previous discretization of the numerical attributes. The procedure is based on a dynamic generation of intervals for each numerical attribute, searching for valid rules satisfying the thresholds *minsup* and *minconf*.

The bounds of the intervals of the numerical attributes are restricted to be existing values in the dataset for each attribute. By doing so, there is no loss of interesting rules, because for each possible rule that can be constructed without that restriction, there is always a rule with all of its bounds being dataset values and with the same support, confidence and lift values.

3.1   Auxiliary Tables

In order to have an efficient way of generating the interval bounds and calculating the rule quality measures, several auxiliary tables are used.

Concretely, a table T_0 is built sorting each attribute ascendingly, a table T_1 holds the corresponding ordered position in T_0 of each dataset value, and another table T_2 holds the corresponding position in the original dataset of each value in T_0.

Equations 4 and 5 show the relationships between T_1 and T_2, and Table 1 shows an example dataset and its associated tables T_0, T_1 and T_2.

$$T_1[\ T_2[\ i\ ][\ j\ ]\ ][\ j\ ] = i\ . \tag{4}$$

$$T_2[\ T_1[\ i\ ][\ j\ ]\ ][\ j\ ] = i\ . \tag{5}$$

Table 1. An example dataset and the corresponding auxiliary tables T_0, T_1 and T_2

A_1	A_2	A_3	A_1	A_2	A_3	A_1	A_2	A_3	A_1	A_2	A_3
29	12	31	13	11	31	4	3	1	2	3	1
13	29	55	14	11	52	1	5	4	3	5	3
14	11	52	18	12	52	2	1	2	4	1	4
18	23	52	29	23	55	3	4	3	1	4	2
32	11	77	32	29	77	5	2	5	5	2	5

By using these auxiliary tables, the bounds of each interval are going to be searched in the range $[1, n]$, where n is the number of instances of the dataset. And when returning the rules, the bounds are transformed into the original values for each attribute, using the table T_0. Also, computing support is done progressively, at the same time that intervals are generated, calculating the support decrease of subintervals derived from previously valid intervals.

So, the method is based on initializing all the attribute intervals to $[1, n]$ and narrowing their bounds in an ordered process, taking into account the minimum thresholds and also the possible repetitions of attribute values.

In the process of generating the intervals, it would be desirable not to built intervals that result in redundant rules. One way of eliminate some redundant rules can be to continue narrowing the bounds of an interval if no loss of support occurred in the last subinterval. This procedure applied to the intervals of attributes for the consequent also gives better lift values, because decreasing the support of the consequent without decreasing the support of the rule, results in a better value for lift and the same confidence.

Table 2 shows an example of this rule generation process applied to the dataset of table 1. Some of the rules extracted for $minsup = 3$ and $minconf = 70\%$ are shown.

In the usual case that the dataset has discrete (categorical) attributes, their treatment can be carried out by first mapping their values into natural numbers. And if there is no interest in obtaining intervals for those attributes, their lower and upper bounds have to be restricted to be the same value in the rule generation process.

Table 2. Some of the rules that can be obtained from the dataset of table 1

rule	sup	conf	lift
$A_1[13, 29] \Rightarrow A_2[11, 23]$	3	75	0.94
$A_1[13, 29] \Rightarrow A_2[11, 23], A_3[31, 52]$	3	75	1.25
$A_1[13, 29] \Rightarrow A_2[12, 29]$	3	75	1.25
$A_1[13, 29] \Rightarrow A_2[12, 29], A_3[31, 55]$	3	75	1.25
$A_1[13, 29] \Rightarrow A_3[31, 55]$	4	100	1.25
$A_1[13, 29] \Rightarrow A_3[31, 52]$	3	75	1.25
$A_1[13, 29] \Rightarrow A_3[52, 77]$	3	75	0.94
$A_1[13, 29] \Rightarrow A_3[52, 55]$	3	75	1.25
$A_1[13, 29], A_2[11, 23] \Rightarrow A_3[31, 52]$	3	100	1.67
$A_1[13, 29], A_2[12, 29] \Rightarrow A_3[31, 55]$	3	100	1.25
$A_1[13, 18] \Rightarrow A_3[52, 55]$	3	100	1.67
$A_1[14, 32] \Rightarrow A_2[11, 23]$	4	100	1.25
$A_1[14, 32] \Rightarrow A_2[11, 23], A_3[31, 55]$	3	75	1.25

3.2 Reducing the Number of Rules

With the objective of reducing the number of rules generated, although probably discarding some rules of good quality, a parameter *delta* $\in [0, 1]$ is also used to control the exhaustivity of the rule searching process.

The parameter *delta* influences the generation of intervals for the numerical attributes, defining dynamically the minimum decrease in support while narrowing the intervals. This minimum decrease in support is evaluated at the beginning of the narrowing of each attribute, by computing (sup-$minsup$)*$delta$, where "sup" is the current support of the antecedent or the consequent (depending on if it is an attribute of the antecedent or the consequent).

Because of this non-exhaustive interval search due to *delta*, in order to fit the rule support to *minsup*, some intervals have also been considered: those that are the final intervals in the narrowing process because the *minsup* limit has been reached.

It is also possible to reduce the number of rules generated by setting a maximum number of attributes in the antecedent and consequent of the rules (parameters *maxAttrAnt* and *maxAttrCon*). Apart from limiting the combinations of attributes, it also makes rules simpler, increasing their comprehensibility. But in the other hand it usually leads to the loss of some rules with good quality measures.

3.3 Algorithm Structure

Algorithm 1 shows the structure of DEQAR (*Deterministic Extraction of Quantitative Association Rules*). The part of the algorithm that generates antecedents (*getNextAntecedent*) employs a depth-first search with backtracking, taking into account *minsup*, *delta* and *maxAttrAnt*. It scans from left to right the attributes, looking for possible valid subintervals, and storing the support reductions due to the current bounds at each interval.

Algorithm 1. DEQAR

Input: Dataset D, *minsup, minconf, delta, maxAttrAnt, maxAttrCon*
Output: Ruleset R
  create the auxiliary tables from D
  $n \leftarrow$ number of instances of D
  initialize all the attribute intervals to $[1, n]$
  while (is possible to obtain a new antecedent) do
    getNextAntecedent()
    while (is possible to obtain a new consequent for the current antecedent) do
      getNextConsequent()
      insert into R the rule obtained
    reset to $[1, n]$ the intervals of the consequent
  transform the rules in R into rules with interval bounds being the original values in D
  return R

The part that generates consequents (*getNextConsequent*) also employs a depth-first search with backtracking, taking into account *minsup*, *delta* and *maxAttrCon*. It also takes advantage of the current support of the rule for pruning consequents, relying on the support of the current antecedent and *minconf*. It scans from left to right the attributes not used in the antecedent, looking for possible valid subintervals, and storing the support reductions (both in the rule support and in the consequent support) due to the current bounds at each interval of the consequent.

4 Experimental Results

The proposed method of association rules extraction has been applied to some datasets. The results of those experiments are shown next.

4.1 Comparison with Apriori

Some experiments have been carried out to analyze the quality of the rules generated by the algorithm DEQAR. The results have been compared with those from the Apriori algorithm, using both equi-frequency and equi-width discretizations with several values for the number of bins employed. Three datasets from the UCI machine learning repository [11] have been used in the experiments, whose characteristics are summarized in table 3.

Table 3. Characteristics of the datasets used in the experiments

Dataset	# instances	# attributes	# discrete	# continuous
abalone	4177	9	1	8
glass	214	10	1	9
wine	178	14	1	13

The parameters *minsup* and *minconf* have been set to 10% and 90% respectively. For DEQAR, a value of 0.5 for *delta* has been used, and the limits for the number of attributes in the antecedent and the consequent have been taken from the combinations 3-2, 3-1 and 2-1. For Apriori, several bins from 2 to 9 were employed in the equi-frequency (EF) and equi-width (EW) discretizations. The Weka software [12] has been used for the Apriori algorithm and the discretization preprocessing.

The results for the *abalone* dataset are shown in tables 4 and 5. The best 10 generated rules after sorting them by their confidence were evaluated for their average support, average confidence and average lift. In case of equal confidence the sorting was based on the lift. The same calculations were repeated for the best 50 and the best 100 rules, and all the process was also repeated after sorting the rules by their lift-confidence values.

As can be seen, the algorithm DEQAR-3-2 presents the best average confidence and lift values both in confidence-lift and lift-confidence arrangements. Its average support values are the lowest, resulting from how DEQAR searches for intervals fitted to *minsup*, and also due to the fact that rules with good lift usually have low support values. The number of rules generated by DEQAR is remarkable higher than that from Apriori, in line with a more exhaustive search.

Table 4. Results for the dataset *abalone* sorting the rules by confidence

Algorithm	# rules	Best 10			Best 50			Best 100		
		sup	conf	lift	sup	conf	lift	sup	conf	lift
APRIORI-EF-6	3102	11.3	**100.0**	6.3	11.8	**100.0**	6.1	11.6	**100.0**	6.0
APRIORI-EF-7	1174	11.6	**100.0**	7.0	11.5	99.7	7.1	11.6	99.3	7.0
APRIORI-EF-8	427	10.4	**100.0**	8.0	10.5	99.2	7.9	10.5	98.3	7.9
APRIORI-EF-9	10	10.3	92.8	**8.4**	-	-	-	-	-	-
APRIORI-EW-6	3463	13.1	**100.0**	3.6	11.7	**100.0**	3.6	12.6	**100.0**	3.4
APRIORI-EW-7	1107	11.3	**100.0**	4.4	11.3	**100.0**	4.4	12.1	**100.0**	3.9
APRIORI-EW-8	548	14.4	**100.0**	3.9	**15.1**	**100.0**	3.8	**15.8**	**100.0**	2.9
APRIORI-EW-9	409	**15.1**	**100.0**	4.5	12.7	99.6	4.4	13.0	99.3	4.5
DEQAR-3-2	436572	10.0	**100.0**	8.3	10.0	**100.0**	**8.1**	10.0	**100.0**	8.0
DEQAR-3-1	72743	10.0	**100.0**	8.0	10.0	**100.0**	7.7	10.1	**100.0**	7.4
DEQAR-2-1	14565	10.0	**100.0**	7.7	10.2	**100.0**	6.9	10.2	**100.0**	6.4

Table 5. Results for the dataset *abalone* sorting the rules by lift

Algorithm	# rules	Best 10 sup	conf	lift	Best 50 sup	conf	lift	Best 100 sup	conf	lift
APRIORI-EF-6	3102	10.1	91.4	6.9	10.2	91.2	6.8	10.5	92.1	6.7
APRIORI-EF-7	1174	11.1	92.9	7.7	11.1	93.2	7.6	11.1	93.8	7.6
APRIORI-EF-8	427	10.1	93.8	8.5	10.2	94.1	8.3	10.3	94.1	8.3
APRIORI-EF-9	10	10.3	92.8	8.4	-	-	-	-	-	-
APRIORI-EW-6	3463	13.9	90.0	5.1	13.9	90.4	5.0	13.8	90.4	5.0
APRIORI-EW-7	1107	10.9	95.7	4.6	11.2	**98.3**	4.5	11.2	**98.9**	4.4
APRIORI-EW-8	548	**15.3**	97.2	4.8	**14.7**	98.2	4.5	**14.9**	98.3	4.4
APRIORI-EW-9	409	12.0	93.4	5.4	13.0	96.5	5.2	12.8	97.0	5.1
DEQAR-3-2	436572	10.0	96.8	**8.6**	10.0	96.8	**8.6**	10.0	97.3	**8.5**
DEQAR-3-1	72743	10.0	96.8	**8.6**	10.0	98.0	8.3	10.0	98.3	8.1
DEQAR-2-1	14565	10.0	**97.8**	8.5	10.1	97.7	8.1	10.1	97.8	7.8

Results from the datasets *glass* and *wine* are shown in tables 6 and 7. They show the averages for the best 10 rules, with both kinds of sorting. In these cases DEQAR also presents better average values than Apriori (except for the average support).

The best values for Apriori in some cases have been obtained with a high number of bins in the discretization (EF-6 and EF-8 in *abalone*) and in others with a low number of bins (EF-2 in *glass* and EW-3 in *wine*). That reflects the difficulty of knowing the best discretization method for a particular dataset.

The effect of the parameter *delta* in DEQAR has been evaluated with some tests using the dataset *wine* with *minsup* = 10%, *minconf* = 90%, *maxAttrAnt* = 3, *maxAttrCon* = 2, and varying *delta* from 0.5 to 0.3. Results for the best 100 rules, sorting them by lift-confidence, are shown in table 8. It also presents the execution times in seconds using a Pentium M 1.86 GHz CPU. As can be seen, lowering *delta* results in a deeper search for possible intervals, generating more rules and usually better quality measures on average.

Table 6. Results for the dataset *glass*

Algorithm	# rules	conf sorting sup	conf	lift	lift sorting sup	conf	lift
APRIORI-EF-2	1481	10.7	**100.0**	7.7	10.6	98.4	7.9
APRIORI-EF-3	300	11.8	**100.0**	3.8	10.7	95.2	5.3
APRIORI-EF-4	102	13.0	**100.0**	2.6	11.5	95.8	4.9
APRIORI-EF-5	53	**13.4**	**100.0**	1.2	**12.9**	97.6	2.8
APRIORI-EW-2	31954	11.4	**100.0**	4.7	10.7	95.6	5.8
APRIORI-EW-3	14139	10.8	**100.0**	2.3	10.7	96.0	3.4
APRIORI-EW-4	7295	11.8	**100.0**	1.8	10.6	94.8	5.5
APRIORI-EW-5	6171	10.9	**100.0**	3.3	10.3	94.4	3.8
DEQAR-3-2	244369	10.5	**100.0**	**9.3**	10.4	**99.1**	**9.3**
DEQAR-3-1	43163	10.6	**100.0**	8.0	10.4	98.3	8.2
DEQAR-2-1	9366	10.4	**100.0**	6.2	10.4	96.2	7.6

Table 7. Results for the dataset *wine*

Algorithm	# rules	conf sorting			lift sorting		
		sup	conf	lift	sup	conf	lift
APRIORI-EF-2	107265	10.7	**100.0**	4.8	11.2	91.0	5.2
APRIORI-EF-3	2148	10.8	**100.0**	4.2	10.5	94.7	4.4
APRIORI-EF-4	172	14.3	**100.0**	3.8	11.5	92.8	4.4
APRIORI-EF-5	38	12.4	**100.0**	3.7	**12.1**	95.6	4.7
APRIORI-EW-2	142214	10.6	**100.0**	4.1	10.1	90.0	4.8
APRIORI-EW-3	10691	**14.5**	**100.0**	5.0	11.1	93.6	5.2
APRIORI-EW-4	686	10.5	**100.0**	4.0	10.4	94.7	4.2
APRIORI-EW-5	198	11.7	**100.0**	3.7	11.0	91.9	4.7
DEQAR-3-2	2258062	10.1	**100.0**	**6.6**	10.1	**96.9**	**6.9**
DEQAR-3-1	259821	10.2	**100.0**	5.1	10.7	95.4	5.3
DEQAR-2-1	35641	10.3	**100.0**	4.3	10.2	96.5	4.5

Table 8. Results for the dataset *wine* using the algorithm DEQAR and several values of *delta*

delta	# rules	sec.	sup	conf	lift
0.50	2258062	12	10.1	96.9	6.2
0.45	7866134	42	10.4	94.8	7.0
0.40	15366188	81	10.3	94.6	7.3
0.35	21043749	104	10.2	94.8	7.2
0.30	48402218	261	10.2	94.8	7.5

4.2 Analysis of Data about Sub-Saharan African Countries

Algorithm DEQAR has also been used for the extraction of association rules from a dataset with information about Sub-Saharan African countries in the 1960s-1980s period. Concretely, the "Easterly and Levine Dataset" [13] was used[1]. Although this dataset covers 160 countries, a selection of the Sub-Saharan African countries was done, resulting in 141 instances (47 countries for three decades). The 21 variables taken into account are shown in Table 9.

First, a search for rules with *minsup* = 10% and *minconf* = 80% was performed, setting *delta* to 0.25, *maxAttrAnt* to 2 and *maxAttrCon* to 1. Some of the best rules sorting them by their confindence and lift values are shown in Table 10. As it can be seen, rules involving a variety of attributes were found, having high values of confidence and lift. For instance, one of those rules associated the school attainment with the real per capita GDP, expressing that "*In the decade of 1980's, all the countries with a value of LSCHOOL in the interval [0.1570, 1.1379], had a value of GYP in the interval [-0.0475, 0.0142]*".

Also, rules concerning the variable WAR either in the antecedent or the consequent were searched for. The parameters setting was *minsup* = 10%, *minconf* = 60% and *delta* = 0.25. Some of the best rules found are shown in Table 11. In many of those rules, the variable BLCK ("black market premium") appears associated to the presence (or absence) of war during the decade. For example, one of the rules

---

[1] This dataset was obtained from http://go.worldbank.org/K7WYOCA8T0

Table 9. Description of the selected variables from a dataset with information about Sub-Saharan African countries in the 1960s-1980s period

Variable	Description
YEAR	Decade
AGOVDEM	Anti-government demonstrations
ASSASS	Number of assassinations per thousand population, decade average
BLCK	Log of 1+ black market premium, decade average
CABCHG	Major Cabinet Changes
COMPOLT	=1 for country with genocidal incident
CONSTCHG	Major Constitutional Changes
DEMOC	Measure of democracy
COUPS	Coups d'Etat
ELF60	Index of ethnolinguistic fractionalization, 1960
GOVTCRIS	Major Government Crises
GYP	Growth rate of real per capita GDP
LLY	Ratio of liquid liabilities of the financial system to GDP, decade average
LRGDP	Log of real per capita GDP measured at the start of each decade
LSCHOOL	Log of 1 + average years of school attainment, quinquennial values
LTELPW	Log of telephones per 1000 workers
PURGES	Any systematic elimination by jailing or execution of political opposition
REVOLS	Any illegal or forced change in the top governmental elite
RIOTS	Any violent demonstration or clash of more than 100 citizens
SURP	Decade average of ratio of central government surplus (+) to GDP
WAR	=1 for war on national territory during the decade

Table 10. Some of the best rules found from the "Easterly and Levine" dataset

Antecedent	Consequent	sup	conf	lift
COMPOLT = 0 LLY [0.2907, 0.5632]	LSCHOOL [0.8372, 1.725]	10.6%	100%	3.36
DEMOC [2, 5] LTELPW [2.2721, 5.1963]	LSCHOOL [0.8372, 1.725]	10.6%	100%	3.36
COMPOLT = 1 GYP [-0.0388, 0.1099]	BLCK [0.1807, 0.9927]	10.6%	100%	3.28
YEAR = 70 SURP [-0.1320, -0.0275]	LLY [0.1542, 0.4481]	10.6%	100%	2.82
YEAR = 60 GYP [-0.0568, 0.0120]	LRGDP [6.2878, 7.0665]	10.6%	100%	2.56
YEAR = 80 LSCHOOL [0.1570, 1.1379]	GYP [-0.0475, 0.0142]	11.3%	100%	1.99
ELF60 [0.62, 0.71] WAR = 0	LLY [0.0553, 0.2297]	17.0%	100%	1.93

expresses that *"The 61.1% of the countries that suffered war on national territory had both a value of BLCK in the interval [0.2066, 1.6781] and an index of ethnolinguistic fractionalization in [0.08, 0.9]"*.

Table 11. Some of the best rules found involving the variable *WAR*

Antecedent	Consequent	sup	conf	lift
BLCK [0.3633, 1.6781] ELF60 [0.04, 0.89] LRGDP [5.438, 8.438]	WAR = 1	10.6%	65.2%	2.55
BLCK [-0.0640, 0.1751] CONSTCHG [0, 1] ELF60 [0.04, 0.82]	WAR = 0	25.5%	100%	1.34
BLCK [-0.0640, 0.1751] ELF60 [0.04, 0.82] GOVTCRIS [0, 4] LLY [0.0286, 0.5632]	WAR = 0	24.1%	100%	1.34
WAR = 1	BLCK [0.2066, 1.6781] ELF60 [0.08, 0.9]	15.6%	61.1%	2.10
WAR = 0	BLCK [-0.0640, 0.4634] COMPOLT = 0 GYP [-0.0382, 0.1099] LRGDP [5.8377, 8.2644]	45.4%	61.0%	1.25
WAR = 0	AGOVDEM [0, 10] COMPOLT = 0 GOVTCRIS = 0 RIOTS [0, 1]	46.8%	62.9%	1.21

5 Conclusions

This paper presents a method based on a deterministic approach to treat the problem of generating association rules without a previous discretization of the numerical attributes. It has been compared with the classical deterministic algorithm Apriori, which needs to discretize the numerical attributes before starting to search for rules.

Several experiments were performed, comparing the average quality of the best rules found. The results show that DEQAR algorithm presented better values of the quality measures (confidence and lift) for the datasets evaluated, in accordance with a more exhaustive search for intervals. The experiments also reflected the difficulty of knowing the best discretization technique for a particular dataset, in order to apply it to a deterministic algorithm like Apriori.

Also, the algorithm DEQAR has been used for the extraction of association rules from a dataset with information about Sub-Saharan African countries in the 1960s-1980s period. The variety of the rules obtained and the high values of their quality measures seem to confirm this approach as a valid alternative in the generation of association rules.

References

1. Han, J., Kamber, M.: Data Mining: Concepts and Techniques. Morgan Kaufmann, San Francisco (2006)
2. Agrawal, R., Imielinski, T., Swami, A.: Mining Association Rules between Sets of Items in Large Databases. In: ACM SIGMOD ICMD, pp. 207–216. ACM Press, Washington (1993)

3. Borgelt, C.: Efficient Implementations of Apriori and Eclat. In: Workshop on Frequent Itemset Mining Implementations. CEUR Workshop Proc. 90, Florida, USA (2003)
4. Bodon, F.: A Trie-based APRIORI Implementation for Mining Frequent Item Sequences. In: 1st International Workshop on Open Source Data Mining: Frequent Pattern Mining Implementations, Chicago, Illinois, USA, pp. 56–65. ACM Press, New York (2005)
5. Srikant, R., Agrawal, R.: Mining Quantitative Association Rules in Large Relational Tables. In: Proc. of the ACM SIGMOD 1996, pp. 1–12 (1996)
6. Wijsen, J., Meersman, R.: On the Complexity of Mining Quantitative Association Rules. Data Mining and Knowledge Discovery 2, 263–281 (1998)
7. Brin, S., Motwani, R., Ullman, J.D., Tsur, S.: Dynamic Itemset Counting and Implication Rules for Market Basket Data. In: Proc. of the ACM SIGMOD 1997, pp. 265–276 (1997)
8. Lee, C.-H.: A Hellinger-based Discretization Method for Numeric Attributes in Classification Learning. Knowledge-Based Systems 20(4), 419–425 (2007)
9. Tsai, C.-J., Lee, C.-I., Yang, W.-P.: A Discretization Algorithm Based on Class-Attribute Contingency Coefficient. Information Science 178(3), 714–731 (2008)
10. Liu, H., Hussain, F., Tan, C., Dash, M.: Discretization: An Enabling Technique. Data Mining and Knowledge Discovery 6(4), 393–423 (2002)
11. UCI Machine Learning Repository, http://archive.ics.uci.edu/ml
12. Hall, M., Frank, E., Holmes, G., Pfahringer, B., Reutemann, P., Witten, I.: The WEKA Data Mining Software: An Update. SIGKDD Explorations 11(1) (2009)
13. Easterly, W., Levine, R.: Africa's Growth Tragedy: Policies and Ethnic Divisions. Quarterly Journal of Economics 112(4), 1203–1250 (1997)

Visualization and Simulation in Data Processing with the Support of Business Intelligence

Milena Janakova

Silesian University in Opava, School of Business Administration in Karvina,
Department of Informatics, Univerzitni nam. 1934,
733 40 Karvina, Czech Republic
mija@opf.slu.cz

Abstract. The paper aim is suggests a way of improvement opportunities for existing solution in Business Intelligence (BI) product architecture. The useful inspirations are links to database and operating systems. BI architecture is too wide, recommended merger leads to simplification on base integration of system sources and available methods for data integration. BI products offer procedures with stored data for future data processing. The benefit is the advantage of a relatively large variety of analyses, although a question remains concerning their utility and the complexity of the implementation. For the evaluation of practical applications, they must accept the dynamic and diverse needs of business and individuals. Presented analysis of selected products is based on Petri Nets with simulation support, and future analysis using an incidence matrix and reachable markings. This analysis helps in search of new perspectives and innovations.

Keywords: Analysis, Business Intelligence, data processing, information, Petri Nets.

1 Introduction

This individual approach to practical implementation of information technology products is important with regards to a number of problems which are different from companies and institutions. The view to the size and business focus of the company is particularly important. Similarly, security, knowledge, time and finance area must be considered. The availability of a creative environment user is growing and is increasingly taking the place of data processing. Suitable inspiration is the requirement and preference of the younger generation. This generation is network-oriented ("net-centered") and is able to use the web to create its own business pathways which are customized to their pace, are available upon request, and are customized to their needs. For example, M. Prensky [13] identifies the main characteristics of net-generation students. They

- are used to getting information quickly,
- are familiar with multitasking,
- prefer graphics over text information,

V. Snasel, J. Platos, and E. El-Qawasmeh (Eds.): ICDIPC 2011, Part I, CCIS 188, pp. 151–159, 2011.
© Springer-Verlag Berlin Heidelberg 2011

- work better if they have a network (and can co-operate),
- are accustomed when work is linked to frequent evaluation and rewards (like in computer games).

The above mentioned characteristics and needs are also useful for the majority of information technology users. All users require information quickly, multitasking, graphics outputs with visualization, and Internet support. Information technology products influence these needs to a greater or lesser extent. The question is "Which implemented solution best suits users?", and "How to improve existing solutions?". The answer is not unique because preferences, users and information technology options exhibit variety. The greatest unknowns are the user preferences which are difficult to estimate. It is problematic that an "average" user does not exist. [17] Practice puts pressure on the characteristics of a good user product [7] and the correct response to given inputs with prevent errors and uncontrolled situations.

Companies and organizations must resist the growing pressures and increased competition in the global information society; it is therefore important to provide information technology support in all activities and businesses. Users have default starting operating systems with future hosting applications for data processing. Database systems and BI products are needed for working with data and information. Database systems are dedicated to storing the data in the database with a system structure for further analysis and decision-making. The base rule is to receive information in time and of adequate quality. The benefits of practical implementation in practice are individual for each individual knowledge and skills. BI products provide a wide spectrum of applications for the automated search of large stores of data for patterns and trends that transcend simple analysis. [12] Users can select from commercial or open-source products. The attractive aim of BI is to provide a basis for informed decisions, and insights into the current market situation with the specifications of new markets.

2 Information Technology for Support Data Processing

Information technology users can select from various database platforms, and specialized platforms for BI application. According to Gartner, the market leaders belong to the database platforms designed for Business Intelligence, Oracle Database, IBM DB2 and Teradata. [15] The Oracle database system is popular because this database system provides elastic and effective ways for information management and application design. Oracle continues the tradition of feature enhancement by making memory management more automated, adding new advisors, and significantly improving availability and failover capabilities. [3] The Oracle Enterprise Manager creates a web site for a management database system with exemplary adaptability. The default management methods were based on a SQL statement that requires the needed syntax, attributes and optimal running. The above mentioned interface Oracle Enterprise Manager builds standard web pages for easy manipulation via the mouse.

BI products provide a similar situation on the market (as with the database systems). Companies and organizations can select from various products of this type. Traditional products are, for example, from Oracle, SAP, IBM, and open-source products such as JasperSoft, or Pentaho. Until recently it was thought that BI is only suitable for large enterprises with hundreds of employees to fully utilize its potential, but recent surveys show that BI is gradually promoted in middle and even small businesses. [11] The reasons for the increase in the use of these products are existence procedures for visibility unexpected and surprising connections based on information.

In addition to the options of BI products, there is the area of advanced data analysis. This includes also data mining with useful links to swarm intelligence. [1] Data mining finds relationships in existing data which are hidden and employing sophisticated mathematical methods. Future objects of analysis are ad-hoc analysis, and reporting. Reporting represent ways of interpreting the information needed for decision support. Ad-hoc analysis enables the searching of data and information related to specific needs.

***

A correct analysis for the specified area of interest is based on a multidimensional methodology MDIS [16] with object access. A multidimensional approach to the solution makes use of all points of view regarding data, function, organization, technology and finance. Future view on the level of abstraction, time, substantive and methodological-organizational dimension are also considered. The standard object approach creates specified objects with data attributes and defines functions over these data. The benefit is the existing relations between the objects, which is considerably more. Practically, the progress of the work is divided into three steps.

The first step was the partition of subject areas at different layers such as the environment user, process management, file system, and security. This approach is verified practically with operating systems. The operating systems are divided into specific layers for better design and future implementation. This type of arrangement reduces the number of inter-dependences, and a lower layer does not make use of any higher layers services.

The second step of the analysis begins with the creation of a model using the principles of Petri Nets. Petri Nets advantage is in a simulation parallel, and concurrent systems with a description of state changes in a system via transitions. The created model shows the characteristic features of a given reality for future superior knowledge of the studied system. Petri Nets are defined as:

$$N = (S^{\otimes}, T, \delta_0, \delta_1), \text{ where} \tag{1}$$

- $S^{\otimes}$ is a free commutative monoid of states,
- T is the set of transitions,
- $\delta_0, \delta_1: T \rightarrow S^{\otimes}$ give the source and target of each transition. [2]

Petri Nets uses a created class of objects such as transition, place, and arc. All objects are defined with attributes and accessible methods. The models are created via drawing of the desired places (the available windows of the selected products), transitions (ways of starting events with the menu, links, or buttons), and oriented edges (connection places and transitions). The places make circles, the transitions make rectangles, and the edges are arcs.

The third step is based on a classic analysis. Classic analysis of Petri Nets for models is realized by matrix representation with incidence matrix and set of reachable markings. The definition incidence matrix is:

$$C = O^T - I^T \ [9].\tag{2}$$

Benefit is easily demonstrated by offered activities and their confrontation. The following rows show a practical application analysis with Petri Nets to create models for BI products and database systems. The analysis is necessitated by the changes in user preferences, needs, and the existing environment. Database systems and BI products need new challenges, and analysis to be able to create an efficient, dynamic, and user-friendly environment. The Oracle database system is selected for analysis, and comparison with a BI product such as JasperSoft suite.

3   Business Intelligence Product Analysis

Business Intelligence products magically attract the interest of users, via vision to reveal unexpected connections and prepare people for upcoming events. The aim is to recognize changes in customer behavior, understand their views, segment customers and create a customized offer. [5] This focus influences BI product architecture. Existing data processing must implement data acquisition, needed cleaning and completion. Future processes are focused on transformation, writing data into data storage, and analysis with reporting, OLAP (On-Line Analytical Processing), or data mining. BI products form the following components and tools [10]:

- Tools for end users

These tools create the given interface of analytical options. This interface creates access to available reports, OLAP structures, and the next analytical work. Users welcome these interfaces in Web sites, but user interface is also integrated into other applications in the form of MS Office. The benefit is that MS Excel provides support for connecting to an OLAP database. This integration allows for simple ways of creating effective reports and dashboards.

- Component analysis

Components create resources for analysis. Data analysis is realized in the following ways: standardized reports, ad-hoc queries, data mining, and OLAP. Data mining provides methods for finding meaningful and previously unknown relationships. The future benefit is from detection dependencies in the data modeling and forecasting.

- Database components

Database components are responsible for the implementation of data storage based on database systems. Database system manages the stored data for BI products. Users can select from various database system spectrums. The desired database structures are Data Mart, DSA (Data Stage Area), ODS (Operational Data Store), Data Store (Data Warehouse). Data Warehousing is based on a central repository of consolidated data, Data Mart is focused on a limited number of users, DSA is the temporary storage of current data (data are created from sources) for processing time, ODS is used, for example, for editing data.

- Components for data transformation and integration.

Data transformation and integration is important when considering the needs of data quality tools and resources. BI products collect data from various sources; they therefore need an optimal method to obtain data. The ETL (Extraction,

Transformation and Load) method realized the obtaining of data from source systems with future transformation into needed forms and import into given structures. Another method EAI (Enterprise Application Integration) works in actual time.

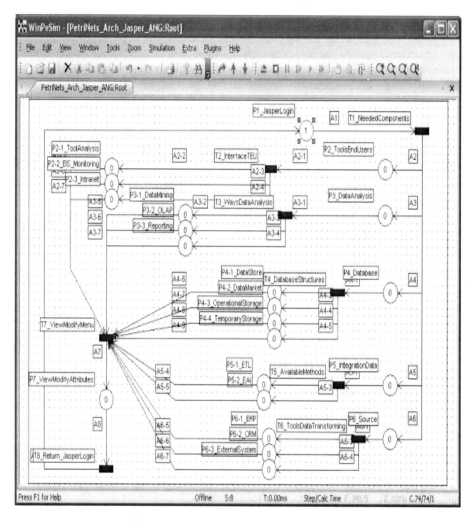

Fig. 1. A model describing Jasper architecture

The future analysis is displayed in Tab. 1 with an incidence matrix and a reachable marking. Rows of this matrix represent specified places, and transitions are needed columns. Intersections of rows and columns represent values to describe the existing inputs (number 1) and outputs (number -1). Second table section is dedicated to reachable marking. This marking shows a sequence of transitions for transfer the Petri Net (symbol →) from marking M to marking M', for example transition t1 converts Petri Net (t1 →M1) to M1 marking (tokens are in p2, p3, p4, p5, p6 places) from M0 marking (token is in p1 place).

- System source.

System sources are centered on tools for extracting and transforming data from source systems.

Users start all the components of the BI products such as JasperSoft from the operating system. A model Jasper architecture is shown in Fig. 1. This model is created in simulating program of Petri Nets HPSim. [14]

Table 1. Analysis of a BI product model with an incidence matrix and reachable marking

| | Incidence matrix | | | | | | | | t1 →M1 | t2, .., t6 →M2 | t7 →M3 | t8 →M0 |
	t1	t2	t3	t4	t5	t6	t7	t8	M0	M1	M2	M3
p1	-1	0	0	0	0	0	0	1	1	0	0	0
p2	1	-1	0	0	0	0	0	0	0	1	0	0
p2-1	0	1	0	0	0	0	-1	0	0	0	1	0
p2-2	0	1	0	0	0	0	-1	0	0	0	1	0
p2-3	0	-1	0	0	0	0	-1	0	0	0	1	0
p3	1	0	-1	0	0	0	0	0	0	1	0	0
p3-1	0	0	1	0	0	0	-1	0	0	0	1	0
p3-2	0	0	1	0	0	0	-1	0	0	0	1	0
p3-3	0	0	1	0	0	0	-1	0	0	0	1	0
p4	1	0	0	-1	0	0	0	0	0	1	0	0
p4-1	0	0	0	1	0	0	-1	0	0	0	1	0
p4-2	0	0	0	1	0	0	-1	0	0	0	1	0
p4-3	0	0	0	1	0	0	-1	0	0	0	1	0
p4-4	0	0	0	1	0	0	-1	0	0	0	1	0
p5	1	0	0	0	-1	0	0	0	0	1	0	0
p5-1	0	0	0	0	1	0	-1	0	0	0	1	0
p5-2	0	0	0	0	1	0	-1	0	0	0	1	0
p6	1	0	0	0	0	-1	0	0	0	1	0	0
p6-1	0	0	0	0	0	1	-1	0	0	0	1	0
p6-2	0	0	0	0	0	1	-1	0	0	0	1	0
p6-3	0	0	0	0	0	1	-1	0	0	0	1	0
p7	0	0	0	0	0	0	1	-1	0	0	0	1

The above-shown model builds specified places (white circles) and transitions (black rectangles). Places and transitions are connected by oriented edges. The required places of the defined model are:

- P1_Jasper_Login – location for standard login to a system with all components; this is the starting point.
- P2_ToolsEndUsers – location displays tools which users can start with for analytical work with reports, OLAP structures, or dashboards.

- P2-1 – P2-3 – items specify user options for selection as tool analysis, EIS monitoring, or Intranet.
- P3_DataAnalysis – locations where users can work with resources for analysis.
- P3-1 – P3-3 – items specify available resources for analysis as reporting, OLAP, and data mining.
- P4_Database – location contains components for needed database structures.
- P4-1 – P4-4 – accesses main structures such as data storage, data market, operation storage, and temporary storage.
- P5_IntegrationData – location shows instruments for data transformation and integration.
- P5-1 – P5-2 – accesses items (methods) for data integration such as ETL and EAI.
- P6_Source – location to specify the system source.
- P6-1 – P6-3 – access system sources items such as ERP, CRM, or the external system.
- P7_ViewModifyAttributes – location for accessing available components and items, for example, via menu, or commands.

The required transitions of the defined model are:

- T1_NeededComponents – JasperSoft system uses defined items. These items must be available for the BI product to function correctly.
- T2_InterfaceTEU – methods of working with tools for end users.
- T3_WaysDataAnalysis – transition specifies analysis options.
- T4_DatabaseStructures – BI product uses the database to store the needed data, for example in the form of data storage, or data market.
- T5_AvailableMethods – allow access to methods for data integration.
- T6_ToolsDataTransforming – create access to important sources.
- T7_ViewModifyMenu – transition enable settings and manipulation with defined components and items.
- T8_Return_JasperLogin – returns to start point P1.

The validity of the defined model is verified by starting the given simulation. A route cycle is built from place P1 via specified transitions and places. Places P2 – P6 create the standard components of the BI products. Places P2-1 – P2-3 specify the items for the tools for the end users. Places P3-1 – P3-3 consist of important analytical options. Places P4-1 – P4-4 create the main database structure. Places P5-1 – P5-2 represent methods for data integration. Places P6-1 – P6-3 specify the important sources. The next route returns to place P1.

4   Links to Database Systems Analysis

Analogue analysis is available in any information technology area, or with any information technology products. Future analysis is interesting from area operating and database systems. The reason is the necessity for an operating system as a host environment for the implemented applications such as BI products, or database systems. The database systems are selected because these systems are directly responsible for the methods of data storage. If an Oracle database system is selected, the analysis shows a similar architecture solution in an extremely sophisticated product. The default components of the Oracle database system [3] make:

- instance,
- database files,
- Oracle Client,
- and Oracle NET.

The Oracle database system creates instances which obtain the main memory structure called SGA (System Global Area), and processes the running in the background. User data are stored into data files. The Oracle database system works with additional files such as redo log files, control files, and parametric files. Oracle client and Oracle Net are utilities for establishing a connection to the database, and transferring data between the client and the server.

***

At first sight, it is apparent that the Oracle database system has four main architectural components. Appropriate solution is to encapsulate the process of working with data in an instance. This method ensures adequate security and stability with links to database files. Existing processes are running in the background and users use automatically offered services. BI products have five architecture components to correct work by user preferences. The needed spectrum interest is caused by a partition to the scope of the analytical work with stored data and issues for work with data source including data integration and database cooperation. From a practical point of view it would be more appropriate to merge components for data integration with system sources. The merger offers simplification of architecture, and the links between data and the way of their acquisition are clarified.

This view allows specification of the characteristics of a good user product. Users have a full view of the existing similarity between the adopted solutions of the selected products. The interest is divided into areas such as efficiency and effectiveness, easy handling, user resiliency and adaptability. Specifically, created models help to determine number of places, transitions, and the necessary links between them.

5 Conclusion

Information technology products have an influence over all areas of business and individual activities. BI products are particularly attractive. The reasons for this situation are the pressure of press market and the need for a competitive advantage. The BI product aims have an influence on architecture. The main architecture components are tools for end users, analysis, database, data integration, and system source. The effective analysis of the adopted solution has been realized by Petri Nets via places and transitions. A presented analysis is based on a multidimensional methodology with object access. The benefits of the realized analysis are options to compare the complexity and scope with another product like Oracle database system.

Results of comparison show that the BI solution architecture takes a broader view in contrast with database systems. The database system architecture needs only four components. The benefit of this architecture is implementation to very sophisticated and consistent resolution. BI products must receive more stability and security in practice for optimal seeking of an answer to user questions about future market development and customer preferences. System source and available methods for data integration are closely tied; therefore, optimal innovation is to merge these components into one object, and simplify the BI implementation in practice.

References

1. Abraham, A., Grosan, C., Ramos, V.: Swarm Intelligence in Data Mining. Studies in Computational Intelligence. Springer, Germany (2006) ISBN 3-540-34955-3
2. Abramsky, S.: Petri Nets, Discrete Physics, and Distributed Quantum Computation. Oxford University Computing Laboratory, Oxford,
   http://www.comlab.ox.ac.uk/files/381/fest.pdf
3. Bryla, B., Loney, K.: Oracle Database 11g DBA Handbook. McGraw-Hill Publishing Company, New York (2008) ISBN 978-0-07-149663-6
4. Černý, J.: Is world information overload?,
   http://pctuning.tyden.cz/index.php?option=com_content&view=article&id=20154&catid=1&Itemid=57
5. Eckerson, W.: Leveraging BI to Create New Value in a Downturn. TDWI (2009)
6. Fletcher, D., Gu, P.: Adaptable Design for Design Reuse. Department of Mechanical and Manufacturing Engineering The University of Calgary, Alberta, Canada (2005),
   http://www.cden.ca/2005/2ndCDEN-conference/data/10061.pdf
7. General characteristics of a good user of the product. Programming Technology,
   http://odkazy.internetshopping.cz/internet/technologie_programovani/otazky.htm
8. Gold, R.: Petri Nets in Software Engineering,
   http://www.haw-ingolstadt.de/fileadmin/daten/allgemein/dokumente/Working_Paper/ABWP_05.pdf
9. Kochaníčková, M.: Petriho sítě. Palacky University, Faculty of Science, Department of Computer Science, Olomouc. Without ISBN (2008)
10. Novotný, O., Pour, J., Slánský, D.: Business Intelligence, Praha. Grada Publishing (2005) ISBN 80-247-1094-3
11. Open-source Business Intelligence, http://www.systemonline.cz/business-intelligence/open-source-business-intelligence.htm
12. Oracle Database Concepts,
    http://www.oracle.com/technology/documentation
13. Prensky, M.: The Reformers Are Leaving Our Schools in the 20th Century,
    http://www.marcprensky.com/blog/
14. Petri Nets Tools Database Quick Overview, http://www.informatik.uni-hamburg.de/TGI/PetriNets/tools/quick.html
15. Trends in the Czech Market for the Second Time BI,
    http://www.dbsvet.cz/view.php?cisloclanku=2008032801
16. Voříšek, J.: Information systems and management. Textbook BIVŠ, Prague (2005)
17. What bring WebExpo, conference. Good site - User experience (2010),
    http://blog.dobryweb.cz/konference-webexpo/

Using Two-Step Modified Parallel SOM for Song Year Prediction

Petr Gajdoš and Pavel Moravec

Department of Computer Science, FEECS, VŠB – Technical University of Ostrava,
17. listopadu 15, 708 33 Ostrava-Poruba, Czech Republic
{petr.gajdos,pavel.moravec}@vsb.cz

Abstract. This paper uses a simple modification of classic Kohonen network
(SOM), which allows parallel processing of input data vectors or partitioning the
problem in case of insufficient memory for all vectors from the training set for
computation of SOM by CUDA on YearPredictionMSD Data Set. The algorithm,
presented in previous paper pre-selects potential centroids of data clusters and
uses them as weight vectors in the final SOM network. The sutability of this
algorithm has been already demonstrated on images as well as on two well-known
datasets of hand-written digits.

Keywords: SOM, Kohonen Network, parallel computation, YearPredictionMSD
Data Set.

1 Introduction

With the massive boom of GPU-based computations, massive parallelism, memory considerations, simplicity of algorithms and CPU-GPU interaction have yet again to play
an important role. In this paper, we present a simple modification of classic Kohonen's
self-organizing maps (*SOM*), which allows us to dynamically scale the computation to
fully utilize the GPU-based approach.

There have already been some attempts to introduce parallelism in Kohonen networks [8,10,9,14,15], however we needed an approach which is simple and easy to
implement. Moreover, it should work both with and without the bulk-loading algorithm [2].

In previous paper [5], we have presented such approach, which divides the training
set into several subsets and calculates the weights in multi-step approach. Calculated
weights with nonzero number of hits serve as input vectors of SOM network in the
following step. Presently, we use a two-step approach, however more steps could be
used if necessary.

The paper is organized as follows: in second section we mention classic SOM
networks and describe the basic variant we have used. In third section we describe
our approach and provide the computation algorithm. The fourth section mentions the
GPU-based computation. Fifth section introduces experimental data and comparison of
results provided by our method with those of classic SOM computation.

V. Snasel, J. Platos, and E. El-Qawasmeh (Eds.): ICDIPC 2011, Part I, CCIS 188, pp. 160–169, 2011.

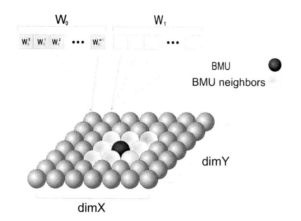

Fig. 1. Kohonen network structure

2   Kohonen Self-organizing Neural Network

In following paragraphs, we will shortly describe the Kohonen self-organizing neural networks (self-organizing maps – *SOM*). The first self-organizing networks were proposed in the beginning of 70's by Malsburg and his successor Willshaw. SOM was proposed by Teuvo Kohonen in in the early 1980s and has been improved by his team since. The summary of this method can be found in [7].

The self-organizing map is one of the common approaches on how to represent and visualize data and how to map the original dimensionality and structure of the input space onto another – usually lower-dimensional – structure in the output space.

The basic idea of SOM is based on human brain, which uses internal 2D or 3D representation of information. We can imagine the input data to be transformed to vectors, which are recorded in neural network. Most neurons in cortex are organized in 2D. Only the adjacent neurons are interconnected.

Besides of the input layer, the SOM contains only the output (competitive) layer. The number of inputs is equal to the dimension of input space. Every input is connected with each neuron in the grid, which is also an output (each neuron in grid is a component in output vector). With growing number of output neurons, the quality coverage of input space grows, but so does computation time.

SOM can be used as a classification or clustering tool that can find clusters of input data which are more closer to each other.

All experiments and examples in this paper respect following specification of the SOM (see also the Figure 1):

– The SOM is initialized as a network of fixed topology. The variables $dimX$ and $dimY$ are dimensions of such 2-dimensional topology.
– V^m represents an m-dimensional input vector.
– W^m represents an m-dimensional weight vector.
– The number of neurons is defined as $N = dimX * dimY$ and every neuron $n \in <$ $0, N - 1 >$ has its weight vector W_n^m

- The neighborhood radius r is initialized to the value $min(dimX, dimY)/2$ and will be systematically reduced to a unit distance.
- All weights vectors are updated after particular input vector is processed.
- The number of epochs e is know at the beginning.

The Kohonen algorithm is defined as follows:

1. **Network initialization**
   All weights are preset to a random or pre-calculated value. The learning factor η, $0 < \eta < 1$, which determines the speed of weight adaptation is set to a value slightly less than 1 and monotonically decreases to zero during learning process. So the weight adaptation is fastest in the beginning, being quite slow in the end.
2. **Learning of input vector**
   Introduce k training input vectors $V_1, V_2, \ldots, V_k$, which are introduced in random order.
3. **Distance computation**
   An neighborhood is defined around each neuron whose weights are going to change, if the neuron is selected in competition. Size, shape and the degree of influence of the neighborhood are parameters of the network and the last two decrease during the learning algorithm.
4. **Choice of closest neuron**
   We select the closest neuron for introduced input.
5. **Weight adjustment**
   The weights of closest neuron and its neighborhood will be adapted as follows:

$$W_{ij}(t+1) = W_{ij}(t) + \eta(t)h(v,t)(V_i - W_{ij}(t)),$$

   where $i = 1, 2, \ldots, dimX$ a $j = 1, 2, \ldots, dimY$ and the radius r of neuron's local neighborhood is determined by adaptation function $h(v)$.
6. **Go back to point 2 until the number of epochs e is reached**

To obtain the best organization of neurons to clusters, a big neighborhood and a big influence of introduced input are chosen in the beginning. Then the primary clusters arise and the neighborhood and learning factor are reduced. Also the $\eta \rightarrow 0$, so the changes become less significant with each epoch.

3   GM-SOM Method

The main steps of SOM computation have already been described above. Following text is focused on description of proposed method, that in the end leads to results similar to the classic SOM (See also Figure 2 for illustration of our approach). We named the method Global-Merged SOM, which suggests, that the computation is divided into parts and then merged to obtain the expected result. Following steps describe the whole process of GM-SOM:

1. **Splitting of input set.** The set of input vectors is divided into a given number of parts. The precision of proposed method increases with the number of parts, however, it has own disadvantages related to larger set of vectors in the final phase of

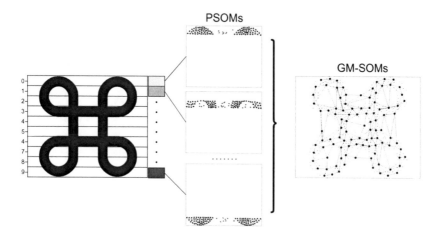

Fig. 2. GM-SOM: An Illustrative schema of the proposed method. All input vectors are divided into ten parts in this case.

computation process. Thus the number of parts will be usually determined from the number of input vectors. Generally, $k \gg N * p$, where k is the number of input vector, N is the number of neurons and p is the number of parts. The mapping of input vectors into individual parts does not affect final result. This will be later demonstrated by the experiments, where all the input vectors were either split sequentially (images) or randomly.

2. **In parts computation.** Classic SOM method is applied on every part. For simplicity sake, an acronym *PSOM* will be used from now on to indicate SOM, which is computed on a given part. All PSOMs start with the same setting (the first distribution of weights vectors, number of neurons, etc.) Such division speeds up parallel computation of PSOMs on GPU. Moreover, the number of epochs can be lower than the the number of epochs used for processing of input set by one SOM. This is represented by a factor f, which is going to be set to $\frac{1}{3}$ in our experiments.

3. **Merging of parts.** Weight vectors, that where computed for each part and correspond to neurons with at least one hit, represent input vectors in the final phase of GM-SOM. The unused neurons and their weight vectors have light gray color in Figure 2. A merged SOM with the same setting is computed and output weights vectors make the final result of proposed method.

The main difference between the proposed algorithm and well known batch SOM algorithms is, that individual parts are fully independent on each other and they update different PSOMs. Moreover, different SOM algorithms can be applied on PSOM of a given part, which makes the proposed algorithm more variable. Next advantage can be seen in different settings of PSOMs. Thus more dense neuron network can be used in case of larger input set. The last advantage consists in a possibility of incremental updating of GM-SOM. Any additional set of input vectors will be processed by a new PSOM in a separate part and the final SOM will be re-learnt. For interpretation see Figure 3.

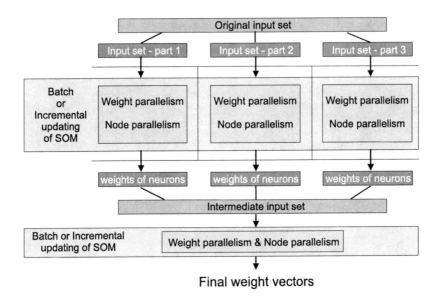

Fig. 3. GM-SOM: Parallelization of the SOM computation by proposed method

4 GPU Computing

Modern graphics hardware plays an important role in the area of parallel computing. Graphics cards have been used to accelerate gaming and 3D graphics applications, but recently, they have been used to accelerate computations for relatively remote topics, e.g. remote sensing, environmental monitoring, business forecasting, medical applications or physical simulations etc. Architecture of GPUs (Graphics Processing Unit) is suitable for vector and matrix algebra operations, which leads to a wide use of GPUs in the area of information retrieval, data mining, image processing, data compression, etc. Nowadays, the programmer does not need to be an expert in graphics hardware because of existence of various APIs (Application Programming Interface), which help programmers to implement their software faster. Nevertheless, it will be always necessary to follow basic rules of GPU programming to write a more efficient code.

Four main APIs exists today. The first two are vendor specific, i.e. they were developed by two main GPU producers - AMD/ATI and nVidia. The API developed by AMD/ATI is called ATI Stream and the API developed by nVidia is called nVidia CUDA (Compute Unified Device Architecture). Both APIs are able to provide similar results. The remaining two APIs are universal. The first one was designed by Khronos Group and it is called OpenCL (Open Computing Language) and the second was designed by Microsoft as a part of DirectX and it is called Direct Compute. All APIs provide a general purpose parallel computing architectures that leverages the parallel computation engine in graphics processing units.

The main advantage of GPU is its structure. Standard CPUs (central processing units) contain usually 1-4 complex computational cores, registers and large cache memory.

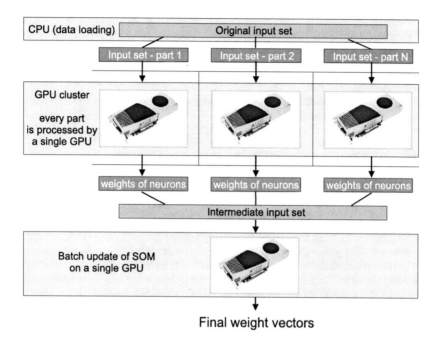

Fig. 4. GM-SOM: Parallelization of the SOM computation by proposed method

GPUs contain up to several hundreds of simplified execution cores grouped into so-called multiprocessors. Every SIMD (Single Instruction Multiple Data) multiprocessor drives eight arithmetic logic units (ALU) which process the data, thus each ALU of a multiprocessor executes the same operations on different data, lying in the registers. In contrast to standard CPUs which can reschedule operations (out-of-order execution), the selected GPU is an in-order architecture. This drawback is overcome by using multiple threads as described by Wellein et al.[6]. Current general-purpose CPUs with clock rates of 3 GHz outperform a single ALU of the multiprocessors with its rather slow 1.3 GHz. The huge number of parallel processors on a single chip compensates this drawback.

The GPU computing has been used in many areas. Andrecut [1] described CUDA-based computing for two variants of Principal Component Analysis (PCA). The usage of parallel computing improved efficiency of the algorithm more than 12 times in comparison with CPU. Preis et al. [13] applied GPU on methods of fluctuation analysis, which includes determination of scaling behavior of a particular stochastic process and equilibrium autocorrelation function in financial markets. The computation was more than 80 times faster than the previous version running on CPU. Patnaik et al. [11] used GPU in the area of temporal data mining in neuroscience. They analyzed spike train data with the aid of a novel frequent episode discovery algorithm, achieving a more than $430\times$ speedup. The GPU computation has also already been used in intrusion detection systems [12] and for human iris identification (for our experiments on this topic see [4]).

The use of our SOM modification on GPU is illustrated in Figure 4.

5   Experiments

Our approach has been already been tested [5] both on a generic set of black-and-white images as well as on two well-known datasets, based on handwritten digits, used for machine learning which were obtained from UCI repository [3]. In this paper we present performance evaluation on a new large data collection. For this task, we have used the new *YearPredictionMSD Data Set* from the UCI repository [3].

5.1   GM-SOM Partitioning Results on 2D Data

The method has been demonstrated on a collection of black-and-white images [5], based on simple geometric shapes and symbols. Coordinates of black pixels were considered the input vectors for this experiment. Given a sufficient number of epochs, the weight vectors of Kohonen self-organizing neural network are known to spread through the image and cover the black areas.

We have compared the original method with our approach on a wide selection of shapes, ranging from simple convex shapes to complicated symbols consisting of several parts. Each symbol was tested several times to reduce the impact of random initiation of the network weights. Some examples are shown in Figure 5.

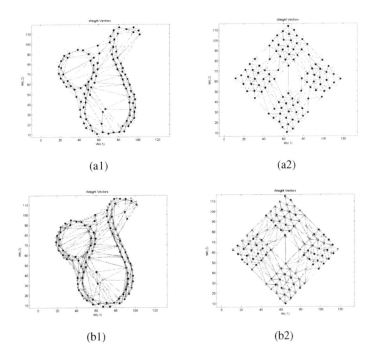

(a1)   (a2)

(b1)   (b2)

Fig. 5. GM-SOM on black-and-white symbols – (a) GM-SOM method, (b) Overlaid results of original and GM-SOM methods

5.2   Data Collection

For the experimental evaluation of our method, we have used a new collection from UCI repository [3]. The *YearPredictionMSD Data Set* is based on the Million Song Dataset, a co-operation of LabROSA (Columbia University) and The Echo Nest, available at http://labrosa.ee.columbia.edu/millionsong/

Table 1. Number of songs from each decade

Years	Number of instances
1920–1929	224
1930–1939	252
1940–1949	356
1950–1959	3102
1960–1969	11739
1970–1979	24745
1980–1989	41814
1990–1999	124713
2000–2009	299003
2010–2011	9397

The data set contains 515,345 instances in 90-dimensional space. The data set is divided into 463,715 training set instances and 51,630 samples for the testing examples. According to its authors, no song from a given artist ends up in both the train and test set.

As suggested by the name, the collection is used for year/decade prediction of given songs[1].

The year prediction data set contains the average and covariance of timbre over all 'segments'. Each segment being described by a 12-dimensional timbre vector. The instance vector has 12 values describing the timbre average and 78 values of timbre covariance values, obtained from the Echo Nest API.

When interpreting the year prediction, one has to take into account that songs from the same year may be more different than say two songs within the same decade. Also, there are usually some revivals, cover versions and "recycled" melodies, used for other songs, which may appear several years or decades later. As a result, the methods may identify the year, where the song would fit based on other songs, instead of the actual year of the song.

Another issue, which one has to take into account when dealing with this collection, is the unequal distribution of the songs, present in the dataset. Even the authors state following: *"Songs are mostly western, commercial tracks ranging from 1922 to 2011, with a peak in the year 2000s."* In Table 1, one can see the number of songs per decade present in the whole collection.

---

[1] This only one of the tasks, defined by MSD authors; for other tasks, please refer to
http://labrosa.ee.columbia.edu/millionsong/pages/tasks-demos

5.3   Performance Evaluation

In the following text, we present examples of such results for a 64×64 rectangular SOM with 300 epochs for both the original SOM network and the final computation. Each partial SOM in our approach used 300 epochs, as well.

Table 2. Computation time (in seconds)

Number of parts	1	5	10	15
Splitting data into parts	3	3	3	3
GPU computation of a single part	1986	397	199	132
Merging data and final updating of SOM	-	87	175	263
Total computation time	1989	487	377	398

The Table 2 shows the different computation times with respect to partitioning of the proposed algorithm. Values on the row *Splitting data into parts* are the same for all partitionings because of the same amount of data that must be loaded and prepared for GPU. The second row – *GPU computation of a single part* – contains different times computation which results from the fact, that greater division leads to smaller parts which are finally processed in shorter time. On the other hand, the third row *Merging data and final updating of SOM* shows, that GPU needs more time to merge more parts together. The last row – *Total computation time* – holds the sum of computation times with the assumption that every single part of SOM is processed on a single GPU and a single GPU merges intermediate results at the end.

There is, however, a limit after which the partitioning performance drops. The automatic determination of the optimal value of partitions has yet to be solved in future.

6   Conclusion

The need of parallel computation of SOM drove us to a new method, that has been also utilized in this paper. Although it has some common features with well known SOM batch or hierarchical algorithms, it is not one of them, as it has its unique properties. The results presented in previous section show that whilst the classic SOM is much faster because of the GPU-based computation, the use of PSOMs and their computation by separate nodes furher improves the computation time.

Firstly, the proposed algorithm can utilize the power of batch processing in all inner parts (PSOMs). Secondly, all PSOMs can have different number of neurons in their networks, which could be found in hierarchical algorithms. Lastly, our method excludes neurons, which do not cover any input vectors in the intermediate phase of GM-SOM.

All experiments suggest, that the results are very close to results provided by classic SOM algorithm. We would like to test the proposed algorithm on more huge data collections in the near future as well as evelute the calculated results in a consistent manner.

References

1. Andrecut, M.: Parallel GPU implementation of iterative PCA algorithms. Journal of Computational Biology 16(11), 1593–1599 (2009)
2. Fort, J., Letremy, P., Cottrel, M.: Advantages and drawbacks of the batch Kohonen algorithm. In: Proceedings of 10th-European-Symposium on Artificial Neural Networks, Esann 2002, pp. 223–230 (2002)
3. Frank, A., Asuncion, A.: UCI machine learning repository (2010)
4. Gajdos, P., Platos, J., Moravec, P.: Iris recognition on GPU with the usage of non-negative matrix factorization. In: 10th International Conference on Intelligent Systems Design and Applications (ISDA 2010), pp. 894–899 (December 29, 2010)
5. Gajdoš, P., Moravec, P.: Two-step modified SOM for parallel calculation. In: Proceedings of DATESO 2010, CEUR Workshop, Štědronín-Plazy, Czech Republic, vol. 567, pp. 13–21 (2010) ISBN 978-80-7378-116-3, ISSN 1613-0073
6. Hager, G., Zeiser, T., Wellein, G.: Data access optimizations for highly threaded multi-core CPUs with multiple memory controllers. In: IPDPS, pp. 1–7. IEEE, Los Alamitos (2008)
7. Kohonen, T.: Self-Organizing Maps, 2nd (extended) edn. Springer, Berlin (1997)
8. Mann, R., Haykin, S.: A parallel implementation of Kohonen's feature maps on the warp systolic computer. In: Proc. of Int. Joint Conf. on Neural Networks, IJCNN 1990-WASH-DC, Hillsdale, NJ, vol. II, pp. 84–87. Lawrence Erlbaum, Mahwah (1990)
9. Nordström, T.: Designing parallel computers for self organizing maps. In: Forth Swedish Workshop on Computer System Architecture (1992)
10. Openshaw, S., Turton, I.: A parallel Kohonen algorithm for the classification of large spatial datasets. Computers & Geosciences 22(9), 1019–1026 (1996)
11. Patnaik, D., Ponce, S.P., Cao, Y., Ramakrishnan, N.: Accelerator-oriented algorithm transformation for temporal data mining. CoRR, abs/0905.2203 (2009)
12. Platos, J., Kromer, P., Snasel, V., Abraham, A.: Scaling IDS construction based on non-negative matrix factorization using GPU computing. In: Sixth International Conference on Information Assurance and Security (IAS 2010), pp. 86–91 (August 2010)
13. Preis, T., Virnau, P., Paul, W., Schneider, J.J.: Accelerated fluctuation analysis by graphic cards and complex pattern formation in financial markets. New Journal of Physics 11(9), 093024 (21pp) (2009)
14. Valova, I., Szer, D., Gueorguieva, N., Buer, A.: A parallel growing architecture for self-organizing maps with unsupervised learning. Neurocomputing 68, 177–195 (2005)
15. Wei-gang, L.: A study of parallel self-organizing map. In: Proceedings of the International Joint Conference on Neural Networks (1999)

Modal Analysis – Measurements versus FEM and Artificial Neural Networks Simulation

David Seidl[1], Pavol Koštial[1], Zora Jančíková[1], Ivan Ružiak[1], Soňa Rusnáková[2], and Martina Farkašová[1]

[1] VŠB - Technical University of Ostrava, Faculty of Metallurgy and Materials Engineering, 17. listopadu 15/2172, 70833 Ostrava - Poruba, Czech Republic
[2] Tomas Bata University in Zlín, Faculty of Technology, T.G. Masaryka 275, 762 72 Zlín, Czech Republic
david.seidl@vsb.cz

Abstract. The article deals with the experimental modal analysis of glass laminates plates with different shape and these results are compared with those obtained by applications of the artificial neural networks (ANN) and finite element method (FEM) simulation. We have investigated the dependence of the generated mode frequency as a function of sample thickness as well as the sample shape (rounding) of glass laminate samples. The coincidence of both experimental and simulated results is very good.

Keywords: Artificial neural network, Glass laminates plate, Finite elements methods.

1 Introduction

The modal analyze plays an important role in civil engineering and construction of means of transport [1].

The glass fabric laminates are widely used when large strength to weight ratios is required. Fibre-reinforced components of various shapes and different boundary conditions (free, clamped, and hinged) commonly occur in practice. Designers need to be able to predict the stiffness parameters and damping values of components for conditions such as aero elasticity, acoustic fatigue, and so on [2,3].

The paper [4] reviews the main developments in the field of electronic speckle pattern interferometry that have been published over the past 20-25 years.

In the work [5] a specimen subjected to uniaxial tensile tests undergoes a thickness reduction that leads to out-of-plane displacements. The combination of the fringe projection technique and the Fourier transform method (FTM) allowed to monitor in real-time the out-of-plane displacement fields, induced on a brass sheet specimen in different regions of the tensile test. These maps enabled us to detect different trends in the deformation process and nonlinear effects linked to the progression of the thickness necking.

The high resolution technique ESPI can be very useful in determining deformation of laboratory specimens and identifying of failure [6].

V. Snasel, J. Platos, and E. El-Qawasmeh (Eds.): ICDIPC 2011, Part I, CCIS 188, pp. 170–175, 2011.
© Springer-Verlag Berlin Heidelberg 2011

Artificial neural networks are suitable for approximating complex mutual relations among different sensor-based data, especially among non-structured data, with a high grade of non-linearity, and with inaccurate and incomplete data. This type of data often occurs in material engineering. A number of applications, which are based on neural network exploitation, occur in material engineering at present. In this field neural networks are applied especially in diagnostics and process modelling and control [7].

Neural networks are capable of simulating behaviour of systems with very complex internal structure and complicated external behaviour, where analytic description is considerably complex; eventually it does not exist at all. They enable to simulate dependences which can be hardly solved by classic methods of statistic data evaluation (e.g. regression analysis) and they are able to express more complex relations than these methods [8, 9].

Neural networks are suitable for modelling of complex systems especially from the reason that their typical property is capability of learning on measured data and capability of generalization. Neural networks are able to appropriately express general properties of data and relations among them and on the contrary to suppress relationships which occur sporadically or they are not sufficiently reliable and strong [10].

The aim of the paper is to outline possibilities of artificial neural networks application for prediction of natural frequencies of glass laminates and to compare obtained experimental results for differently shaped glass laminate samples with those of artificial neural networks and FEM simulation.

2 Experimental Technique and Methods

For the mode frequency measurements the standard ESPI device was used [11]. In the first step we have tested the mode frequency generation as a function of the sample thickness. The Table 1 describes the sample shape and dimensions for experiments with a different rounding. Sample with r = 0 is tetragonal and sample with r = 87,5mm is a disc. The sample thickness is presented in the Table 2 together width generated mode frequencies.

Table 1. Sample rounding values

Sample Number	1	2	3	4	5	6	7	8	9
Sample Rounding [mm]	0	10	20	30	40	50	60	70	87,5

Neural networks were created in software STATISTICA – Neural Networks. This system enables among others a choice of most suitable with the best performance, it contains efficient investigative and analytic techniques and enables to achieve summary descriptive statistics, to execute sensitive analysis and to create response graphs. For particular neural network models a quality of network adaptation to the submitted patterns and generalization scale were observed.

Table 2. Resonance frequencies obtained by ESPI

		Sample thickness h [mm]			
	ESPI mode shape	0,8	1,05	1,35	1,65
Resonance frequency [Hz]	1	61	78	93	112
	2	138	187	228	293
	3	179	248	309	378
	4	374	522	663	800
	5	432	620	758	919
	6	498	694	861	1058

The rate of inaccuracy between predicted and actual output represent a prediction error. In technical applications the error is mainly represented by following functions: relation for RMS error (Root Mean Squared), relation for REL_RMS error, R^2 – determination index [8].

The rate of inaccuracy between predicted and actual output represent a prediction error. In technical applications the error is mainly represented by following relations [4]:

- RMS error (Root Mean Squared) – it does not compensate used units

$$RMS = \sqrt{\frac{\sum_{i=0}^{i=n-1}(y_i - o_i)^2}{n-1}} \tag{1}$$

- REL_RMS error – it compensates used units

$$REL\_RMS = \sqrt{\frac{\sum_{i=0}^{i=n-1}(y_i - o_i)^2}{\sum_{i=0}^{i=n-1}(y_i)^2}} \tag{2}$$

- R^2 (Determination Index):

$$R^2 = 1 - \frac{SSE}{SST} \tag{3}$$

where:
n - number of patterns of a training or test set,
y_i - predicted outputs,

o_i - measured outputs,
SSE   - sum of squared errors,
SST   - total sum of squared errors.

3   Results and Discussion

In the first step of our analysis we focus an attention on the finite element method application and its comparison with ESPI mode measurements. Results are collected in the Tables 2 (ESPI) and 3 (FEM). Corresponding mode shapes are presented in all cases.

Table 3. Resonance frequencies obtained by FEM

		Sample thickness h [mm]			
	FEM mode shape	0,8	1,05	1,35	1,65
Resonance frequency [Hz]	1	48	63	81	99
	2	167	219	282	345
	3	210	276	355	434
	4	403	530	681	832
	5	512	672	864	1055
	6	515	676	869	1062
	7	626	821	1056	1290

The measured ESPI values are higher than computed ones (FEM) in the first mode only. These observations could be caused by model imperfections as well as material's constants indefinites of a model and real body respectively. A maximum observed percentage difference for the first mode is 27 percent (thickness 0.8). All other differences are smaller than this value.

For prediction of the resonance frequency in the dependence of the sample thickness data about sample thickness and type of mode (7 types of modes) were used as an input vector (8 neurons in the input layer). Output vector represented the resonance frequency (1 neuron in the output layer). The best results of prediction proved multilayer feed forward neural network with topology 8-3-1. Above mentioned prediction errors for this neural network are: RMS = 13,668 Hz, REL_RMS = 0, 0226, R^2= 0, 9983.

The regression equation in the case of the thickness dependence of generated modes has a form y=0, 9862x+4, 3736. It is clearly seen an excellent agreement of predicted values by ANN and experimental data.

For prediction of the resonance frequency in dependence of sample rounding data about sample rounding and type of mode (9 types of mode) were used as an input vector (10 neurons in the input layer). Output vector represented the resonance frequency (1 neuron in the output layer). The best results of prediction represented multilayer feed forward neural network with topology 10-7-1. Prediction errors for this neural network are: RMS = 2,743 Hz, REL_RMS = 0, 0031, R^2= 0, 9999.The regression equation has a form y= 0,999x-0,453. The FEM simulation data for the sample rounding are collected in the Table 4.

Table 4. FEM simulation for the rounding

	FEM mode shape	Sample rounding r [mm]								
		0	10	20	30	40	50	60	70	87,5
Resonance frequency [Hz]	1	91	93	96	99	104	111	117	126	145
	2	69	69	71	72	74	77	80	85	
	3	132	133	133	133	133	134	136	138	145
	4	303	308	320	338	361	391	425	466	546
	5	580	580	580	578	574	569			
	6	736	739	743	748	753	762	777		
	7	740	740	742	747	757	775	798	825	877
	8	899	924	977	1049	1134	1227	1325	1426	

4 Conclusion

The models of artificial neural networks for prediction of resonance frequencies of glass laminates were created. These models enable to predict glass laminates resonance frequencies with a sufficiently small error. Obtained experimental results for differently shaped glass laminate samples were compared with those of artificial neural networks and finite element method (FEM) simulation. The coincidence of both experimental and simulated results was very good.

References

1. Babic, B.: Modal analyze in dynamic of building constructions (in Slovak) ISBN 978-80-969595-1-8
2. Ma, C.C., Lin, C.C.: Experimental Investigation of Vibrating Laminated Composite Plates by Optical Interferometry Method. AIAA J. 39(3), 491–497 (2001)
3. Lin, D.X., Ni, R.G., Adams, R.D.: Prediction and Measurement of the vibration Damping Parameters of Carbon and Glass Fiber-Reinforced Plastics Plates. J. Compos. Mater 18, 132–152 (1984)
4. Mujeeb, A., Nayar, V.U., Ravindran, V.R.: Electronic Speckle Pattern Interferometry techniques for non- destructive evaluation: a review. Insight - Non-Destructive Testing and Condition Monitoring 48(5) (2006)
5. Cordero, R.R., Martinez, A., Rayas, J.A., Labbe, F.: Necking progression in tensile specimens monitored in real-time by using fringe projection. Optics and Lasers in Engineering 48(12), 1285–1290 (2010)
6. Haggerty, M., Qing Lin, Ć., Labuť, J.F.: Observing Deformation and Fracture of Rock with Speckle Patterns. Rock Mech. Rock Eng. 43, 417–426 (2010)
7. Badeshia, H.K.D.H.: Neural Networks in Material Science. ISIJ International 39(10), 966–979 (1999)
8. Jančíková, Z.: Artificial Neural Networks in Material Engineering, p. 81. GEP ARTS, Ostrava (2006)
9. Švec, P., Jančíková, Z., Melecký, J., Koštial, P.: Implementation of Neural Networks for Prediction of Chemical Composition of Refining Slag. In: International Conference on Metallurgy and Materials, Rožnov, pp. 155–159 (2010) ISBN 978-80-87294-17-8
10. Jančíková, Z., David, J., Vrožina, M.: Aplikace neuronových sítí v materiálovém inženýrství. Hutnické listy LXI(1), 88–94 (2008) ISSN 0018-8069
11. Rusnáková, S., Kopál, I., Koštial, P.: The applications of waveprocess for the study of glass fibre reinforced laminates. Current topics in acoustical research 4 (2006) ISSN 0972-4818

View from Inside One Neuron

Luciana Morogan

Military Technical Academy,
81-83 George Cosbuc Bd., 050141 Bucharest,
Romania
morogan.luciana@gmail.com

Abstract. Neural networks started to be developed around the idea of creating models of real neural systems because of the existing need in understanding how biological systems work. New areas of neural computing are trying to make at least one step beyond what digital computing means. The key point is based on learning rather than programming. We designed a mathematical model for information processing. The neuron model is viewed from inside as a feedback system that controls the information flow. The process of learning at "molecular" level (internal neural learning), under the form of a computational algorithm inspired by a real brain functioning, has been introduced.

Keywords: Neural networks, natural computing, evolutionary computing.

1 Introduction

From the biological hypothesis about the functionality of certain subsystems of the nervous system arise the field of neural networks. There already are many models that are used in the field, each one of them being defined at a different level of abstraction. They were designed in the desire of modeling different aspects of real neural systems. In the beginnings of this field, research was concentrated around the electrical characteristics of neurons (mostly, around electrical information exchange between neurons in a neural network). In recent years, new investigations were focused over mechanisms for synaptic plasticity or the exploration of the role of neuromodulators over behavior and learning. Applications pointed toward both computer science and neuroscience.

Our work focuses on designing a system called the *prion neural system* as part of an ambitious project to build models of complex systems into a bottom up approach. The system construction started with the molecular level and continued with the synaptic level, both of them creating the upper level of a neuron. In the diagram presented in figure 1, there can be seen all the levels that make up the entire system: molecular, synaptic, neuron, networks, maps, systems and the central nervous system level.

The prion neural system belongs to the hybrid dynamic systems category. Why? The answer is that we needed to encompass a larger class of systems

V. Snasel, J. Platos, and E. El-Qawasmeh (Eds.): ICDIPC 2011, Part I, CCIS 188, pp. 176–188, 2011.
© Springer-Verlag Berlin Heidelberg 2011

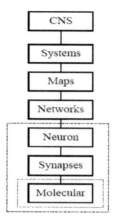

Fig. 1. The seven levels of a *prion neural system*: molecular, synaptic, neuron, networks, maps, systems and the central nervous system level

within the system structure. This way we gain more flexibility in modeling a dynamic biological phenomena (introduced in [1]). It works as a parallel machine at the level of its own systems, but also in a parallel manner at the level of each neuron. We are abstracting a computing model from the structure and the functioning of a living neuron as an evolutionary multi-functional computing system. In designing the model of such a system we used some interdisciplinary interplay because it involves not only the neural networks fields, but also membrane computing under the framework of DNA computing.

From the computational point of view, regarding the neuroarchitecture and functionality, one neuron device was designed to be directly dependent on its anatomical and functional "metabolism" (to be seen [1]). One neuron is viewed as a mechanisms for processing data. The support for computational processes is provided by what we called "protein" objects. The inspiration came from membrane computing areas where some objects are being used as playing the same role as the one played by biological protein molecules in a living cell ([1], [2]). Such a devise is also capable of transforming an input signal into an output one following the tradition of classical neural networks (read [3], [4], [5], [6] and [7] for specific details; novel neural network architectures are presented in papers like [8] and [9]).

Placing a finite set of such neuron devices in the nodes of a finite directed graph we are creating a network (see [10]). What we called a neural-like system structure is the ensemble of all network units, a parallel distributed communication network of networks of neurons. In such a system two different types of interactions are being defined. These are local interactions defined between neurons and global ones defined between networks or neurons of different networks. All these interactions are translated as neural communication realized by means of a set of directed links between neurons in the entire graph. Such a directed link between two neurons is called a *synapse*. As the communication with the

surrounding environment is necessary for the model, we will also refer with the
term *synapse* to a directed communication channel from one neuron to the environment and vice-versa. The evolution or the involution of the entire system will
be directly dependent on the synaptic creation or "deletion" from one network
during the computations. Also of biological inspiration was the idea of designing
binding affinities between neurons (fully described in [15]) as not any neuron can
bind to any other neuron. Connections in a network are dependent on sufficient
quantities of the corresponding substrates inside the neurons and the compat-
ibilities between the type of the transmitters in the pre-synaptic neurons and
receptors types in the posts-synaptic neurons. The transmitters and receptors
are specific "protein" objects in the pre and post-synaptic neurons respectively,
in accordance with the real biological transmitters and receptors proteins ([11],
[12], [13]). Synapse weights, representing degrees of the binding affinity, are assigned to each synapse. For neurons with no synapse between them the value
of the binding affinity degree is considered to be zero. Also assigned to zero
are the affinity degrees of some special "synapses", those between neurons and
the environment. This article is focused on some changes (mutations), that may
occur into one neuron, that can influence the expression of its "genetic material". Those changes, as in real biological cases, will influence the the binding
degrees (between neurons and between neurons and the environment). Analyzing the neuron activity rate we can control the flow of information and the effect
of the events that can induce both modified synaptic communications and, finally, modification into the network structure. Another result will reside in the
fact that modifications into the synaptic communications will also determine
the neuron to adapt to its inputs and modeling this way its behavior (first time
mentioned in [14]). The neuron ability to adapt to its inputs leads to a process
of learning at the molecular level and defines the neuron as a *feedback control
system*. An algorithm of the learning process at a molecular level is presented
within the pages of this article. As it requires some special attention our future
work will be concentrated around modification that can occur into the network
architecture and the implications involved by such a dynamic system over the
information processing.

2   Background

At the lowest level (molecular level), the neuron device is viewed as a system
for information processing offering objects, playing the role of biological protein
molecules, as a support for computational processes. The *tree - like architecture*, fully described in [15], of one neuron device n is defined as a structure
$\alpha(n) = \langle \alpha_{0,j_0}, \alpha_{1,j_1}, \ldots, \alpha_{r,j_r} \rangle$ where the finite number of r compartments are
structured as an hierarchical tree-like arrangement. Their role is to delimit pro-
tected compartments as finite spaces and to represent supports for chemical
reactions of some chemicals embedded inside ([1] is recommended for more details). α_{0,j_0} found at the $j_0 = 0$ level of the "tree root" corresponds to the
inner finite space of the neuron (containing all the other compartments). The

inner hierarchical arrangement of the neuron is represented by the construction $\alpha_{1,j_1}, \ldots, \alpha_{r,j_r}$ such as for $j_1, \ldots, j_r$ natural numbers, not necessarily disjoint, with $j_k \leq r$ for $k \in \{1, \ldots, r\}$ we define the proper depth level of the k - th compartment. We may have a maximum of r inner depth levels. *Initial configuration* defines the initial neuronal architecture of n along with the objects found in each of its compartment regions. Formally, this is represented by

$$(\alpha_{0,j_0} : o_0, \alpha_{1,j_1} : o_1, \ldots, \alpha_{r,j_r} : o_r)$$

For each α_{k,j_k} with $k \in \{1, \ldots, r\}$, o_k may be written under the form of the string objects $a_1^{m_1} a_2^{m_2} \ldots a_p^{m_p}$ where $p \in \mathbf{N}$, finite. Each $a_i^{m_i}$ represents the quantity m_i ($m_i \in \mathbf{N}$) of a_i found in the region α_{k,j_k} of the neuron n. If $m_i = *$, then we say that a_i is found in an arbitrary finite number of copies in that compartment.

A naive model of synaptic formation was presented in [14] and [15]. We kept in mind a restriction coming from biology field: not any neuron can bind to any other neuron. For N a finite set of neurons of a network from the entire system structure, a few finite sets are defined. OC_{n_i} is the set of all classes of organic compounds/organic complexes for the neuron n_i and OC_{n_j} the set of all classes of organic compounds/organic complexes for the neuron n_j ($OC_{n_i} \cap OC_{n_j} \neq \emptyset$). We know $OC_{nt_i} \subset OC_{n_i}$ the set of all neurotransmitters for n_i and $OC_{r_j} \subset OC_{n_j}$ the set of all receptors for n_j. For an easier way of handling those sets we will refer to the set of neurotransmitters for n_i by OC_{nt} and the set receptors for n_j by OC_r. A finite set of labels over the English alphabet is denoted by L. There is a labeling function of each organic compound/organic complex defined by $l : OC_n \rightarrow L$ where n is ether n_i or n_j. $T_r = l(OC_{nt}) \subseteq 2^L$ is the set of labels of all neurotransmitters for n_i and $R = l(OC_r) \subseteq 2^L$ the set of labels of all receptors for n_j.

It is considered the set $T = \{i \cdot \mu | i \in \mathbf{N}, \mu = \frac{1}{k}, k \in \mathbf{N}^* fixed\}$ of discrete times. For all $a_i \in OC_n$ found in the region α_{k,j_k} of n and m_i its multiplicity, the *quantity found into the substrate (in the region α_{k,j_k} of neuron n) of one organic compound/organic complex a_i* at the computational time $t, t \in T$ is the function $C_{n:\alpha_{k,j_k}} : T \times OC_n \rightarrow \mathbf{N} \cup \{*\}$, defined by

$$C_{n:\alpha_{k,j_k}}(t, a_i) = \begin{cases} m_i, \text{ if } m_i \text{ represents the number of} \\ \quad \text{copies of } a_i \text{ into the substrate} \\ *, \text{ if there is an arbitrary finite number} \\ \quad \text{of copies of } a_i \text{ into the substrate .} \end{cases}$$

A few properties of quantities of organic compounds/organic complexes into the substrate are presented below:

1. The *quantity of substrate*, at the computational time $t, t \in T$ found into α_{k,j_k} is

$$C_{n:\alpha_{k,j_k}}(t) = C_{n:\alpha_{k,j_k}}(t, a_1) + C_{n:\alpha_{k,j_k}}(t, a_2) + \ldots +$$

$$+ C_{n:\alpha_{k,j_k}}(t, a_p) = \sum_{i=1}^{p} C_{n:\alpha_{k,j_k}}(t, a_i) = \sum_{i}^{p} m_i, \tag{1}$$

for all $m_i \in \mathbf{N}$. If there is $i \in \{1, ..., p\}$ such as $C_{n:\alpha_{k,j_k}}(t, a_i) = *$, then $C_{n:\alpha_{k,j_k}}(t) = *$.

2. If at the moment t we have $C_{n:\alpha_{k,j_k}}(t, a_i) = m_i$ and at a later time t' a new quantity m_i' of a_i was produced, supposing that in the discrete time interval $[t, t']$ no object a_i was used (one may say consumed), then

$$C_{n:\alpha_{k,j_k}}\left(t', a_i\right) = C_{n:\alpha_{k,j_k}}(t, a_i) + m_i' = m_i + m_i'. \tag{2}$$

3. If at the moment t we have $C_{n:\alpha_{k,j_k}}(t, a_i) = m_i$ and at a later time t' the quantity m_i' of a_i was consumed, supposing that in the discrete time interval $[t, t']$ no object a_i was produced, then

$$C_{n:\alpha_{k,j_k}}\left(t', a_i\right) = C_{n:\alpha_{k,j_k}}(t, a_i) - m_i' = m_i - m_i'. \tag{3}$$

We make the observation that $m_i - m_i' \geq 0$ ($m_i \geq m_i'$) because it can not be consumed more than it exists.

4. If at the moment t we have $C_{n:\alpha_{k,j_k}}(t, a_i) = m_i$ and at a later time t' we have $C_{n:\alpha_{k,j_k}}\left(t', a_i\right) = m_i'$, supposing that in the discrete time interval $[t, t']$ no object a_i was produced or consumed, then

(a) if $m_i < m_i'$ we say that there is a rise in the quantity of a_i;
(b) if $m_i > m_i'$ we say that there is a decrease in the quantity of a_i;
(c) if $m_i = m_i'$ we say that no changes occurred in the quantity of a_i.

The *binding affinity* depends on a sufficient quantity of substrate and the compatibility between the type of transmitter and receptor type at time t of synaptic formation ($t \in T$).

The *sufficient quantity of substrate* is a fair ratio admitted r between the number of neurotransmitters released by n_i into the synapse and the number of receptors of the receiver neuron n_j. Without restraining generality, we consider the sufficient quantity of substrate at time t ($t \in T$) of synaptic formation as a boolean function of the assessment ratio evaluation. For $trans \in T_r$ with m its multiplicity (where for $a \in OC_{nt}$ with $l(a) = trans$ and $trans \in T_r$ we have $C_{n_i:\alpha_{0,0}}(t, a) = m$) and $rec \in R$ with n its multiplicity (where for $b \in OC_r$ with $l(b) = rec$ and $rec \in R$ we have $C_{n_j:\alpha_{0,0}}(t, b) = n$), we define $q^t : T_r \times R \to \{0, 1\}$,

$$q^t(trans, rec) = \begin{cases} 0, & \text{if } m/n \neq r \\ 1, & \text{if } m/n = r \end{cases}.$$

The *compatibility function* is a subjective function $C^t : T_r \times R \to \{0, 1\}$ such as for any $trans \in T_r$ and any $rec \in R$,

$$C^t(trans, rec) = \begin{cases} 0, & \text{if } trans \text{ and } rec \text{ are not compatible} \\ 1, & \text{otherwise} \end{cases}.$$

The *binding affinity function* is the one that models the connection affinities between neurons by mapping an affinity degree to each possible connection. We consider $W^t \subset \mathbf{N}$ the set of all affinity degrees (at time t),

$$W^t = \left\{ w_{ij}^t \middle| w_{ij}^t \in \mathbf{N}, \forall i,j \in \{1,2,\ldots,|N|\}, n_i, n_j \in N \right\}.$$

For any $n_i, n_j \in N$, $trans \in T_r$ (the transmitters type of neuron n_i), $rec \in R$ (the receptors type in neuron n_j), $\mathcal{C}^t(trans, rec) = x$ with $x \in \{0,1\}$ and $q^t(trans, rec) = y$ with $y \in \{0,1\}$, we design the binding affinity function as a function $A_f^t : (N \times N) \times (T_r \times R) \times \mathcal{C}^t(T_r \times R) \times q^t(T_r \times R) \to W$ where

$A_f^t((n_i, n_j), (trans, rec), x, y) =$

$$= \begin{cases} 0, \text{ if } x = \mathcal{C}^t(trans, rec) = 0, \forall y \in \{0,1\} \\ 0, \text{ if } (x = \mathcal{C}^t(trans, rec) = 1) \wedge \\ \quad (y = q^t(trans, rec) = 0) \\ w_{ij}^t, \text{ if } (x = \mathcal{C}^t(trans, rec) = 1) \wedge \\ \quad (y = q^t(trans, rec) = 1) \wedge (w_{ij}^t \neq 0). \end{cases}$$

Theorem 1 (The binding affinity theorem). *For $P_i \in P_{b_{n_i}}$ a finite set of biochemical processes of neuron n_i by which it produces a multiset of neurotransmitters of type trans (trans $\in T_r$), at the computational time t ($t \in T$), and, in the same time, for $P_j \in P_{b_{n_j}}$ a finite set of biochemical processes of neuron n_j by which it produces a multiset of receptors of type rec (rec $\in R$), we say that there is a binding affinity between n_i and n_j with the binding affinity degree w_{ij}^t ($w_{ij}^t \neq 0$) if and only if there is $w_{ij}^t \in W^{t^*}$ such as $A_f^t((n_i, n_j), (trans, rec), 1, 1) = w_{ij}^t$.*

Definition 1. *For any $n_i, n_j \in N$, trans $\in T_r$ (the transmitters type of neuron n_i) and rec $\in R$ (the receptors type in neuron n_j) at time t, if there is a binding affinity between n_i and n_j with the binding degree w_{ij}^t ($w_{ij}^t \in W^t$) and $w_{ij}^t \neq 0$ then we say that **there is a connection** formed from n_i to n_j. This connection is called the **synapse between the two neurons** and it is denoted by syn_{ij}. Each synapse has a **synapse weight** $w_{ij}^t = w, w \in \mathbf{N}^*$. If instead of n_i we have e then the synapse syn_{ej} represents the directed link from the environment to the neuron n_j and if instead of n_j we have e then the synapse syn_{ie} represents the directed link from the neuron n_i to the environment. The synapses weighs are considered to be zero ($w_{ej}^t = w_{ie}^t = 0$).*

Definition 2. *We say that there is **no connection** from neuron n_i to neuron n_j if and only if $w_{ij}^t = 0$.*

Theorem 2 (One way synaptic direction theorem). *For $P_i \in P_{b_{n_i}}$ a finite set of biochemical processes of neuron n_i by which it produces a multiset of neurotransmitters of type trans and receptors of type rec', at the computational time t ($t \in T$), and in the same time for $P_j \in P_{b_{n_j}}$ a finite set of biochemical processes of neuron n_j by which it produces a multiset of receptors of type rec and neurotransmitters of type trans', if there is w_{ij}^t in W^t with $w_{ij}^t \neq 0$ such as $A_f^t((n_i, n_j), (trans, rec), 1, 1) = w_{ij}^t$, then there is no w_{ji}^t in W^t with $w_{ji}^t \neq 0$ such as $A_f^t((n_j, n_i), (trans', rec'), 1, 1) = w_{ji}^t$. (If there is w_{ji}^t in W^t such as $A_f^t((n_j, n_i), (trans', rec'), 1, 1) = w_{ji}^t$, then $w_{ji}^t = 0$.)*

3   Information Control in Modeling the Neuron Behavior

The electrical information exchange between neurons in a neural network is viewed here as the physical information. For our model this was not enough. We also needed some molecular information for dealing with the internal processes taking place into one neuron device. In order to materialize this kind of information we introduced the "molecular" objects viewed as both computational and information carrying elements. In this manner, one neuron device represents a system for information processing making use of object "molecules" that offer support for computational processes. Applied to these objects, some processes are transforming the input signal(s) into an output signal.

We define the *neuron genome* as a memory register of the result of the previous information processing and the effect of events. The temporary memory of all informations of both the cellular and surrounding environment and the partially recording of the results of the previous computations are translated as DNA sequences. From the information processing point of view, for each neuron in N we have to define:

- the neuron architecture along with the processes defined for each of the compartments in the initial neuron configuration;

- the initial quantity found into the substrates of each compartment;

- neuron *genome* as totality of all genes encoders of genetic information contained in DNA (denoted G);

- *genetic information* represented by all information about the cellular and external environment;

- *genetic code*: represented as a set of genes ($G = (g_1, \ldots g_k), k \in \mathbb{N}$) along with the appropriate expressions and the controllers of genes expression as a set of objects representing the genes controllers ($c = (c_1, \ldots c_q), q \in \mathbb{N}$).

There is an internal timing that sets up the neuron activity rate. It must not be confound with the computational timing representing the time unit for both internal processing and external electrical exchanges of spikes between neurons[1]. The internal timing is characterized by an intracellular feedback-loop. It is measured between consecutive activations of groups of genes. On activation, the expression of a group of genes encode proteins after which they will be turned off until the next activation. The computational timing is defined as the set $T = \{i \cdot \mu | i \in \mathbb{N}, \mu = \frac{1}{k}, k \in \mathbb{N}^* fixed\}$ meanwhile the internal timing that sets up the neuron activity rate as $T_{nR} = \{T_k | k \in \mathbb{N}, T_k \stackrel{notation}{=} t_i, i \in \mathbb{N}, t_i \in T$, where T_k represents the moment of a gene (group of genes) activation$\}$, $T_{nR} \subset T$. Corresponding to the computational time $t_i, i \in \mathbb{N}$, in parallel, we may deal with an activation of a gene (group of genes) at time T_k ($T_k \stackrel{notation}{=} t_i$) and then the gene (group of genes) is turned off at a later moment in time $t_{i+p}, 0 < p < j, p, j \in \mathbb{N}$. It is possible that not only one computation may take place until the next activation ether of the same gene (group of genes) or a different one (group) at T_{k+1}

---

[1] One may say that the computational timing may be the "real time" because, in biology, molecular timescale is measured in picoseconds (10^{-12}s). On such timescales chemical bonds are forged or broken and the physical process called "life" develops.

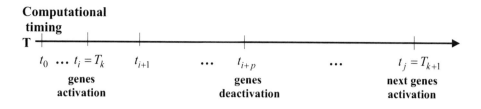

Fig. 2. Internal timing that sets the neuron activity rate is not the computational timing which represents the time unit for both internal processing and external electrical exchanges

$(T_{k+1} \stackrel{notation}{=} t_j)$. The internal timing is measured between consecutive activation of the same gene (group of genes). If in the discrete time interval $[T_k, T_{k+1}]$ the neuron device computes starting from t_i to t_j $(t_i, t_{i+1}, \ldots t_j)$, then the time interval will represent the internal neuron timing characterizing the gene (group of genes) that were activated at T_k. This can be illustrated in Figure 2.

For generalizing the above statements, we present two successive activations of all genes of genome G. We make the observation that if the arrangement of the genes into the genome is $(g_1, \ldots g_k)$, bellow they will be arranged fallowing the moment of their expression. We denote by T_g^i the time of the activation of the gene g. For $k_1 + k_2 \ldots + k_r = k$ and for each g_{jl} (with $j \in \{1, \ldots, r\}$ and $l \in \{1, \ldots, k_j\}$) representing genes that are activated in the same time T^{i_j}, we have:

- at one activation of all genes:
  - at time T^{i_1}, the activated genes will be: $(g_{11}, g_{12}, \ldots, g_{1k_1})$ at their corresponding activation times $(T_{g_{11}}^{i_1}, T_{g_{12}}^{i_1}, \ldots, T_{g_{1k_1}}^{i_1})$ (representing in fact the same T^{i_1})
  - at time T^{i_2}, the activated genes will be: $(g_{21}, g_{22}, \ldots, g_{2k_2})$ at their corresponding activation times $(T_{g_{21}}^{i_2}, T_{g_{22}}^{i_2}, \ldots, T_{g_{2k_2}}^{i_2})$ (representing in fact the same T^{i_2})

    ...

  - at time T^{i_r}, the activated genes will be: $(g_{r1}, g_{r2}, \ldots, g_{rk_r})$ at their corresponding activation times $(T_{g_{r1}}^{i_r}, T_{g_{r2}}^{i_r}, \ldots, T_{g_{rk_r}}^{i_r})$ (representing in fact the same T^{i_r})
- at the next activation of all genes:
  - at time T^{i_1+1}, the activated genes will be: $(g_{11}, g_{12}, \ldots, g_{1k_1})$ at their corresponding activation times $(T_{g_{11}}^{i_1+1}, T_{g_{12}}^{i_1+1}, \ldots, T_{g_{1k_1}}^{i_1+1})$ (representing in fact the same T^{i_1+1})
  - at time T^{i_2+1}, the activated genes will be: $(g_{21}, g_{22}, \ldots, g_{2k_2})$ at their corresponding activation times $(T_{g_{21}}^{i_2+1}, T_{g_{22}}^{i_2+1}, \ldots, T_{g_{2k_2}}^{i_2+1})$ (representing in fact the same T^{i_2+1})

    ...

- at time T^{i_r+1}, the activated genes will be: $(g_{r1}, g_{r2}, \ldots, g_{rk_r})$ at their corresponding activation times $(T^{i_r+1}_{g_{r1}}, T^{i_r+1}_{g_{r2}}, \ldots, T^{i_r+1}_{g_{rk_r}})$ (representing in fact the same T^{i_r+1}).

We make the observation that for $i \in \{i_1, \ldots, i_r\}$, the gene g_{jl} activated at time $T^i_{g_{jl}}$ is not necessarily the same gene g_{jl} activated at $T^{i+1}_{g_{jl}}$ (case of gene mutation that will be discussed later within the pages of this article). The *neuron activity rate* for neuron n is a mapping $nRate : T_{nR} \times \mathbf{N} \to \mathbf{N} \times \ldots \times \mathbf{N}$ (k times) defined by $nRate(T_{i+1}, i + 1) = (T^{i+1}_{g_1} - T^i_{g_1}, T^{i+1}_{g_2} - T^i_{g_2}, \ldots, T^{i+1}_{g_k} - T^i_{g_k})$, for all genes $(g_1, \ldots g_k)$ composing the neuron genome. One observation arises from here: some values in the array may be equal for genes that are activated at the same step (from the same group). If $nRate(T_{i+2}, i + 2) = (T^{i+2}_{g_1} - T^{i+1}_{g_1}, T^{i+2}_{g_2} - T^{i+1}_{g_2}, \ldots, T^{i+2}_{g_k} - T^{i+1}_{g_k})$ and there are some values $T^{i+1}_{g_j} - T^i_{g_j} = T^{i+1}_{g_l} - T^i_{g_l}$ (meaning that g_j and g_l were activated at the same step of the iteration), then it is not necessarily that at the next step of the iteration $T^{i+2}_{g_j} - T^{i+1}_{g_j} = T^{i+2}_{g_l} - T^{i+1}_{g_l}$. This is the case when some changes may occur into the neuron functionality (case of mutation of at least one of the genes involved in that process). Also, if $T^{i+1}_{g_j} - T^i_{g_j}$ differs from $T^{i+2}_{g_j} - T^{i+1}_{g_j}$ we are dealing with some changes of neuron activity. In conclusion, there can be detected some changes into the neuron functionality by analyzing the differences that may occur into the neuron activity rate values.

In biology, there are processes that lead to internal neuronal changes in case of indirectly activation of the transfer channels of the post-synaptic neuron. To explain the biological phenomena, we must say that the transmitters action into the post-synaptic neurons are not dependent on their chemical nature, but the properties of the receptors of the binding neurons. There are the receptors that determine if the synapse is excitatory or inhibitory. An excitatory synapse is a synapse in which the spike in the presynaptic cell increases the probability of a spike occurring in the postsynaptic cell. The receptors are also determining the way transfer channels are activated. In case of direct gating they are quickly producing synaptic actions. In case of indirect gating the receptors are producing slow actions that usually serve for neuron behavior modeling by modifying the affinity degree of the receptors. From our point of view, we chose for our model precisely this second case. In this manner, we define the neuron ability to adapt to its inputs by altering gene expression as *a process of learning at a molecular level*. The neuron device will be viewed as a *feedback control system*.

We suppose T_k time of expression of the gene g, encoding "protein" object a. After expression, g will be deactivated. For each controller object $c \in OC_n$ there is a gene $g \in G$ such as we define the gene expression function in relation to the internal timing T_k as a function $Exp(T_k) : G \times OC_n \to OC_n \times OC_n \times \ldots OC_n$,

$$Exp(T_k)(g, c) = a^{var}$$

where $c \in OC_n$ is the controller of the gene expression, a is the produced object and var its multiplicity (representing the quantity of a produced at the expression of gene g). There are three remarks to make about the definition of this function:

Remark 1. At a specific moment in time the expression of a gene under the influence of a controller encode only one type of object. (At a specific moment in time one gene controlled by a controller can encode only one "protein" object.)

Remark 2. At consecutive activations a controller can influence the expression of different genes from a group. (After the deactivation of a gene that encoded one type of object, the same controller can activate (at the next iteration) another gene in the sequence of genes from the same group.)

Remark 3. In the same time, there are controllers that activate different genes, each one encoding different objects. (There is a set of genes that can be activated in the same time, each one of them being under the influence of different controllers and encoding different types of objects).

Considering $T_1 \in T_{nR}$ the time of a gene (group of genes) activation, we present bellow some properties of the genes expressions (expressed as moments of T_1):

1. At time $T_1 \in T_{nR}$, different controllers of different genes from the group of genes activated in the same time will lead to different results of the gene expression functions. Formally, for all $c_i \neq c_j$ and for all $g_i \neq g_j (i \neq j)$ such as c_i controllers the expression of g_i and c_j controls the expression of g_j, we have $Exp(T_1)(g_i, c_i) \neq Exp(T_1)(g_j, c_j)$.

2. One gene controlled by different controllers at different moments in time will lead to different results of the gene expression function. Formally, for all $c_i \neq c_j (i \neq j)$ controllers of the same gene g and for all $T_k \in T_{nR}, k \neq 1$ such as $T_1 < T_k$, we have $Exp(T_1)(g, c_i) \neq Exp(T_k)(g, c_j)$.

3. Different genes controlled by the same controller at different moments in time will lead to different results of their gene expression functions. Formally, for all c that can control different genes $g_i \neq g_j$ and for all $T_k \in T_{nR}, k \neq 1$ such as $T_1 < T_k$, we have $Exp(T_1)(g_i, c) \neq Exp(T_k)(g_j, c)$.

4. One gene controlled by the same controller at different consecutive times leads to the same result of the gene expression function. Formally, for all c that controllers a gene g, we have $Exp(T_1)(g, c) = Exp(T_2)(g, c)$.

5. For all c and for all g, the expression of gene g being controlled by c, if at time T_1 we have $Exp(T_1)(g, c) = a^{var_1}$ and at time T_2 (such as $T_2 - T_1$ is a positive value not necessarily $T_2 = T_1 + 1$) we have $Exp(T_2)(g, c) = b^{var_2}$ such as for $var_1 \neq var_2$ we obtain two different object types ($a \neq b$), then we say that the gene g *was mutated (underwent a genetic mutation).*

Algorithm of Learning at Molecular Level

The way one neuron have the ability to adapt to its inputs by altering gene expression along with the conditions of this to occur, we chose to present in the fallowing algorithm. We make the assumption that the region of the neuron n in which the objects are encoded will be α_{p,j_r}. The steps in this algorithm correspond to some discrete internal times of activation of one group of genes. The gene considered to suffer a mutation (at step m) is $g, g \in G$. Its controller is considered to be c. We make the observation that *Step 0* is not actually the first step of this algorithm computation, but a previous step in which the controller of g was produced.

Step 0. (Step of internal time T_0 of the group of genes activation): The controller c is produced. It will be able to control the expression of gene g at a next activation of the group of genes from which g belongs to.

Step 1. (Step of internal time T_1 of the group of genes activation, $T_0 < T_1$): The gene g controlled by c will encode object a in a var_1 number of copies:

$$Exp(T_1)(g, c) = a^{var_1}.$$

Step j. (Step of internal time T_j of the group of genes activation such as $T_1 < T_j \leq T_{m-1}$, for $m \in \mathbb{N}, m > 1$): The gene g controlled by c will encode the same object a in a var_1 number of copies (as from *Step 1* to *Step j*). We have:

– the neuron activity rate:

$$nRate(T_j, j) = (T_{g_1}^j - T_{g_1}^{j-1}, \ldots, T_g^j - T_g^{j-1}, \ldots, T_{g_k}^j - T_{g_k}^{j-1})$$

– $Exp(T_j)(g, c) = a^{var_1}$
– the quantity found into the substrate in the region α_{p,j_p} of neuron n:

$$C_{n:\alpha_{p,j_p}}(T_j) = C_{n:\alpha_{p,j_p}}(T_j, a) + \sum_{i, a_i \neq a} C_{n:\alpha_{p,j_p}}(T_j, a_i) =$$

$$= var_1 + \sum_{i, a_i \neq a} C_{n:\alpha_{p,j_p}}(T_j, a_i)$$

Step m. (Step of internal time T_m of the group of genes activation): If in the discrete time interval (T_{m-1}, T_m) some changes occurred and the gene g suffered a mutation, then this fact involves some changes that can be detected by analyzing the differences in the neuron activity rate. The results will be seen as fallows:

– the neuron activity rate:

$$nRate(T_m, m) = (T_{g_1}^m - T_{g_1}^{m-1}, \ldots, T_g^m - T_g^{m-1}, \ldots, T_{g_k}^m - T_{g_k}^{m-1})$$

and $T_g^m - T_g^{m-1} \neq T_g^j - T_g^{j-1}$ for $1 \leq j \leq m - 1$. This fact will involve the next two items bellow:
– $Exp(T_m)(g, c) = b^{var_2}$
– the quantity found into the substrate in the region α_{p,j_p} of neuron n:

$$C_{n:\alpha_{p,j_p}}(T_m) = C_{n:\alpha_{p,j_p}}(T_m, b) + \sum_{i, a_i \neq a, a_i \neq b} C_{n:\alpha_{p,j_p}}(T_m, a_i) =$$

$$= var_2 + \sum_{i, a_i \neq a, a_i \neq b} C_{n:\alpha_{p,j_p}}(T_m, a_i)$$

As at time T_j in the neuron substrate there is no b^{var_2} then $\sum_{i,a_i \neq a} C_{n:\alpha_{p.j_p}}(T_j, a_i) = \sum_{i,a_i \neq a, a_i \neq b} C_{n:\alpha_{p.j_p}}(T_m, a_i)$ and from the properties above $var_1 \neq var_2$ we obtain that $C_{n:\alpha_{p.j_p}}(T_j) \neq C_{n:\alpha_{p.j_p}}(T_m)$.

Step $m+1$. (Step of internal time T_{m+1} of the group of genes activation): the same biochemical processes that led to c at the internal time T_0, produces, at step $m+1$, a different controller $\bar{c}$ ($c \neq \bar{c}$). This way, the new substrate will undergo some changes (into the receptors conformations) inducing modified binding affinity degrees of the neuron.

Consequences. Changes of the binding affinity degrees induce modified synaptic communications between neuron devices in a network. Because of the alteration of the genetic expression, modifications of the binding affinities degrees determine the neuron ability to adapt to its inputs. It determines the modeling of the behavior of one neuron device. By memorizing the new state into the memory of DNA the definition of the learning process at the molecular level along with the view over the neuron device as a feedback control system are justified.

4   Conclusion

In the present paper we presented an algorithm of how information can be controlled and monitored in modeling one neuron (from a network of neurons) behavior. The neuron behavior is viewed also from inside (molecular point of view) and not only from the outside point of view as the neurons from an usual neural network. One may say that we tried to take a glimpse at how things can be viewed and analyzed from inside to outside one neuron. There are some obvious conclusions arise from the model. Changes into the neuron functionality can be detected by analyzing the differences that may occur into the neuron activity rate values measured between consecutive activations of groups of genes. The internal timing is the one that sets up the neuron activity rate. Changes occurred during the evolution of the neuron device induce modifications of the binding affinity degrees (between neuron devices or between neurons and the environment). In their turn, this fact will lead to modifications of the "synaptic" communications and even into the network structure where communication between devices could be interrupted. Modifications of the binding affinities degrees will also determine the neuron ability to adapt to its inputs by memorizing the new state and modeling its behavior. Due to the fact that the entire complex system structure and functionality is still in its early stages of a theoretical model, experiments to test the proposed technique have not been done yet. The purpose of this paper was to create a stronger background for our future directions of work in analyzing the behavior at a network level. This background represents the platform on which one neuron device develops as a feedback control system by its ability to adapt to its own inputs. This ability was defined as a learning process at the molecular level.

References

1. Morogan, L.M.: Prion Neural Systems, Why Choosing a Hybrid Approach of Natural Computing? In: Elefterakis, G., et al. (eds.) 4th Annual South-East European Doctoral Student Conference on Infusing Research and Knowledge in South-East Europe, Thessaloniki, vol. 1, pp. 381–391 (2009)
2. Morogan, L.M.: Coding Information in New Computing Models. DNA Computing and Membrane Computing. In: Analele Universitatii Spiru Haret, vol. 2, pp. 59–73. FRM, Bucharest (2006)
3. Maass, W.: Networks of Spiking Neurons: The Third Generation of Neural Network Models. Neural Networks 10(9), 1659–1671 (1997)
4. Maass, W., Schmitt, M.: On the Complexity of Learning for Spiking Neurons with Temporal Coding. Information and Computation 153(1), 26–46 (1999)
5. Maass, W., Natschlager, T.: Associative Memory with Networks of Spiking Neurons in Temporal Coding. In: Smith, L.S., Hamilton, A. (eds.) Neuromorphic Systems: Engineering Silicon from Neurobiology, pp. 21–32. World Scientific, Singapore (1998)
6. Natschlaeger, T.: Efficient Computation in Networks of Spiking Neurons - Simulations and Theory. Ph.D. thesis, Institute for Theoretical Computer Science, Technische Universitaet Graz, Austria (1999)
7. Natschlager, T., Maass, W.: Finding the Key to a Synapse. In: Leen, T.K., et al. (eds.) Advances in Neural Information Processing Systems. NIPS 2000 Conference, vol. 13, pp. 138–145. MIT Press, Cambridge (2001)
8. Ghazali, R., Mohd Nawi, N., Mohd Salikon, M.Z.: Forecasting the UK/EU and JP/UK Trading Signals Using Polynomial Neural Networks. International Journal of Computer Information Systems and Industrial Management Applications 1, 110–117 (2009)
9. Ciarelli, P.M., Oliveira, E., Badue, C., De Souza, A.F.: Multi-Label Text Categorization Using a Probabilistic Neural Network. International Journal of Computer Information Systems and Industrial Management Applications 1, 133–144 (2009)
10. Morogan, L.M., Barza, S.: Algoritmica Grafurilor. FRM, Bucharest (2008)
11. Alberts, B., Johnson, A., Lewis, J., Raff, M., Roberts, K., Walter, P.: Molecular Biology of the Cell, 4th edn. Garland Science, New York (2002)
12. Benga, G.: Biologia Moleculara a Membranelor cu Aplicatii Medicale. Dacia, Cluj-Napoca (1979)
13. Israil, A.M.: Biologie Moleculara. Prezent si Perspective. Humanitas, Bucharest (2000)
14. Morogan, L.M.: Prion Neural Systems: Synaptic Level. In: Psychogios, A., et al. (eds.) 5th Annual South-East European Doctoral Student Conference on Infusing Research and Knowledge in South-East Europe, Thessaloniki, pp. 436–444 (2010)
15. Morogan, L.M.: Prion Neural System: Modeling the Binding Affinities Between Neurons of a Network. In: Abraham, A., et al. (eds.) Proceeding of International Conference on Computer Information Systems and Industrial Management Applications with Applications to Ambient Intelligence and Ubiquitous Systems, pp. 143–147. IEEE Press, Krakow (2010)

A Fault Tolerant Scheduling Algorithm for DAG Applications in Cluster Environments

Nabil Tabbaa, Reza Entezari-Maleki, and Ali Movaghar

Department of Computer Engineering, Sharif University of Technology,
Tehran, Iran
{tabbaa,entezari}@ce.sharif.edu, movaghar@sharif.edu

Abstract. Fault tolerance is an essential requirement in systems running applications which need a technique to continue execution where some system components are subject to failure. In this paper, a fault tolerant task scheduling algorithm is proposed for mapping task graphs to heterogeneous processing nodes in cluster computing systems. The starting point of the algorithm is a DAG representing an application with information about the tasks. This information consists of the execution time of the tasks on the target system processors, communication times between the tasks having data dependencies, and the number of the processor failures (ε) which should be tolerated by the scheduling algorithm. The algorithm is based on the active replication scheme, and it schedules $\varepsilon+1$ replicas of each task to achieve the required fault tolerance. Simulation results show the efficiency of the proposed algorithm in spite of its lower complexity.

Keywords: Cluster Environment, Task Scheduling Algorithms, DAG Tasks, Fault Tolerance.

1 Introduction

Cluster environments consist of an array of diverse computers connected by high-speed networks to achieve powerful platforms. Cluster computing systems are widely deployed for executing computationally intensive parallel applications with various computing requirements [1]. Although the field of parallel computing has existed for many years, programming a parallel system to execute a single application is still a challenging problem, strongly more challenging than programming a single processor, or a sequential system. Allocation of the tasks to the processors and specifying the order of the execution is one of the most important steps in parallel programming. This step, named scheduling, fundamentally determines the efficiency of the application's parallelization. The parallelization in parallel programming shows the speedup of the execution in comparison to a single processor system [2].

There are two well-known types of scheduling algorithms; dynamic and static scheduling. In dynamic scheduling, the decision as to which processor executes a task and when is controlled by the runtime system. This is mostly practical for independent tasks. In contrast, static scheduling means that the processor allocation, often called mapping, and the ordering of the tasks are determined at compile time.

V. Snasel, J. Platos, and E. El-Qawasmeh (Eds.): ICDIPC 2011, Part I, CCIS 188, pp. 189–199, 2011.

The advantage of static scheduling is that it can include the dependences and communications among the tasks in its scheduling decisions. Furthermore, since the scheduling is done at compile time, the execution is not burdened with the scheduling overhead [3]. The main goal of most scheduling strategies is to minimize the scheduling length, which is the total completion time of the application tasks. An alternative designation for schedule length, which is quite common in the literature, is makespan [4] and [5].

Resource failures may frequently occur in distributed computing systems and have undesired effects on applications. Consequently, there is an increasing need for developing techniques to achieve fault tolerance [6] and [7]. Fault tolerance is an important property in distributed computing as the dependability of individual resources may not be guaranteed. A fault tolerant approach may therefore be useful in order to potentially prevent a malicious node affecting the overall performance of the application. This subject is very important in distributed computing systems because the size and complexity of the applications are increased dramatically to take advantage of such system resources. Actually, the probability of error occurrence may be increased by the fact that many cluster applications will perform long tasks that may require several days of computation. Hence, the cost and difficulty of recovering from faults in distributed applications are higher than those of traditional applications [6]. If fault tolerance is not provided, the system cannot survive to continue when one or several processors fail. In such situation, the entire program crashes. Therefore, a technique is needed to enable a system to execute critical applications even in the presence of one or more processor failures. Both the task scheduling and fault tolerance within distributed systems are difficult problems in their own, and solving them together makes the problem even harder. Concretely, the main goal of fault tolerant task scheduling algorithms is to find a static schedule of application tasks on the processing elements of a cluster computing system and tolerate a given number of processor failures. The input of the fault tolerant scheduling algorithm is a specification of the application tasks, the computation power of the processing elements, and some information about the execution times of the tasks on the system processors and the communication times between the tasks. In this paper, a fault tolerant task scheduling algorithm is proposed, which aims at tolerating multiple processor failures and tries to achieve a minimum possible makespan. The proposed algorithm uses active replication scheme to mask failures.

The remainder of this paper is organized as follows. Section 2 presents a review of the related works. A brief description of the task graph and the multiprocessor models is given in Section 3. Section 4 presents the proposed algorithm. The simulation results are presented in Section 5. Finally, Section 6 concludes the paper and presents future work.

2   Related Works

A large number of task scheduling algorithms for DAG applications have been proposed in the literature. But most of the available algorithms assume that the processors of the system are completely safe, so they do not tolerate any failure in the system components. Fault tolerance can be achieved in distributed computing systems by scheduling multiple copies of each task on different processors. In the follow, a brief survey of two well-known types of fault tolerant task scheduling algorithms named primary/backup scheduling and active replication scheduling are presented.

Oh et al. [7] have proposed an algorithm in which each of the submitted tasks are assumed to be independent and non-preemptive. The algorithm considers the case where the backup copies are allowed to be overlapped in time of their execution on a processor; if the primary copies are scheduled on different processors. Ghosh et al. [8] present techniques to provide fault tolerance for non-preemptive, aperiodic and real-time tasks having deadline. The goal of the presented techniques is to achieve high acceptance ratio, percentage of accepted arriving tasks. Manimaran et al. [9] have presented an algorithm to dynamically schedule real-time tasks. This algorithm handles resource constraints, where a task might need some resources, such as data structures, variables, and communication buffers for its execution. Al-Omari et al. [10] have proposed an algorithm which uses the Primary-Backup (PB) overloading technique to be as an alternative to the usually used Backup-Backup overloading. The algorithm is presented to improve schedulability and achieve fault tolerant scheduling of real-time tasks in multiprocessor systems. Zheng et al. [11] and [12] have proposed two techniques, called the Minimum Replication Cost with Early Completion Time (MRC-ECT) and the Minimum Completion Time with Less Replication Cost (MCT-LRC), to schedule backups of independent and dependent jobs, respectively.

The main disadvantage of all of the previous algorithms is that only two copies of the task are scheduled on different processors. Based on this assumption, the task can be completed only when one processor fails. So, these algorithms cannot tolerate more than one failure at a time.

In active replication scheme, multiple copies of each task are mapped on different processors, which are run in parallel to tolerate a given number of failures. Hashimito et al. [13] have proposed a new approach to achieve fault tolerance by scheduling DAG applications on identical processing elements. This algorithm exploits implicit redundancy, which is originally introduced by task duplication to reduce the execution times of parallel programs. Girault et al. [14] have presented an algorithm with the goal of automatically obtain a distributed and fault tolerant task scheduling in embedded systems. The proposed algorithm considers timing constraints on tasks execution, and indicates whether or not the real-time constraints are satisfied. In order to tolerate N failures, the algorithm allows at least $N+1$ replicas of a task to be scheduled on different processors.

3   The Directed Acyclic Graph Scheduling Problem

The objective of Directed Acyclic Graph (DAG) scheduling is to minimize the overall program finish-time by proper allocation of the tasks to the processors and arrangement of execution sequence of the tasks. Scheduling is done in such a manner that the precedence constraints among the program components are preserved.

3.1   The DAG Model

A parallel program can be represented by DAG, $G = (V, E)$, where V is a set of v nodes and E is a set of e directed edges. Each node n_i in the DAG denotes a task, and its weight represents the computation cost and is indicated by $w(n_i)$. The edges in the DAG, each of which is denoted by (n_i, n_j), correspond to the communication messages and precedence constraints between the nodes. The weight of an edge is called the communication cost and is indicated by $c(n_i, n_j)$. The communication has no cost if two nodes are mapped to the same processor. For a node n_i in G, $pred(n_i)$ is the set of immediate predecessors and $succ(n_i)$ denotes its immediate successors. A node having no parent is called an entry node and a node having no child is called an exit node [3]. The precedence constraints of a DAG dictate that a node cannot start execution before it gathers all of the messages from its parent nodes. A critical path (CP) of a DAG is a longest path traversed from an entry node to an exit node. Obviously, a DAG can have more than one CP. Consider the task graph shown in Fig. 1. In this task graph, nodes n_1, n_7, and n_9 are the nodes of the only CP. The edges on the CP are shown with thick arrows. The communication-to-computation-ratio (CCR) of a parallel program is defined as its average edge weight divided by its average node weight [15]. Hereafter, the terms node and task are used interchangeably.

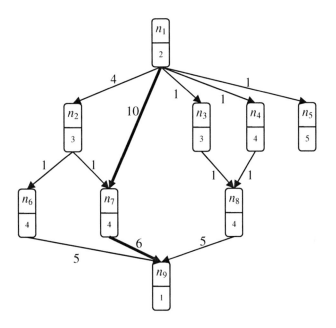

Fig. 1. Directed Acyclic Graph

3.2 The Multiprocessor Model

In DAG scheduling, the target system is represented by a finite processor set $P = \{P_1, P_2, \ldots, P_m\}$. The processors may be heterogeneous or homogeneous. The heterogeneity of the processors means that they have different speeds or processing capabilities. However, it is assumed that every task of the application can be executed on any processor even though the completion times on different processors may be different. The heterogeneity of processing capability is modeled by a function

$C:P{\to}R^+$, so the completion time of task n_i on processor P_k equals to $C(P_k){\times}w(n_i)$ [15]. The processors are assumed to be fully connected.

4   The Proposed Algorithm

The objective of the proposed algorithm is to map the tasks of DAG represented application to processors with diverse capabilities in a cluster computing system. The algorithm aims to minimize the schedule length while tolerating a given number of ε fail-silent (fail-stop) processor failures. To achieve this, active replication scheme is used to allocate ε +1 copies of each task to different processors.

4.1   Scheduling Heuristic

The proposed algorithm mainly uses the well-known heuristic technique encountered in scheduling algorithms that is called list scheduling. In its general form, the first part of list scheduling sorts the nodes of the application graph to be scheduled depending on a priority scheme, while respecting the precedence constraints of the nodes. In the second part, each node of the list is consecutively scheduled to a processor chosen for the node [3]. In our algorithm each node is scheduled to multiple processors to achieve the required fault tolerance. An important characteristic of list scheduling is that it guarantees the feasibility of all partial schedules, and the final schedule, by scheduling only free nodes and choosing an appropriate start time for each node [3]. The nodes are processed in precedence order (i.e., in topological order), so at the time a node is scheduled all ancestor nodes have already been processed.

4.2   Priority Scheme

List scheduling algorithms establish the scheduling order of the nodes before the scheduling process. During the node scheduling in the second part, this order remains unchanged, so the node priorities are static. To achieve most efficient schedules, it is better to consider the state of the partial schedule when the order of the remaining nodes is established. In this case, the priorities of the nodes are considered to be dynamic. Additionally, the node order must be compatible with the precedence constraints of the application graph, which is achieved if only free nodes are scheduled.

In the proposed algorithm free nodes are ordered by a priority value equals to *tlevel+blevel* of the node, where *tlevel* and *blevel* denote the *dynamic top level* and the *static bottom level* of the node respectively. The word *dynamic* implies that the value *tlevel* depends upon the nodes which have already been mapped, and the word *static* implies that the value *blevel* remains unchanged during the scheduling process.

Taking the computational heterogeneity of the system into account, the average execution time of a node on all processors can be used when calculating *blevel*, since the processor on which a node will be assigned is not known. So *blevel* can be computed using (1).

$$blevel\,(n_i) = \max_{n_j \in succ\,(n_i)} \{\overline{w(n_i)} + c(n_i, n_j) + blevel\,(n_j)\} \ . \tag{1}$$

Where $\overline{w(n_i)}$ is the average execution time of node n_i and $c(n_i,\ n_j)$ is the communication cost between node n_i and node n_j (a successor of n_i).

The *tlevel* is calculated dynamically for each of the free nodes at each step by (2).

$$tlevel(n_i) = \max_{n_j \in pred\,(n_i)} \{FT(n_j, \mathrm{Proc}(n_j)) + c(n_i, n_j)\} \ . \tag{2}$$

Where $FT(n_j, \mathrm{Proc}(n_j))$ is the finish time of node n_j (a predecessor of n_i) which has been previously scheduled on processor $\mathrm{Proc}(n_j)$.

This priority value provides a good measure of the node importance, since the nodes that have the maximum value of *tlevel+blevel* compose the critical path of the application graph. The greater the priority, the more work is to be performed along the path containing that node.

4.3 Processor Choice

At each step the scheduling process selects the free node n that has the highest priority and tries to schedule it on all processors to calculate its expected finish time on each processor using (3)

$$FT\,(n, P_l) = w(n, P_l) + \max\{ \max_{n_j \in pred\,(n)} [\min_{1 \leq k \leq \varepsilon+1} (FT\,(n_j^k, \mathrm{Proc}(n_j^k)) + c(n_j, n), r(P_l)]\} \cdot \tag{3}$$

Where $r(P_l)$ is the ready time of the processor P_l, and the predecessor nodes are already scheduled onto $\varepsilon +1$ processors, and n_j^k denotes the replicas of node n_j.

Then, the node n is scheduled on the $\varepsilon +1$ processors which deliver the minimum finish time for that node using (3). Actually, (3) determines the finish time of the node n if no processor fails during the execution of the application, since the minimum of all replicas is used. In this case, the lower bound of the schedule length $SL_{\min}$ can be computed using (4).

$$SL_{\min} = \max_{n \in V} \{ \min_{1 \leq k \leq \varepsilon+1} [FT\,(n^k, \mathrm{Proc}\,(n^k))]\} \ . \tag{4}$$

While for the worst case, in the presence of ε failures, the finish time would be given by (5).

$$FT\,(n, P_l) = w(n, P_l) + \max\{ \max_{n_j \in pred\,(n)} [\max_{1 \leq k \leq \varepsilon+1} (FT(n_j^k, \mathrm{Proc}(n_j^k)) + c(n_j, n), r(P_l)]\} \cdot \tag{5}$$

Then, to compute the upper bound of the schedule length $SL_{\max}$, (6) can be used.

$$SL_{\max} = \max_{n \in V} \{ \max_{1 \leq k \leq \varepsilon+1} [FT\,(n^k, \mathrm{Proc}\,(n^k))]\} \ . \tag{6}$$

4.4 The Algorithm

The main steps of the proposed scheduling algorithm can be written as follows:

1) Compute *blevel* for each task in the graph,
2) Mark all entry tasks as free tasks,
3) **While** still have unscheduled tasks do
4)   Compute *tlevel* for each free task,
5)   Update the priorities of all free tasks,
6)   Select a free task n with highest priority,
7)   Compute the finish time $FT(n, P_l)$ of the task n on all of the processors,
8)   Schedule the task n on $\varepsilon + 1$ processors that allow the minimum finish time,
9)   Add free successors of n to the free tasks,
10) **End while**

5 Simulation Results

To evaluate the proposed fault tolerant scheduling algorithm, this algorithm is simulated and compared to the FTBAR algorithm [14] which is the closest to our algorithm found in the literature. The goal of our simulations is to evaluate the fault tolerance overhead of the proposed algorithm and compare it with the overhead of FTBAR algorithm.

The proposed algorithm and FTBAR are simulated with a set of randomly generated graphs. Different methods of generating random DAGs for simulation can be found in [16]. In this paper, the method of Layer-by-Layer is used in simulation phase. A random graph is generated as follows: given the total number of tasks, we randomly generated a set of levels with a random number of tasks such that the sum of the number of tasks in all of the levels is equal to the total number of tasks. Consequently, the tasks at a given level are randomly connected to the tasks at higher levels. The execution times of the tasks and communication times between them are randomly selected from uniform distributions with chosen ranges. The number of processors is set to 10 and each point in the shown figures in this paper represents an average over 60 random graphs. The most important metric of the performance of the algorithm is the fault tolerance overhead caused by the active replication scheme. The overhead is computed using the following formula.

$$overhead = \frac{FTSL - nonFTSL}{FTSL} \times 100 \ . \tag{7}$$

Where *FTSL* is the fault tolerant schedule length and the *nonFTSL* is the schedule length produced when the number of failures ε is set to zero.

The average fault tolerance overhead is plotted in Fig. 2 as a function of the number of tasks which is varied uniformly in the range [20, 200]. The communication to computation ratio (*CCR*) is set to 1 and the number of failures ε is set to 2 and 5. This figure shows that the average overhead increases with the number of tasks. This is due to the replication of all tasks and communications.

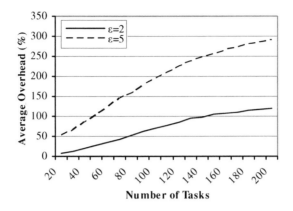

Fig. 2. Average overhead for *CCR*=1

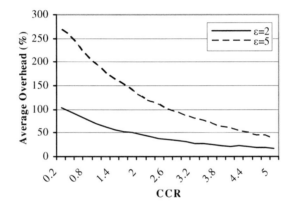

Fig. 3. Average overhead for *Number of Tasks*=100

In Fig. 3 the average fault tolerance overhead is plotted as a function of the *CCR* which is varied uniformly in the range [0.2, 5]. The number of tasks is set to 100 and the number of failures ε is set to 2 and 5. One can see in this figure that the average overhead decreases when the *CCR* increases, since the replication of tasks has a positive effect in withdrawing many of the communications required among the tasks.

Fig. 4 and Fig. 5 show the comparison of the overhead between the proposed algorithm and the FTBAR algorithm as a function of the number of tasks which is varied uniformly in the range [20, 200]. The *CCR* is set to 1 and the number of failures ε is set to 2 and 5 in Fig. 4 and Fig. 5, respectively. It can be seen that the proposed algorithm shows better results compared to FTBAR algorithm for any number of tasks.

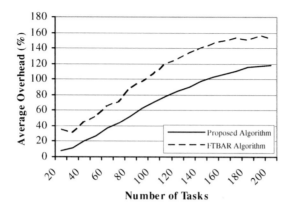

Fig. 4. Average overhead for $CCR=1$ and $\varepsilon =2$

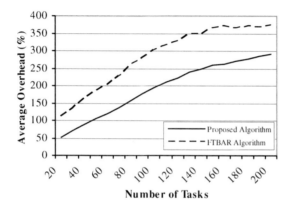
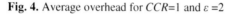

Fig. 5. Average overhead for $CCR=1$ and $\varepsilon =5$

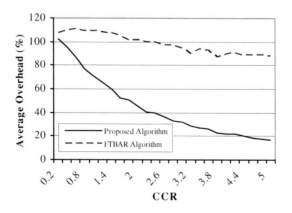

Fig. 6. Average overhead for *Number of Tasks*=100 and $\varepsilon =2$

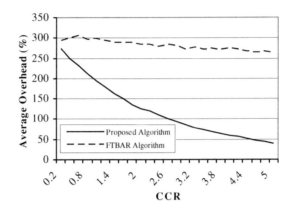

Fig. 7. Average overhead for *Number of Tasks*=100 and ε =5

In Fig. 6 and Fig. 7 the comparison of the overhead is shown as a function of the *CCR* which is varied uniformly in the range [0.2, 5]. The number of tasks is set to 100 and the number of failures ε is set to 2 and 5 in Fig. 6 and Fig. 7, respectively. We can see that for small values of *CCR* there is a little difference between the proposed algorithm and the FTBAR. But for higher values of *CCR*, the proposed algorithm performs significantly better than FTBAR algorithm.

6   Conclusions and Future Work

A large number of algorithms for scheduling and partitioning DAGs have been proposed in the literature, either with an unbounded or with a limited number of processors. Most of these algorithms assume that the processors in the systems are completely safe, so they do not achieve fault tolerance. Some techniques for supporting fault tolerant systems have been proposed, but only few of them are able to tolerate multiple failures at a time. In this paper, a fault tolerant task scheduling algorithm is proposed for mapping DAG tasks on cluster computing systems with heterogeneous processor capabilities. The algorithm is based on active replication, and it schedules $\varepsilon+1$ replicas of each task on different processors to tolerate a given number ε of processor failures. Despite its lower complexity, simulation results demonstrate that the proposed algorithm has an efficient performance in the term of schedule length overhead. It outperforms the closest available algorithm FTBAR, especially in the case of high communication to computation ratio.

Scheduling $\varepsilon+1$ replicas of each task on different processors results in replicating the communications between tasks $(\varepsilon+1)^2$ times. This is due to the fact that each of $\varepsilon+1$ replicas of each task will receive the same message from the $\varepsilon+1$ replicas of each one of its predecessors. Future work on this algorithm might try to reduce the total number of communications. Additionally, in the proposed algorithm, the processors are considered fully connected with non-faulty links. While this can be appropriate in cluster environments, extensions might be added to this algorithm to take communication link failures into account, and make it relevant to other distributed computing systems such as grid environments.

References

1. Buyya, R.: High Performance Cluster Computing: Architectures and Systems, 1st edn. Prentice Hall PTR, Upper Saddle River (1999)
2. Buyya, R.: High Performance Cluster Computing: Programming and Applications, 1st edn. Prentice Hall PTR, Upper Saddle River (1999)
3. Sinnen, O.: Task Scheduling for Parallel Systems, 1st edn. John Wiley and Sons Inc, New Jersey (2007)
4. Entezari-Maleki, R., Movaghar, A.: A genetic-based scheduling algorithm to minimize the makespan of the grid applications. In: Kim, T., Yau, S., Gervasi, O., Kang, B., Stoica, A. (eds.) Grid and Distributed Computing, Control and Automation. Communications in Computer and Information Science, vol. 121, pp. 22–31. Springer, Heidelberg (2010)
5. Parsa, S., Entezari-Maleki, R.: RASA: A new grid task scheduling algorithm. International Journal of Digital Content Technology and its Applications 3(4), 91–99 (2009)
6. Sathya, S.S., Babu, K.S.: Survey of fault tolerant techniques for grid. Computer Science Review 4(2), 101–120 (2010)
7. Oh, Y., Son, S.H.: Scheduling real-time tasks for dependability. Journal of Operational Research Society 48(6), 629–639 (1997)
8. Ghosh, S., Melhem, R., Mosse, D.: Fault-tolerance through scheduling of aperiodic tasks in hard real-time multiprocessor systems. IEEE Transactions on Parallel and Distributed Systems 8(3), 272–284 (1997)
9. Manimaran, G., Murthy, C.S.R.: A fault-tolerant dynamic scheduling algorithm for multiprocessor real-time systems and its analysis. IEEE Transactions on Parallel and Distributed Systems 9(11), 1137–1152 (1998)
10. Al-Omari, R., Somani, A., Manimaran, G.: A new fault-tolerant technique for improving schedulability in multiprocessor real-time systems. In: The 15th International Parallel and Distributed Processing Symposium, pp. 32–39 (2001)
11. Zheng, Q., Veeravalli, B., Tham, C.K.: Fault-tolerant scheduling of independent tasks in computational grid. In: The 10th IEEE International Conference on Communications Systems, pp. 1–5 (2006)
12. Zheng, Q., Veeravalli, B., Tham, C.K.: On the design of fault-tolerant scheduling strategies using primary-backup approach for computational grids with low replication costs. IEEE Transactions on Computers 58(3), 380–393 (2009)
13. Hashimito, K., Tsuchiya, T., Kikuno, T.: A new approach to realizing fault-tolerant multiprocessor scheduling by exploiting implicit redundancy. In: The 27th International Symposium on Fault-Tolerant Computing, pp. 174–183 (1997)
14. Girault, A., Kalla, H., Sighireanu, M., Sore, Y.: An algorithm for automatically obtaining distributed and fault-tolerant static schedules. In: International Conference on Dependable Systems and Networks, pp. 159–168 (2003)
15. Kwok, Y.K., Ahmad, I.: Static scheduling algorithms for allocating directed task graphs to multiprocessors. ACM Computing Surveys 31(4), 406–471 (1999)
16. Cordeiro, D., Mouni, G., Perarnau, S., Trystram, D., Vincent, J.M., Wagner, F.: Random graph generation for scheduling simulations. In: The 3rd International ICST Conference on Simulation Tools and Techniques, pp. 60:1-60:10 (2010)

A Bee Colony Task Scheduling Algorithm in Computational Grids

Zohreh Mousavinasab[1], Reza Entezari-Maleki[2], and Ali Movaghar[1,2]

[1] Department of Information Technology, Sharif University of Technology,
International Campus, Kish Island, Iran
[2] Department of Computer Engineering, Sharif University of Technology, Tehran, Iran
mousavinasab@kish.sharif.edu, entezari@ce.sharif.edu,
movaghar@sharif.edu

Abstract. The efficient scheduling of the independent and sequential tasks on distributed and heterogeneous computing resources within grid computing environments is an NP-complete problem. Therefore, using heuristic approaches to solve the scheduling problem is a very common and also acceptable method in these environments. In this paper, a new task scheduling algorithm based on bee colony optimization approach is proposed. The algorithm uses artificial bees to appropriately schedule the submitted tasks to the grid resources. Applying the proposed algorithm to the grid computing environments, the maximum delay and finish times of the tasks are reduced. Furthermore, the total makespan of the environment is minimized when the algorithm is applied. The proposed algorithm not only minimizes the makespan of the environment, but also satisfies the deadline and priority requirements of the tasks. Simulation results obtained from applying the algorithm to different grid environments show the prominence of the algorithm to other similar scheduling algorithms.

Keywords: Task scheduling, grid computing, bee colony optimization, makespan, delay time.

1 Introduction

Grid computing [1] is a large scale distributed environment designed for solving the computational- and data-intensive problems in science and industry. Actually, the grid is an infrastructure which supplies a mechanism to run the applications over computational resources which are heterogeneous and geographically distributed. The computational resources within the grid environments may belong to the various individuals and institutions [1], [2]. Bringing the computational resources together from various administrative domains provides a tremendous computational environment to execute the tasks submitted to the environment. In order to execute the tasks, two factors are of great importance in the grid computing environments: resource management and task scheduling [1], [3]. Resource management provides the possibility to have access to all of the resources within the grid environment, regardless of their platforms and hardware architectures. Task scheduling algorithms

V. Snasel, J. Platos, and E. El-Qawasmeh (Eds.): ICDIPC 2011, Part I, CCIS 188, pp. 200–210, 2011.
© Springer-Verlag Berlin Heidelberg 2011

are needed to effectively use the tremendous capabilities of the grid computing environments. Grid managers apply task scheduling algorithms to dispatch the submitted tasks among the grid resources appropriately. Generally, the grid tasks are submitted to the grid managers by grid users and then the manager schedules the tasks within the available resources [4].

In order to schedule the tasks to the multiple resources distributed within the grid environments, the need for an efficient and proper scheduling algorithm is sensed. Since the scheduling is an NP-complete problem, many heuristic approaches have been proposed to appropriately schedule the tasks within the grid resources. Heuristic algorithms produce a good solution by solving a simpler problem that contains or intersects with the solution of a more complex problem.

Due to the study of the behavior of social insects, a source of inspiration for the design and manipulation of optimization algorithms has been found by computer scientists recently. Nature-inspired algorithms are considered by the ability of biological systems to efficiently regulate the mostly changeable environments. These algorithms include evolutionary computation, neural networks, ant colony optimization, particle swarm optimization, artificial immune systems, and bacteria foraging algorithm [5], [6]. Swarming and showing the different characteristics and behaviors are the main specifications of the various colonies of social insects such as bees, wasps, ants and termites. The behavior of the social insects is first and foremost characterized by autonomy, distributed functioning and self-organizing [5]. Swarm intelligence is the part of the artificial intelligence that is based on the study of actions of individuals in various decentralized systems [7]. Recently, the bee colony optimization (BCO) has been introduced as a new horizon in the discussion of swarm intelligence [4]. Artificial bees stand for agents, which are collaborative solutions to solve the complex combinatorial optimization problems. The impression BCO suggests a multi agent system (colony of artificial bees) to solve the complex optimization problems [5]. The study of bee colonies proved to be interesting enough for developing problem-solving algorithms. For this reason, a new task scheduling algorithm inspired by bee colonies is presented in this paper.

The rest of this paper is organized as follows. Section 2 presents the related works done in the field of task scheduling algorithms and optimization problems using BCO. In Sect. 3, the concepts of the BCO are introduced. Section 4 proposes the new task scheduling algorithm based on BCO. Section 5 presents the simulation results and compares the proposed algorithm against the well-known scheduling algorithms in a hypothesis grid environment. Finally, Sect. 6 concludes the paper and presents future work.

2 Related Works

Since the BCO is a meta-heuristic and can be displayed as a general algorithmic framework, it has been able to apply various optimization problems in management, engineering, and control [5], [6]. On the other hand, the problem of task scheduling in distributed systems and especially in grid environments has been souled by various heuristic methods such as genetic algorithms (GAs), particle swarm optimization (PSO), simulated annealing (SA), ant colony and so forth [8], [9]. In the below, some of the algorithms related to the task scheduling problem are introduced. Also, the several research works which use the BCO as an optimization technique in various optimization problems are introduced.

Parsa et al. [3] have presented a new task scheduling algorithm which is called RASA in grid environments with the goal of reducing the makespan of the grid resources. RASA takes advantages of two algorithms, Min-min and Max-min [10], and avoids their drawbacks. Entezari-Maleki et al. [11] have proposed a genetic-based scheduling algorithm to reduce the makespan of the grid applications.

The proposed algorithm in Ref. [11] schedules the submitted tasks to the grid resources considering the completion time of the tasks on each of the resources. The simulation results show that the proposed algorithm reaches a good level of throughput in comparison with the others. But, none of the algorithms presented in Refs. [3] and [11] consider the deadline and arriving rate of the tasks, as well as the cost of the task execution on each of the resources.

Zheng et al. [8] have offered a model that combines two optimal schemes, genetic algorithm (GA) and simulated annealing (SA), based on the probability distribution. Actually, the algorithm uses the benefits of the genetic algorithms and simulated annealing and provides a parallel genetic-simulated annealing algorithm to solve the task scheduling problem in grid environments. Liu et al. [9] have proposed an improved ant colony algorithm which is called adaptive ant colony algorithm for grid task scheduling which can balance the loads of the resources within the grid environment. The algorithm has avoided impressively the phenomena of hunger and starvation on the resources due to the fighting for preponderant resources by more tasks.

Davidovic et al. [12] have presented the BCO heuristic algorithm which is inspired by bees behavior for task scheduling problem on homogeneous processors. This algorithm has the ability to obtain the optimal value of the objective function in all small to medium size test problems. However, there is no theoretical background at the moment that could support the presented approach.

Wong et al. [13] have presented a BCO algorithm for traveling salesman problem (TSP). The BCO algorithm is made based on the collective intelligence shown in bee foraging behavior. In Ref. [13] both approaches are integrated to solve TSP; the BCO model and the 2-opt heuristic. Actually, the BCO model is further improved by using a local search approach, named 2-opt heuristic, that increased the performance of the algorithm significantly.

Chong et al. [14] have offered a novel approach that uses the honey bees for aging model to solve the job shop scheduling problem. In the construction industry, job shop scheduling is an important task for improving machine utilization and decreasing cycle-time. The proposed algorithm is based on self-organization of a honey bee colony. Although the algorithm has better performance of ant colony algorithm, Tabu search heuristics work more efficient than the proposed algorithm. Quijano et al. [15] have proposed the algorithm based on foraging habits of honey bees to solve a class of optimal resource allocation problems. The algorithm uses the strategy of evolutionarily stable strategy where several such algorithms compete in the same problem domain. In addition, the authors have proved that they can achieve an ideal free distribution for a single hive or multiple hives in this problem.

3   Bee Colony Optimization

On study of individuals in multiple decentralized systems, swarm intelligence is thought to constitute part of artificial intelligence. As a new horizon, the BCO meta-heuristic has been introduced as one of the approaches in swarm intelligence. Artificial bees represent agents which form collaborative solutions to issues of complex combinational optimization. The artificial bee colony behaves partly similar to and partly different from bee colonies in nature. They search the state space of the problem to seek the possible solutions. Artificial bees work with each other and exchange information to attain the suitable solutions [13]. In order to use BCO in grid scheduling algorithms, the required preliminaries should be mentioned. To do this, first the behavior of the bees in nature is briefly introduced and then, a short introduction of a general BCO algorithm is given.

3.1   Bees in the Nature

Bee system consists of two essential components: food sources and foragers [5]. Food sources depend on different parameters such as its proximity to the hive, richness of the energy and ease of extracting this energy. Foragers consist of two types: *unemployed* and *employed foragers* [12].

If it is assumed that a bee has no knowledge about the food sources in the search field, bee initializes its search as an unemployed forager. There are also two types of unemployed foragers: *scout* and *recruit* bees [13]. If the bee starts searching spontaneously without any knowledge, it will be a scout bee. The percentage of scout bees varies from 5% to 30% according to the information into the hive. The mean number of scouts averaged over conditions is about 10%. The scout bee returns to hive and announce the found locations as well as the amount and the quality of pollen, nectar and propolis. The scout bee exchanges this information by a special sort of dancing called *waggle dance*. *Waggle dance* is done in a special area of the hive called *dance floor* to expand the sources of food. If the unemployed forager attends to a waggle dance done by some other bees, the bee will start searching by using the knowledge from waggle dance. These types of the unemployed foragers are named recruit bees. When a recruit bee finds and exploits the food source, it will raise to be an employed forager who memorizes the location of the food source. After the employed foraging bee loads a portion of nectar from the food source, it returns to the hive and unloads the nectar to the food area in the hive [12].

Considering the above mentioned bee types and their jobs, three different situations are possible for a foraging bee: 1. the bee can discard the food source and become again an uncommitted follower, 2. it can continue to forage at the food source without recruiting the nestmates, 3. it can recruit other bees with the dance to return to the food location. The bee decides to choose one of these three options due to the quality and quantity of the food resource as well as its distance from the hive.

3.2   BCO Algorithm

Lucic and Teodorovic [5], [16] are the first researchers who applied the basic principles of collective bee intelligence in figuring out combinational optimization problems. The BCO is an algorithm based on population in which the population of the artificial bees seeks the best solution to which every artificial bee contributes. After the bees partly attain solutions, which is in fact the first phase of their job called *forward pass*, they get back to the hive, beginning the second phase called *backward pass*. During the latter phase, the bees exchange all information and solutions. While the dancing process of bees in nature is aimed at telling other bees how much food exists and how far the source is to the hive, the bees do this in the search algorithm to announce the quality of the solution. In fact, every bee decides with a certain probability whether it will advertise its solution or not. Those with better solutions are more successful in advertising their solutions. The rest of the bees either keep exploring their own solutions in the next so called forward pass or proceed to explore the neighborhood of one of the advertised solutions. Thus, the best solutions have always more chance of attracting attentions to be explored. The two phases are performed iteratively until a condition such as the maximum total number of forward/backward passes is met to stop the whole process.

4 The Proposed Algorithm

The task scheduling algorithm proposed in this paper is based on BCO. The general scheme of the algorithm is presented in Fig. 1.

As shown in Fig. 1, requests or tasks are entered to the system by grid users. When a task is delivered to the system, the priority of the task toward the others and also the deadline of the task is specified. After the arrival of the tasks, a unique ID is assigned to each of the tasks by pre-scheduler. Then, the task is sent to a resource named Priority Based Bee Scheduling (PBBS). All of the tasks are queued inside PBBS to be dispatched within grid resources.

After that, PBBS selects a task considering its priority and deadline. A task with the highest priority and the lowest deadline is selected firstly. Then, the PBBS randomly assigns an algorithm to the task and sends the task information to the Knowledge Base which uses the bee colony algorithm. The Knowledge Base includes one table with the following fields about the task: ID, arrival time, priority, dead time, data size, start time, execution time, finish time, delay time, execution algorithm and the destination resource allocated to the task.

All required information for each task should be saved in the table. The tasks are sorted in the table considering the mixed value called objective function value. The objective function considers the data and computational size of each of the tasks. Actually, the position of a task in the table totally depends on its objective function value. In other words, the algorithm searches the table to find the best position for the new submitted task based on its objective function value.

After finding a best possible position for a submitted task, the Knowledge Base selects a suitable algorithm considering the minimum finish time of the tasks inside the table in that acceptable range. This range can vary based on the implementation of the algorithm, e.g. in our algorithm, the best position for a task with computational size equal to MI is the range of $\left[MI - \frac{1}{10}MI, MI + \frac{1}{10}MI \right]$. Then, the Knowledge Base

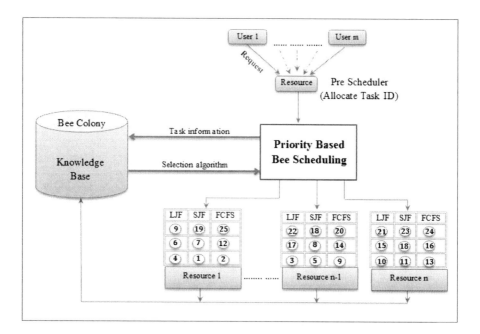

Fig. 1. The general scheme of the proposed algorithm

sends the best algorithm to the PBBS to calculate the p value of the algorithm using Eq. 1.

$$p_{tID}^{u+1} = e^{-\frac{f_{max} - f_{min}}{u}} \tag{1}$$

Where u shows the number of the forward passes in the BCO which is equal to one in our algorithm, tID denotes the ID of the task and f_{max} and f_{min} denote the maximum and minimum value for the finish time of the task, respectively.

Finally, the PBBS attaches the selected algorithm to the task considering its p value. The p value is more efficient when the numerator in the formula (i.e. the difference between the maximum finish time and the minimum finish time) is a large number.

There is a need to save some information about the resources inside PBBS. Actually the ID number of the resources, the bandwidth of the communication links corresponding to each of the resources and the computational power of the resources should be saved in PBBS. The PBBS calculates the computation and data transmission time of the tasks for all of the existing resources. After that, PBBS selects the best resource by the minimum computation time to execute the task. In the proposed BCO algorithm, three algorithms, First Come First Served (FCFS), Shortest Job First (SJF) and Longest Job First (LJF), in each of the resources are implemented. When the PBBS selects a resource to execute a specified task, one of these three algorithms is also specified to be assigned the task. This assignment is made by considering the logs existing in the Knowledge Base. Therefore, the PBBS sends the task to the specific queue (related to the selected algorithm) on the chosen resource. Each resource executes the tasks in its own queues considering the deadline of the tasks, so the task with the nearest deadline has higher priority than others inside a resource. After executing the task inside the resource, the resource sends all of the tasks information such as finish time, delay time and execution time to the Knowledge Base. Then, the Knowledge Base updates the task table by the new data.

In the beginning of the algorithm, some random tasks are entered into the PBBS. Later, an algorithm is randomly assigned to each task for training the system. The more random tasks we have in the training process, the more noticeably optimized will be the Knowledge Base. The main steps of the proposed algorithm are illustrated below.

- **While** there is any unscheduled task **do**

  1. Select task T based on maximum priority and minimum deadline and then update tasks table,
  2. For each of the resources calculate the computation and data transmission times and then compute the task completion time,
  3. Select the minimum completion time,
  4. **Until** the number of the tasks existing in the training set is less than the pre-specified number **do**

     a. Randomly select the scheduling algorithm between FCFS, SJF and LJF algorithms,
     b. Send the information of task T to the Knowledge Base,
     c. Go to step 7.

  5. For each task (or bee) do the forward pass (in the initialization phase, randomly select one of the scheduling algorithms, FCFS, SJF and LJF, and assign it to the task),
  6. For each task do the backward pass:

     a. Send the information of task T to the Knowledge Base (This step is equal to the returning of all of bees to the hive),
     b. Sort the tasks' table by the value of tasks' objective functions,
     c. Considering the objective function of the tasks, choose a suitable algorithm for each of the tasks which results in the lowest finish time,
     d. Each task decides with probability p_{tID}^{u+1} to continue its own algorithm. The value of p_{tID}^{u+1} can be calculated using Eq. 1.

  7. Attach the selected algorithm to task T,
  8. Send task T to the selected queue on the resource R,
  9. Execute task T on the resource R based on the nearest deadline,
  10. Update Knowledge Base after finishing the execution of the task.

- End **While**.

5 Simulation Results

To measure the performance of the proposed algorithm and compare the algorithm to the other algorithms, FCFS, SJF and LJF, various case studies have been considered. To achieve more realistic results, several sample grid environments with different number of the resources and tasks have been simulated and the important metrics such as tasks delay times, tasks finish times and total makespan of the environment have been evaluated on these environments. For the sake of brevity, only one scenario is discussed and the related plots showing the comparison results are demonstrated in this section. The other results in various situations which are not presented here emphasize the following statements more.

Assume there is a grid environment with two different resources. The processing speed of the grid resources and their related bandwidth are shown in Table 1. All of these values are generated randomly.

Table 1. Specification of the grid resources

Resources	Processing Speed (MIPS)	Related Bandwidth (Mbps)
R_1	150	175
R_2	225	200

To simulate different loads on the grid resources, various numbers of the tasks are entered to the environment and the required metrics are evaluated when the tasks are dispatched and executed on the resources. Figures 2 and 3 show the delay times of the tasks when the four mentioned algorithms are applied to the submitted tasks. As shown in Fig. 2 and Fig. 3, the BCO algorithm shows lower maximum and average delay times in comparison to the other algorithms. Figures 4 and 5 show the finish times of the tasks for each of the algorithms. As shown in Fig. 4 and Fig. 5, the maximum finish time of all the submitted tasks which can be considered as makespan of the environment, is lower than other algorithms' makespans.

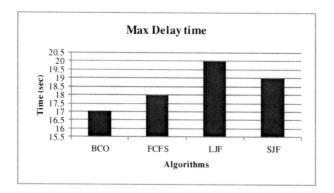

Fig. 2. Maximum delay times of the algorithms

It is necessary to mention that all of the tasks' properties such as arrival times, priorities, execution times and other specifications mentioned earlier have been generated randomly in all of the case studies.

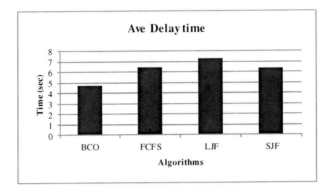

Fig. 3. Average delay times of the algorithms

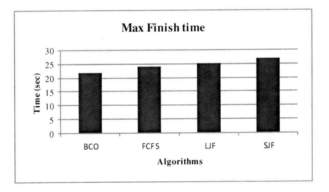

Fig. 4. Maximum finish times of the algorithms

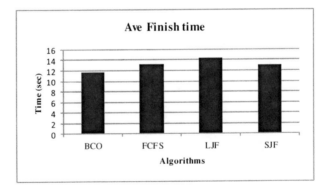

Fig. 5. Average finish times of the algorithms

6 Conclusions and Future Work

To solve the scheduling problem in grid environments, a new algorithm inspired from BCO is presented in this paper. The proposed algorithm can be applied to schedule grid tasks considering their priorities and deadlines to reduce the maximum and average delay and finish times of the tasks. Reducing the maximum finish times of the tasks, the total makespan of the grid environment can be minimized and thereby the throughput of the environment increases. The algorithm proposed in this paper not only uses very simple method to represent the resource allocation using BCO, but also exposes lower makespan values in comparison with the standard scheduling algorithms. Furthermore, the proposed algorithm converges to the suitable solution for the large number of tasks submitted to the grid environment.

There are numbers of research issues remaining open for future work. One can use other QoS measures (instead of finish and delay times of the tasks) to evaluate the bees behavior and find the best possible match between the tasks and resources. Taking into account other criteria (e.g. cost of the scheduling, performance and reliability of the grid environment and so forth) may result in new scheduling algorithms in grid environment. In addition, we expect to improve the algorithm selection mechanism within Knowledge Base by using new methods and probability formulas. Also, improving the behavior of bees to recognize and eliminate the wrong actions is one of the open problems in this algorithm which can be considered in future work.

References

1. Foster, I., Kesselman, C.: The Grid 2: Blueprint for a New Computing Infrastructure, 2nd edn. Elsevier and Morgan Kaufmann Press (2004)
2. Khanli, L.M., Analoui, M.: Resource Scheduling in Desktop Grid by Grid-jqa. In: The 3rd IEEE International Conference on Grid and Pervasive Computing, pp. 63–68 (2008)
3. Parsa, S., Entezari-Maleki, R.: Rasa: A New Grid Task Scheduling Algorithm. International Journal of Digital Content Technology and its Applications 3(4), 91–99 (2009)
4. Ferreira, L., Berstis, V., Armostrong, J., Kendzierski, M., Neukoetter, A., Takagi, M., Bing-Wo, R., Amir, A., Murakawa, R., Hernandez, O., Magowan, J., Ieberstein, N.: Introduction to Grid Computing with Globus, 2nd edn, IBM International Technical Support Organization (2003)
5. Teodorovic, D., Davidovic, T., Selmic, M.: Bee colony optimization: The Applications Survey. ACM Transactions on Computational Logic (Published online)
6. Bonabeau, E., Dorigo, M., Theraulaz, G.: Swarm intelligence, 1st edn. Oxford University Press, Oxford (1997)
7. Yanli, H., Lining, X., Weiming, Z., Weidong, X., Daquan, T.: A knowledge-based ant colony optimization for a grid workflow scheduling problem. In: Tan, Y., Shi, Y., Tan, K.C. (eds.) ICSI 2010. LNCS, vol. 6145, pp. 241–248. Springer, Heidelberg (2010)
8. Zheng, S., Shu, W., Gao, L.: Task Scheduling Using Parallel Genetic Simulated Annealing Algorithm. In: IEEE International Conference on Service Operations and Logistics, and Informatics, pp. 46–50 (2006)

9. Liu, A., Wang, Z.: Grid Task Scheduling Based on Adaptive Ant Colony Algorithm. In: International Conference on Management of e-Commerce and e-Government, pp. 415–418 (2008)
10. He, X., Sun, X.H., Laszewski, G.V.: Qos Guided Min-Min Heuristic for Grid task Scheduling. Journal of Computer Science and Technology 18(4), 442–451 (2003)
11. Entezari-Maleki, R., Movaghar, A.: A Genetic-Based Scheduling Algorithm to Minimize the Makespan of the Grid Applications. In: Kim, T., Yau, S., Gervasi, O., Kang, B., Stoica, A., Slezak, D. (eds.) GDC and CA 2010. CCIS, vol. 121, pp. 22–31. Springer, Heidelberg (2010)
12. Davidovic, T., Selmic, M., Teodorovic, D.: Scheduling independent tasks: Bee Colony Optimization Approach. In: 17th Mediterranean Conference on Control and Automation, pp. 1020–1025 (2009)
13. Wong, L.P., Low, M.Y.H., Chong, C.S.: A Bee Colony Optimization Algorithm for Traveling Salesman Problem. In: 6th IEEE International Conference on Industrial Informatics, pp. 1019–1025 (2008)
14. Chong, C.S., Low, M.Y.H., Sivakumar, A.I., Gay, K.L.: A Bee Colony Optimization Algorithm to Job Shop Scheduling Simulation. In: Perrone, L., Wieland, F., Liu, J., Lawson, B., Nicol, D., Fujimoto, R. (eds.) The Winter Simulation Conference, pp. 1954–1961 (2006)
15. Quijano, N., Passino, K., Univ, M.: Honey Bee Social Foraging Algorithms for Resource Allocation. In: American Control Conference, pp. 3389–3394 (2007)
16. Lucic, P., Teodorovic, D.: Computing with Bees: Attacking Complex Transportation Engineering Problems. International Journal on Artificial Intelligence Tools 12(2), 375–394 (2003)

Interaction Distribution Network

Shun-Yun Hu

Institute of Information Science
Academia Sinica, Taiwan, R.O.C.

Abstract. Content Distribution Network (CDN) has been effective in accelerating the access and growth for web content such as web pages and streaming audio and video. However, the relatively static and bulky data CDNs are designed to serve makes them unsuitable to support latency-sensitive interactive streams such as network games or real-time conferencing. In this position paper, we describe the concepts for an Interaction Distribution Network (IDN), which supports small, interactive data streams in a scalable manner.

An IDN shares certain concepts similar to a CDN in that end-user clients connect to the closest serving proxies for accessing and updating interaction data packets. However, the key differences lies in the bi-directional nature of the interaction streams, and that the data streams may belong to a certain "interaction group," within which some additional processing on the data are possible. An IDN may support existing instant messenger (IM) services and Massively Multiplayer Online Games (MMOGs), while enabling new usage scenarios. We discuss the key challenges, potential solutions, and implications of IDNs in this paper.

1   Introduction

The Internet was designed to disseminate data packets to a large number of audience, and the invention of World Wide Web (WWW) has provided very effective means to distribute information. Subsequently, the serving of static content was augmented by dynamic (e.g., dynamic web pages) and streaming content (e.g., video and voice). As the size of Internet users increases, so have solutions to serve content to them on a large scale. Content Distribution Networks (CDNs) [12] have been designed to offload the requests from popular web-sites so that both the number of concurrent users and the quality of user experience can be improved.

However, in addition to the relatively static (and possibly bulky) content data, another important type of data are *interaction data*, which are bi-directional, and often come in short bursts of small packets, for the purpose to facilitate real-time human-to-human interactions. Such data, except in certain special cases, have yet found general solutions to support many millions of users. For example, although technically feasible with dedicated resources, it is still uncommon for thousands of people listen to a *live* online speech, while asking live questions afterwards. Or, in emergency diaster reliefs, to gather groups of rescuers and volunteers in groups up to hundreds or thousands, to brief them online for the

V. Snasel, J. Platos, and E. El-Qawasmeh (Eds.): ICDIPC 2011, Part I, CCIS 188, pp. 211–221, 2011.

tasks ahead, or to discuss quickly what to do (currently this is only feasible by a physical gathering within a big hall).

Even though Internet services such as instant messenger (IM) networks have been deployed for many years, where a user can send real-time messages to one or a group of contacts. Their usage scenario is limited to text or voice chat messages with a few other users (e.g., most IM sessions are between two persons, and a practical Skype discussion group is generally under 10 people). Interaction groups with a large group size have yet appeared on the Internet.

In recent years, Massively Multiuser Online Games (MMOGs) [1] have spawned out a new generation of Internet applications, where millions of concurrent users are joining in the same virtual world, to interact with one another in real-time. MMOGs provide a glimpse as to what future online interactions might look like, as they provide settings similar to what we experience in the real world, with spaces and gathering places. However, due to limited client-side bandwidth and server-side resources, interactions among a single group of people generally are limited to below 100 users. On the other hand, we are interested in interactions that may allow thousands or more participants, to hold events similar to real-world graduation speeches, holiday parades, rock concerts, and even political rallies.

We observe that while disseminating content (e.g., web pages, audio and video streams) is very matured, the dissemination of interaction (e.g., chat, online editing, gaming actions), have yet found a general mechanism for large-scale dissemination. In this paper, we term a mechanism that can serve this purpose as an *Interaction Distribution Network* (IDN), and describe why an IDN may allow new applications to develop, and help to scale existing interactions on the Internet. We describe an initial proposal for how an IDN may be implemented, and discuss some of its key issues and application scenarios.

2 Background

2.1 Content Distribution Network

CDNs [12] have been put in place soon after WWW took off. The main problem CDNs try to address is the *flash crowd* effect of popular content. For example, when a significant news event just happens, an online news site may suddenly receive traffics several times over the normal. In such case, a single service point would quickly be overwhelmed and ceased to provide services.

CDNs try to replicate the content onto several *edge servers* that could serve similarly as the main site to potential visitors. A request sent to the main server will be redirected to one of the *best* edge server so that the loading on the main site is distributed. The best selection may be based on a number of different criteria, such as latency experienced by the user, content availability, or the current load of the edge server.

Note that because CDNs serve relatively static content, the key issues in CDNs are content placement and request re-direction. Maintaining latency guarantee is not of primary concern (e.g., it is acceptable for a video stream to have a couple of seconds of start-off delay, as long as the bandwidth is enough to smoothly stream the video subsequently), nor is supporting potential processing on the data stream (e.g., as needed by MMOGs to update game states).

2.2   Interest Management

To support scalable user interactions in MMOGs, a basic approach is to limit the amount of data sent to each user. Ideally, only data most relevant to the user's current interaction should be delivered. The most basic interest management thus is for a server to gather all data streams, then filter the data individually for each user. For example, in a MMOG, the server may only deliver messages on events occurring within the receiving user's view, or the user's *area of interest* (AOI) [10].

To scale up such function, a common approach is to partition the virtual environment spatially into regions, and assign each region a channel (i.e., either a physical or application-layer multicast address). A user would subscribe to the channels that represent or overlap with its AOI, in order to receive only the relevant information. While such a basic technique would work, how to partition and load balance the virtual space then becomes the main challenge. Due to the often uneven user distribution across geographic or time of day [7], the proper partitioning becomes the major challenge in keeping the approach scalable yet economical.

2.3   Publish/Subscribe

To realize interest management, a common method is via the publish / subscribe (pub/sub) model, of which there are two main types: channel-based and content-based [2]. Channel-based pub/sub allows any user subscribed to a channel to receive messages sent to the channel. For example, chatrooms can be realized by having all users subscribed a given chat channel, and publish their respective chat text to the channel. Content-based pub/sub on the other hand, would deliver messages only if the message content matches certain pre-specified criteria (called *interest expressions*) specified by the subscribers. For example, for messages that have x and y coordinates, a user with a subscription request of $[100 < x < 200]$ and $[250 < y < 450]$ would only receive messages with coordinates that fall within the specified range.

A useful form of content-based pub/sub is spatial publish / subscribe (SPS) [4]. In SPS, a user specifies only a subscription area (on a 2D space), other users may then publish messages to either a point or an area. Only if the published area overlaps with the subscribed area(s), will the subscriber receive the message. Additionally, each subscriber can move its subscribed area continuously, which helps to automatically receive the most spatially relevant messages, without having to query continuously. For spatial interactions such as those within MMOGs, SPS can be a more useful primitive than channel-based pub/sub.

3   Interaction Distribution Network

3.1   Basic Definition

We now describe what constitute as an IDN, and highlight its main character-istics. In contrast to a CDN, an IDN should serve interaction data instead of content data. By interaction data, we mean small packets that are generated by human operators, which can come in short bursts, and need to be delivered to intended targets in sub-second time-scale (e.g., the results of a user's action should reach other users in 250 milliseconds for an online action game). Another requirement is that the number of interacting entities within a group should be scalable, potentially in the range of thousands of more.

Existing real-time interactions on the Internet include IM networks, MMOGs, and some forms of collaborative editing (e.g., Google Docs that allow sharable online documents). When the supportable number of concurrent users are high, the infrastructures used can be seen as specialized instances of IDNs (e.g., large IM networks supporting tens of millions of concurrent users). However, an ideal IDN should be able to serve a generic audience, regardless of application types, much like how CDN can serve any web content (be it files or streaming media). Another important aspect is that an IDN should keep the interaction latency bounded within certain reasonable limits, while delivering only relevant data to users.

In terms of functionality, IDN should support a general data path, which can be best summarized as an "event → processing → update" path. We define the messages generated by the human operators as *event*, which are delivered (via the IDN) to some *state managers* for *processing*, according to application-specific rules, the results are then delivered to users who may be interested or are affected by the changes via *update* messages. For IM services, the *processing* stage is missing (unless for backup or analysis purpose at the server), and the messages only go through an "event → update" data path. However, MMOGs are more general and do indeed need the *processing* stage for calculating new game states based on rules of the game (i.e., the *game logic*). So existing data path in MMOGs can serve as good examples of the full interaction data path for an IDN.

We summarize some key requirements as follows:

Interactivity. For any given interaction, there exists an *interaction group* where bi-directional communications are possible and are of mutual interest to the participants. The bi-directionality distinguishes *interactions* from the familiar *broadcasting* (e.g., Internet radio or YouTube streaming). Because interactions are between human participants, the delay between the generation of events and the receival of updates should be within application-specified limits. This is mostly application-specific, for example, the latency requirement for voice communication should be less than 100ms, but for IM text it can be a couple of seconds.

Scalability. There are two types of scalability: scalability in terms of the total number of concurrent users (which may be termed *system scalability*)and another is scalability within the same interaction group (which may be called *group scalability*). So while existing IM services can already scale to tens of millions of concurrent users (i.e., achieving system scalability), the number of participants is at most a few tens, and we do not yet see thousands of people within the same interaction group. A similar situation exists for MMOGs, where even though the size of the concurrent users in a game may be a few millions, each interaction group is often less than 100 people.

Generality. While existing architectures may already support some form of IDN (e.g., IM networks and MMOGs), we consider that they are not yet generic enough to support different application types *on the same infrastructure*. This requires a generic design such that not only existing IM or MMOG services can be deployed, new classes of applications can also be enabled (e.g., large-scale interactive online lectures or rallies).

To compare with existing online interactions: an IDN is different from instant messenger services in that in addition to the simple "sender $\rightarrow$ receiver" data path, some optional processing can be placed on this path, enabling a complete "event $\rightarrow$ process $\rightarrow$ update" cycle. On the other hand, while current MMOGs already support such data path, they are not yet scalable enough so that thousands of people can be inside the same interaction group. In other words, although we already have scalable solutions for content distribution (via CDNs), we do not yet have scalable solutions for interaction distribution, thus the need for new designs.

3.2   Key Challenges

The requirements for an IDN can translate to certain challenges:

Bounded Delay (Interactivity). To support interactions, the key here is that the interaction delay should be bounded, though not necessarily minimized. In order to provide an upper bound for interaction delays, the time spent on the data path from the sender to receiver of an interaction message should be predictable and controllable, regardless of the current scale of the system or the interaction group. As the data path consists of event $\rightarrow$ processing $\rightarrow$ update, all three main stages should have predictable durations. While it is easy to control such latency in small group interactions (e.g., we can assign one available server to handle the message relay between two IM participants), it becomes more problematic if the interaction group size is large, and if processing is involved on the event messages. The main challenge then is whether the system can deliver to a large interaction group, while keeping processing delay within certain limits.

Load Distribution (Scalability). In order for the interaction to scale, some form of load distribution may be needed. This can be done in the form of having *proxy servers*, where users can connect to the closest proxies to avoid over-connecting a single server, or in the form of having multiple processing servers (i.e., multiple state managers) so that the system is not brought down by overloaded processing. In general, both CPU and I/O operations on a IDN should be distributed across the available IDN nodes as to maximize scalability.

Dynamic Grouping (Generality). For any given interaction, an *interaction group* is formed among the participants, where members of the group can communicate with one another (pending some intermediate processing). In order to allow for a generic architecture, the membership of the group should be able to adjust dynamically based on application requirements. For example, new members can join and old members can leave for an IM discussion group, or users can walk in and out of an on-going battle field in an MMOG. While the rules of the group formation may be application-specific, interactions within the group should still adhere to the interactivity and scalability requirements mentioned above.

3.3   A Potential IDN Design

Recent research on scalable MMOG systems have shown that by separating different tasks traditionally located on a single server, group scalability may improve. For example, Lake et al. [6] show that by separating the network I/O function of a MMOG region server into a separate component (called a *client manager*, which is responsible to handle all incoming and outgoing traffic with user clients), they are able to scale the number of users in a Second Life region (256m x 256m) from 100 to 1000. In works such as DarkStar [11] and Najaran and Krasic [8], it is shown that if the function of message filtering (also called *interest management*) is made into a separate component from normal processing tasks, then message processing may become more scalable. In other words, by separating *interest management* from *state management*, we can improve the scalability of the system by: 1) lessening the load on state managers, and 2) utilizing more state managers in parallel to improve overall scalability when the processed tasks are independent from one another. We thus suggest the following components in a generic IDN:

Proxies: These are servers which the user clients directly connect to, and function much like web proxy or the edge servers in CDNs (e.g., the *client manager* component as proposed by Lake et al. [6]). A connected client will have a user instance created at the proxy to participate in the IDN on behalf of the user. Users should connect to physically closest proxy to minimize latency. Connections among proxies and between proxies and other servers are assumed to be high-speed. This way, overall latencies on the data paths can be reduced.

Matchers: These are servers that perform *interest management* for the user clients. So users (via their proxy instance) can specify interest subscription or requests to the matchers, who will then perform the necessary filtering of unwanted messages and deliver only messages with relevance back to the user proxies. The matchers can simply support channel-based pub/sub functions (i.e., all users subscribed to a given channel will receive messages sent to that channel, for example, in Najaran and Krasic [8], a *Scribe* P2P overlay is used to perform channel subscription on a per-user basis), or spatial publish / subscribe (SPS) functions [4] (i.e., subscriptions and publications are specified as areas that can move with users, which is more suitable for MMOG-style interactions).

Managers: These are servers that perform *state management*, which is also the *processing* part in the "event → processing → update" data path. The events generated by users are used as inputs to further calculate and refine certain object states, based on the input events and some pre-defined rules. The results of the calculations (in the form of updated state variables) may then be communicated back to the users via the matchers and proxies.

From another view, proxies are the system's entry-points, and are representatives acting on users' behalf to participate in the IDN, for security and latency-reduction purposes; matchers form a communication layer, where messages within the IDN are passed; while managers form a computing layer, where tasks that require further computations (e.g., game state and logic calculations) are done.

The basic *"event → processing → update"* data path may then be realized in such a manner: a user-generated *event* is first sent to the user's proxy, which is then delivered to the respective matcher currently handling the interaction group(s) of the user (e.g., a chatroom in case of IM service, or a small region in case for a MMOG). If the event requires processing, for each interaction group, there is a respective manager subscribed to the group, in order to receive any events sent to the group. If the interaction group is large, it can be partitioned and handled by multiple managers. A manager may also query relevant states from other managers, in order to perform the correct *processing* (e.g., a manager that handles a given region in an MMOG may want to know the status of other users who reside in a neighboring region). Once the states are modified by the manager, the manager would publish the *update* messages to the matchers, who will deliver the updates to the respective subscribers (i.e., proxies on behalf of their users). The proxies then deliver the updates back to the users, completing the data path. In other words, the data path will look something like: user A → proxy A → matcher A → manager → matcher B → proxy B → user B.

It should be noted that when the processing stage is involved, only managers are allowed to subscribe for the user events, and user proxies can only subscribe for update messages. So the matchers responsible for delivering events (to managers) and updates (to users) are logically different, and can be hosted on different physical machines. Note that even though the data path involves six network hops, four of which are within the server cluster, which is assumed to be connected via high-speed networks. As the two external hops (i.e., between users and proxies) are also assumed to have low latencies (users should connect to their closest proxies), overall latency can be controllable.

3.4   IDN Variations

The above outlines the basic designs for an IDN, however, variations exist that can either improve performance or make IDN more customized to specific applications. For example, existing IM networks can be supported with only proxies and matchers, as chat messages generally do not require further processing (unless real-time analysis is required). A scalable channel-based pub/sub mechanism is sufficient for running the matchers. To support group communication, a chat channel is set up for all participants to join, each message sent to the channel is then delivered to all active participants (i.e., subscribers) of that channel. In another variation, the roles of proxies and matchers may be combined or run on the same physical machines. This will have the interesting effect that events in an MMOG that require processing can be separately handled from those that do not. For example, when the proxies have received a trade or attack event message (which may need to be processed based on current game states and game logic), the message should be forwarded to the manager. However, if the message is simply a movement or a chat, the matchers can deliver the messages directly to relevant proxies, without going through the managers, thus saving both processing and delivery time. If the proxies and matchers reside on the same machines, delivery can be quite efficient (e.g., user A → proxy A → proxy B → user B), given the assumed low latencies among proxies, and between users and their proxies.

4   Discussions

One important question is how interaction groups up to thousands of participants can be supported, while keeping delay bounded. The answer depends on both mechanism and hardware performance. For mechanism, the simplest delivery is based on channel-based pub/sub, where a given channel is hosted on a certain matcher, and all potential users interested in group interactions send subscription requests to the matcher. Whenever a message is sent to the matcher, the matcher will forward it to the subscribers. This mechanism faces a limitation when the subscriber size is large and beyond a single matcher's upload capacity. A simple extension is to allow the matchers to first forward the messages to some helper matchers, which can then forward the message to subscribers on their own. Certain application-layer multicasts such as Scribe (as used by Najaran and Krasic [8]) or VoroCast [5] can be used for this purpose. While there is latency penalty for the forwarding among the matchers, the cost should be small as it occurs within a LAN. As each additional helper matcher contributes its own processing capability, overall delivery time can be improved for many recipients. Whether the overall latency can be bounded is determined by the depth and speed of the forwarding among matchers. Actual hardware limit and latency thus will determine the maximum size of an interaction group.

Another important question is how to ensure that the processing time at the managers is also bounded. We note that for state management, the most generic form is that some existing object states are updated based on some new events and pre-existing rules. For example, the processing of a trade event from user A to user B in an MMOG would check the following: 1) whether user A has the trading item (e.g., money); 2) whether user B has the traded item (e.g., some clothes); and 3) whether user A has enough space to carry the new item, etc.

Such a transaction requires the knowledge of the game states of both user A and user B, as well as certain rules regulating the transaction (e.g., user A must have enough money and space for the trade to be successful). Afterwards, if the trade is successfully concluded, both user A and user B should be notified of the new states. We note that in such case, each transaction is quite localized and requires only a few states. It is thus possible to conduct many such interactions in parallel, independent from each other. If there are conflicting updates to a certain state, existing consistency techniques such as locking or synchronization model (e.g., primary-replica objects) can be employed. The key to scalable processing thus lies in ensuring that each individual state managers can have access to the relevant states and events in time [11].

Assuming that the update rules are already stored at the managers, the relevant question then is whether existing object states can be accessed within a given time constrain. This involves certain query operations of either key-value queries (e.g., access the object states for user 'John'), or spatial queries (e.g., find all objects within a 3 meters range that this rocket might collide). We note that key-value lookup can be done in $O(log\ n)$ time, where n is the number of searchable objects (e.g., using CAN [9]). While spatial query can be done within constant time (by using geographically partitioned overlay such as a VON [3] or on extensions of CAN). As long as the query time can be independent from the total number of objects searchable, or at least those key-value queries (which takes $O(log\ n)$ time) are few for a given event, the processing operations can spread out on different processors, independent of where the event takes place (e.g., as used by Project DarkStar [11]). State processing thus may become parallelizable on a massive scale.

In summary, the keys to support scalable interactions within the same group are: whether the message delivery and event processing time within the IDN can be bounded. For the former, we consider that using multiple matchers for forwarding will distribute messages to a larger set of subscribers, while incurring small latency overhead within the IDN's high-speed LAN environment. For the latter, we consider that as long as the query time for accessing existing object states can be constant, and that event processing generally involves only a few objects, it is possible to process a large number of events in parallel such that the processing is distributed on multiple machines and finished within a bounded time.

5   Application Scenarios

While webcast already enables up to hundreds to thousands of people to watch a live or recorded event on video over the Internet (delivered via CDNs), we do not yet see scenarios where the audiences can ask live questions afterwards and still be heard by all other participants. This can be seen as an extended form of a large chatroom, except that the number of participants may be too large for a single server to deliver all out-bound messages.

With an IDN, the speaker's voice or video will go through the speaker's proxy first, then it will reach the one of the matchers responsible for the speech publication. The first matcher could then forward the data stream to a number of helper matchers, which then could forward the speech stream to the subscribing users' proxies. The depth of the internal forwarding can be adjusted according to the number of total participants (e.g., the more participants, the higher the depth and width of the forwarding). The data stream finally will reach the participants via their respective proxies.

If any participant wishes to ask a question afterward, his or her data stream will go through exactly the same procedure as the speaker's (i.e., asker → asker's proxy → asker's matcher → helper matchers → audiences' proxies → other audiences). The only problem that will prevent the system to scale is if too many users are all speaking simultaneously. However, given that only one participant will be asking questions at a time in this scenario (provided that a moderator exists), the situation should be scalable to thousands of users.

6 Conclusion

This paper presents the concept for an Interaction Distribution Network (IDN). Although aspects of IDN already exist in today's instant messenger networks and MMOG systems, current systems can still improve in their group scalability and generality. We show that by integrating the separate components into a coherent design, scalability under bounded delay may become possible. The main difference between an IDN and existing systems is the separation of interest management from state management, so that message delivery and processing time may be bounded. We identify three components at the server side as proxies, matchers, and managers. Not only existing systems can be supported by using a combination of these components, new classes of applications can become feasible from the improved scalability and generality. While we have identified the basic IDN layout and how we can approach to build one, works remain on actually constructing one. This will provide a step towards supporting truly dynamic interactions on a massive scale on the Internet, and possibly new types of applications.

References

1. Alexander, T.: Massively Multiplayer Game Development. Charles River Media, Hingham (2003)
2. Bharambe, A.R., Rao, S., Seshan, S.: Mercury: A scalable publish-subscribe system for internet games. In: Proc. NetGames, pp. 3–9 (2002)
3. Hu, S.Y., Chen, J.F., Chen, T.H.: Von: A scalable peer-to-peer network for virtual environments. IEEE Network 20(4), 22–31 (2006)
4. Hu, S.Y., et al.: A spatial publish subscribe overlay for massively multiuser virtual environments. In: Proc. International Conference on Electronics and Information Engineering (ICEIE 2010), pp. V2-314–V2-318 (2010)
5. Jiang, J.R., Huang, Y.L., Hu, S.Y.: Scalable aoi-cast for peer-to-peer networked virtual environments. In: Proc. ICDCS Workshop Cooperative Distributed Systems (CDS), pp. 447–452 (2008)

6. Lake, D., Bowman, M., Liu, H.: Distributed scene graph to enable thousands of interacting users in a virtual environment. In: Proc. NetGames 2010 (MMVE session) (2010)
7. Lee, Y.T., Chen, K.T.: Is server consolidation beneficial to mmorpg? In: Proc. IEEE Cloud (2010)
8. Najaran, M.T., Krasic, C.: Scaling online games with adaptive interest management in the cloud. In: Proc. NetGames 2010 (2010)
9. Ratnasamy, S., Francis, P., Handley, M., Karp, R., Shenker, S.: A scalable content-addressable network. In: Proc. SIGCOMM (2001)
10. Singhal, S., Zyda, M.: Networked Virtual Environments. ACM Press, New York (1999)
11. Waldo, J.: Scaling in games & virtual worlds. ACM Queue, New York (November/December 2008)
12. Wang, L., Park, K., Pang, R., Pai, V., Peterson, L.: Reliability and security in the codeen content distribution network. In: Proceedings USENIX Annual Technical Conference, ATEC 2004 (2004)

Bi-relational P/T Petri Nets and the Modeling of Multithreading Object-Oriented Programming Systems

Ivo Martiník

VŠB-Technical University of Ostrava, Faculty of Economics,
Sokolská strret 33, 701 21 Ostrava 1, Czech Republic
ivo.martinik@vsb.cz

Abstract. Bi-relational P/T Petri nets are the newly introduced class of Petri nets, whose implementation and definitions are the main topics of this paper; they feature certain new and original concepts when compared with conventional P/T Petri nets, which can be successfully used at a design, modeling and verification of multithreading object-oriented programming systems executing in parallel or distributed environment. In this paper basic characteristics of bi-relational P/T Petri nets are very briefly presented including possibilities in their definition of newly introduced net static pages and dynamic pages, net dynamic pages instances and their possible dynamic creation and destruction, functionalities of multiarcs and the mechanism of the execution of transitions at the modeling of object-oriented programming systems. The concept of subpages of net pages and its application in the modeling of the declared static and non-static variables and methods including the class inheritance and polymorphism, is also of an interest. Basic principles of bi-relational P/T Petri nets could be then further applied when defining the bi-relational object Petri Nets.

Keywords: Petri nets, bi-relational, net page, multiarc, object-oriented modeling, class.

1 Introduction

Place/Transition Petri net (see [1], [2], [3]) is a tuple $PTN = (P, T, A, AF, IF)$, where P is a non-empty finite set of *places*, T is a finite set of *transitions*, disjoint from P (i.e. $P \cap T = \varnothing$), A is the finite set of *arcs* (flow relation), $A \subseteq (P \times T) \cup (T \times P)$, AF is the *arc function*, $AF: A \rightarrow N$, where N is the set of all natural numbers and $IF: P \rightarrow N_0$ is the *initialization function* (*initial marking*), where N_0 is the set of all non-negative integer numbers.

P/T Petri nets represent a popular formalism connecting advantages of the graphic representation of a modeled system with possibilities of its simulation and the formal analyzability. The system is then described with a bipartite graph containing a finite non-empty set of places P used for expressing of conditions of a modeled system (we usually use circles for their representation), a finite non-empty set of transitions T describing changes in the system (we usually draw them in the form of rectangles), a finite set of arcs A being principally oriented while connecting the place with transition or transition with place and we usually draw them as lines with arrows, the arc function

V. Snasel, J. Platos, and E. El-Qawasmeh (Eds.): ICDIPC 2011, Part I, CCIS 188, pp. 222–236, 2011.

AF assigning each arc with a natural number (such number has the default value of 1, if not explicitly indicated in the net diagram) expressing the number of removed or added tokens from or to the place associated with that arc when executing a particular transition, and the initial marking *IF* expressing the current status of the modeled system with so called *tokens* considered as mutually unidentifiable and we usually represent them in the form of small circles in particular places of the net.

As P/T Petri nets arcs are directed, each place or transition of the net can be referred to as a set of *input arcs,* i.e. the set of arcs terminated at a given place or transition, and a set of *output arcs,* i.e. the arcs which on the contrary initiate at a given place or transition. Similarly as in case of input and output arcs we can refer to *input and output elements* of the studied place or transition. For example the set of input places of the given transition are all places associated with input arcs of transition and the set of its output places is created by all places associated with output arcs of the transition. Similar principles apply for input and output transitions of the particular place.

As it has been stated, with P/T Petri nets not only the current condition of the modeled system can be detected, but dynamics of transitions between its individual states, too. In P/T Petri nets that dynamics is illustrated by *firing of transitions* of the net. The transition is enabled (can be fired) if at each input place of the transition is at least as many token as required by the value of the arc function of the particular input arc of the transition. The firing of transition itself consists in the removal of as many tokens from each input places of the transition, as required by the value of the arc function of the particular input arc of the transition and adding of as many tokens into each of the output places of the transition as required by the value of the arc function of the particular output arc of the transition.

Fig. 1a shows P/T Petri net modeling the situation known from the area of the multithreading programming systems development in which three programming threads represented by tokens in **P1** place of the net require the input into the critical section of the program (place **P2** of the net) protected by the program lock (token in **P4** place of the net). The input into the critical section (firing of the transition **T1**) is then enabled to one of the programming threads only (see Fig. 1b).

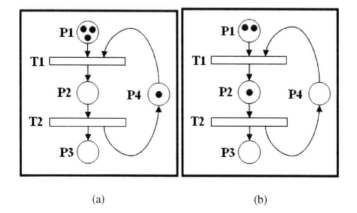

(a)   (b)

Fig. 1a, b. P/T Petri Net

Currently, there are a lot of various types of Petri nets, starting with C-E nets (*Condition-Event nets*), P/T nets (*Place/Transition nets*) and their sub-classes (see [6]), followed by *High-Level nets* (see [7]), such as *Predicate-Transition nets* and *Coloured nets* (see [4]), enabling to model apart from the management structure of the system even data processing, and in connection with modeling of object-oriented programming systems it is *Object nets* (see [5]), which are being studied lately.

The existence of various types of Petri Nets is connected with strive for increasing their modeling and descriptive capability for a certain type of the studied system. Unfortunately it holds that mainly higher classes of Petri nets are more difficult to be analyzed. High-level Petri Nets can be also understood as special programming languages analyzable with formal mathematic methods.

But practical usability of Petri Nets (in their original form) in the role of the parallel programming language is mainly impeded by the static nature of their structure. They are missing standard mechanisms for description of methods alone, programming modules, classes, data types, hierarchic structures, etc. Positive characteristics of Petri nets demonstrate only in not too much large-scale modules at high abstraction level. That is why Petri Nets are often understood as the theoretical abstract module only, whose applicability for analyses, design and verification of extensive program systems is limited. Therefore, this article briefly describes a special class of bi-relational P/T Petri Nets, which eliminates the stated shortcomings required for design, analysis and verification of object-oriented program system in several directions.

2   Bi-relational P/T Petri Nets

Bi-relational P/T Petri nets are a newly introduced class of Petri nets in this article stemming from the concepts of P/T Petri nets class. Their implementation was motivated mainly by a need of designing, modeling, analyzing and verifying the parallel or distributed object-oriented programming system in all phases of their life cycle.

Bi-relational P/T Petri net consists of a finite set of net *static pages*, *dynamic pages* and *dynamic pages instances*. For the sake of graphic differentiation of individual types of bi-relational P/T Petri net pages, we will display dynamic pages by dotted line edges while dynamic pages instances will be displayed with double dotted line edges (see Fig. 2).

At the modeling of object-oriented programming systems the net *static page* represents typically static part of declared class (ie. static variables and methods), the net *dynamic page* represents the object part of declared class (ie. object variables, methods and events), of the object-oriented programming system while *dynamic page instance* represents the class instance (object). Therefore, it applies that for each dynamic page of the net any finite number of net dynamic page instances of that net dynamic page can be created and destroyed. Each of the created net dynamic page instances of the net dynamic page obviously contains all elements of the particular net dynamic page which net dynamic page instance is associated with.

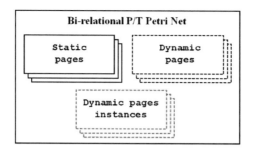

Fig. 2. Bi-relational P/T Petri net structure

Bi-relational P/T Petri net is an ordered triple $BPN = (\Sigma, \Delta, \Gamma)$, where

- Σ is the finite set of net ***static pages*** of net *BPN*,
- Δ is the finite set of net ***dynamic pages*** of net *BPN*,
- Γ is the finite set of net ***dynamic pages instances*** of net *BPN*.

All net pages and page instances can include elements implemented in conventional P/T Petri nets, i.e. each net page can include the finite number of places, transitions, arcs connecting place with transition or transition with place, while with each arc a value of its arc function is associated with and the initialization function of net page is implemented. Next elements which can be included in net page and page instance compared to conventional P/T Petri nets are presented in the following definition.

Let $BPN = (\Sigma, \Delta, \Gamma)$ is bi-relational P/T Petri net, ***IDENT*** is the set of all identifiers over some alphabet. Net ***static page*** of the bi-relational P/T Petri net *BPN* is touple $PG = (PID, P, IP, OP, T, EI, A, MA, AF, MAF, IPF, OPF, SSP, DSP, IF)$, where:

- *PID* is unique ***page identifier***, $PID \in \textbf{\textit{IDENT}}$,
- *P* is finite set of ***places***,
- *IP* is finite set of ***input places***, $P \cap IP = \varnothing$,
- *OP* is finite set of ***output places***, $P \cap OP = \varnothing$,
- *T* is finite set of ***transitions***, $(P \cup IP \cup OP) \cap T = \varnothing$,
- *EI* are unique ***element identifiers***, $EI: (P \cup IP \cup OP \cup T) \rightarrow \textbf{\textit{IDENT}}$,
- *A* is finite set of ***arcs***, $A \subseteq ((P \cup IP) \times T) \cup (T \times (P \cup OP))$,
- *MA* is finite set of ***multiarcs***, $MA \subseteq ((P \cup IP) \times T) \cup (T \times (P \cup OP))$, $A \cap MA = \varnothing$,
- *AF* is ***arc function***, $AF: (A \cup MA) \rightarrow N_0$, such that $AF(x, y) \neq 0 \Leftrightarrow (x, y) \in A$, $AF(x, y) = 0$ otherwise, where $x, y \in P \cup IP \cup OP \cup T$,
- *MAF* is ***multiarcs function***, $MAF: MA \rightarrow N_0$, such that $MAF(x, y) \neq 0 \Leftrightarrow (x, y) \in MA$, $MAF(x, y) = 0$ otherwise, where $x, y \in P \cup IP \cup OP \cup T$,

- *IPF* is **input place function** of multiarcs, *IPF*: $(T \times (P \cup OP)) \rightarrow AllInputPlaces$, where $(T \times (P \cup OP)) \subseteq MA$, $AllInputPlaces = \{p \mid \exists \gamma \in (\Sigma \cup \Gamma): p \in IP \in \gamma\}$, so, that the following is true: $\forall a \in MA \ \forall b \in MA \ \forall p \in P \ \forall q \in P \ \forall t \in T: (a = (t, p) \land b = (t, q) \land p \neq q) \Rightarrow (IPF(a) \neq IPF(b))$,
- *OPF* is **output place function** of multiarcs, *OPF*: $((P \cup IP) \times T) \rightarrow AllOutputPlaces$, where $((P \cup IP) \times T) \subseteq MA$, $AllOutputPlaces = \{p \mid \exists \gamma \in (\Sigma \cup \Gamma): p \in OP \in \gamma\}$, so that the following is true: $\forall a \in MA \ \forall b \in MA \ \forall p \in P \ \forall q \in P \ \forall t \in T: (a = (p, t) \land b = (q, t) \land p \neq q) \Rightarrow (OPF(a) \neq OPF(b))$,
- *SSP* is the finite set of **static subpages of page**, $SSP \subseteq \Sigma$,
- *DSP* is the finite set of **dynamic subpages of page**, $DSP \subseteq \Delta$,
- *IF* is **initialization function**, *IF*: $(P \cup IP \cup OP) \rightarrow N_0$.

PID is within the given bi-relational P/T Petri net the unique net static page identifier, being an element of the set **IDENT** of all identifiers. The set *P* of places is of the same significance as in case of conventional P/T Petri nets and in the layout of the net we represent them with circles. *IP* is a set of input places of net static page representing its input interface. Additionally, no net static page input place can be identical with any place of net static page. Input places are represented in the page layout with circles of highlighted upper semicircle. Then, *OP* is a set of output places of net static page representing its output interface. Additionally, no net static page output places can be identical with any place of net static page. The definition admits even such possibility that the selected input place is identical with any of output places of the given net static page. Output places are represented in the net static page layout with circles of highlighted lower semicircle.

The set of transitions *T* is of the same significance as in case of conventional P/T Petri nets and in the net layout it is represented by rectangles, similarly as a set of arcs *A*, represented in the net layout with directed arrows drawn in full line. It is worth considering that none of its input arc can be associated with any input place of net static page, and none of its output arc can be associated with any output place of net static page.

Each place, input place, output place and transition must be identified with the unique identifier from the set **IDENT** of all identifiers within net static page. If `page_identifier` is the identifier of the selected net static page and `element_identifier` is the identifier of place, input place, output place or transition of net static page, we call the combined identifier (being also an element of **IDENT** set) in the form of `page_identifier.element_identifier` so called *distinguished identifier of net static page element*, which uniquely identifies it within the given bi-relational P/T Petri net.

MA is a set of so called multiarcs, newly introduced type of arc in bi-relational P/T Petri nets. Multiarcs are represented in layouts of the net with oriented arrows drawn with dash line. The set of arcs of the given page is disjoint with the set of its multiarcs, hence it is not allowed the existence of the ordered pair (*place, transition*) or (*transition, place*) connected by both types of oriented arcs.

Each arc and multiarc of net static page is associated with a value of its arc function *AF*, being of the same significance as in case of conventional P/T Petri nets.

If the value of arc function *AF* of the given arc or multiarc is 1, that value is not usually explicitly displayed in the net layout. Each multiarc of net static page is then associated with a value of its multiarc function *MAF* assigning the given multiarc with natural number expressing the quantity of removed or added tokens from output or input place of the selected net static page or net dynamic page instance, being the value of output place function *OPF* or input place function *IPF* of the particular multiarc. If the value of multiarc function of a given multiarc is number 1, again we do not explicitly display that value in the net layout. Regarding the fact that each multiarc of net static page is associated with the value of its arc function and also the value of its multiarc function, we display those two values in the net layouts by the form of ordered pair of numbers separated by vertical line.

The input place function *IPF* of multiarc assigns to each multiarc connecting the ordered pair (*transition, place*) a selected *input place* of a certain net static page or net dynamic page instance of the given net. Additionally, the definition for any transition of the given net page does not admit such option that values of two or more input place functions of selected output arcs of that transition are identical. The output place function *OPF* of multiarc assigns to each multiarc of net static page connecting the ordered pair (*place, transition*) a selected *output place* of a certain net static page or net dynamic page page instance of the net and its features are similar as in the case of the input place function.

A part of each net static page of bi-relational P/T Petri net can be a finite set *SSP* of its static subpages, which are in themselves static pages of given net (i.e. elements of set Σ), and a finite set *DSP* of its dynamic subpages, which are in themselves dynamic pages of given net (i.e. elements of set Δ). The initialization function *IF* assigns to each place including input and output places of net static page of the bi-relational P/T Petri net with a non-negative integer number expressing the number of tokens of the given place at the initial state of net. If that number is not explicitly indicated by the given place, it is considered to be equal to 0. We illustrate tokens with small circles at discrete places of net static page; if the quantity of circles is large, it is possible to illustrate marking of the given place of net static page with a natural number. In literature, M_0 identification has been also applied for that function.

Let *BPN* = (Σ, Δ, Γ) is bi-relational P/T Petri net. Net **dynamic page** of the bi-relational P/T Petri net *BPN* is touple *DPG* = (*PID, P, IP, OP, T, EI, A, MA, AF, MAF, IPF, OPF, SSP, DSP, IF*), where:

- *IP* is **input place**, $P \cap IP = \varnothing$,
- *OP* is **output place**, $P \cap OP = \varnothing$,
- *IF* is **initialization function**, $IF: (P \cup IP \cup OP) \rightarrow 0$,
- *PID, P, T, EI, A, MA, AF, MAF, IPF, OPF, SSP, DSP* have the same meaning as in the net static page definition.

Net dynamic page has the only one input place *IP*, the only one output place *OP* and the initialization function *IF* assigns to each place including input and output place of net dynamic page of the bi-relational P/T Petri net with the zero number of tokens.

Let $BPN = (\Sigma, \Delta, \Gamma)$ is bi-relational P/T Petri net and $DPG \in \Delta$, $DPG = (PID, P, IP, OP, T, EI, A, MA, AF, MAF, IPF, OPF, SSP, DSP, IF)$ is dynamic page of bi-relational P/T Petri net BPN.

Net *dynamic page instance* of bi-relational P/T Petri net BPN is ordered n-tuple $IDPG = (IID, PID, P, IP, OP, T, EI, A, MA, AF, MAF, IPF, OPF, SSP, DSP, IF)$, where $IID \in \textbf{\textit{IDENT}}$ is the unique identifier of net dynamic page instance within bi-relational P/T Petri net BPN, other elements of net dynamic page instance $IDPG$ have identical significance as in the case of the net dynamic page DPG of net BPN.

If PID is the unique identifier of net dynamic page DPG and IID unique identifier of net dynamic page instance $IDPG$, we call the combined identifier (which is also an element of the set of identifiers **IDENT**) in the form $IID{:}PID$ *distinguished identifier of net dynamic page instance* and again, we require its uniqueness within the bi-relational P/T Petri net BPN.

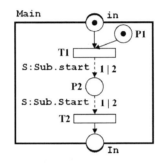

Fig. 3. Net static page of bi-relational P/T Petri net

Fig. 3 shows net static page of a certain bi-relational P/T Petri net, where $PID = $ **Main**, $P = \{$**P1, P2**$\}$, $IP = \{$**in**$\}$, $OP = \{$**In**$\}$, $T = \{$**T1, T2**$\}$, $EI = \{($**in, in**$)$, $($**In, In**$)$, $($**P1, P1**$)$, $($**P2, P2**$)$, $($**T1, T1**$)$, $($**T2, T2**$)\}$, $A = \{($**in, T1**$)$, $($**P1, T1**$)$, $($**T2, In**$)\}$, $MA = \{($**T1, P2**$)$, $($**P2, T2**$)\}$, $AF = \{(($**in, T1**$)$, $1)$, $(($**P1, T1**$)$, $1)$, $(($**T1, P2**$)$, $1)$, $(($**P2, T2**$)$, $1)$, $(($**T2, In**$)$, $1)\}$, $MAF = \{(($**T1, P2**$)$, $2)$, $(($**P2, T2**$)$, $2)\}$, $IPF = \{(($**T1, P2**$)$, **S:Sub.start**$)\}$, $OPF = \{(($**P2, T2**$)$, **S:Sub.Start**$)\}$, $SSP = \varnothing$, $DSP = \varnothing$, $IF = \{($**in**, $1)$, $($**P1**, $1)$, $($**P2**, $0)$, $($**In**, $0)\}$.

Let $BPN = (\Sigma, \Delta, \Gamma)$ is bi-relational P/T Petri net, $PG \in \Sigma$ is its net static page, $IDPG \in \Gamma$ is its net dynamic page instance.

Marking M of net static page PG (or net dynamic page instance $IDPG$) is understood as notation $M: (P \cup IP \cup OP) \rightarrow N_0$, where $P \in PG$ (or $IDPG$), $IP \in PG$ (or $IDPG$), $OP \in PG$ (or $IDPG$).

Initial marking M_0 of net static page PG (or net dynamic page instance $IDPG$) is understood as the initialization function IF of net static page PG (or net dynamic page instance $IDPG$).

Final marking M_F of net dynamic page instance $IDPG$ is understood as marking of $IDPG$ with the following properties: $\forall p \in (P \cup IP)$: $M_F(p) = 0$ and $M_F(OP) \neq 0$ (ie. in the final marking M_F the tokens can be associated only with the output place OP).

Marking of net *BPN* net is understood as marking of all net static pages and net dynamic page instances of that net, while ***initial marking of net*** *BPN* is understood as initial marking of all net static pages and net dynamic page instances of that net.

If $BPN = (\Sigma, \Delta, \Gamma)$ is bi-relational P/T Petri net, $PG \in \Sigma$ is net static page of net BPN, $IDPG \in \Gamma$ is its net dynamic page instance, we introduce in the subsequent text the following net element sets:

- Set $InputMultiArcs(x) = \{a \in MA \mid \exists y \in (P \cup IP \cup T) : a = (y, x)\}$ is a set of all input multiarcs of the selected place, output place or transition x,
- Set $OutputMultiArcs(x) = \{a \in MA \mid \exists y \in (P \cup OP \cup T): a = (x, y)\}$ is a set of all output multiarcs of the selected place, input place or transition x,
- Set $InputNodes(x) = \{y \in (P \cup IP \cup T) \mid \exists a \in (A \cup MA): a = (y, x)\}$ is a set of all places, input places and transitions y, connected with the given place, output place or transition x by the directed arc or multiarc (y, x). We denote $InputNodes(x)$ set in short as •x,
- Set $OutputNodes(x) = \{y \in (P \cup OP \cup T) \mid \exists a \in (A \cup MA): a = (x, y)\}$ is a set of all places, output places and transitions y, connected with the given place, input place or transition x by the directed arc or multiarc (x, y). We denote $OutputNodes(x)$ set in short as x•.

As the firing of transitions in bi-relational P/T Petri nets is in many aspects different than it is in the case of conventional P/T Petri nets, we will firstly introduce its formal definition.

Let $BPN = (\Sigma, \Delta, \Gamma)$ is bi-relational P/T Petri net, $PG \in \Sigma$ is its net static page, $IDPG \in \Gamma$ is its net dynamic page instance

(i)   Transition $t \in T \in PG$ (or $t \in T \in IDPG$) is ***enabled*** in the marking M of net BPN, if the following is concurrently true:

- $\forall p \in$ •$t : M(p) \geq AF(p, t)$,
- $\forall a \in InputMultiArcs(t): M(OPF(a)) \geq MAF(a)$,   if $OPF(a) \in NP \in \Sigma$,
- $\forall a \in InputMultiArcs(t): M_F(OPF(a)) \geq MAF(a)$,   if $OPF(a) \in NP \in \Gamma$,

(ii)   If transition $t \in T \in PG$ (or $t \in T \in IDPG$) is enabled in the marking M, then by its firing we will obtain the marking M' of the net BPN defined as this:
$\forall p \in (P \cup IP \cup OP) \in PG$ (or $\forall p \in (P \cup IP \cup OP) \in IDPG$):
$$M'(p) = M(p) - AF(p, t) + AF(t, p),$$
$\forall a \in InputMultiArcs(t):$ $M'(OPF(a)) = M(OPF(a)) - MAF(a)$,
$\forall a \in OutputMultiArcs(t):$ $M'(IPF(a)) = M(IPF(a)) + MAF(a)$,

Transition t of net static page (or of net dynamic page instance) is then enabled, if the following is concurrently true:

- all its input places connected with it by arc or multiarc contain in the given marking M of net at least as many tokens as required by value of arc function AF of the relevant connecting arcs,
- all output places of net static pages associated with all input multiarcs of the transition t being enabled in a given marking M of net contain at least as many

tokens as required by the value of multiarc function *MAF* of relevant input multiarcs,

- all output places of net dynamic pages instances associated with all input multiarcs of the transition *t* being enabled in a **final marking M_F** of net contain at least as many tokens as required by the value of multiarc function *MAF* of relevant input multiarcs.

Firing of transition will result in new marking *M'* of bi-relational P/T Petri net, which we will obtain using the following procedure:

- from all input places of the transition *t* being enabled which are connected with it by arc or multiarc, we will remove such number of tokens which is equal to the value of arc function *AF* of relevant arc or multiarc,
- to all output places of the transition *t* being enabled which are connected with it by arc or multiarc we will add such number of tokens which is equal to the value of arc function *AF* of relevant arc or multiarc,
- for all input multiarcs of the transition *t* being enabled on the basis of values of output place function *OPF* of multiarcs, we will remove from all output places of net static pages (or net dynamic page instances in their final marking) of net associated with those input multiarcs such number of tokens which is equal to the value of multiarc function *MAF* of relevant input multiarc,
- for all output multiarcs of the transition *t* being enabled on the basis of values of input place function *IPF* of multiarcs we will add to all input places of net static pages (or net dynamic page instances) of net associated with those output multiarcs such number of tokens which is equal to the value of multiarc function *MAF* of relevant output multiarc.

We will briefly informally deal with the description of the life cycle of net dynamic pages instances, which can be dynamically created and destroyed in connection with changes in marking of a particular bi-relational P/T Petri net. Instance of the dynamic page is created at the moment when it is necessary to put at least one token to its input place as a consequence of performance of any transition of the net, among whose input arcs is also found multiarc, while the value of its input place function *IPF* is relevant input place *IP* of the given net dynamic page instance. The net dynamic page instance ends up its life cycle after obtaining its final marking M_F, if all tokens are removed from its only output place *OP* as a consequence of performance of the particular transition.

The mechanism of enabling transitions included in the definition will be now informally illustrated using an example. Fig. 4 shows net static page **Main** of a certain bi-relational P/T Petri net. So now, let us investigate if transition **Main.T1** is enabled in the current marking *M*. To do so, it is necessary, based on the definition, that input place **Main.in** and place **Main.P1** must contain at least one token in the given marking *M* of net.

Both conditions have been met and thus transition **Main.T1** is in the given marking *M* of net enabled. Its firing will result in marking *M'* of the net in the following way (see Fig. 4):

- we will remove from input place **Main.in** and place **Main.P1** always one token,
- we will add to place **Main.P2** one token,
- with transition **M:Main.T1** no its input multircs are associated,
- with transition **Main.T1** is associated just one output multiarc whose value of its input place function *IPF* is the input place **S:Sub.start** and hence in our case we will create the net dynamic page instance **S:Sub** and to its input place **S:Sub.start** we will add 2 tokens.

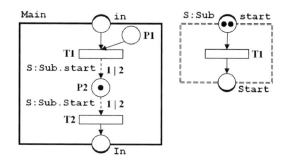

Fig. 4. Firing of transition in bi-relational P/T Petri net

Multiarcs functionalities in the process of transitions firing in the given bi-relational P/T Petri net can be simply demonstrated by *symbolic* substitution of every of its multiarc with the pair of standard net arcs. In our example it is possible to *symbolically* substitute the multiarc (**Main.T1, Main.P2**) by the pair of arcs

- (**Main.T1, Main.P2**) with the value of the arc function *AF* equals to 1,
- (**Main.T1, S:Sub.start**) with the value of the arc function *AF* equals to 2 (this is the original value of the multiarcs function *MAF* of the multiarc (**Main.T1, Main.P2**)),

and the multiarc (**Main.P2, Main.T2**) by the pair of arcs

- (**S:Sub.Start, Main.T2**) with the value of the arc function *AF* equals to 1 (this is the original value of the multiarcs function *MAF* of the multiarc (**Main.P2, Main.T2**)),
- (**Main.P2, Main.T2**) with the value of the arc function *AF* equals to 1.

Resulting net can be seen on fig. 5 and the principles of transition firing in the bi-relational P/T Petri nets can be then simply demonstrated.

Final marking M_F of the net dynamic page instance **S:Sub** is illustrated in Fig. 6 (it is worth mentioning that in this marking M'' of the net, transitions **Main.T2** is enabled and after its firing the net dynamic page instance **S:Sub** will be destroyed).

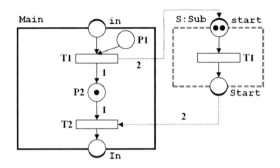

Fig. 5. Symbolic representation of the multiarcs in bi-relational P/T Petri net

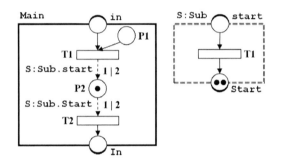

Fig. 6. Final marking of the net dynamic page instance in bi-relational P/T Petri net

3   Main Principles for Object-Oriented Programming System Modeling at the Use of Bi-relational P/T Petri Nets

Next sections will very shortly cover main principles applied at the modeling of object-oriented programming systems by bi-relational P/T Petri nets.

Every declared class of given object-oriented programming system is generally represented by two net pages:

- *Net static page*, that contains declared static (class) data variables and static (class) methods of given class declaration. It is not possible to create the instance of this net static page. This net static page is called the ***class page***.
- *Net dynamic page*, that contains declared object (non-static) data variables, object (non-static) methods and events. It is possible to dynamically create and destroy instances of every net dynamic page (ie. create and destroy *net dynamic page instances*) representing instances of the declared class (ie. objects). This net dynamic page is called the ***object page***. The only one input place and the only one output place of the object page are then the entry and the exit of the appropriate object constructor.

Declared data variables (both static and non-static) are typically represented by the places and tokens in their initial markings of the appropriate net *static subpage* of the given class page or object page. Static subpage then typically contains also *setter* and *getter* of the modeled data variable that encapsulate its value. Declared methods (also both static and non-static) and events that are synchronously called during the program execution are typically represented by the net *dynamic subpages* of the given class or object page. When there is a synchronous call of this method by some programming thread, net dynamic page instance is then created and so every thread has its own net dynamic page instance representing given declared method. So every programming thread has also its own instances of method local variables and local parameters during the appropriate method call.

If it is no possible to create the new net dynamic page instance representing the declared method during its calling by the given programming thread (eg. given method is called asynchronously, given method contains the programming critical section, the subpage representing given method contains its initial marking, etc.), it is possible to represent declared method also by net *static subpage* of class or object page.

The possibility of the net subpages existence in the frame of all the kind of net pages gives us also the possibility of the class inheritance mechanism representation. For instance if the class **Subobj** is the subclass of the class **Obj**, then it is possible to express this inheritance relation by the following way (see Fig. 7):

- class **Obj** will be represented by the (static) class page with the identifier **Obj** and the (dynamic) object page with the identifier **Obj_O**,
- class **Subobj** will be represented by the (static) class page with the identifier **Subobj** and the (dynamic) object page with the identifier **Subobj_O**,
- class page **Obj** will be the static subpage of the class page **Subobj** and the object page **Obj_O** will be the dynamic subpage of the object page **Subobj_O**.

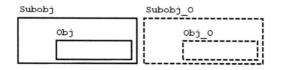

Fig. 7. Representation of class inheritance in bi-relational P/T Petri net

Polymorphism of the classes and the simple example of its representation in the bi-relational P/T Petri nets can be seen on fig. 8. In this example the object method **method** declared in the class **Subobj** is represented by the dynamic subpage **Subobj_O.dp** of the object page **Subobj_O**. This method then overrides the object method with the same name declared in the superclass **Obj** of the class **Subobj**.

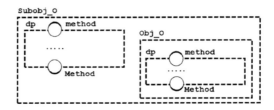

Fig. 8. Representation of class polymorphism in bi-relational P/T Petri net

4   An Example of Bi-relational P/T Petri Nets Application at the Modeling of Multithreading Object-Oriented Programming Systems

In the following example we will develop a design of a (very) simple bi-relational P/T Petri net modeling the programming system operating on the side of the application server and realizing reading and writing procedures from the given database system on the basis of user requests. Individual requests are executed via a finite set of programming threads (in our model of that system we assume availability of totally three programming threads) stored in the created pool of threads. In so doing it is required, that in the case of realization of the request on the writing into the database, no other thread can access the database in the course of execution of that writing; in the case of the request of reading operation in the database any number of other threads can concurrently carry out the operation of reading, yet no thread can concurrently realize the writing operation into the database.

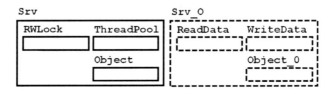

Fig. 9. Structure of declared classes of the programming system

Structure of declared classes of the programming system is very simple and consists only from the class **Srv**, that is subclass of the top class **Object** (see Fig. 9). Class page **Srv** of the class contains two net static subpages **RWLock** and **ThreadPool** (and of course net static subpage **Object** representing class page of the declared superclass **Object**), object page **Srv_O** contains two net dynamic subpages **ReadData** and **WriteData** (and of course net dynamic subpage **Object_O** representing object page of the declared superclass **Object**).

Net static page **ThreadPool** can be seen on Fig. 10. In the place **ThreadPool.ThreadPool** of the net static page, three tokens representing three accessible programming threads are applied in the initial marking of the net (initial marking is possible for any net static page). Static method **getThread** allows the allocation of one randomly chosen programming thread from the pool, static method **returnThread** specifies the mechanism of returning of the allocated programming thread back into the shared thread pool.

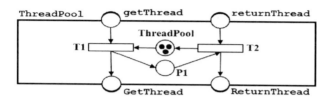

Fig. 10. Net static page `ThreadPool`

Net static page **RWLock** represents simple read-write lock implementing methods of the class determined for obtaining and releasing of the relevant type of lock. Those methods of the class are again accessible via input places of net static page **RWLock** (see Fig. 11) determined for obtaining the exclusive access of the thread to the database for realization of writing and shared access to the database in case of reading of the database content jointly with other threads. In the place **LockPool** of the net static page, three tokens representing access locks for three accessible programming threads are applied in the initial marking of the net. Programming thread requiring exclusive access for writing into the database enters on the net static page via its input place **wLock** Following completion of the operation of writing the thread must release all locks, which can be realized by input of thread on net static page via input place **wUnlock**. And similarly, via input place **rLock** it is possible to request the lock for access to read the database content, yet that lock is not exclusive and can be shared by other threads realizing operation of reading over database. By using input place **rUnlock** discrete threads can release the obtained lock for reading.

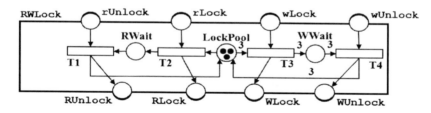

Fig. 11. Net static page **RWLock**

Net dynamic page **ReadData** (the subpage of net dynamic page **Srv_O**) can be seen on Fig. 12 and represents object method determined for reading data from given database. This method is called by the client of the programming system (more precisely by the client programming thread) and the every call of this method will evoke the net dynamic page instance creation. Net dynamic page **WriteData** will be implemented similarly, for writing to the database it is of course necessary to obtain non-shared write lock for the programming thread.

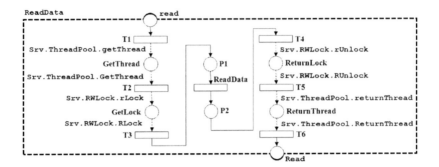

Fig. 12. Net dynamic page **ReadData**

5 Conclusions

Bi-relational P/T Petri nets represent an interesting modification of conventional P/T Petri nets, which can be applied at design, modeling, analysis and verification of generally distributed multithreading object-oriented programming systems. A newly introduced term of multiarc significantly supports modularization of homogenous P/T Petri nets into formats of net static pages, net dynamic pages, net dynamic pages instances and their subpages which represent classes, their instances, methods, events and other components and relations of elements of an object-oriented programming system. Representation of basic characteristics of encapsulation, inheritance and polymorphism of the object-oriented programming while using modeling capabilities of bi-relational P/T Petri nets, is also quite interesting.

In the article we did not discuss many interesting aspects of bi-relational P/T Petri nets like asynchronous method calling, the events mechanism, etc. Additionally, the given bi-relational P/T Petri net can be transformed to the equivalent P/T Petri net and at study of its properties, existing results in the area of P/T Petri net theory can be then used.

References

1. Reisig, W., Rozenberg, G.: Lectures on Petri Nets I: Basic Models. Springer, Heidelberg (1998)
2. Diaz, M.: Petri Nets: Fundamental Models, Verification and Applications. John Willey & Sons, ISTE Ltd (2009)
3. Reisig, W.: Elements Of Distributed Algorithms. Springer, Heidelberg (1998)
4. Jensen, K., Kristensen, L.M.: Coloured Petri Nets: Modelling and Validation of Concurrent Systems. Springer, Heidelberg (2009)
5. Agha, G.A., De Cindio, F., Rozenberg, G.: Concurrent Object-Oriented Programming and Petri Nets: Advances in Petri Nets. Springer, Heidelberg (2001)
6. David, R., Alla, H.: Discrete, Continous and Hybrid Petri Nets. Springer, Heidelberg (2010)
7. Jensen, K., Rozenberg, G.: High-Level Petri Nets: Theory And Application. Springer, Heidelberg (1991)

Developing Parallel Applications Using Kaira

Stanislav Böhm, Marek Běhálek, and Ondřej Garncarz*

Department of Computer Science
FEI VŠB Technical University of Ostrava
Ostrava, Czech Republic
{stanislav.bohm,marek.behalek,ondrej.garncarz.st}@vsb.cz
http://verif.cs.vsb.cz/kaira/

Abstract. We are developing a tool named Kaira. This tool is intended for modelling, simulation and generation of parallel applications. Modelling is based on the variant of Coloured Petri Nets. Coloured Petri Nets provide the theoretical background and we use their syntax and semantics. Moreover our tool can automatically generate standalone parallel applications from the model. In this paper we present how to develop parallel applications in Kaira. Like an example we use two dimensional heat flow problem solved by Jacobi finite difference method. We present different aspects and different approaches how to model this problem in Kaira on different levels of abstraction.

Keywords: modelling and simulation, Coloured Petri Nets, code generation, high level tool.

1 Introduction

Parallel and distributed systems play an important role in the rapid development of information technologies and their applications. A concrete example of this trend is the increasing use of parallel algorithms for scientific and engineering computations. However, it is generally felt that the potential of the current hardware is in reality far from being fully exploited. The reason is that design, analysis, verification and implementation of parallel systems are inherently much more difficult than dealing with sequential systems. A possible solution can be a tool focused on systematic, well-arranged modelling, analysis, and verification of these complex systems. The main goal of this paper is to introduce such tool named *Kaira* that we are developing. The current version of Kaira is available at http://verif.cs.vsb.cz/kaira/.

For the first time Kaira was introduced in [1]. The referenced paper describes Kaira properties in general and introduces it like a modelling/simulation tool that is able to generate standalone parallel applications using threads or Message Passing Interface (MPI) [2] on a lower level. The current paper presents new features in Kaira that allows to model problems on a high level of abstraction.

---

* Authors have been partially supported by the Czech Ministry of Education, project No. 1M0567, GACR P202/11/0340 and students research project SP2011/25.

V. Snasel, J. Platos, and E. El-Qawasmeh (Eds.): ICDIPC 2011, Part I, CCIS 188, pp. 237–251, 2011.

Generally the paper describes how to develop parallel applications using Kaira. It is demonstrated by the two dimensional heat flow problem that is solved using Jacobi finite difference method.

2   Basic Principles of Coloured Petri Nets

The model in Kaira is based on Coloured Petri Nets (CPN) [3]. They are the extension of standard Petri Nets [4]. Tokens can have different *colours* in this extension. For practical reasons we are not using sets of *colours* but types like numbers, strings etc. If *integer* is used as a data type then tokens have values like $1, 2, \ldots$ etc. Following examples use common types `Int` (32-bit signed integer) and `Double` (double precision floating-point number).

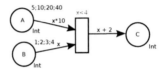

Fig. 1. The example of Coloured Petri Net

Let us consider the network in the figure 1. There are three places and one transition. All places have the type `Int` so tokens representing integers can be stored in them. Tokens $5, 10, 20$ are the initial marking of the place A and tokens $1, 2, 3, 4$ are the initial marking of the place B. There is also the guard expression $x < 4$.

We use terms *input* and *output* edges. An input (output) edge means an edge from a place (transition) to a transition (place). A transition is enabled if all input edges are able to pick a token from the place and the guard expression is true. The transition in our example in the initial marking is enabled in two variable bindings: $x = 1$ or $x = 2$. If there is at least one variable binding enabling a transition then the transition can be fired. Let us say that our transition is fired with $x = 1$. When expressions on output edges are evaluated then new tokens are added into output places and tokens used on input edges are consumed from input places. It means that 3 is added into the place C and 10 is removed from A and 1 is removed from B.

3   Related Works

Parallel or distributed applications [5] are still normal applications and we can use common tools and methods for their development. On the other hand there are specific problems related to the development of these applications and there are also tools that try to solve them.

First, Kaira is a modelling tool. The model is based on CPN. As an alternative we can use for example Unified Modelling Language (UML). UML is a standardized general-purpose modelling language widely used in the field of software engineering. There are different approaches how to use UML for modelling of parallel or distributed applications. One possibility is described in [6]. On the other hand CPN have formally defined not only the syntax but also semantics and they are more useful when we want to reason about created models. Also the automatic code generation is easier and more straightforward for CPN. Modelling tools used for parallel applications are rarely able to automatically generate a working implementation from a model.

Second, Kaira is a simulation tool. It is possible to simulate executions of modelled systems on high level of abstraction (captured by CPN models). Kaira also helps in the process of the debugging. Standalone applications generated by Kaira have still well defined connections to the original model. Execution states or different errors can be later visualized using the original CPN model.

There are different tools and technologies targeted to parallel and distributed systems [7]. These tools are suitable for different tasks, they work on different levels of abstraction and they are designed for different platforms or technologies. The paper [8] presents a good overview. It references many available tools and categorizes them. We found *CPN Tools* [9,3] and *Renew* [10] as the most inspiring and closest to Kaira from all tools that we are familiar with.

CPN Tools is one of the most famous tools for designing CPN. We got inspired by this tool. CPN ML (the variant of Standard ML) is used as the network inscription language. The strong points of this tool are simulations, the state space analysis and the performance analysis. The *CPN Tools* is (for example) very good at modelling protocols. The main difference from Kaira is the absence of a code generation. So a user can model applications but when he wants to get executable codes he needs to write them by hand from scratch. *CPN Tools* is freely available at `http://cpntools.org/`.

Renew is the tool for designing reference nets. These nets try to combine the object oriented programming with Petri nets. Java is used as the inscription language and any Java library can be used in models. Renew is also good at modelling parallelism. Communication between networks' instances is ensured by synchronization of firing transitions, instead of the flow of tokens like in Kaira. The simulation in Renew can run simultaneously on more processors but it is restricted to symmetric multiprocessing machines. Any program generated by Kaira can also run on parallel computers without shared memory due to MPI. Moreover Renew cannot generate stand-alone applications. The typical usage of Renew is designing multi agent systems. It is not designed for the high performance computing. The latest version is available at `http://renew.de/`.

If we want to target low-level hardware issues we can for example use Reconfigurable computing [11]. It is a computer architecture that combines some of the flexibility of software with the high performance of hardware by processing with very flexible high speed computing fabrics like field-programmable gate arrays (FPGAs). We can for example use Handel-C. It is a high level programming language which targets low-level hardware, very often used in the programming of FPGAs. It is a rich subset of C, with non-standard extensions to control hardware instantiations with an emphasis on parallelism.

4   Introduction to Kaira

Kaira was first introduced in [1]. The original motivation was the implementation of different mathematical numerical methods as algorithms intended to be run on parallel computers. These algorithms were implemented in C/C++ using MPI. A programmer spends a large effort on communication and synchronization of processes while solving problems like these. We feel that there is a well-motivated space for a more high-level form of the description of parallel programs that allows simpler and a more reliable way of the programming. The developed tool is focused on solving problems with following characteristics:

- The problems where a user has some input data and wants to compute some output; the typical example is scientific and technical computations. It is possible to create applications like HTTP server in Kaira but we are not focused on this kind of problems.
- The problems with nontrivial data flows and communication.

The model is based on our own variant of Coloured Petri Nets (CPN) [3] with the extensions making modelling of parallel algorithms easier. The goal is to separate the computational parts of a modelled algorithm from the parts dealing with a communication between parallel processes. Communication is modelled by a CPN while the sequential computational parts are implemented directly in a suitable programming language. Right now we are using C/C++. The very essence of our extension of CPN is the ability to add any C++ code by a user into transitions. This code is executed when such transitions are fired. Kaira also provides possibility to integrate any C/C++ library. For example a user has a C++ library that provides a fast implementation of matrix operations. He can use matrices and operations from this library directly in the inscription language in the CPN model.

Besides modelling and simulation the presented tool is also intended for transformation of a model into a standalone parallel application. Currently our tool can generate standalone parallel applications using threads or MPI, hence they can be executed on parallel computers. We are led by the idea that visual models allow an easy modelling and debugging of algorithms. The automatic generation removes errors that may occur during a hand-made transformation of a source model to a real program. Also in the future we plan to use formal verifications to rule out some types of errors. To summarize, CPN model represents data flows and parallelisms and the sequential parts are "hidden" in transitions in the form of C++ code.

In the following sections we speak about two programming languages, inscription language (NeL) and C++. The former is the simple language developed to describe expressions on edges and places. The language was developed as a part of Kaira. The latter can be inserted into the transitions and places or it can be used to extend NeL. There are specific constructions that are easier to express using specific inscription language. That is main reason why we are not using C++ as an inscription language. It is also important that common things used in a network can be written by short expressions, so a picture of a network stays well-arranged. Moreover a further analysis of the network's behaviour is easier with a domain specific language.

4.1 Inserting a Code into the Model

Kaira uses CPN enriched with constructions that helps with modelling parallel algorithms. They are namely the integration with C++ and concept of areas. The easiest way how to integrate C/C++ code with a model in Kaira is inserting a code into transitions and places. A code in a transition is executed every time when the transition is fired. A code in place serves for its initialization and it is called only once at the beginning, the typical usage is loading some data from a file. Assume that we want to add code into the transition in the figure 1. The following code is generated by Kaira:

```
struct Vars {
    int x;
};
void function (CaContext *ctx, Vars &var)
{

}
```

The editor in Kaira does not allow to edit this code but a user can write any code as the body of the function. The structure *Vars* always contains variables that occur on edges of the transition. When the network is changed a generated code is automatically regenerated to reflect a new state of the network. Places and transitions with inserted codes are drawn with double borders.

Other way how to integrate C++ code is to extend NeL types with C++ types, hence a user can use those types as types for tokens. Own serialize/unserialize functions can be defined so even complicated data structures can be used in the model. NeL can be also extended by C/C++ functions in similar way so these functions can be used in inscriptions of edges.

4.2 Network Areas

In parallel algorithms we often want many concurrent running instances of one program processing different data. Because we do not want to draw the same network repeatedly so we introduce concept of *network areas*. A user can select a part of a network and set a number of standalone copies of this part by one expression. Network areas are depicted as blue rectangles and the number of replications is an expression in the left top corner. The example can be seen in the figure 2. There can be more blue areas in the model. Each area generates copies of the network enclosed by the rectangle. We call these networks as *instances* of the area. Each instance has own transitions and edges and each instance runs concurrently with other instances. Transitions in one instance do not run in parallel to each other. If more of them are enabled simultaneously then only one is fired. There is a simple scheduler in each process that ensures fairness of firing transitions. So two transitions cannot be constantly enabled but only one is fired. Let us repeat that this holds for transitions in the same instance, transitions in different instances (even of the same area) are fully concurrent. Instances of each area are numbered from zero. We call this identification as *iid* (instance's id).

There can be transitions and places outside any area. The network in the figure 1 is also such case because there is no area. All such places and transitions are part of *the default area* and there is only one instance of this area.

4.3   Example: Workers

In this section we describe some other features and give the overall impression how to create models in Kaira. We model the following problem. We want to perform some computations for an interval of numbers. We can divide our task to separate subtasks (subintervals) but the computation time of each subtask are notably different and we cannot guess these times before the computation. It is ineffective to simply divide all subtasks to working nodes at the beginning, because some of them may finish their subtasks earlier and they do not do anything useful for the rest of the computation. We introduce the *master node* that divides the work to other nodes. When a working node finishes a computation of a subtask, it sends results to the master node and waits for a new subtask. For the sake of simplicity we fix the number of working nodes to five. The network solving this problem is shown in the figure 2.

A user is able to use parameters in the model. The syntax of parameters is: #NAME. A user specifies values of parameters when a program or a simulation is started. Our example has two parameters: #LIMIT (the length of computed intervals) and #SIZE (the size of subintervals).

We start with five tokens in the place *ready*, this place represents idling nodes. All nodes have nothing to do at the beginning. The place *counter* stores an integer representing start of a next assigned interval. When the transition *divide* is fired then we take iid of an idling worker and assign a new subinterval. Because the area represents more networks we have to specify the iid on the output edge from *divide* to the place in the area. It is achieved by the expression after the sign "@". The second output edge from *divide* returns a token to the place *counter* with a new bigger value. The guard at this transition ensures that dividing work stops when #LIMIT is reached.

The function in the transition *Compute* does the main job. When the transition is fired then the token is placed to the place *ready* to indicate that the instance is ready for a new task. Results of the computation are also sent to the master node. The sign "∼" in the front of the variable *results* changes the meaning of the variable. It is not an integer but an array of integers, so we can transfer an arbitrary number of tokens.

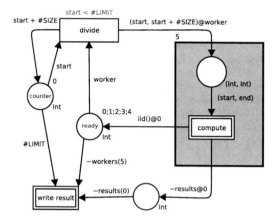

Fig. 2. The network for example in the section 4.3

Results can be written only when and the place *counter* has token that equals to #LIMIT and the place *ready* contains five tokens, so there is no working nodes. The second condition is ensured by the expression $\sim workers(5)$. The meaning of this construction is to express that transition should consume all tokens from the place but there should be at least five of them.

5   Modelled problem

In this section we start with the description of the modelled problem. Inspired by [12], we have selected the heat flow problem using the two dimensional grid. We solve this problem by Jacobi's method. We have chosen this method because it is simple and we can focus on the modelling of the problem in Kaira. We do not want to discuss mathematical properties of this method.

The principle of the method is following: for each point in the grid we compute a new temperature as an average value of temperatures of the point and its four surrounding points in the previous step. For the points that are not on the borders we can use the following formula where $T_{i,j}(t)$ is a temperature value at the position (i, j) in time t:

$$T_{i,j}(t+1) = \frac{4 \cdot T_{i,j}(t) + T_{i-1,j}(t) + T_{i,j-1}(t) + T_{i+1,j}(t) + T_{i,j+1}(t)}{8}$$

The scheme of computation of such point is depicted in the picture 3. We assume that temperature in the outside area is a fixed zero value. Therefore elements at the borders of the grid (the first and last row and the first and last column) receive zero from the outside space. Moreover, we will use a fixed value of temperature for the middle point in the grid. The following parameters for the computation are used in our models:

– SIZE_X, SIZE_Y are sizes of the grid.

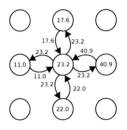

Fig. 3. The example of communication in Jacobi's method

- TEMP is the fixed temperature of the point in the middle.
- LIMIT means the number of the iterations.

The common methodology how to design parallel programs is Foster's methodology [12]. It contains following four steps: Partitioning, Communication, Agglomeration and Mapping. The first two steps are quite straightforward for our problem. The problem can be naturally decomposed by points in the grid. The value of each point in the grid can be computed in parallel. The communication analysis is also simple because we have simple local communication between a node and its four neighbours. We also need communication to gather the results from each node at the end. The goal of the agglomeration is to make the model more suitable for real computation. In this step we join the atomic tasks into bigger tasks. The mapping of tasks to physical resources is left for the backend to process. It is an operating system for threads and MPI daemon for MPI.

5.1 Fine-Grained Model

In this section we use the fine-grained model, so we model parallel tasks on very abstract level and the phase of agglomeration is proceeded by Kaira.

First we focus on the elements in the inner area. The figure 4 shows the network with the model of these points. In this network there are SIZE_X×SIZE_Y instances of the area, one instance for each point in the grid. Because iid is an integer and a position in the grid is a two dimensional value we use the mapping: $iid = x + y \cdot$SIZE_X where (x, y) is position in the grid. The following two functions are used in source codes for the conversion: *iid_to_position* and *position_to_iid*.

The place named a contains a current temperature of a point. Places u, d, l and r contain values from top, bottom, left and right neighbours. The transition *Compute* implements the execution of a single iteration. When the transition is fired then one token is consumed for each place and the computation is performed. The C function inside the transition is very simple:

```
void function(CaContext *ctx, Vars & var) {
    var.newvalue = (4*var.value + var.up + var.down
        + var.left + var.right) / 8;
}
```

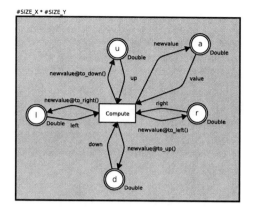

Fig. 4. The model of computation for values in grid's inner points

The result of the computation is stored in the variable *newvalue*. This value is now transmitted back to the place *a* and it is also sent to the neighbour's places *u*, *d*, *l* and *r*. The function *to_up* is the user defined function with the following code:

```
int to_up(CaContext *ctx)
{
    int x, y;
    iid_to_pos(ctx->iid(), x, y);
    return pos_to_iid(x, y - 1);
}
```

Functions *to_down*, *to_left*, *to_right* are defined similarly. We will refer them as *to_**-functions. Note that when the token is sent to the left neighbour then it has to be placed in the place *r* because it is data "from right" in the view of the neighbour.

5.2   Borders

The above described network models behaviour of inner points in the grid. This is sufficient if the grid is unbounded. In other words if the leftmost column is connected with rightmost and the top row is connected with the bottom row. In such case we have to modified only *to_** functions and the changed coordinate has to be taken by modulo SIZE_Y(or SIZE_X).

In our original setting we have borders hence points laying there communicate only with three neighbours (or with two neighbours in the corners). We demonstrate several ways how to solve this problem. The simplest solution is to use same approach as for unbounded area but we create a grid (SIZE_X + 1) × (SIZE_Y + 1) and we force these elements on the new extra column and row will always have zero values. It can be easily achieved by a condition in the *Compute*'s function. Note that only one row and column suffices because of connection between the first and last column and the first and last row.

The main advantage of this approach is the minimal effort to achieve this model from the previous one. On the other hand the important aspect of the model is hidden inside the C function. The other disadvantage is the creation of new artificial connections between the leftmost column and the rightmost column and between the top row and the bottom row). There is no such thing in our setting. These needless connections can cause problems while automatically processed agglomeration.

The other way is to use several versions of *Computation* for each position type (inner points, top border, bottom border, left border, right border + 4 corners). Hence we make a new transition for each type and by transition's guards we can choose right transition in dependence on the point's position. Each transition has own edges so it can be connected only to necessary places. This model lacks some disadvantages of the previous one. The different behaviours on the borders are caught directly by the Petri net and there are not needless connections between borders. The disadvantage is nine transitions in the area so the model is not as transparent as previous one.

The problem with too many transitions in one area can be solved by concept of heterogeneous areas. This concept allows us to design different transitions and edges for instances of one area. The model stays well-arranged and still has same advantages as previous one. This concept is not fully implemented yet, so we do not describe it here. We believe that this will be the most general solution for these types of problems. The following subsections contain another possibilities with the changed networks.

5.3   Remodelled Network

The model in this approach is based on the following observation: we are summing the values from neighbours, so we do not need to remember if a token comes from the left or right neighbour. We join places l, r, u and d into the one place c. This place is used for communication with all four neighbours. The network is depicted in the figure 5. The final version of this model can be found in the Kaira's repository in the directory `samples/jacobi1`.

Each instance takes four tokens from the place c and binds the values in variables $v1, v2, v3$ and $v4$. The instance sends a new value to neighbours into their places c after the computation. The borders can be established quite easily in this model by the modification of *to_*-functions*. Consider *to_up*, it returns iid for an instance at the position $(x, y - 1)$. We change the function's behaviour in the following way. If the current position is at the top border then return own iid else return iid of an instance at the position $(x, y - 1)$. We change other three functions in the same sense. After this change our model works quite well, instances at the borders (in the corners) communicate with three (two) neighbour. The only problem is fixing zero in border instances because from one direction it receives own value instead of zero. We can introduce new variables and fill them with zero or *newvalue* based on the position. But because

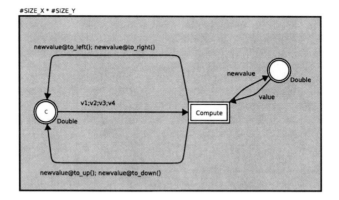

Fig. 5. The model where places u, d, l, r are joined into one place c

of the summing in the computation we can use the following simplification. We computes $4x + v_1 + v_2 + v_3 + v_4$ but in one v_i we receive x and we need 0, so we can change computation to $3x + v_1 + v_2 + v_3 + v_4$. Analogously for the corners the constant 3 is changed to 2.

This new approach shares the same disadvantage as the first proposed solution: something important is hidden in C functions. Contrary to the first solution there are no needless connections between border instances. Moreover the model stays still small and transparent. Note that we cannot make such change of to_*-functions in the first model (the figure 4). Tokens send via these "loopbacks" end in the wrong (opposite) places.

Another problem that we have neglected so far is asynchronous aspect of the whole computation. Some instance may compute it's values faster than the other. So it sends two tokens to neighbour instance even there is yet no token from other neighbour. Hence we can fire the transition with bad values. It can be solved by a "clock" storing a sequence number of a current iteration. Moreover

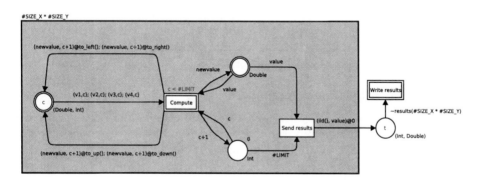

Fig. 6. The final model for the section 5.3

it will be useful for detecting the end of the computation. The final network is shown in the figure 6. The clock is modelled by one place with one token and the value of this token is incremented by one every execution of *Compute*. Instead of sending only values of temperature to neighbours we send a pair containing the temperature and the "time". If we want to fire the transition *Compute* then we need again four tokens from the place c but now the time values have to correspond with the current state of the clock.

At the end we also need to gather the results from all nodes. There is the transition *Send results* that can be executed only if values of the clock is equal to LIMIT. This transition has no code inside and only transfers results from the instance to the place t as pair of iid and the temperature value. The transition *Compute* is blocked by guard when value of the clock reaches LIMIT. When all results arrived to t then the transition *Write results* do its job.

5.4   Automated Agglomeration

The goal of this paper is to show how can be a problem modelled on different levels in Kaira. The implementation of the automated agglomeration itself is now limited, but it works and models with a large number of instances can be executed. In the previous version of Kaira there was a limitation that every instance has to run in separated process. We use term process in the meaning of something that runs concurrently to other processes. The true form of processes depends on the chosen backend. Processes can be threads or MPI processes. In the current version there can be more instances in one process and we can use this feature for the agglomeration.

The number of processes is not hard-wired into the generated program but it can be specified at start-up of the program. The current implementation allows two strategies of distributing instances to processes. Both of them try to assign the equal number of instances to each process. The first strategy tries to assign to each process different instances as much as possible. The second one tries to assign instances from same area and with continuous interval of iids. The both are simple but they are sufficient for a large number of problems. The second strategy is suitable for our problem.

In the future we plan to add more complex agglomeration procedures based on static analysis of the network. Other option is to use the dynamic monitoring of running programs. The gathered information can be used for the real-time redistribution of instances or as hints for following generating of programs.

5.5   Model with Manual Agglomeration

In the previous case we left the agglomeration on Kaira. In this section we use lower level of abstraction and we solve the model's agglomeration *by hand*. In our problem there is a natural agglomeration by rectangle subareas of the grid. We split the grid by horizontal cuts as it is shown in the figure 7. Subareas have to exchange top and bottom edges each of iterations with neighbour areas.

In this case we do not work directly with temperatures in the model but we use more complex structures. We use two C++ classes *Data* and *Row*. The

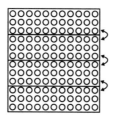

Fig. 7. The agglomeration on the grid (arrows show exchanging rows)

former represents a rectangle subarea of the grid. The latter represents one row of the grid and it will be used for communication. We use Kaira's ability to bind external types and we will use them directly as tokens types.

The network for this case is shown in the figure 8. This model can be found in the Kaira's repository in the directory `samples/jacobi2`. The reader can find full source used for this example there. We introduce the new parameter WORKERS, it specifies the number of subareas of the grid, in other words it is number of working nodes computing the temperatures in the grid. The structure is similar to the previous case. We have here one place to store worker's part of the grid (the place m), two places for receiving rows from the upper (place u) and lower (place b) neighbour and one place that serves as a clock. Moreover there is the transition *Init* that performs initial interchange of rows. For the same reason as in the previous case we do not send only rows between instances but we send pairs containing time and the row.

In this model we have to solve the similar problem with borders as in the fine-grained model. Both the top subarea and bottom subarea have only one neighbour. The solutions are very the same as in the previous case, but we have only three types of position in the grid (top, inner, bottom), so the solution with more transitions is much more acceptable. For the sake of simplicity we show here the performance suboptimal solution where instances on the borders are connected but they ignore one of received rows. It introduces needless connection between first and last instance, but the drawback is not so big because this model is planned for the setting *one worker instance per CPU*. The function inside the transition *Compute* is following:

```
void transition_function (CaContext *ctx, Vars & var)
{
    if (ctx->iid () == 0) {
        var.up.set_zero ();
    }
    if (ctx->iid () == ctx->instances () - 1) {
        var.down.set_zero ();
    }
    var.data.compute(var.up, var.down);
}
```

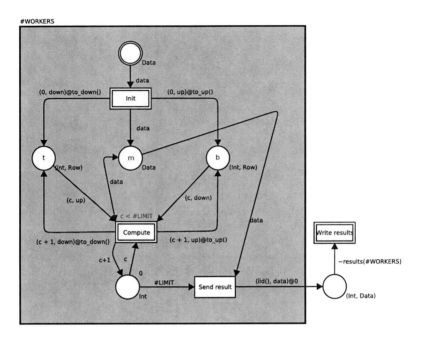

Fig. 8. The model for the section 5.5

6   Contribution and Conclusion

Kaira was first introduced in [1]. It contains an overall description and basic principles of the tool. This paper is focused on developing of parallel applications using Kaira. The main contribution of this paper is that we show different approaches to parallelization. We use heat flow problem as an example and using this example we show how can be different aspects of an algorithm catch into a model. The example also demonstrates solutions to issues that are common in the process of parallel applications development. Other contribution is the usage of features newly implemented in Kaira. For example features related to agglomeration. Now more instances of network areas can be mapped into a single process. Presented models are on different levels of abstraction and we can left the agglomeration on the tool or we can do it *by hand*.

In the future we plan to extend our tool to support more complex strategies how to map instances to processes, as it is described in the section 5.4. We also plan to extend our tool to support more language backends (for instance Haskell or Python). We believe that it can be very useful especially for developing prototypes of parallel applications. The next goal is to use visual models more intensively during debugging and testing of parallel applications.

References

1. Bohm, S., Behalek, M.: Kaira: Modelling and generation tool based on petri nets for parallel applications. In: 13th International Conference on Computer Modelling and Simulation (UKSim 2011), Cambridge, United Kingdom (2011)
2. Snir, M., Otto, S., Huss-Lederman, S., Walker, D., Dongarra, J.: MPI-The Complete Reference, 2nd (revised) edn. The MPI Core, vol. 1. MIT Press, Cambridge (1998)
3. Jensen, K., Kristensen, L.M.: Coloured Petri Nets: Modelling and Validation of Concurrent Systems, 1st edn. Springer Publishing Company, Incorporated, Heidelberg (2009)
4. Reisig, W.: Petri nets: an introduction. Springer-Verlag New York, Inc., New York (1985)
5. Bazewicz, J., Trystram, D., Ecker, K., Plateau, B.: Handbook on Parallel and Distributed Processing, 1st edn. Springer-Verlag New York, Inc., Secaucus (2000)
6. Hughes, C., Hughes, T.: Parallel and Distributed Programming Using C++. Prentice Hall Professional Technical Reference (2003)
7. Reisig, W.: Elements Of Distributed Algorithms: Modeling and Analysis with Petri Nets. Springer, Heidelberg (1998)
8. Delistavrou, C.T., Margaritis, K.G.: Survey of software environments for parallel distributed processing: Parallel programming education on real life target systems using production oriented software tools. In: Panhellenic Conference on Informatics, pp. 231–236 (2010)
9. Jensen, K., Kristensen, L., Wells, L.: Coloured Petri Nets and CPN Tools for modelling and validation of concurrent systems. International Journal on Software Tools for Technology Transfer (STTT) 9, 213–254 (2007)
10. Kummer, O., Wienberg, F., Duvigneau, M., Schumacher, J., Köhler, M., Moldt, D., Rölke, H., Valk, R.: An extensible editor and simulation engine for petri nets: Renew. In: Cortadella, J., Reisig, W. (eds.) ICATPN 2004. LNCS, vol. 3099, pp. 484–493. Springer, Heidelberg (2004)
11. Buell, D., El-Ghazawi, T., Gaj, K., Kindratenko, V.: Guest editors' introduction: High-performance reconfigurable computing. Computer 40, 23–27 (2007)
12. Foster, I.: Designing and Building Parallel Programs: Concepts and Tools for Parallel Software Engineering. Addison-Wesley Longman Publishing Co., Inc, Boston (1995)

Context-Aware Task Scheduling for Resource Constrained Mobile Devices

Somayeh Kafaie, Omid Kashefi, and Mohsen Sharifi

School of Computer Engineering,
Iran University of Science and Thechnology,Tehran, Iran
so_kafaie@comp.iust.ac.ir,kashefi@{ieee.org,iust.ac.ir},
msharifi@iust.ac.ir

Abstract. Nowadays, mobile devices are very popular and accessible. Therefore users prefer to substitute mobile devices for stationary computers to run their applications. On the other hand, mobile devices are always resource-poor in contrast with stationary computers and portability and limitation on their weight and size restrict mobile devises' processor speed, memory size and battery lifetime. One of the most common solutions, in pervasive computing environments, to resolve the challenges of computing on resource constrained mobile devices is cyber foraging, wherein nearby and more powerful stationary computers called surrogates are exploited to run the whole or parts of applications. However, cyber foraging is not beneficial for all circumstances. So, there should be a solver unit to choose the best location either the mobile device or a surrogate to run a task. In this paper, we propose a mechanism to select the best method between local execution on the mobile device and remote execution on nearby surrogates to run an application by calculating the execution cost according to the context's metrics such as mobile device, surrogates, network, and application specifications. Experimental results show the superiority of our proposed mechanism compared to local execution of the application on the mobile device and blind task offloading with respect to latency.

Keywords: Pervasive Computing, Cyber Foraging, Mobile Computing, Task Offloading, Latency.

1 Introduction

These days, the users of mobile devices are increasing from day to day. On a planet with around 6.8 billion people, the number of people with cell phone subscriptions worldwide has reached 4.6 billion at the end of 2009 and is expected to reach five billion by the end of 2010 [1]. People all over the world are increasingly using their cell phones for daily tasks such as Internet banking, emailing, and emergencies.

However, mobile devices are always resource-poor. At any level of cost and technology, considerations such as weight, size, battery lifetime, ergonomics, and heat dissipation impose severe restrictions on computational resources such as processor speed, memory size and disk capacity [2]. Although mobile device technology is evolving but mobile devices always remain more resource constrained than traditional stationary computers [2, 3].

V. Snasel, J. Platos, and E. El-Qawasmeh (Eds.): ICDIPC 2011, Part I, CCIS 188, pp. 252–261, 2011.
© Springer-Verlag Berlin Heidelberg 2011

Due to these restrictions, execution of some applications on mobile devices is impossible or along with low and undesirable performance. For example, imagine a person who has a complete and smart map on his mobile device and is going to find the best path to go to a destination. Scientific calculator [4], speech recognizer [5, 6], language translator [5, 6] and image manipulator [2, 7] are some more examples of such applications that their execution may need more energy or memory than available in mobile device or impose an unacceptable latency to the system and users.

Satyanarayanan has introduced cyber foraging [8] or task offloading as a solution to resolve the challenges of executing resource intensive applications on resource constrained mobile devices in pervasive computing environments. In this approach, the nearby stationary computers, called Surrogates, are used to execute the whole or some parts of resource-intensive application on behalf of the mobile device. As computers become cheaper and more plentiful, cyber foraging approaches become more reasonable to employ in pervasive computing. However, there is a challenge: "Is cyber foraging approach reasonable in all situations?"

In this paper, we exploit cyber foraging approach to improve the performance on mobile devices. We introduce a solver unit that is responsible to determine the best location to run the task that would be the mobile device (i.e. local execution of the task) or best surrogate(s) around (i.e. remote execution of the task) by calculating the cost of executing the task on each location according to the context's metrics such as mobile device, surrogates, network, and application specifications.

The remainder of the paper is organized as follows. Related works on cyber foraging are discussed in Section 2. Section 3 presents our proposed solver and describes its implementation detail. The results of experimental evaluations are depicted in Section 4, and Section 5 concludes the paper.

2 Related Work

There are several approaches with different objectives that have used the offloading of applications on resource constrained mobile devices in pervasive computing environments. Spectra [6] is one of the first proposed cyber foraging systems is focused on reducing the latency and energy consumption. Chroma [5, 9] tries to improve spectra's idea and reduce the burden on the programmers. Both of these works suppose the application is installed on the surrogates and there is no need to send the application code. But it is evident that this assumption decreases the flexibility and their approach does not work on new surrogates and tasks.

While, Gu et al. [10] have used a graph model to select offloading parts of the program to improve memory constraint of the mobile device, Ou et al. [4, 11] have used a similar method to address the CPU and bandwidth constraint, too. Song et al. [12, 13] has proposed a middleware architecture, called MobiGo for seamless mobility to choose the best available service according to the bandwidth and latency, and Kristensen [14] has introduced Scavenger as a cyber-foraging framework whose focus is on CPU Power of mobile devices and decreases latency.

All mentioned works have used adaptive history-based approach and dynamic profiling to estimate execution time on mobile device and surrogates and select the best location to execute a task. In fact, they use previous runs to estimate execution time on future ones. Therefore, in first executions, there is no valid estimation of execution time to use by the solver and solver's decisions are probably wrong. Furthermore, the effect of input size on execution time is not considered or doesn't have enough precision, and also history-based approach imposes dynamic profiling overhead to the system.

On the contrary, as it will be shown in next Section, we don't need to save information of previous runs and we estimate execution time in terms of input size with high precision simply, by defining two factors as *Function* and *InstructionPmSecond* for every task and much less dynamic profiling overhead.

3   Proposed Solver

3.1   Necessity of the Solver

Cyber foraging combines the mobility of small devices with high computing capability and extensive resources of nearby static servers by offloading the tasks from mobile devices to surrogates for remote execution [6]. Nevertheless, there is a challenge. Is task offloading reasonable in all situations?

To benefit from cyber foraging, some application related data, such as input parameters and application codes, must be sent from the mobile device to the surrogate and also the output results should be received.

Let us consider T_M as the time of running a program on a mobile device and T_S as the time of running the program on a surrogate. If D_T is the size of input data and code, D_R is output size, and B is the network bandwidth, the offloading time can be defined as $T_{offload} = (D_T + D_R)/B + T_S$.

It is obvious that the offloading is effective only when T_M is more than $T_{offload}$. As usually $T_M >> T_S$, It is evident that if the cost of data transmission (i.e. communication cost) is more than the cost of local execution or computation cost, task offloading is not beneficial and local execution of application is superior to remote execution by cyber foraging. Therefore, a solver unit is needed to manage the trade-off between communication cost and computation cost of offloading the task, schedule the task, and select the best location to run it.

To augment the resources of mobile devices, we introduce a solver that is responsible for task scheduling and select the best location to run a task by calculating the cost of task execution for each location.

When a task is going to run, the solver calculates the cost for every available machine (i.e. the mobile device and surrogates). Then the solver makes a decision to offload the task to one of the nearby surrogates or runs the task locally. Actually, the solver chooses a location that has the minimum cost to run the task. Figure 1 shows an overview of the proposed solver's flowchart.

3.2   Definition of Execution Cost

To define the execution cost, we have to determine the goal of task offloading. In general, Cyber foraging tries to augment some resources of mobile devices in terms of effective metrics to achieve more efficient application execution. The most important factors that have been considered in offloading approaches are as follows:

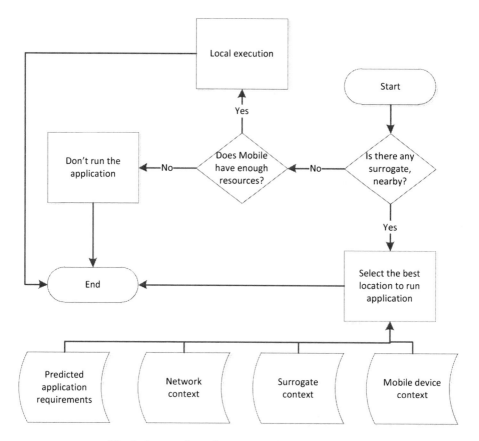

Fig. 1. An overview of our proposed solver's flowchart

- *Latency.* The processing power of mobile devices is considerably lower than static computers. Task offloading exploits powerful surrogates to decrease latency.
- *Energy.* One of the most important constraints of mobile devices is energy consumption because energy cannot be replenished [15]. Therefore the best location to run a task may be the one with minimum energy consumption.
- *Memory and storage.* Memory intensive applications cannot usually run on mobile devices and they need to be offloaded. Therefore execution cost can be calculated according to the required memory and storage of the tasks.

In this paper, we have defined execution cost according to the latency metric. Because latency is an important factor for users and as the programs usually execute on the mobile device by user's demand, the preference of the user is an important metric. We define latency as the delay time between receive of application's input from the user and presentation of application's output to the user.

Therefore, we define the execution cost function to improve an important factor of mobile devices, latency. We calculate the cost value for each machine including surrogates and mobile device itself and the machine with the minimum cost value would be the offloading target.

3.3 Effective Parameters in Execution Cost

In this paper, the most important effective parameters which influence the execution cost function can be categorized into three classes, as follows:

- *Mobile and surrogate context* include current processor power of surrogates and mobile device.
- *Application context* include application code, input and output size. Furthermore some parts of applications are not transferable to the surrogate, e.g. codes that interact with I/O devices [11, 16, 17], and native methods of a language with different implementations on different platforms [10].
- *Network context* include type and bandwidth of the communication network.

Solver uses this context information to calculate execution cost (latency) for every location and select the best one.

3.4 Latency Estimation

Latency is the delay between receiving the application's input from the user and delivering the application's output to the user. We estimate the latency or execution cost for two cases: (1) a surrogate is selected as execution location, and (2) local execution which means the mobile device runs the task itself.

The latency time in the mobile device is equal to execution time of the application on the mobile device but the latency of offloading the task to the surrogates includes three parts: (1) the time is taken to send related data such as input data and application code to the surrogate, (2) execution time on the surrogate, and (3) the time of receiving the output data from the surrogate. Equation 1 shows the latency of offloading the task to the surrogates.

$$\text{Latency}_{\text{surrogate}} = \text{Time}_{\text{send}} + \text{ExecutionTime}_{\text{surrogate}} + \text{Time}_{\text{receive}} \quad (1)$$

$\text{Time}_{\text{send}}$ and $\text{Time}_{\text{receive}}$ are calculated in terms of *Data Transmission Rate* and *Transmission Data Size* by Equation 2.

$$\text{Time}_{\text{Send/receive}} = \frac{\text{Transmission Data Size}}{\text{Data Transmission Rate}} \quad (2)$$

We defined *Data Transmission Rate* as a constant value and the results in Section 4 show the constant value works good enough. On the other hand, *Transmission Data* usually includes input, output and code of the task. The size of code and input is available, because making decision is just before task execution. Output size is usually a constant value with a definite size or it can be estimated in terms of input value or input size.

To estimate execution time, we defined a *Function* for every task which is calculated simply, according to the time complexity order of the task. For example, the value of *Function* is *N!* for *finding matrix determinant* application, where N is the row count, or is N^2 for *selection sort* application, where N is the array size. We calculated *InstructionPmSecond* value for every task and machine as Equation 3.

$$\text{InstructionPmSecond} = \frac{\text{Function(N)}}{\text{Execution Time}} \tag{3}$$

This information is measured for every task and the mobile device, in advance and is available before task execution in application context descriptor. To calculate the execution time for different input values on mobile device, solver calculates the Function score for the input value of the application presented in the application context descriptor. The result is then divided by *InstructionPmSecond* of mobile device which is also presented in application context descriptor to estimate the *execution time* of the application for the specific input value.

To estimate execution time on a surrogate, if the *InstructionPmSecond* was not presented for the corresponding application and surrogate (i.e. the surrogate was not profiled for that application before), we need to estimate *InstructionPmSecond* for that surrogate. Therefore, we generated a task profiler for the application which is sent to the surrogate to run the application. This profiler contains application code with a comparatively small input data, runs the application on the surrogate, calculates *InstructionPmSecond* for the surrogate by Equation 3, and sends back the calculated *InstructionPmSecond* factor to the solver. It takes about one second time for the tasks which are introduced in *Experiments* Section of this paper.

Although calculating *InstructionPmSecond* in this way imposes a little latency to the system for the first run, the experimental results in Section 4 shows that the precious effect of this factor to have a good estimation of execution time can well cover the imposed overhead. Also, by using this factor there is no need to monitor and save the execution time of task runs, as it was discussed in *Related Work* Section in more details.

4 Experiments

4.1 Experimental Platform

For our experiments, we used one HTC Touch 2 smartphone as the mobile device with a QualcommMSM7225™528 MHz processor and 256 MB RAM running Windows Mobile 6.5 Professional. The surrogate in this platform is a laptop running Windows 7 Professional. The surrogate's processor is Intel(R) Core(TM)2 Duo 2.5 GHz and its memory size is 4 GB. The mobile device is connected to the surrogate via 802.11b/g WLAN.

4.2 Test Applications

To quantify our proposed solver we used several applications that all of them are almost CPU-intensive tasks. We categorized these applications into three categories according to their usage, as follows: (1) scientific calculator operations such as calculating *matrix determinant*, (2) statistical applications such as sorting an array (*selection sort*), (3) daily applications such as *finding shortest path* between a source and a destination node in a map. Table 1 describes the detailed information about these applications.

The second and third columns of Table 2 (i.e. Function and InstructionPmSecond) have been used to calculate execution time on the mobile device by Equation 3. Output size is constant or is calculated in terms of input size and "N Description" column describes the *N* value in the *Function*.

Table 1. Detailed information about test applications

Name	Matrix determinant	Selection sort	Shortest Path
Function	N!	N^2	N^3
InstructionPmSecond	90	4400	550
Output Size	500B	INPUT	Sqrt (INPUT)
Output Type	Constant	Variable	Variable
N Description	Row count	Array size	Node count

4.3 Latency Evaluation

Latency is defined as the amount of time is taken to respond upon a user-triggered request. Usually, less latency causes more users' satisfaction. We evaluated our proposed mechanism with regard to the latency in 3 scenarios as follow.

a) Local execution where the mobile device executes the task itself
b) Remote execution or blind offloading where the mobile device always sends application code and input data to a surrogate to execute the task on behalf of it (without managing the trade-off between computation and communication costs)
c) Using our proposed mechanism to find the best execution plan between local execution (scenario 1) and remote execution (scenario 2) according to the current situations and input data of the task and run it.

We evaluated the benefits of our proposed mechanism on 20 iterations of running mentioned applications in terms of different inputs. We measured latency on three mentioned scenario in 20 iterations. Figure 2-4 show the average latency for three applications of *matrix determinant*, *selection sort*, and *shortest path* respectively.

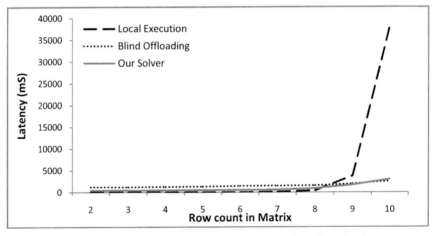

Fig. 2. Latency comparison for "matrix determinant" application

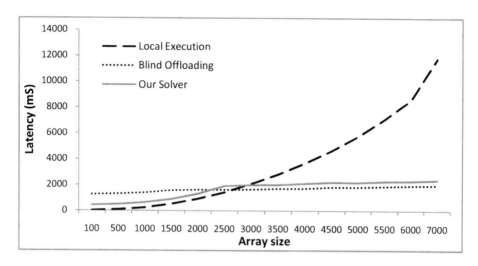

Fig. 3. Latency comparison for "selection sort" application

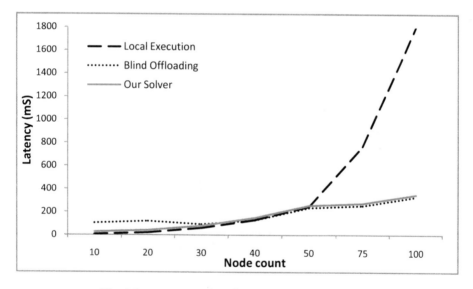

Fig. 4. Latency comparison for "shortest path" application

As it is clear in Figures 2-4, local execution on the mobile device is the best choice for small input values, due to communication overhead. On the contrary, for larger input values, remote execution (task offloading) is a better choice. Our proposed mechanism is almost always able to choose the best one between local execution and remote execution in terms of input value, with a small overhead.

5   Conclusion

These days, due to popularity of mobile devices, users intend to run more complex tasks on them and they expect to get the same performance as if they used to run their applications on powerful stationary computers. But it is evident that mobile devices are always resource poor in contrast with non-mobile computers.

Cyber foraging is one of the most common solutions for resource constraint in mobile devices. It augments mobile devices' capabilities by task offloading to nearby idle surrogates. Although powerful surrogates with more processing power and resources run tasks faster than resource constrained mobile devices, task offloading imposes communication overhead on the system. Because task information (e.g. code and input data) should be sent to the surrogate and output results should be received. Therefore task offloading is not beneficial in all situations.

In this paper, we meant to decrease latency by choosing the right one between local and remote execution. We proposed a solver unit that estimates latency of running the task on each location (i.e. the mobile device and surrogates) and selects the best location to run the task according to the context information such as processing power of every machine, code, input and output size of the task and network information.

Also, we introduced a good solution to have an acceptable estimation of execution time, before real execution. The experimental results show that our proposed mechanism is superior to local execution and blind task offloading in respect of latency.

References

1. The Global Partnership for Development at a Critical Juncture. United Nations, New York, MDG GAP Task Force Report (2010)
2. Satyanarayanan, M., Bahl, P., Cáceres, R., Davies, N.: The Case for VM-Based Cloudlets in Mobile Computing. IEEE Pervasive Computing 8, 14–23 (2009)
3. Oh, J., Lee, S., Lee, E.-s.: An Adaptive Mobile System Using Mobile Grid Computing in Wireless Network. In: Gavrilova, M.L., Gervasi, O., Kumar, V., Tan, C.J.K., Taniar, D., Laganá, A., Mun, Y., Choo, H. (eds.) ICCSA 2006. LNCS, vol. 3984, pp. 49–57. Springer, Heidelberg (2006)
4. Ou, S., Yang, K., Zhang, Q.: An Efficient Runtime Offloading Approach for Pervasive Services. In: IEEE Wireless Communications & Networking Conference (WCNC 2006), Las Vegas, pp. 2229–2234 (2006)
5. Balan, R.K., Gergle, D., Satyanarayanan, M., Herbsleb, J.: Simplifying Cyber Foraging for Mobile Devices. In: 5th USENIX International Conference on Mobile Systems, Applications and Services (MobiSys), San Juan, Puerto Rico, pp. 272–285 (2007)
6. Flinn, J., Park, S., Satyanarayanan, M.: Balancing Performance, Energy, and Quality in Pervasive Computing. In: 22nd International Conference on Distributed Computing Systems (ICDCS 2002), Austria, pp. 217–226 (2002)
7. Chen, G., Kang, B.T., Kandemir, M., Vijaykrishnan, N., Irwin, M.J., Chandramouli, R.: Studying Energy Trade Offs in Offloading Computation/Compilation in Java-Enabled Mobile Devices. IEEE Transactions on Parallel and Distributed Systems 15, 795–809 (2004)

8. Satyanarayanan, M.: Pervasive Computing: Vision and Challenges. IEEE Personal Communication 8, 10–17 (2001)
9. Balan, R.K., Satyanarayanan, M., Park, S., Okoshi, T.: Tactics-Based Remote Execution for Mobile Computing. In: 1st International Conference on Mobile Systems, Applications and Services, San Francisco, pp. 273–286 (2003)
10. Gu, X., Messer, A., Greenbergx, I., Milojicic, D., Nahrstedt, K.: Adaptive Offloading for Pervasive Computing. IEEE Pervasive Computing Magazine 3, 66–73 (2004)
11. Ou, S., Yang, K., Liotta, A.: An Adaptive Multi-Constraint Partitioning Algorithm for Offloading in Pervasive Systems. In: 4th Annual IEEE International Conference on Pervasive Computing and Communications (PERCOM 2006), Pisa, Italy, pp. 116–125 (2006)
12. Song, X.: Seamless Mobility in Ubiquitous Computing Environments. PhD Thesis, Georgia Institute of Technology (2008)
13. Song, X., Ramachandran, U.: MobiGo: A Middleware for Seamless Mobility. In: 13th IEEE International Conference on Embedded and Real-Time Computing Systems and Applications (RTCSA 2007), Daegu, pp. 249–256 (2007)
14. Kristensen, M.D.: Empowering Mobile Devices through Cyber Foraging:The Development of Scavenger, an Open Mobile Cyber Foraging System. PhD Thesis, Department of Computer Science, Aarhus University, Denmark (2010)
15. Satyanarayanan, M.: Avoiding Dead Batteries. IEEE Pervasive Computing 4, 2–3 (2005)
16. Othrnan, M., Hailes, S.: Power Conservation Strategy for Mobile Computers Using Load Sharing. Mobile Computing and Communications Review 2, 19–26 (1998)
17. Cuervo, E., Balasubramanian, A., Cho, D.K., Wolman, A., Saroiu, S., Chandra, R., Bahl, P.: MAUI: Making Smartphones Last Longer with Code Offload. In: ACM MobiSys, San Francisco, USA, pp. 49–62 (2010)

An Application for Singular Point Location in Fingerprint Classification

Ali Ismail Awad[1] and Kensuke Baba[2]

[1] Graduate School of Information Science and Electrical Engineering,
Kyushu University, Japan
[2] Research and Development Division, Kyushu University Library, Japan
{awad,baba}@soc.ait.kyushu-u.ac.jp

Abstract. Singular Point (SP) is one of the local fingerprint features, and it is used as a landmark due its scale and rotation immutability. SP characteristics have been widely used as a feature vector for many fingerprint classification approaches. This paper introduces a new application of singular point location in fingerprint classification by considering it as a reference point to the partitioning process in the proposed pattern-based classification algorithm. The key idea of the proposed classification method is dividing fingerprint into small sub images using SP location, and then, creating distinguished patterns for each class using frequency domain representation for each sub-image. The performance evaluation of the SP detection and the proposed algorithm with different database sub-sets focused on both the processing time and the classification accuracy as key issues of any classification approach. The experimental work shows the superiority of using singular point location with the proposed classification algorithm. The achieved classification accuracy over FVC2002 database subsets is up to 91.4% with considerable processing time and robustness to scale, shift, and rotation conditions.

Keywords: Fingerprint Classification, Singular Point, Texture Patterns.

1 Introduction

Biometrics technology is keep growing substantially in the last decades with great advances in biometric applications. An accurate automatic personal authentication and identification have become crucial steps in a wide range of application domains such as national ID, Electronic Commerce, and Automated Banking. The recent developments in the biometrics area have led to smaller, faster, and cheaper systems, which in turn has increased the number of possible areas for biometric usage [1].

Fingerprint as a kind of human biometrics on the finger tip is the dominant trait between many biometrics like iris, retina, and face. It is widely used for personal recognition in forensic and civilian applications because of its uniqueness, immutability, and low cost. Therefore, large volumes of fingerprints are collected and stored everyday by different meanings for a wide range of applications. In Automated Fingerprint Identification System (AFIS) with a large database, the input image is matched with all fields inside the database to identify the most potential identity. Recently, AFIS

V. Snasel, J. Platos, and E. El-Qawasmeh (Eds.): ICDIPC 2011, Part I, CCIS 188, pp. 262–276, 2011.
© Springer-Verlag Berlin Heidelberg 2011

that supporting instant identification or recognition is increasingly used, and the matching time for this system is an important research field. Although satisfactory performances have been reported for 1:1 matching, both the time efficiency and the matching accuracy deteriorate seriously for simple extensions of the 1:1 matching procedure to a 1:N matching [2]. For addressing the problem, fingerprint classification has become an indispensable operation toward reducing the search time through large fingerprint databases. Fingerprint classification refers to the problem of assigning fingerprint to one of several pre-specified classes. It presents an interesting problem in pattern recognition, especially in real applications that require small response time. The classification process works on narrowing the search domain into smaller database subsets, and hence, speeds up the total matching time of the AFIS.

A typical fingerprint classification algorithm usually extracts a representative feature set to capture the individuality of each fingerprint, and then does some processes to determine the fingerprint class. The first attempt to classify fingerprint was done by Sir Henry in 1900 [3], he classified fingerprints into five classes (Arch, Tended Arch, Left Loop, Right Lop, and Whorl) based on the global ridge characteristics. Fig. 1 shows an example of these classes. In recent years, the most of fingerprint classification approaches use one or more of the following features: singular points (SPs, which are core or delta points), orientation field, ridge flow, and the Gabor filter responses [1]. Processing the extracted features from singularities fall under one of strategies such as rule-based classifiers [4, 5], structural and statistical approaches [6], and learning-based and multi classifier system [1], [7]. More recently, Neural Networks [8] and Wavelet-based classifiers [9] are also considered. The performance of any classification approach highly depends on the preprocessing steps where various ways to extract and represent distinguishable features among classes can be applied. Most of the available classifications methods are dominated by the nature of preprocessing steps that require a high processing time which slow down the overall response time.

This paper presents a new fingerprint classification algorithm that uses the fingerprint texture (periodicity and directionality) property to create distinguished patterns for each fingerprint class shown in Fig. 1. In order to emphases the texture property usage and avoid the intraclass problem of using full fingerprint image, a partitioning process is proposed to generate different patterns for each sub-image. The prototype of the presented algorithm [10] uses the (x, y) lengths to divide fingerprint into equally four sub-images. Driven from scale and rotation invariant property of the SP, thus it will be used in our algorithm in different way as reference point for image division process. The frequency patterns are scale and rotation invariant since it is limited to the texture orientation inside each block. Therefore, using SP location guarantees that the process of creating all sub-images will be also robust for image scale and rotation. The constructed patterns are then processed by Gabor Filter to extract their directions. Finally, classification process is carried out by matching the ensemble four patterns of the input fingerprint with the ensemble patterns of the four labeled classes.

The reminder part of this paper is organized as follows: Section 2 describes in details fingerprint global structure, fingerprint classes, and the state of the art of using singular point for solving fingerprint classification problem. An accurate and reliable method for singular point localization using complex filters is described in Section 3. Section 4 explains the classification algorithm, patterns extraction, and patterns matching techniques.

The experimental results, performance evaluation, and classification results are reported in Section 5. Finally, conclusions and future work are drawn in Section 6.

2 Fingerprint Structure

Fingerprint structure is defined by the interleaved ridges and furrows constructed on the finger tip. Fingerprint structure falls under two categories, local and global structures. Local structure is described by ridge ending and bifurcation (minutiae). It is also compact, and captures a significant component of individual information in fingerprints for matching process. Global structure is considered as a coarse level structure, and it highly depends on the ridge flow orientation inside the overall fingerprint image. Fingerprint classification uses the coarse level structure to label fingerprint images into classes. Fig. 1 shows labeled fingerprint classes with their corresponding singular points.

The singular points or singularities, shown also in Fig. 1 (Circle – core, Triangle – delta), are the most important global characteristics of fingerprint images. Singular point area is defined as a region where the ridge curvature is higher than normal and where the direction of the ridge changes rapidly. The core point is defined as the topmost point of the innermost curving ridge, and the delta point is the center of triangular regions where three different direction flows meet [11]. Singularities have both global and local properties. Globally, a singularity is a region of a fingerprint where the ridge pattern makes it visually prominent. Locally, a core point is the turning point of an inner-most ridge, and a delta point is a place where two ridges running side-by-side diverged. Many classification algorithms have used singularity characteristics as features for classification process due their rotate and scale immunities, however, the singularities detection is sensitive to different conditions such as noise, sensor type, and the fingerprint status which result in the difficulty of consistent and reliable classification. In our implementation, we neither consider the number of SPs, nor any other extra supporting features. The location of the maximum curvature change is only considered, and hence the Arch class may have one singular point.

Principal axes technique [12] has been used as a secondary stage of singularity-based classification algorithm. This algorithm takes into account not only the number of singular points, but also the relation between them, and their orientations on (x, y) coordinates. Pseudo ridge tracing [13] have used the ridge tracing beside the orientation field analysis as a supplement to compensate the missing singularities and improves the classification process. A Gaussian–Hermite moment [11] detects different type of singularities that depends on the core and delta structures and relationships.

Singular points features have been also used by different learning approaches including Multilayer Preceptron (MPL) Neural Networks [14], and Bidirectional Associative Memory (BAM) Neural Networks [15]. One can expect that using singular point location for fingerprint image partitioning can dramatically increase the robustness of the proposed fingerprint classification algorithm.

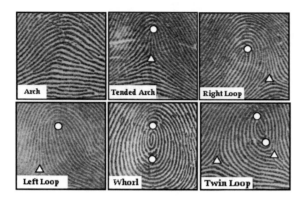

Fig. 1. Global structure of fingerprint with a representation of common singular points

3 Singular Point Localization

Poincaré index [16] is the common method for singular point detection. Complex filter with Gaussian window [17] is another existing method that applies the complex filter on complex directional field to extract singular points in fingerprint image. An advantage of using complex filter over the traditional Poincaré index is the possibility to detect both location and direction of the singular point. Another advantage is that the complex filter can be designed to extract core or delta point individually, where Poincaré index should perform all calculations first, and then decide the singular type. Therefore, the complex filter method is more suitable to our algorithm due to its small computational time [18]. The main steps of the complex filter implementations are orientation field estimation, complex filter construction, and the convolution between both complex filter and directional image.

3.1 Complex Orientation Field Estimation

Many proposed approaches for complex orientation field estimation can be found in the literature [19]. In order to construct the complex directional image, assume that $G_x(i, j)$ and $G_y(i, j)$ are the pixel derivations at point (i, j) in x and y directions, respectively. Then, the complex directional image can be calculated as:

$$z(x, y) = (G_x + iG_y)^2, \tag{1}$$

where i is the imaginary unit. Fig. 2(b) shows the original input image and the final extracted directional image corresponding to the input image in Fig. 2(a).

3.2 Complex Filter Construction

Another advantage of using complex filter instead of the traditional Poincaré index is the possibility to speed up the process by applying a separate filter for each singular type. In this research, we are interested only in core point detection, since most of fingerprints have this type of singularity. Therefore, we will neglect the filter design for delta point. The polynomial explanation of the complex filter for core point with order m at point (x, y) is mathematically represented as [17]:

$$(x + iy)^m g(x, y),\qquad(2)$$

where $g(x, y)$ is a Gaussian window, and it is mathematically expressed as:

$$g(x, y) = \exp\left(-\frac{x^2 + y^2}{2\sigma^2}\right),\qquad(3)$$

where σ is the variance of Gaussian window. Since Gaussian function is the only function which is orientation isotropic and separable, it does not introduce any orientation dependency. Fig. 3(a) shows the 3D complex filter response in spatial domain

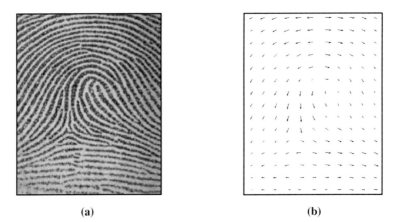

(a)   (b)

Fig. 2. Complex orientation field estimation: (a) original input image, and (b) corresponding complex directional image of (a)

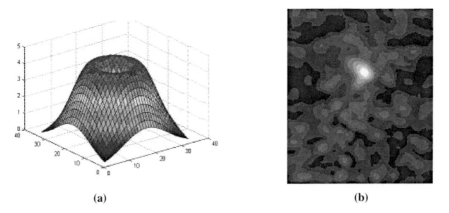

(a)   (b)

Fig. 3. Complex filter and its output response: (a) 3D spatial domain representation of a first order complex filter, and (b) magnitude of the resulted output after convoluting the complex filter with the orientation image shown in Fig. 2(b) with selected filter size as (32×32) pixels. Fig. 3(b) points out the magnitude image of convoluting the complex filter with the directional image. By Fig. 3(b) the maximum filter response at the core point can be visualized as a bright area, and then it can be consistently extracted by calculating the maximum points inside the convolution output array.

4 Proposed Classification Algorithm

Many fingerprint classification approaches use the information extracted from frequency domain representation to exclusively classify fingerprint. Some of frequency-based methods [20], [14] use the information extracted from the full image transformed into frequency domain. Fig. 5 shows the resulted frequency representation of a full fingerprint image. These methods failed to achieve good results due to the resulted classes overlapping.

The proposed algorithm overcomes the classes overlapping problem, and facilitates the texture property of fingerprint image by building four different patterns for each class using image division process. Fig. 6(c) points out the gained difference of using four sub images over full image patterns. The accuracy of the algorithm highly depends on the patterns generation and extraction processes. Beside its immutability to scale, shift, and rotation conditions, fingerprint partitioning based on singular point location provides the ability to process fingerprint image as four individual sub- images, and makes each image/block has its own texture as ridge frequency and direction. Therefore, each sub-image is considered as a stand alone pattern, and the

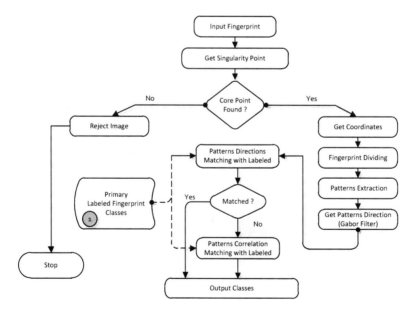

Fig. 4. A Flowchart of the proposed pattern-based classification algorithm

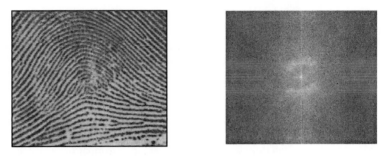

Fig. 5. Frequency components of full fingerprint image: full input fingerprint image (left), and corresponding 2D-FFT output (right)

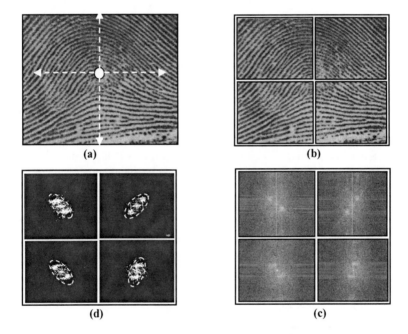

(a)   (b)

(d)   (c)

Fig. 6. Implementations of the proposed algorithm: (a) singular point detection, (b) dividing image into sub-images using singular point coordinates, (c) corresponding frequency representations of sub-images in (b), and (d) final extracted patterns from frequency domain in (c)

Fig. 7. Patterns rotation invariant: normal sub-image with its corresponding pattern (left), and rotated sub-mage with (180°) and its corresponding pattern (right)

ensemble of the four individual patterns forms the final class pattern. The number of blocks (four) has been selected due to processing time and computational complexity considerations. Four blocks selection compromising the trade offs between processing time and accepted performance of the algorithm.

As shown in the algorithm flowchart in Fig. 4, the first step (marked with 1) is to build the patterns of the labeled/standard four classes and hold them for the further matching processes. Gabor filter has been used for processing patterns and extract their directions. To reduce the total response time, matching process was first applied over patterns directions. In case of failing in direction matching, the matching process will be extended further to include patterns shape using 2D correlation mechanism.

4.1 Pattern Extraction and Shaping

Prior to the pattern extraction, an accurate image partitioning has been done based on the singular point location. The advantage of image partitioning is to facilitate the fingerprint texture for each resulted sub-image. To ensure the correctness of image partitioning, image padding has been also implemented on all images to make sure that all sub images are individual square blocks. Patterns of each class are constructed from the frequency components of the four sub-images. There are two types of patterns: (i) Labeled (Standard) classes' patterns, and (ii) Input image patterns. Patterns of standard classes are extracted once and stored in system buffer to be used later for the matching process. The first step toward pattern extraction is frequency domain representation. Two dimensional fast Fourier transform (2D-FFT) [14, 21] is a simple method to transform fingerprint images from spatial domain into frequency domain. 2D-FFT has been applied individually on each sub-image. The resulted patterns are defined by both direction and shape. Fig. 6 shows the outputs each step in pattern extraction process, and moreover, it points out the difference between using full image patterns and partitioned image patterns in terms of pattern shape and direction.

The second step of pattern extraction is making an adaptive threshold to the FFT output components. This step aims to primary segment the foreground components in each sub-image. Fig. 6(d) shows an example of the final extracted patterns after we perform an adaptive threshold process. As an advantage of the proposed algorithm, Fig.7 shows how the extracted pattern from individual block is robust for image rotation which is not possible when using full image pattern. By a simple visual inspection on Fig. 5(b) and Fig. 6(c), one can realize how much the 2D-FFT outputs are different from using the full image and the partitioned image. More investigations on Fig. 6(c) prove that the extracted patterns are different in shape and direction from one sub image to another. It is worth to say that the final class pattern is the ensemble of the individual four sub-image patterns. Fig. 6(d) shows the final pattern of Arch class. The proposed algorithm uses these distinguished patterns in shapes and directions as features for future fingerprint classification.

4.2 Pattern Direction Estimation

The extracted patterns in the previous subsection can be used by different matching techniques such as absolute image difference, and 2D image correlation. In order to increase classification accuracy of the pattern-based algorithm, pattern orientation has been corporate as first step of the pattern matching process. Due to the texture properties of the extracted patterns, Gabor filter [22] has been selected to separate patterns into lines like parallel ridges and valleys, and then the pattern direction can be extracted using simple gradient methods such as "Sobel" or "Prewitt" filters [21].

Gabor filter is considered as very useful tool for direction extraction due to its optimal frequency and orientation selectivity properties in both spatial and frequency domains. A general form of 2D Gabor can be split into odd and even symmetric components. Since we need to reduce the computational time as much as possible, the odd-symmetric components will be considered. The odd-symmetric components of the Gabor filter can be calculated as [23]:

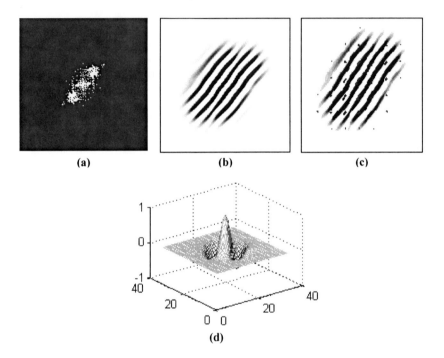

(a)   (b)   (c)

(d)

Fig. 8. Extraction of pattern direction using Gabor filter: (a) sample pattern image, (b) output of Gabor filter implementation, (c) extracted pattern direction using simple "Sobel" gradient method, and (d) the 3D representation of Gabor filter components with (45°) orientation of x-axis

$$g(x, y) = \exp\left(-\frac{1}{2}\left[\frac{x_\phi^2}{\sigma_x^2} + \frac{y_\phi^2}{\sigma_y^2}\right]\right)\sin\left(\frac{2\pi x_\phi}{T}\right), \tag{4}$$

where ϕ is the filter orientation, T is the filter wavelength, and

$$x_\phi = x\cos\phi + y\sin\phi, \quad y_\phi = -x\cos\phi + y\sin\phi. \tag{5}$$

One of the Gabor filter properties is the performing of low pass filtering along the orientation ϕ and band pass filtering orthogonal to that orientation. We got the result in Fig. 8(b) by configuring the Gabor filter as $T = 10$ pixels, $\phi = 45°$, and $\sigma = 1$ for both x and y coordinates. The final result has been produced by implementing Gabor filter using 2D convolution on the extracted patterns. Fig. 8(d) shows the spatial representation of 2D Gabor filter with orientation 45°. Final Gabor output has been processed further using "Sobel" filter to detect the maximum pattern direction with block size configuration as (16×16) pixels. Fig. 8(c) represents the detected direction plotted over the output of Gabor filter implementation. The Gabor filter orientation is different from one sub image to another. It has been empirically set by visually inspecting the ridge orientation of each sub-image in the four pre-defined classes.

4.3 Pattern Matching

The extracted patterns of the input image have been matched with patterns of the pre-labeled classes in terms of the directions and the shapes of patterns. Since the fingerprint ridge periodicity and directionality are fixed over shifting and rotation, the extracted patterns will be accordingly related to the local features of each sub-image. The pattern matching has been implemented in two steps, direction matching based on previously calculated directions and 2D correlation for spatial pattern shape. In this regard, it is worth mentioning that the matching process is being performed on each sub-image of the input fingerprint and its corresponding one in pre-extracted classes. The final matching result is then accumulated as a summation of the four sub-images matching. To increase the direction matching flexibility, a direction range is used instead of hard direction matching. For example, for matching two patterns on one direction, a 5° tolerance is used. Finally, the matching results are forwarded to the decision step to detect the class of the input fingerprint image.

5   Experimental Results and Evaluations

The application of singular points in fingerprint classification has two main steps, singular point detection and fingerprint classification. During our experiments, both steps have been evaluated individually and incorporated in terms of the processing time, the accuracy, and the classification results. DB1_B, DB2_B, and DB3_B are subsets of Fingerprint Verification Competition 2002 (FVC2002) [1] which have been captured by optical sensor "TouchView II" by Identix and "FX2000" by Biometrika and capacitive sensor "100 SC" by Precise Biometrics, respectively. The total images in all subsets are 3×80 fingerprints, and all of them have been used in the evaluation.

5.1   Accuracy of Singularity Detection

The accuracy of singular point detection is measured as the images with the correctly detected singular related to the total images in the database. Table 1 shows the results of the accuracy measurements over all contents of the selected subsets. In Table 1, the total detection accuracy is up to 91.25%, 95.0%, and 90.0% measured upon the three FVC2002 subsets. The difference between "Incorrect" detection and "Rejected" images is that the core point in the rejected fingerprint can not be detected by human expert. Therefore, the rejected images have been removed from the accuracy calculations. Fig. 9 shows some samples of correctly and incorrectly detected singular points.

Table 1. Accuracy measurement of singular point detection method

Databases	(240) Fingerprint images			
	Detected	Incorrect	Rejected	Total Accuracy %
DB1_B (80)	73	7	0	91.25
DB2_B (80)	76	4	0	95.00
DB3_B 80)	63	7	10	90.00

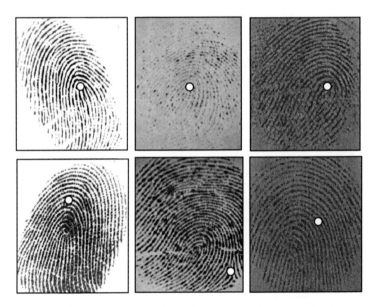

Fig. 9. Accuracy of singularity detection: fingerprints with correctly detected singular points (Top), and fingerprints with incorrectly detected singular points (Down) in all subsets, respectively

5.2 Processing Time of Singularity Detection

The key issue of any classification algorithm is reducing the total processing time inside the large database. Therefore, the processing time of the algorithm must be minimized as much as possible to avoid any impact of the singular point detection on the overall system performance. All experimental work have been performed on Intel® Core ™ 2 Due Processor (T9300, 2.5 GHz), 3 GB of RAM, Windows XP® Pro 32 bit, and Matlab® R2009b. Table 2 summarizes the minimum, the maximum, and the mean processing times of the singular point detection method over all images in the selected databases subsets. By Table 2, the processing time is related to image size due to filter convolution, and it is also in an acceptable range for individual fingerprint images. From this section, we conclude that the complex filter works as a lightweight method for singular point detection, and it imposes only a very small amount of time compared to the other processes in the algorithm.

Table 2. Processing time measurements of singular point detection algorithm

Database	(240) Fingerprint images			
	Min time / Fingerprint	Max time / Fingerprint	Mean time / Fingerprint	Total time / Database
DB1_B (80)	0.11 sec	0.140 sec	0.120 sec	09.96 sec
DB2_B (80)	0.12 sec	0.155 sec	0.134 sec	10.50 sec
DB3_B (80)	0.08 sec	0.091 sec	0.083 sec	06.95 sec

5.3 Classification Accuracy

In term of classification accuracy, we have evaluated our classification algorithm over the same above databases. Table 3 shows the resulted confusion matrix of the classification process of DB1_B. Visually inspecting DB1_B, we found that the ambiguous fingerprints are 10, and hence, the total algorithm accuracy has been calculated over 70 images. The classification accuracy of that subset is 91.4 % with 12.5% rejection.

Table 3. Confusion matrix of pattern-based classification algorithm with (BD1_B)

True Classes	Assigned Classes				
	Arch	R. L.	L. L.	W	T. L.
Arch (0)	0	0	0	0	0
R Loop (20)	0	19	1	0	0
L Loop (34)	1	2	30	1	0
Whorl (8)	0	0	1	7	0
Twin Loop (8)	0	0	0	0	8

Table 4. Confusion matrix of pattern-based classification algorithm with (BD2_B)

True Classes	Assigned Classes				
	Arch	R. L.	L. L.	W	T. L.
Arch (0)	0	0	0	0	0
R Loop (26)	0	23	1	2	0
L Loop (22)	1	0	18	1	2
Whorl (16)	0	0	1	15	0
Twin Loop (6)	0	0	0	0	6

Table 5. Confusion matrix of pattern-based classification algorithm with (BD3_B)

True Classes	Assigned Classes				
	Arch	R. L.	L. L.	W	T. L.
Arch (17)	13	0	1	3	0
R Loop (8)	0	6	0	2	0
L Loop (1)	0	0	0	0	0
Whorl (32)	1	0	1	29	1
Twin Loop (0)	0	0	0	0	0

Table 4 and Table 5 are the confusion matrices for the other two database subsets. Analogy to Table 1, the first column shows the class index detected by visual inspection, and the first row gives the assigned class using the proposed method. Because of the subtle differences between the Tented Arch and the Arch, it is reasonable to combine them into one class as Arch in all confusion matrices. By visual investigations of both datasets, we have found that the DB2_B and DB3_B have ambiguous fingerprints as 10 and 22, respectively. From both tables, the classification accuracies for these two subsets are 88.5% and 82.7% with rejection rates as 12.5% and 27.7%, respectively. The classification accuracies of the proposed algorithm in the first two subsets are higher than that one achieved by using full fingerprint image in frequency domain representation (85% measured over 40 fingerprint images) reported in [20].

5.4 Processing Time of Fingerprint Classification

Table 6 represents the elapsed time for processing the full patterns (four sub-images) of single input image including all algorithms steps from singular point detection to the final matching step. From that Table, we could extrapolate that the total consumed time for processing single fingerprint image is relatively small comparing to the other classification methods. The total evaluation of combining singular point with pattern-based classification algorithm introduces good classification results for different databases subsets regardless of the image quality, and with a relatively small processing time. Our previous experiments drown the fact that the singular point detection method does not affected by any image shift and rotations. Therefore, the patterns created from fingerprint sub-images are also robust for these two conditions. The final algorithm evaluation drives us to use the extracted patterns for building a new features vector for future Neural Networks implementations.

Table 6. Consumed time for sequential algorithm steps (four sub-images considered)

	Sequential algorithm steps				
	Singular point	Partitioning	Patterns extraction	Matching	Total time
Time/Fingerprint	0.110 sec	0.020 sec	0.083 sec	0.071 sec	**0.283 sec**

6   Conclusions and Future Work

Fingerprint singular point is considered as a landmark of fingerprint image due to its scale, shift, and rotation immutability. This paper presented a new application of the detected singular point in the classification process by considering its coordinates as the original point of fingerprint partitioning process in the proposed patterns based classification algorithm. The key contributions of this work are two-folds: Firstly, implementation of a new singular point detection method using complex filters and complex tensor orientation images with high accuracy and reliability. Moreover, complex filtering with Gaussian window has also been tuned for low computational cost. Secondly, we developed the pattern-based classification algorithm that generates a distinguished classification patterns from ridge frequency and orientation. The partitioning process introduces some extra processing time, however the extracted patterns from four sub images are completely different from using a full image patterns with intraclass avoidance. Gabor filter has been also applied in a different way to convert pattern shape into ridge like parallel flow lines to easily calculate its direction. The overall performance evaluation of both contributions proves that both of them are working well for different database subsets. Therefore, our research continues into improving their processing time, accuracy, and efficiency.

Acknowledgement

This work was partially supported by CREST program of Japan Science and Technology Agency (JST) from 2008 to 2012 and the Grant-in-Aid for Young Scientists (B) No. 22700149 of the Ministry of Education, Culture, Sports, Science and Technology (MEXT) from 2010 to 2012.

References

1. Maltoni, D., Maio, D., Jain, A.K., Prabhakar, S.: Handbook of Fingerprint Recognition. Springer, Heidelberg (2009)
2. Liu, M.: Fingerprint Classification based on Adaboost Learning from Singularity Features. Pattern Recognition 43, 1062–1070 (2010)
3. Henry, E.: Classification and uses of Fingerprints. Routledge & Sons, London (1900)
4. Jain, A.K., Minut, S.: Hierarchical Kernel Fitting for Fingerprint Classification and Alignment. In: Proceedings of IEEE 16th International Conference on Pattern Recognition (ICPR 2002), p. 20469. IEEE, Quebec City (2002)
5. Cappelli, R., Maio, D., Maltoni, D.: A Multi-Classifier Approach to Fingerprint Classification. Pattern Analysis & Applications 5, 136–144 (2002)
6. Maltoni, D., Maio, D.: A Structural Approach to Fingerprint Classification. In: Proceedings of 13th International Conference on Pattern Recognition (ICPR). IEEE Computer Society, Vienna (1996)
7. Cappelli, R., Maio, D., Maltoni, D., Nanni, L.: A Two-stage Fingerprint Classification System. In: Proceedings of the 2003 ACM SIGMM workshop on Biometrics methods and applications (WBMA 2003), pp. 95–99. ACM, Berkley (2003)
8. Senior, A.: A Combination Fingerprint Classifier. IEEE Transactions on Pattern Analysis and Machine Intelligence 23, 1165–1174 (2001)
9. Wang, W., Li, J., Chen, W.: Fingerprint Classification Using Improved Directional Field and Fuzzy Wavelet Neural Networks. In: Proceedings of the IEEE Sixth World Congress on Intelligent Control and Automation, pp. 9961–9964. IEEE, Dalian (2006)

10. Awad, A.I., Baba, K.: Toward An Efficient Fingerprint Classification. In: Albert, M. (ed.) Biometrics - Unique and Diverse Applications in Nature, Science, and Technology, InTech (2011)
11. Wang, L., Dai, M.: Application of a New Type of Singular Points in Fingerprint Classification. Pattern Recognition Letters 28, 1640–1650 (2007)
12. Klimanee, C., Nguyen, D.T.: Classification of Fingerprints Using Singular Points and Their Principal Axes. In: Proceedings of IEEE International Conference on Image Processing (ICIP 2004), pp. 849–852. IEEE, Singapore (2004)
13. Zhanga, Q., Yan, H.: Fingerprint Classification based on Extraction and Analysis of Singularities and Pseudo Ridges. Pattern Recognition 37, 2233–2243 (2004)
14. Sarbadhikari, S.N., Basak, J., Pal, S.K., Kundu, M.K.: Noisy Fingerprints Classification with Directional Based Features Using MLP. Neural Computing & Applications 7, 180–191 (1998)
15. Kristensen, T., Borthen, J., Fyllingsnes, K.: Comparison of Neural Network based Fingerprint Classification Techniques. In: International Joint Conference on Neural Networks (IJCNN 2007), pp. 1043–1048. IEEE, Orlando (2007)
16. Kawagoe, M., Tojo, A.: Fingerprint Pattern Classification. Pattern Recognition 17, 295–303 (1984)
17. Nilsson, K., Josef, B.: Localization of Corresponding Points in Fingerprints by Complex Ffiltering. Pattern Recognition Letters 24, 2135–2144 (2003)
18. Awad, A.I., Baba, K.: Fingerprint Singularity Detection: A Comparative Study. In: Proceeding of the Second International Conference on Software Engineering and Computer Systems (ICSECS 2011). LNCS, Springer, Kuantan (to appear, 2011)
19. Hou, Z., Yau, W., Wang, Y.: A Review on Fingerprint Orientation Estimation. Security and Communication Networks (2010)
20. Green, R.J., Fitz, A.P.: Fingerprint Classification using a Hexagonal Fast Fourier Transform. Pattern Recognition 29, 1587–1597 (1996)
21. Gonzalez, R.C., Woods, R.E., Eddins, S.L.: Digital Image Processing Using Matlab. Prentice Hall, Englewood Cliffs (2003)
22. Gabor, D.J.: Theory of Communication. IEE 93, 429–457 (1946)
23. Yang, J., Liu, L., Jiang, T., Fan, Y.: A Modified Gabor Filter Design Method for Fingerprint Image Enhancement. Pattern Recognition Letters 24, 1805–1817 (2003)

A Classification-Based Graduates Employability Model for Tracer Study by MOHE

Myzatul Akmam Sapaat, Aida Mustapha, Johanna Ahmad, Khadijah Chamili, and Rahamirzam Muhamad

Faculty of Computer Science and Information Technology, Universiti Putra Malaysia, 43400 UPM Serdang, Selangor, Malaysia
angahmyz@yahoo.com, aida@fsktm.upm.edu.my, johanna@esyariah.gov.my, khadijah@usim.edu.my, raha_muhd@yahoo.com

Abstract. This study is to construct the Graduates Employability Model using data mining approach, in specific the classification task. To achieve it, we use data sourced from the Tracer Study, a web-based survey system from the Ministry of Higher Education, Malaysia (MOHE) since 2009. The classification experiment is performed using various Bayes algorithms to determine whether a graduate has been employed, remains unemployed or in an undetermined situation. The performance of Bayes algorithms are also compared against a number of tree-based algorithms. In conjunction with tree-based algorithm, Information Gain is used to rank the attributes and the results showed that top three attributes that have direct impact on employability are the job sector, job status and reason for not working. Results showed that J48, a variant of decision-tree algorithm performed with highest accuracy, which is 92.3% as compared to the average of 90.8% from other Bayes algorithms. This leads to the conclusion that a tree-based classifier is more suitable for the tracer data due to the information gain strategy.

Keywords: Classification, Bayes methods, Decision tree, Employability.

1 Introduction

Tracer Study is a web-based survey system developed by the Ministry of Higher Education, Malaysia (MOHE). It is compulsory to be filled by all students graduating from polytechnics, public or private institutions before their convocation for any level of degree awarded. The sole purpose of the survey is to guide future planning and to improve various aspects of local higher education administrative system. The survey also serves as a tool to gauge the adequacy of higher education in Malaysia in supplying manpower needs in all areas across technical, managerial or social science. Data sourced from the Tracer Study is invaluable because it provides correlation about the graduate qualifications and skills along with employment status.

Graduates employability remains as national issues due to the increasing number of graduates produced by higher education institutions each year. According to statistics generated from the Tracer Study, total number of graduates at diploma and bachelor

V. Snasel, J. Platos, and E. El-Qawasmeh (Eds.): ICDIPC 2011, Part I, CCIS 188, pp. 277–287, 2011.

level produced by public universities alone in 78,165 in 2008. In 2009, the volume has increased to 89,290 graduates. Nonetheless, the system reports only 61.5% of degree holders are working within the first six months after finishing their studies. Previous research on graduate employability covers wide range of domain such as education, engineering, and social science. While the researches are mainly based on surveys or interviews, little has been done using data mining techniques.

Bayes' theorem is among the earliest statistical method that is used to identify patterns in data. But as data sets have grown in size and complexity, data mining has emerged as a technology to apply methods such as neural networks, genetic algorithms, decision trees, and support vector machines to uncover hidden patterns [1]. Today, data mining technologies are dealing with huge amount of data from various sources, for example relational or transactional databases, data warehouse, images, flat files or in the form World Wide Web. Classification is the task of generalizing observations in the training data, which are accompanied by specific class of the observations.

The objective of this paper is to predict whether a graduate has been employed, remains unemployed or in an undetermined situation within the first six months after graduation. This will be achieved through a classification experiment that classifies a graduate profile as employed, unemployed or others. The main contribution of this paper is the comparison of classification accuracy between various algorithms from the two most commonly used data mining techniques in the education domain, which are the Bayes methods and decision trees.

The remainder of this paper is organized as follows. Section 2 presents the related works on graduate employability and reviews recent techniques employed in data mining. Section 3 introduces the data set and the experimental setting. Section 4 discusses finding of the results. Finally Section 5 concludes the paper with some direction for future work.

2   Related Works

A number of works have been done to identify the factors that influenced graduates employability in Malaysia. It is as an initiative step to align the higher education with the industry, where currently exists unquestionable impact against each other. Nonetheless, most of the previous works were carried out beyond the data mining domain. Besides, data sources for previous works were collected and assembled through survey in sample population.

Research in [2] identifies three major requirements concerned by the employers in hiring employees, which are basic academic skills, higher order thinking skills, and personal qualities. The work is restricted in the education domain specifically analyzing the effectiveness of a subject, English for Occupational Purposes (EOP) in enhancing employability skills. Similar to [2], work by [3] proposes to restructure the curriculum and methods of instruction in preparing future graduates for the forthcoming challenges based on the model of the T-shaped professional and newly developed field of Service Science, Management and Engineering (SSME).

More recently, [4] proposes a new Malaysian Engineering Employability Skills Framework (MEES), which is constructed based on requirement by accrediting bodies and professional bodies and existing research findings in employability skills as a guideline in training package and qualification in Malaysia. Nonetheless, not surprisingly, graduates employability is rarely being studied especially within the scope of data mining, mainly due to limited and authentic data source available.

However, data mining techniques have indeed been employed in education domain, for instance in prediction and classification of student academic performance using Artificial Neural Network [5, 6] and a combination of clustering and decision tree classification techniques [5]. Experiments in [7] classifies students to predict their final grade using six common classifiers (Quadratic Bayesian classifier, 1-nearest neighbour (1-NN), k-nearest neighbor (k-NN), Parzen-window, multilayer perceptron (MLP), and Decision Tree). With regards to student performance, [8] discovers individual student characteristics that are associated with their success according to grade point averages (GPA) by using a Microsoft Decision Trees (MDT) classification technique. Among the related work, we found that work done by [9] is most related to this research, whereby the work mines historical data of students' academic results using different classifiers (Bayes, trees, function) to rank influencing factors that contribute in predicting student academic performance.

3   Materials and Methods

The main objective of this paper is to classify a graduate profile as employed, unemployed or undetermined using data sourced from the Tracer Study database for the year of 2009. The data set consists of 12,830 instances and 20 attributes related to graduate profiles from 19 public universities and 138 private universities. Table 1 shows the complete attributes for the Tracer Study data set.

In preparing the data set, we performed pre-processing including data cleaning, data reduction, and data transformation as described in Section 3.1. During the experiment, a number of algorithms under Bayes and tree methods were built on the training set of the Tracer Study as described in Section 3.2. Finally, their predictive performances were compared on the validation set and the results will be reported in Section 4.

3.1   Data Preprocessing

The raw data retrieved from the Tracer Study database required pre-processing to prepare the data set for the classification task. First, cleaning activities involved eliminating data with missing values in critical attributes, identifying outliers, correcting inconsistent data, as well as removing duplicate data. From the total of 89,290 instances in the raw data, the data cleaning process ended up 12,830 instances that are ready to be mined. For missing values (i.e., age attribute), we replaced them with the mean values of the attribute.

Second, data discretization is required due to the fact that most of attributes from the Tracer Study are continuous attributes. In this case, we discretized the values into interval so as to prepare the data set into categorical or nominal attributes as below.

- cgpa previously in continuous number is transformed into grade range
- sex previously coded as 1 and 2 is transformed into nominal

- age previously in continuous number is transformed into age range
- field of study previously in numerical code 1-4 is transformed into nominal
- skill information (i.e., language proficiency, general knowledge, interpersonal communication etc) previously in numerical 1-9 is transformed into nominal
- employment status previously in numerical code 1-3 is transformed into nominal

Table 1. Attributes from the Tracer Study data set after the pre-processing is performed

No.	Attributes	Values	Descriptions
1	sex	{male, female}	Gender of the graduate
2	age	{20-25, 25-30, 30-40, 40-50, >50}	Age of the graduate
3	univ	{public_univ, private_univ}	University/institution of current qualification
4	level	{certificate, diploma, advanced_diploma, first_degree, postGraduate_diploma, masters_ thesis, masters_courseWork& Thesis, masters_courseWork, phd_ thesis, phd_courseWork&Thesis, professional}	Level of study for current qualification
5	field	{technical, ict, education, science, art&soc_science }	Field of study for current qualification
6	cgpa	{2.00-2.49, 2.50-2.99, 3.00-3.66, 3.67-4.00, failed, 4.01-6.17}	CGPA for current qualification
7	emp_status	{employed, unemployed, others}	Current employment status
8	general_IT skills	{satisfied, extremely_satisfied, average, strongly_not_satisfied, not_satisfied, not_applicable}	Level of IT skills, Malay and English language proficiency, general knowledge, interpersonal communication, creative and critical thinking, analytical skills, problem solving, inculcation of positive values, and teamwork acquired from the programme of study
9	Malay_lang		
10	English_lang		
11	gen_knowledge		
12	interpersonal_ comm		
13	cc_thinking		
14	analytical		
15	prob_solving		
16	positive_value		
17	teamwork		
18	job_status	{permanent, contract, temp, self_ employed, family_business}	Job status of employed graduates
19	job_sector	{local_private_company, multinational_ company, own_company, government, NGO, GLC, statutory_body, others}	Job sector of employed graduates
20	reason_not_ working	{job_hunting, waiting_for_ posting, further_study, participating_skills_ program, waiting_posting_of_study, unsuitable_job, resting, others, family_ responsibilities, medical_ issues, not_ interested_to_work, not_going_to_work, lack_of_confidence, chambering}	Reason for not working for unemployed graduates

3.2 Classification Task

The classification task at hand is to predict the employment status (employed, unemployed, others) for graduate profiles in the Tracer Study. The task is performed in two stages, training and testing. Once the classifier is constructed, testing data set is used to estimate the predictive accuracy of the classifier. To avoid overfitting, we employed hold-out validation method with 70-30 percentage split, whereby 70% out of the 12,830 instances is used for training while the remaining instances are used for testing.

Various algorithms from both Bayes and decision tree families are used in predicting the accuracy of the employment status. All the classifiers were constructed using the Waikato Environment for Knowledge Analysis (WEKA), an open-source data mining tool [10].

Bayes Methods. In Bayes methods, the classification task consists of classifying a class variable, given a set of attribute variables. It is a type of statistical in which the prior distribution is estimated from the data before any new data are observed, hence every parameter is assigned with a prior probability distribution [11]. A Bayesian classifier learns from the samples over both class and attribute variables.

The naïve Bayesian classifier works as follows: Let D be a training set of tuples and their associated class labels. As usual, each tuple is represented by an n-dimensional attribute vector, $X = (x_1, x_2, ..., x_n)$, depicting n measurements made on the tuple from n attributes, respectively, $A_1, A_2, ... , A_n$.

Suppose that there are m classes, $C_1, C_2, ..., C_m$. Given a tuple, X, the classifier will predict that X belongs to the class having the highest posterior probability, conditioned on X. That is, the naïve Bayesian classifier predicts that tuple X belongs to the class C_i if and only if

$$P(C_i|X) > P(C_j|X) \text{ for } 1 \leq j \leq m; j \neq i$$

Thus, we maximize $P(C_i|X)$. The class C_i for which $P(C_i|X)$ is maximized is called the maximum posteriori hypothesis. Under the Bayes method in WEKA, we performed the experiment with five algorithms, which are AODE, Bayes Network, HNB, Naïve Bayesian, and Naïve Bayesian Simple. AODE, HNB and Naïve Bayesian was also used in [9] and the rest algorithms were chosen to further compare the results from the Bayes algorithm experiment using the same data set.

Tree Methods. Tree-based methods classify instances by sorting the instances down the tree from the root to some leaf node, which provides the classification of a particular instance. Each node in the tree specifies a test of some attribute of the instance and each branch descending from that node corresponds to one of the possible values for this attribute [12]. Figure 1 shows the model produced by decision trees, which is represented in the form of tree structure.

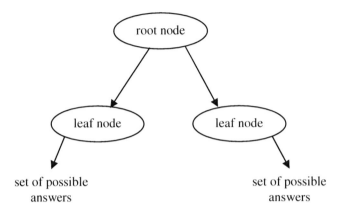

Fig. 1. In a tree structure, each node denotes a test on an attribute value, each branch represents an outcome of the test, and tree leaves represent classes or class distributions. A leaf node indicates the class of the examples. The instances are classified by sorting them down the tree from the root node to some leaf node.

Under the tree method in WEKA, we performed the classification experiment with five algorithms, which are ID3, J48, REPTree, J48graft, and RandomTree. J48 and REPTree was also used in [9], but we did not managed to use NBTree and BFTree because the experiment worked on large amount of data sets, thus incompatible with the memory allocation in WEKA. In addition, we employed ID3, J48graft and RandomTree to experiment with other alternative algorithms in decision tree.

4   Results and Discussion

We segregated the experimental results into three parts. The first is the result from ranking attributes in the Tracer Study data set using the Information Gain. The second and third parts presents the predictive accuracy results by various algorithms from the Bayes method and decision tree families, respectively.

4.1   Information Gain

In this study, we employed Information Gain to rank the attributes in determining the target values as well as to reduce the size of prediction. Decision tree algorithms adopt a mutual-information criterion to choose the particular attribute to branch on that gain the most information. This is inherently a simple preference bias that explicitly searches for a simple hypothesis. Ranking attributes also increases the speed and accuracy in making prediction.

Based on the attribute selection using the Information Gain, the job sector attribute was found the most important factor in discriminating the graduate profiles to predict the graduate's employment status. This is shown in Figure 2.

```
=== Attribute Selection on all input data ===

Search Method:
        Attribute ranking.

Attribute Evaluator (supervised, Class (nominal): 21 employment_status):
        Information Gain Ranking Filter

Ranked attributes:
 0.773246   19 job_sector
 0.773206   18 job_status
 0.711698   20 reason_not_working
 0.032441    5 field
 0.027959    3 state
 0.02775     2 age
 0.007128   10 Other_lang
 0.005547    6 cgpa
 0.003567    9 Eng_lang
 0.002275    1 sex
 0.001378    8 Malay_lang
 0.000813    7 general_ITskills
 0.000563   11 interpersonal_comm
 0.000513   17 gen_knowledge
 0.000493   12 cc_thinking
 0.000376   14 analytical
 0.000287   13 prob_solving
 0.000191    4 univ
 0.000144   16 positive_value
 0.000117   15 teamwork
```

Fig. 2. Job sector is ranked the highest by attribute selection based on Information Gain. This is largely because the attribute has small set of values, thus one instance is easily distinguishable than the remaining instances.

4.2 Bayes Methods

Table 2 shows the classification accuracies for various algorithms under Bayes method. In addition, the table provides comparative results for the kappa statistics, mean absolute error, root mean squared error, relative absolute error, and root relative squared error from the total of 3,840 testing instances.

Table 2. Classification accuracy using various algorithms under Bayes method in WEKA

Algorithm	Accuracy (%)	Error Rate (%)	Kappa Statistics	Mean Absolute Error	Root Mean Squared Error	Relative Absolute Error (%)	Root Relative Squared Error (%)
AODE	91.1	8.9	0.827	0.069	0.208	19.5	49.6
Naïve Bayesian	90.9	9.1	0.825	0.072	0.214	20.5	51.3
Naïve Bayes simple	90.9	9.1	0.825	0.072	0.214	20.5	51.3
BayesNet	90.9	9.1	0.824	0.072	0.215	20.5	51.4
HNB	90.3	9.7	0.816	0.091	0.214	25.7	51.1

The AODE algorithm achieved the highest accuracy percentage as compared to other algorithms. Basically, AODE achieved high accuracy by averaging all of smaller searching-space in alternative naive Bayes-like models that have weaker and hence less detrimental independence assumptions than naive Bayes. The resulting algorithm is computationally efficient while delivering highly accurate classification on many learning tasks.

4.3   Tree Methods

Table 3 shows the classification accuracies for various algorithms under tree method. In addition, the table provides comparative results for the kappa statistics, mean absolute error, root mean squared error, relative absolute error, and root relative squared error from the total of 3,840 testing instances.

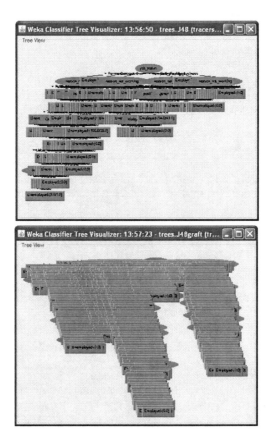

Fig. 3. The top figure is the tree structure for J48 and the bottom figure is the tree structure for grafted J48. Grafting adds nodes to the decision trees to increase the predictive accuracy. In the grafted J48, new branches are added in the place of a single leaf or graft within leaves.

Table 3. Classification accuracy using various algorithms under Tree method in WEKA

Algorithm	Accuracy (%)	Error Rate (%)	Kappa Statistics	Mean Absolute Error	Root Mean Squared Error	Relative Absolute Error (%)	Root Relative Squared Error (%)
J48Graft	92.3	7.7	0.849	0.078	0.204	22.1	48.7
J48	92.2	7.8	0.848	0.078	0.204	22.2	48.8
REPTree	91.0	9.0	0.825	0.080	0.213	22.8	50.9
RandomTree	88.9	11.1	0.787	0.081	0.269	23.0	64.4
ID3	86.7	13.3	0.795	0.072	0.268	21.1	65.2

The J48Graft algorithm achieved the highest accuracy percentage as compared to other algorithms. J48Graft generates a grafted C4.5 decision tree, whether pruned or unprunned. Grafting is an inductive process that adds nodes to the inferred decision tree. Unlike pruning that uses only information as the tree grows, grafting uses non-local information to provide better predictive accuracy. Figure 3 shows the different tree structure in a J48 tree as well as the grafted J48 tree.

Comparing the performance of both Bayes and tree-based methods, the J48Graft algorithm achieved the highest accuracy of 92.3% using the Tracer Study data set. The second highest accuracy is also under Tree method, which is J48 algorithm with an accuracy of 92.2%. Bayes method only falls to number three using AODE algorithm with prediction accuracy of 91.1%.

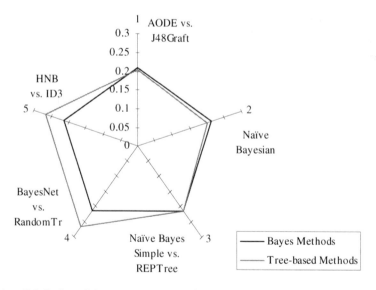

Fig. 4. A radial display of the root mean squared error across all algorithms under both Bayes and tree-based methods relative to accuracy. The smaller the mean squared error, the better is the forecast. Based on this figure, three out of five tree-based algorithms indicate better forecast as compared to the corresponding algorithms under the Bayes methods.

Nonetheless, we found that both classification approaches were complementary because the Bayes methods provide better view of association or dependencies among the attributes while the results from the tree method are easier to interpret. Figure 4 shows the mapping of root mean squared error values that resulted from the classification experiment. This knowledge could be used in getting insights on the employment trend of graduates from local higher institutions.

5 Conclusion and Future Works

As the education sector blooms every year, graduates are facing stiff competitions to ensure their employability in the industry. The sole purpose of the Tracer Study system is to aid the higher educational institutions in preparing their graduates with sufficient skills to enter the job market. This paper focussed on indentifying attributes that influenced graduates' employability based on actual data from the graduates themselves after six month of graduation. Nonetheless, assembling the data set was difficult because only 90% of the attributes made their way to the classification task. This is due to confidentiality and sensitivity issues, hence the remaining 10% of the attributes are not permitted by the data owner.

This paper attempts to predict whether a graduate has been employed, remains unemployed or in an undetermined situation within the first six months after their graduation. The prediction has been performed through a series of classification experiments using various algorithms under Bayes and decision methods to classify a graduate profile as employed, unemployed or others. Results showed that J48, a variant of decision-tree algorithm yielded the highest accuracy, which is 92.3% as compared to the average of 90.8% across other Bayes algorithms.

As for future work, we are hoping to expand the data set from the Tracer Study with more attributes and to annotate the attributes with information like correlation factor between the current employer and the previous employer. We are also looking at integration data set from different sources of data, for instance graduate profiles from the alumni organization in the respective educational institutions. Having this, next we plan to introduce clustering as part of pre-processing to cluster the attributes before attribute ranking is performed. Finally, other data mining techniques such as anomaly detection or classification-based association may be implemented in order to gain more knowledge on the graduates employability in Malaysia.

Acknowledgments. Special thanks to Prof. Dr. Md Yusof Abu Bakar and Puan Salwati Badaroddin from Ministry of Higher Education Malaysia (MOHE) for their help with data gathering as well as expert opinion.

References

1. Han, J., Kamber, M.: Data Mining: Concepts and Techniques. Morgan Kaufman, San Francisco (2006)
2. Shafie, L.A., Nayan, S.: Employability Awareness among Malaysian Undergraduates. International Journal of Business and Management 5(8), 119–123 (2010)

3. Mukhtar, M., Yahya, Y., Abdullah, S., Hamdan, A.R., Jailani, N., Abdullah, Z.: Employability and Service Science: Facing the Challenges via Curriculum Design and Restructuring. In: International Conference on Electrical Engineering and Informatics, pp. 357–361 (2009)

4. Zaharim, A., Omar, M.Z., Yusoff, Y.M., Muhamad, N., Mohamed, A., Mustapha, R.: Practical Framework of Employability Skills for Engineering Graduate in Malaysia. In: IEEE EDUCON Education Engineering 2010: The Future Of Global Learning Engineering Education, pp. 921–927 (2010)

5. Wook, M., Yahaya, Y.H., Wahab, N., Isa, M.R.M.: Predicting NDUM Student's Academic Performance using Data Mining Techniques. In: Second International Conference on Computer and Electrical Engineering, pp. 357–361 (2009)

6. Ogor, E.N.: Student Academic Performance Monitoring and Evaluation Using Data Mining Techniques. In: Fourth Congress of Electronics, Robotics and Automotive Mechanics, pp. 354–359 (2007)

7. Minaei-Bidgoli, B., Kashy, D.A., Kortemeyer, G., Punch, W.F.: Predicting Student Performance: An Application of Data Mining Methods with an Educational Web-based System. In: 33rd Frontiers in Education Conference, pp. 13–18 (2003)

8. Guruler, H., Istanbullu, A., Karahasan, M.: A New Student Performance Analysing System using Knowledge Discovery in Higher Educational Databases. Computers & Education 55(1), 247–254 (2010)

9. Affendey, L.S., Paris, I.H.M., Mustapha, N., Sulaiman, M.N., Muda, Z.: Ranking of Influencing Factors in Predicting Student Academic Performance. Information Technology Journal 9(4), 832–837 (2010)

10. Hall, M., Frank, E., Holmes, G., Pfahringer, B., Reutemann, P., Witten, I.H.: The WEKA Data Mining Software: An Update; SIGKDD Explorations 11(1) (2009)

11. Jaynes, E.T.: Probability Theory: The Logic of Science. Cambridge University Press, Cambridge (2003)

12. Mitchell, T.: Machine Learning. McGraw Hill, New York (1997)

Improving Network Performance by Enabling Explicit Congestion Notification (ECN) in SCTP Control Chunks

Hatim Mohamad Tahir[1], Abas Md Said[2], Mohammed J.M. Elhalabi[1],
Nurnasran Puteh[1], Azliza Othman[1], Nurzaid Muhd Zain[1], Zulkhairi Md Dahalin[1],
Muhammad Hafiz Ismail[1], Khuzairi Mohd Zaini[1], and Mohd Zabidin Hussin[1]

[1] College of Arts and Sciences
FTM Building
University Utara Malaysia
06010 UUM Sintok, Kedah, Malaysia
{hatim,nasran,zabidin}@uum.edu.my
[2] Universitiy Teknologi Pertronas,
Bandar Seri Iskandar, 31750 Tronoh, Perak, Malaysia
abass@petronas.com.my

Abstract. The need for a reliable transmission protocol that can cover the Transport Control Protocol (TCP) and User Datagram Protocol (UDP) has prompted the Internet Engineering Task Force (IETF) to define a new protocol called the Stream Control Transmission Protocol (SCTP). This paper proposes adding Explicit Congestion Notification (ECN) mechanism into SCTP chunks (INIT chunk, and INIT-ACK chunk) to reduce the delay of transferring important data during congestion as compared with the TCP and UDP protocols. This paper also discusses the details of adding ECN, and the reason for choosing Random Early Detection (RED). Through the experimental analysis, we compare SCTP enabled ECN in INIT-ACK chunk to SCTP without ECN enabled in INIT-ACK chunk and demonstrate the result of ECN impact on SCTP delay time.

Keywords: Network performance, TCP, UDP, SCTP, ECN.

1 Introduction

In the OSI model, the first two protocols (TCP and UDP) are the most employed protocols for data transfer where they have served the internet well for many years, but do not ideally satisfy all application needs. Therefore, the birth of a new protocol Stream Control Transmission Protocol (SCTP) came to significantly cover that lack left behind by TCP and UDP. SCTP is defined by the Internet Engineering Task Force (IETF) to provide a reliable, full-duplex connection and control network congestion mechanism as similar as TCP. SCTP also offers new delivery options that are particularly desirable in multimedia applications and telephony signaling. The SCTP connection provides novel services such as multi-homing and multi-streaming that allow the end points of a single association to have multiple IP addresses and allow independent delivery among data streams.

V. Snasel, J. Platos, and E. El-Qawasmeh (Eds.): ICDIPC 2011, Part I, CCIS 188, pp. 288–297, 2011.

SCTP is a connection-oriented protocol, where before starting to send and receive data, it must first establish a connection through four-way handshaking between end hosts. The four-way handshake consists of four chunks which are INIT chunk, INIT-ACK chunk, COOKIE-ECHO chunk, and COOKIE-ACK chunk. In comparison with TCP, there are just two packets in TCP for connection setup phase which are TCP SYN and TCP SYN-ACK packets [8,12]. In addition, this four-way handshake makes SCTP resistant to malicious attacks and thus improves overall protocol security.

However, these control packets and chunks in TCP and SCTP both may drop in the case of congestion. The loss of any of these chunks leads to significant increase in Delay Time (DT). Recently, the research done by [11] proposed the enablement of the Explicit Congestion Notification (ECN) in TCP SYN-ACK packets to prevent this packet from being dropped, in the aim to improve delay time. The results showed that by enabling ECN in TCP SYN-ACK packet, it can dramatically reduce the delay time. In this work, we attempt to improve delay time by enabling the ECN in the SCTP chunks. Specifically, our objective is to propose the usage of ECN in the INIT and INIT-ACK chunks in the SCTP header.

The structure of the paper is as follows. In Section 2, we explain the background concept for this work. In Section 3, we discuss some related works. In Section 4, we give description about our methodology. In Section 5, we present the experimental results. In Section 6, we conclude with a summary of our work..

2   Related Work

2.1   Transmission Control Protocol (TCP)

TCP is a connection-oriented protocol. It creates a virtual connection between two TCPs to send data. In addition, TCP uses flow and error control mechanisms at the transport level. TCP offers multiple services to the process at the application layer such as process-to-process communication, Stream Delivery Services, Sending and Receiving Buffers, Segmentation, Full-Duplex Communication, Connection-Oriented Service, Reliable Service [9]. In the TCP connection setup, the TCP sender must send the TCP SYN packet, and the receiver must reply with TCP SYN-ACK packet. When the sender receives TCP SYN-ACK packet, the negotiation part is finished and the data transmission is ready to begin as shown in the figure 1[7].

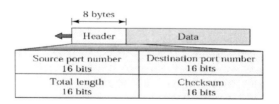

Fig. 1. TCP segment format [7]

2.2 User Datagram Protocol (UDP)

The User Datagram Protocol (UDP) is called a connectionless, unreliable transport protocol as it does not make a connection setup or negotiation part between end hosts and does not add anything to the services of IP except to provide process-to-process communication instead of host-to-host communication. UDP is used in the application that does not need the TCP reliability such as Network File System (NFS), Simple Network Management Protocol (SNMP), Domain Name System (DNS) and Trivial File Transfer Protocol (TFTP). UDP packet format consists of source and destination ports, length, and checksum field as shown in figure 2.

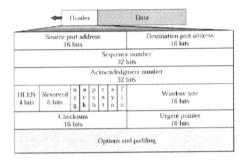

Fig. 2. User datagram format [7]

Source and destination ports contain the16-bit UDP protocol port numbers used to de-multiplex datagram for receiving application-layer processes. A length field specifies the length of the UDP header and data. Checksum provides an (optional) integrity check on the UDP header and data.

2.3 Stream Control Transmission Protocol (SCTP)

SCTP is a connection-oriented protocol that exists at the same level to the TCP and UDP to provide all the TCP and UDP features in addition to cover all the limitations by TCP and UDP [1,10].
     SCTP offers many other features such as:

- Multi-homing support.
- Through sending data in multiple streams, delay time will decreased.
- Using data fragmentation to discover and conform to the Maximum Transmission Unit (MTU) size.
- Although data delivery is done by sending the data in multiple streams but the streams of messages are delivered in sequence.
- SCTP provides a bundling option to the user messages into SCTP packets.
- Protection against SYN flood attack.

The SCTP is designed to overcome the lack of both TCP and UDP where it uses the four-way handshake to resist DoS attack and defines packet format that contains

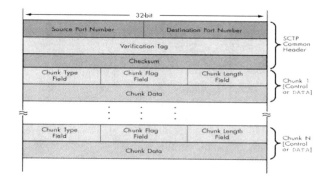

Fig. 3. SCTP Packet format [9]

additional header such as cookie and verification tag to avoid SYN flooding. In addition to using a progress congestion control algorithm (refer to figure 3). SCTP is also a connection oriented protocol that ensures data delivery to the end hosts [1].

2.4 UDP, TCP, and SCTP Comparisons

SCTP takes the benefit of the two other protocols (UDP, TCP) to offer novel services such as multi-homing, that allows each end point to have multiple IP addresses, and multi-streaming, that allows independent delivery among data streams. SCTP also has its own four-way handshake to establish an association, which makes it resistant to attacks and thus improves overall protocol security [9].

2.4.1 Multi-homing
One of the most critical problems in TCP is the path failure as a result of congestion during connection phase or data transmission which leads to head-of-line blocking (HOL). SCTP overcome this problem by providing uninterrupted service during resource failure by using multiple IP addresses, which is called multi-homing. A multi-homed SCTP sender still can send its data through the other IP addresses in case if one of its IP addresses fails due to interface, link failure or congestion. The multi-homed SCTP receiver still can receives data through the other IP addresses. In contrast to SCTP, TCP does not support the multi-homing where it uses a single IP address at each end point.

2.4.2 Multi-streaming
In a single SCTP association, SCTP can send more than one stream in each association using different IP addresses. Each single association is unidirectional and needs to negotiate application requested streams during association setup that exist for the life of the association [9].

Table 1 below summaries the comparison between TCP, UDP and SCTP.

Table 1. TCP, UDP and SCTP comparisons

STCP	TCP	UDP
Reliable	Reliable	Unreliable
Connection-oriented	Connection-oriented	Connectionless
Segment retransmission and Flow control through windowing	Segment retransmission and Flow control through windowing	No windowing or retransmission
Acknowledge segments	Acknowledge segments	No Acknowledge segments
Mult-ihoming	No Multi-homing	No Multi-homing
Multi-streaming	No Multi-streaming	No Multi-streaming

2.5 Congestion Control in SCTP

The SCTP congestion control combines the same TCP mechanism with extensions to be compatible with multi-homing and the modification for the message transfer rather than stream of bytes transfer. The sliding window control was specified with a modified version of TCP slow-start, congestion avoidance, fast retransmit and recovery mechanisms. Due to the similarity in congestion control mechanisms between TCP and SCTP, many works [6,8,9,10] were done on SCTP congestion control in order to combine some of TCP control mechanism into SCTP control mechanism such as congestion window validation where it is also incorporated with SCTP. Another optional mechanism for TCP incorporated with SCTP is the use of Selective Acknowledgments (SACKs). Like TCP, SCTP supports ECN mechanism as an optional feature as a congestion notification [1,10].

2.6 Active Queue Management (AQM)

AQM is the most important technique in Packet-Switched Networks which obtains high throughput with low average delay. In addition to using the Random Early Detection (RED) algorithm that drops packets randomly toward maintaining the average queue size in between of lower threshold (minthreshold) and upper threshold (maxthreshold). The use of RED is more useful than using Drop-Tail (DT), where it provides an equal dropping probability to all packets that are in the flow. Even if it is possible to avoid the DT mechanism, there are many applications that are still sensitive to delay time. Therefore, the need to use the ECN mechanism is required in both routers and end points (hosts) [10].

RED is one of the popular algorithm used by AQM for congestion avoidance to tell the sender about congestion before a queue gets full. RED tries to avoid congestion by dropping packets randomly before congestion take place. These dropped packets must be in the RED Zone when it is dropped. RED Zone is an interval of minthreshold (min th) and maxthresold (max th) over the queue length [9]. Average Queue Length (AvgQlen) is a weighted moving average and it is used as a marker that moves over the queue length when RED zone activates prognostic actions. It is calculated as follows:

$$AvgQlen = (i\text{-}wq)AvgQlen\text{-}i + w q \; Qlen\ldots\ldots\ldots \qquad (1)$$

where:

wq is the weight factor = 0.002 ....[2,3,4].

The basic RED flow are as follows:

```
If (avg.qlen < min th)
Forward all incoming packets
If (avg.qlen > max th)
Drop all incoming packets.
Else
Mark the packet with a drop probability 'p drop'
If the packet is not dropped, forward the
packet.
```

Where P drop is a result of Bernoulli Trails and is calculated as follows:

$$P\ drop = P\ temp\ /\ (1\text{-}\ count) \times P\ temp \qquad (2)$$

and P temp is calculated as follows:

$$P\ temp = max\ p \times (AvgQlen - min\ th)\ /\ (max\ th - min\ th) \qquad (3)$$

RED algorithm is sufficient to use with ECN because RED algorithm marks the packets before queue size becomes full which in return will reduce delay time. In contrast to DT, the marking of the packets is done after the queue size is full which increase the delay time [5,6].

2.7   Explicit Congestion Notification (ECN)

ECN coupled with AQM will enforces RED to mark packets with ECN instead of dropping these packets as an indication of congestion [11]. In TCP/IP, ECN introduces new fields such as a Congestion Experienced bit (CE) CodePoint and ECN Capable Transport bit (ECT) that are defined in the IP Header, whereas ECN-Echo bit (ECE) is in TCP headers, and ECN nonce in SCTP chunk. As mentioned earlier, ECN mechanism used the negotiation part to look at the ability of using ECN mechanism at the end points. Here it is important for any senders that is identified to be ECN Capable to respond to the marked packets as an indication of congestion, and half its congestion window as a reaction to the instance congestion. ECN, unlike other notifications mechanisms, such as DECBit, does not wait until it receives second notifier. It reacts immediately when it receives the first marked packet [3].

A number of researchers [8,9] have done on ECN mechanism such as using ECN in TCP, IPv4 and IPv6. Recently, some researchers [9, 11] have considered using ECN in TCP SYN-ACK packet. There was a proposal of using this mechanism in TCP SYN-ACK packet waiting to be admitted [10]. One of the equivalent related research to this paper is the ECN impact on SCTP four-ways handshake which is the contribution of this paper. The recent works on ECN mechanism advice the use of ECN mechanism in TCP SYN-ACK packet and the future work is to enable ECN in

SCTP INIT-ACK chunk for the same purpose where in the both cases aims to improve the delay time [8, 10, 11]

3 Methodology

This section gives explanation on the adding of ECN into the SCTP control chunks as well as on the experiments that have been conducted.

3.1 ECN Mechanism on SCTP Control Chunks

The SCTP control has four chunks; SCTP INIT chunk, SCTP INIT-ACK chunk, COOKIE-ECHO chunk, and COOKIE-ACK chunk. These four chunks are also used to negotiate the connection between two end hosts. They are also exposed to be lost in many ways, either in the case of a full router buffer or in the path failure condition. The question to be asked is that what is the suitable place to deploy the ECN mechanism in? We have determined that the SCTP INT-ACK chunk is the suitable place of the SCTP control chunks after taking into account the following:

- SCTP provides an effective protection against malicious attacks through using the Cookie mechanism and despite the use of state resources that is used in the TCP, the use of ECN mechanism is not advisable in the SCTP INIT chunk because it will open to the attackers to find suitable way to infect the host victim.
- In the second chunk (SCTP INIT-ACK), the use of ECN mechanism will be more appropriate than the SCTP INIT chunk where there is no obstacle that can degrade the network performance. In addition, the implementation of ECN in SCTP INIT-ACK will increase the network performance especially in a short life term.
- Since the ECN mechanism was implemented in the second chunk (SCTP INIT-ACK), there is no need to look for other chunks, because they will be ECN-capable (since SCTP INIT-ACK has been enabled).

3.2 Experimental Topology and Parameters

The topology used for all experiments is shown in figure 4 which were simulated using ns-2 simulator and ran under Linux environment.

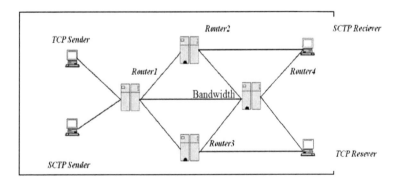

Fig. 4. Experiment Topology

The parameters' values setting for the simulation experiment topology are as follows:

  i.   The bottleneck bandwidth with the values of: 1Mbps and 2Mbps
  ii. The load on both of sender's links is 2Mbps.
  iii. The queue management at the router Router1 and Router2: RED will be used.

For each experiment, two similar simulation scenarios have to be run with the above defined set of values (Load) to get statistically valid results. The starting time of the SCTP associations will be fixed for each simulation run. The collected metrics will be as:

  i.   All the outcome packets from the sender (Ns).
  ii. All the received packets at the receiver (Nr).
  iii. The average rate of these packets.
  iv. The delay time for each of SCTP chunks (INIT, INIT-ACK, ECHOO-COOKIE and COOKIE-ACK).

3.3 Experimental Procedures

The following are the steps taken in the experiment scenarios:

  i.   TCP sender starts generating traffic load with 1Mbps to prepare a congested environment.
  ii. SCTP sender start to initiate association in TCP congested environment through sending the first initiate chunk.
  iii. Measuring the SCTP control chunks delay time without enabling ECN mechanism and the sent/received packets for the SCTP connection as well.
  iv. Enable the ECN mechanism in both of SCTP hosts and repeat step 2 and 3.

4 Experiment Results

The performance of SCTP in the experimental topology is tested for two scenarios as explained in previous section, and shown below in table 2 and 3. Varying terms are used in the result tables such as the number of the packets that sent from the SCTP sender to the SCTP sink (defined by Ns), the number of the real packets that received by the sink (Nr), and the average rate (Avg), which equals to Ns/Nr.

Table 2. SCTP performance without ECN mechanism

Trafic Load (Mbps)	Bottleneck Size (Mbps)	Ns	Nr	Average Rate
2	1	24000	1650	14.5
2	2	6000	1650	3.6

Table 3. SCTP performance with ECN mechanism enabled

Trafic Load (Mbps)	Bottleneck Size (Mbps)	Ns	Nr	Average Rate
2	1	24000	3200	7.5
2	2	6000	3960	1.5

The delay time of control chunks as shown in the following table 4:

Table 4. SCTP chunks delay time

Bit rate (Mbps)	Bottle neck size	INIT chunk Delay time (ms)	INIT-ACK chunk Delay time (ms)	COOKIE-ECHO chunk Delay time	COOKIE-ACK chunk Delay time
2	1	0.030	0.060	0.090	0.120
2	2	0.030	0.090	0.120	0.150

The difference of the delay time between the Chunks is (+ 0.030 ms). As shown in Table 1 and 2, ECN has an obvious impact on SCTP performance in case of congestion compared with SCTP performance without using ECN in the same conditions. The implementing of ECN mechanism in both INIT and INIT-ACK chunks can improve delay time by preventing these packets from being dropped.

5 Conclusion

This paper describes the reason of using the SCTP instead of the TCP. Moreover, the available benefits in applying ECN itself in SCTP (INI, INI-ACK) chunks clarifying the reason behind applying such a mechanism. The congestion control in the routers and the use of Random Early Detection (RED) as Active Queue Management (AQM) algorithm. The reason of choosing this algorithm in presences of other algorithms was also discussed. An explanation on how the Explicit Congestion Notification (ECN) could be added in both the SCTP/IP and to the (INI and INI-ACK) chunks headers was also discussed. The research contains the simulation part which proved that the implemention of ECN mechanism in both the INIT and INIT-ACK chunks can improve delay time by preventing these packets from being dropped.

Acknowledgments. We would like to express our gratitude to the Ministry of Science, Technology and Innovation (MOSTI), Government of Malaysia under e-Science Grant No. 01-01-07-SF0018.

References

1. Caro Jr., A.L., Iyengar, J.R., Amer, P.D., Heinz, G.J., Stewart, R.R.: Using SCTP multihoming for fault tolerance and load balancing. ACM SIGCOMM Computer Communication Review 32(3), 23–23 (2002)
2. Floyd, S., Jacobson, V.: Random Early Detection Gateways for Congestion Avoidance. IEEE/ACM Transaction on Networking 1(4) (1993)
3. Floyd, S.: Ramakrishnan.K.K.: A proposal to add Explicit Congestion Notification to IP. RFC 2481 (1999)
4. Floyd, S.: TCP and Explicit Congestion Notification. ACM Computer Communication review 24(5), 10–23 (1994)
5. Floyd, S., Ramakrishnan, K.K., Black, D.: The Addition of Explicit Congestion Notification (ECN) to IP. RFC 3168 (2001),
   http://www.iciri.org/floyd/REDparameters.txt
6. Floyd, S.: Adding Explicit Congestion Notification (ECN) Capability to TCP's SYN/ACK Packets. IETF Internet-Draft, draft-ietf-tsvwg-ecnsyn.text (2008)
7. Antonopoulos, N.: Network Technologies: The TCP/IP Protocol Suite, Department of Computing, University of Surrey (2006)
8. Pentikousis, K., Badr, H.: An Evaluation Of TCP With Explicit Congestion Notification. Annals of Telecommunications (2004)
9. Rajamani, R., Kumar, S., Gupta, N.: SCTP versus TCP: Comparing the performance of transport protocols for web traffic. University of Wisconsin-Madison (2002)
10. Stewart, R., Xie, Q.: Stream Control Transmission Protocol, SCTP (2002)
11. Stewart, R., Xie, Q., Morneault, K., Sharp, C., Schwarzbauer, H., Taylor, T., Rytina, I., Ramakrishnan, K.K., Floyd, S.A.: Proposal to add Explicit Congestion Notification (ECN) to IPv6 and to TCP. Internet draft draft-kksjf-ecn-00.txt (1997),
    http://www.icir.org/floyd/talks/sf-ecn-DCietf.pdf

Obtaining Knowledge in Cases with Incomplete Information

Sylvia Encheva

Stord/Haugesund University College, Bjørnsonsg. 45, 5528 Haugesund, Norway
sbe@hsh.no

Abstract. Providing students with timely feedback on their level of concepts understanding, learning and skills mastering is time consuming. One way to resolve this issue is to involve computer based assessment tools. When optional tests are considered educators have to address the problem of incomplete information.

The research described in this paper aims at facilitating the process of drawing conclusions while working with incomplete information. The approach is based on formal concept analysis and six valued logic. The Armstrong axioms are further applied to obtain knowledge in cases with incomplete information.

Keywords: formal concept analysis, incomplete information, logic.

1   Introduction

Computer based tools for knowledge evaluation are often designed to operate with complete information, see f.ex. [20], [21], and [22]. As a consequence of that missing information is treated as a negative response. Some models suggest ways to treat contradictory and incomplete information but the problem of extracting knowledge from incomplete information is not very well addressed. "Therefore it is useful to have tools around to obtain as much of 'certain' knowledge as possible in as many situations as possible. And in cases of incomplete knowledge it is desirable to be able to 'measure' what is missing", [2].

According to the principle of bounded rationality a decision-maker in a real-world situation will never have all information necessary for making an optimal decision.

In [2] authors suggest treatment of incomplete knowledge based on the theory of formal concept analysis, [6]. Involvement of the three valued Kleene's logic [5] is briefly mentioned. This three-valued logic has three truth values, truth, unknown and false, where unknown indicates a state of partial vagueness. These truth values represent the states of a world that does not change. The Kleene's logic might be useful if one operates with one source of information. If however information is provided by two sources one needs six truth values.

In this paper we present an approach to extract knowledge from incomplete data by applying the theory of formal concept analysis, six valued logic and Armstrong axioms.

V. Snasel, J. Platos, and E. El-Qawasmeh (Eds.): ICDIPC 2011, Part I, CCIS 188, pp. 298–308, 2011.

The rest of the paper is organized as follows. Related work and supporting theory may be found in Section 2. The model of the proposed system is presented in Section 3. The paper ends with a conclusion in Section 4.

2   Related Work

Intelligent systems usually reason quite successfully when they operate with well defined domains. If a domain is partially unknown a system has to extract and process new knowledge with adequate reasoning techniques. A methodology addressing the issues of automatically acquiring knowledge in complex domains called automatic case elicitation is presented in [13]. The method relies on real-time trial and error interaction.

Case-based reasoning solves new problems exploring solutions of similar past problems. In order to begin case-based reasoning needs a set of training examples. It then creates some general cases and a solution is finally presented based on a comparison between one of the obtained general cases and the current one.

Inspired by the Aristotle writing on propositions about the future - namely those about events that are not already predetermined, Lukasiewicz has devised a three-valued calculus whose third value, $\frac{1}{2}$, is attached to propositions referring to future contingencies [10]. The third truth value can be construed as 'intermediate' or 'neutral' or 'indeterminate' [14].

A three-valued logic, known as Kleene's logic is developed in [9] and has three truth values, truth, unknown and false, where unknown indicates a state of partial vagueness. These truth values represent the states of a world that does not change.

A brief overview of a six-valued logic, which is a generalized Kleene's logic, has been first presented in [11]. The six-valued logic was described in more detail in [8]. The six-valued logic distinguishes two types of unknown knowledge values - permanently or eternally unknown value and a value representing current lack of knowledge about a state [7].

Two kinds of negation, weak and strong negation are discussed in [17]. Weak negation or negation-as-failure refers to cases when it cannot be proved that a sentence is true. Strong negation or constructable falsity is used when the falsity of a sentence is directly established.

Let P be a non-empty ordered set. If $sup\{x,y\}$ and $inf\{x,y\}$ exist for all $x, y \in P$, then P is called a *lattice* [3]. In a lattice illustrating partial ordering of knowledge values, the logical conjunction is identified with the meet operation and the logical disjunction with the join operation.

The meaning of the elements true, false, unknown, unknown$_t$, unknown$_f$, contradiction is

- true - possible to prove the truth of the formula only
- false - possible to prove the falsity of the formula only
- unknown - not possible to prove the truth or the falsity of the formula
- unknown$_t$ - intermediate level of truth between unknown and true
- unknown$_f$ - intermediate level of truth between unknown and false
- contradiction - possible to prove both the truth and the falsity of the formula

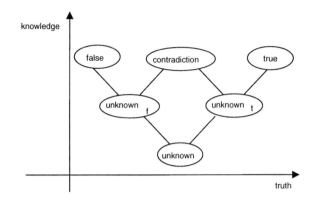

Fig. 1. Partial ordering of truth values

A lattice showing a partial ordering of the elements true, false, unknown, unknown$_t$, unknown$_f$, contradiction by degree of knowledge is presented in Fig. 1. The logical conjunction is identified with the meet operation and logical disjunction with the join operation.

A lattice showing a partial ordering of the elements true, false, unknown, unknown$_t$, unknown$_f$, contradiction by degree of truth is presented in Fig. 2. The logical conjunction is identified with the meet operation and logical disjunction with the join operation.

For describing six-valued logic we use notations as in [8]. Thus

- t denotes true - it is possible to prove the truth of the formula (but not its falsity)
- f denotes false - it is possible to prove the falsity of the formula (but not its truth)

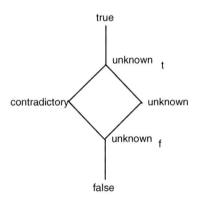

Fig. 2. Degree of truth

- $\bot$ denotes unknown - it is not possible to prove the truth or the falsity of the formula (there is not enough information)
- $\bot_t$ denotes unknown$_t$ - intermediate level of truth between $\bot$ and t
- $\bot_f$ denotes unknown$_f$ - intermediate level of truth between $\bot$ and f
- $\top$ denotes contradiction - it is possible to prove both the truth and the falsity of the formula

The six-valued logic distinguishes two types of unknown knowledge values - permanently or eternally unknown value and a value representing current lack of knowledge about a state [7]. The epistemic value of formula when it is known that the formula may take on the truth value t is denoted by $\bot_t$ and by $\bot_f$ when it is known that the formula may take on the truth value f.

Truth tables for the six-valued logic as shown in [7] and [8] are presented in Table 1, Table 2, and Table 3.

Table 1. Truth table for the connective '$\neg$' in six-valued logic

$\neg$	
t	f
f	t
$\top$	$\top$
$\bot_t$	$\bot_f$
$\bot_f$	$\bot_t$
$\bot$	$\bot$

Table 2. Truth table for the connective '$\wedge$' in six-valued logic

$\wedge$	t	f	$\top$	$\bot_t$	$\bot_f$	$\bot$
t	t	f	$\top$	$\bot_t$	$\bot_f$	$\bot$
f	f	f	f	f	f	f
$\top$	$\top$	f	$\top$	$\top$	$\bot_f$	$\bot_f$
$\bot_t$	$\bot_t$	f	$\top$	$\bot_t$	$\bot_f$	$\bot$
$\bot_f$	$\bot_f$	f	$\bot_f$	$\bot_f$	$\bot_f$	$\bot_f$
$\bot$	$\bot$	f	$\bot_f$	$\bot$	$\bot_f$	$\bot$

The '$\twoheadrightarrow$' implication shown in Table 4 is not an implication in the traditional sense since it does not satisfy *modus ponens* and the deduction theorem. These principals however hold for '$\twoheadrightarrow$' whenever the premises are not contradictory.

Armstrong axioms for arbitrary sets of attributes A, B, C and D to be applied:

If $\alpha \rightarrow \gamma$, then $\alpha \cup \beta \rightarrow \gamma$

If $\alpha \rightarrow \beta$ and $\beta \cup \gamma \rightarrow \delta$, then $\alpha \cup \gamma \rightarrow \delta$

The Armstrong axioms, [1] are sound in that they generate only functional dependencies in the closure of a set of functional dependencies (denoted as F^+) when applied to that set (denoted as F). They are also complete in that repeated application of these rules will generate all functional dependencies in the closure F^+, [19].

Table 3. Truth table for the connective '∨' in six-valued logic

∨	t	f	T	$\perp_t$	$\perp_f$	$\perp$
t	t	t	t	t	t	t
f	t	f	T	$\perp_t$	$\perp_f$	$\perp$
T	t	T	T	$\perp_t$	T	$\perp_t$
$\perp_t$	t	$\perp_t$	$\perp_t$	$\perp_t$	$\perp_t$	$\perp_t$
$\perp_f$	t	$\perp_f$	T	$\perp_t$	$\perp_f$	$\perp$
$\perp$	t	$\perp$	$\perp_t$	$\perp_t$	$\perp$	$\perp$

Table 4. The '→' implication

→	f	$\perp_f$	$\perp$	T	$\perp_t$	t
f	T	T	T	T	T	T
$\perp_f$	T	T	T	T	T	T
T	T	T	T	T	T	T
$\perp$	$\perp_f$	$\perp_f$	$\perp$	T	$\perp_t$	$\perp_t$
$\perp_t$	$\perp_f$	$\perp_f$	$\perp$	T	$\perp_t$	$\perp_t$
t	f	$\perp_f$	$\perp$	T	$\perp_t$	t

3   The Decision Process

The decision making process is based on students' responses to Web-based tests. A test consists of two questions requiring understanding of a single term (skill, rule, etc.) or several terms. A test considering a single term is denoted by a and b or c while a test considering two terms is denoted by ab and ac or bc respectively. Response options to a single question can be correct, incorrect or left unanswered.

Thus the possible outcomes of a test are:
tt - two correct responses
ff - two incorrect responses
uu - neither of the two questions is answered
tf - one correct and one incorrect response
tu - one correct response and the other question is left unanswered
fu - one incorrect response and the other question is left unanswered

Questions in a single test are not ordered since they are assumed to have similar level of significance.

Once students' responses are registered in a database we apply Armstrong axioms in order to extract maximal knowledge in the presence of incomplete information. Responses to tests concerning ab, ac, and bc before and after application of Armstrong axioms are presented in Table 6 and Table 8 in terms of six valued logic. The last columns in both tables illustrate a summary of these responses after

Table 5. Responses to optional tests with incomplete information

	a	b	c	ab	ac	bc
S1	tt	uu	tt	tt	tf	tt
S2	tu	tt	tf	uu	tt	tt
S3	tu	tu	tu	tt	uu	tt
S4	tf	tu	uu	tu	tt	tt
S5	tu	tf	tf	tf	tu	uu
S6	fu	tu	fu	tf	fu	ff
S7	ff	fu	tu	fu	fu	ff
S8	ff	uu	ff	ff	tu	ff
S9	fu	ff	tf	uu	ff	ff
S10	fu	fu	fu	ff	uu	ff
S11	fu	fu	uu	fu	ff	ff
S12	fu	tu	fu	fu	tf	tu

Table 6. Results for responses to optional tests in terms of six valued logic based on Table 5

	ab	ac	bc	$\wedge$
S1	t	$\top$	t	$\top$
S2	$\bot$	t	t	$\bot$
S3	t	$\bot$	t	$\bot$
S4	$\bot_t$	t	t	$\bot_t$
S5	$\top$	$\bot_t$	$\bot$	$\bot_f$
S6	$\top$	$\bot_f$	f	f
S7	$\top$	$\top$	f	f
S8	f	$\bot_t$	f	f
S9	$\bot$	f	f	f
S10	f	$\bot$	f	f
S11	$\bot_f$	f	f	f
S12	$\bot_f$	$\top$	$\bot_t$	$\bot_f$

$\wedge$ operation. Fig. 3 and Fig. 4 are knowledge lattices for six valued logic visualizing the truth values for objects $S1, ..., S12$ with respect to the tests ab, ac, bc.

The Armstrong axioms are applied to obtain new knowledge from incomplete information, Table 5. The results can be seen in Table 7.

Note that Table 7 shows cases where entrances with incomplete information like f. ex uu or fu are filled with precise data. The initial data from Table 5 related to $S5$ and $S12$ does not allow drawing of conclusions according to the Armstrong axioms. The initial data from Table 5 related to $S6$ and $S7$ is used to fill in missing responses to single questions and in the rest of the cases missing responses to single tests have been deduced. Bullets in Table 7 indicate entrances with decreased incomplete information.

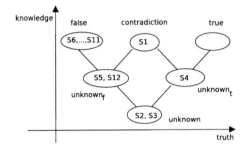

Fig. 3. Positioning of objects $S1, ..., S12$ in a knowledge lattice based on Table 6

Table 7. Results concerning responses to optional tests with decreased incomplete information

	a	b	c	ab	ac	bc
S1	tt	tt •	tt	tt	tf	tt
S2	tu	tt	tf	tt •	tt	tt
S3	tu	tu	tu	tt	tt •	tt
S4	tf	tu	tt •	tu	tt	tt
S5	tu	tf	tf	tf	tu	uu
S6	ff •	tu	uf	tf	fu	ff
S7	ff	fu	tu	ff •	fu	ff
S8	ff	ff •	ff	ff	tu	ff
S9	fu	ff	tf	ff •	ff	ff
S10	fu	fu	fu	ff	ff •	ff
S11	fu	fu	ff •	fu	ff	ff
S12	fu	tu	fu	fu	tf	tu

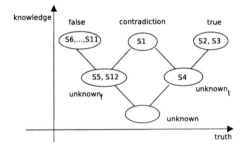

Fig. 4. Positioning of objects $S1, ..., S12$ knowledge lattice based on Table 8

The six valued logic is afterwords applied to interpret unprecise and contradictory information with respect to the values of ab, ac and bc, Table 8.

Table 8. Results for responses to optional tests in terms of six valued logic based on Table 7

	ab	ac	bc	$\wedge$
S1	t	$\top$	t	$\top$
S2	t	t	t	t
S3	t	t	t	t
S4	$\bot_t$	t	t	$\bot_t$
S5	$\top$	$\bot_t$	$\bot$	$\bot_f$
S6	$\top$	$\bot_f$	f	f
S7	$\top$	$\bot_f$	f	f
S8	f	$\bot_t$	f	f
S9	f	f	f	f
S10	f	f	f	f
S11	$\bot_f$	f	f	f
S12	$\bot_f$	$\top$	$\bot_t$	$\bot_f$

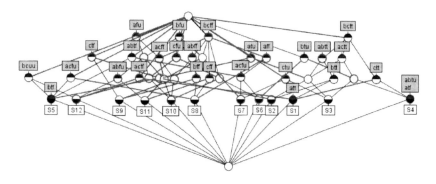

Fig. 5. Concept lattice based on Table 7

A comparison of Fig. 3 and Fig. 4 shows that after applying the Armstrong axioms and six valued logic for objects $S1, ..., S12$ and attributes ab, ac, bc, objects $S2$ and $S3$ obtain new truth values.

Data obtained from Table 7 is used to build a concept lattice, Fig. 5. Fig. 6 and Fig. 7 show paths between attribute bc taking truth values tt and ff respectively and all objects and attributes related to them.

Concept lattices provide detailed information about sets of objects sharing sets of attributes. Such information facilitates the process of finding evidence based explanations for certain happenings.

Fig. 6 shows that objects $S1, S2, S3$ and $S4$ share exactly one attribute with value tt, i.e. bc. Further more, objects $S1$ and $S2$ share attribute b with value tt, while objects $S1$ and $S4$ share attribute c with value tt, and attribute a with value tt is possessed only by object $S1$.

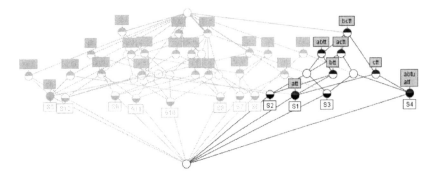

Fig. 6. Concept lattice based on Table 7 focussing on attribute bc with value tt

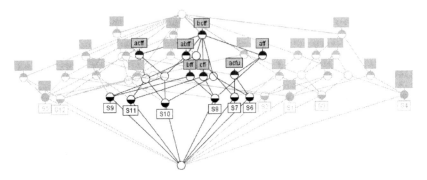

Fig. 7. Concept lattice based on Table 7 focussing on attribute bc with value ff

Fig. 7 shows that objects $S6, S7, S10$, and $S11$ share exactly one attribute with value ff, i.e. bc. Objects $S6, S7$, and $S8$ share attribute a with value ff, while objects $S6$ and $S7$ share attribute ac with value fu. Objects $S9, S10$ and $S11$ share attribute ac with value ff. Attributes b, c with value ff are shared by objects $S8$ and $S9$, and $S8$ and $S11$ respectively.

3.1 Accumulation of Responses

Data obtained from accumulation of responses received from other groups of students can be incorporated by f. ex. applying Yager's weights.

The problem of aggregating a set of numerical readings in order to obtain a mean value is addressed in [16].

If $x_1, x_2, ..., x_n$ is a set of readings then the aggregating process is denoted as

$$Agg(x_1, x_2, ..., x_n) = a$$

The weights must satisfy the following conditions

$$\sum_{j=1}^{n} w_{nj} = 1 \ \forall \ n \ \text{and} \ w_{nj} \geq 0 \ \forall \ n, j$$

For the case with n arguments

$$Agg(x_1, ..., x_n) = \sum_{j=1}^{n} w_{nj} x_n$$

The weights w_{nj} are uniquely determined by the formula

$$w_{ni} = w_{n1} \left(\frac{1}{w_{i,1}} - \frac{1}{w_{i-1,1}} \right), \ \ 2 \leq i \leq n$$

and the ratio

$$\frac{w_{n1}}{w_{n-1,1}}$$

between the first element in the current iteration and the first element in the previous iteration, [16].

4   Conclusion

The presented approach can be used for drawing conclusions based on incomplete data. Experience from working with optional tests taken by a group of learners can be used for providing hints and early diagnostic reports for forthcoming students.

References

1. Armstrong, W.W.: Dependency Structures of Data Base Relationships. IFIP Congress, 580–583 (1974)
2. Burmeister, P., Holzer, R.: On the Treatment of Incomplete Knowledge in Formal Concept Analysis. In: Ganter, B., Mineau, G.W. (eds.) ICCS 2000. LNCS, vol. 1867, pp. 385–398. Springer, Heidelberg (2000)
3. Davey, B.A., Priestley, H.A.: Introduction to Lattices and Order. Cambridge University Press, Cambridge (2005)
4. Dubois, D., Prade, H.: A Review of Fuzzy Sets Aggregation Connectives. Information Science 36, 85–121 (1985)
5. Fitting, M.: Kleene's Logic, Generalized. Journal of Logic and Computation 1(6), 797–810 (1991)
6. Ganter, B., Wille, R.: Formal Concept Analysis - Mathematical Foundations. Springer, Heidelberg (1999)
7. Garcia, O.N., Moussavi, M.: A Six-Valued Logic for Representing Incomplete Knowledge. In: Proceedings of the 20th International Symposium on Multiple-Valued Logic (ISMVL), pp. 110–114. IEEE Computer Society Press, Charlotte (1990)

8. Garca-Duque, J., Lpez-Nores, M., Pazos-Arias, J., Fernndez-Vilas, A., Daz-Redondo, R., Gil-Solla, A., Blanco-Fernndez, Y., Ramos-Cabrer, M.: A Six-valued Logic to Reason about Uncertainty and Inconsistency in Requirements Specifications. Journal of Logic and Computation 16(2), 227–255 (2006)

9. Kleene, S.: Introduction to Metamathematics. D. Van Nostrand Co., Inc., New York (1952)

10. Lukasiewicz, J.: On Three-Valued Logic. Ruch Filozoficzny, vol. 5 (1920); English translation in Borkowski, L. (ed.) (1970), Lukasiewicz, J.: Selected Works. North Holland, Amsterdam (1920)

11. Moussavi, M., Garcia, O.N.: A Six-Valued Logic and Its Application to Artificial Intelligence. In: Proceedings of the Fift Southeastern Logic Symposium (1989)

12. Polkowski, L., Skowron, A.: Rough Mereological Approach to Knowledge-based Distributed AI, Soeul, Korea, pp. 774–781 (February 5-9, 1996)

13. Powell, J.H., Hauff, M., Hastings, J.D.: Evaluating the effectiveness of exploration and accumulated experience in automatic case elicitation. In: Muñoz-Ávila, H., Ricci, F. (eds.) ICCBR 2005. LNCS (LNAI), vol. 3620, pp. 397–407. Springer, Heidelberg (2005)

14. Sim, K.M.: Bilattices and Reasoning in Artificial Intelligence: Concepts and Foundations. Artificial Intelligence Review 15(3), 219–240 (2001)

15. Yager, R.R.: OWA Aggregation over a Continuous Interval Argument with Applications to Decision Making. IEEE Transactions on Systems, Man, and Cybernetics, Part B, 34(5), 1952–1963 (2004)

16. Yager, R.R., Rybalov, A.: Noncommutative Self-identity Aggregation. Fuzzy Sets and Systems 85, 73–82 (1997)

17. Wagner, G.: Vivid Logic. LNCS (LNAI), vol. 764. Springer, Heidelberg (1994)

18. Wille, R.: Concept Lattices and Conceptual Knowledge Systems. Computers Math. Applications 23(6-9), 493–515 (1992)

19. http://en.wikipedia.org/wiki/Armstrongs_axioms

20. http://www.edtechsystems.com

21. http://www.exampro.co.uk/

22. http://www.softwareamerica.net

23. http://www.vantage.com

Complete Graphs and Orderings

Sylvia Encheva

Stord/Haugesund University College, Bjørnsonsg, 45, 5528 Haugesund, Norway
sbe@hsh.no

Abstract. Ranking of help functions with respect to their usefulness is in the main focus of this work. In this work a help function is regarded as useful to a student if the student has succeeded to solve a problem after using it. Methods from the theory of partial orderings are further applied facilitating an automated process of suggesting individualised advises on how to proceed in order to solve a particular problem. The decision making process is based on the common assumption that if given a choice between two alternatives, a person will choose one. Thus obtained partial orderings appeared to be all linear orders since each pair of alternatives is compared.

Keywords: Ordered sets, help functions, intelligent systems.

1 Introduction

Artificial intelligence techniques are widely used for facilitating a learning process tailored to a student's individual needs. Among the most successful computer-based instructional tools, seriously relying on such techniques, are intelligent tutoring systems.

An intelligent tutoring system is defined in [20] as a "computer system" based on "artificial intelligence" designed to deliver content and provide feedback to its user. In [21] an intelligent tutoring system is considered to be a software agent that provides customised and adaptable instructions and feedback to learners. The topic received a lot of attention from the research community since the 1980's. However it seems that the process of providing adequate help to users based on their individual responses is still open.

Usually the level of usefulness of a service is established by sending users questionnaires and summarising the obtained responses. Naturally new students lack in-depth understanding of the subject they study and cannot really judge to which extend a particular help function is facilitating the learning process. What they actually express is their overall likings of the tool. Among other factors that influence their responses are friends' opinions on the matter, student's degree of interest in that subject, honesty, i.e. are their responses anonymous or a sender can be tracked down and so on. Usability issues of a Web-based assessment system are discussed in [18].

This work is intended to facilitate automated provision of help functions via an intelligent tutoring system, applying mathematical methods from partially ordered sets. Our approach to evaluate help functions will avoid the influence of the above mentioned

V. Snasel, J. Platos, and E. El-Qawasmeh (Eds.): ICDIPC 2011, Part I, CCIS 188, pp. 309–319, 2011.

subjective factors since a help function in this work is regarded as useful to a student if the student has succeeded to solve a problem after using it.

The rest of the paper is organised as follows. Section 2 contains definitions of terms used later on. Section 3 is devoted to ordered sets. Section 4 explains how to rank help functions according to personal responses. Section 5 contains the conclusion of this work.

2   Background

A personalized intelligent computer assisted training system is presented in [15].

Ordering of knowledge spaces is discussed in [9]. A trend based prediction model for Web user behaviour without extra information is proposed in [11]. Applying many-valued logic in practical deductive processes related to knowledge assessment, evaluating propositions being neither true nor false when they are uttered, [10].

Learning management systems (LMS) facilitate sequencing of content and creation of a practical structure for teachers and students. While being very useful with respect to content delivery they appear to be insufficient for developing higher level thinking skills. LMS are educational software that among other things should track students' progress and provide tailored feedback. They however cannot make reasonable inferences and provide personalized assistance.

A serious step forward satisfying such requirements is the involvement of intelligent software agents. Generally speaking they are supposed to achieve particular goals in an autonomous fashion, taking responsibility for its own actions, the creation of its own plans, and the establishment of its own sub-goals.

The Cognitive Tutor, [5] is able to understand student knowledge and problem-solving strategies through the use of a cognitive model. A cognitive model represents the knowledge that an ideal student would possess about a particular subject.

Developing a cognitive tutor involves creating a cognitive model of student problem solving by writing production rules that characterize the variety of strategies and misconceptions students may acquire.

Cognitive Tutors have been successful in raising students' mathematical test scores in high school and middle-school classrooms, but their development has traditionally required considerable time and expertise, [6].

Learning styles describe the influence of cognitive factors where learning orientations describe the influence of emotions and intentions.

In [12] learning styles are defined as the "composite of characteristic cognitive, affective, and physiological factors that serve as relatively stable indicators of how a learner perceives, interacts with, and responds to the learning environment," while in [17] they are considered to be the "educational conditions under which a student is most likely to learn. Learnings styles theorists refer humans' tendency to perceive and process information differently depending on heredity, upbringing, and current environmental demands. In this respect individuals are often classified as being concrete, abstract, active or reflective.

Learning styles group common ways that people learn, [7]. The following seven learning styles are presented there:

Type	Description
- Visual (spatial)	prefer using pictures, images, and spatial understanding,
- Aural (auditory-musical)	prefer using sound and music,
- Verbal (linguistic)	prefer using words, both in speech and writing,
- Physical (kinesthetic)	prefer using your body, hands and sense of touch,
- Logical (mathematical)	prefer using logic, reasoning and systems,
- Social (interpersonal)	prefer to learn in groups or with other people,
- Solitary (intrapersonal)	prefer to work alone and use self-study.

The learning orientations model in [14] refers to four categories of learning orientations:

Type	Description
- Transforming learners	highly motivated, passionate, highly committed,
- Performing learners	self-motivated in learning situations that interest them,
- Conforming learners	short-term, detail, task-oriented,
- Resistant learners	lacking a fundamental belief that academic learning and achievement can help them achieve personal goals or initiate change.

Learning orientations describe an individual's disposition to approach, manage, and achieve learning intentionally and differently from others, [23]. The following factors having impact on intentional learning success and influence individual learning differences are listed:

Type	Description
- Conation/ Affective Learning Focus	refers to the individual's desire or striving to learn
- Learning Independence	considers focus and control
- Committed Strategic Planning and Learning Effort	refers to the degree that learners persist and commit deliberate, strategic effort to accomplish learning and achieve goals.

Student navigation in an automated tutoring system should prevent students from becoming overwhelmed with information and losing track of where they are going, while permitting them to make the most of the facilities the system offers, [8].

3 Sets

Two very interesting problems are considered in [3], namely the problem of determining a consensus from a group of orderings and the problem of making statistically significant statements about ordering.

Two elements a and b where $a \neq b$ and $a, b \in P$ are comparable if $a \leq b$ or $b \leq a$, and incomparable otherwise. If $\forall a, b$ where $a, b \in P$ are comparable, then P is a chain. If $\forall a, b$ where $a, b \in P$ are incomparable, then P is an antichain.

3.1 Orderings

A relation I is an *indifference* relation when given AIB neither $A > B$ nor $A < B$ has place in the componentwise ordering. A partial ordering whose indifference relation is transitive is called a *weak ordering*.

Let w_1, w_2, w_3 be weak orderings. Then w_2 is between w_1 and w_3 if each decision made by w_2 is made by either w_1 or w_3 and any decision made by both w_1 and w_3 is made by w_2, i.e. $w_1 \cap w_3 \subseteq w_2 \subseteq w_1 \cup w_3$.

The distance $d(w_1, w_3)$ is defined as $d(w_1, w_2) + d(w_2, w_3) = d(w_1, w_3)$. The distance is a metric in the usual sense, it is invariant under permutation of alternatives, and the minimum positive distance is 1. Further more if two weak orderings agree except for a set of alternatives which is an open interval in both, then the distance may be computed as if the alternatives in this set were the only objects being ranked.

3.2 Voting Paradox

If given two alternatives, a person is finally choosing only one. The natural extension to more than two elements is known as the 'majority rule' or the 'Condorcet Principle'.

A relation $R(L_1, L_2, ..., L_k)$ is constructed by saying that the pair $(a, b) \in R$ if (a, b) belong to the majority of relations L_i.

Next three linear orderings a b c, b c a and c a b

leading to $R = \{(a,b),(b,c),(c,a)\}$ (three-way tie), illustrate the 'paradox of voting'.

The probability of the voting paradox for weak orderings is calculated analytically for the three-voter-three-alternative case. It appears that the probability obtained this way is considerably smaller than in the corresponding case for linear orderings, [19].

Another interesting paradox is related to $m, m > 2$ persons and $n, n > 2$ alternatives, [13]. For each person a preference relation is transitive if a is preferred to b, b is preferred to c, and a is preferred to c. A voting pattern yielding an intransitive social ordering can be either of the form

1st person a b c
2nd person c a b
3rd person b c a

or

1st person a b c
2nd person b c a
3rd person c a b

Thus the majority of the involved people has the following preferences

a is preferred to b
b is preferred to c
a is preferred to c.

Note that transitivity along single criterion does not prevent occurrences of intransitive individual preferences.

3.3 Social Welfare Function

A 'social welfare function' maps k-tuples of the set of linear orderings of any $b \subset A$ to single linear orderings of B, where A is a set of at least three alternatives. In order to be reasonable, a 'social welfare function' should satisfy the following conditions: Axiom I - positive association of individual and social values, Axiom II - independence of irrelevant alternatives, Axiom III - citizen's sovereignty, and Axiom IV - nondictatorship. Note that there is no social welfare function satisfying Axioms I-IV.

A social welfare function acts on k-tuples representing either weak or linear orderings of k individuals for m alternatives. The representation of an individual's ordering can be thought of as a column vector in which an integer in position i represents the preference level the individual assigns to alternative i. Thus k individuals presented with m alternatives can illustrated by k-tuples of orderings in a $m \times k$ matrix A of integers of preference levels

Theorem 1 along with *Axioms 0-4*, [3] provide an existing social welfare function.

- *Axiom 0* - (Any state of information is possible) The domain of social welfare function consists of all matrices with negative integer entries.
- *Axiom 1* - (Pareto Optimality) If no individual prefers alternative i to alternative j and some individual prefers alternative j to alternative i, then j is preferred to i by the social welfare function.
- *Axiom 2* - (Symmetry) Permuting columns of a ranking matrix A does not change the value of the social welfare function.
- *Axiom 3* - (Translation invariance) Adding the same row vector C to row i and row j of A will not change the ordering of i and j by the social welfare function.
- *Axiom 4* - (independence of unavailable candidates once given a state of information) Deleting a row other than i or j from A will not change the ordering of i and j by the social welfare function.

Theorem 1. *There is a unique social welfare function satisfying Axioms 0-4. It is given by: i is preferred to j if and only if the sum of the row of A corresponding to j is larger than the the sum of the row of A corresponding to i, and otherwise the social ordering is indifferent between i and j.*

4 Main Results

Note that the set a, b, c is neither a chain no an antichain, i.e. a pair of different elements can be either comparable or incomparable. The graph of all partial orderings of a 3-element set is presented in Fig. 1.

Students are suggested to solve problems presented to them via an intelligent tutoring system. The system provides assistance in a form of help functions on a user request. Three types of help functions called a, b, and c respectively are available. They can contain f. ex. theoretical rules, hints and solutions of similar problems. All students' responses are saved in a database. The goal is to find out in which order help functions related to a particular problem should be presented to a new student and in which order help functions should be presented to a student who has been using the system when the student is requesting help with respect to a new problem.

The expressions an 'element a' and a 'function a' are used interchangeably in this content.

Based on students' responses content providers can follow the process of responses clustering and make appropriate adjustments in contents of a problem or the related help functions or both. This can be used to track down the effect of help functions on each student and thus provide better individualized assistance.

Example 1. Let a particular study unit exhibit these pattern of clustering (ab(c)) - 50%, (a(bc)) - 10%, and (c(ab)) - 20%, and the rest of the 20% are distributed to other orderings and are therefore not significant, when the significant factor is 10% or above.

With this distribution one can clearly conclude that help function 'a' has been helpful. Another interesting observation is that help function 'c' is helpful to 20% of the students. Since the distance from (ab(c)) or (a(bc)) to (c(ab)) is 4, we can safely conclude that there are two types of students with different knowledge background in relation to the learning process of this particular study unit. Such observations are very useful for future tuning of help functions.

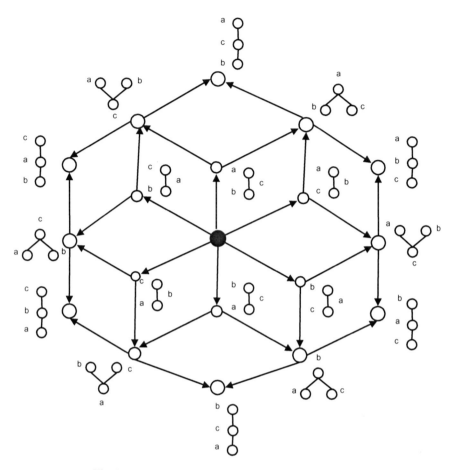

Fig. 1. The graph of all partial orderings of a 3-element set

When a pattern of clustering does not show any significant value but is evenly distributed amongst the twelve ordering pattern then one can conclude that none of the
help functions were helpful for the students study progress. The help functions need to
be redesigned.

Discussions on distances between two orderings are enclosed along with the rest
of the orderings on the path between the two discussed orderings, Subsection 4.1 and
Subsection 4.2.

4.1   Two of the Functions Are Considered to Be Equally Helpful

The observed distances between two orderings in a case two of the functions are considered to be equally helpful are either 2 or 4. Illustration details for the following three
cases:

Case 1 - The path between ordering (a(bc)) and ordering ((ac)b) is
$\{(a(bc)), (a(c(b))), ((ac)b)\}$ and the distance is 2, Fig. 2.

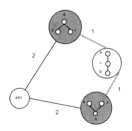

Fig. 2. The path between ordering (a(bc)) and ordering ((ac)b)

Case 2 - Flipping the structure results in all functions changing their levels of belonging. The path between ordering (a(bc)) and ordering ((ac)b) is $\{(ab(c)), abc, (c(ab))\}$ and the distance is 4, Fig. 3.

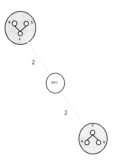

Fig. 3. The path between ordering (ab(c)) and ordering (c(ab))

Case 3 - Both orderings have the same structure. The path between ordering (a(bc)) and ordering ((ac)b) is $\{(ab(c)), (a(b(c))), (ab(c)), (b(a(c))), (c(ab))\}$ and the distance is 4, Fig. 4.

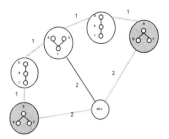

Fig. 4. The path between ordering (a(bc)) and ordering (b(ac))

4.2   All Functions Have Different Level of Helpfulness

The observed distances between two orderings where all functions are considered to have different levels of helpfulness. Illustration details follow.

Case 1 - Both orderings have the same structure. The path between ordering (a(c(b)))
and ordering (c(a(b))) is {(a(c(b))), (ac(b)), (c(a(b)))} and the distance is 2, Fig. 6.
   Case 2 - The path between ordering (a(c(b))) to ordering (c(b(a))) is
(a(c(b))), (ac(b)), (c(a(b))), (c(ab)), (c(b(a))) and the distance is 4, Fig. 5.

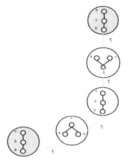

Fig. 5. The path between ordering (a(c(b))) and ordering (c(b(a)))

Fig. 6. The path between ordering (a(c(b))) and ordering (c(a(b)))

Case 3 - Both orderings have the same structure. The path between ordering (a(c(b)))
and ordering (b(c(a))) is
{(a(c(b))), (ac(b)), (c(a(b))), (c(ab)), (c(b(a))), (bc(a)), (b(c(a)))}, Fig. 7.

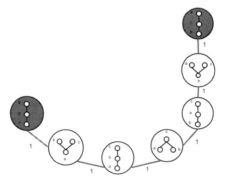

Fig. 7. The distance between ordering (a(c(b))) and ordering (b(c(a)))

5 Conclusion

The presented approach is a response to the increased demand for the necessity of developing effective learning tools that can be smoothly integrated in the educational process.

Further research is needed in order to find an appropriate approach to separate cases currently ranked as equally important. Methods based on rough sets ans grey theory are likely to be used.

References

1. Berg, S.: Condorcet's Jury Theorem and the Reliability of Majority Voting. Group Decision and Negotiation 5(3), 229–238 (1996)
2. Boboila, C., Iordache, G.V., Boboila, M.S.: An Online System for Testing and Evaluation. WSEAS Transactions on advances in Engineering Education 5(1), 20–28 (2008)
3. Bogart, K.P.: Some Social Sciences Applications of Ordered Sets. In: Rival, I. (ed.) Ordered Sets, pp. 759–787. Reidel, Dordrecht (1982)
4. Breuker, J.: Components of Problem Solving and Types of Problems. In: Steels, L., Van de Velde, W., Schreiber, G. (eds.) EKAW 1994. LNCS, vol. 867, pp. 118–136. Springer, Heidelberg (1994)
5. http://www.carnegielearning.com/web_docs/Whitepaper_Edweek.pdf
6. http://ctat.pact.cs.cmu.edu/
7. http://www.learning-styles-online.com/overview/
8. Encheva, S., Tumin, S.: Automated discovering of what is hindering the learning performance of a student. In: Zhou, X., Li, J., Shen, H.T., Kitsuregawa, M., Zhang, Y. (eds.) APWeb 2006. LNCS, vol. 3841, pp. 521–531. Springer, Heidelberg (2006)
9. Encheva, S., Tumin, S.: Ordering of Knowledge Spaces. WSEAS Transactions on Advances in Engineering Education 3(10), 895–900 (2006)
10. Encheva, S., Tumin, S.: Uncertainties in Knowledge Assessment. WSEAS Transactions on Advances in Engineering Education 5(4), 895–900 (2008)
11. Jan, N., Lin, S.-C., Lin, N.P., Chang, C.: A Trend-based Prediction System for Web User Behavior. WSEAS Transactions on Advances in Engineering Education 5 (2008)
12. Keefe, J.W.: Learning Style: An Overview. In: NASSP's Student Learning Styles: Diagnosing and Proscribing Programs, pp. 1–17. National Association of Secondary School Principles, Reston, VA (1979)
13. Klahr, D.A.: Computer Simulation of the Paradox of Voting. The American Political Science Review LX (2), 384–390 (1966)
14. Martinez, M.: Building Interactive Web Learning Environments to Match and Support Individual Learning Differences. Journal of Interactive Learning Research 11(2) (2001)
15. Pecheanu, E., Segal, C., Stefanescu, D.: Content Modelling in Intelligent Instructional Environment. LNCS (LNAI), vol. 3190, pp. 1229–1234. Springer, Heidelberg (2003)
16. Schworm, S., Renkl, A.: Learning by Solved Example Problems: Instructional Explanations Reduce Self-explanation Activity. In: Gray, W.D., Schunn, C.D. (eds.) Proceeding of the 24th Annual Conference of the Cognitive Science Society, pp. 816–821. Erlbaum, Mahwah (2002)
17. Stewart, K.L., Felicetti, L.A.: Learning Styles of Marketing Majors. Educational Research Quarterly 15(2), 15–23 (1992)
18. Yeum, Y., Lee, W.: Usability Issues of Web-Based Assessment System for K-12 and Implementation of PAS System. WSEAS Transactions on Advances in Engineering Education 9(4) (2007)

19. Van Deemen, A.: The Probability of the Paradox of Voting for Weak Preference Orderings. Social Choice and Welfare 16(2) (1999)
20. http://design.test.olt.ubc.ca/Intelligent_Tutoring_System
21. http://www.cs.ualberta.ca/zaiane/courses/cmput605/2008-3.html
22. http://www.engsc.ac.uk/journal/index.php/ee/article/view/62/97
23. http://www.trainingplace.com/source/research/learningorientations.htm

Communications in Computer and Information Science: Assumptions for Business and IT Alignment Achievement

Renáta Kunstová

University of Economics, Faculty of Informatics and Statistics,
Department of Information Technology
W. Churchill sq. 4, Prague 3, Czech Republic
kunstova@vse.cz

Abstract. A key factor for a successful organization, in a current dynamic environment, is effective information technology (IT) supporting business strategies and processes. Aligning IT with business depends on many factors, including the level of communication and cooperation between top management of organizations and top management of IT departments. This paper builds on the rules published in [5] which create prerequisites for the achievement of business and IT alignment. The paper discusses the outcomes of the survey realized in six hundred organizations operating on the Czech market. The survey aimed to determine whether the organization meets the basic assumptions, for it to be potentially mature in business/IT alignment, in order to select such organizations for future research into this matter. Characteristics of such organizations were deduced from the survey data. Survey results and analyses provide the base and direction for further business/IT alignment maturity research.

Keywords: Business/IT alignment, strategic alignment maturity model, strategic decision.

1 Introduction

The fact that information technology became a competitive advantage has been discussed for many years. At the beginning, only the existence of information systems, and information and communication technologies (IS/ICT, in short IT), in a company was a competitive advantage. Once IT had become ubiquitous, companies gained a competitive advantage from a portfolio of available applications and their unique functionality, followed by rapid implementation of applications that support decision making based on currently available information. In 2003 N. G. Carr published a controversial article "IT Doesn't Matter" [4]. This article provoked a lot of discussions [7, 17, 23]. Despite the contrary view that IT does not matter, reality shows that a competitive advantage was gained by those companies which proactively worked with business needs [6]. In recent times the alignment between business needs and IT capabilities is a main area of concern. It is evidenced by numerous articles [16, 19, 21] and surveys [5, 15, 25]. Alignment means that IT is in harmony with the business and conversely, or in other words, that IT investments generate business value.

V. Snasel, J. Platos, and E. El-Qawasmeh (Eds.): ICDIPC 2011, Part I, CCIS 188, pp. 320–332, 2011.
© Springer-Verlag Berlin Heidelberg 2011

Luftman described [11] an approach for assessing the maturity of business and IT alignment. His strategic alignment maturity model involves five levels of maturity. Each of the five levels is described in terms of six evaluation criteria (i.e. communications, competency/value measurement, governance, partnership, scope & architecture, skills). The model involves the following levels of maturity (basic characteristics of single levels are stated in parentheses):

- Initial/Ad Hoc Process (minimum communication between business and IT managers, IT metrics are not related to business and strategic planning is random, IT managers are not present in decision-making, no integration, no staff motivation),
- Committed Process (limited awareness about mutual understanding of business and IT, metrics are unlinked, planning is realized at the functional level, IT is emerging as an asset, early attempts at integration, innovation and changes are dependent on functional organization),
- Established Focused Process (regular meetings business and IT managers, business and IT metrics are typically financial and are linked, some inter-organizational planning is performed, IT is seen as an asset, enterprise standards are emerging, a need for change is recognized),
- Improved/Managed Process (knowledge sharing and mutual understanding of business and IT, IT metrics are focused on cost-effectiveness and business metrics are focused on customers, strategic planning is managed across the enterprise, IT is seen as a driver/enabler, enterprise standards and enterprise architecture are defined, management style is based on profit and is focused on changes and innovations),
- Optimized Process (communication between business and IT managers is ubiquitous, IT and business metrics are extended to external partners, IT strategic planning process is integrated with the strategic business process, risks and rewards are shared, business strategy is seen as a driver/enabler, management style is based on partnership).

This model was verified on 25 companies in November 2000 [11]. Over 80 % of the companies were at Level 2 maturity with some characteristics of Level 3 maturity. These results were a basis for anticipated follow-up surveys.

A European research [5], based on Luftman's strategic alignment maturity model, was performed by an international team of over 641 companies from seven countries in 2007. The goal of this research was to find rules of alignment, and to specify a guideline, that can help to understand how alignment can be achieved in practice. The team examined 18 IT management practices belonging to six evaluation criteria defined by Luftman. The results of the research indicated that business and IT alignment is a complex and a multidimensional matter. "A combination of 4 or 5 different processes or structures is needed for organizations to score high on the alignment capability variable. Furthermore, there is not one alignment competence that dominates the rules. Both rules are a combination of what Luftman calls partnership, communications, governance, architecture and value measurement competencies. This is an important result for practitioners. Investing in only one of these alignment competencies will not lead to better business/IT alignment. Our results clearly indicate that the combination of these different competencies makes for high alignment. [5] The research results were two rules inferred by the AntMiner+ algorithm from research data. These rules were represented by an if-then-else statement.

Final conclusions were not surprising but they confirmed results published in literature [8, 14, 21]: the most important prerequisites of a highly aligned organization are that business and IT planning and management processes are tightly connected and integrated, and that business has a good understanding of the impact of IT.

These prerequisites have become the basis of our hypotheses, reviewed in the survey, in the Czech business environment.

2   Concept and Survey Hypotheses

The team of the Department of Information Technology, at the University of Economics, deals with new principles and models for enterprise IT management. Our recent project on the enhancement of the Enterprise IT Management Model, which results were published in [1, 2, 3, 9, 10, 12, 13, 20] as well as other works in this area, e.g. best practices model ITIL v. 3, audit model CobiT, enterprise architecture framework [24], styles of IT Management [22], give numerous new insights into enterprise IT management. Now we are working on the proposal of the overall conceptual model, of corporate performance management, based on the results of the survey and current business requirements. We have identified several research issues in our current grant project, "Advanced Principles and Models for Enterprise ICT Management". One of them is: "How and under what conditions can IT help the enterprise to effectively react to adverse economic situations (e.g. present economic downturn)?"

Based on literature retrieval, and results of other surveys (as discussed above), we assume that the basic aspect of IT efficiency is business/IT alignment. As it is mentioned above, if the most important prerequisite of business/IT alignment organization is integrated business and IT planning, and business has to have a good understanding of the impact of IT, then business and IT managers must be close in strategic decision making. In this context we formulated the following hypotheses:

1. Hypothesis: IT strategy and its implementation are discussed in top management meetings.
2. Hypothesis: Business managers and IT managers participate in decision making about IT investments and about application architecture.

A confirmation of these hypotheses means that the prerequisites for achieving business/IT alignment are satisfied. In other words, if the organization operates in line with these hypotheses, it has the potential to be at some level of business/IT alignment maturity.

Within the survey, which will be described below, we investigated whether organizations operating on the Czech market meet assumptions for business/IT aligning. We investigated the probability of a confirmation of these hypotheses, and a relationship with external factors arising from the characteristics of the organization and the respondent.

The conceptual model of our investigation is shown in Fig. 1. Shortcuts H1 and H2 symbolize the hypotheses, shortcuts Q1 to Q4 symbolize the questions from the survey. Responses to question 4 are not directly related to the hypotheses, but may affect the responses to questions 1 – 3.

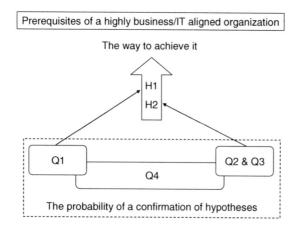

Fig. 1. The conceptual model of the survey objectives

3 Methodology

The analysis of how different enterprises respond to the current economic downturn, and the outcomes of their management decisions, can provide valuable information for research into the efficiency of various technological and sourcing solutions, and for the conditions under which they improve business performance.

Implementation of an extensive national survey was therefore the starting point of our new Enterprise IT Management Model. At the beginning of the survey realization we had to specify:

- form of data collection,
- professional company which will perform data collection,
- structure of interviewed organizations sample,
- questionnaire content.

In this paper the author only focuses on the very small part of the survey related to the above mentioned hypotheses.

3.1 Data Collection

We decided to realize data collection through a professional company. To this end, we contacted several companies. Based on incoming offers we chose the Czech company Ipsos Tambor, s.r.o. (http://www.ipsos.cz), which is a part of the Ipsos corporation (http://www.ipsos.com) – an independent company which has offices in 66 countries and ranks fifth among global research companies.

The Ipsos Tambor Company used the CATI (Computer–Assisted Telephone Interviewing) method for data collection in our survey. "Using CATI increases the accuracy and comparability of data, allowing complex questionnaires to be programmed, and, by linking CATI to dialers, enables significant increases in the speed and efficiency of data collected. The dialer technology also allows for the offering of full voice recording and remote monitoring of interviews." [18] All interviewers received the questionnaire with detailed instructions. The Ipsos Tambor

Company always ensures the highest quality of its interviewing through control mechanisms and practices. Interviews took place in October 2010.

3.2 Sample of Interviewed Organizations

The total number of surveyed organizations was limited by time and financial demands of data collection. The survey involved respondents, from 600 organizations, whose characteristics were very different.

Expected users, of our survey results, influenced our recommendations regarding the structure of surveyed organizations. Interviewed organizations were selected, by quota sampling, with the following criteria:

- the survey had to cover the following sizes of organizations based on the number of employees: 10 – 49, 50 – 249, 250 and more,
- the survey had to cover all industry sectors except organizations operating in the IT industry. Among industry sectors, in which the organization operates, should be preferred: banking and insurance, telecommunications, utilities, government and public services. These organizations, so-called highly dependent on IT, should be about a third of all surveyed organizations.

According to data published by the Czech Statistical Office, nearly 1,4 million organizations were registered in the Czech Republic in 2010, but 1,3 million organizations from this number are organizations that have only one to nine employees. For such small organizations, results of our work are not meaningful. Our sample could not therefore respect the structure of the statistical distribution of the respondents. So we modified structure of the sample, in anticipation of the use of outputs, and we have given preference to organizations with 50 – 249 employees.

We deliberately did not include organizations operating in the IT industry. These organizations could skew the results with respect to their own specific relationship of IT and IT as a business. We have preferred organizations from branches which business has a high dependency on IT.

3.3 Structure of the Questionnaire

The questionnaire had six sections. The author focuses on selected questions, from the first and second section, which are related to this paper.

The first section included questions designed to detect characteristics of examined organizations and their respondents: number of employees, organization's industry, establishment of the organization and respondent's job position.

The second section included questions to test hypotheses. As shown in Fig. 1, Q1 was related to H1, Q2 and Q3 were related to H2, and Q4 monitored the impact of the position of IT units in organizations.

1. Question: How often is IT strategy and its implementation discussed in top management of your organization?
2. Question: Who makes decisions about financial investments in IT in your organization?
3. Question: Who makes decisions about the application's architecture, i.e. which applications will be developed and purchased in your organization?
4. Question: IT unit reports to whom?

Respondents always marked one item from the list. Responses to the second and the third question were the same, responses to the first and fourth questions were diverse.

4 Analysis and Results

The survey was taken by respondents, from 600 organizations, operating on the Czech market. Respondents were first contacted, after their agreement to participate in the survey, they received a questionnaire and then answered questions in a controlled phone call.

We have received collected data in the form of a Microsoft Excel table. The analysis was performed using statistic functions of this software.

4.1 Characteristics of Organizations and of Respondents

Survey respondents represented organizations of three sizes. The size of organizations was measured by number of employees. Organizations with 250 and more employees represented 20 % of respondents (in absolute numbers it was 120 organizations), and mid-size organizations of 50 – 249 employees represented the largest group of respondents – 63 % (in absolute numbers it was 380 organizations). The remaining 17 % of respondents were from small organizations with 10 – 49 employees (in absolute numbers it was 100 organizations).

The survey involved representatives from all industry sectors except the IT industry (as justified above). Due to the fragmentation of organizations in different industry sectors, the numbers of organizations from various industry sectors were accumulated according to the dependence on IT. Numbers of respondents from different sectors, and their accumulation, are described in Table 1.

Table 1. Distribution of respondents by industry sectors

Industry Sector	Total	Dependence on IT	Total	Percentage
Banking, Insurance	23			
Telecommunication Services	24	High	204	34 %
Utilities	44			
Government and Public Services	113			
Retail Business	19			
Real Estate	32			
Accommodation and Catering	23	Medium	202	34 %
Wholesale Business	44			
Manufacturing	60			
Healthcare	24			
Transportation and Stocking	18			
Culture and Recreation	39			
Construction	45	Small	194	32 %
Education	43			
Mining Industry	3			
Agriculture, Forestry and Fishing	46			
Total	600		600	100 %

Original Czech organizations, without offices abroad, have high participation in the survey (81 %). 13 % of organizations were affiliates of multinational organizations, and the remaining 6 % were original Czech organizations now with offices abroad.

Results of the survey were also analyzed from the point of view of who answered the questionnaire, meaning, what job position the respondent has in the organization. Number of respondents according to their job positions is in Table 2.

Table 2. Number of respondents according to their job positions

Job Position of Respondents	Total	Percentage
Member of Top-Management (non IT)	232	39 %
Member of Mid-Level Management (non IT)	98	16 %
CIO	148	25 %
IT Specialist	122	20 %
Total	600	100 %

4.2   Analyses of Respondents Answers

In the second section respondents answered the above mentioned four questions. The following text will analyze the responses on single questions and their interaction.

IT strategy discussion. Respondents had the following list of answers on the question, "How often is IT strategy and its implementation discussed by top management of your organization?":

- At almost every meeting.
- Regularly according to the schedule, at least once a year.
- Sometimes - depending on the status of IT projects.
- Never.
- IT strategy is not established.

Four of five organizations have developed IT strategy, and discuss it at least once a year, or occasionally according to the status of IT projects, or in almost every meeting. (see Fig. 2).

An account of manager decisions, in IT strategy and IT projects, is important for achieving business/IT alignment (see e.g. [5]). More often the strategy is being discussed, so better alignment between IT and business can be expected. The survey showed that the larger organization, the greater the chance that the top management will also work with IT strategy.

Sixteen percent of surveyed organizations have not established IT strategy yet or do not work with it. More detailed analysis showed that more then half of them were small organizations. A connection with the industry sector does not come out. A probability, that the IT strategy is developed and is discussed (with varying regularity), is higher for organizations that have offices abroad or that are an affiliation of a multinational organization.

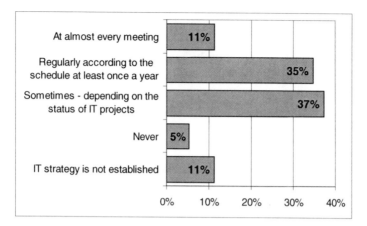

Fig. 2. The frequency of IT strategy discussing at the top management of an organization

IT investment decisions. At the question, "Who decides on financial investments in IT in your organization?", respondents had the following list of possible answers:

- CEO (chief executive officer) or top management of organization.
- CIO (chief information officer) or top management of IT department.
- Managers of business departments.
- Top management, in cooperation with the business management department concerned.
- IT management and business management department concerned.
- Different managers take decision in different situations.

Seventy five percent of respondents chose the first answer – CEO or top management of organization. The other 9 % of respondents answered that it is top management, in cooperation with the business management department concerned. The remaining 16 % of answers evenly split among other options.

The survey showed that the increasing number of employees reduces the probability that the CEO or top management make decisions on IT investments. In terms of who answered the question, different perceptions appeared among respondents who are members of top management, or who are heads of IT departments. CEO respondents more often answered, that they make decisions on IT investments, contrary to CIO respondents who more often answered that they make decisions about IT investments (see Fig. 3). Maybe it is a coincidence, but it is certainly appropriate to follow in future surveys, i.e. "what is the respondent's job position?".

According to respondents' answers, an absolute minimum of business managers is involved in decision making about IT investments. If the organization is not an affiliation of a multinational company, the probability that the CEO makes decisions about IT investments is doubled. For multinational organizations, much more decision making is moved from CEO to lower levels of management (see Fig. 4).

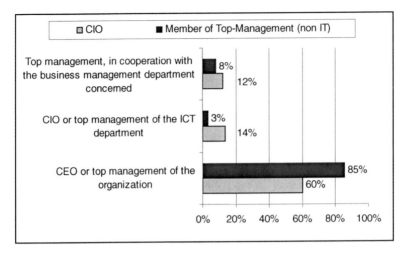

Fig. 3. Comparison of responses by respondents to the question "Who makes decisions about financial investments in IT in your organization?"

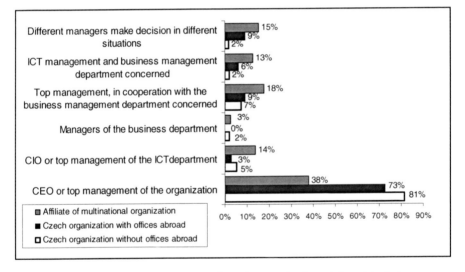

Fig. 4. Decision on IT investments from the organization origin point of view

Application architecture decision. On the third question, "Who decides on the application architecture, i.e. which applications will be developed and purchased in your organization?", respondents chose answers from the same list as with the previous questions. "CEO or top management of organization" was the most common answer again (with 55 %). But the survey showed that the proportion of CEOs decreases with an increasing number of employees, and on the contrary a proportion of CIOs, or top management of IT departments, increases.

The analysis, from the view of who answered the question, showed the following relations. Members of top management level assume that it is just them who decide.

Members of the middle-management level accept a greater share of CIO or IT top-managers. CIO more often state that the decisions on the application architecture are contributed by CIOs and IT management, rather than by the management of the organization.

Significant differences result from respondents' answers in relation to the dislocation of the organization. CEOs make decisions in 61 % of Czech Republic based organizations, while CIOs make decisions only in 14 % of organizations. CIOs have the largest share (27 %) in organizations that are part of multinational companies, CEOs make decisions in 20 % of these organizations.

Position of IT department in the organizational structure. Sixty two percent of respondents answered that their CIO reports to the CEO, and while 14 % of CIOs report into the CFO, 24 % of CIOs report to other senior executives. The smaller the number of employees, the more probability that the CIO reports to the CEO. If the IT department reports to some senior executives, then the larger the number of employees, the more CIOs report to the CFO than any other senior executives (see Fig. 5).

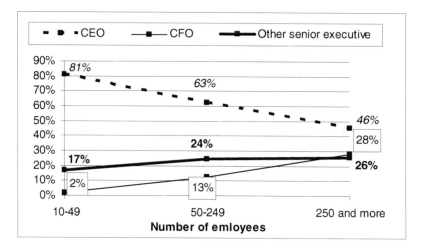

Fig. 5. The relationship between the subordination of the CIO and the size of the organization

Differences are apparent depending on the location of the organization. While in the Czech organizations, without offices abroad, CIOs report to the CEOs (67 %), and respondents from the affiliates of multinational organizations answered that their CIO reports to the CFO or to any other senior executives (60 %).

The survey confirmed the link between the position of the IT department, in the organizational structure, and decision making on IT investments. If a CIO reports to the CEO, then the CEO also makes decisions on IT investments. If a CIO reports to the CFO, or any other senior executives, then the proportion of CEO decision-making is decreasing, while the proportion of CIO and CEO in cooperation with middle-management is increasing.

5 Discussion

Regarding the complexity of the strategic alignment maturity model, we focused on the existence of two of the most important prerequisites of a highly aligned organization. These prerequisites have been published in [5]. On their basis we have formulated two hypotheses. The hypotheses were tested through an extensive survey realized among Czech organizations.

The first hypothesis that, "IT strategy and its implementation are discussed in top management meetings", was proved in 84 % of surveyed organizations. It means that some level of maturity in business/IT alignment can be expected in these organizations.

More detailed analysis, of the remaining 16 % of organizations, showed that more then half of them were small organizations with a number of employees up to 49. One hundred small organizations, which participated in our survey, were selected randomly and covered all industry sectors. A third of them do not work with the IT strategy at all. The probability that these organizations are at Level 1 business/IT alignment maturity is very high.

The second hypothesis that, "Business managers and IT managers participate in decision making about IT investments and about application architecture", was proved in 73 % of organizations.

The surveyed organizations, that are part of multinational organizations, differed significantly, from local organizations in the shift, from centralized decision-making of top management, to decision-making of cooperative business teams and IT top managers. This cooperation, between different management groups in IT decision making, shows that a certain level of business/IT alignment maturity can be expected in these organizations.

Organizations, which confirmed both hypotheses, create a group with a high probability that more than a Level 1 of business/IT alignment maturity is achieved there. Future surveys should focus specifically on this group of organizations.

In order to specify this group of organizations, we identified them, according to their answers, leading to hypotheses confirmation. We determined that answers to the research questions 1 - 3 are important for achieving business/IT alignment maturity. We selected organizations with following answers:

- IT strategy is developed and is discussed at top management meeting (with varying regularity),
- CEO and/or top management of organization (in cooperation with the business management department concerned) make decisions about IT investment,
- CIO and/or CEO and/or top management of organization (in cooperation with the business management department concerned) make decisions about application architecture.

In our survey 369 respondents (62 %) chose a combination of these answers. These organizations had the following characteristics:

- organization with 50 and more employees,
- organization without offices abroad or affiliates of multinational organizations,
- organization operating in any industry sector (i.e. dependence on IT disproved).

Although this study is not without limitations, the research provides sufficient data to show that organizations, with the combination of these characteristics, are well positioned to achieve maturity in business and IT alignment. From that follows the recommendation on how to compile a sample of organizations for future surveys focused on business/IT alignment.

Future surveys should be directed to provide conclusions, for business support and strategy, on how to achieve maturity in business/IT alignment which has a serious impact on business success and the financial efficiency of IT investment. Such surveys should focus on a clearly identified group of organizations, so that time and resources are best used.

This recommendation is only appropriate for organizations operating on the Czech market as the base survey is limited to this area.

6 Conclusion

This paper describes our investigation into whether organizations operating on the Czech market meet assumptions for business/IT aligning. The results of the survey show that the maturity level of business/IT aligning is rather low in Czech organizations, but we identified characteristics of organizations which can achieve higher maturity levels. Our future surveys should focus on this group of organizations, identified on the basis of found characteristics.

Determining what level of maturity the organization is at may be a good driver for future business/IT alignment strategy.

Acknowledgments. This paper was supported by the "Advanced Principles and Models for Enterprise ICT Management" grant, from the Czech Science Foundation, under the number P403/10/0092.

References

1. Basl, J., Gála, L.: The Role of ICT in Business Inovation. In: IDIMT 2009 System and Humans – A Complex Relationship, pp. 67–76. Trauner, Linz (2009)
2. Basl, J., Pour, J., Šimková, E.: The Survey of the Main Trends of the ERP Applications in the Czech Republic and their Business Effects. In: Research and Practical Issues of Enterprise Information Systems II, pp. 1311–1318. Springer, New York (2008)
3. Buchalcevová, A.: Research of the Use of Agile Methodologies in the Czech Republic. In: Barry, C., Conboy, K., Lang, M., Wojtkowski, W.G., Wojtkowski, W. (eds.) Information Systems Development - Challenges in Practice, Theory, and Education, vol. 1, pp. 51–64. Springer, New York (2009)
4. Carr, N.G.: IT Doesn't Matter. Harvard Business review 81(5), 41–49 (2003)
5. Cumps, B., et al.: Predicting Business/ICT Alignment with AntMiner+, KBI0708, Research paper. K.U. Leuven - Faculty of Economics and Applied Economics, Belgium (2007), https://lirias.kuleuven.be/handle/123456789/120533
6. EcomNets. Corporate IT Governant Process, http://www.ecomnets.com/ecomnets-innovations/it-governance.html
7. Gourvennec, Y.: IT Doesn't Matter or Does IT, Really?, http://www.visionarymarketing.com/articles/it-doesnt-matter.html

8. Kearns, G.S., Lederer, A.L.: The Effect of Strategic Alignment on the use of IS-Based Resources for Competitive Advantage. Journal of Strategic Information Systems 9(4), 265–293 (2000)
9. Kunstová, R.: Barriers and Benefits of Investments into Enterprise Content Management Systems. Organizacija 43(5), 205–213 (2010)
10. Kunstová, R.: Enterprise Content Management and Innovation. In: IDIMT 2010 Information Technology – Human Values, Innovation and Economy, pp. 49–56. Trauner, Linz (2010)
11. Luftman, J.: Assessing Business-IT Alignment Maturity. Communications of the Association for Information Systems 4, article 14, 1–50 (2000)
12. Maryška, M.: Model for Measuring and Analysing Costs in Business Informatics. In: The Eighth Wuhan International Conference on E-Business (CD-ROM), pp. 1–5. Alfred University Press, Sigillum (2009)
13. Novotný, O.: ICT Performance Reference Model in the Context of Corporate Performance Management. In: IDIMT 2009 System and Humans – A Complex Relationship, pp. 13–16. Trauner, Linz (2009)
14. Reich, B.H., Benbasat, I.: Factors that Influence the Social Dimension of Alignment between Business and Information Technology Objectives. MIS Quarterly 24(1), 81–113 (2000)
15. Sabherwal, R., Chain, Y.E.: Alignment Between Business and IS Strategies: A Study of Prospectors, Analyzers, and Defenders. Information Systems Research 12(1), 11–33 (2001)
16. Silvius, A.J.G.: Business and IT Alignment: What we Know and What we Don't Know. In: International Conference on Information Management and Engineering, Malaysia, pp. 558–563 (2009)
17. Smith, H., Fingar, P.: IT Doesn't Matter – Business Processes Do: A Critical Analysis of Nicholas Carr's I.T. Article in the Harvard Business Review, 128 (2003)
18. Telephone (CATI) Surveys. Corporate web sites, http://www.ipsos-mori.com/researchtechniques/datacollection/telephone.aspx
19. Ula, M.: Aligning IT with the Business (2010), http://www.i-data-recovery.com/it-governance/itil/aligning-it-with-the-business
20. Voříšek, J., et al.: Principles and Models of Enterprise IT Management, p. 446. Oeconomica, Prague (2008)
21. Voříšek, J., Feuerlicht, G.: The Impact of New Trends in the Delivery and Utilization of Enterprise ICT on Supplier and User Organizations. In: St. Amant, K. (ed.) IT Outsourcing: Concepts, Methodologies, Tools, and Application. Infromation Science Reference, pp. 2303–2316 (2009)
22. Weill, P., Ross, J.W.: IT Governance on One Page, Center for Information Systems Research, CISR WP No. 349 and Sloan WP No. 4516-04, pp. 1–15 (2004)
23. Wybolt, N.: Some Thoughts on IT Doesn't Matter, http://www.infoed.com/Open/PAPERS/SomeThoughtsonITDoesntMatter.pdf
24. Zachman, J.A.: A Framework for Information Systems Architecture. IBM Systems Journal 26(3), 276–292 (1987)
25. Zhu, X., Yan, Y.: Does IT Matter in China? Empirical Study on Information Technology, Organization Structure and Performance of Chinese Firms. In: International Conference on Information Management, Innovation Management and Industrial Engineering, vol. 2, pp. 395–398 (2009)

Measuring Students' Satisfaction in Blended Learning at the Arab Open University – Kuwait

Hassan Sharafuddin and Chekra Allani

Arab Open University-Kuwait
AlArdia, 92400, Kuwait
{sharafha,c.allani}@aou.edu.kw

Abstract. Blended learning is widely used in higher education institutions. The global prominence of this emerging trend is the result of the technological revolution that offered new possibilities of interactivity. The integration of e-learning as a complement rather than a substitute for traditional learning created the hybrid approach to learning called Blended learning. This paper attempts to measure the students' satisfaction they receive from their studies at The Arab Open University – Kuwait Branch within a blended system. Student satisfaction is reliant on factors such as the academic support provided by the tutors, teaching materials, teaching pedagogy, the range of the academic subjects taught, the IT infrastructure, the curriculum, e-library and the different assessment provided by the institution. The aim of this paper is three-fold: first, to measure student satisfaction by developing an appropriate questionnaire that covers most of the sources of satisfaction and dissatisfaction areas; second, to identify the constructs that are critical to a satisfying blended learning experience; and finally, to provide a feedback to the AOU officials on the effect of environmental factors to be used as a guide for further extension of regional branches in some other Arabic countries. To achieve these goals, a questionnaire was conducted containing fourteen items. Students responded from different programs and different courses ($n=165$).Data Analysis showed that AOU- Kuwait Branch enjoys a high rate of student satisfaction.

Keywords: e-learning, blended learning.

1 Introduction

The Arab Open University is Pan Arab Project with seven branches in different Arab countries. Its rapid growth is a hallmark of its success in creating new learning communities. The AOU is affiliated with the Open University, United Kingdom (UKOU) with four validated programs (Faculty of Language and Literature (FLL), Faculty of Business Studies (FBS), Faculty of Information Technology and Computing (FITC) and Faculty of Education (FED)). AOU Kuwait branch completed almost 9 years of operations with nearly 5000 thousands. It aims is to provide higher education for all citizens and expatriates. It created such a multicultural society that it encompassed 45 nationalities. AOU is planning to expand its branches to cover more countries, this expansion comes from the fact that open learning can improve the

V. Snasel, J. Platos, and E. El-Qawasmeh (Eds.): ICDIPC 2011, Part I, CCIS 188, pp. 333–341, 2011.
© Springer-Verlag Berlin Heidelberg 2011

quality of education. The increase in demand for open learning is expected to grow rapidly during the next five years and AOU is investing in more e-infrastructure to meet this ascending demand.

Gathering students' feedback is an important part for any university seeking expansion or to measuring program outcomes. Measuring blended programs outcomes can be efficiently and effectively done through the use of survey research. It is critical when conducting survey research that the instrument is more than a series of questions and that it measures what it is intended to measure. Therefore the *Student Satisfaction Survey* instrument was developed as a tool that could be used to evaluate student satisfaction.

The authors went through many surveys conducted in different educational systems and tailored a paper-based survey upon the most crucial elements of a blended educational system that enhance the students' learning experience. At the beginning of the spring semester 2011, the survey was passed over to colleagues from three different programs who handed the survey during their face-to-face meetings with their students. The initiative was taken based on the encouragement of the AOU Research and Development Department to conduct institutional research in an endeavor to promote quality in higher education.

2 Objectives

The following are the main objectives of the study:

1. To measure student satisfaction by developing an appropriate questionnaire that covers most of the sources of satisfaction and dissatisfaction areas and to suggest positive reforms accordingly.
2. To identify the constructs that are crucial to a satisfying blended learning experience.
3. To offer suitable recommendations and suggestions for the enhancement of effective teaching performance.
4. To provide a feedback to the AOU officials on the effect of environmental factors to be used as a guide for further extension of regional branches in other Arab countries.

3 Rationale

There are very limited studies that have been conducted to analyze the quality of academic programs submitted by AOU-Kuwait. One of these studies is Sharafuddin and Allani (2010). They have tried to analyze the strength and weaknesses of the blended learning provided by AOU-Kuwait using SWOT analysis, they reported that AOU strengths overweigh all as it provides equal opportunity of learning and proves that the system of learning at AOU-Kuwait is highly effective as it provides quality higher education by making use of the technology [1]. However, in spite of the highly controversial exposition of e-learning and the quality learning it provides, little effort has been devoted to learning outcomes and quality learning provided. Students' satisfaction is a crucial issue facing academic departments which stems from the AOU endeavor to ensure quality education by gauging the contentment of our students with the blended system and AOU services. It is this lacking evaluation that we propose to address in this study.

4 Blended Learning

The AOU – Kuwait branch is applying a blended learning system. This system is a mixing of multiple approaches to teaching. Though it has been called mixed, hybrid or blended, it essentially involves the application of e-learning techniques and tools along with face-to-face tutorials.

In spite of the controversial exposition on e-learning, the educational trend of the new millennium has a strong penchant towards a blended approach to learning. The convergence between the two platforms of e-learning with traditional learning has been expanding rapidly, due to its potential to ease the learning experience. (Allen et al, 2007) stated that among over 1000 American institutions of higher education, over half of them offered blended courses [2]. (Garrison & Vaughan, 2008) asserted that one should make use of the advantages of both systems to promote the learning outcomes. The enthusiasm and spontaneity of the traditional system can be balanced with the scheduling flexibility and interactivity of online forums [3]. Marc Rosenberg (Barbian 2002) argued: "The question is not if we should blend. Rather the question is what are the ingredients?" [4].

At the AOU, the blended system is tailored upon the nature of the course content, the goals of the course and the technology that has been constantly updated. Due to local accreditation requirements, the system was tailored to include face-to-face tutorials. This newly-created system is a blend of traditional and open learning whereby it is mandatory for AOU students to attend no less than 75% of tutorials and to sit Midterm and Final Exams [5]. AOU is a non-profit academic institution, and as its name connotes, it is open to all. It provides education to students regardless of their age, gender and nationality. 60% of Kuwait Branch students come from over 40 nationalities and 40% are Kuwaiti nationals. Their age is predominantly 20-24; with around 30% more mature students. As for the gender division, statistics show over 2/3 of the enrolled students are females [6]. As the figure shows, the total number of AOU students throughout the seven branches exceeded 30000 students in 2009 [7].

4.1 Analytical Tools

The study surveyed 165 AOU students from Kuwait Branch in the three major programs namely: Information Technology (IT), Business Studies (BS) and English Language and Literature (ELL). The survey is meant to gauge the students' satisfaction level about their learning experience at the AOU. As a result of the initial research activities, 9 areas were identified as the most possible sources of student satisfaction and dissatisfaction:

- *Quality of the courses offered.*
- *Open learning study experience.*
- *Good value for money.*
- *Academic support provided by tutors.*

- *Teaching materials.*
- *Learning outcomes.*
- *Teaching pedagogy in blended learning.*
- *E- library.*
- *Assessment.*
- *Use of the LMS.*

Respondents were asked to show their overall satisfaction with the above factors using five-point Likert's scale anchored by 1 (Strongly Disagree) and 5 (Strongly Agree) [8]. In order to analyze these factors in a Blended Education System, the writers have applied statistical tools such as Descriptive Statistics and percentages. Table 1 presents means and standard deviations of each measured facet of satisfaction. The survey was not passed extensively through the four levels of learning because freshman and sophomore may not have acquired the required experience that qualifies them to respond efficiently and adequately to the survey. Therefore, the data sample represents the more senior students who have become familiar with the blended learning system and who have been exposed to UKOU core courses. Response from students can provide important information about the level of improvement in higher education institutions and this can be accounted as an important role in university management. The following table shows the distribution of sample students.

4.2 Discussing the Findings

Table 1 shows that for most of the items related to the blended learning experience, an average score of over 3.5 is obtained, specifically with the quality of the courses, the new blended learning study experience, the good value for money and teaching materials. These results are similar to the findings reported by Donnelly, R. (2010) [9] and Alexander, S. (1999) [10]. This assessment did not take into consideration the GPA of the students who responded to this survey, we followed the findings of Marsh and Roche (1979) who suggest that students' evaluations of teaching are relatively unaffected by grading leniency [11].

Table 1. Frequency of Respondents' Answers to the Survey

Question	SA	A	N	D	SD	Mean	S.D.
Q1. Overall, I am satisfied with the quality of the courses offered at the AOU	35	90	29	11	0	3.90	0.81
Q2. Overall, I am satisfied with my new blended learning study experience	33	90	18	24	0	3.80	0.93
Q3. The courses provided good value for money (the fees are affordable and the quality of learning is good)	24	83	35	12	10	3.60	1.02

Table 1. (*Continued*)

	SA	A	N	D	SD	Mean	S.D.
Q4. I was satisfied with the academic support provided by my tutor/study advisor.	49	84	22	8	2	4.03	0.85
Q5. Overall, I was satisfied with the teaching materials provided.	34	91	26	14	0	3.88	0.83
Q6. The courses met their stated learning outcomes.	24	74	52	15	0	3.65	0.84
Q7. I got along well with the new teaching pedagogy in blended learning	20	78	49	16	2	3.60	0.84
Q8. I would recommend this university to other students.	20	78	49	16	2	3.73	1.26
Q9. The courses met my expectations	18	85	39	19	4	3.60	0.92
Q10. I enjoyed studying these courses.	53	71	25	12	4	3.95	0.99
Q11. The workload on my courses was higher than I expected.	42	53	35	29	6	3.60	1.15
Q12. Making use to the LMS helped me in my study experience.	55	58	27	17	8	3.82	1.15
Q13. The e-library was useful for the review of the literature in my research	16	33	29	42	45	2.60	1.33
Q14. The assessment is fair and justified.	22	63	43	33	4	3.4	1.03

SA= Strongly Agree,   A=Agree, N= Not Agree nor Disagree,   D=Disagree, SD=Strongly Disagree
S.D. = Standard Deviation

The following is a detailed analysis for the scales measured:

(1=Strongly Disagree, 2=Disagree, 3=Neutral, 4=Agree, 5=Strongly Agree)

1. Students were first asked to rate the overall courses offered at the AOU. As the Figure shows, 75% of the students agreed and strongly agreed upon their overall satisfaction with courses. The quality of the courses stems from the UKOU philosophy to develop and to update its courses from its on set in 1969 until the present. Obsolete courses have thus been supplanted by new ones that meet the requirements of a changing labour market.

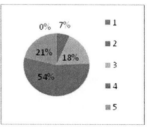

2. Though all of our students are the product of traditional brick and mortar schools, they integrated so dexterously into their new open learning study experience and are quite satisfied with it (75%) as the graph shows with a strong penchant towards agreement with their new experience. This is attributed to the blended nature of the system whereby students are closely guided by their tutors in their face-to-face meeting and remotely instructed through the LMS.

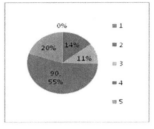

3. The AOU provides state-of-the art curriculum supported by cutting-edge technology. However, its fees are so affordable as they constitute nearly 20% of the charges of other local private universities. This pertains to the fact that the founder, HRH Prince Talal Bin Abdulaziz, established the AOU as a non-profit academic institution. The survey reflects the students' satisfaction and appreciation of the affordability of the fees and the rapid growth of AOU adherents is a further emblem of this satisfaction about good value for these subsidized fees.

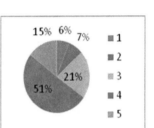

4. The result of the students' satisfaction with academic support provided by their tutors and advisers is the highest in the survey, with a mean being 4.03. Academic staff members realize the novelty of the system and therefore do not throw students in the middle of the ocean without life jackets and ask them to swim ashore. We rather lend a hand and put them on the rails through recurrent inductions and workshops tutorials and office hours and through discussions forums and communications tools embedded in the LMS.

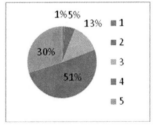

5. Through a partnership agreement with the UKOU, the AOU is entitled to use the UKOU teaching materials. ¾ of the students agree and strongly agree about the efficiency of the teaching materials. These consist of books, course guides and audiovisual aids. Indeed, they constitute one of the points of strength in the success of the AOU academic experience. The comprehensive, and at times challenging, features of these materials are eased by the academic support provided by the tutors.

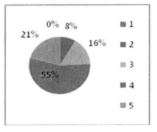

6. Tutors at the AOU do not act as the sage on the stage but rather as the guide on the side. The teaching pedagogy in blended learning relies on technology use in and beyond the class-room. In their new virtual environment, the presence of the tutor in synchronous learning provides an instant feedback to students while asynchronous communication allows a scope for developing thinking skills and organizing ones thoughts before posting them. At AOU- Kuwait, 60% of our students got along with this new pedagogy since it offers a relative flexibility that compromises between their personal, professional and academic life. Whereas 30% of the students do not seem to have fully adjusted to the new teaching pedagogy. They could have got used to be spoon fed and may need further instructions on the partial autonomy and the guided self study and the consequent self confidence it bestows upon the learner.

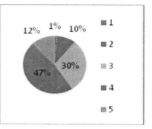

7. The only unsatisfactory factor this study found is that students do not appear to be as satisfied with the e-library facilities. The survey indicates that e-library was not useful for the review of the literature in research for about 50% of the students. Possible explanation exists for this finding that AOU is currently experimenting with different e-library providers and to share license for all AOU campuses rather than having a license for one campus. More focused investigation into this finding is needed to determine the reasons behind the delay of inauguration of e-library facility.

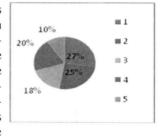

8. Students' evaluation is carried out through continuous assessment in the form of TMAs, Mid-term Assessment (MTA) and a final assessment. To ensure fairness and non-bias, anonymous and group marking are devised in final exams. The student is entitled to file a complaint to the Grievance Committee within 2 weeks of dispatching final exam results. Tutors provide comprehensive feedback to students in their continuous assessment. These are all monitored by the External Examiners assigned by the UKOU. As the graph shows, over 50% of the students strongly believe in the fairness of the assessment. A fourth takes the neutral side. The remaining 1/4th seem to be unsatisfied with the fairness of the

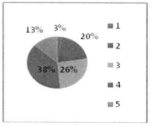

assessment. Tutors have recently been inducted to consecrate more time for written and verbal feedback to students who are lagging behind their studies.

9. LMS (Moodle) has proved to be an important tool between tutor and students. High percentage of students is satisfied with its components (68%). LMS supports students in many activities such as keeping track of grading, attendance, access to the latest information about the course, tutor advice and announcement, teaching material, course plan, power points, tutor's guides and manuals, forums, discussions, training modules in using software, feedback for individual papers, emails, etc. Above all, it is the main communication tool between teachers and learners at the AOU and it is subject to updating by our ICT officials.

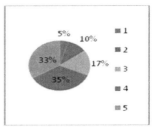

5 Conclusion

This paper concludes that most of students are satisfied with their new blended learning study experience and with the quality of the courses offered at the AOU. Academic support provided by tutors/advisors appears to be the highest factor generating a sizeable amount of satisfaction. The survey results support also the help of LMS in students' experience; this became a very important factor especially for those students involved at their official works. In addition, most respondents do appear to agree that the courses met their stated learning outcomes along with the new teaching pedagogy in blended learning (open – learning as well as face-to-face tutorials) to the extent that they are ready to recommend this university to other students.

We at the AOU believe that students are not mere by-passers who passively go through their academic experience. Their involvement into the managerial decision-taking that arise from recommendations of survey findings gives them a strong emotional bond with the AOU. Therefore, introducing this type of survey may have produced what is called a "Hawthorne Effect", whereby student satisfaction improves due to the survey itself.

In summary, this survey and its assessment technique provides a valid step to measure the student satisfaction across a range of factors and across a large number of students from different programs. In addition, programs are changing and post graduate programs are going to be implemented soon, and we feel that this survey will provide a solid base for faculty for further annual surveys and to express their ideas towards providing further improvement for graduate studies in blended learning system.

References

1. Sharafuddin, H., Allani, C.: The Efficiency of E-Learning System, Case study: Arab Open University-Kuwait. In: International Conference on Education and New Learning Technologies, EDULEARN 2010, Barcelona, Spain (July 5-7, 2010)
2. Allen, I.E., Seaman, J., Farrett, R.: Blending in: The extent and promise of blended education in the United States (2007),
   `http://www.sloan-c.org/publications/survey/`
   `pdf/Blending_In.pdf`
   (retrieved May 12, 2007)
3. Garrison, D.R., Vaughan, N.: Blended learning in higher education: Framework, principles and guidelines. Jossey-Bass, San Francisco (2008)
4. Barbian, J.: Blended Works: Here's Proof. Online Learning Magazine (July 2002),
   `http://www.onlinelearningmag.com/onlinelearning/magazine/`
   `article_display.jsp?vnu_content_id=1526767` (retrieved)
5. AOU- Student Handbook (2008)
6. ibid. p:4
7. `http://www.agfund.org/en/about/flagships/pages/thearabopenun`
   `iversity.aspx` (accessed April 11, 2011)
8. Hall, S.: How to use the Likert Scale in Statistical Analysis,
   `http://www.ehow.com/how_4855078_use-likert-scale-`
   `statistical-analysis.html` (accessed April 7, 2011)
9. Donnelly, R.: Harmonizing technology with interaction in blended problem-based learning. Computers & Education 54, 350–359 (2010)
10. Alexander, S.: An evaluation of innovative projects involving communication and information technology in higher education. Higher Education Research & Development 18(2), 173–183 (1999)
11. Marsh, H.W., Roche, L.A.: Making students' evaluations of teaching effectiveness effective: The critical issues of validity, bias, and utility. American Psychologist 52, 1187–1197 (1979)

Educational Technology Eroding National Borders

Khalid J. Siddiqui[1,2], Gurmukh Singh[1], and Turhan Tunali[2]

[1] SUNY Fredonia, Computer and Information Sciences,
Fredonia, NY, USA 14063
[2] Izmir University of Economics, Computer Engineering, Izmir, Turkey
{Siddiqui,Singh}@cs.fredonia.edu

Abstract. Businesses are continuously forced to reeducate and train their new workforce before they can be productive. The existing employees also need to improve their skills or retrain for promotion/growth. To cater to this breed of students "schooling business" is also faced with an inescapable demand to design new programs/courses. The growth in educational technology is also influencing academic institutions to redefine their endeavors in terms of producing learning while providing instructions. With the growing demand for higher education such endeavors are crossing the physical boundaries of many countries. We are using online and hybrid learning models to attract traditional, distance and international students. A major component of this model is the web-based course management system that provides an environment for teaching/learning and interaction 24/7. This model optimally combines interactive-classroom, web-based lectures and traditional instructions and has successfully offered courses at SUNY-Fredonia with students registering from around the globe. This model is presented and the opportunities and challenges of web technologies in education are discussed.

Keywords: Course Management System, Face-2-Face model, Higher education, Synchronous and Asynchronous learning.

1 Introduction

To be competitive and to maximize the productivity of their employees the businesses are continuously forced to reeducate and train or retrain their workforce before they can be integrated into normal business routine and become productive. This is particularly true of new starters and fresh graduates. Often existing employees are also required to take refresher courses to update their knowledge or to pursue higher education either for promotion or personal growth. In addition, many traditional students have to juggle between classes and work to get them through the school years. Thus with the changing times, both men and women are continuously forced to improve their academic and vocational know-how in order to gain economic stability and progress. These individuals often seek evening classes and frequently request universities to offer evening, continuing education or vocational programs at their own available times. To compromise between work and family responsibilities, these individuals need flexible and loosely structured ways of instruction and learning. With the introduction of web-based educational technology, we see software vendors and

V. Snasel, J. Platos, and E. El-Qawasmeh (Eds.): ICDIPC 2011, Part I, CCIS 188, pp. 342–355, 2011.

commercial organizations are also entering the education business. Their primary outlook is to profit, and we consider this may compromise the educational integrity. With these external pressures, the educators, in the real "schooling industry," are faced with continuous demand to redefine their endeavors in terms of producing learning and training rather than providing instruction alone.

Another demand on instructors, particularly in technology, engineering and science education, is to include additional topics in courses as industry and the scientific community frequently introduces newer material to their respective fields. This is particularly true for computer science, IT, engineering and other emerging sciences. Often existing courses are revised every calendar (academic) cycle and newer or more material is added into the same three credit hours courses or new courses are introduced without additional hours to the program. Due to the large number of topics in subjects like computer networking, software engineering, problem-solving, research-oriented courses [3], etc., it has become difficult to squeeze evolving new material into courses without overwhelming the students with information overload and keeping them focused during the lectures. As a result, classroom management has become more demanding. Also, given the large size of classes and continuously increasing workload of instructors, it is very difficult to closely monitor for cheating, plagiarism and use of other unfair means in homework and projects [24]. The instructors are faced with the challenge of assuring that students learn the key concepts, and that they are able to apply those concepts to practice and discovery when they enter the real world.

The recent information and technology explosion is also challenging the teaching process that has been the same for centuries [22]. Until recently, the only aspect that has changed over time is the way we store the information – writing on stones, leaves, leather, cloth, etc. was changed to using slates, blackboards, books and now the electronic media. In the traditional face-to-face (f2f) teaching, the learning process is often not emphasized. Web-based technology is fostering a shift from a teaching to a learning paradigm with outcomes that could be measurable. The online and blended (hybrid) model that we are suggesting provides a smooth transition between the two paradigms and in fact, complements the traditional face-to-face classroom as well [23].

The composition of the student body with increasing number of ethnically diverse, non-traditional and international students is changing the class dynamics. The structure of the classroom is also changing with time and the influence of educational technology is deepening in the instructional process. The technologies of social networking, videoconferencing, smart boards, clickers and web-based education have made their way into the classroom. These technologies along with course management systems have made it possible to offer classes in a virtual setting. Thus time, distance, location and physical presence (in the classroom) like restrictions are quickly disappearing. A student who cannot travel to the campus can take a course through videoconferencing (supplemented with social networking tools, e.g., YouTube, Chat, etc.) and the internet from any institution and location of their choice. Similarly, a student who cannot attend the class at the designated day and time can logon to the course site on the web and attend the lecture interactively through the posted lecture notes and online delivery and still able to interact with the instructor and classmates. These traditional courses are supplemented with an assortment of web technologies. There is no doubt, a growing interest in combining the evolving web technologies with the traditional classroom in order to make the learning process more interactive and effective without undermining the necessity for human touch.

There is also a need to comprehensively address the role of educational technology and globalization on higher education. Since 1995 with the introduction of Lotus-Notes [11] which was successfully used until summer of 2009 many new systems have emerged, e.g., WebCT, Angel, BlackBoard, Moodle, Sakai to name a few [5], [8]. At SUNY Fredonia (FSU) we have been using Angel for over four years for online offerings. We discuss the application of Angel educational technology in this paper. We developed hybrid learning model that integrates both the synchronous and asynchronous learning. We focus on these two approaches to make Computing Sciences education more effective without compromising the rigor and quality. First, we reviewed the evolving educational technologies in Section 2. Section 3 presents the asynchronous e-learning model and it is devoted to an effective design and creation of online course modules using Angel. The conventional synchronous instruction delivery model along with the techniques to enhance the learning in this setting is presented in Section 4. Section 5 presents the hybrid learning model and shows how instructors can take advantage of new web and multimedia technologies in offering distance-learning (online or e-learning) classes. In Section 6 we discuss our international collaboration and how it is eroding the national borders. We particularly elaborated the joint Dual Diploma programs that one of the authors established with many institutions in Turkey and elsewhere and it is bringing new meanings to higher education without borders. We discuss our experience in distance e-learning at FSU in Section 7and concluded the article.

2 Educational Technology

The 1950s led to two major designs pertaining to instruction: "programmed instruction" and "rewarding correct responses early and often," [28]. The "programmed instruction" focused on the formulation of behavioral objectives, breaking instructional content into small units and "rewarding correct responses early and often" focused on immediately recognizing the mastery of the subject achieved. Bloom [6] endorsed instructional techniques that varied both instruction and time according to learner requirements. These initial observations paved the way to "computer-based training (CBT)" and "computer-aided instruction (CAI) in the 1970s through 1990s." The focus of these early efforts was "e-contents" that basically forms the core of "e-learning."

These digital advances brought numerous changes to teaching and learning processes. Its impact is obvious on students learning and instructor's teaching and delivery of instruction. The World Wide Web, Wikipedia, WebEncyclopedia, etc. have become the reference library of the world with thousands of online publications, discussions and tutorials available round the clock and more added every day. The technologies of social networking, videoconferencing, podcasting and web-based education technology, for example, HTML and Javascript, etc., have made their way into the classroom. They facilitated the learning and improved the student performance by creating, using and managing appropriate technological processes and resources [16]. These technologies along with course management systems have made it possible to offer classes in a virtual setting. These advances led to the creation of course management software systems.

Today many course management software systems are available. The first one no doubt was the LotusNotes from IBM that remained dominant until 2008. It was mainly a text-based system and SUNY-SLN decided to consider other options. From the beginning of 2002 many new systems emerged [8]. Many more systems for example, Angel, Blackboard, WebCT, click-2-learn [5], [8], and more recently Moodle and Sakai have appeared with new promises [13], [19]. Using these course management software systems instructors create a course web-site and post lecture notes, course work, assemble links to external sources of information about the course and include any additional material that may be needed for the course. As the course progresses, more material and links are added. Students may be given assignments to explore these links and complete the assigned tasks from time to time. As an example, in introductory courses, the Abacus simulator [18] was explored and the students were asked to use Abacus simulator in performing arithmetic computations. Another example of online mathematics education is given in [1]. In courses with assembly language programming, Intel's programming manuals [12] could be downloaded and specific programming exercises could be designed around the manuals. In addition to classroom enhancement, other learning technologies also play a major role in the full-time distance learning and teaching. While most quality offers still rely on f2f engagement, e-learning is gaining both popularity and recognition.

From this point on we will focus mainly on Angel as this is the course management tool currently being used at SUNY Fredonia and most SUNY campuses in the New York state. It can be used to communicate with the students. It has facilitated the learning and improved the performance by creating, using and managing appropriate technological processes and resources. In section 3 we will show how it is being used for course development and delivery. With the help of new software systems in traditional classroom setting as well as in an online teaching/learning environment a classroom can be transformed into a 24/7 class benefitting both the student and instructor. We take advantage of these information resources on the web in our curriculum.

3   The Online Asynchronous Delivery Model

Since 1995 many SUNY campuses joined the newly formed SUNY Learning Network (SLN) – a SUNY wide course delivery and management environment that has been used to create on-line courses [29]. SUNY Fredonia joined the network in 1998 [25]. Until summer 2009 other course management tools used were Angel and CourseSpace [5]. To review an example of the use of World Wide Web in developing exercises for classroom, the reader is referred to the URL in [14].

Since summer 2009, the SLN and many SUNY campuses switched to Angel software package. Angel is an e-learning course management software system that has been extensively employed in many educational institutions across the USA [20]. This software is the product of an Indiana based software company [5]. Angel is a web-based teaching/learning management system which offers instructors to manage their course materials for f2f as well as online (asynchronous) teaching. It can serve two fundamental functions: (a) an instructor is able to use it in a traditional face-to-face setting as a supplemental tool for posting assignments, study guides, reference material, etc., and (b) it offers an effective online instruction delivery system, i.e., a web-site for full-time distance e-learning.

Angel allows an instructor to post documents, such as the course syllabus, announcements, student work/data files, slides embedded with audio-voice, video clips, etc. It can be used to administer student surveys, student evaluations, etc. In addition, one can establish links or hyperlinks to any external URLs (web addresses) that can be useful for the course. Another advantage of Angel is that it can be used as an assessment tool, which is useful for designing online and f2f quizzes/ examinations and course evaluations. This is due to the fact that once a student submits a quiz or examination, the instructor has an immediate access to the answers which can be graded and automatically tabulated using Angel grade-book along with their statistical analysis and even representation in graphical or tabular forms. An instructor can then transfer the grades manually or automatically to either the built-in grade-book or a spreadsheet if s/he is keeping records of grades in such a manner. An instructor can send and receive course e-mail through Angel e-mail facility. S/he can establish and monitor discussion/threaded discussion forum [17] and chat-room, receive and grade uploaded or posted take-home assignments using online drop-boxes, create group/ team for discussions or special projects and much more. The course "Calendar" can be used to post live office hours and assignment due dates as well as the date on which a given quiz and examinations will be held. Precisely, it is a wholesome package that provides most teaching and learning tools 24/7. In a recent investigation, it has been found that online learning continued to grow at a much higher pace in comparison to traditional f2f course enrollment [2]. Therefore, it is important to assess the new teaching/learning software systems and strategies to achieve productive and satisfying experience for the online learners.

3.1 Creation of Course Modules

For an effective online course design, it is important to use a modular structure. In general, these modules reside in Angel's "Lessons" nugget since most e-contents of the course sit in "Lessons" tab. We briefly discuss some of the major modules that we developed in "Lessons," which is normal for online courses at FSU [21].

The first component in "Lessons" nugget should be a "Course Map," which outlines the overall structure of the course and provides instructions for navigating through the course. Its component and structure are normally course dependent. For example, two course maps are presented in Fig. 1; one for the two week intersession course, which is taught during Christmas break and other for a summer session course, which ran for five weeks. The Course Map for a two-week course comprised of eight Modules in "Lessons" tab.

For a five-week summer course, the structure is modified to deliver the course in five weeks. The basic structure of Course Map remains the same, but the course material is distributed over five weeks. A screen-shot of Course Map for a five-week online summer course is shown in Fig. 2. Students were advised to explore these modules and to familiarize themselves with the course setup. At the end of the Course Map, an instructor may thank the students for registering in his/her course and may include acknowledgements, description of copyright laws, disciplinary rules, academic integrity policies, etc.

3.2 Welcome Message and Introduction of Class

This Module is contained in a folder and can be created using several options present in "Add Content" toolbox in Angel. Primarily, an instructor introduces himself/herself to the students, gives a brief overview of the course and elaborates on assessment, policies and scope of the course. Although there are multiple choices such as "Discussion Forum" we used a Blog. Here students were advised to post their profiles. Instructor may set some ground rules for students' open postings to the class to control substandard language and scripts. In addition instructor may establish some useful links to resource, e.g., department website, relevant course material, library, course tutorials on internet where students can practice or test their knowledge set, solve exercises concerning the course work, etc.

3.3 Angel Nuggets and Their Functions

Angel Graphical User Interface (GUI) provides eight major tabs or nuggets for e-contents development, delivery and management. Seven tabs which are commonly used are briefly described in the sections below.

3.3.1 "Lessons" Nugget

The most important tab is "Lessons," which may contain several folders, e.g., Course Map, Welcome Message from Instructor, Self Introduction and Some Useful Links, Student Data files (if any), Instructions: How to Submit Assignment, Course Flow: Week1, Week 2, Week 3, Week 4 and Week 5 folders, where each week's folders contains two modules, slides, lecture notes, assignment handouts, examinations/quizzes, assignment Drop-Boxes, etc.

3.3.2 Other Nuggets

Other useful nuggets Angel provides are: Course, Calendar, Communicate, Report, Resources and Manage. The first tab "Course," comprised of two windows called "Activity at a Glance" and "Course Announcements." "Activity at a Glance" provides a snapshot of student activities in the course with the statistics on: Logons, Mail Messages, Discussion Posts, and Submissions. All important course announcements are posted in the "Course Announcements" and they may also be posted in "Calendar." The second tab is "Calendar," which contains information of all important due dates of assignments and the dates on which an Examination or Quiz shall be held. Students shall be advised to visit the "Calendar" frequently.

The next tab is "Resources," which houses "Syllabus," link to "Wikipedia," "Google," "Online (resources)" and "Course Resources." The Communication Links has five options, using any one of them students can communicate with the instructor or fellow students. An instructor may advise a preferred mode of communication. In case students do not have an access to these preferred communication options, they may be allowed to use other communication links to interact with the instructor or classmates. The Links could be used to access university resources and some other pertinent information. The fifth tab is "Communicate," which has five choices: Mail, Roster, News and Events, Discussion Forums, and Communication Links. The next tab is "Report" nugget which provides access to several reports to help instructor monitor student progress. "Learning Profile" offers a unique opportunity to instructor to know learner's performance measures and statistics. The last tab "Manage" nugget composed of three windows: Course Management, Course Settings and Data Management. Course Management window has four links: Grade-book, Roster, Teams and Attendance. The most important link is Grade-book, which instructor is required to link with Assignments, Quizzes, Examination DropBoxes or the Assessment Editor in case an Examination/Quiz is created using the editor. Grade-Book will not show students the letter grades unless instructor has associated the grade scale with the letter grades. "Course Settings" window has five options: General Course Settings, Course Theme Selector, Tab Settings, Environment Variables and Mail Settings. The last window in Manage tab is called "Data Management," which has several database management options: Course Files Manager, Backup and Restore, Import and Export Consoles, Data Maintenance, Date Manager, Keyword Manager, Assessment Question Bank Manager, Survey Question Bank Manager, and Rubric Manager. These components may be used for course management.

3.4 Course Flow: Week 1 ... Week N

One way to structure a course is to organize the material in the form of weekly modules. For the first week of a summer course students are expected to go through a main Module called Week 1 which is further subdivided into two Sub-Modules: Module 1 and Module 2. Module 1 must start with a list of items or materials required for a given course. It may contain several folders including, 1) optional welcome message from instructor, 2) module map, and 3) the Course Syllabus. The subsequent weeks could follow the similar structure. Student should be required to read modules carefully as all course policies explained therein. Further, student can download Course Syllabus. In this manner students will be comfortable about the course. They would know the textbook to be used and amount of work involved along with the grading scale and course policies. It is important to provide advance information to the students about what is to be done once they open a given Module or sub Module. Sub Module 2 is composed of optional five items/links, 1) lecture notes, 2) handout for homework, 3) a Discussion Forum to discuss selected topics, 4) guidelines for creating or submitting a file of their work, 5) the DropBox where a homework file could be submitted.

Two Weeks Course	Five Weeks Course
1. Course Map	1. Course Map
2. Welcome Message from Your Instructor	2. Welcome Message from Your Instructor
3. Introduce Yourself & Useful Links	3. Introduce Yourself & Useful Links
4. An Introduction to ANGEL Nuggets	4. An Introduction to ANGEL Nuggets
5. Student Data files	5. Student Data files
6. How to Submit Your Assignment	6. How to Submit Your Assignment
- Week 1	- Week 1
Module 1	Module 1
Module 2	Module 2
...	- Week 2
Module 5	Module 1
- Week 2	Module 2
Module 1	...
Module 2	- Week 5
...	Module 1
Module 5	Module 2

Fig. 1. Course Map for a two week and a five weeks course

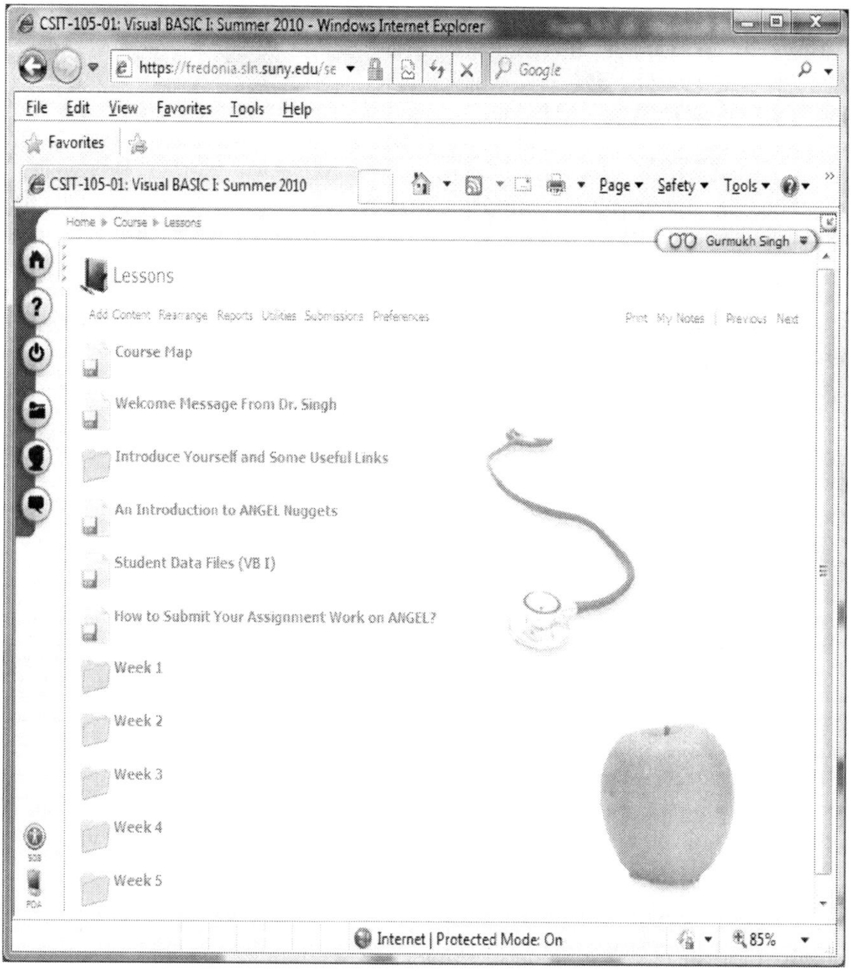

Fig. 2. A screen-shot of Module 1 of Week 1

4   Educational Technology in Traditional Classroom

To generate interest and excitement in a classroom a number of methods have been tested and found useful. One such method is called the "mini-lecture" technique [7], [24] using which the course material is divided into several modules and every class period is subdivided into optional two or three slots. At the end of a few modules or slots, students are tested about the material covered so far. The selective mini-lecture material is posted on the discussion board where students discuss their answers and opinions with fellow classmates and make any revisions before they are asked to answer questions on assignments or examinations. This methodology enhances the participation of students as those students who are afraid of being proven wrong in public can see peer reaction before presenting their own viewpoint to the class. Depending upon the nature of the questions, the instructor can sometimes pose short questions directly without allowing any discussion. Another avenue to encourage participation and getting a useful feedback is to provide students with multiple channels of communication [24]. The question-answer session in the classroom is formal for many students who are afraid of public speaking. A candid and informal forum may be needed where everyone can participate at any given time. This is where the internet and the web help in traditional classroom. The mini-lectures are available on the internet as well. We create discussion groups, for example, subgroups, chat sessions, and on-line project partners (see more details in Sec. 5).

Another channel of communication is the problem solving sessions in an informal classroom setting, such as fishbowl (Angel also simulates fishbowl as well as provides options such as private, specific users, teams, post-first). In fishbowl sessions, students are free to choose the questions that are to be solved by the instructor in the class. It is advisable to prepare the list of problems ahead of the actual session so that the instructor can plan on explaining and solving the problems in a particular and optimized order.

5   The Hybrid Course Delivery Model - Activities Involved

The hybrid delivery model for courses that we developed at FSU is a composite of three components: traditional classroom, web-based internet technology and course management systems. The traditional (or web enhanced) classroom and virtual classroom can be used independently as well, as discussed in sections 3 and 4. Additional components may be added as various disciplines or even courses adopt the model. To combine the two paradigms into a hybrid model, suitable adjustments in the classroom component have been made – they restructured to complement each other. The contributions these components make are discussed in the following sections.

5.1   Hands-On Exercises or Experiments

Hands-on experiments are vital to learning as they reinforce and strengthen concepts covered in classes. Simulated experiments are now common and instructors use simulators and kits to supplement their courses. Examples include language translators, tools for network-modeling, computer architecture-simulating, computer-aided software design and engineering, and tools that run various algorithms including hardware kits with which the students build small machine architectures. Many Java applets are available for educational purposes. Some of these tools simulate several mathematical and engineering concepts, e.g., the dining philosophers problem [15], comparison of sort algorithms [10], etc. Some authors have included full logic level simulators such as bill_gates [9] in their books. These tools can be used in the classroom and assignments can be given based on their use. As new learning tools become available, course structures would become more involved and intense.

5.2   Team Building, Group Projects and Presentations

Another avenue to encourage participation is to provide students with group projects and peer- discussions [23]. We created subgroups, chat sessions, and on-line group projects. These components may be created at the start of the class and students are asked to subscribe to the subgroups. Instructor sets the agenda of the subgroup by declaring it to be an informal link among the students taking the course. Topics to be discussed can range from problems or concerns about the course to hobbies, results of the latest football game, etc. The instructor may assign a portion of the grade towards participation. This activity helps keeping interest in the course.

5.3 Web, Video, On-line Resources and Course Management Systems

The World Wide Web has become the largest reference library in the world with thousands of online publications, discussions and tutorials available every day. We take advantage of these information resources in our curriculum.

Using the web resources such as Flash or HTML or the course management software such as Angel, instructors create a course homepage and assemble links to additional sources of information about the course. As the course progresses, more links are added. Students are given assignments to explore these links and complete the assigned tasks from time to time, for example, the Abacus simulator [18] was explored in introductory courses. In courses with assembly language programming specific programming exercises were designed around Intel's programming manuals [12].

Until summer 2009 we were using SUNY Learning Network (SLN) – a SUNY wide course delivery and management environment to create on-line courses [29]. The reader may review an example of using World-Wide-Web in developing exercises for classroom in [14]. The modules provide preliminary discussion and present several web links for additional reading. Also refer to the URL (www.sln.suny.edu) for a sample course completely run under internet methodology using Angel course management software. In order to further strengthen the concepts covered in the classroom, video resources related to the material are used. Such models have been used by others as well [4].

6 Ed-Tech Based Educational Programs – Eroding Borders

The first distance learning courses at SUNY Fredonia were offered in Fall 1998. Two instructors, Siddiqui and Leslie developed courses on Operating Systems, and Paradigms of Programming Languages [25]. The courses were supported by a grant from the SUNY Learning Network. The courses were offered through the SUNY-wide SLN system and over thirty students enrolled. The courses were successful as most students liked the new delivery method and teaching and in particular the fact that they can study at their own pace, at a time convenient to them regardless of the rigid class schedule they had during the day. Later, other departments on campus started offering courses over SLN, e.g., Political Sciences, Business, Biology, etc.

During 1999-2010, the Department of Computer and Information Sciences (CIS) offered over 20 different distance learning courses through SLN and some were offered through both the Angel and SLN. Almost all other courses include some elements of on-line communication: on-line handouts, e-mail connection with the students, password protected system for uploading homework assignments, and others.

Based on twelve year experience of distance learning we can make several conclusions (see Sec. 7).

The CIS is also among the pioneers of developing collaborative programs both nationally and internationally. Among the international initiatives several Dual-Diploma programs were created [26], [27]. The first program with the Ege University [26], Izmir, Turkey which began in fall 2005 with the cohort of twenty students started at Ege in fall 2006 of which ten arrived at Fredonia in fall 2008 and four the following year. The first batch will graduate from FSU at the end of spring 2011. The program with Izmir University of Economics (IUE) [27] was signed in 2005 with its first student arrived at FSU in fall 2009. To optimize the time and to provide student not even a degree from the USA but also to transform them into effective international workforce the course equivalency and their mutually transferability agreements among institutions were established. In addition students are required to complete the general education programs of two universities. The general education (Gen-Ed) program at FSU is designed to prepare students better citizens. The Gen-Ed program requires an integral component of general education which includes courses in arts, humanities, social sciences, natural sciences, literature, history, study-abroad, speaking-intensive, etc. These courses which are unique to US system to education help provide a well-rounded education and make student better citizen of the world. The multidisciplinary curriculum of Computer and Information Sciences program train students in several subject for example, economics, accounting, business systems development, etc. that businesses need across the globe. The students registered in Dual Degree diploma program are able to earn two bachelor degrees, one from the IUE and the other from FSU in four years as well as they are able to receive vocational training in the USA.

These programs are structured such that Turkish students will study at FSU during their sophomore and senior years, while in the freshman and junior year they will study at their home university in Turkey. Obviously, if some of these students need to take a course while at the home campus, or to repeat a course, or to take additional courses, the most suitable alternative is through the distance learning courses. Thus, the program structure provides students enormous opportunities for defining their own interests while taking cross-discipline courses in multiple delivery formats, so much so that a student may be able to take a course in the USA while studying at IUE. A reciprocal program is being developed for US students to study abroad.

7   Conclusion and Our Experience with the New Paradigm

The rapid development in computing sciences and technology field has resulted in an increased number of topics to be covered in classrooms. In order to educate students effectively with the necessary concepts, active learning techniques need to be explored. Instructors can adapt discussion and interaction techniques in the classroom and supplement such efforts with the use of subgroups, world-wide-web resources and instructional video material. Some suggestions are presented in this article with the goal of effective science and technology education without compromising the rigor and quality.

The hybrid learning model combines interactive classroom, web-based lectures and traditional instructions in an optimal way to provide classroom 24/7 for learning and interaction, achieving high quality education. The model is suitable even for instructors who prefer offering a traditional f2f course work, they can prepare one or two distance learning lectures while away from campus for a conference. Some courses have such a nature that does not allow to be offered as completely distance courses such as lab-based courses, speaking intensive courses, and courses where the exams need to be done on-site, there the hybrid format will be appropriate.

The online or asynchronous (distance) learning part of the program is effectively used to offer courses which students are able to take regardless of their location or the international boundaries. Asynchronous distance education which still simulates the typical full-time classroom is appropriate to students since it gives them more flexibility in combining their classes, work and other commitments.

Distance learning courses are efficient for summer and inter-sessions. They allow students to be with their families or to work or have an internship in another city, state or country while taking the course at FSU. Our summer and intersession classes are usually filled with off-campus students residing across the New York state, some from other states and many international students. Students have taken courses from various parts of the US, Japan and Turkey. However, distance education is suitable for highly motivated students capable of working without being closely supervised. At the same time, it is not a suitable learning environment for students needing personal interaction with the professor or the classmates.

Over last twelve years more than 700 students at FSU alone and many faculty members have embraced the new online emerging technology, making classes available to every student around the globe, anywhere and anytime. With the ability to study more effectively, students are showing signs of improvement in grades, retention and graduation rates. Through this model one can create a virtual classroom for students of all ages under any daily-life circumstances – from youngsters to doctoral candidates, from corporate workers to military personnel. The result of course, an instructor can reach across borders more economically and effectively than ever before. The program also reduces overheads and simplifies support services. It expands faculty use of presentation tools, motivates and engages students and above all increases class participation and discussion and opens the doors for collaborative teaching. From administration point of view, there is a significant cost saving in running such programs as no new infrastructure is needed to run online programs and no strain on existing physical resources of educational institution. Finally, under current economic recession existing throughout the world, students can save a large amount of money spent on boarding, lodging and commuting by taking online courses. It is also beneficial to students who have to commute to the college/ university campuses to attend f2f classes as they could be selective in attending traditional classes.

Acknowledgements

The institutional support from FSU from the beginning of e-learning initiative in 1998 and IUE since 2005 is highly appreciated, particularly the support from Drs. Ewing, Karnes, Kijinski, Hefner and Horvath and Mrs. Sasso of FSU and Drs. Esen, Gokce, Sezgin of IUE and many colleagues at SLN are acknowledged. The authors are also grateful to Prof. Leslie who contributed in structuring the distance learning program in early stages of its development.

References

1. Akdemir, O.: Teaching Math Online: Current Practices in Turkey. Journal of Educational Technology Systems 39(1), 47–64 (2010-2011)
2. Allen, I.E., Seaman, J., Sloan, C.: Online Nation: Five years of growth in online learning, Sloan-Center for Online Education, Report No, 181156262, Needham, MA (2007)
3. Almstrum, V., Guzdial, M., Hazzan, O., Petre, M.: Challenges to computer science education research. In: Proc. SIGCSE – The 36th Technical Symposium on Computer Science Education, St. Louis, Missouri, pp. 191–192 (2005)
4. Bilali, E., Erol, M.: Influence of Hybrid Teaching Approach on Attitude and Success Concerning Electrostatics. Journal of Turkish Science Education 6(2), 63–74 (2009)
5. BlackBoard (2011),
   http://www.blackboard.com/Teaching-Learning/Learn-Resources/ANGEL-Edition.aspx
6. Bloom, B.S.: Taxonomy of Educational Objectives. In: Handbook I: The Cognitive Domain. David McKay Co., New York (1956)
7. Bonwell, C., Eison J.: Active Learning: Creating Excitement in the Class Room. ASHE-ERIC Higher Education Report No. 1. GWU, School of Education and Human Development, Washington DC (1991)
8. Curtin, J.: WebCT and online tutorials: New possibilities for student interaction. Australian Jr. of Educational Technology 18(1), 110–126 (2002),
   http://www.ascilite.org.au/ajet/ajet18/curtin.html
   (retrieved January 24, 2004)
9. Decker R., Hirshfield S.: The Analytical Engine: An Introduction to Computer Science Using the Internet. PWS Publishing (ITP), Lab 7.2, (file:///Dl/course/7/2/index.html) on accompanied CD (1998)
10. Harrison, J.: Sorting Algorithms Demo (2001),
    http://www.cs.ubc.ca/~harrison/Java/sorting-demo.html
    (available on March 31, 2011)
11. IBM (2005), http://www.ibm.com/developerworks/lotus/library/ls-NDHistory/ (available on March 31, 2011)
12. Intel: Developer's Manual,
    http://www.intel.com/p/en_US/business/design?iid=subhdr+devctr (available on March 31, 2011)
13. Moodle (2011), http://www.moodle.org (available on March 31, 2011)
14. NSF: Ethics & Computing (1998),
    http://www.figment.csee.usf.edu/~kwb/nsf-ufe/exercises-overview.html
15. Oracle, Dining Philosophers Problem,
    http://www.oracle.com/technetwork/testcontent/tha-using-deadlock-141272.html (available on March 31, 2011)
16. Richey, R.C.: Reflections on the 2008 AECT Definitions of the Field. Tech. Trends 52(1), 24–25 (2008)
17. Rizopoulos, L.A., McCarthy, P.: Using Online Threaded Discussions: Best Practices for the Digital Learner. Journal of Educational Technology Systems 37(4), 373–383 (2009)

18. Ryerson, F.: The Abacus (2010),
    `http://www.ee.ryerson.ca:8080/~elf/abacus/index.html`
    (available on March 30, 2011)
19. Sakai (2011), `http://www.sakaiproj.org` (available on Mach 31, 2011)
20. Shively, M., Ketcham, G.: The ANGEL Difference: Simple, Powerful, Open. In: Conference on Instructional Technologies (CIT 2009), SUNY Oswego, p. 32 (May 19-22, 2009)
21. Singh, G., Siddiqui, K.: Optimum Course Design Methodology for Effective Online Teaching/Learning on ANGEL Server, accepted at the CIT-2011 to be held at SUNY Oneonta, NY, (May 24-27, 2011)
22. Siddiqui, K.J., Tunali, T.: Educational Technology Eroding Borders – Collaborative Higher Education Programs Between Izmir University of Economics and SUNY Fredonia, submitted to Higher Education Conference, Istanbul, Turkey (2011)
23. Siddiqui, K.J., Barneva, R.: Distance Learning at SUNY Fredonia. In: ICCSE (2006)
24. Siddiqui, K.J., Zubairi, J.: Distance Learning Using Web-Based Multimedia Environment. In: Proc. IEEE/ ACM Int. Conf. on Next Generation Enterprises: Virtual Organization and Mobile/ Pervasive Technologies, AIWORC 2000, Buffalo (April 2000)
25. Siddiqui, K.J., Rupprecht, R.: Online BS in Computer Information Systems. SUNY Learning Network (Sloan Foundation grant) (1998)
26. Siddiqui, K.J.: Dual BS Degree Program in Computer Information Sciences between Department of Computer and Information Sciences, SUNY Fredonia and Department of Computer Engineering, Ege University Program Description (2005)
27. Siddiqui, K.J.: Dual BS Degree Program in Computer Information Sciences between Department of Computer and Information Sciences, SUNY Fredonia and Departments of Computer Engineering and Software Engineering, Izmir University of Economics Program Description (2007)
28. Skinner, B.F.: The Science of Learning and the Art of Teaching. Harvard Educational Review 24, 86–97 (1954); Teaching Machines. Science 128, 969–977 (1958)
29. Sln, The SUNY Learning Network, Faculty Development Guide, State University of new York, Albany, NY (2010), `http://sln.suny.edu` (available on November 30, 2010)

Multimedia Distance E-Learning System for Higher Education Students

Nedhal A. Al Saiyd[1] and Intisar A. Al Sayed[2]

[1] Computer Science Department, Faculty of Information Technology,
Applied Science University, Amman- Jordan
[2] Software Engineering Department, College of Information Technology,
Al-Isra University, Amman-Jordan
Nedhal_alsaiyd@asu.edu.jo, Intisar@ipu.edu.jo

Abstract. The recent advances in information technologies with the increasing interest of large number of individuals in the developing countries to get higher education have led to the evolution of online distance education. Distance e-learning has a possibility to offer education to students who are busy or being unable to attend face-to-face classroom lectures. This study focuses specifically on how distance learning will impact the learning of students taking online software engineering course that includes a lab. It examines the ways that the teacher and the students will perceive the online course so as to be an effective and positive educational experience. The system effectively integrates the multimedia contents of the study materials with the virtual lab and simulation of computer-generated diagrams and models that enhances the productivity of educational process.

Keywords: Distance e-Learning, Multimedia, Asynchronous Model, Blended Learning, Teaching Process, Learner-Centered Design.

1 Introduction

The term "open and distance learning" appeared in 1991.The word "open" meant that people do not need a diploma in order to enroll at a distance education [1], [2]. The increasing use of computer networks over an Intranet or through the Internet, and the acceleration of globalization had supported the educational system with effective methods that ensure the growth of knowledge and information, and shifted the organizational structure towards decentralization. The distinction between distance education and local education is disappearing [3]. The integration of technology into education systems increases the quality, diversity, and availability of information, and is altering the teacher-student relationship. E-learning provides education, teaching, learning or training materials using electronic technology via computers or electronic devices. E-Learning is a subset of two large domains, specifically, "information technology" and "education and training" [4].

E-learning is widely implemented in all levels of human education and it has directed the scientific research in the field of blended learning and distance e-learning systems in order to provide higher quality services towards the end users [5].

V. Snasel, J. Platos, and E. El-Qawasmeh (Eds.): ICDIPC 2011, Part I, CCIS 188, pp. 356–367, 2011.
© Springer-Verlag Berlin Heidelberg 2011

The main reason is to personalize the functionalities and to introduce features that satisfy the end users. It allows students to study with more convenience and lower costs because they receive their learning at the place and time that is well-suited to their time or work schedule. The learner can achieve learning qualification at the same time he can perform his work or family commitments [5, 6].

Distance education has special advantages for adult learning in higher education, where the online courses are becoming normal part of college life. The students can do online learning on their own time and at their own pace [7]. Distance education and blended learning allow universities to better control educational process and provide higher quality services for students. It is an opportunity to offer education to the students who are working or who are mothers of little children and frequently unable to attend face-to-face university lectures and tutorials given at classrooms [8]. However, it is essential to adapt the university courses to the needs of these kinds of learners [9, 10, and 11].

In this paper, we introduce an attempt to move the center of attention from the traditional teaching approach to a student-centered e-learning approach using asynchronous communication. Students in online courses learn asynchronously – at different times. This research focuses specifically on how distance learning will impact the learning of students studying software engineering course that includes theoretical subjects and a practical laboratory. It examines the ways that the teacher and the students will grasp the online course within an effective and positive educational experience. An empirical system that applies distant online learning of 'software engineering' course is developed to investigate how e-learning is used to promote the learning practice of lectures to third year software engineering students in the faculty of Information Technology. The students in a particular course section take their lectures in the same classroom, which is identified by classroom number and is fixed throughout the semester. The weekly time schedule for the semester courses is prespecified earlier before the semester begins. The course name, lecture start time, instructor's name, semester number, and year are all specified for each classroom. This data is useful in defining the scope of the proposed system as it is considered a prerequisite for storing and retrieving the course contents resources.

The rest of the paper is organized as follow: The types of long distance e-learning are introduced in section; section 3, presents e-learning development process; the proposed system structure is introduced in section 4. In section 5, we discuss the evaluation scheme for the proposed system and finally, we give some conclusions and recommendations for future work in section 6.

2 Types of Long Distance E-Learning

Long distance e-learning systems become of its era because there is an increasing need for the higher education and information in addition to the high progress in communication technology. It can be categorized into [12]:

   a. *Asynchronous* distance e-learning system: Most e-learning systems today are asynchronous in nature that is pre-recorded or available to learners at any time of the day or from any location. It is not synchronized with the teacher or any another learner. It allows a learner to start and stop whenever they want. It is to learn professional knowledge without the constraint of time and space [13, 14]. Most commonly available web-based learning (WBL) systems are asynchronous in nature.

b. *Synchronous* distance e-learning system: Less common is *synchronous* e-learning, or e-learning that is 'live' and that requires all learners to be in front of their computers at the same time. Synchronous e-learning involves real time sessions. Synchronous WBL systems are used to create a virtual classroom environment where all students are accessing the same information [15].

The integrated teaching and learning environment helps in studying at home according to the learner time and learning pace. It is available to students at any time of the day, potentially from any location. There are different types of online e-learning [16]:

a. *Individualized online self-paced* e-learning refers to situations where an individual learner is accessing learning resources such as a database or course content online via an Intranet or the Internet.

b. *Group-based e-learning asynchronously* refers to situations where groups of learners are working online over an Intranet or the Internet); where exchanges among participants occur with a time delay (i.e., not in real time).

c. *Group-based e-learning synchronously* refers to situations where groups of learners are working together in real time via an Intranet or the Internet.

In higher education, the blended classes, or 'blended learning' which use some combination of technology-based learning and classroom-based learning is becoming very popular [4]. Blended learning has been widely accepted as a very important key-factor in the field of learning. The basic idea is to apply and use several learning mediums in the learning process, which is usually a combination of instructor-led learning, with tools supported by web services. It is partially web-based that enables the distant learning process and partially classroom-based that is the traditional means. It is clear that it does not exclude or isolate existing educational methods and technologies. On the contrary, it is a useful tool that complements them.

3 E-Learning Development Process

Research shows that up to 60% of e-learning implementations failed, despite improvements in technology, content development and increased knowledge [4, 5]. The role of e-learning and the true value that it can present and perform are carefully considered. The results of the current technological and market trends have led to the production of new categories of products that include new capabilities and other products that combine existing functionalities into new and promising product configurations. It is a great challenge to identify the interrelation of these systems and how they can complete the e-learning objectives.

The e-learning development process can be divided into two main phases: development, and maintenance; that effectively support multimedia distance e-learning system objectives. A typical e-learning development process has the following stages:

a. Project scoping and system conceptualization.
b. System requirement analysis and specification of system requirements.
c. Architectural design, using modular design.
d. Unit design.
e. Unit coding.
f. System integration and testing.
g. System testing.
h. Evaluating and maintenance.

The chosen e-learning development process model is incremental iterative development process [17]; it is consistent with the nature of the proposed e-learning system. Although evaluation is a separate stage of the e-learning process, evaluation for system improvement should always be embedded within each stage to ensure improvement.

The divide-and-conquer paradigm is employed as a very general approach for solving large and complex problems. It is called problem decomposition/solution-integration [18]; which is applicable in a wide range of domains. In this approach, a complex problem is successively decomposed into smaller manageable sub-problems, recursively solve these problems, and then these solutions are successively composed, from bottom up, until the solution is obtained. To reveal the problem-solving, the system is structured into a relatively small loosely-coupled modules and a set of problem-solving rules are identified. The problem decomposition rule expresses how is decomposed into smaller and simpler generic problems and under what conditions. Another type of rule is the solution integration rule which expresses how the solutions of generic sub problems can be integrated into the solution of a generic problem and under what conditions.

4 Proposed System Structure

The development of a distance e-learning system is influenced by the structure of the learning-centered educational processes; evaluating of the existing course content, structuring of the course materials and analyzing the needs of the potential learners. The asynchronous self-paced e-learning system should support the learners to follow their lectures and move through the semester at the same pace. The students work through a series of measurable activities at specified times, and the students undergo a compulsory final examination at the end of faculty courses to reveal a comprehensive understanding of the subject matter. The customization of the system will also be considered, it involves the definition of different types of users; who has the supported roles in a typical e-learning environment (e.g. learner, teacher, and administrator) with rights to access only certain modules. Accordingly, the system has three main subsystems: administrator subsystem, learner supporting subsystem and teacher supporting subsystem. Fig. 1 shows distant e-learning system structure.

We consider a prerequisite data for learner–content interaction and teacher-learners communication as an important element of the structure. Interface design aspect includes designing of home page that directs to teacher and student pages with database accessibility to course contents offering interactive navigation and usability of user interfaces as a primary requirement. If the e-learning system interface is not usable, the student could spend more time learning how to use the system rather than learning the educational content, because poorly designed interface will make the student confused and lost. Thus, issues of usability will assume greater significance. In this direction, there should be integration between the learning process and the student's interaction with the course content. The accessible course contents can be searched and made available as needed by learners, content developers, and administrator.

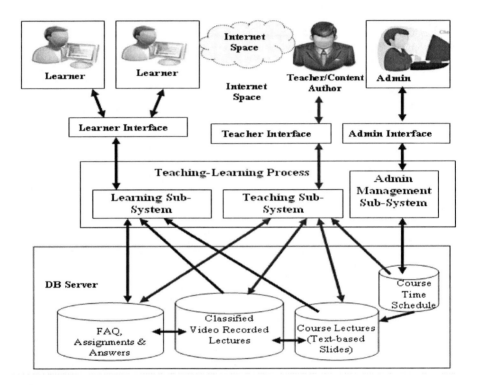

Fig. 1. Distant E-Learning System Structure

4.1 E-Learning Course Content Resources Management

E-learning management system is used to deliver all course content resources, including notes, schedules, assignments, announcements, and instructions for the theoretical lectures and the practical laboratory material that must to be easy to use and flexible enough to accommodate the learning objectives. Following these easy steps:

1. Identifying the scope of the course, learners, and task objectives.
2. Organize the course content: Gather the course content and develop the flow of content.
3. Identify the best way to present the content.
4. Identify the interaction with the course content.
5. Review and evaluate the course content.

Course content instructors usually have to assign additional time other than their normal teaching hours to transform their original classroom course materials; that are not fully well-suited with the e-learning settings, into the e-learning course content [19]. Instructors who teach in-class courses may also choose to use a 'blended' approach and the courses are called 'hybrid courses' by combining in-class time with online components. The design focuses on learning tasks which are associated with the planned learning outcomes and its assessment to allow students to complete their learning tasks. Using a delicate balance between course structure and interaction between the instructor and learners is critical for e-learning success [20].

Nevertheless, the designers give dedicated effort for the course content design. The content experts (i.e. university teachers) need to prepare and supply:

a. Course name, course objectives, course structure, course content specifications (theoretical and laboratory using rational tools), schedule time, homework plan, course syllabus; which define the course learning intellectual outcomes, topics, lecture titles.
b. Microsoft PowerPoint slides posted on a website.
c. Text-based course materials.
d. Simulations with graphics for the practical laboratory.
e. Series of video recorded lectures are prepared while they are teaching the normal face-to-face courses.
f. Quizzes, discussion topic/questions, glossary, assignments questions, case studies, lab exercises, etc.

A multimedia approach takes advantage of the e-learning system by incorporating not only text, but also graphics, audio, video and animations in an interactive format. The video recorded lectures help the students to create reasonable and intellectual pictures of lecture topic, provide integrated pictures and to give more unforgettable knowledge than the text-based lectures do. The students have the opportunity to watch the videoed courses as many times as desired. If the student finds the course material difficult, or the student misses a class, then the video possibly will provide a useful learning tool. Distance students may take a break when tired by stopping the video, whereas students in a traditional course do not have the same features. Because the material is always available, students have control over the pace of learning.

4.2 Administrator Supporting Subsystem

It manages the interface between the system and the administrator. After logging into the system, a system administrator has the responsibility to manage (e.g. add, modify and/or delete) teacher and student data, as well as the accounts and passwords for the teacher and the student subsystems respectively. With these two subsystems, the administrator can also query, sort teachers and students by name, course and manage time scheduling. This subsystem can access to the all databases and managing other subsystems.

4.3 Teacher Supporting Subsystem

The teacher subsystem has a series of systematic related activities that help him to achieve the instructional goals. The whole-class group is applied for Teacher-Led instruction to introduce the course materials, meeting the common whole-class needs. It is used to introduce new concepts for the entire course, which can build common experiences and basis for further explanation, problem solving and skills development.

The subsystem provides a means to manage the profile of the teacher, present an interface between the system and the human teacher and has the role of a tutor of the learner.

In the *video creation module*, the teacher can record his lecture when he is giving his regular face-to-face lecture at the same classroom that is allocated to give his lectures. The teacher start his lecture by writing the title of the lectures, describing the lecture goals, and reviewing the previous related topics from the previous given lectures to build common knowledge, then he presents the new concept of the new lecture. He can also pause recording (e.g. to stop recording unwanted video footage), resume recording and ending to save the recorded lecture on the database.

The time schedule that is pre-specified and stored in the database for all classrooms in the faculty, identifies classroom number, course name, section number, teacher name, day of the week, start lecture time, and end lecture time. Each classroom has a personal computer that is equipped with a camera and the computer is connected through LAN. All of the required data are retrieved from the database and the system suggests the path and the file name, where the recorded video lecture will be stored. The teacher can insert the lecture title; which is considered as the filename, set and direct camera towards him at the front area of the classroom to record the lecture, record white board notes, in addition to displaying Power Point slides. Video recording lectures is done by a teacher needs only minimal technical knowledge and he did not require any additional time allocated for creating the recordings other than the time to give the lecture. Providing that there is a video camera installed in the classroom and an attached microphone. This technology will record the lecture and then add it to course directory in a database.

It allows the on-line students to watch the lecture face-to-face, and can start, pause, replay and stop the videoed lecture according to their requests, as it is shown in fig. 1. A teacher can assign new tasks to students, edit assignments, add new quizzes or select existing questions from the system database.

4.4   Learner-Centered Design (LCD)

Learner-centered design plays a fundamental role in determining the success of e-learning. And according to [21]; it is considered as a bridge between usability, accessibility of information and distance learning system. This will allow applying the Human Computer Interaction (HCI) principles. A main challenge for designers and HCI researchers is to develop a software tools to interact with learners and support their learning process [22].

Students-centered learning is focused on students needs and learning styles of the teacher. Students get access to the system via learning interface; which provides the interface to the individual students, as it is shown in fig. 2. The students; who can not attend the classroom lecture but exist in the faculty, can watch the given lecture at the same time but with a slight delay. The student outside university can retrieve the stored lecture and watch the lecture later via the university site. The *Query Module* allows the student to search for the intended course lecture materials by classroom number, course name, date and time, as it is shown in fig. 3. The student can play, pause or end the lecture at the place and time that is well-suited to their time or work schedule. There is asynchronous interaction between the student and the teacher (online response) when the student needs the teacher help, the teacher answers the student's question only by e-mail. The teaching system must be effective in meeting the instructor's pedagogical objectives and the student's needs.

Besides being usable, interface elements and functionalities, information quality and pedagogical content should support students to learn in various contexts according to selected pedagogical objectives

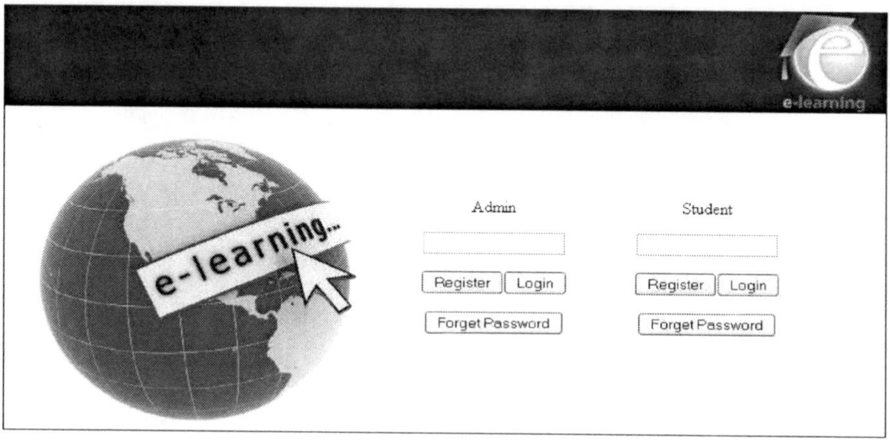

Fig. 2. System Log-in Page

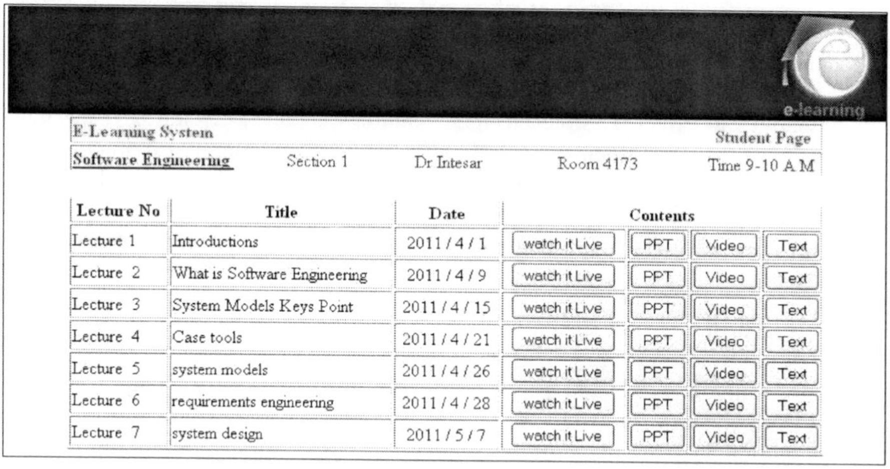

Fig. 3. Learner-Centered Design (LCD): Student Page

5   Evaluation

The evaluation for distance e-learning system includes both assessment of learners
and evaluation of the instruction and learning environment. Assessment can be part of
evaluation but not synonyms [23]. E-learning evaluation has the important role in
measuring the effectiveness. We determine some of the evaluation indicators that influence the cognition of learners:

1. The advantages of using blended strategy.
2. The benefits from the utilization of e-learning.
3. What are the relative advantages and disadvantages of taking an online software
   engineering course?
4. Is the course suitable for an e-learning?
5. To what extent are students satisfied with their experiences in the online lab
   class.
6. Learner interface.
7. How the system allow the students to understand the 'laboratory of software engineering' course material.
8. How the system allow the students to understand the 'theory of software engineering' course material.
9. Is student-teacher interface reflects the learner needs.
10. System interaction.
11. Is the course content structure consistent and enough.
12. Is displaying or playing the instruction materials clear and useful.

The teacher's role is limited that he cannot interact directly with the students at the
time the student need them to answer questions.

The problems that are faced: There is lack of immediate feedback and the student
can not hear the questions of other students.

Usability evaluation technique is done using samples of real students, in which usability properties are assessed by observing how the system is actually used by few
representatives to detect possible misunderstandings about the system and the interface elements. Every participant worked individually to find usability problems in the
application, record the description of the problem, and the location of problem. The
resultant information from evaluation process is used in identifying whether the students reach the learning objectives and in maintaining the system and to enhance it.

6   Conclusion

Distance learning is considered as an active force that move the developing countries
forward in an attempt to offer life long learning and to increase the quality of educational opportunities. In this paper, we proposed an empirical distance e-learning
system that effectively incorporates text, audio and video materials in conjunction
with e-learning for the third year software engineering course from information technology courses. The multimedia course content materials are combined with asynchronous e-learning approach to provide the teachers and the students an opportunity

to rise above the obstacles that face the students and prevent them from attending face-to-face classroom lectures or from continuing their academic education.

The system has three main subsystems: administrator supporting subsystem, learner-centered subsystem and teacher supporting subsystem. Instructors who have recorded multimedia lectures from prior semesters may use these recordings in future classes. The system will relatively improve the course content quality, increase the numbers of higher educated students, improve their qualifications and to bring their skills up. The a blended approach from incorporating the online e-learning system with the traditional face-to-face teaching helps to achieve the intellectual learning outcomes and to promote learning for IT courses.

In addition to determining the relative advantages of taking an online 'software engineering' course that include laboratory, the disadvantages are also stated. The teacher's role is limited that he cannot interact directly with the students (e.g. there is lack of immediate feedback) at the time the student need them to answer questions. The student cannot hear the questions of other students as it is regular in the traditional learning. The system needs to be improved to have synchronous interaction among learners and between the teacher and his students when the students need help.

Acknowledgements. The authors are grateful to the Applied Science University in Amman, Jordan for the partial financial support granted to cover the publication fee of this research article.

References

1. Inoue, Y.: Theoretical and Practical Challenges of Online Education for Life-Long Learning, pp. 624–628. IMECS (2007)
2. Koper, R., Battersall, C.T.: New Directions for Lifelong Learning Using Network Technologies. British Journal of Educational Technologies 35(6), 689–700 (2004)
3. Howell, S.L., Williams, P.B., Lindsay, N.K.: Thirty-Two Trends Affecting Distance Education: An Informed Foundation for Strategic Planning,
   http://www.westga.edu/~distance/ojdla/fall63/howell163.html
4. Giotopoulos, K.C., Alexakos, C.E., Beligiannis, G.N., Likothanassis, S.D.: Computational Intelligence Techniques and Agents Technology in E-learning Environments. International Journal of Information Technology 2(2)
5. Giotopoulos, K.C., Alexakos, C.E., Beligiannis, G.N., Likothanassis, S.D.: Integrating Agents and Computational Intelligence Techniques in E-learning Environments. World Academy of Science, Engineering and Technology 7 (2005),
   http://www.waset.org/journals/waset/v7/v7-45.pdf
6. Richardson, A.: An Ecology of Learning And The Role Of E-learnin. The Learning Environment, A Discussion Paper, Global Summit (2002),
   http://www.citeseerx.ist.psu.edu/viewdoc/
   download?doi=10.1.1.120.1435.pdf
7. Maureen, M., McMahon, M.S.: E-Learning in Higher Education,
   http://web.ebscohost.com/ehost/pdfviewer/pdfviewer?vid=4&hid
   =111&sid=60b52a7e-12c2-4a28-8e14-
   3f0bd745eec0%40sessionmgr104

8. Signor, L.: Virtual Lectures Versus Face-To-Face Lectures: A Four-Year Study Exploring The Impact On Students Results. In: Proceedings of the 20th Annual Conference of the Australasian Society for Computers in Learning in Tertiary Education (ASCILITE), Australia, pp. 700–703 (December 7-10, 2003)
9. Pohl, M., Rester, M., Judmaier, P., Stöckelmayr, K.: Ecodesign - Design and Evaluation of an E-Learning System for Vocational Training,
   http://www.citeseerx.ist.psu.edu/10.1.1.136.2737.pdf
10. McMahon, M.S.: E-Learning in Higher Education. EBSCO Publishing Inc. (December 1, 2009), EBSCO online database
    http://web.ebscohost.com/ehost/pdfviewer/pdfviewer?vid=4&hid
    =106&sid=9287069d-907e-4131-8ce8-
    734c97e9af78%40sessionmgr110
11. Desai, M.S., Hart, J., Richards, T.C.: E-learning: Paradigm shift in education. Education 129(2), 327–334 (2008), EBSCO online database, Academic Search Premier
    http://search.ebscohost.com/login.aspx?direct=true&db=aph&AN
    =35732425&site=ehost-live (retrieved September 28, 2009)
12. Welsh, E.T., Wanberg, C.R., Brown, K.G., Simmering, M.J.: E-learning: emerging uses, empirical results and future directions. International Journal of Training and Development 7, 245–258 (2003) ISSN 1360-3736,
    http://kanjiteacher.googlecode.com/svn-history/r62/
    Non-Code/Papers/Learning/welsh_E-learning.pdf
13. Chao, R., Chen, Y.: Evaluation of the criteria and effectiveness of distance e-learning with consistent fuzzy preference relations. Expert Systems with Applications 36, 10657–10662 (2009), http://www.elsevier.com/locate/eswa
14. Coppola, N.W., Hiltz, S.R., Rotter, N.G.: Becoming a Virtual Professor: Pedagogical Roles and Asynchronous Learning Networks. Journal of Management Information Systems 18(4), 169–189 (2002)
15. Lansari, A., Tubaishat, A., Al-Rawi, A.: Using an Outcome-Based Information Technology Curriculum and an E-Learning Platform to Facilitate Student Learning. Issues in Informing Science and Information Technology 4 (2007),
    http://web.ebscohost.com/ehost/pdfviewer/pdfviewer?vid=4&hid
    =106&sid=9287069d-907e-4131-8ce8-
    734c97e9af78%40sessionmgr110
16. Naido, S.: E-Learning: A Guidebook of Principles, Procedures and Practices, 2nd revised edn. CEMCA, Australia (2006),
    http://www.cemca.org/e-learning_guidebook.pdf
17. Sommerville, I.: Software Engineering, 8th edn. Addison Wisely, UK (2007)
18. Baase, S., Gelder, A.V.: Computer Algorithms: Introduction to Design and Analysis, 3rd edn. Addison-Wesley, Reading (2000)
19. Wenchao He, R.: Enterprise architecture roadmap for the development of distance online learning programs in tertiary education. In: Proceedings ASCILITE, Sydney, pp. 416–442 (2010),
    http://ascilite.org.au/conferences/sydney10/procs/
    He-concise.pdf
20. Benson, R., Samarawickrema, G.: Addressing the context of e-learning: using transactional distance theory to inform design. Distance Education 30(1), 5–21 (2009),
    http://web.ebscohost.com/ehost/pdfviewer/pdfviewer?vid=4&hid
    =111&sid=d052c84b-ffe5-44c4-9a4c-
    8b2bedd49ee9%40sessionmgr114

21. Pennaa, M.P., Stara, V.: The failure of e-learning: why should we use a learner centered design. Journal of e-Learning and Knowledge Society 3(2), 127–135 (2007)
22. Benson, R., Samarawickrema, G.: Addressing the context of e-learning: using transactional distance theory to inform design. Distance Education 30(1), 5–21 (2009),
    http://web.ebscohost.com/ehost/pdfviewer/pdfviewer?vid=4&hid
    =111&sid=d052c84b-ffe5-44c4-9a4c-
    8b2bedd49ee9%40sessionmgr114
23. Lockee, B., Moore M., Burton J.: Measuring successes: Evaluation Strategies for Distance Education. Eeducase Quarterly (2002),
    http://www.net.educause.edu/ir/library/pdf/eqm0213.pdf

Analysis of Learning Styles for Adaptive E-Learning

Ondřej Takács[1], Jana Šarmanová[1], and Kateřina Kostolányová[2]

[1] VSB - Technical university of Ostrava, Department of Computer Science,
17. Listopadu 15, 70833 Ostrava, Czech Republic
{ondrej.takacs,jana.sarmanova}@vsb.cz
[2] University of Ostrava, Department of Information and Communication Technologies,
Dvořákova 7, 70103 Ostrava, Czech Republic
katerina.kostolanyova@osu.cz

Abstract. In adaptive e-learning we try to make learning more efficient by adapting the process of learning to students' individual needs. To make this adaptation possible, we need to know key students characteristics – his motivation, group learning preferences, sensual type and various learning styles. One of the easiest ways to measure these characteristics is to use questionnaires. New questionnaire was created because there was no questionnaire to measure all these characteristics at once. This questionnaire was filled by 500 students from different fields of study. These results were analyzed using clustering, decision tree and principal component analysis. Several interesting dependencies between students' properties were discovered using this analysis.

Keywords: Learning styles, e-learning, data mining.

1 Introduction

Learning process can be influenced by a number of aspects. For our field of interest, let us choose those which characterize learning style, preferences, motivation and the way particular students learn using e-learning materials. Our aim is to prepare a learning environment in e-learning domain respecting students' differences and adapting to them accordingly.

In a traditional teaching process, the educator teaches all of the students in the same way despite the fact that the educator realizes that each student is different. Each student is talented for different subjects, has a different level of previous knowledge, possesses different learning styles, different memory, motivation for learning, different family background, different habits concerning when and how to learn, etc. Unfortunately, a teacher in the class lacks the capacity to respect and consider such preferences as well as the instant dispositions of all individuals in the class [1].

This can be different in e- learning. In this learning form the student studies through the Internet and represents an individual person to a tutor, who communicates with the student individually, gives advice and guides the student through the learning process. The tutor is thus able to adapt to the preferences of the student. Ideal assistants for such adaptation are modern information and communication technologies, vast databases, multimedia equipment, internet, etc. We asked ourselves a question, if

V. Snasel, J. Platos, and E. El-Qawasmeh (Eds.): ICDIPC 2011, Part I, CCIS 188, pp. 368–376, 2011.
© Springer-Verlag Berlin Heidelberg 2011

it is possible to simulate the process of going through a course, which would suit each student with his individual properties. Our intention is to find methodology and algorithms to search for the optimum procedure. This procedure shall respect the differences among students on the basis of detected learning style and also consider the altering level of knowledge and skills of each individual student in the course. On the basis of students' personal characteristics identification, they will be provided with learning material in the form which shall be most convenient to them.

The model of learning being created is based on a new paradigm – the personalization of learning environment. In an ideal case, this environment consists of three parts: a student part, a learning materials database part and a part representing the system of adaptive algorithm.

Our goal is to create adaptive e-learning environment – an environment in which the student learns through directed self-study form. Suitable instruments for this form of teaching are so called LMS. These are systems incorporating teaching supports, features to support learning management and, finally, an information system registering students, their activities and results [2].

For an adaptive system being able to respect the diversity of users, it cannot be anonymous [3]. The collection of data about a student will be implemented in several phases. The most important part is the student self-assessment, i.e. testing before entering the course. The second type of students testing during the study course (testing will be classified as dynamic changing characteristics, crucial for adjustments of the proposed course route).

In such an extensive project we first concentrated on students and their characteristics, as they are the key subjects. Especially their learning preferences which will influence the creation of the adaptive course route the most.

2 Student Part of Adaptive System

To enable the learning management system to react on different students, we have to choose, describe and suitably store the student's qualities and other attributes, which influence the process of his/her learning.

We can gain one group of qualities straight from students with the help of a suitable questionnaire and the second group of qualities we gain by long time monitoring of their study activities. The second group can serve as feedback not only during the current learning, but also for the alteration of the student's qualities, possibly for monitoring of his/her development.

It can be generally said that each person is a true individuality out of various points of view. There is an abundant literature available dealing with learning styles and also describing their classification. By analyzing and studying the already published classifications by various authors we have come to the following characteristics that may be taken into account in the area of e-learning. We have divided these characteristics into several groups:

The group of characteristics called the sensual perception describes the form of information most convenient for the student – visual type, auditive type, kinaesthetic type and verbal type. For this group of characteristics we used the VARK questionnaire [4].

Another group of characteristics called the social aspects deals with the company most convenient to the student within the learning process – whether the student prefers learning with his classmates, with a teacher or by himself. For his group of characteristics the LSI questionnaire was used [5].

The group of characteristics called the affective characteristics deals with student's feelings and attitude which influence the learning process. The most important characteristic of this category is motivation. For this group a part of the LSI questionnaire was used [5].

The most extensive group of characteristics is called the tactics of learning. These describe the „technology"of the way the student learns. The method of the student's learning is described by the order of learning, which can be done either subsequently in mutually related blocks (pole rule) or in almost random manner, without connections, with large skipping (pole latitude). To describe this characteristic a part of the ILS questionnaire was used [6].

According to the way of learning we divide the tactics to theoretical deduction and experimentation. To describe these characteristics a part of the ILS questionnaire was used [6].

According to the order of learning there can be either detailistic or holistic tactics. For this characteristic a part of the TSI questionnaire was used [7].

The conception of student's learning can be divided into three levels: deep, strategic and surface. This characteristic is tested by ASSIST questionnaire [8].

The learning auto-regulation defines, to which extent the student is able to manage his learning independently. This implies his need of external supervision of the processes of learning where, on one side, there are those who appreciate punctual instructions and on the other side those who prefer to manage the learning processes themselves. For this characteristic a part of the LSI questionnaire was used [5].

To measure aforesaid characteristics, it is best to use questionnaires. In the pilot phase we used the above mentioned questionnaires, but their combination wasn't applicable due to their length. This led to inaccurate filling of the questionnaires, shown by the results of their analysis [9]. These reasons led to compiling a new shorted questionnaire LPQ [10]. The usual duration of filling the LPQ is only ten minutes while measuring all properties needed.

Most questions in the LPQ questionnaire are made of statements together with scales of agreement to this statement. These scales are usually from 1 (I don't agree) to 5 (I agree). Some questions have four variants, one for each sensual type.

This questionnaire was converted into electronic form. Before filling the questionnaire, its purpose was introduced to the students. A group of university students from different fields of study were asked to fill this questionnaire, as well as a group of high school students. Total of 508 students filled this questionnaire, 190 from those being grammar school students, 196 pedagogical university students, 68 high school students and 62 informatics university students. The duration of filling the questionnaires varied between two minutes and half an hour. To exclude suspiciously fast filling students we sat aside 45 questionnaires filled in less than five minutes.

From filled questionnaires we saved data about students' answers and questionnaire results that were computed according to a scoring key of this questionnaire. Values of all properties ranged from 0 to 100, zero meaning that the student does not possess this characteristic and one-hundred meaning that he does.

For the data analysis association rules method, which looks for dependencies between attributes and conveys them in form of rules, was used. Each rule consists of a condition and a conclusion and is assigned with reliability and support. Reliability provides information about how many percent of records found with this condition being true meet also the conclusion. Support provides information about for how many percent of records the condition is true.

Decision tree analysis was also performed. This analysis finds numbers of interesting rules for one goal attribute. Rules are then represented in a form of a tree. Leafs gives value of the goal attribute, nodes are conditions of rules and branches are values of conditions. Finally, a cluster analysis was performed, which tries to find groups of similar objects that are different from other group's objects in data.

3   Results of Learning Style Analysis

Here are described results by methods of analysis they were obtained.

Association rules found many dependencies between properties. We were looking for rules with minimal support of 10% and minimal reliability of 70% and found total of 147 rules. Majority of these rules have very low level of depth learning in conclusion. Conclusions also contained visual type, strategic learning and motivation. Some of these rules are shown in Table 1. Most interesting are the rules with high support.

Table 1. Picked rules with 70% minimal *reliability* and 10% minimal *support*, ordered by *support*

Num	Condition	Conclusion	Support	Reliability
1	visual = very low	depth = very low	43%	71%
2	strategic = very low	depth = very low	38%	76%
3	social (alone - group) = middle	depth = very low	38%	72%
4	verbal = low	depth = very low	31%	73%
5	theoretical – experimental = high	depth = very low	31%	76%
...	...	...	...	...
32	motivation = high, theoretical – experimental = high	depth = very low	17%	73%
33	social (alone - group) = middle, verbal = low	depth = very low	17%	75%
34	auditive = middle	visual = very low	16%	80%
...	...	...	...	...
69	depth = very low, systematic (sequential - random) = very low	strategic = very low	13%	72%
70	visual = very low, motivation = high, strategic = very low	depth = very low	13%	73%
...	...	...	...	...
87	depth = very low, visual = very low, field = University, pedagogical	motivation = high	12%	70%
88	strategic = very low, visual = middle	depth = very low	12%	79%
...	...	...	...	...
107	depth = very low, surface = very low, autoregulation = low	visual = very low	11%	71%
...	...	...	...	...
147	autoregulation = low, social (alone - group) = low	depth = very low	10%	87%

For example almost half of non-visual type of students mostly don't possess depth learning style (see rule number 1). Unfortunately 70% of all students don't possess depth learning style, so many of these rules are deformed by this fact. Because of this we can't make any valid conclusions based on this analysis. But we can use its results to determine goal attributes for the decision tree analysis: depth and strategic learning, visual perception and motivation.

This method was used for four goal attributes based on the association rule analysis results: depth and strategic learning, visual perception and motivation. Further on we describe results of these analyses.

By analyzing depth learning (see Fig. 1) we found out that holistic, group learning students mostly have depth learning style. Other results derived from this tree can't be unfortunately used because 70% of students in this data sample don't have depth learning style.

The analysis of strategic learning style revealed (see Fig. 2) that most experimenting students, not learning alone and randomly don't possess the strategic learning style. Other rules provided by this tree cannot unfortunately be used because of their low reliability.

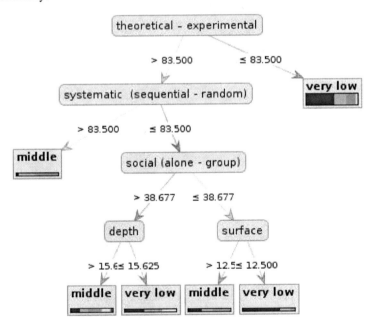

Fig. 1. Decision tree for depth learning

By analyzing motivation (see Fig. 3) we discovered that students have high motivation if they:

- don't possess surface learning style,
- possess surface learning but don't have high auto-regulation,
- possess neither surface learning style, nor high auto-regulation nor strategic learning style.

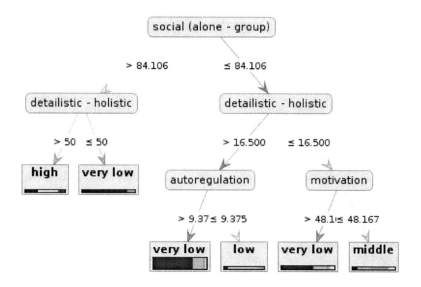

Fig. 2. Decision tree for strategic learning style

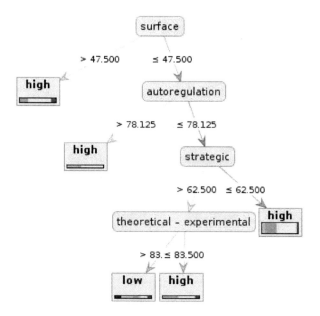

Fig. 3. Decision tree for motivation

Through the analysis of visual perception (see Fig. 4) we found out that students don't possess visual perception if they:

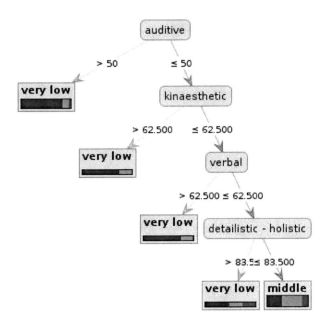

Fig. 4. Decision tree for visual perception

Fig. 5. Dendogram of agglomerative clustering analysis

- are auditive types,
- are not auditive and are kinesthetic types,
- are neither auditive nor kinesthetic, but are verbal types.

Agglomerative clustering didn't find any significant clusters. The out-coming dendogram (see Fig. 5) only showed isolated points that gradually clustered to one global cluster.

4 Conclusion

Newly created LPQ questionnaire has many advantages over previously used group of questionnaires. Its main benefit is five times lower filling time that led to more honest filling. Analysis of filled questionnaires found only minor dependencies between chosen students' learning properties.. That's why it's suitable to use formerly defined set of measured properties. One potential problem is that very few students possess the depth learning style. This can be explained by wrongly designed questions in the questionnaire or by the composition of the set of the tested students where most of them couldn't really possess the depth learning style.

Another important conclusion derived from the cluster analysis is that students can't be divided in several groups that have similar properties. This is an important result for the design of the adaptive learning system. If we want to deal with every student individually we can't adapt learning to only several groups and simply test every student and assign him to one of the groups because every student have properties very different from the properties of other students.

LPQ questionnaire proved to be suitable for using directly in adaptive learning process because of his short filling time. It will be presented to untested students at the beginning of the lecture. We plan to do more analysis of results of this questionnaire on students that will participate in adaptive learning.

Acknowledgements

This publication is supported by the ESF project OP VK CZ.1.07/2.2.00/07.0339 title Personalization of Teaching through E-learning.

References

1. Šarmanová, J., Kostolányová, K., Takács, O.: Intelligent Tutoring in E-Learning System. In: 9th European Conference on e-Learning, Porto, pp. 794–796 (2010)
2. Kostolányová, K., Šarmanová, J., Takács, O.: Learning Characteristics. In: Proceedings of the 9th European Conference on e-Learning, Porto, p. 107 (2010)
3. Takács, O., Kostolányová, K., Šarmanová, J.: The use of adaptive individualized e-learning at teaching. In: IMSCI 2010, Florida, pp. 147–152 (2010)
4. Fleming, N.D., Mills, C.: Not Another Inventory. Rather a Catalyst for Reflection, To Improve the Academy 11, 137 (1992)

5. Mareš, J., Skalská, H.: Česká verze dotazníku LSI, zjišťující styly učení u žáků základních škol. Pedagogický výzkum a transformace české školy, 54 (1993)
6. Felder, M.R., Soloman, A.B.: Index of Learning Styles (2009), http://www.ncsu.edu/felder-public/ILSpage.html
7. Sternberg, J.R.: Thinking styles, p. 192. University Press, Cambridge (1999)
8. Tait, H., Entwistle, N.: Identifying students at risk through ineffective study strategies. Higher Education 31, 99–118 (1996)
9. Takács, O., Šarmanová, J., Kostolányová, K.: Results of analysis of learning styles. In: ICTE 2009, Ostrava, pp. 205–210 (2009)
10. Novotný, J.S.: Individualization of teaching through e-learning: Development of Students? Learning Profile Questionnaire. Theoretical and Practical Aspects of Distance Learning, Cieszyn, 58–67 (2010)

A Cloud Service on Distributed Multiple Servers for Cooperative Learning and Emergency Communication

Yoshio Moritoh[1], Yoshiro Imai[2], Hiroshi Inomo[2], and Wataru Shiraki[2]

[1] Kagawa Junior College,
10 Hama-ichiban Utazu-cho, Ayauta-gun, Kagawa, 769-0201, Japan
[2] Graduate School of Engineering, Kagawa University,
2217-20 Hayashi-cho, Takamatsu, Kagawa, 761-0396 Japan
moritoh@kjc.ac.jp
{imai,inomo,shiraki}@eng.kagawa-u.ac.jp

Abstract. A distributed multiple server system is designed and implemented with Web-DB based services, which can play an important role not only to provide an environment for cooperative learning but also to support a function for emergency communication. In many instances, such an environment or a function used to be designed as so-called dedicated system, which can perform only single purpose. In other words, these different functions frequently seem to be mutually exclusive so that they may be realized independently with absolutely different methodologies. In our case, however, two different specifications have been accomplished by one identical system. The system has employed multiple servers located in a distributed campus network environment. Each server has multi-core processors. With virtualized CPUs by server virtualization, some programs are executed in parallel (on the virtual servers) so that our system can efficiently perform several functions. Based on our related works, two major applications are realized as a Cloud services on the system. It can provide a cooperative learning environment for educational tool as well as Web-based surveillance functions with emergency contact.

Keywords: Web-DB based multiple server system, Server virtualization, Cooperative learning, Emergency communication.

1 Introduction

Nowadays, it becomes very much necessary for several types of users to take advantages of efficient information exchange among many distributed systems, such as network servers, control systems, educational systems and so on. It is also important to design and achieve more suitable mechanism for cost-effective services of information sharing and exchanging environment. There are a lot of researches and works to propose and provide educational systems in order to utilize distributed cooperative learning environments [1] [2].

V. Snasel, J. Platos, and E. El-Qawasmeh (Eds.): ICDIPC 2011, Part I, CCIS 188, pp. 377–390, 2011.
© Springer-Verlag Berlin Heidelberg 2011

In the case of ourselves, for example, we have already obtained good analytical results for our educational tool in the cooperative learning field through real education[3]. Based on the above successful background, we have been going to design and implement information server system in order to realize a distributed information-processing environment for cooperative learning. This system employs a configuration of distributed environment with multiple servers connected and located in the three campuses initially.

In addition, with information exchange concurrently, it is possible to provide both effective structures of cooperative learning and efficient methods of emergency contact. In real education, such a strategy may be very much useful to maintain practically robust schooling (i.e. one of Business Continuity Plans in Schools / Universities / other educational institutes).

This paper describes a distributed multiple server system for cooperative learning at normal times as well as emergency contact with out-of-hours communication. It introduces our distributed campus network environment and design concept of distributed multiple server system in the next (second) section. It illustrates the system configuration and development with our related works in the third section. It demonstrates some applications by means of our multiple server system in the fourth section. And finally it summarizes some conclusions and future problems in the last (fifth) section.

2   Design of Distributed Multiple Server System

This section describes our distributed campus environment and the current situation of our network. They include some special conditions but all of them are the given assumption for distributed multiple server system as our target. And the section also explains design concepts to design our multiple server system.

Kagawa University has four major campuses and six faculties and some institutes/ centers. They are connected one another by means of dedicated high-speed campus network. Tele-conference and remote(distance) education can be performed with interconnection through such network. In order to keep network security of the whole university, we have the external (first-level) firewall at the connected point with the internet backbone and some UTMs (Unified Threat Managements) at the interconnected points for the all the campuses, which are called as internal (second-level) firewalls. And we have anti-virus mail servers and spam firewalls (i.e. Barracudas) in addition.

In the case to carry out remote education, we have introduced some educational systems in our university. It is necessary to operate and modify the according UTMs for smooth communication between the target campuses as well as systems. In the case of tele-conference, well-known "PolyComs" and "Live Meetings/Round Table" by Microsoft have been introduced and utilized by several users of our university. We have some problems in tele-conference, and they are sometimes related to file sharing, so we think that it must be important how to realize and manage remote file sharing suitably and seamlessly.

Almost all users of our university depend on using WWW and e-mail services in order to perform information transfer and exchange. Not only students but also staffs of university do like to utilize simple functions and manipulations in daily operations. There are additional merits because almost Firewalls and UTMs allow to pass the above HTTP/SMTP-based communication without any problems. Such a case is suitable for several types of network security policies, so that it can avoid needless confusion before some incidents happen.

Based on the above discussion, we think that information transfer and exchange could be limited to HTTP and SMTP protocols from the viewpoints of network managements and security policies. In this case, an above HTTP includes HTTPS protocol and an above SMTP includes POP3/IMAP4 ones. It must be better for us to implement information transfer and exchange services based on the above protocols. Especially, employment of SMTP protocol is suitable to link up with spam firewall and other security devices.

It is necessary to have an affinity to existing network facilities when we develop new information server system and try to start its services in our real situation. Our system has employed multiple server configuration located in the distributed campuses.And then we must decide to choose suitable protocols and communication procedures in order to be consistent with our network facilities and security services.

From the above discussion and our experiences, our multiple server system has employed the following configurations and specifications.

- Our system has the three or more homogeneous information servers which are located in our distributed network environment.
- Each information server can provide mirroring function against the specific server for the sake of reliable information exchange.
- Sampling rate of mirroring function between pair of servers can be adjusted to cumulate users information and learning contents in desirable reliability level.
- Registered users can access any server of the multiple server system so that they can choose the most convenient access point of the system.
- Collaborative communication and information exchanging are available between users who login the system from any server.
- Our system can inquire after its users based on users information, even if damages partly happen (for example, a server becomes dysfunctional, or it ceases to function properly in the cooperation between specific servers).
- Our system can provide communication method such as information transfer and exchange between users at a normal condition as well as extraordinary one.
- Our system can support user collaboration environment for not only cooperative learning but also emergency contact.

PC, PDAs (or smart phones) and cellular phones are expected as clients of our distributed multiple server system. Each information server of the system must treat with multimedia information including image and voice. It must be also designed to support cooperative learning between users in distributed environment, asynchronous information sharing, and emergency communication between clients at any extraordinary condition.

3 System Configuration and Development

This section illustrates our related works to implement a new information server, overview of the system configuration for our distributed multiple server system, and specifications of the target clients in sequence.

3.1 Our Typical Related Work(I)

In order to learn computer system, it is very important to understand the internal behavior and structure of computer. In such a case, it is effective for learners to utilize some educational tools with visualization facility. For example, learners use such tools to simulate a sample program graphically in the register-transfer level. If learners want to know a role of a specific register, PC (Program Counter), they can stop the simulation at any point, change the value of PC, and then restart the simulation in the register-transfer level. An effect of simulation increases more and more with such a visualization facility. Figure 1 shows our educational tool, which has been designed and developed to provide such educational environment[4].

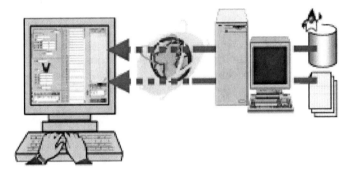

Fig. 1. Visual Computer Simulator on Web-browser

Online help functions are necessary for learners to utilize some tools by themselves. Instructors want to prepare some information about their tools for learners through message of online help. For the sake of providing such a message, instructors have written message on specific text files, the relevant Web server transfers such files according to requests from clients, and our Web-based educational tool reads the files for learners through HTTP connection. In the same manner, the educational tool can read sample programs for learners from its Web server according to learner's request. Such a mechanism is very good for instructors to provide suitable information for the understanding level of each learner at any time.

When learners use our educational tool and want to correspond with others, they can invoke e-mail sending or receiving module which is built together in the tool itself. These modules can be utilized whenever our tool is invoked as a Java stand-alone application as well as a Java applet. "SMTP-client" is a Simple

Mail Transfer Protocol-based sending module, which transfers e-mail from the tool to the server.

With SMTP-client, the tool provides e-mail sending service to allow learners to transfer information including the current state of the tool itself to others.

With the above service using SMTP-client, the tool can make the copy of itself onto another instance of it. There is a particular condition or limitation about capability of SMTP-client as follows, whenever the tool executes as a Java applet. Namely, Java applets can access to their Web server only, which do download such applets. Therefore, SMTP-client can only transfer its e-mail to the mail server which must play a role of the Web server at the same time. In the other words, Our educational tool works as a Java applet, its built-in SMTP-client should be invoked as a child process of such an applet so that it can only communicate with the mail server which is the same machine of the Web server for our tool itself.

On the other hand, transferring of e-mail needs both sending and receiving modules. "POP3-client" is a Post Office Protocol3-based receiving module, which obtains e-mail from the server to the tool. POP3-client is able to transfer e-mail including the current state of some tool from the server to the tool.Of course, as described above, there is the same condition for POP3-client to access the server just like STMP-client does. Two users of our educational tool can communicate with each other, throw an e-mail including some information from one to another through the intermediary of the mail server, and finally share the same information related to educational tool between each other.

Figure 2 shows a schematic relation between SMTP-client, POP3-client and our educational tool. This communication scheme in Figure 2 illustrates a typical story that a learner downloads the tool, invokes SMTP-client, adds the current state of his/her tool into an e-mail, and easily send such an e-mail to the mail/Web server.

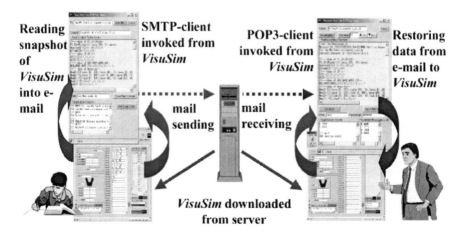

Fig. 2. Schematic Relation of our Web-based educational tool "Visual Computer Simulator" and Communication Functions for Cooperative Learning

At the same time, this scheme also illustrates another typical story that an instructor asynchronously downloads the tool, invokes POP3-client, receives an e-mail with other internal status of relevant learner's tool, restore such a status onto own his/her tool, and readily shares the same status of other tool of his/her learner.

It will be a good example of useful interdependence by means of our educational tool. In such a case, each learner is held accountable for doing his/ her share of given problems and for mastery of all of the jobs to be learned. In order to exchange frequently several information and idea among learners and instructors, some facilities of our Web-based educational tool described above are very efficient and effective for a pair of learners as well as a couple of learner and instructor. And these facilities can support users to study in a cooperative learning environment[6].

3.2   Our Typical Related Work(II)

An information server has been developed in order to work as the kernel of Web-based surveillance system. Web, mail, and database facilities are integrated in the server function. The picture information is obtained from the network camera, accumulated in the server, and transferred to its clients according to their requests. In addition to the remote monitoring function, our server can provide a service for household appliance control.

As GUI client of the surveillance system, the server has utilized some kinds of mobile phones, and employed CLDC[1]-based Java programming to realize the function of clients. For the sake of enhancement of our monitoring function, change from an acquisition picture to another can be analyzed by means of image processing. A service of urgent connection between clients and server is also adopted based on the result of image processing[5]. Figure 3 show a schematic organization of our Web-based surveillance system.

3.3   Overview of System Configuration

As our previous works illustrate, we have obtained some kinds of experiences and skills from information server configuration, their applications, and continuous managements. It seems to be an effective strategy to combine and integrate individual functions into a new solution for complicated problems. So it is employed that multiple servers are located in the distributed campus network and they work together with existing facilities and services.

Figure 4 shows an overview of the system configuration for our distributed multiple server system. The system has been implemented in our distributed campus network environment. And each sub-system includes rack-mounted server, UPS and a few kinds of clients, such as usual PC, PDA/mobile phone and

---

[1] The Connected Limited Device Configuration (CLDC) defines the base set of application programming interfaces and a virtual machine for resource-constrained devices like mobile phones, pagers, and mainstream personal digital assistants. http://java.sun.com/products/cldc/

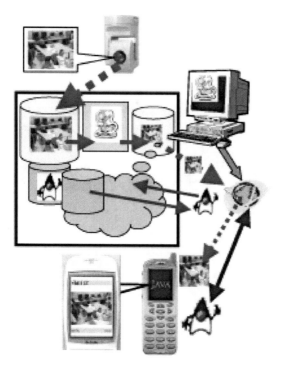

Fig. 3. Schematic Organization of Web-based Surveillance System

multimedia input/output devices. Sub-systems are linked and interconnected with campus network by means of Giga high speed and/or Wi-Fi wireless LAN.

Each information server also employs multi-core processor architecture[7] [8] and virtualized server technology, namely Virtual Machine Scheme, named Citrix Xen Server Virtualization[2]. It is very efficient to realize parallel programs execution and smart management of concurrent services. If some applications need more powerful CPU services, the information server and its hypervisor can adjust its facilities to migrate (assign) virtualized server and related resources to relevant specific applications according to dynamic demand changing and/or configure modification.

One of multi-core processors has been designed to execute most useful Linux-based Web-DB software fundamentals. This is a basic layer (i.e. platform) for usual and classical applications. One of others is sometimes assigned to multimedia information processing modules, such as image understanding, video transmission, voice generation and so on. Some of them are potentially adjusted to carry out asynchronous information sharing functions and support for emergency contact and/or urgent situation changing.

This approach coincides with our basic principle for realization of information transmission and exchanging with HTTP and/or SMTP protocols. In general,

2 http://www.xen.org/

Fig. 4. Overview of Distributed Multiple Server System for Campus Network

the real educational situation needs Windows server and Windows-based information sharing so that our system must prepare for the according requests and specification. The system may provide some platforms in order to let Windows server software be executed in one of multi-core processors.

With such a mechanism described before, it is possible for system designer/developer to configure one information server including two or more functions or services, which clearly differ from one another in their objectives to realize. Each function or service can be executed sometimes in parallel and concurrently.

In the former case, function or service is assigned and executed in the different processor, while they are assigned to the single processor and executed in turn in the latter case.

3.4   Specifications of Target Clients

Client devices for our system are normal PCs, note PCs (mobile PCs), PDAs, smart phones, mobile phones and similar digital devices. It is assumed that specific characteristics of clients have wired / wireless network connectivity and Web browsing functions. E-mail handling is one of desirable functions for clients, but it seems to be fungible by means of browsing functions.

It is useful that clients can perform multimedia information processing such as signal input, image display, voice/music generation and so on. The system requests some kinds of clients to obtain such information from the specific server with previously registered and dedicated software and carry out suitable handling, operating and manipulating sometimes semi-automatically.

If special requirements are necessary, our policy allows the system to prepare the according software and equipments. For example, our system has prepared special-purpose modules of Java application program, let it be downloaded on clients and invoked it to be executed on the target client. So users can utilize their necessary services without special preparation and limitation. Of course, such a case needs the condition that clients already have Java virtual machine in side of them.

4   Applications of Multiple Server System

This section explains two types of applications of distributed multiple server system, namely, implementation of cooperative learning environment and distributed surveillance system for emergency communication.

4.1   Cloud Service for Cooperative Learning

In order to manage our educational tool effectively, it is indispensable to design and implement a special-purpose information server which can provide some kinds of information-exchanging environment for the tool and its users. With such a server, the tool can play the very important role to carry out communication among users. Built-in e-mail handlers of the tool realize such communication between users, for example, a learner and an instructor.

In such a case, learners using our educational tool, visual computer simulator, can obtain their necessary information from the special-purpose information server through its communication supporting functions according to their understanding levels. So the information server needs the following three basic functions.

- Web service function: They are very much essential to deliver the program (executable) code of Simulator and sample (source) programs for Simulator. They correspond to HTTP-based communication with 3-way hand-shaking procedure. Additionally, They support FTP-based data transferring service.
- e-Mail service function: Simulator can support information-sharing mechanism among users by means of SMTP-and/or POP3-based modules.It is necessary for the server to be implemented to provide SMTP-transferring server function and POP3-receiving server ones. So SMTP-sending function and POP3-receiving one must be implemented in the server.
- User management service function: There must be user management functions in the server, not only because of POP3-service but also because of user identification to recognize user's understanding level. The former is necessary to realize POP3-service, while the latter is essential to specify user's level to utilize simulator more effectively.

With these functions, the special-purpose information server prepares necessary and minimal conditions to realize communication supporting and information-exchanging environment for the educational tool and its users.

Cooperation among multiple servers : The previous information server simply employed one server system for all the users' management, user identification with serial number, so that there were some regulations such as not so good two-way authentication among users, not so efficient information transmission and/or sharing between different level of users, etc.

Now we have employed a new resolution of Cloud Service to group all the users into cluster and assign such a cluster to one server as one of temporary expedients for management of users among multiple servers. Of course, the above palliative treatment is not effective for cooperation among multiple servers. Figure 5 shows implementation of cooperative learning environment for our educational tool with a distributed multiple server system.

It is necessary to establish more effective methods to organize and cooperate different servers. One of those is to utilize e-mail function of the educational tool and communication facilities between its users. And then all the users of educational tool are registered on the shared user database, their mail spool area and users' home directories are created in the shared volume area by means of NIS/NFS or SAMBA (or Network-Attached Storage) facilities.

User management for multiple servers : Flexible identification for user management is necessary to allow hierarchical user naming. With introduction of LDAP (Lightweight Directory Access Protocol) based authentication, it is relatively smooth to manage the users among multiple servers and easy to implement flexible user authority for such servers.

Although this is a useful method for user management, it will be suffering from some dangerous intrusion without closed network based characteristics and benefits. Security problems are very serious and expensive to protect correctly and urgently. Additional facilities such as NAT/NAPT (Network Address

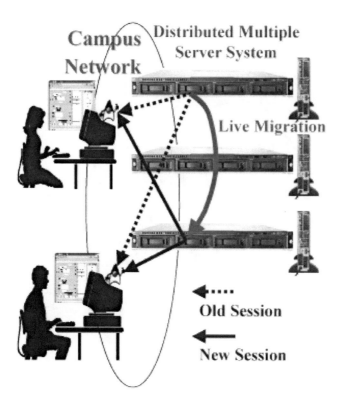

Fig. 5. Cooperative Learning Environment for the Educational Tool with Distributed Multiple Server System

(& Port) Translation) mechanism will be implemented into a new information server simultaneously.

4.2   Cloud Service for Surveillance and Emergency Contact

One server obtains image from network camera and cumulates it into database. The image is sometimes one of object for image processing in the server. For example, one server performs image processing for a series of sampling images by means of background difference method. Figure 6 shows urgent communication between clients and servers on the distributed multiple server system.

Users of such an application can utilize facilities of surveillance and emergency contact without cognition about detail of servers. So the relevant services have been realized as a kind of Cloud computing results. If some accidents happen to one server and it terminates performing, our system can switch such relevant service from the according server to another.

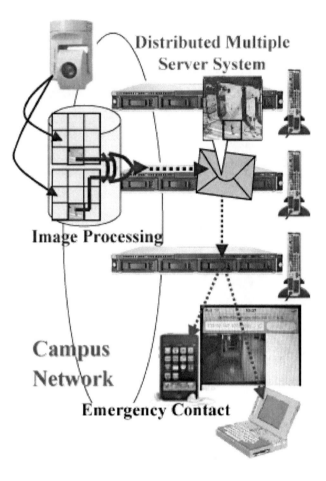

Fig. 6. Urgent Communication between Clients and Servers

5   Conclusion

This paper has described a multiple server system with Web-DB based services for both of cooperative learning and emergency communication. Such a system has been designed and developed to provide effective environment for cooperative learning as well as efficient methods for emergency contact.

In the case of application for cooperative learning, the system can realize multiple users collaboration through multiple server configuration in a distributed environment. It facilitates asynchronous information exchange among its constitutive servers and/or virtualized servers, because it employs virtual server mechanism and always invokes communication-oriented procedure.

In other case of application, our system can assign and run limited surveillance program into one of its virtual servers. Such a program always monitors its target place, recognize it whenever registered conditions happen at the place, and transfer such information to the specified clients by means of mobile communication. The above applications can be easily installed and work suitably in the multiple server system. So we can summarize our work as follows;

1. Our multiple server system employs a virtual server scheme with Xen mechanism so that several applications can work easily and concurrently.
2. An educational tool can be executed in one of such virtual servers together with Web and DB services. And it provides cooperative learning environment effectively.
3. At the emergent condition, the multiple server system can automatically switch surveillance program into foreground and realize emergency contact and transfer suitable information between specified users.

In the future works, we will try to evaluate the performance and significance of our multiple server system in a real application field. And we will tune up and improve this prototype of our system into more fruitful one through some more practical usages and tough situation.

Acknowledgment

The authors would like to express sincere thanks for Professor Masaki Nakagawa and Professor Keiichi Kaneko of Tokyo University of Agriculture and Technology for valuable comments and useful suggestions. And they are very much delightful to Professor Shinji Tomita of Kyoto University (the previous dean of graduate school of informatics) for his constructive supervision. They are also thankful to our anonymous Reviewers for their contributions. This study was partly supported by Grand-in-Aid for scientific research from the Ministry of Education, Culture, Sports, Science and Technology under the contract No. 19500044. And it was also partly supported by Research for Promoting Technological Seeds from Japan Science and Technology Agency (JST).

References

1. Nguyen, D., et al.: CoMobile: Collaborative Learning with Mobile Devices. In: Proc. 6th IEEE Int'l Conf. Advanced Learning Technologies (ICALT 2006), pp. 355–359 (July 2006)
2. Shoul, L., et al.: Collaborative Online Examinations: Impacts on Interaction, Learning, and Student Satisfaction. IEEE Trans. Sys. Man, Cyb.-Part A: Systems and Humans 36(6), 1045–1053 (2006)
3. Imai, Y., Tomita, S.: A Web-based Education Tool for Collaborative Learning of Assembly Programming. In: Proc. 2nd IADIS Int'l Conf. WWW/Internet 2003, vol. 1, pp. 703–711 (November 2003)
4. Imai, Y., Kaneko, K., Nakagawa, M.: Application of a Visual Computer Simulator into Collaborative Learning. J. of Computing and Information Technology 14(4), 267–273 (2006)

5. Imai, Y., Hori, Y., Masuda, S.: A Mobile Phone-Enhanced Remote Surveillance System with Electric Power Appliance Control and Network Camera Homing. In: Proc. 3rd Int'l Conf. Autonomic and Autonomous Systems, 6 pages (June 2007)
6. Imai, Y., Kaneko, K., Nakagawa, M.: A Web-based Visual Simulator with Communication Support and its Application to Computer Architecture Education. In: Proc. 7th IEEE Int'l Conf. Advanced Learning Technologies (ICALT 2007), pp. 147–151 (July 2007)
7. Hill, M.D., Marty, M.R.: Amdahl's law in the multicore era. IEEE Computer 41(7), 33–38 (2008)
8. Sun, X.-H., Chen, Y.: Reevaluating amdahl's law in the multicore era. Journal of Parallel and Distributed Computing 70(2), 183–188 (2010)

Analysis of Composite Indices Used in Information Society Research

Michał Goliński

Warsaw School of Economics, Department of Business Informatics,
Al. Niepodległości 162, 02-554 Warszawa, Poland
mgol@sgh.waw.pl

Abstract. The problem of measurement is the Achilles heel of the information society research. Despite this, or possibly for this reason, one can find a lot of different quantitative studies of this issue. Broader media popularity gain studies using composite indices for such examination. The paper presents the results of the analysis of most popular composite indices used in the information society research. Discussed are the basic methodological problems as well as the strengths and weaknesses of using such tools.

Keywords: information society, information society measuring, composite indices.

1 Introduction

None of the theories concerning the Information Society (IS) have not managed to deal with two fundamental, connected – and probably insurmountable problems: definition and measurement. There is not any satisfying and widely accepted definition of the IS [1], [2], [3], [4]. It entails a subsequent problem – it is difficult to decide which characteristics should measure, a practically indefinable concept. Question what and how should it be measured to monitor the development of IS is one of the most important (if not fundamental) and the most difficult (if not impossible to solve) problem of IS studies. This paper presents analysis of the chosen aspects of this „Grand Challenge" [5], [6], taking into special consideration popular tools of such measurement – composite indices (CI).

2 Measuring the Information Society

The presence of IS issues in public discourse in the last two decades has provoked a rising demand for tools allowing to quantify occurring processes. Lots of studies have been carried out aiming to measure different aspects of information and communication technologies (ICT) and IS.

The main tool of IS' quantitative description are proper indexes providing information about different aspects of ICT usage in society and economics. They allow us to assess the level of IS development in geographical regions, social groups and

V. Snasel, J. Platos, and E. El-Qawasmeh (Eds.): ICDIPC 2011, Part I, CCIS 188, pp. 391–405, 2011.

branches of economy. They are necessary to plan public and commercial projects and investments as well as to assess their implementation. They are essential part of creation, implementation and evaluation of development policies [7], [8], [9].

In the early 1990s quantitative IS studies were rare and pioneering. Currently there are lots of studies concerning different IS aspects, maybe even too many. The studies are conducted by national statistics offices, regulatory authorities, international organizations (e.g. Eurostat, UN, OECD, ITU, WB), research institutions, universities, non-governmental organizations (e.g. Orbicom, Bridges.org, GISW), commercial companies (e.g. WEF, EIU, Siemens/Nokia) and many other subjects.

Authors of such studies concentrate on different IS aspects and use different research methods, creating their own sets of data and measuring tools. IS statistics is a new area. There are still disputes concerning source data, indicators and methodology as well as interpretation of results. For many years, standardization efforts have been made. Not even the limits of IS statistics could be determined. It seems that, because of significant dynamics of IS issues stiff limits will never be conclusively defined.

One of the possible models of IS statistics was suggested in 2005 by OECD [10]. It describes the complex and wide field of potential research areas. Complexity is even greater because of rapid nature of these issues. It is not possible to set and monitor IS characteristics permanently. Apart from that, one set of indicators should not be used to assess countries in different stages of development. OECD suggests using a model, that includes three stages of IS development: e-readiness, e-intensity and e-impact. They have different, leading problems and need different methods of measurement.

Monitoring of such a wide and complex field requires the use of many indicators. How many of them are necessary shows a list of more than 80 basic (not potential!) indicators prepared by Partnership on Measuring ICT for Development [11].

It seems that working on numerous sets of indicators is the only responsible way to monitor the IS issues. This method is used by most "official" institutions, including statistics offices, government bodies or international organizations (e.g. Eurostat).

Such researches provide essential and thorough information. Their factual value depends mainly on accuracy of the process of indicators selection and is generally high. However, they have an important drawback. Many indicators in use are only clear for professionals. For others they are too hermetic, difficult and simply boring. Ongoing mediatization of our world has contributed to the popularization of different research trend – composite indicators (CI). Growing popularity of IS issues forced to create tools that are simple to interpret, fit to popularize IS among wider audience and ready to use it in marketing and politics.

CIs enable a simpler interpretation of data acquired from the analysis of socio-economic phenomena. They substitute a large set of attributes with a single one - a synthetic variable. Transition from a multidimensional set of attributes to a single dimensional one is achieved by variable aggregation. It enables us to arrange objects according to the value of aggregated variable. What makes the CIs so attractive is the fact that they are easy to interpret – the audience is presented with impressive rankings showing the development of IS in countries or regions. CIs became a subject of interest for the media and the public and this popularity was used by their creators.

3 Analysis of CIs Used in the IS Studies - Research Methodology

The results of the analysis of the most popular CIs, used in current IS discourse are presented below (Table 1). It should be emphasized that the analysis does not include all studies of this type. Such a task would be virtually impossible because of the large number of such researches. We will present studies that meet the following conditions:

- Methodology applied uses CI.
- Survey was available online and can be arbitrarily considered as significant, mainly decided by the reputation of its creator (this requirement was not explicitly met in the case of two CIs, created by the author of this paper).
- The last edition of the survey took place after 2000.

Eighteen studies were found that meet these conditions (Table 1).

Table 1. Analyzed composite indices of information society

No.	Symbol	Name of the CI	Creator	First ed.
1	ISI/IDC	Information Society Index	IDC	1997
2	IIDLI/Goliński	II Development Level Index	Goliński	1997
3	ERI/EIU	E-Readiness Index	EIU/IBM	2000
4	TAI/UNDP	Technology Achievement Index	UNDP	2001
5	E-GOV RI/UNPAN	UN e-Government Readiness Index	UNPAN	2002
6	NRI/WEF	Networked Readiness Index	WEF	2002
7	M/II/ITU	Mobile/Internet Index	ITU	2002
8	DAI/ITU	Digital Access Index	ITU	2003
9	IS/Orbicom	Infostates	ORBICOM/ ITU	2003
10	NRPI/Goliński	Net Readiness Perception Index	Goliński	2004
11	ICT-OI/ITU	ICT Opportunity Index	ITU	2005
12	DOI/ITU	Digital Opportunity Index	ITU	2005
13	eE/INSEAD	eEurope 2005	INSEAD/ SAP	2005
14	KEI/WB	Knowledge Economy Index	WB	2005
15	IKS/UNPAN	Index of Knowledge Societies	UNPAN	2005
16	ICT-DI/UNCTAD	ICT Diffusion Index	UNCTAD	2006
17	CSC/Waverman	Connectivity Scorecard	Waverman	2008
18	IDI/ITU	ICT Development Index	ITU	2009

In literature, one can meet a lot of analysis of CIs and methodology of their creation [12], [13], [14]. OECD defines the reference sequence of ten stages of construction and use of CIs [15]. Booysen [16], in his analysis, identifies seven.

Below is the author's methodology, created by using selected elements of both those methodologies. This assessment consists of six elements: theoretical foundations, composite indices structure, quality of data used, interpretation, ability to be verify, and popularization and marketing.

As the work is not an econometric evaluation it does not include elements related to technical aspects of CI's construction, such as factor analysis, standardization, weighting, aggregation or sensitivity testing. The analysis is limited to the six factors outlined above.

4 Analysis of CIs Used in the IS study – Results

Review of the release years of the studies deserves a brief analysis. Surprisingly, the majority of studies (16) made their debut after the end of the e-euphoria of the late twentieth century. The late 90s was a period in which a naive faith in the limitless potential of the ICT and IS was common. Despite this, there were few relevant studies. Breakthrough occurred after the dotcom bubble burst. In later years, a new study was created almost every year (except 2007). 2002 (three new studies) and 2005 (five studies) were the most productive years. After 2006 the number of new studies has declined. It is difficult to explain both phenomena. The increase after 2000 may be due to the growing popularity of CIs, as tools to analyze all aspects of reality [17], [18]. The decrease after 2005 is probably the result of the standardization works and international understandings[1] - Organizations that previously competed with one another, began working on one common tool.

Summary of main characteristics of the structure of CIs are shown in Table 2.

Table 2. Key characteristics of the analyzed CIs

No.	CI	Num. of countries	Sub-indices	2nd.Sub-indices	Partial indic.	Hard indic.	Soft indic.	ICT indic.	Others indic.
1	ISI/IDC	53	4	0	15	13	2	11	4
2	IIDLI/Goliński	29	0	0	7	7	0	7	0
3	ERI/EIU *(est.)	70	6	0	100	50	50	20	80
4	TAI/UNDP	72	4	0	8	8	0	2	6
5	E-GOV RI/UNPAN	182	3	0	8	8	0	6	2
6	NRI/WEF	134	3	3	68	27	41	29	39
7	M/II/ITU	206	3	0	26	20	6	26	0
8	DAI/ITU	178	5	0	8	8	0	6	2
9	IS/Orbicom	183	2	2	10	10	0	8	2
10	NRPI/Goliński	49	4	0	12	0	12	5	7
11	ICT-OI/ITU	183	2	2	10	10	0	8	2
12	DOI/ITU	181	3	0	11	11	0	11	0
13	eE/INSEAD	28	5	0	39	34	5	39	0
14	KEI/WB	140	4	0	12	9	3	3	9
15	IKS/UNPAN	45	3	0	15	14	1	2	13
16	ICT-DI/UNCTAD	180	2	0	8	8	0	6	2
17	CSC/Waverman	50	6	0	28	28	0	28	0
18	IDI/ITU	154	3	0	11	11	0	8	3

In the group of CIs creators are almost all those involved in the statistical monitoring of IS. There are both international organizations, commercial firms and individual researchers. Only one but very important group is missing - the official statistical offices. Neither Eurostat nor any of the national offices conduct researches using CIs. This is despite the fact that this organizations collect data concerning IS, which are often used by the CIs creators.

---

[1] Establishment of Partnership on Measuring ICT for Development - 2004, World Summits on the Information Society in Tunis – 2005, the first version of a basic set of ICT indicators and the appointment of the Global Alliance for ICT and Development (GAID) - 2006.

Authors declare different goals for their tools. Some indication should be provided by the names given to CIs. However, marketing character of the names means that they are often exaggerated and therefore misleading. An example would be the oldest of the investigated tools: Information Society Index (ISI/IDC), which despite of the most promising name, measures only the level of information infrastructure.

Analyzed CIs can be, quite arbitrarily, arranged in three groups, which are characterized by increasingly ambitious objectives and, often, increasing complexity of its structure (Table 3):

- CIs analyzing information infrastructure, its availability and use: IIDLI/Goliński, DAI/ITU, ICT-DI/UNCTAD, IS/Orbicom, ICT-OI/ITU, DOI/ITU, IDI/ITU, ISI/IDC, M/II/ITU, CSC/Waverman, eE/INSEAD, E-GOV RI/UNPAN,
- studies trying to assess also the readiness to use the infrastructure: NRPI/Goliński, NRI/WEF, ERI/EIU,
- tools aspiring for measuring wider and more abstract issues, defined as the information/ knowledge society or the knowledge economy: TAI/UNDP, KEI/WB, IKS/UNPAN.

Table 3. Share of different types of partial indicators in the structure of analyzed CIs

No.	CI	Partial indic.	Hard indic. %	Soft indic. %	ICT indic. %	Others indic. %
			infrastructure indices			
1	IIDLI/Goliński	7	100%	0%	100%	0%
2	DAI/ITU	8	100%	0%	75%	25%
3	ICT-DI/UNCTAD	8	100%	0%	75%	25%
4	E-GOV RI/UNPAN	8	100%	0%	75%	25%
5	IS/Orbicom	10	100%	0%	80%	20%
6	ICT-OI/ITU	10	100%	0%	80%	20%
7	DOI/ITU	11	100%	0%	100%	0%
8	IDI/ITU	11	100%	0%	73%	27%
9	ISI/IDC	15	87%	13%	73%	27%
10	M/II/ITU	26	77%	23%	100%	0%
11	CSC/Waverman	28	100%	0%	100%	0%
12	eE/INSEAD	39	87%	13%	100%	0%
			readiness indices			
13	NRPI/Goliński	12	0%	100%	42%	58%
14	NRI/WEF	68	40%	60%	43%	57%
15	ERI/EIU *(est.)	100	50%	50%	20%	80%
			society/economy indices			
16	TAI/UNDP	8	100%	0%	25%	75%
17	KEI/WB	12	75%	25%	25%	75%
18	IKS/UNPAN	15	93%	7%	13%	87%

Ordering basic information about the structure of the examined CIs according to the proposed division allows us to formulate several conclusions. Research focused on infrastructure using a relatively small number of partial indicators, dominated by hard data (their share exceeds 75%) and data related to ICT (share above 70%).

Readiness assessment tool uses the largest number of variables, with the largest share of soft data and the majority of not ICT-related variables. Indexes aspiring to evaluate the society and the economy are using more variables than the indices of infrastructure, among which dominate hard variables (share above 75%), with the highest share of not ICT-related variables (share above 75%).

One can observe a certain regularity. With rising aspirations of the authors, seeking to extend their study to the widest range of IS issues, increase the complexity of the CI, share of soft data and share of not ICT-related data. This trend interferes with two readiness indices (NRI/WEF and ERI/EIU).

4.1 Theoretical Foundations

It is difficult to assess the theoretical foundation of CIs. One should determine what aspects of the IS should be investigated and assess how the CI are performing this task. The lack of universally accepted definition of IS makes such an assessment virtually impossible. The analyzed indices vary considerably depending on the understanding of IS by their authors. Definitional deficit means that virtually every logic solution is equitable and justified. The development of unambiguous evaluation criteria is impossible. The only criterion can be a common sense, which allows the elimination of the elements that have only a weak relationship with the IS issues.

It is also difficult to assess the quantity, type and structure of the components of CI. Each creator has the right to his own selection of partial indicators, and possible clustering of these into the sub-indices in a manner appropriate to his vision of IS. This phase of construction of the CI should be based on recognized theories (but there are many of them), empirical analysis, research pragmatism and intuition of the author. In practice a combination of all these elements with a predominance of intuition and arbitrary decisions of the author will be used. The political context or needs of influential stakeholders can also play important roles. Often, the ultimate determinant of the selection of partial indicators is the limited availability of data.

4.2 Composite Indices Structure

A desirable characteristic of CI is the simplicity of its construction. This facilitates the understanding and interpretation of the results. However, the complexity, multidimensionality and interdisciplinary character of IS issues result in understandable tendency to increase the number of partial indicators. A small number of partial indicators can lead to a situation in which important aspects of IS are being missed. Another factor that may affect a significant increase in the complexity of the CI may be the use of sophisticated statistical methods. Hence a compromise to ensure simplicity of design while maintaining the descriptive ability of the CI is needed.

The analyzed studies use significantly different number of partial indicators (Fig. 1), ranging from seven to about one hundred. The largest group is the eight CIs that consist of 10 to 20 partial indicators, five contain less than 10 and five over 20 partial indicators.

Record holders are: ERI/EIU -about 100 (EIU does not give the exact methodology of his study, therefore the number of partial indicators was estimated on the basis of other CIs created by this organization.) and NRI/WEF - 68. This raises the question what is actually measured by a CI composed of so many components.

Interestingly, these indices have been developed by a commercial firm and by an organization which - in the author's opinion - the commercial nature dominates the declared scientific objectives.

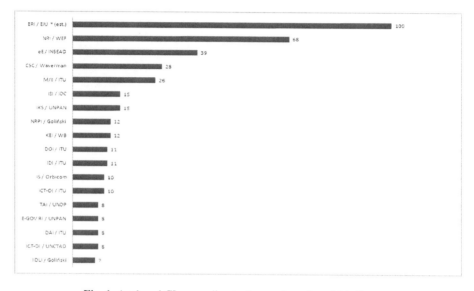

Fig. 1. Analyzed CIs according to the number of partial indicators

Analyzed CIs include both hard data as well as soft data. Miscellaneous is the share of these two groups in the design of synthetic tools (Fig. 2).

Ten of the CIs use only hard statistical data and one (NRPI/Goliński) only soft data. The other seven studies used both types of data. Five of these show the share of the soft data under 25%. Only two have a larger share of such components. In the case of NRI/WEF it is 60% and in the case of ERI/EIU this share is estimated at 50%. In these cases soft indicators prevalent in the construction of composite indices.

A record share of soft data appears in the CIs done by commercial organizations (WEF and EIU). This is a deliberate strategy of both organizations. A specific "CIs manufacturer's business model" is cyclical conducting extensive survey among managers in many countries. A matching subset of the results of this survey, combined with hard statistical data derived from public sources (UN, ITU, etc.), can be used to construct composite tools concerning virtually any trendy and contemporary problems.

In this way, the WEF publishes periodically 10 researches and a number of additional, occasional reports on specific countries or regions. The thematic span range from "Latin America, Private Investment in Infrastructure" to the "Gender Gap Report" [19]. Just follow the EIU. It is a clever strategy of selling repeatedly the same information to different customers in different distribution channels. One can argue that this is the essence of business in the information economy. There is of course nothing reprehensible in such activities, but such a standardized assembly line production of CIs, affects the quality of these tools and their descriptive potential.

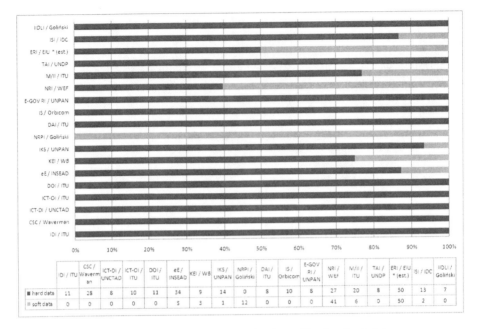

	IDI / ITU	CSC / Waverman	ICT-DI / UNCTAD	ICT-OI / ITU	DOI / ITU	eE / INSEAD	KEI / WB	IKS / UNPAN	NRPI / Goliński	DAI / ITU	IS / Orbicom	E-GOV RI / UNPAN	NRI / WEF	M/II / ITU	TAI / UNDP	ERI / EIU * (est.)	IS / IDC	IIDLI / Goliński
■ hard data	11	28	8	10	11	34	9	14	0	8	10	8	27	20	8	50	13	7
▧ soft data	0	0	0	0	0	5	3	1	12	0	0	0	41	6	0	50	2	0

Fig. 2. Analyzed CIs according to the share of hard and soft data

Data from the surveys can obviously be used in the construction of CI. They enrich the study of an analysis of IS issues, which hard statistical data does not reflect. However, soft data should not dominate the structure of CI. This is particularly important when the procedures of the survey are not clear and the survey itself is not verifiable. This is precisely the case for NRI/WEF and ERI/EIU.

The survey itself is not problematic. It is the nature of the questions ask there. Surveys are widely used, for example, Eurostat periodic studies about ICT used by businesses and citizens [20]. However, the results of these surveys are quantitative data telling us, for example, what percentage of companies purchased online within the last year [21]. Let us compare the descriptive value of such information with data obtained from responses to the question: "Companies in your country use the Internet extensively for buying and selling goods, and for interacting with customers and suppliers (1 = strongly disagree, 7 = strongly agree)". Firstly, the question is very vague. Secondly, the answers given by respondents from 134 countries, coming from different cultural backgrounds, having radically different experiences and points of references do not bring relevant information, but rather an unintended, comic element[2].

For early quantitative IS studies a focus on monitoring the information infrastructure was characteristic. The complexity and multidimensionality of IS issues caused increasing use of the variables which are not directly related to the dissemination and use of ICT. Among analyzed CIs, five use only partial indicators concerning ICT and other combine them with indicators describing other socio-economic characteristics.

---

[2] NRI Variable 8.05 - Extent of business Internet use. One can be surprised by 83th. position of Italy, overtaken by Azerbaijan (68) and Senegal (43) [22, p. 364].

In this group, in the case of seven CIs prevails ICT indicators and in six CIs dominate other variables (Fig. 3).

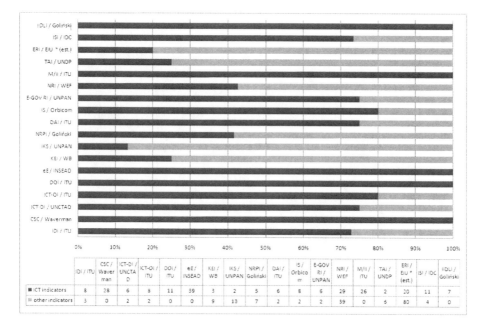

	IDI / ITU	CSC / Waverman	ICT-DI / UNCTAD	ICT-DI / ITU	DOI / ITU	eE / INSEAD	KEI / WB	IKS / UNPAN	NRPI / Goliński	DAI / ITU	IS / Orbicom	E-GOV RI / UNPAN	NRI / WEF	M/II / ITU	TAI / UNDP	ERI / EIU * (est.)	ISI / IDC	IIDLI / Goliński
ICT indicators	8	28	6	3	11	39	3	2	5	6	8	6	29	26	2	20	11	7
other indicators	3	0	2	2	0	0	9	13	7	2	2	2	39	0	6	80	4	0

Fig. 3. Analyzed CIs according to the share of ICT and not-ICT indicators

Use of variables, which are not strictly related to ICT, is sometimes referred to as the "analog noise" [23, p.75]. However, it is necessary and justified by the multidisciplinary nature of IS issues. According to the author, characteristics not directly related to ICT - such as the level of education – can be more decisive for the success in the use of ICT-related opportunities, than purely digital characteristics.

The CIs creators willingly use the variables characterizing the "analog sphere". The smallest share of ICT related variables show: IKS/UNPAN and ERI/EIU (less than 20%) along with TAI/KEI and UNDP/WB (below 30%). Such a low share of ICT indicators in the tools designed to explore IS issues may be controversial. However, increasing dissemination and availability of ICT justifies this conduct. The role of infrastructure is likely to decline in favor of characteristics that describe the potential of the society to use, more and more accessible infrastructure. Turning "analog elements" into IS research is therefore reasonable, but specific solutions may raise eyebrows. Thus, NRI/WEF uses variables such as: "Extent and effect of taxation", "Time required to start a business" or "Local supplier quality" [22].

A consideration on the structure of the partial indicators summarizes Fig. 4. The largest group is 12 CIs, which construction is dominated by hard indicators and indicators related to ICT (right, upper part of the figure). According to the proposed typology they can be defined as indices of infrastructure. In case of three CIs dominates hard and not-ICT indicators (right, lower part) - society/economy indices. In the other three CIs dominates soft and not- ICT indicators (left, lower part) - indices of readiness. In the analyzed group there are no CIs, in which dominated soft indicators and indicators related to ICT (left, upper part).

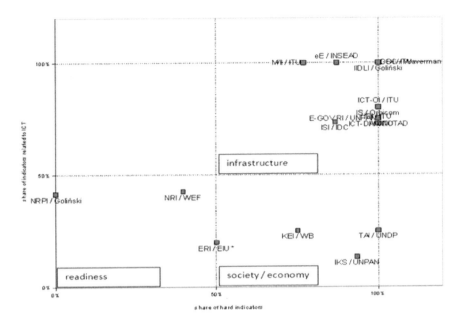

Fig. 4. Analyzed CIs according to categories of partial indicators and by proposed typology

All analyzed CIs aggregate partial indicators first into sub-indices, which are then aggregated (in three cases) into the sub-indices of higher level or immediately into the composite measures (Fig. 5). The number of sub-indices used is different: two CIs using 6 sub-indices, two 5, four 4, seven 3 and three 2 sub-indices. Three of the tested tools (NRI/WEF, IS/Orbicom and ICT-OI/ITU) use two levels of sub-indices.

The number of countries surveyed in these studies is different - it varies from 28 to 206 (Fig. 6). One can highlight eight studies focused on comparing the restricted group of countries and ten studies having global aspirations.

If the aim of the CI is a research on a global scale, its components should be significant for the IS issues in the whole world. They should ensure comparability of results for countries at different stages of development and in different cultural contexts [16, p. 119]. Therefore one could consider using distinct characteristics for different groups of countries. Such grouping, though desirable from the methodological point of view, reduces the attractiveness of the CI, making impossible to make striking comparisons on a global scale.

The uniform assessment of all countries dominates in the analyzed CIs. According to the author, such assessment model is usually drawn on the basis of experience of most developed countries. Only one CI uses different measurement methods - CSC/Waverman divides countries in two, treated differently, groups.

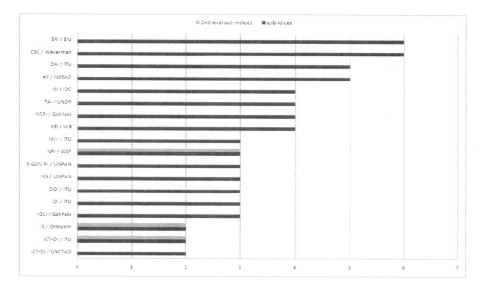

Fig. 5. Analyzed CIs by the number of sub-indices

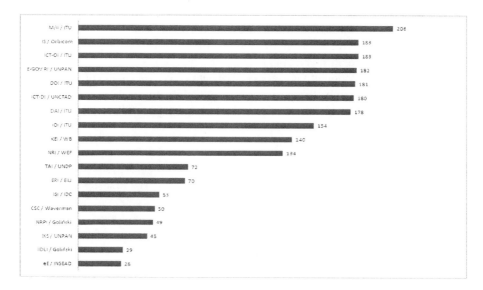

Fig. 6. Analyzed CIs according to the number of the countries surveyed

4.3 Quality of Data Used

Next element of the CI evaluation is the quality of data used. CIs creators willingly use public available external data, from reputable sources, such as the ITU, Eurostat or the World Bank. The nature of these organizations allows the assumption that the data are reliable. In some cases, these external data are supplemented by data from surveys conducted by the CIs creators (NRI/WEF and ERI/EIU). The results of these studies and fragmentary information about the methodology of the survey tend to be skeptical about their descriptive potential.

4.4 Interpretation

All studies present the results at the aggregate level. They are then interpreted and commented in detail. The vast majority of studies (except CSC/Waverman and ISI/IDC) also presents an analysis of the CI disaggregation at the sub-indices level and often at particular indicators level. All levels of analysis are then interpreted and analyzed. Often the correlation of CI with various external variables is tested. This happens in twelve of the analyzed studies. GDP per capita is a variable whose correlation with the composite indices is the most tested. In some cases, also the correlation with HDI (Human Development Index) is examined.

4.5 Ability to Be Verify

An important feature of CI is the possibility to verify its results - which is a condition of his credibility. It is possible for the majority of analyzed CIs. Preconditions for such validation are transparency of the methodology and data sources. The studies, which prevent such verification, are ISI/IDC and ERI/EIU, in which the description of the methodology is fragmentary. Another is in the case of NRI/WEF. This study provides a detailed description of the methodology but in the construction of CI also data from a survey conducted by the WEF partners around the world are used. The inability to replicate this study for anyone else makes verifying the results impossible.

4.6 Popularization and Marketing

Analyzed CIs enjoy differentiated popularity. Table 4 shows the results of the Google search of strings containing the names of individual studies. The first search relates to the whole Internet and the second to the Internet with the exception of home domain of study creator. This is obviously only a rough approximation of the actual popularity of the study, however, it allows to draw a few conclusions.

The absolute leader is the NRI/WEF. Recognition deserves the second place of IDI/ITU - achieved despite the short history of this tool (published in 2009). Third place is taken by ERI / EIU. The high position of the two "commercial" CIs is a result of a skillfully executed marketing strategy of the WEF and EIU, which is a core competency of these organizations. WEF and EIU well promote their products in the media with the marketing effect that far exceed, according to the author, the real merit of theirs tools. Other indexes enjoyed much less popularity, and some of them have only a historical or local character (both author indexes.)

Table 4. The popularity of analyzed studies on the Web [Google search – 2011-01-29]

No.	Searched string	Whole Internet	Whole Internet – home domain
1	Networked Readiness Index	330000	-weforum.org: 329000
2	ICT Development Index	142000	-itu.int: 138000
3	E-readiness rankings	111000	-eiu.com: 105000
4	Mobile/Internet Index	92500	-itu.int: 92200
5	Knowledge Economy Index	80800	-worldbank.org: 79700
6	e-Government Readiness Index	52300	-unpan.org: 52200
7	Connectivity Scorecard	43900	-connectivity...org: 43700
8	Infostates	31900	-itu.int: 29000
9	Digital Opportunity Index	25100	-itu.int: 22900
10	Digital Access Index	19600	-itu.int: 18600
11	Information Society Index	12800	-idc.com: 12600
12	ICT Diffusion Index	10100	-unctad.org: 8710
13	ICT Opportunity Index	9230	-itu.int: 7910
14	eEurope 2005	7980	-insead.edu: 6830
15	Technology Achievement Index	6930	-undp.org: 6840
16	Index of Knowledge Societies	6830	-unpan.org: 6830
17	Poziom rozwoju infrastruktury ...	2450	-sgh.waw.pl: 2440
18	Postrzegana gotowość do ...	3	-sgh.waw.pl: 3

5 Conclusion

Presented analysis of CIs used in information society research allows us to formulate the following assessments of this type of measuring tools:

- All analyzed CIs, despite high-sounding titles, explore only selected elements of the IS issues. None of them can aspire to become a comprehensive tool for measuring the information society. This is not a complaint. Because of the dynamics and multi-dimensionality of the studied phenomena, defining the universal tool is, quite simply, impossible.
- CIs are affected by the subjective choices done by its creators, virtually at all stages of their design [16, p. 141]. Thus, all are inherently subjective.
- It seems that in many cases the choice of partial indicators is caused not by the theoretical assumptions but rather by the availability of statistical data.
- The global comparability of some data is questionable. For example: participation in various levels of education - data readily used in IS studies.
- The numerical value of the CI themselves do not have a clear and unequivocal meaning [16, p. 142], which significantly reduces their value as a tool of analysis and interpretation. So, CIs do not provide practical findings, needed for decision making.

Despite these allegations one must accept that CIs have also several advantages:

- CIs are popular tools of presenting the complex characteristics of the contemporary world in an attractive and accessible to a wider audience way.
- CIs are important complements to the multi-criteria analysis.

- CIs focus on the analysis of IS issues at the highest level of generality. They integrate elements of various economic, social and political characters. This is their essential advantage. Comprehensive analysis of IS issues using large collection of partial indicators is "not for sale" from a marketing point of view.
- The complexity and ambiguity of CI corresponds to the complexity and ambiguity of the IS issues and a character of partial indicator is contrary to the complex and interdependent nature of IS phenomena.

CIs truly fulfill its central role of drawing public attention to the significance of IS issues in an effective way. However, for responsible decision-making (often forced by the publication of research results using CI) one needs to use an in-depth, multi-criteria analysis, using a set of numerous partial indicators - deeply characterizing the investigated phenomenon. The growing diversity of the IS issues and the significant dynamics of the processes that shape them, necessitate the simultaneous use of both groups of tools. This enables both effective and readable for the public IS analysis.

The use of CIs for measuring the information society is often an attempt to count the uncountable. However, their contribution to the popularization of this important issue is difficult to overestimate.

References

1. Webster, F.: What Information Society. In: Alberts, D.S., Papp, D.S. (eds.) The Information Age: An Anthology on Its Impact and Consequences (1997),
   http://www.dodccrp.org/files/Alberts_Anthology_I.pdf
2. Webster, F.: Theories of the Information Society, 3rd edn. Routledge, London (2006)
3. Mullan, P.: Information society: frequently un-asked questions, Spiked (2000),
   http://www.spiked-online.com/Printable/0000000053AA.htm
4. Goliński, M.: Spór o pojęcie społeczeństwa informacyjnego. In: Czarnacka-Chrobot, B., Kobyliński, A., Sobczak, A. (eds.) Ekonomiczne i społeczne aspekty informatyki – wybrane zagadnienia, SGH, Warszawa (2009)
5. Menou, M.J., Taylor, R.D.: Grand Challenge Measuring Information Societies. In: The Information Society, vol. 22, Taylor & Francis Group, Abingdon (2006)
6. Taylor, R.D.: The nature and measurement of information: Two grand challenges for the field. Paper presented at the16th Biennial Conference of the International Telecommunications Society, Beijing, China (June 2006),
   http://intramis.net/iip_infometrics_papers/
   ITS2006NatureofInformation.doc
7. Mahan, A.K.: ICT indicators for advocacy, In: Global Information Society Watch 2007, APC, Hivos and ITeM (2007),
   http://www.giswatch.org/files/pdf/GISW_2007.pdf
8. Goliński, M.: ICT Development Index – nowe narzędzie pomiaru poziomu rozwoju społeczeństwa informacyjnego. In: Babis, H., Buko, J., Czaplewski, R. (eds.) Rynki przesyłu i przetwarzania informacji – stan obecny i perspektywy rozwoju, Uniwersytet Szczeciński, Szczecin (2009)
9. Goliński, M.: Indeksy złożone jako narzędzie analizy społeczeństwa informacyjnego. In: Babis, H. (ed.) E-gospodarka w Polsce – Stan obecny i perspektywy rozwoju, Uniwersytet Szczeciński, Szczecin (2010)

10. OECD Guide to Measuring the Information Society - 2009, Working Party on Indicators for the Information Society OECD (2009),
    http://www.itu.int/ITU-D/ict/conferences/rio09/material/
    5-Guide-measuringIS09-E.pdf
11. UNCTAD Revisions And Additions To The Core List Of ICT Indicators, UNCTAD - Partnership on Measuring ICT for Development (2009),
    http://unstats.un.org/unsd/statcom/doc09/
    BG-ICTIndicators.pdf
12. Nardo, et al.: Tools for Composite Indicators Building, European Commission, JRC Ispra (2005),
    http://composite-indicators.jrc.ec.europa.eu/Document/
    EUR%2021682%20EN_Tools_for_Composite_Indicator_Building.pdf
13. Jacobs, R., Smith, P., Goddard, M.: Measuring performance: An examination of composite performance indicators. Centre for Health Economics. University of York, York (2004),
    http://www.york.ac.uk/inst/che/pdf/tp29.pdf
14. Freudenberg, M.: Composite Indicators of Country Performance: A Critical Assessment, OECD, Paris (2003),
    http://www.oecdilibrary.org/oecd/content/workingpaper/
    405566708255
15. OECD Handbook on Constructing Composite Indicators - Methodology and User Guide, OECD (2008),
    http://browse.oecdbookshop.org/oecd/pdfs/browseit/
    3008251E.PDF
16. Booysen, F.: An Overview and Evaluation of Composite Indices of Development. In: Social Indicators Research, vol. 59. Kluwer Academic Publishers, Dordrecht (2002),
    http://composite-indicators.jrc.ec.europa.eu/Document/
    booysen_2002.pdf
17. Bandura, R.: Measuring Country Performance and State Behavior: A Survey of Composite Indices. UNDP, New York (2005),
    http://www.thenewpublicfinance.org/background/measuring.pdf
18. Bandura, R.: A Survey of Composite Indices Measuring Country Performance: 2008 Update. UNDP, New York, (2008)
    http://www.undp.org/developmentstudies/docs/
    indices_2008_bandura.pdf,
19. World Economic Forum:
    http://www.weforum.org/en/initiatives/gcp/index.htm
20. Eurostat,
    http://epp.eurostat.ec.europa.eu/cache/ITY_SDDS/en/isoc_ci_e
    sms.htm
21. Eurostat,
    http://nui.epp.eurostat.ec.europa.eu/nui/show.do?dataset=iso
    c_ec_ebuy&lang=en
22. The Global Information Technology Report 2008–2009 - Mobility in a Networked World, World Economic Forum, Geneva (2009)
23. Pena-Lopez, I.: Measuring digital development for policy-making: Models, stages, characteristics and causes, Universitat Oberta de Catalunya, Barcelona (2009)

A Survey on Image Steganography Algorithms and Evaluation

Arash Habibi Lashkari[1], Azizah Abdul Manaf[1],
Maslin Masrom[2], and Salwani Mohd Daud[1]

[1] Advanced Informatics School, Universiti Technologi Malaysia (UTM),
Kuala Lumpur, Malaysia
[2] Razak School of Engineering and Advanced Technology, Universiti Technologi Malaysia
(UTM), Kuala Lumpur, Malaysia
a_habibi_1@hotmail.com, {azizah07,maslin,salwani}@ic.utm.my

Abstract. The technique of hiding confidential information within any media is known as Stegonography. Since both stegonography and cryptography are used to protect confidential information, the two are used interchangeably. This is wrong because the appearance of the output from the two processes is totally different; the output from a stegonography operation is not apparently visible while for cryptography the output is scrambled such that it easily draws attention. The detection of the presence of stegonography is referred to as Steganlysis. In this article we have attempted to elucidate the main image steganography approaches, and then we will evaluate the techniques and result will show in a table and discuss.

Keywords: Steganography, Image steganography, Least Significant Bit (LSB), Pseudorandom permutations (PP), Patchwork technique (PW), Palette-based Techniques, Discrete Cosine Transform (DCT), Perturbed Quantization (PQ), Spread spectrum (SS).

1 Introduction

Just like cryptography, steganography offers a way of communicating secrets. However where as cryptography jumbles up a message in such a way that it is visible but cannot be understood, steganography obscures the very existence of the message. This is achieved by hiding private or sensitive information within a medium which on the surface looks innocent. Since the main use of both steganography and cryptology is to secure important information the two are normally confused with each other. The distinction between the two is that Steganography obscures information in such a way that it appears as though nothing is hidden at all. When a stego object is viewed the person viewing it with a naked eye will have no way of knowing whether it contains any hidden information. Thus no attempt will be made to decrypt the information. The term steganography is derived from two Greek words Steganós (Covered) and Graptos (Writing). Steganography is commonly used as a means of hiding a file within another file called a carrier. To add further security the file that is hidden within a carrier file is normally encrypted with a password.

V. Snasel, J. Platos, and E. El-Qawasmeh (Eds.): ICDIPC 2011, Part I, CCIS 188, pp. 406–418, 2011.
© Springer-Verlag Berlin Heidelberg 2011

Simply put "steganography" means concealing one piece of data inside another". Contemporary steganography has made it possible to hide information within both digital multimedia files and a at the network packet level.

2 Structure of Steganography

In order to hide information within media the following elements are required:

- The cover media(C) that contains the hidden data
- The secret message (M), which could be in form of plain text, cipher text or any type of data
- The stego function (Fe) and its inverse (Fe-1)
- An optional stego-key (K) or password could be utilised to conceal and show the message.

The cover media and the message (to be hidden) along with a stego-key (optionally) are operated on by the stego function to produce a stego media (S). A diagrammatic representation of the steganographic operation is depicted below (Figure 1).

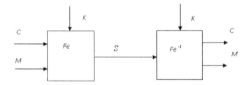

Fig. 1. The Image Steganographic Process

Despite the functional difference between Steganography and Cryptography in practice they are usually used conjointly.

3 Techniques of Steganography

Images can be used in diverse ways to hide information. Messages can either be inserted straight into or scattered randomly throughout the cover image. Nearly all image steganography techniques are image format dependent. This implies that each of these can be applied to various images, with varying levels of success or be affected by the operations like cropping or decreasing of the color depth of the image.

4 Four Categories of Image Steganography

When we research on all steganography techniques, it is possible to find that everything is done to keep secret messages; naturally, these actions or techniques can be categorised and classify based on what is happening during the whole process. The four categories of steganography are possible to define:

- **Substitution system techniques:** Replaces redundant or unneeded bits of a cover with the bits from the secret message
- **Statistical method techniques:** Embeds one bit of information only in a digital carrier, and then creates a statistical change
- **Transform domain techniques:** Hide message data in the "transform space" of a signal
- **Spread spectrum techniques:** The stream of information to be transmitted is divided into small pieces

From the most available techniques in these categories, this paper shall focus on six main techniques that can placement in above categories such as below:

Substitution system techniques: Least Significant Bit (LSB) and Palette-based images Techniques

Statistical method techniques: Pseudorandom Permutations (PP), Patchwork Technique (PW)

Transform domain techniques: Discrete Cosine Transform (DCT)

Spread spectrum techniques: Spread spectrum (SS)

4.1 Least Significant Bit (LSB)

For this technique the LSBs of each pixel in the cover medium are replaced with the binary equivalent of the message that is to be hidden. Least significant bit (LSB) is not only a common but, simple approach for embedding information in a cover medium. Regrettably, it is susceptible to even tiny image manipulations. The conversion a GIF or BMP image that reconstructs the initial message into a JPEG (no lossy compression) using lossless compression) may easily ruin the information hidden in the LSBs [10].

24-bit images: 3 bits in each pixel of a 24-bit image can be stored in the LSBs of each byte. It is thus possible to hide information that is 2,359,296 bits (294,912 bytes) in size in a 1,024 * 768 image. Additionally compressing the message to be hidden beforehand permits the hiding of larger amounts of information. When the resulting stego-image is viewed with human eyes, both the stego and cover image show no difference. For instance, the character A, when no compression is used, can be hidden in three pixels. The initial formation data for 3 pixels (9 bytes) could be as follows:

```
00100111 11101001 11001000
00100111 11001000 11101001
11001000 00100111 11101001
```

In the event that A is a binary value represented as 10000011 which is inserted in the three pixels it would be appear as follows:

```
00100111 11101001 11001000
00100111 11001000 11101001      + 10000011=
11001000 00100111 11101001
```

```
00100111 11101000 11001000
00100110 11001000 11101000
11001000 00100111 11101001
```

Only the underlined bits (three of them) out of the 8 bytes used are actually modified. For a message to be hidden in the least and second least significant bits and still not be visible to the human eye it should only occupy half or less than half the bits in an image to be changed.

8-bit images: 8-bit images are not as tolerant to LSB manipulation due to their color limitations. There has be various approaches with varying success levels that Steganography software authors have come up with to hide information in 8-bit images. To start with the chosen cover image should be one that will not broadcast the existence of an embedded message within it. The only drawback with this method is that it is highly susceptible image compression and formatting to attacks [8] [10].

4.2 Pseudorandom Permutations (PP)

This technique is more complex since all the cover bits can be accessed during the embedding process, and the bits in the secret message can be randomly dispersed within the cover. A random number generator whose output is utilized as indices is used in the encoding process. To avoid relying on the secrecy of the algorithm only for the protection of the system, the use of a stego-key should not be overlooked. It is important to point out that the same index could appear twice or more times in a sequence, because the end results from the pseudorandom number generator is not limited in any way. Its occurrence is referred to as a "collision". A collision can be avoided by keeping track of all cover bits which have already been utilized in a list. In the event that in course of embedding a particular cover-element which has not been used before, it's index can be included on the list so that it can be used. Where the index of the cover element already exists on the list, the element should be gotten rid of and another one pseudo-randomly chosen as a cover element. The same method can be applied at the receiving end as well. This technique ensures that subsequent message bits are not embedded in the same order thus making it even harder for an attack to succeed. As LSB, some of data which is stored randomly stored in LSB could disappear also it may generate a high noisy image if it stored large bits in MSBs [9]. For instance:

Pseudo Random Numbers: 1, 5, 9, 11, 17, 24, 29, 32...

00100111 11101001 11001000		01100011 10101001 10001000
00100111 11001000 11101001	+ 10000011=	00100111 11001000 11101001
11001000 00100111 11101001		11001000 00100111 11101001

4.3 Patchwork Technique (PW)

This is a method based on a pseudorandom, statistical process. Patchwork imperceptibly inserts a host image with a particular statistic using a Gaussian distribution. Iteration in the Patchwork method is depicted in figure 2. A pseudo randomly selection of two patches is carried out where the first one is A and the second is B. Patch A image data is brightened where as that of patch B is darkened (for purposes of this illustration this is magnified). This statistic unilaterally shows the existence or lack of a signature.

The contents of the host image are independent of the Patchwork process. It also exhibits a fairly high tolerance to a lot of geometric image alterations. The following are the steps involved in the Patchwork algorithm:

- Generate a pseudo-random bit stream to select pairs of pixels from the cover data.
- For each pair, let d be the difference between the two pixels.
- Encode a bit of information into the pair. Let d < 0 represent 0 and d > 0 represent Given that the pixels are not ordered correctly, swap them.
- In the event that d is greater than a predefined threshold or if is equal to 0, ignore the pair and proceed to the next pair.

Patchwork being statistical methods uses redundant pattern encoding to insert a message within an image. The algorithm adds redundancy to the concealed information and thereafter scatters it all over the image [8] [11].

Fig. 2. Patchwork technique with two areas or patchworks

A reasonable amount of damage to the image may occur due to the fact that there is pixel swapping involved in the algorithm and making this algorithm suitable just for embedding little amounts of data. This major disadvantage can be overridden but by increasing when a lot more information is hidden within an image one has to make a trade off on secrecy. However in the event that the message is redundantly embedded the main advantage is its resilience against lossy compression or unplanned image manipulation when Patchwork is used. If a stego image that is using patchwork is cropped or rotated, a few bits from the message might be discarded but since the message is repeatedly embedded in the image, most of the information will still be present. Therefore the best type of data to transmit with Patchwork is small amounts of a highly sensitive nature [8] [11].

4.4 Palette-Based Technique

Included in the palette-based image are a palette and an index image. Palettes are typically made up of a set of color vectors and an 8 bit unique index is allotted to each. A pixel value in an index image is equivalent to an index on a palette. Given that we have three images namely R, G, and B that we can consider to be equivalent to the intensities of the R, G, and B color components of the color images [4].

An image which is colored might be depicted using a different color model, for instance, YCbCr, where the elements indicate luminance, chrominance blue and chrominance red respectively. The index could include information such as the location of each color in the palette. A small block of the index which is expanded it in order to show the pixels is shown in figure 3 [5] [6] [7] [12] [13].

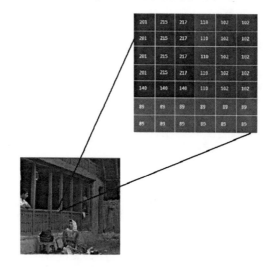

Fig. 3. This figure shows the indices of the image
(This indices point to colors in the palette that shows in figure 4)

Then again the palette includes an array of three columns and N rows, where N is the number of unique colors. Included also is every color used in the image; each of the three columns in the palette corresponds to the color components. The symbols NR, NG and NB are used to denote the color layers which are dependent on the color representation used. Every one of these colors is a collection of normalized RGB values ranging from 0 to 1.

	NR	NG	NB
0			
110	0.254	0.145	0.122
111	0.102	0.188	0.652
112	0.458	0.854	0.755
113	0.492	0.568	0.843
114	0.754	0.496	0.492
115	0.689	0.872	0.569
255			

Fig. 4. Shows the palette of the image
(The palette is an array that contains all of the colors used in the image.)

The images illustrated in such a model are changed into palette based color representations that are commonly used on the Internet. Palette based steganography is able hides the steganographic message into bits of the palette and/or the indices. It is however important to make sure that the number of colors does not go over the required amount. [5] [6] [7] [12] [13].

Palette-based using the palette order (PO)
Small amounts of secret information are able to be concealed into the palette using this method. PO is simple to follow through and does not distort the image in any way. All the same, this method is not resilient enough because an adversary simply reorders the color vectors in the palette (figure 5) [4].

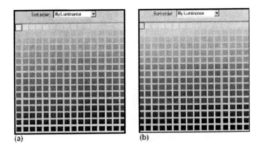

Fig. 5. (a) Palette of original 8 bit GIF (b) Palette of 8 bit GIF of stego image

Palette-based using the image data (PI)
The secret information is concealed within the index image. This technique is generally dependent on the order of the color vectors which have no restriction in the order, and color vectors. The palette easily draws attention thus security wise this causes problems [4].

4.5   Discrete Cosine Transform (DCT)

JPEG compression is achieved by using DCT coefficients through separating the image into portions of varying importance. A signal or image is changed from the spatial domain to the frequency domain. DCT demarcates an image into high, middle and low frequency components for instance an image being broken into 8x8 blocks of pixels. Additionally a 512x512 image can initially be segmented into non-overlapping 8 pixels x 8 pixels (8x8) blocks. The end result being a total of 64x64 blocks. DCT is then applied to each block of the image moving from left to right and top to bottom. Every single block is compressed through the quantization table to scale the DCT coefficients and message is embedded in DCT coefficients [14] [15] [18] [24].

Basically the idea behind JPEG steganography is discribed below in five steps while figure 6 shows the process.

1   Convert image to YIQ color space
2   Every color plane is divided into 8x8 blocks
3   Apply DCT to every block
4   Values are quantized by dividing with preset quantization values (in a table)
5   Values are then rounded to the nearest integer

The location for the two DCT coefficients in the 8 x 8 block and Middle frequencies with same quantization value is agreed upon before hand by both the sender and receiver. In this case   Location 1 is (4, 1) & Location 2 is (3, 2). Table 1 depicts the detail of one 8*8 block and it chosen locations.

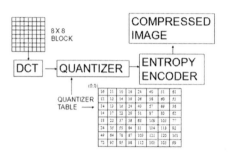

Fig. 6. Process of DCT in JPEG format images

Table 1. one 8*8 block selected in DCT method

16	11	10	16	24	40	51	61
12	12	14	19	26	58	60	55
14	13	16	24	40	57	69	56
14	17	22	29	51	87	80	62
18	22	37	56	68	109	103	77
24	35	55	64	81	104	113	92
49	64	78	87	103	121	120	101
72	92	95	98	112	100	103	99

This is followed by the DCT being applied to every 8 x 8 block in the image to come up with a block Bi and every block will encode a single bit. In the event that the message bit is a 1 then the larger of the two values Bi (4, 1) and Bi (3, 2) is allocated to location (4, 1). When the message bit is a 0, the smaller of the two values is allocated to location (4, 1). In order to extract the data at the destination, the DCT is performed on every block. The coefficient values at locations (4, 1) and (3, 2) are compared if $B^i(4, 1) > B^i(3, 2)$ to determine if the message bit is a 1, or a 0.

Modulating the relative size of two DCT coefficients (MD)
According to Johnson and Katzenbeisser [17] in an image steganographic system within the DCT domain, the message is embedded by modulating the relative size of two specific DCT coefficients with the same quantization value in the middle frequencies, like coefficients in the location (1, 2) and (3, 0) or in (4, 1) and (3, 2). This technique is similar to the one proposed by Zhao and Koch [18]. It's shortcoming arises when particular image blocks for a desired relation of DCT coefficients is not able to be enforced without seriously ruining the image data. To overcome this Zhao and Koch [19] proposed an improved technique. In their method the relations between three quantized DCT coefficients are used, since these image blocks mentioned above can be gotten rid of.

Manipulating the LSB's of the DCT coefficients (ML)
When a low resolution image with 8 bit color is used the effects of manipulating the LSB can cause evident shifts in colors. However with increasing resolution and depth of color in an image the effects of LSB manipulation lessens. Undoubtedly high resolution images will be chosen over low resolution ones as cover images. A gray scale is an exception to this rule since uses 8 bits to define 256 shades of gray

between white and black. Apart from this each shade in the pallet represents an increment (or decrement) of 1 bit from the preceding shade. Therefore manipulation of the LSB is less liable to generate a "new" or previously unused shade within the pallet. A good number of the stego-tools on hand today utilize bit wise methods for hiding information [20].

4.6 Spread spectrum (SS)

Since the hidden data is spread all over the cover-image in spread spectrum techniques, it is more difficult to detect. Marvel et al. integrates spread spectrum communication, error control coding and image processing to hide information in images. Spread spectrum communication is the process of distributing the bandwidth of a narrow band signal over a wide band of frequencies. This can be achieved by aligning the narrowband waveform with a wideband waveform, like white noise. The energy of the narrowband signal in any one frequency band is low after being spread, making hard to detect. For spread spectrum image steganography the message is first embedded in noise and then combined with the cover image to come up with the stego image. The embedded signal is a lot lower than that of the the cover image, thus making the embedded image not suspicious to the naked human eye or by computer analysis in the absence the initial image.

Spread Spectrum Image Steganography (SSIS) involves storing a message as Gaussian noise within an image [16].The impact of low noise power levels on the image is not noticeable by the human eye, but once the scale is tipped to the other side (higher levels the noise) the effects are as "white as snow". The main steps involved in this process consist are illustrated in figure 7:

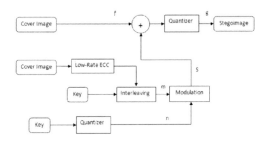

Fig. 7. Simplified Steganography Embedder

From figure 7 it is clear that it is not necessary to be in possession of the original image to recover the hidden message during the decoding process. In order to extract the noise from the Stegoimage a filter is used which results in an approximation of the original image.

5 Test and Evaluation

The aforementioned image steganography algorithms have varying strong and weak points and it is crucial to ascertain that the most suitable algorithm for an application is chosen. Every steganographic algorithms must adhere to a few basic requirements, out of which imperceptibility is the most important [1] [25]. Regarding to the most of steganography research, the evaluation criteria is magic triangle (Figure 8) which focus on Imperceptibility, Capacity and Robustness. Now, in this paper we try to sustain the current evaluation by insert three more evaluation aspects (Magic Hexagon) and then evaluate steganography techniques based on this criterion (figure 9).

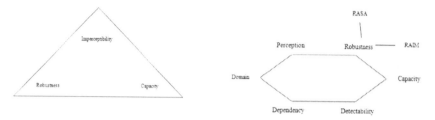

Fig. 8. Magic Triangle evaluation criteria   **Fig. 9.** Magic Hexagon Evaluation criteria

Perception (Level of Visibility) (Per): A Steganographic technique is meant to embed information such that the embedded data leaves no traces its use. The level of perceptibly is dependent on the size of the secret message, the format and the content of the carrier image. In the comparison table it is denoted as PER and is made up of three levels "Low", "Medium" and "High" respectively[1]

Robustness (Rob): The embedded data should endure any reprocessing operation that cover may be subjected to and still remain intact [1]. There are two types of robustness namely Robustness against statistical attacks (RASA) and Robustness against image manipulation (RAIM) [8].

Capacity (Cap): This is the amount of information that can be carried in a cover image without obvious damage. A compromise is usually taken between the capacity (message size) and robustness. For example in the case of the LSB techniques which have the capacity to hide huge amounts of information in a cover image, but just a little manipulation will result in an image that is completely destroyed, this is inevitable [1].

Detectability (Det) or Security (Sec): This is an important criterion that determines the success of a technique as a result of the complexity involved in detecting the hidden data in the carrier [2] [3].

Domain Type (Dom): DOM is Spatial (S) /Image (I) or Transform (T).In some research the categories named Image (I) or Transform(T).The techniques that use transform domain conceal in significant areas of the cover images and could prove to be less vulnerable to attackers. Even though they offer complexity, such techniques are limited to only to lossy format with varying quality factors. In the comparison table "Tran" stands for transform and "Spa" for Spatial [2]

File Format Dependency (FFD): Some techniques are dependent on a particular carrier file format while others are flexible [2] [10] [23].

6   Discussion

Table 2 tabulates the comparison of the steganographic methodologies based on the proposed evaluation criteria. The levels of conformity to the requirements by the algorithms have been defined as high, medium or low. A high indicates that algorithm totally meets the requirement, while a low level indicates that the algorithm has some shortcomings in this requirement. A medium level indicates that the requirement is dependent on external factors [8] [9] [21] [22] [23] [24].

Table 2. Evaluation of the Image Steganography techniques

	Per	RASA	RAIM	Cap	Sec	Dom	FFD
LSB (BMP)	High	Low	Low	High	Low	Spa	Yes
LSB (JPG)	Medium	Low	Low	High	High	Tran	Yes
PP	High	Medium	Medium	Low	High	Spa	No
PW	High	High	High	Low	High	Tran/Spa	No
PO	Low	Low	Low	Low	High	Spa	Yes
PI	Low	Low	Low	Low	High	Spa	Yes
MD	High	Medium	Medium	Low	Low	Tran	Yes
ML	High	Medium	Medium	Medium	High	Tran	Yes
SS	High	High	Medium	Medium	High	Tran/Spa	No

7   Conclusion

This paper was only able to discuss the main image steganography techniques and evaluation criteria, however today there is a wide choice of approaches to hiding information in images in existence. Undoubtedly each one of the image file formats has various methods of hiding messages, with varying strengths and weaknesses. The eight discussed techniques of steganography evaluated by evaluation criteria and the results of evaluation show in a table (Table 2). In this evaluation we observed that where one technique is deficient in payload capacity, the other is deficient in robustness. Indeed from our tabulation of the patchwork approach in the table, it is evident that it has a very high level of robustness against most kinds of attacks, but can hide only very small amounts of information. Even though least significant bit (LSB) in both BMP and GIF is able to overcome this, the end result in both cases is a suspicious file that is easily susceptible to detection by an adversary. Therefore in deciding which steganographic algorithm to use, the type of application to be used must be considered and a trade off on some features to ensure the security is inevitable.

References

1. Zhang, H.-J., Tang, H.-J.: A Novel Image Steganography Algorithm Against Statistical Analysis. In: Proceedings of The Sixth International Conference on Machine Learning and Cybernetics. IEEE, Hong Kong (2007)
2. Mathkour, H., Al-Sadoon, B., Touir, A.: A New Image Steganography Technique. In: 4th International Conference on IEEE Wireless Communications, Networking and Mobile Computing, WiCOM (2008)
3. Babu, S., Raja, K.B., Kiran Kumar, K., Manjula Devi, T.H., Venugopal, K.R., Patnaik, L.M.: Authentication of Secret Information in Image Steganography. IEEE, Los Alamitos (2008)
4. Niimi, M., Noda, H., KaWaguchi, E., Eason, R.: High Capacity and Secure Digital Steganography to Palette-Based Images. IEEE, Los Alamitos (2002)
5. Chen, M.-C., Agaian, S., Chen, P.: Generalized Collage Steganography on Images. In: IEEE International Conference on Systems, Man and Cybernetics (SMC), IEEE, Los Alamitos (2008)
6. Johnson, N.F.: Steganography Software (2008),
   http://www.jjtc.com/Steganography/tools.html
7. Niimi, M., Noda, H., Kawaguchi, E., Eason, R.: Luminance quasipreserving color quantization for digital steganography to palette-based image. In: Proceeding of the Sixteenth International Conference on Pattern Recognition, vol. 1, pp. 251–254 (2002)
8. Morkel, T., Eloff, J.H.P., Olivier, M.S.: An Overview of Image Steganography. University of Pretoria, South Africa (2002)
9. Al-Sadoon, B., Mathkour, H., Assassa, G.: On the Development of Steganographic Tools. KSU Journal, Computer and Information Sciences, King Saud University Magazine, Saudi Arabia
10. Wang, H., Wang, S.: Cyber Warfare: Steganography vs. Steganalysis. Communications of the ACM 47(10) (2004)
11. Bender, W., Gruhl, D., Morimoto, N., Lu, A.: Techniques for data hiding. IBM Systems Journal 35(3-4) (1996)
12. Niimi, M., Noda, H., Kawaguchi, E., Eason, R.: Luminance Quasi-preserving Color Quantization for Digital Steganography to Palette-Based Images, 1051-465UO2. IEEE, Los Alamitos (2002)
13. Agaian, S., Perez, J.: New Pixel Sorting Method for Palette Based Steganography and Color Model Selection. In: International Workshop on Spectral Methods and Multirate Signal Processing (SMMSP), Latvija, Riga (2005)
14. Walia, E., Jain, P., Navdeep: An Analysis of LSB & DCT based Steganography. Global Journal of Computer Science and Technology 10(1) (Ver 1.0) (April 2010)
15. Manikopoulos, C., Shi, Y.-Q., Song, S., Zhang, Z., Ni, Z., Zou, D.: Detection of block DCT-based Steganography in gray-scale images. IEEE, Los Alamitos (2002) 0-7803-7713-3/02
16. Brundick, F., Marvel, L.: Implementation of Spread Spectrum Image Steganography. Army Research Laboratory ARL-TR-2433 (March 2001)
17. Katzenbeisser, S., Petitcolas, F.A.P.: Information Hiding Techniques for Steganography and Digital Watermarking. Artech House, Boston (2000)
18. Zhao, J., Koch, E.: Towards robust and hidden image copyright labeling. In: Proceeding IEEE Work on Nonlinear Signal and Image Processing (1995)

19. Zhao, J., Koch, E.: Embedding robust labels into images for copyright protection. In: Proceeding International Conference on Intellectual Property Rights for Information, Knowledge and New Techniques (1995)
20. Silman, J.: Steganography and Steganalysis: An Overview. InfoSec Reading Room. SANS Institute (2001)
21. Anderson, R., Petitcolas, F.: On the Limits of Steganography. IEEE Journal on Selected Areas In Communications 16(4) (May1998)
22. Dickman, S.: An Overview of Steganography. James Madison University Infosec Techreport, JMU-INFOSEC-TR-2007-002 (2007)
23. Kumari, M., Khare, A., Khare, P.: JPEG Compression Steganography & Crypography Using Image-Adaptation Technique. Journal of Advances in Information Technology 1(3) (2010)
24. Cheddad, A., Condell, J., Curran, K., Kevitt, P.M.: Enhancing Steganography In Digital Images. In: Canadian Conference on Computer and Robot Vision. IEEE, Los Alamitos (2008)
25. Johnson, N., Duric, Z., Jajodia, S.: Information Hiding: Steganography and Watermarking-Attacks and Countermeasures. Kluwer Academic Publishers, Boston (2001)

Real-Time Monitoring Environment to Detect Damaged Buildings in Case of Earthquakes

Yasar Guneri Sahin, Ahmet Oktay Kabar, Bengi Saglam, and Erkam Tek

Izmir University of Economics, Faculty of Engineering and Computer Sciences,
Sakarya Cad. No:156, Balcova, Izmir-Turkey
yasar.sahin@ieu.edu.tr,
{aoktaykabar,bengisaglam,erkamtek}@gmail.com

Abstract. Detection of damaged buildings in case of an earthquake is a vital process for rapid response to casualties caused by falling debris before their health deteriorates. This paper presents a system for real time detection of damaged buildings in the case of an earthquake, using video cameras to supply information to national disaster management centers. The system consists of video cameras which monitor buildings continuously, an algorithm to detect damaged buildings rapidly using video images, and a database to store data concerning sound and damaged buildings. The detection method used in the system is applicable for local areas only (several small buildings or one big building), but it may provide accurate information about the buildings immediately after a disaster.

Keywords: Real time monitoring; disaster management; decision making; image processing.

1 Introduction

Earthquakes cannot be predicted, and they are likely to be most destructive disasters. Moreover, they have been the foremost reason of mass destruction and people death in a very short time for ages. While earthquakes cannot be prevented, the influences and consequences of them can be reduced using several methods, such as new construction techniques and new settlement plans.

Everyone agrees that there is no more important thing than a human life. Thus, saving people is the most critical operation in case of a disaster, especially an earthquake. In addition, the elapsed time between disaster and succoring to casualties is also very critical. If the rescue services are informed urgently about damaged buildings (debris) and their locations, they would reach them rapidly, and then they may rescue many people from debris.

Although many different solutions have discovered to rapidly detect damaged buildings after an earthquake, some disadvantages make them infeasible for local applications. Satellite imaging techniques provide very accurate results, but they are very expensive. Laser scanners can provide reasonably accurate results, however they are rather costly and are quite hard to be installed. Several video camera based solution proposals can be found in the literature, however, most of them don't provide real-time data about buildings.

V. Snasel, J. Platos, and E. El-Qawasmeh (Eds.): ICDIPC 2011, Part I, CCIS 188, pp. 419–425, 2011.
© Springer-Verlag Berlin Heidelberg 2011

This paper presents a low cost real-time monitoring system to detect damaged buildings immediately after an earthquake. The information about damaged buildings (debris) and the volume of damages are gathered by real-time monitoring the environment using video cameras.

2 Related Works

Monitoring environment to assess the effects of disasters is not a new idea, and it has been a major assessment method for years. Furthermore, many different methods have been developed to detect damaged buildings, type and amount of damages using different sensing techniques and sensors, such as wireless sensors, video cameras, lasers and satellites. However, too few of these methods realize the monitoring operation in real-time with low cost.

In a study, Fawzy and Sahin proposed a real-time hazard reporting system using wireless sensors [1]. In the proposal, wireless displacement sensors are placed to particular locations on the buildings, and if any displacement is sensed by the sensors, the amount of change in distance between sensors is assessed and the result is used to calculate the amount of damage in building. Another study simply explains the benefits of SAR imaging techniques and how airborne laser scanning can be used to acquire digital surface modeling [2]. The authors have tried to collect accurate information about affected regions after the earthquake using SAR images. Although, they stated that airborne sensors could provide information quickly (not-real time), locating sensors to whole city might not be feasible.

In another study, Chen and Hutchinson focus on statistical experiments on the satellite imagery. They use high-resolution satellite (Quickbird-Digital Globe Inc. and Ikonos-Space Imaging Inc.) optics to capture land images of Bam-Iran (Dec 26, 2003 earthquake) before and after the earthquake, and they use these images for three object-based change detection methods based on histogram-based classification to detect damaged buildings [3]. Another airborne remote sensing method is offered by Suzuki and Yamazaki (2008) [4]. They used airborne remote sensing instead of satellite remote sensing after 16 July 2007 Niigata-Ken Chuetsu-Oki, Japan earthquake. They stated that spatial resolution in the airborne remote sensing is higher than satellite remote sensing, and they assessed the damage according to pixel and object based classifications. However, there were some salt and pepper noise in all of the images because of the high resolution.

Ozisik and Kerle (2004) tried to find buildings damaged by Kocaeli earthquake using remote sensing technology [5]. Their proposal depends on comparison of before and after images of regional areas to detect changes on buildings. In the proposal, vertical satellite and oblique airborne imagery methods are used, but they state several problems in damage assessments due to "vertical viewing characteristic, spatial and temporal resolution. There are a lot of damage detection methods based on satellite imaginary and airborne laser scanning in the literature, and several examples of them can be found in [6]-[10].

Video imaging based techniques have also been used to detect damages of earthquakes and to estimate the possible changes caused by earthquakes in land structure.

Kanda et al. have developed an interesting method to detect structural collapse and overturning of interior elements, and they used shaking table tests to assess the method's abilities in damage detection [11], [12]. Their proposal's results showed that the method has a great potential to detect small to large deformations. Another creative solution is to use aerial television images taken with a digital video camera from a light plane to assess damage of earthquake. They used these images to detect damaged buildings using multi level slice method and the maximum likelihood classifier [13].

Although many methods have developed, still there is a necessity of cheap and locally applicable real-time damage detection method. This paper addresses a possible solution to this necessity.

3   The Proposed System

The proposed system in this study is based on real-time monitoring buildings and comparison of before and after images captured by local video cameras located on watchtowers. Fig 1 shows the proposed system design.

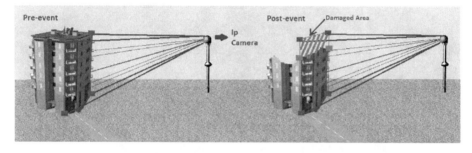

Fig. 1. Monitoring buildings using video cameras

In the proposed system, IP video cameras located on watchtowers scan the buildings' images (several medium size buildings –about 10 floors- or one huge building) continuously and send the video file to the command center. Next, the software at the command center captures images from video frames (capturing frequency is configurable and depends on the resolution and color quality of the video frames, default value is considered 1 frame/sec.), and it compares the images with the buildings' original images previously recorded to a database. Finally, if the software detects any change in volume of the buildings, it gives alert to national disaster management center. Fig 2 shows a screenshot from the computer program user interface written for the system.

Fig 3 demonstrates the comparison of before and after images method used in this study. Image comparison for finding the differences has been investigated for years, and several accurate models have discovered. Most of the comparison models are based on texture, shape-color and thresholds of images [14]-[16].

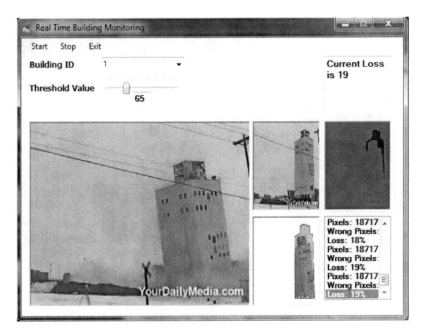

Fig. 2. A user interface of building monitoring software (simulation videos were downloaded from YourDailyMedia.com)

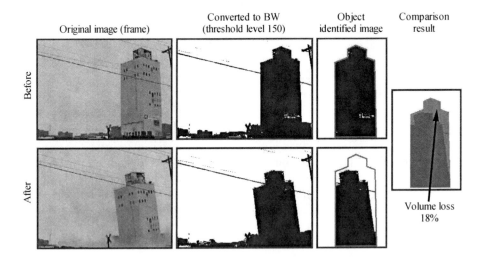

Fig. 3. Comparison of before and after images and detection simulation

Our proposal uses thresholds and color changes of images in comparing them. A clear image of and several information about the building, such as building id, location, size and type of building (residential, hospital etc.) are firstly stored in the system's database. The software converts the building image to black and white (BW) with a threshold level

150, and adds this new image to the database for future use. While video cameras at watchtowers in real-time provides new images (at a certain frame rate –usually 1frame/sec.) to the command center. The software converts these images into BW forms (at threshold level 150) continuously, and pushes into an image histogram (first in - first out), as shown Fig. 4. Next, comparison process is started.

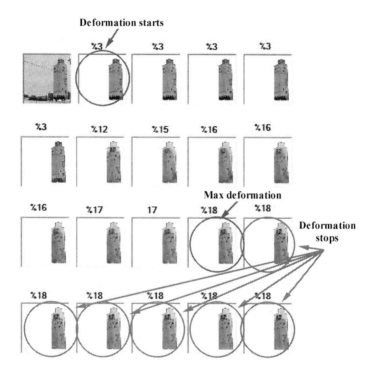

Fig. 4. Comparison histogram

The comparison results are calculated as the ratio of the deformation (% of change in volume or shape) on the building. If any deformation is detected on the building, then the software checks the delta value between two deformation ratios (current and previous values). This process continues until all the delta ratios become zero for last ten images, this means that there is no more change in volume and the building deformation is stable. Next, the last deformation ratio is considered as the total damage (percentage of volume loss) on the building. If this value is greater than 10% (this percentage is configurable), then the building is marked as collapsed building, and an alert is given.

4   Conclusions and Future Works

In this study, several different simulations have been done with building destruction video files. The results showed that the proposed system accurately detects all the damages on buildings and calculates the percentage of damage in normal weather conditions. However, at nights without a light-source, the system has failed several times in real-time detection of damages. Therefore the system requires a light source or a video camera with night vision ability in dark weather to operate properly, otherwise the accurate results can only be available after awhile (sun rise, or a light source supplied). Besides, cloudy weather conditions may affect the reliability of the system negatively because of noises in the images; therefore the system may have to be corrected manually. Furthermore, the system is operable only for local applications because of limited scanning capability of video cameras, and needs to be improved for wide area implementations.

Even though the system has a few disadvantages, it is very cheap, and it can be installed easily and quickly in a particular region. In addition, security and traffic control cameras can be used by the system without additional requirement as well as the system can be used for security and traffic control purposes. Moreover, the operational and maintenance cost of the system are reasonable low.

This paper presents a low cost real-time building monitoring system to detect damaged buildings in case of disasters, and it may be very useful for assessing the hazard, and for accelerated succoring casualties.

Acknowledgements

This study is a part of "HaReS: Real-time hazard reporting and loss estimation system" project, and it is also a part of graduation project supervised by Assoc. Prof. Dr. Yasar Guneri SAHIN. The authors would like to thank the staff of Izmir/Turkey Governorate for their valuable contributions.

References

1. Fawzy, D.E., Sahin, Y.G.: RT-HRLE: A System Design for Real-Time Hazards Reporting and Loss Estimation Using Wireless Sensors. In: International Conference on Education and Management Technology (ICEMT 2010), pp. 205–209 (2010)
2. Schweier, C., Markus, M., Steinle, E.: Simulation of earthquake caused building damages for the development of fast reconnaissance techniques. Natural Hazards and Earth System Sciences 4, 285–293 (2004)
3. Chen, Z.Q., Hutchinson, T.C.: Urban damage estimation using statistical processing of satellite images. Journal of Computing in Civil Engineering, 187–199 (May-June 2007)
4. Suzuki, D., Yamazaki, F.: Extraction of Building Damages in the 2007 Niigata-Ken Chuetsu-Oki Earthquake Using Digital Aerial Images. In: Proceedings of Asian Association on Remote Sensing, ACRS 2008 TS26.7 (2008)
5. Ozisik, D., Kerle, N.: Post - earthquake damage assessment using satellite and airborne data in the case of the 1999 Kocaeli earthquake, Turkey. In: ISPRS 2004-Proceedings of the XXth ISPRS congress: Geo-imagery bridging continents, pp. 686–691 (2004)
6. Yamazaki, F., Suzuki, D., Maruyama, Y.: Detection of damages due to earthquakes using digital aerial images. In: 6th International Workshop on Remote Sensing for Disaster Applications (2008)

7. Markus, M., Fiedrich, F., Gehbauer, F., Hirschberger, S.: Strong Earthquakes, Rapid Damage Assessment and Rescue Planning. In: Proceedings of the Seventh Annual Conference of the International Emergency Management Society, pp. 369–378 (1999)

8. Steinle, E., Kiema, J.B.K., Leebmann, J., Bähr, H.P.: Laser scanning for Analysis of Damages caused by Earthquake Hazards. In: Proceedings of OEEPE Workshop on Airborne Lasers canning and Interferometric SAR for Detailed Digital Elevation Models, vol. (40) (2001)

9. Sidar, Y., Bayram, B., Helvaci, C., Bayraktar, H.: Research the Change of the Buildings Before and After Earthquake by Using Airborne Photographs. In: XXth Congress International Society for Photogrammetry and Remote Sensing, Commission VII, WG VII/5, pp. 639–641 (2004)

10. Rehor, M.: Classification of Building Damages Based on Laser Scanning Data. In: ISPRS Workshop on Laser Scanning and SilviLaser 2007, pp. 326–331 (2007)

11. Kanda, K., Miyamoto, Y., Kondo, A., Oshio, M.: Monitoring of earthquake induced motions and damage with optical motion tracking. Smart Materials & Structures 14(3), S32–S38 (2005)

12. Kanda, K., Miyamoto, Y., Kondo, A., Oshio, M.: Seismic damage monitoring with optical motion tracking. Structural Health Monitoring and Intelligent Infrastructure 1, 521–528 (2003)

13. Mitomi, H., Saita, J., Matsuoka, M., Yamazaki, F.: Automated damage detection of buildings from aerial television images of the 2001 Gujarat, India earthquake. In: IEEE International Symposium on Geoscience and Remote Sensing (IGARSS), pp. 147–149 (2001)

14. Kelly, P., Cannon, M.: Experience with Candid - Comparison Algorithm for Navigating Digital Image Databases. In: Proceedings of the Society of Photo-Optical Instrumentation Engineers (SPIE), vol. 2368, pp. 64–75 (1995)

15. Rosin, P.L.: Thresholding for change detection. Computer Vision and Image Understanding 86(2), 79–95 (2002)

16. Rosin, P.L., Ioannidis, E.: Evaluation of global image thresholding for change detection. Pattern Recognition Letters 24(14), 2345–2356 (2003)

Face Recognition Algorithm Using Two Dimensional Principal Component Analysis Based on Discrete Wavelet Transform

Venus AlEnzi[1], Mohanad Alfiras[2], and Falah Alsaqre[2]

[1] Department of Electrical and Electronic Engineering, Gulf University
[2] Department of Computer Communication Engineering, Gulf University
ve_al@hotmail.com, dr.muhanned@gulfuniversity.net,
dr.Falah@gulfuniversity.net

Abstract. The roles of this paper is to improve the face recognition rate by applying different levels of discrete wavelet transform(DWT) as to reduce the high dimensional image into a low dimensional image. Two dimensional principal component analyze (2DPCA) is being utilized to find the face recognition accuracy rate, processing it through the ORL image database. This database contains images from 40 persons (10 different images for each) in grayscale and resolution of 92x112 pixels. An evaluation between 2DPCA and multilevel-DWT/2DPCA has been done. These have been assessed according to the recognition accuracy, recognition rate, dimensional reduction, computing complexity and multi-resolution data approximation. The results show that the recognition rate across all trials was higher using 2-level DWT/2DPCA than 2DPCA with a time rate of 4.28 sec. Also, these experiments indicate that the recognition time has been improved from 692.91sec to 1.69sec. with recognition accuracy from 90% to 92.5% .

Keywords: Face Recognition (FR), Two Dimensional Principle Component Analysis (2DPCA), Discrete Wavelet Transform (DWT).

1 Introduction

In our century, face recognition has received increased attention because of its benefit of being an appropriate conventional system to verify a person's identity in a natural and friendly way. It has various potential application sites, ranging from access control, to security monitoring to observation systems. Building face recognition systems is yet a sophisticated and complex issue, since faces have numerous variations and may be located in diverse environments. Due to the wide variety of illumination in pattern recognition and facial expressions with pose variations, it is considered among the most demanding research topics.

There are many approaches to evaluate face images. The methods used in face recognition can be generally classified into, image feature based and geometry feature based methods [1]. In feature geometry based approach, recognition is based on the relationship between human facial features such as eye(s), mouth, nose and face boundary and Subspace analysis approach attempts to capture and define the face as a

V. Snasel, J. Platos, and E. El-Qawasmeh (Eds.): ICDIPC 2011, Part I, CCIS 188, pp. 426–438, 2011.
© Springer-Verlag Berlin Heidelberg 2011

whole [2]. The subspace method is the most fames technique for face recognition. In this method the face treated as two-dimensional pattern of intensity variation. Yang et al. proposed a technique called two-dimensional PCA (2DPCA), which directly computes the Eigenvectors from an image covariance matrix avoiding the matrix-to-vector conversion [3]. Because of that the covariance matrix in 2DPCA can be computed more accurately and easily than that in PCA [1]. 2DPCA is a face recognition method that uses the Feature Subspaces technique within the field of signal & image analysis, the wavelet transform has emerged as a cutting edge technology [4]. The discrete wavelet transform (DWT) is a linear, invertible and fast orthogonal operation [5]. Wavelets are a good mathematical tool for hierarchically decomposing occupations [4]. Without degrading the quality of the image to an unacceptable level image compression minimizes the size in bytes of a graphics file. The reduction in file size permits more images to be stored in a certain amount of disk or memory space [6]. This is, considering that the wavelet transformation will take a place spatially over each image band, while the 2DPCA transform will take place spectrally over the set of images. Wavelet decomposition is a multilevel dimension reduction process that makes time–space–frequency analysis. In this study we investigate the effect of the DWT and two-dimensional selecting Eigenfaces 2DPCA on face recognition efficiency and the time rate using the ORL database.

The remainder of this paper is organized as follows: section 2, Discrete Wavelet Transform; Section 3: Two-Dimensional Principle Component Analysis; Section 4: Experimental Results and Analysis; Section 5: Conclusion.

2 Discrete Wavelet Transform

The discrete wavelet transform (DWT) is a prompt, linear, invertible and orthogonal method, just similar to the Discrete Fourier transform (DFT) The central idea lying under the DWT is to classify a time-scale representation of a signal (contrasting Short Time Fourier Transform (STFT), which defines a time-frequency signal representation) by decaying it onto a set of basic occupations, called wavelet[5]. Wavelet analysis is a local time frequency analysis technique, in which the low frequency has high frequency resolution and low time resolution, but the high frequency operates vice versa. Therefore, in the time frequency domain has a strong ability to represent local signal characteristics [7]. Wavelet transform develops both the spatial and frequency correlation of data by dilations (or contractions) and translations of mother wavelet on the input data [6]. The mother wavelet is designed to generate all the basic functions of a particular one. The one dimensional continuous wavelet transform (CWT) can be defined as follows:

$$CWT(s, \tau) = \frac{1}{\sqrt{s}} f(t) \Psi_{s, \tau}(t) \tag{1}$$

Where Ψ is called mother wavelet and the basis function can defined as:

$$\Psi_{s, \tau} = \frac{1}{\sqrt{s}} (\frac{t - \tau}{s} dt) \tag{2}$$

The parameter s represent the scaling and τ is the shift parameter. Wavelets are a mathematical tool to provide an efficient decomposition of signals prior to compression for hierarchically decomposing functions [8]. The decomposition can be applied at different levels repeatedly on low frequency channel (LL) to obtain next level decomposition [9]. The original image of size NxN will decomposed in to four sub band image of size $N/2 * N/2$ (Figure 1), when it pass through a series of high pass filters and low pass filters as it shown in Figure 2. The LL sub band corresponds to low frequency components of an image, and HL, LH and HH are high frequency components of an image.

LL	LH
HL	HH

Fig. 1. One grade wavelet decomposition for image of size NxN to for sub band of size $N/2*N/2$

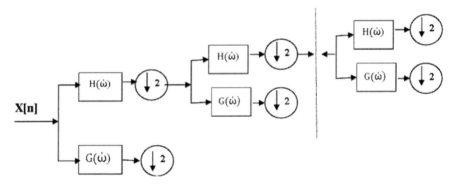

Fig. 2. Multi – level wavelet decomposition tree composed of low pass filter H and high pass filter G

They correspond respectively to vertical, horizontal and diagonal sub bands [9], only the sub image LL is further decomposed. Discrete wavelet transform (DWT) can be mathematically given as in equation (3):

$$DWT\ x(n) = \begin{cases} a_{p,q} = \sum x(n) g_p(n - 2^p q) \\ d_{p,q} = \sum x(n) h_p(n - 2^p q) \end{cases} \qquad (3)$$

The coefficient $d_{p.q}$ gives the frequency component details to the wavelet function, where as $a_{p.q}$ gives approximation components of the image. The functions $h(n)$ and $g(n)$ in the Equation (3) gives the coefficients of high pass and low pass filters respectively. The parameters p and q refers to wavelet scale and translation factors.

The one dimensional wavelet decomposition is applied first along the images rows, and then their results are further decomposed along the columns of the images [10]. Figure 3. shows DWT decomposition at 5 levels.

Fig. 3. First level DWT up to Fifth level DWT applied on ORL first image

$$H(w) = \frac{1}{2} + \frac{1}{2}e^{-jw}$$

$$G(w) = \frac{1}{2} + \frac{1}{2}e^{-jw}$$

(4)

Where $G(w)$ is a high pass filter, and $H(w)$ is a low pass filter. Low pass analysis coefficients of Haar Wavelet is $\begin{bmatrix} \frac{1}{2} & \frac{1}{2} \end{bmatrix}$. High pass analysis coefficients of Haar Wavelet is $\begin{bmatrix} \frac{-1}{2} & \frac{1}{2} \end{bmatrix}$. High pass synthesis coefficients of Haar Wavelet is $\begin{bmatrix} \frac{1}{2} & \frac{-1}{2} \end{bmatrix}$ low pass synthesis coefficients of Haar Wavelet is $\begin{bmatrix} \frac{1}{2} & \frac{1}{2} \end{bmatrix}$ [4]. The advantages of Haar wavelet transform:

1. The computation time has the best performance.
2. The computation has high speed.
3. HWT is efficient decomposition method.
4. The signal can be divided into a low and a high frequency part and filters enabling the splitting without duplicating information.
5. Haar transform is a very fast transform.

3   Two – Dimensional Principal Component Analysis (2D PCA)

Principal component analysis (PCA) has been known as an Eigenfaces method for face recognition. The two dimensional face image in the PCA must be previously transformed into one dimensional vector, which leads to high dimensional image space. Therefore, it becomes difficult to compute the covariance matrix. Moreover, finding the Eigenvectors from a large size covariance matrix is highly time- consuming. To overcome those difficulties, a new technique known as two-dimensional principal component analysis (2DPCA) is appropriate. Two dimensional -PCA is a method that uses the 2D features, which are features, obtained directly from original vector space of a face image rather than from a vector sized 1D space [1]. The idea of 2DPCA is to find directly the Eigenvectors of the covariance matrix without converting matrix-to-vector. Due to the fact that the size of the image covariance matrix is equal to the size of each element matrix of the data set, which is very small compared to the size of a covariance matrix in PCA, the two dimensional -PCA finds the corresponding Eigenvectors and the covariance matrix more efficiently more accurately than PCA [5].

In order to apply the 2DPCA consider A as m x n random image matrix.

$$A = \begin{pmatrix} a_{11} & \cdots & a_{12} \\ \vdots & \ddots & \vdots \\ a_{m1} & \cdots & a_{mn} \end{pmatrix} \tag{5}$$

Projecting A onto x yields an M- dimensional vector y.

$$Y = Ax \tag{6}$$

Calculate the mean row matrix $\overline{A}$, of matrix A using equation 7, (Figure 4. Shows the mean face)

Fig. 4. Mean face for the ORL database

$$\overline{A} = \frac{1}{m} \sum_{i=1}^{m} A_i \tag{7}$$

The main idea of 2DPCA is to select good projection vectors X. To evaluate good projection vectors, the total scatter of the projected samples S_x, which can be denoted by the trace of the covariance matrix of the projected feature vectors, so the following equation 8.

$$J_{(x)} = \text{tr}(S_x) \tag{8}$$

Where S_x is the covariance matrix of the projected feature vectors, determining by equations 9 and 10. Figure 5. shows the Eigen covariance matrix :

$$S_x = E(y - Ey)(y - Ey)^T = E[(A - EA)x][(A - EA)]^T \tag{9}$$

Hence

$$J_{(x)} = \text{tr}(S_x) = x^T E[(A - EA)^T (A - EA)]x \tag{10}$$

Fig. 5. Eigen covariance matrix

Given a set of training images A(1), A(2), … , A(n), criterion (10) becomes

$$J(x) = x^T [\sum_{i=1}^{m} (A_i - \overline{A})^T (A_i - \overline{A})]x \tag{11}$$

Let

$$G = \frac{1}{M} \sum_{i=1}^{m} (A_i - \overline{A})^T (A_i - \overline{A}) \tag{12}$$

Where G is alternatively, the criterion in (8) can be expressed by

$$J(x) = X^T G_i X \tag{13}$$

This criterion is called the generalized total scatter criterion, where X is a unitary vector that maximizes the criterion is called the optimal projection axis J(X). i.e. the eigenvector of G corresponding to the largest Eigenvalue.

In general, it is not enough to have only one optimal projection axis Xopt. It's usually needed to select a set of projection axis. X_1 ,… , X_d as it showed in equation (14)

$$\{X_1........X_d\} = \arg\max J(x)$$
$$X_1^T X_j = 0, i \neq j \quad i, j = 1........c$$

(14)

Where Xopt are the orthogonal Eigenvectors of G_i corresponding to the first d largest Eigenvalues. Figure 6. shows the Eigenvectors with 2DPCA in ORL database.

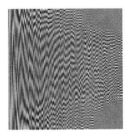

Fig. 6. Show Eigenvectors using 2DPCA

A feature matrix is obtained for each image, after a transformation by 2DPCA, [11]. Then a nearest neighbor classifier is used for classification. Here the distance between two arbitrary feature matrices Ai and Aj is defined by using Euclidean distance as follows:

$$d(A_i, A_j) = \sqrt{\sum_{u=1}^{k}\sum_{v=1}^{d}(A_i(u,v) - A_j(u,v))^2}$$

(15)

Given a test sample At,

if $d(A_t, A_c) = \min_j d(A_j, A_t)$) , then the resulting decision is At belong to the same class as A_c [11].

4   Experimental Result and Analysis

The experiment is performed using ORL face database from AT&T (Olivetti) Research Laboratories, Cambridge [2]. The ORL data base contain images with grayscale and normalized to a resolution of 112x92 pixels from 40 individuals, each have ten different images with different facial expression such as open/closed eyes and smiling/non smiling face. Also facial details variation is included. All images have the same dark homogeneous background with frontal position and tolerance for some side movement. This data base has been divided for training and testing class, five images for each. Thus the total number for the training samples and testing sample were both 200. The aim of this experiment was to compare the performance of different six methods (2DPCA without using DWT, first level DWT/2DPCA second level DWT/2DPCA, third level DWT/2DPCA, forth level DWT/2DPCA and fifth level DWT/2DPCA) on face recognition and investigating the recognition rate according to the size of Eigenfaces space selection considering the time rate for the recognition operation. Table 1 shows the results of the 2DPCA recognition assay. It demonstrates that the recognition rate was best at 90.5%, with an Eigenvalue of 50% and a timing of 177.11 sec. Moreover, it shows that the recognition value did not change, (90%) at Eigenvalues of 100%, 75% and 25%. Also, the time rate decreased as the Eigenvalue decreased from 692.91 sec to 49.56sec. In order to get the best recognition rate in the least time, an Eigenvalue of 25% is better (90% recognition in 49.56 sec). Figure7. shows the relation between the face recognition and the Eigenfaces on 2DPCA technique.

Table 1. Recognition rate 2DPCA

Technique	Eigen value selection	Recognition Rate %	Test time In second
2DPCA (112x92)	100%	90	692.91
	75%	90	396.98
	50%	90.5	177.11
	25%	90	49.56

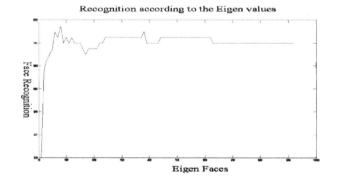

Fig. 7. Show the recognition rate at different Eignfaces using 2DPCA

In table2 the recognition rate was improved with first level DWT/2DPCA technique on the same time the recognition time was increase also up to 6.87 esc   with the 25% of the Eigenvalues coefficient and recognition rate of 94%. While it will take 88.80 sec for the full coefficient Eigenvalues and recognition rate of 92.5%. it can be observed that the performance of decreasing the Eigenvalue selection will give better recognition rate and time with images of size (56x46). Figure 8. shows the relation between the face recognition and the Eigen faces on 1-level of DWT/2DPCA technique.

Table 2. Recognition rate 1-level DWT

Technique	Eigen value selection	Recognition Rate %	Test time In second
1-level DWT/2DPCA (56x46)	100%	92.5	88.80
	75%	93.5	51.31
	50%	93	25.37
	25%	94	6.87

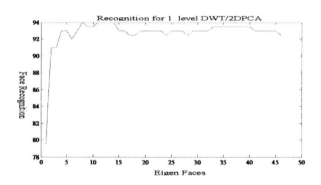

Fig. 8. Show the recognition rate at different Eigenfaces using 1-level DWT/2DPCA

Table 3 shows the different values obtained when using second level DWT/2DPCA. At the 50% selection of Eigenvalue, the highest recognition rate value of 94.5% was reported with a best recognition time of 4.28 sec. When changing the Eigenvalue selection to the fullest only the time rate increased up to 12.34sec, while the recognition rate stayed the same. Figure 9. illustrates the relation between the face recognition and the Eigenfaces on 2- level DWT/2DPCA technique.

Table 3. Recognition rate 2-level DWT

Technique	Eigen value selection	Recognition Rate %	Test time In second
2-level DWT/2DPCA (28x23)	100%	94.5	12.34
	75%	94	7.07
	50%	94.5	4.28
	25%	92.5	1.69

In the third level DWT/2DPCA technique, it was found that the best recognition rate (85.5%) is given by a full Eigenvalue with a timing of 2.61 sec, as shown in table 4. However, in order to reduce recognition time in 0.70 sec, it is appropriate to select an Eigenvalue of 25%, for which the recognition rate wouldn't decrease significantly (81.5%). Figure 10. shows the relation between the face recognition and the Eigenfaces on a 3-level DWT/2DPCA technique.

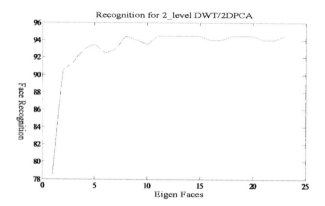

Fig. 9. Show the recognition rate at different Eigenfaces using 2-level DWT/2DPCA

Table 4. Recognition rate 3-level DWT

Technique	Eigen value selection	Recognition Rate%	Test time In second
3-level DWT/2DPCA (14x12)	100%	85.5	2.61
	75%	85.5	1.89
	50%	84	1.29
	25%	81.5	0.71

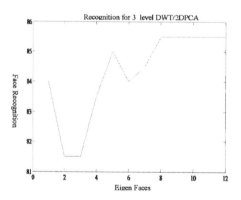

Fig. 10. Show the recognition rate at different Eigenfaces using 3-level DWT/2DPCA

In table5 the recognition rate was drop off to 30.5% with the 4-level DWL/2DPCA technique and the recognition time was 2.61 sec with the full Eigenvalues coefficient. It is also can be seen that when the selection of the Eigenfaces decrease the recognition rate also decrease. Figure 11. Present the relation between the face recognition and the Eigenfaces on 4-level DWT/2DPCA technique.

Table 5. Recognition rate 4-level DWT

Technique	Eigenvalue selection	Recognition Rate %	Test time In second
4-level DWT/2DPCA (7x6)	100%	30.5	2.61
	75%	30.5	1.89
	50%	30	1.29
	25%	23	0.71

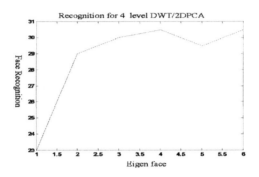

Fig. 11. Show the recognition rate at different Eigenfaces using 4-level DWT/2DPCA

Table 6. Fifth level DWT/2DPCA technique in the ORL data base lead to low efficiency in recognition rate, it decreases to 2.5% with a time rate for 0.29 sec. Figure 12. shows the relation between the face recognition and the Eigenfaces on fifth level DWT/2DPCA technique. It can be observed that the performance of Eigenvectors selection in image of size 3x4 it getting worse and it fixed the recognition rate to very low level.

Table 6. Recognition rate 5-level DWT

Technique	Eigen value selection	Recognition Rate %	Test time In second
5-level DWT/2DPCA (4x3)	100%	2.5	0.57
	75%	2.5	0.44
	50%	2.5	0.29
	25%	0	0.15

Comparing the recognition performances of two dimensional principal component analysis (2DPCA) with the various discrete wavelet transform (DWT) shows that accuracy average of only 2DPCA is 90.13% whereas the average accuracy of 1-level DWT/2DPCA is 93.25%. The average accuracy of 2-level DWT/2DPCA is 93.88% knowing that 2-level DWT/2DPCA have a fast time rate of about 1.8 sec. For 3-level DWT/2DPCA the average accuracy is 84.13% whereas that of 4-level DWT/2DPCA is 28.5%, and of 5-level DWT/2DPCA is 1.88%

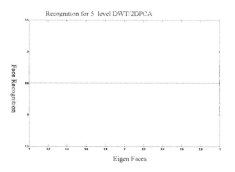

Fig. 12. Show the recognition rate at different Eigenfaces using 5-level DWT/2DPCA

5 Conclusion

In this paper we proposed a face recognition method by coalescing the histogram equalization discrete wavelet transform (DWT) subband representation and two dimensional principal component analysis (2DPCA). We have been scrutinizing the relationship between the Eigenfaces selection and the efficiency of the face recognition and we found that the more Eigenfaces selected, the more efficiency we get. However, in certain selections it does not change or it can decrease as well. As a result of applying DWT on the ORL database, face images are decomposed and choosing a lower resolution subband image considerably reduces the calculation complexity. Using the DWT with a different level will enable high compression ratios with good quality of reconstruction, which helps us decrease the time rate and speed up the recognition operation from 692.91 sec to 0.70 sec, with a high quality of face recognition (81.5%). Implementing WDT/2DPCA based recognition gave us better results than the 2DPCA approach. Experimental results show that the higher recognition accuracy with 2DPCA method is 90.5% with 50% of Eigenvalues selection and a time rate of 177.11 sec. On the other hand, combining 2-level DWL technique with 2DPCA method gave us the highest recognition accuracy (94.5%) with a time rate of 4.28 sec using the same Eigen values selection. Analyzing the recognition performances of various wavelets at 5 levels, 1 to 5, the recognition accuracy average was convenient up to the third level of wavelet. The numbers were 93.25%, 93.88% and 84.13% accuracy average, respectively, but there was significant uncertainty with the forth and the fifth level of wavelet, as it was 28.5% and 1.88% respectively.

References

1. Radha, V., Pushpalatha, M.: Comparison of PCA Based and 2DPCA Based Face Recognition Systems. International Journal of Engineering Science and Technology 2(12), 7177–7182 (2010)
2. Kinage1, K.S., Bhirud2, S.G.: Face Recognition based on Two- Dimensional PCA on Wavelet Subband. International Journal of Recent Trends in Engineering 2(2) (November 2009)

3. Koerich, A.L., de Oliveira, L.E.S., Britto Jr, A.S.: Face Recognition Using Selected 2DPCA Coefficients. In: 17th International Conference on Systems, Signals and Image Processing-IWSSIP (2010)
4. Ashok, V., Balakumaran, T., Gowrishankar, C., Vennila, I.L.A., Nirmal kumar, A.: The Fast Haar Wavelet Transform for Signal & Image Processing (IJCSIS). International Journal of Computer Science and Information Security 7(1) (2010)
5. Liu, C.-C., Chin, S.-Y.: A Face Identification Algorithm using Two Dimensional Principal Component Analysis Based on Wavelet Transform. In: International Conference on Advanced Information Technologies, AIT (2010)
6. Talukder, K.H., Harada, K.: Haar Wavelet Based Approach for Image Compression and Quality Assessment of Compressed Image. IAENG International Journal of Applied Mathematics 36(1), 36-1-9 (2007)
7. Dongcheng, S.H.I., Qinqing, W.: A Face Recognition Algorithm Based on Block PCA and Wavelet Transform. Applied Mechanics and Materials 40, 523–530 (2011)
8. Stollnitz, E.J., Derose, T.D., Salesin, D.H.: Wavelets for Computer Graphics- Theory and Applications Book. Morgan Kaufmann Publishers, Inc., San Francisco
9. Ramesha, K., Raja, K.B.: Gram-Schmidt Orthogonalization Based Face Recognition Using DWT. International Journal of Engineering Science and Technology (IJEST) 3 (2011) ISSN : 0975-5462
10. Murugan, D., Arumugam, S., Rajalakshmi, K., Manish, T.I.: Performance Evaluation of Face Recognation Using Gabor Filter, Log Gabor filter and Discrete Wavelet Transform. International journal of computer science & information Technology (IJCSIT) 2(1) (February 2010)
11. Nhat, V.D.M., Lee, S.: Kernel-based 2DPCA for Face Recognition. In: IEEE International Symposium on Signal Processing and Information Technology 978-1 -4244-1 835-0/07 (2007)

Construction and Interpretation of Data Structures for Rotating Images of Coins

Radoslav Fasuga, Petr Kašpar, Martin Šurkovský, and Martin Němec

VŠB - Technical University of Ostrava
Department of Computer Science
17. listopadu, Ostrava - Poruba, Czech Republic
{radoslav.fasuga,petr.kaspar.st4,martin.surkovsky.st1,
martin.nemec}@vsb.cz

Abstract. This article is oriented to the processing of multimedia data. This is a proposal for a rapid and computationally efficient method that is applicable in the Internet environment with the minimum requirements for hardware and software. The article mapping the current state of the recognition of multimedia data independent of the rotation and deformation. Proposes its own solution for pre-processing, storing and indexing images in the form of vectors. Here are discussed various methods of searching in image data. For the purposes of detecting commemorative coins, the approach was chosen based on edge detection and subsequent indexing. Directions are outlined to further development of the whole project. A particular focus on effective pre-processing and indexing large collections of data.

Keywords: Coin, image processing, indexing, searching.

1 Introduction

Coins are one of the most frequently used legal tender in the world. First coins were used thousands of years before Christ. Non-cash payment system is very popular nowadays, but coins are still in use today.

The search and indexing of multimedia data in the past few years has growing interest. The main goal of this project is to create complex internet catalogue of monetary and commemorative coins or medals with recognition system based on images. The main purpose of this work is to provide tools for easy identification of unknown coins. The system can be used also to identify fake coins.

In the first part of the article describes the methods suitable image preprocessing. Where the largest part is devoted to standardizing the method of rotation of the coin. It is one of the most important steps in the preprocessing, which then allows for efficient storage templates in the database. Ideally, a single model for one coin.

The second part of a larger article is devoted to methods for storing models in a database and subsequent search. For each of the methods are published and search results.

V. Snasel, J. Platos, and E. El-Qawasmeh (Eds.): ICDIPC 2011, Part I, CCIS 188, pp. 439–447, 2011.
© Springer-Verlag Berlin Heidelberg 2011

2   State of the Art

We can access the description of the image by several possible ways. The first division is to describe the categories, either text or image content, respectively combination of both. Then is possible to precise them. This work deals with the description of the image according to its content [1], specifically by the shapes in the image.

More options image recognition based on color or texture are unsuitable for us. Color because it is too dependent on the quality of acquired images and the quality of the coin itself. We removed a detection area (region based shapes), as the images on the coins are often very detailed and it is better to use edge detection. Methods for edge detection, there are several. We chose Canny edge detector which is generally recognized as one of the best and most accurate. Results of GFD were not for our purpose too convincing. This method is more suitable for the area, the edges form a very small piece of information for recognition. The other possibility is using of Neural Networks [2] or Gabor wavelets [3].

3   Preprocessing

Preprocessing aims at the beginning of the image of the coin properly prepare for the subsequent edge detection. This is meant to eliminate adverse effects early, such as might be: different image size, different lighting, etc. The procedure is as follows: Selection of the relevant area, scale standardization, transfer to grayscale, standardization brightness.

3.1   Problems That May Arise

Perhaps the most problems comes with atypical forms of coins. This group comprises the old, such as ancient coins [4]. They has often (develop) an irregular shape, are often falsely embossed a piece of the coin is missing.

Often the problem is not just to identify the center of the coin, which is needed in further processing, but also to select the relevant area. To select the relevant area is then possible to proceed in two ways: copy the image of a coin or take

Fig. 1. Center issue   **Fig. 2.** Oxidation

Fig. 3. Camera   **Fig. 4.** Scanner

the circle as much of the central motif (Fig. 1). Also for coin detection is very negative oxidation of the coin (Fig. 2).

Other problems can cause a type of device, which is a picture taken. Very large difference can be seen as using the scanner and camera (Fig. 3 and 4). It was one of the main reasons why we preferred edge detection method.

4   Rotation Normalization

The algorithms we use for processing and indexing of images depends on the orientation of images. The ideal is that all (same) coins are standardized into one rotation variant. To this end, we tested several possible approaches, some of them brings satisfactory results and others are later proved to be unsuitable.

4.1   Rotation Normalization Using CG Image

The fundamental task of this method is to find the value of gravity image with which it can calculate the angle by which you need to rotate the picture. Center of gravity can be calculated from the moments. Moment the image is defined by:

$$m_{p,q} = \iint_{\Omega} x^p y^p f(x,y) dx dy \tag{1}$$

The function $f(x,y)$ is image function - shows the brightness of the coordinates, p, q indicate the degree of Ω brings part of the image. To calculate the center of gravity of the picture is necessary to know the moments m_{00}, m_{01} and m_{10}, from which we calculate the center of gravity by relations:

$$x_T = \frac{m_{10}}{m_{00}} , y_T = \frac{m_{01}}{m_{00}} \tag{2}$$

Angle φ is calculated as the deviation of direction vectors $\boldsymbol{s}$ a $\boldsymbol{t}$ lines SS_1 and ST (picture below) according to the formula:

$$\cos \alpha = \cos \left(\widehat{\boldsymbol{s},\boldsymbol{t}} \right) = \frac{\boldsymbol{s} \cdot \boldsymbol{t}}{|\boldsymbol{s}| \, |\boldsymbol{t}|} \tag{3}$$

According to the quadrant in which lies the center of gravity, make correct orientation (Fig. 5). If the center of gravity T found in quadrants $II.$ or $III.$ we make a rotation of the coin about a point S with the angle $-\alpha$. Conversely, if the center of gravity T found in quadrants I or $IV.$ We make a rotation of the coin about a point S with the angle $+\alpha$.

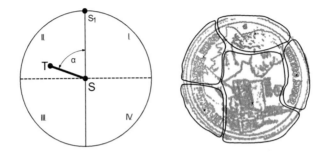

Fig. 5. Calculation of angles   **Fig. 6.** Cluster scatter plot

This method of normalization of rotation is not worked in practice too, because the results were very inconsistent. Some coins were standardized orientation relatively successful, in other coins, however, differences appear in the order to tens of degrees. These errors are caused by the center of gravity was near the geometric center of the whole coin, and the deviation of the number of pixels causes a deviation in the order of tens of degrees.

4.2   Normalization Rotation Using Clustering Algorithms

Normalization rotation method using clustering algorithm [5] works on a similar idea as the previous method. In this case, however, does not focus the image, but by grouping algorithms try to identify the most important areas of the coin (the largest clusters) and on those areas of standardization for rotation, similar as in the previous method (Fig. 6).

Here was tested several grouping algorithms and several metrics, the results were very inconsistent. It follows that even this method is not suitable for standardization rotation of commemorative coins.

4.3   Normalization Rotation Method Extended Histogram

The last method is based on the coin image in polar coordinates. The problem of rotation in polar coordinates replaced by the problem of displacement.

The first step is to convert the image from Cartesian coordinates (Fig. 3) to polar coordinates and subsequent implementation of precalculation - histogram equation, edge detection, thresholding (Fig. 7 Bottom).

Subsequently, we calculate the frequency of edge points in each column image in polar coordinates. Visualization of the frequency in the form of a histogram can be seen in Fig. 7 Bottom.

Fig. 7. Polar coordinates + preprocessing + basic histogram

The first variant of this algorithm to work with the histogram. On the basis of the detected minima and maxima, under which was subsequently carried out standardization displacement (rotation). These results were not very accurate, as minima and maxima in the histogram there are more even minor variations in the number of points will introduce inaccuracies in the result. Therefore, we developed this idea further and created a method called the extended histogram.

The principle is as follows. For each coordinate axis x to calculate the basic frequency histogram of all points on the coordinate and add N frequencies of x-ary points on the following positions. The resulting frequency is placed into the new histogram. The advantage of this scheme is that the new histogram has expanded coherent course than the basic histogram. There is elimination of undesirable deviations and errors in the calculation.

Normalization shift is based on extended histogram. Figuratively speaking, the histogram is interleaved by line so that a certain percentage of the points below this line. During the experiments, we used a value of 85%. Consequently, we find the largest contiguous area, which will be defined as the beginning point of reference for the normalization shift.

It is important not to remove a non-important areas that could affect the largest contiguous area. Perform this step in two sub-steps. First, remove all areas whose width is less than 10 points (approximately 2.5% across the width of the histogram). It is also removed on the basis of their area. Removes all the tips and slumps, the surface is negligible (for example, the width may be sufficient, but the depth is only 1 pixel).

5 Getting Image Descriptive Vector – Masks

The result of image processing methods is the final theme of the coin without the irrelevant data is standardized and the rotation of Cartesian coordinates. This template should be stored in the database.

The first way to distribute the resulting processed motif segments in the form of 4×4 matrix (Fig. 8). Total is 16 square segments. Each of them has a size of 64×64px in size of the input image 256×256px. The database stores the number of (edge) points in each segment and the total number of points. In the first search process sought the input of the coin, which is also divided into segments, and calculate the respective numbers of points. After that the actual selection of similar coins was made with SQL (Structured Query Language) query. First, compare the total number of points in the model and then there matching count of points in each segment.

It is unlikely that the same two coins have the same pixel counts, it is necessary to establish tolerance in the search. Tolerance for the total number of points is set to 2000. Overall, the picture may be 51468 points. Tolerance of points in each segment is 250 points. Overall, the segment may be 4096 points. These values emerged from the practical tests.

Since the 4×4 matrix contains large segments, we used to compare the mask of the size of 8×8. In principle, this method works identically as the previous method. Results were 8×8 matrix better, but we also store more information in the database.

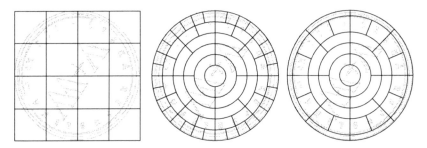

Fig. 8. Square mask 4×4 **Fig. 9.** Circular 63 seg.   **Fig. 10.** Circular 39 seg.

Type of segments can also be based on the shape of coins. These are usually in the shape of a circle, the perimeter usually contains some text and motive in the middle, and so on.

On Fig. 9 is seen dividing of a coin into 63 segments. These are created equal, distribution of the coin for a few rings and they are also evenly divided into specific segments. Segments in each ring sizes are different. Numbers of points in segments in each ring (from center): 1429, 2071, 1824, 1228, 793 and 518. Segments are numbered in ascending order by value 1 from the center in a clockwise direction.

On Fig. 10 the right to see an improved shape of segments. The outer ring is thinner to the other ring by 50%. At the same time in the outer ring of the lower number of segments (8 instead of the original 32). Second extended ring is better for text (content) values that are usually located in this part of the coin. The total number of segments with this approach reduced at the 39.

All the methods have their advantages and disadvantages. The experiments are used by all. These masks are also used as a tool for defining critical areas on a coin (Fig. 11), which can also be used to refine search results.

Fig. 11. Tool for defining critical areas on a coin

5.1   Test Search by Quantity of Pixels in Each Segment of the Mask

The success of this method was verified by the following test. There is a test set
of images A. This is a set of 50 images, each of which is turned by a random angle
between $0°$ to $359°$ (compared to the models in the database). Images come at
random from 2 different sources (scanners). Searching the database with a total
of 358 coins. Used all four types of masks. Rotation normalization is performed
using the extended histogram, which is discussed above. To calculate the most
similar coins is chosen algorithm City Block Distance:

$$CBD = |seg_1 - tseg_1| + \ldots + |seg_n - tseg_n| \qquad (4)$$

We compare our input vector $S = (seg_1, \ldots, seg_n)$ with vectors of all models
in the database $T = (tseg_1, \ldots, tseg_n)$.

In Table 1 are the results for different types of masks. The results show that
the use of all types of masks was at least 80% of cases found the required coins
in 10 first ten places in the search results. When using a uniform mask of 63
segments was the success of finding the right coins to 10 times even 90%. The
previous figure (Fig. 12) results are shown graphically.

Table 1. Searching test

Mask	Place						
	1st	2nd	3rd	4th	5th	6th - 10th	> 10th
4×4	64%	2%	6%	4%	2%	4%	18%
8×8	76%	2%	2%	4%	0%	0%	16%
63	78%	2%	0%	4%	0%	6%	10%
39	76%	2%	4%	2%	0%	4%	12%

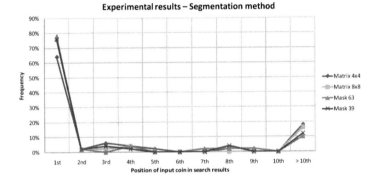

Fig. 12. Test search by pixel frequency

6   Conclusion and Future Work

Presented methods for processing, storage and retrieval of coins are only the first step in searching in this specific field of images. Proposed tests suggest that they might be sufficient for initial search, especially the method with circular masks. In the near future we plan to run a test on a much larger collection of data around 100000 images. Furthermore, we want to focus on identification of important data on the coins, such as the year, the nominal value or name of natural origin. The database proposed to use sophisticated data structures. At the current time, we consider to use of M-tree structures.

Work is partially supported by Grant of GACR No. P202/10/0573, and SP2011/172.

References

1. Vassilieva, N.S.: Content-Based Image Retrieval Methods. Program. Comput. Softw. 35(3), 158–180 (2009)
2. Khashman, A., Sekeroglu, B., Dimililer, K.: Rotated Coin Recognition Using Neural Networks. Analysis and Design of Intelligent Systems using Soft Computing Techniques, 290–297 (2007)

3. Shen, L., Jia, S., Ji, Z., Chen, W.S.: Statictics of Gabor Features for Coin Recognition. In: IEEE International Workshop on Imaging Systems and Techniques IST 2009, pp. 295–298 (2009)
4. Kampel, M., Zaharieva, M.: Recognizing ancient coins based on local features. In: Bebis, G., Boyle, R., Parvin, B., Koracin, D., Remagnino, P., Porikli, F., Peters, J., Klosowski, J., Arns, L., Chun, Y.K., Rhyne, T.-M., Monroe, L. (eds.) ISVC 2008, Part I. LNCS, vol. 5358, pp. 11–22. Springer, Heidelberg (2008)
5. Malyszko, D., Stepaniuk, J.: Adaptive Rough Entropy Clustering Algorithms in Image Segmentation. Fundam. Inf. 98(2-3), 199–231 (2010)

Digitalization of Pixel Shift in 3CCD Camera-Monitored Images

Yoshiro Imai[1], Hirokazu Kawasaki[1], Yukio Hori[1], and Shin'ichi Masuda[2]

[1] Graduate School of Engineering, Kagawa University
2217-20 Hayashi-cho, Takamatsu, Kagawa, 761-0396 Japan
[2] CMICRO Corporation
269-1 Hayashi-cho, Takamatsu, Kagawa, 761-0301, Japan
imai@eng.kagawa-u.ac.jp

Abstract. This paper describes a phenomenon "pixel shift" which sometimes occurs in images monitored by 3CCD Cameras and others. If there is such a pixel shift in the image, a user is suffering from a lack of precision of the image to be measured or utilized for image recognition and other image understanding. In a conventional approach, a specialist has determined whether pixel shift occurs or not in the image and he/she has reported performance evaluation for the relevant camera which monitors the image. This paper proposes a numerical method to detect occurrence of pixel shift in the image with Lagrange interpolation function, calculates the values of the level for occurrence of pixel shift quantitatively, and then compares the calculated results with the determination by specialist for 20 sample image files. The comparison results have good scores and support probability of a proposed approach to detect occurrence of pixel shift in the image without help from specialist. This paper calls the below sequence of procedure "digitalization of pixel shift", namely, 1) reading the values of R, G, and B signals from the target image, 2) selecting some sample values, 3) interpolating a suitable approximation function with the previous sample values, and 4) calculating numerically phase difference of R, G, B signals as the level for occurrence of pixel shift.

Keywords: Digitalization of pixel shift, Determination for occurrence of pixel shift, Numerical methods with function interpolation.

1 Introduction

Nowadays, several applications with monitoring and surveillance become essential and very much necessary because of accident detection, crime prevention, disaster avoidance and so on[1][2][3]. Web Cameras and digital image understanding with related technologies have been essential and playing one of the most important roles for the above activities.

As several kinds of digital cameras become more popular, users of such cameras want to apply them into various fields. Some of applications include image

V. Snasel, J. Platos, and E. El-Qawasmeh (Eds.): ICDIPC 2011, Part I, CCIS 188, pp. 448–459, 2011.

understanding, image-based measuring, objects detecting, and so on. These procedures assume the precision of camera's resolution. Such procedures should check resolution precision of their cameras in order to achieve good performance for image recognition. Some cameras, especially 3CCD color cameras, cannot always provide good images in practical cases. Images sometimes have blur or color bleeding. In such a case, this paper defines that there occurs a phenomenon "pixel shift" in the target image which has been monitored by the potentially incorrect camera.

It is very important to detect occurrence of pixel shift based on not only visual judgment by specialist but also mechanical/electronic examination by suitable method for the sake of correct monitoring with the camera. This paper describes determination whether a phenomenon "pixel shift" occurs in images monitored by 3CCD Cameras or not, calculating the value/level for occurrence of such pixel shift in the image by means of interpolating methods, and comparing the a proposed approach with a certain conventional one by specialist.

This paper explains such a phenomenon and determines whether "pixel shift" occurs or not through the following procedures; namely recognizing occurrence of pixel shift in the monitored images obtained from 3CCD camera, Web camera, etc., calculating relevant values of pixel shift with interpolating method of approximation function, and visualizing corresponding results by means of numerical methods and graphical ones. A series of the above procedures are called "digitalization of pixel shift" within the paper.

In order to formulate a determination procedure efficiently, this paper includes the following sections; The next section introduces a phenomenon "pixel shift" of the images obtained from 3CCD cameras and proposed approach to detect occurrence of pixel shift without relying on specialist's contribution. The third section explains how to analyze pixel shift and compute it into digital values. Numerical methods with function interpolation are utilized to calculate the digital values systematically. The fourth section demonstrates digitalization for the real images of 3CCD camera, comparison the digitalized results with determination by specialist, classification of those images with specialist's determination and proposed digitalization approach, and mentions future works. And finally, the last section concludes some summaries of this paper.

2   Research Background

This section introduces a phenomenon "pixel shift" in the image monitored by potentially incorrect Camera in the first subsection. And it shows proposed approach for efficient detection of occurrence of pixel shift by means of numerical method instead of visual judgment by specialist.

2.1   A Phenomenon "Pixel Shift" in Camera-Monitored Images

This subsection introduces a phenomenon, which is called "pixel shift" in this paper, in the images obtained from 3CCD color cameras. Recently, 3CCD cameras become popular in the fields of image-based measuring and object detecting.

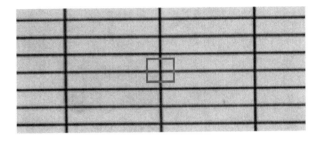

Fig. 1. Image for Fiducial Grids of Standard Target for Camera Calibration

Performance of such cameras has played a dominate role for reliability of measurement and detection. Precision of resolution is also very much important for 3CCD color cameras. Figure 1 shows an image for fiducial grids of standard target for camera calibration and focuses an orange-line square for one of its grids. This is a very important baseline for camera calibration as well as detection of target objects.

If a camera is designed to work correctly and generate suitable images for several applications such as image understanding, it can provide normal images, one of which is expressed in the Figure 2.

At manufacturing lines of 3CCD color camera in Japanese corporation, a few specialists must check quality and performance of their corporation-produced cameras, unit by unit in the literature, in a relatively short period in order to improve efficiency of corporation's production. Such a process sometimes needs time-consuming procedures and almost always suffers from a lack of human resources, for example, power, capability, working time and so on.

On the other hand, if cameras may unfortunately be designed/manufactured not to work correctly, they cannot provide images just like Figure 2. Some of those cameras used to provide images shown in Figure 3.

Fig. 2. Normal Digital Image for an Orange-line Square in Figure 1

Fig. 3. Non-suitable Digital Image for an Orange-line Square in Figure 1

In such a case, there may be a clear detection of a phase difference among R, G, and B signals provided from the relevant 3CCD digital color camera.With comparison between Figure 2 and Figure 3, the latter is clearly recognized to include occurrence of a phenomenon "pixel shift" in contradistinction to the former.

2.2 Proposed Approach to Detect Occurrence of Pixel Shift

As mentioned before, pixel shift can be defined as phase difference among R, G, and B signals for color images. A specialist has been able to find and recognize such a phenomenon in the color image while adjusting 3CCD camera by means of visual judgment. However, this procedure sometimes gets to be a skillful, patient and time-consuming tasks so that other staffs can do neither in the short period nor in an accurate way.

If monitoring and measuring are carried out with such a camera, their performance will be not good and degree of precision will become poor because of pixel shift. It is necessary for users to have certain criteria to determine whether such a "pixel shift" really occurs or not in target color image. In the other hand, objective criteria could provide well-defined level to utilize the relevant camera for image recognition/measurement or not. At the macro level, there does not seem to be pixel shift in the relevant image, but there sometimes may be some pixel shifts in it when examined microscopically.

It is very much important to know whether pixel shift occurs or not, namely whether such pixel shift remains within the range of allowance (= tolerance level) or outside. This paper focuses how to analyze characteristics of pixel shift, work out(i.e. calculate or derive) reasonable (and useful) criteria, and propose an efficient procedure to get numerical value and tolerance level according to the relevant pixel shift. It may be difficult to express R, G, and B signals for color image, which are generated from 3CCD digital camera, as general periodic functions such as $A(t)sin(\omega t + \phi)$. Because such a case needs some necessary conditions to demonstrate that these signals are periodic. Therefore, this paper will employ not periodic functions but general polynomial functions to formulate the relevant R, G, and B signals simply. This study has employed several numerical methods by reference of many books such as "Numerical Recipes[4]".

In order to calculate efficiently phase difference among the relevant R, G, and B signals defined with polynomial functions, certain baseline has been utilized where all the values of R, G, and B signals would become to zeros simultaneously if there were no pixel shift at the target image. The formulation of proposed procedure is described as follows;

1. the R, G, and B signals are expressed and approximated as the according three polynomial functions.
2. The (three) minimal values of x-coordinate for the above functions are calculated by means of analytic methods.
3. The phase difference among the R, G, and B signals is obtained by means of the three differences of the above minimal values.
4. Pixel shift is digitalized and visualized to utilize the above phase difference.
5. This is a trial to introduce an objective criteria whether the pixel shift occurs or not.

3   Digitalization of Pixel Shift

This section explains graphical characteristics of pixel shift as preparation of digitalization of pixel shift, demonstrates a procedure of digitalization through calculation of the value for occurrence of pixel shift, and describes algorithm for digitalization of pixel shift including function interpolation and others.

3.1   Graphical Characteristics of Pixel Shift

This subsection prepares graphical characteristics of pixel shift before practical calculation of the value of pixel shift and derivation the level of occurrence of pixel shift.

In the case of normal image, which includes no pixel shift or few and indistinctive one, for example, Figure 2, it is suitable for users to utilize the relevant image for image recognition and measurement. Some applications of image handling need efficient detection of outline and contour. And others, especially, perform image processing in order to determine outlines/borders of target objects. Such application users really want to use normal and sharply-defined images and avoid unclear focused ones.

Figure 2 is a good example for normal image with very little or almost no pixel shift. If our approach of digitalizing pixel shift is applied to that image, the according result must be indicated with low level of pixel shift. Figure 4 shows graphical characteristics of Figure 2.

With reference of Figure 4, there looks like no phase difference among R, G. and B signals and the values of those get down to zeros simultaneously according to the fiducial grid. Such a case can provide sharply-defined images and efficient determination of outlines/borders of target objects.

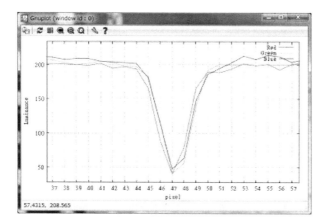

Fig. 4. Graphical Characteristics for Figure 2 with No Pixel Shift

By the way, in the case of incorrect image, which includes certain distinguished pixel shift(s), for example, Figure 3, it is difficult for users to utilize such an image for image recognition and measurement. Because it is vaguely-outlined, it is considered not to be suitable for almost applications of image understanding and so on. If a user did not know his/her camera generates image including some serious pixel shifts, his/her remote monitoring and surveillance might not be successful and could not provide suitable information for decision making.

For the next discussion about digitalization of pixel shift, it will be useful for readers to investigate and understand graphical characteristics of Figure 3. Figure 5 shows the relevant characteristics clearly and points out distinguished phase difference among R, G. and B signals. And it illustrates that R, G, and B signals do "not" get down to zeros simultaneously according to the fiducial grid.

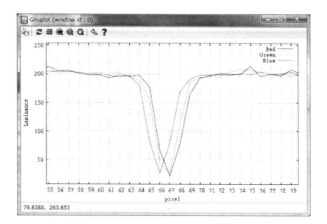

Fig. 5. Graphical Characteristics for Figure 3 with certain Pixel Shift

As it is mentioned before, we are willing to focus attention on its phase difference among R, G, and B signals to define occurrence of pixel shift to be analyzed
later in this paper. We will provide a useful numerical procedure to digitalize
pixel shift to obtain the level for occurrence of pixel shift in the next subsections.

3.2   Demonstration of Digitalization of Pixel Shift

This subsection demonstrates how to digitalize the value of pixel shift by means
of Lagrange function interpolation. Assuming that three points of x-coordinate
are given, for example, (x_0, y_0), (x_1, y_1), (x_2, y_2), Lagrange interpolation coefficient function $L_i(x)$ can be defined as follows;

$$
\begin{aligned}
L_0(x) &= (x - x_1)(x - x_2)/(x_0 - x_1)(x_0 - x_2) \\
L_1(x) &= (x - x_2)(x - x_0)/(x_1 - x_2)(x_1 - x_0) \\
L_2(x) &= (x - x_0)(x - x_1)/(x_2 - x_0)(x_2 - x_1)
\end{aligned}
\tag{1}
$$

With the above functions(1), the relevant Lagrange interpolation polynomial
$P_2(x)$ can be defined as follows;

$$
\begin{aligned}
P_2(x) &= \Sigma_{i=0}^{2}\{y_i L_i(x)\} \\
&= y_0 L_0(x) + y_1 L_1(x) + y_2 L_2(x) \\
&= y_0(x - x_1)(x - x_2)/(x_0 - x_1)(x_0 - x_2) + \\
&\quad y_1(x - x_2)(x - x_0)/(x_1 - x_2)(x_1 - x_0) + \\
&\quad y_2(x - x_0)(x - x_1)/(x_2 - x_0)(x_2 - x_1)
\end{aligned}
\tag{2}
$$

Using expression (2), we can calculate the value of x-coordinate which gives
the minimal value of $P_2(x)$. After differentiating $P_2(x)$, we can derive the relevant value of x-coordinate with equation $dP_2(x)/dx = 0$. In this case, $P_2(x)$
is quadratic function so that the above value of x-coordinate can be derived as
follows;

$$
\begin{aligned}
dP_2(x)/dx &= y_0\{2x - (x_1 + x_2)\}/(x_0 - x_1)(x_0 - x_2) + \\
&\quad y_1\{2x - (x_2 + x_0)\}/(x_1 - x_2)(x_1 - x_0) + \\
&\quad y_2\{2x - (x_0 + x_1)\}/(x_2 - x_0)(x_2 - x_1) \\
&= 0
\end{aligned}
$$

$$
\begin{aligned}
&2x\{y_0(x_1 - x_2) + y_1(x_2 - x_0) + y_2(x_0 - x_1)\} \\
&= y_0(x_1 - x_2)(x_1 + x_2) + y_1(x_2 - x_0)(x_2 + x_0) + y_2(x_0 - x_1)(x_0 + x_1)
\end{aligned}
$$

$$
\begin{aligned}
x &= \frac{y_0(x_1 - x_2)(x_1 + x_2) + y_1(x_2 - x_0)(x_2 + x_0) + y_2(x_0 - x_1)(x_0 + x_1)}{2\{y_0(x_1 - x_2) + y_1(x_2 - x_0) + y_2(x_0 - x_1)\}} \\
&\equiv minf(x_0, y_0, x_1, y_1, x_2, y_2)
\end{aligned}
\tag{3}
$$

In the case of giving the three pixel points for R, G, B signals, we can easily calculate the minimal values for Lagrange-interpolated functions according to R, G, B signals using the above expression (3) as follows;

$$min(x_R) = minf(x_{0R}, y_{0R}, x_{1R}, y_{1R}, x_{2R}, y_{2R}) \tag{4}$$
$$min(x_G) = minf(x_{0G}, y_{0G}, x_{1G}, y_{1G}, x_{2G}, y_{2G}) \tag{5}$$
$$min(x_B) = minf(x_{0B}, y_{0B}, x_{1B}, y_{1B}, x_{2B}, y_{2B}) \tag{6}$$

With the above three equations (4), (5) and (6), we can compute numerical value for the pixel shift as follows;

$$DigitalizedPixelShift$$
$$\equiv max\{|min(x_R) - min(x_G)|, |min(x_G) - min(x_B)|, |min(x_B) - min(x_R)|\}$$

Through calculating in the above way, we can digitalize pixel shift to determine whether pixel shift occurs or not. Of course, that is for the case of using the three pixel points, but other cases can do like this. In the other words, we will be able to determine whether pixel shift occurs or not semi-automatically without ability from specialist, with reference to the relevant value for digitalized pixel shift limited in an allowance range.

As you know, Lagrange interpolation can be easily expanded to more multiple pixel points in the case that four or more pixel points become necessary to obtain more suitable value for digitalized pixel shift. In such a case, $min(x_R)$, $min(x_G)$ and $min(x_B)$ can be calculated by means of famous Newton-Raphson numerical method to resolve efficiently an equation: $dP_n(x)/dx = 0$, where $n \geq 3$.

3.3   Algorithm for Digitalization of Pixel Shift

This subsection discusses how to digitalize suitable pixel shift for given target images. In the normal case, digital cameras provide JPEG images so that the target image is in the JPEG format from now on.

1. exaction of R, G, B color signals from a specified area of the target JPEG image.
   exacting module can read the JPEG image and write the relevant R, G and B pixel data sequences onto files.
2. selection of a necessary pixel points according to the specification.
   selecting module can get the three, four and more pixel points for the below function interpolation.
3. definition of Lagrange interpolation coefficient function and introduction of Lagrange interpolation polynomial.
   defining interpolation function for its minimal value within the specified range must be fixed because the algorithm for calculating the minimal values is static and never change during digitalization of pixel shift.
4. calculation of the minimal values of x-coordinates for interpolation functions for R, G, and B signals.
   calculating module can generate the minimal values by means of interpolation function scheme and characteristic.

5. digitalization of pixel shift using calculated minimal values for R, G, and B signals.

digitalizing module can generate numerical value for measuring pixel shift and provide its level to determine whether pixel shift occurs or not without capability and/or experience of specialists.

We practically calculate $min(x_R)$, $min(x_G)$ and $min(x_B)$ for Figure 5 and generate absolute differences for $|min(x_R) - min(x_G)|$, $|min(x_G) - min(x_B)|$ and $|min(x_B) - min(x_R)|$. The results are shown in Table 1.

Table 1. Calculation of Absolute Differences for Digitalization of Pixel Shift

$|min(x_R) - min(x_G)|$	$|min(x_G) - min(x_B)|$	$|min(x_B) - min(x_R)|$
0.72(pixel)	0.29(pixel)	1.01(pixel)

In the case of Table 1, the maximal value among $|min(x_R) - min(x_G)|$, $|min(x_G) - min(x_B)|$ and $|min(x_B) - min(x_R)|$ is $|min(x_B) - min(x_R)| = 1.01$. So the digitalized value for pixel shift can be calculated as 1.01 pixel. In the comparison with the next section's discussion, the level of pixel shift is relatively large because of being more than 0.5 pixel.

4 Performance Evaluation and Future Works for Digitalization of Pixel Shift

This section tries to carry out performance evaluation of our approach to digitalize pixel shift for determination of occurrence of pixel shift in the target image. And it also mentions some future works about digitalization of pixel shift.

4.1 Performance Evaluation of Digitalization

We have made an attempt to compare results for digitalization of pixel shift with determination by specialist as performance evaluation of our approach. As it is mentioned before, the conventional approach is to determine whether pixel shift occurs or not through visual judgment achieved by specialist. In ordinary cases, the above procedure sometimes becomes one of the most time-consuming tasks and used to be suffering from a lack of power and working time of specialist.

With our approach to digitalize pixel shift, it might be improved and specialist would be set free for this procedure. (Of course, such excellent specialist must be waited for other hard jobs, we think :-) We have obtained 20 images which have been already determined whether pixel shift or not and classified based on visual judgment by specialist into two groups explained below. We have tried to apply "digitalization of pixel shift" into the relevant 20 images and derived their values of the levels for occurrence of pixel shift according to the images. Table2 shows

Table 2. Comparison between Visual Judgment by Specialist and Digitalization of Pixel Shift

image file	determination by specialist	calculated value of pixel shift	image file	determination by specialist	calculated value of pixel shift
image#01	OK	0.25	image#11	NG	1.01
image#02	OK	0.25	image#12	NG	1.73
image#03	OK	0.25	image#13	NG	0.93
image#04	OK	0.28	image#14	NG	0.68
image#05	OK	0.40	image#15	NG	0.73
image#06	OK	0.38	image#16	NG	0.63
image#07	OK	0.40	image#17	NG	1.00
image#08	OK	0.45	image#18	NG	0.88
image#09	OK	0.15	image#19	NG	0.73
image#10	OK	0.35	image#20	NG	0.88

comparison between determination by specialist and calculated value through "digitalization of pixel shift".

In Table2, the notation "OK" means that a specialist determines there is no pixel shift in the relevant image. And the notation "NG" means that the same specialist determines there are some pixel shifts in the relevant image.

From comparison in Table2, we can have some useful knowledge about relation between specialist's determination and approach to digitalization of pixel shift as follows;

- The value of digitalization for the image, which has been determined as "OK" by specialist, is less than 0.45 pixel. And the value of digitalization for the image, which has been determined as "NG" by specialist, is more than 0.63 pixel.
- The table of comparison indicates a high likelihood of determination as "OK" by specialist where digitalization of pixel shift is less than 0.5 pixel and also determination as "NG" by him/her where the results of digitalization is more than 0.5 pixel.

It is one of useful evidences that our approach can reply the same determination of occurrence of pixel shift as visual judgment by specialist. And it can be considered that our approach is one of useful solution to overcome the time-consuming problem without help of specialist.

4.2 Future Works

We will describe our future works for digitalization for pixel shift in a short period. We must improve the precision of digitalization and think about some near future perspectives.

First of all, we will check which degrees of Lagrange interpolation function is suitable for digitalization of pixel shift. The previous section shows 2 degrees of Lagrange interpolation function, namely "quadratic" function. So we will try to 3 or more degrees of Lagrange interpolation function in order to obtain more effective and efficient results.

Of course, we must change other interpolation methods except of Lagrange one. Some periodic function such as $A(t)sin(\omega t + \phi)$ might be one of potential candidates for approximation function. We need to obtain some criteria for judging which is better, Lagrange method, periodic one and others.

Secondary, we want to specify more clear level to determine whether pixel shift or not. Digitalization of pixel shift must be only one step to define more suitable judgment and determination level for semi- or full-automatic procedure to check performance of target 3CCD cameras. Pixel shift will be one of testing items for such cameras. *As our Reviewer's suitable comments,* we should investigate and evaluate our approach through precise comparison with potentially existed algorithms and/or approaches among related works.

At the beginning of checking 3CCD cameras, results of performance evaluation test had carried out feedback to design stage very lately due to delay for specialist's determination of pixel shift and other checking items. If it realized semi-or full-automatic determination of pixel shift, a whole performance test would be much more shortly than the current state.

In a relatively longer period, namely next stage, we will challenge to develop realtime digitalization and adjustment of pixel shift during such cameras working. That might be one of some anti-aliasing and self-tuning for 3CCD cameras. With such facility equipped in the target cameras, those camera can provide non-stop working suitably and free for maintenance during termination. It must be very much convenient for users to utilize such camera and apply them into 24-hours monitoring and surveillance.

5   Conclusions

This paper describes a phenomenon "pixel shift" in the image which is monitored by potentially incorrect camera. And it introduces a sequence of procedures as "digitalization of pixel shift". Such procedures are summarized as follows;

1. Reading the values of R, G, and B signals from the target image.
2. Picking up specified sample value for efficient approximation.
3. Interpolating a suitable Lagrange-based approximation function with picked-up pixel points.
4. Calculating the minimal values of the above interpolated functions for R, G, and B signals respectively according to the fiducial grid image where all the color signals, namely interpolated functions, become to zeros simultaneously.
5. Deriving phase difference among interpolated R, G, and B signals with mutual absolute differences of the above minimal values and defining that phase difference as the level for occurrence of pixel shift.

And we have compared the above-defined level for occurrence of pixel shift with visual judgment for pixel shift by specialist. Compared results is good and make it possible to replace conventional method of Visual judgment for pixel shift by specialist with our approach to detect occurrence of pixel shift with digitalized value/level of pixel shift.

And finally, we describe our future works to improve digitalization of pixel shift and semi- and/or full-automatic determination of pixel shift. Then we mention realtime digitalization and adjustment of pixel shift as our more future plans.

Acknowledgments. The authors would like to express sincere thanks to the members of CMICRO-ImaiLab joint Research project, especially, Mr. Masanori Fujisawa (Vice President of CMICRO), Mr. Mitsuru Saeki and Mr. Hirofumi Kuwajima (Managers of CMICRO), Mr. Yutaka Iwamoto (Senior Engineer of CMICRO), and Mr. Makoto Ooga (Engineer of CMICRO) for their great contributions and comments to this study. They are also thankful to our anonymous Reviewer for his/her kind contributions. This work was partly supported by the 2009 Special Science Fund from CMICRO Corporation.

References

1. Gelbord, B., Roelofsen, G.: New surveillance techniques raise privacy concerns. Com. ACM 45(11), 23–24 (2002)
2. Yuan, X., Sun, Z., Varol, Y., Bebis, G.: A distributed visual surveillance system. In: Proceedings of the IEEE Conf. on Advanced Video and Signal Based Surveillance, pp. 199–204 (July 2003)
3. Hu, W., Tan, T., Wang, L., Maybank, S.: A survey on visual surveillance of object motion and behaviors. IEEE Trans. Systems, Man, and Cybernetics -Part C 34(3), 334–352 (2004)
4. Press, H., Teukolsky, S., Vetterling, W., Flannery, B.: Numerical Recipes, The Art of Scientific Computing, 3rd edn. Cambridge University Press, Cambridge (2007)

Combination of Wavelet Transform and Morphological Filtering for Enhancement of Magnetic Resonance Images

Akansha Srivastava, Alankrita, Abhishek Raj, and Vikrant Bhateja

Department of Electronics and Communication Engineering,
Shri Ramswaroop Memorial Group of Professional Colleges,
Lucknow-227105 (U.P.), India
{akanshas2412,iamalankrita,abhishekraj1989,
bhateja.vikrant}@gmail.com

Abstract. Brain tumor is an abnormal mass of tissue with uncoordinated growth inside the skull which may invade and damage nerves and other healthy tissues. Limitations posed by the image acquisition systems leads to the inaccurate analysis of magnetic resonance images (MRI) even by the skilled neurologists. This paper presents an improved framework for enhancement of cerebral MRI features by incorporating enhancement approaches of both the frequency and spatial domain. The proposed method requires de-noising, enhancement using a non-linear enhancement function in wavelet domain and then iterative enhancement algorithm using the morphological filter for further enhancing the edges is applied. A good enhancement of Region Of Interest(ROI) is obtained with the proposed method which is well portrayed by estimates of three quality metrics. Contrast improvement index (*CII*), peak signal to noise ratio *(PSNR)* and average signal to noise ratio *(ASNR)*.

Keywords: brain tumor, contrast improvement index, daubechies wavelet, discrete wavelet transform, logistic function, magnetic resonance imaging, morphological filter.

1 Introduction

Human beings have battled cancer since their existence. In the United States, every year more than 200,000 people are diagnosed with a primary or metastatic brain tumor. The full repertoire of numbers reported till date reflects the enormous complexity and diversity of cancer. Malignant solid brain tumors are masses of tissues formed inside skull as a result of abnormal and uncoordinated growth due to proliferation of atypical cells. The grown mass may evolve in a more complex manner, once it starts affecting the neighboring healthy tissues and nerves. Neuro-radiologists classify brain tumors into two groups, namely: glial tumors (gliomas) and non-glial tumors. There are more than 120 different types of brain tumors, which further increase the complexity of the effective treatment [1]. MR images are noisy and suffer from poor contrast. Due to these miscellanea in tumor characteristics for

V. Snasel, J. Platos, and E. El-Qawasmeh (Eds.): ICDIPC 2011, Part I, CCIS 188, pp. 460–474, 2011.
© Springer-Verlag Berlin Heidelberg 2011

different patients, coupled with the limitations posed by the various image acquisition devices, analysis of MR images, becomes a complex task, even for the skilled neurologists. The comprehensive survey indicates the exponential increase in the number of research work going on in the medical world for brain cancer indicating the fatal traits of brain tumor. An efficient image contrast enhancement module is the primary pre-requisite of any computer aided detection system employed for medical diagnosis. In this paper, a new method is proposed for the enhancement of cerebral MRI features which will aid in the detection and diagnosis of tumor patients.

2 Review of Literature Survey

Common methods for image contrast enhancement include techniques such as histogram equalization [2], mathematical morphology [3], and transform domain techniques such curvelet transform [4]. There are two possible approaches to enhance image features. One is the removal of background noise; the other is to increase the contrast on suspicious areas by linear or nonlinear operations. However, these conventional enhancement techniques pose limitations such as inappropriate enhancement of the desired ROI, thereby complicating the process of image segmentation. The present work proposes a combination of these traditional contrast enhancement algorithms to enhance the targeted lesion with respect to its background without enhancement of noise and other artifacts. Wavelet analysis serves as an important tool for the practical implementation of image de-noising and enhancement in the frequency domain. Significant amount of design flexibility can be obtained using wavelet transform. Choice of requisite level of decomposition, selection of wavelet family, spatial frequency tiling coupled with various thresholding techniques can be well optimized for enhancement as well as background noise suppression in the region of interest. Kim *et al.* used partially overlapped sub-block histogram equalization (POSHE) technique [2] for image enhancement. The technique used a blocking effect reduction filter (BERF) for suppression of the blurring effect. But, this in turn leads to a trade-off problem between visual quality and computational speed-up. Kharrat *et al.* proposed a morphological filter [3] for contrast enhancement of magnetic resonance images using structuring element of radius 30 pixels. However, usage of large sized structuring elements poses the problem of image blurring leading to loss of useful information. Also, the hardware implementation of large sized structuring element is cumbersome. Starck *et al.* proposed an algorithm [4] for enhancement of gray and color images using curvelet transform. This transform based approach works better than the wavelet transform in case of noisy images, however for near noiseless images this transform is not well suited. In case of noise free images, the results of curvelet enhancement are not much better than wavelet based enhancement as the enhancement function tends towards Velde's approach in cases of weak noise. The edges and contours can be detected effectively using wavelets in such cases. Yang *et al.* proposed an algorithm [5] for medical image de-noising by soft thresholding using wavelet transform followed by enhancement using non linear histogram equalization. Besides enhancing the ROI, histogram equalization also enhances the noise contents of the image which is undesirable. Sardy *et al.* proposed a robust wavelet based estimator for image de-noising [6]. However, the authors have used a universal threshold parameter for image de-noising. Universal threshold computes a global threshold value for the image without emphasizing on local details. As a consequence, undesired blurring is observed. Chen *et al.* proposed image denoising using neighborhood wavelet coefficients [7]. This approach is based on the assumption that adjacent wavelet coefficients have similar value. Hence, this algorithm will not produce optimal results for images with sharp edges and variations. Arulmozhi *et al.* proposed three spatial domain filters [8] for contrast enhancement. These algorithms were application specific, but the author has not mentioned in particular that, which technique works best for which specific application. In addition to this, the author suggests to apply histogram equalization on the final enhanced output, which could lead to over enhancement. Pisano *et al.* proposed a methodology [9] to determine whether contrast limited adaptive histogram equalization (CLAHE) helps to improve the detection of simulated spiculations in dense mammograms. CLAHE can provide subtle edge information but might degrade performance in the screening setting by enhancing the visibility of nuisance information. With the discussed literature review, it can be inferred that combination of non-linear filtering techniques in the transform domain, known as multiscale analysis techniques, can catalyze the performance of image contrast enhancement algorithms by providing remarkably improved results for image denoising along with feature enhancement. This paper presents an improved framework for contrast enhancement of cerebral MRI features by incorporating multiscale analysis, thereby assisting neurologists in early detection of cerebral cancer. The proposed method requires denoising and enhancement using a non-linear enhancement function in wavelet domain followed by the application of an iterative enhancement algorithm using the morphological filter to further enhance the edges and filter out the residual noise. The proposed morphological filter uses a variable sized structuring elements (not exceeding, a symmetric size of 5×5), thereby providing a consistent enhancement of ROI along with suppression of background noise.

3 Wavelet Transform and Multi-scale Analysis

The primary aim of wavelet analysis is to decompose a given input signal on a set of 'basis functions'. To capture the frequency evolution of a non-static signal, it is necessary that the basis function should have a compact support in both time and frequency domain [10]. A continuous wavelet transform decomposes an input signal over dilated and translated wavelet function. The wavelet transform of a signal at time u and scale s is performed as

$$Wf(u,s) = \langle f, \Psi_{u,s} \rangle = \int_{-\infty}^{+\infty} f(t) \frac{1}{\sqrt{s}} \Psi^* (\frac{t-u}{s}) dt = 0 \qquad (1)$$

Assuming that the energy of $\Psi^*(\omega)$ is concentrated in a positive frequency interval centered at η, the time-frequency support of a wavelet atom $\Psi_{u,s}(t)$ is symbolically represented by a Heisenberg rectangle centered at $(u, \eta/s)$ with time and frequency supports spread proportional to s and $1/s$ respectively. An orthogonal (non-redundant wavelet transform) can be constructed by dicretising the dilation parameters on an exponential sampling using fixed dilation steps, on the other hand, the translation parameter can be varied in integral multiples of a dilation dependent step [11]. For the purpose of medical imaging one has to generally deal with the discrete pixel intensities. Therefore, the focus centers on discrete wavelet transform. Wavelets find extensive applications in image processing. Since an image is two dimensional, so the dimensionality of wavelet transform for images is also increased by one. Hence, wavelet transform for an image is given by:

$$W_t\left(p;q_1,q_2\right) = f\left(y_1,y_2\right),\varphi_{a;q_1,q_2}\left(y_1,y_2\right)$$

$$= \frac{1}{p}\iint f\left(y_1,y_2\right)\varphi\left(\frac{y_1-q_1}{p},\frac{y_2-q_2}{p}\right)dy_1 dy_2 . \tag{2}$$

where: translation in two dimensions is given by q_1 and q_2. Similarly, the inverse wavelet transform can be computed as:

$$f\left(y_1,y_2\right) = \frac{1}{r_\varphi}\int_0^\infty \frac{dp}{p^3}\iint W_t\left(p;q_1,q_2\right)\varphi\left(\frac{y_1-q_1}{p},\frac{y_2-q_2}{p}\right)dq_1 dq_2 . \tag{3}$$

$$\text{where: } r_\varphi = \frac{1}{4\pi^2}\iint\frac{|\varphi(\omega_1,\omega_2)|^2}{|\omega_1^2+\omega_2^2|}d\omega_1 d\omega_2, \tag{4}$$

$$\varphi_{a;q_1,q_2}\left(y_1,y_2\right) = \frac{1}{p}\varphi(\frac{y_1-q_1}{p},\frac{y_2-q_2}{p}). \tag{5}$$

and $\varphi_{a;q1,q2}(y_1,y_2)$ is basic wavelet function in two dimension [12].

4 Proposed Enhancement Framework

This paper proposes an improved framework for enhancing the contrast of cerebral MRI features by incorporating enhancement approaches of both the frequency and spatial domain. Multiscale analysis techniques are employed, which decomposes an image signal using wavelets followed by enhancement and de-noising of only those sub images which contain the necessary information. Morphological filter is then applied to the reconstructed image to further enhance the features along with filtering of residual noise. The block diagram of the proposed framework for enhancement of cerebral MRI features is shown in figure 1.

4.1 Wavelet Based Sub-band Coding

In wavelet transform, an image is represented at different resolution levels. It decomposes any image into low frequency approximation coefficients and high frequency detail coefficients, viz. horizontal, vertical and diagonal coefficients, at any resolution. Discrete Wavelet Transform (DWT) transforms the image into an array of wavelet coefficients. These coefficients are then modified as per the requirement and the image is reconstructed from these modified coefficients by using Inverse Discrete

464 A. Srivastava et al.

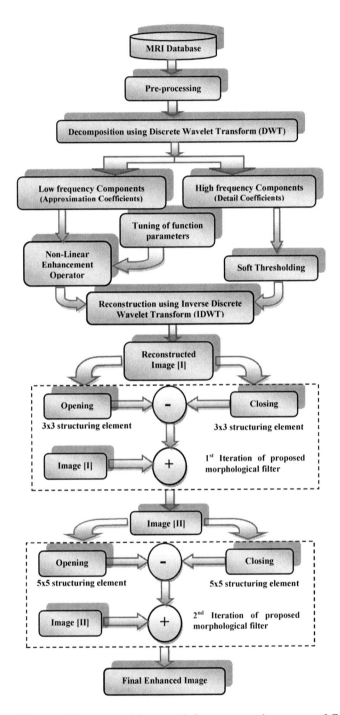

Fig. 1. Block diagram of the proposed framework for contrast enhancement of Cerebral MRI Features

Wavelet Transform (IDWT). In the proposed method, a two-level decomposition of the input signal is performed using daubechies wavelet family. In the higher frequency spectrum, with the increase in the information content, noise also increases. Therefore, de-noising is performed by doing soft thresholding of the high frequency coefficients.

Soft Thresholding [5] can be mathematically defined as:

$$f(t) = \begin{cases} t - T_h; t \geq T_h \\ t + T_h; t \leq -T_h \\ 0; |t| < T_h \end{cases}.$$ (6)

As in different high frequency sub-images, the noise properties are different, different threshold levels are used for each sub-image. The threshold T_h is defined as:

$$T_h = \sigma\sqrt{2\log N_i}.$$ (7)

where: σ is the noise standard deviation and N_i is the size of sub-image. After accessing the coefficients at the fine level, IDWT is applied for reconstructing the image back into the spatial domain. The non-linear enhancement operator is then applied to the approximation coefficients.

4.2 Non Linear Enhancement Operator

The fundamental problem posed in the enhancement of brain tumor images is the inability to emphasize the desired features without the enhancement of noise. This drawback is overcome by the global enhancement techniques equipped with multistate Adaptive Gain [13]. A logistic function is real-valued, differentiable, and monotonically increasing function given by:

$$logistic(x) = \frac{1}{1 + e^{-x}}.$$ (8)

This is also the requirement of the non-linear transformation function for conventional histogram equalization. The graphical variation for $logistic(x)$ is shown in figure 2(a). Linear combination of logistic functions with an adaptive gain factor is used for the preparation of non-linear mask for contrast enhancement of cerebral MRI features. This mask is spatially moved over the ROI to produce the enhanced image. The function modifies the gray levels by suppression of pixel values of very small amplitude, and enhancement of only those pixels larger than a certain threshold within each level of the transform space. The non-linear enhancement operator [14] (as shown in figure 2(b)) used to accomplish the above operation is given by:

$$y(x) = a[logistic\{k(x-b)\} - logistic\{-k(x+b)\}].$$ (9)

where: x denotes the gray level value of the original ROI at co-ordinate (i, j). k and b are the parameters for control of enhancement and the threshold respectively and a is given by:

$$a = \frac{1}{logistic\{k(1-b)\} - logistic\{-k(1+b)\}}.$$ (10)

where: the parameters $b \in$ R while $k \in$ N.

The enhancement operator $y(x)$ is differentiable as well as continuous, hence it is monotonically increasing within the interval [-1, 1]. This further ensures that the enhancement using $y(x)$ does not include any discontinuities into the enhanced image. In this approach, the threshold parameter b controls the noise level of the ROI during the process of enhancement. All the pixel intensity values above the threshold level are enhanced while the ones below it are suppressed. This threshold level can be calculated by solving the equation $y(x)-x=0$ or by finding the standard deviation of pixel values.

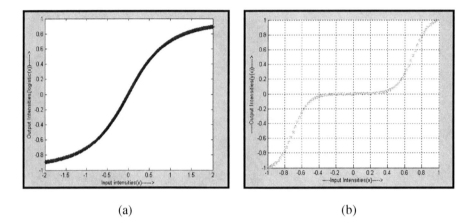

(a)   (b)

Fig. 2. (**a**) Graphical variation of Logistic Function [*logistic(x)*], (**b**) Graphical variation of Non-Linear Enhancement operator $y(x)$

However, with the above function (9), the threshold is controlled through the parameter b (where $0<b<1$, $b \in R$) while, the effective contrast enhancement can be controlled through the parameter k.

4.3 Morphological Filter

Morphological filters are non-linear filters commonly used as a tool for noise filtering, contrast enhancement as well as edge detection. This is achieved by the application of basic morphological operations using a structuring element. Flat and symmetric structuring elements of larger size are primarily used for noise removal, while contrast enhancement of small sized objects can be achieved by using small sized structuring elements, although it might be comparatively difficult to suppress noise. Image features similar in shape to that of the structuring element remains unaltered, while others are either extracted or suppressed. So the choice of structuring element depends on the type of information to be retrieved [15]. Erosion, dilation, opening and closing are among the common morphological operations. Dilations and erosions can be combined in a variety of ways to solve wide range of problems involving non linear filtering [16]. As the names suggests, erosion shrinks an image while dilation expands it. In erosion, when the structuring element passes over an image then the intensity of the neighborhood pixel with minimum value is considered. This reduces the brightness and hence the size of the image. On the contrary, dilation selects the pixel with maximum intensity value thereby increasing its brightness and size. Another set of morphological operations used are opening and closing. Opening is defined as erosion followed by dilation. Small islands and thin filaments of object pixels are removed by this operation. Mathematically, opening is expressed as:

$$A \circ B = (A \ominus B) \oplus B . \tag{11}$$

Likewise, islands and thin filaments of background pixels are removed by closing. It is dilation followed by erosion [17].

$$A \bullet B = (A \oplus B) \ominus B . \tag{12}$$

Contrast improvement coupled with edge enhancement in digital images can be developed by approximating morphological derivatives with discrete differences. A difference of morphological opening and closing yields the image boundary by providing an asymmetric treatment between the image foreground and its background. Local contrast enhancement can be achieved by adding the original image to the difference between morphological open and close transformed image. A two stage iterative morphological filter using variable flat structuring elements is proposed in this work. The flat structuring element used during the first iteration of this filter (15) is a disk shaped structuring element of radius 2 or size 5×5 (13). Similarly the second iteration of this filter (17) utilizes a flat disk shaped structuring element of order 3×3 (14).

$$S_1 = \begin{bmatrix} 0 & 0 & 1 & 0 & 0 \\ 0 & 1 & 1 & 1 & 0 \\ 1 & 1 & 1 & 1 & 1 \\ 0 & 1 & 1 & 1 & 0 \\ 0 & 0 & 1 & 0 & 0 \end{bmatrix} \tag{13}$$

$$S_2 = \begin{bmatrix} 0 & 1 & 0 \\ 1 & 1 & 1 \\ 0 & 1 & 0 \end{bmatrix} \tag{14}$$

1st Iteration:

$$I^{10}(x) = [y(x) \circ R_1] - [y(x) \bullet R_1] , \tag{15}$$

$$I^{11}(x) = [I^{10}(x) + y(x)] , \tag{16}$$

2nd Iteration:

$$I^{20}(x) = [F^{11}(x) \circ R_2] - [F^{11}(x) \bullet R_2] , \tag{17}$$

$$I^{21}(x) = [I^{20}(x) + y(x)] , \tag{18}$$

A symmetric flat structuring element of approximately 30 pixels is sufficient to trap brain lesions while smaller sized structuring elements serve to trap small sized features. This justifies the usage of two-stage iterative morphological filter. The duo-iterations of the proposed morphological filter provide significant preservation of the lesion edges along with the removal of noise. The results of the proposed enhancement method are improved in comparison to the morphological top-hat transformation which has been used for fingerprint segmentation [17] as well as for brain tumor detection.

5 Objective Evaluation of Proposed Method

The ultimate goal of a contrast enhancement algorithm is to reduce distortion in such a manner that some low contrast feature can be visualized by a human observer. It is although difficult to evaluate effectively the effect of image enhancement. *PSNR* (in dB) is a common tool for objective evaluation but it fails to quantify the errors as per the human visual system (HVS) [18]. The degree of contrast improvement provided by the enhancement method is adjudged by the fact that it should enhance the difference between the average gray scale values lying in the background and the foreground regions. *CII, PSNR* and *ASNR* are the three quality metrics used in this work for the objective evaluation of the proposed method for contrast enhancement.

5.1 Contrast Improvement Index (*CII*)

This parameter for evaluation is performed using the local region of interest (region containing the tumor, referred to as foreground) and the artifacts present in the original as well as the enhanced images. The contrast 'C' of an object is given by [19]:

$$C = \frac{m_f - m_b}{m_f + m_b} \tag{19}$$

where: m_f is the mean gray-level value of the foreground and m_b is the mean gray-level value of the background. The quantitative measure of contrast improvement, defined as 'Contrast Improvement Index *(CII)*'

$$CII = \frac{C_E}{C_O} \tag{20}$$

where: C_E and C_O are the contrasts of regions of interest in the enhanced and original images respectively. As *CII* does not contain enough information to quantize the background, the two other parameters used are *PSNR* and *ASNR*.

5.2 *PSNR* (Peak Signal to Noise Ratio) and *ASNR* (Average Signal to Noise Ratio)

These parameters are based on general medical physics measurement and accepted by radiologists for detection of abnormalities. *PSNR* and *ASNR* are defined as:-

$$PSNR = \frac{m_f^m - m_b}{\sigma} \tag{21}$$

$$ASNR = \frac{m_f - m_b}{\sigma} \tag{22}$$

Here, σ is the standard deviation, which gives the measurement of the level of noise in the background, m_f^m is the maximum gray level value of the foreground. m_f is the mean gray level value of the foreground and m_b is the mean gray level value of the surrounding background region. Higher the value of *CII, PSNR* and *ASNR*, more promising is the method for contrast enhancement.

6 Experimental Results

The cerebral magnetic resonance images used for simulation are taken from the 'Whole Brain Atlas' by Keith A. Johnson and J. Alex Becker [20]. This is a registered database which provides the brain image datasets acquired from various techniques; although in this work MR-T2 and MR-GAD images are used for simulation. The contrast of selected ROI is computed by manually selecting the foreground and

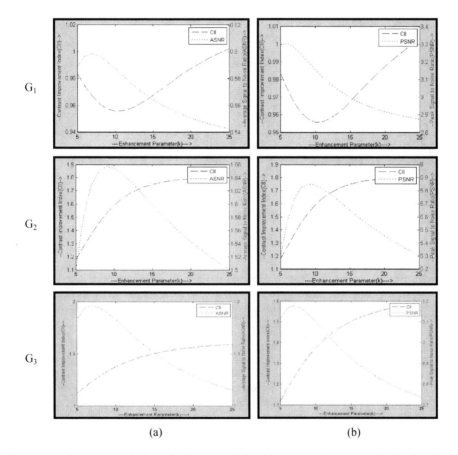

(a)   (b)

Fig. 3. (a) Graphical variation of *CII* and *ASNR* with against changes in k, **(b)** Graphical variation of *CII* and *PSNR* against change in k
G_1=Graphical variation for image with Tumor Glioma MR- GAD (I_2), G_2=Graphical variation for image with Tumor Glioma MR- GAD(I_3), G_3=Graphical variation for image with Tumor Sarcoma MR- T2(I_5)

background with the help of the radiologist markings in the database. The cerebral images obtained from the MRI database are normalized followed by extraction of ROI of size 128×128. The graphical variations of *CII, ASNR* and *PSNR* for various ROI against changes in k are plotted in figure 3 (a) and figure 3 (b) respectively. The non-linear function parameters k and b are tuned in such a range yielding high values of quality metrics. Values of enhancement factor (k) $2 < k < 20$ and control of threshold $0.60 < b < 0.90$ are optimally chosen in the mentioned bounds to produce visually improved results coupled with high values of quality metrics. The proposed methodology incorporates wavelet decomposition at two levels. Multiple wavelet combinations have been tested and the daubechies wavelet family yields the most optimal visual results. Hence, DWT has been implemented using daubechies wavelet family at both the levels of decomposition. The selection of wavelets is performed, based on the results mentioned under table 1 and results of objective evaluation (*PSNR, ASNR* and *CII*) on different cerebral images using the proposed enhancement method are shown in table 2 and 3 respectively. Figure 4 (a) shows the original cerebral MRI and the extracted ROI are shown in figure 4 (b). Figure 4 (c) shows the ROI after wavelet reconstruction and figure 4 (d) shows the enhanced ROI resulting from the two stage recursive application of the proposed morphological filter with variable size structuring elements.

Table 1. Tabulated values of *PSNR* for different wavelet combinations

Wavelet Family at Level 1	Wavelet Family at Level 2	*PSNR*
db2	db2	4.1726
db2	haar	3.6158
haar	haar	4.0929
sym2	sym2	3.6298
db1	db1	4.1677
sym2	db2	9.9623
coif2	coif2	3.2672
haar	db2	3.8384

Table 2. Tabulated values of *PSNR* and *ASNR* for the proposed enhancement method

Input Cerebral Images	PSNR			ASNR		
	Original	After Wavelet Reconstruction	After Morphologi-cal Filter	Original	After Wavelet Reconstru-ction	After Morphologi-cal Filter
I_1	2.7735	3.6571	4.1726	1.1367	1.1472	1.1817
I_2	3.5773	3.9361	4.4598	1.0789	1.1634	1.1669
I_3	2.3340	2.3345	2.3716	0.6794	0.6914	0.7270
I_4	1.5359	2.3615	2.3711	0.8045	0.9041	0.9272
$I_5(i)$	2.0277	2.0373	2.0764	0.5207	0.5518	0.5682
$I_5(ii)$	3.0263	3.1564	3.2804	0.8055	0.8305	0.8804
I_6	1.8555	2.3657	2.3674	0.5247	0.5861	0.6110
I_7	2.1995	3.6353	3.8183	0.6252	0.7140	0.7902

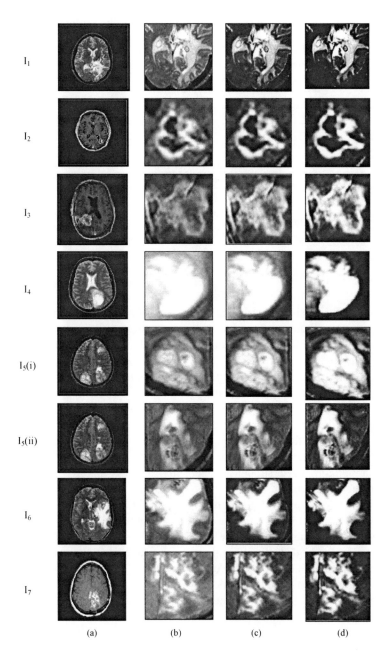

Fig. 4. Enhanced MRI images obtained with proposed enhancement method. (a) Input cerebral MRI images, (b) Preprocessed ROI, (c) ROI obtained after wavelet reconstruction, (d) Final enhanced ROI.

I_1= Tumor Glioma MR-T2, I_2= Tumor glioma MR- GAD,I_3= Tumor Glioma MR- GAD, I_4= Tumor Glioma MR- T2, I_5= Tumor Sarcoma MR- T2, I_6 =Tumor Metastatic Bronchogenic Carcinoma, I_7= Tumor Glioma MR- GAD

Table 3. Tabulated values of *CII* for the proposed enhancement method

Input Cerebral Images	CII	
	After Wavelet Reconstruction	After Morphological Filter
I_1	1.3755	1.6504
I_2	1.3045	1.5582
I_3	1.4748	1.5736
I_4	2.3294	2.3834
$I_5(i)$	1.5107	1.5695
$I_5(ii)$	1.3166	1.4133
I_6	1.4448	1.5372
I_7	2.0793	2.2632

I_1= Tumor Glioma MR-T2, I_2= Tumor glioma MR- GAD,I_3= Tumor Glioma MR- GAD, I_4= Tumor Glioma MR-T2, I_5= Tumor Sarcoma MR- T2, I_6 =Tumor Metastatic Bronchogenic Carcinoma, I_7= Tumor Glioma MR- GAD

7 Conclusion

For the proper diagnosis and early stage treatment of brain tumor, a precise study of MRI is the primary requisite. Thus, this paper presents a novel framework for contrast improvement of cerebral MRI features using combination wavelet transform and morphological filtering approach. Wavelet transform serves as a powerful tool for image processing and is widely applied to the domain of medical images. Such diverse applications are attributed to the versatility of wavelet tools, especially with respect to their localization properties in transform domain. The proposed recursive morphological filter uses variable sized structuring elements to enhance the targeted ROI with respect to the non-homogeneous background of the brain tissues. The iterative morphological filtering approach produces rapid convergence without application of large sized structuring elements, thereby simplifying the hardware implementation. Simulation results show significant improvement in contrast of cerebral features as depicted by increment in the values of the three quality metrics (*CII, PSNR* and *ASNR*). The aggregate value of *CII* obtained with the above results is 1.7436 whereas the maximum *CII* reached is 2.3834. The average *CII* obtained by Kharrat *et al.* [3] is 1.5073. But the author has no where suggested whether the given value is aggregate or maximum value obtained. Moreover, this technique may lead to efficient segmentation and classification at later stages, thereby producing optimization in therapies for the patients suffering from brain tumor.

8 Future Work

The performance of the proposed non-linear transformation function can be further increased by applying any mathematical optimization techniques. Features extraction as well as classification of brain anomalies can be done so that the tumor can be diagnosed as benign or malignant. However, for further studies, it seems important to develop algorithms to find optimal number of levels at which wavelet decomposition has to be performed when using soft thresholding and non linear enhancement operator.

References

1. Revolution Health,
   http://www.revolutionhealth.com/conditions/cancer/
   brain-cancer/facts-statistics
2. Kim, J.Y., Kim, L.S., Hwang, S.H.: An Advanced Contrast Enhancement Using Partially Overlapped Sub-Block Histogram Equalization. IEEE Transactions On Circuits and Systems for Video Technology 11(4) (2001)
3. Kharrat, A., Messaoud, M.B., Benanrane, N., Abid, M.: Detection of Brain Tumor in Medical Images. In: Proceedings of International Conference on Signals, Circuits and Systems, pp. 1–6 (2009)
4. Starck, J.L., Murtagh, F., Candès, E.J., Donoho, D.L.: Gray and Color Image Contrast Enhancement by the Curvelet Transform. IEEE Transactions on Image Processing 12(6) (2003)
5. Yang, Y., Su, Z., Sun, L.: Medical Image Enhancement Algorithm Based on Wavelet Trnsform. Electronics Letters 46(2), 120 (2010)
6. Sardy, S., Tseng, P., Bruce, A.: Robust Wavelet De-noising. IEEE Transactions on Image Processing 49(6) (2001)
7. Chen, Y.G., Bui, T.D., Krzyzak, A.: Image Denoising Using Neighbouring Wavelet Coefficients. In: Proceedings of the ICASSP, vol. 2, pp. 917–920 (2004)
8. Arulmozhi, K., Perumal, S.A., Kanna, K., Bharathi, S.: Contrast Improvement of Radiographic Images in Spatial Domain by Edge Preserving Filters. IJCSNS International Journal of Computer Science and Network Security 10(2) (2010)
9. Pisano, E.D., Zong, S., Hemminger, B.M., DeLuca, M., Johnston, R.E., Muller, K., Braeuning, M.P., Pizer, S.M.: Contrast Limited Adaptive Histogram Equalization Image Processing to Improve the Detection of Simulated Spiculations in Dense Mammograms. SpringerLink Journal of Digital Imaging 11(4), 193–200 (1998)
10. Mallat, S.: A Wavelet Tour of Signal Processing. Academic Press, London (1998)
11. Daubechies, I.: Ten Lectures on Wavelets, Philadelphia, PA, Siam (1992)
12. Tian, D.Z., Ha, M.H.: Applications of Wavelet Transform in Medical Image Processing. In: Proceedings of the Third International Conference on Machine Learning and Cybemetics, Shanghai (2004)
13. Laine, A.F., Schuler, S., Fan, J., Huda, W.: Mammographic Feature Enhancement by Multiscale Analysis. IEEE Transactions on Medical Imaging 13(4), 725–752 (1994)
14. Quintanilla, D.J., Sanchez, G.M., Gozalez, R.M., Vega, C.A., Andina, D.: Feature Extraction using Coordinate Logic Filters and Artificial Neural Networks. In: 7th IEEE International Conference on Industrial Informatics, pp. 645–649 (2009)
15. Maragos, P.: Differential Morphological and Image Procssing. IEEE Transactions on Image Processing 5(6), 922–937 (1996)
16. Jian, L.: Research on Morphological Filter Algorithms Based on Mathematical Morphology. Harbin Institute of Technology, Harbin (2006)

17. Mosorov, V.: Using Tophat Transformation for Image Fingerprints Segmentation. In: Proceedings of the International Conference on Signals and Electronic Systems, Lodz, Poland, pp. 241–246 (2001)
18. Wharton, E., Panetta, K., Agaian, S.: Human Visual System Based Similarity Metrics. In: Proceedings of IEEE International Conference on Systems, Man and Cybernetics, pp. 685–690 (2008)
19. Morrow, W.M., Paranjape, R.B., Rangayyan, R.M., Desautels, J.E.L.: Region Based Contrast Enhancement of Mammograms. IEEE Transactions on Medical Imaging 11(3), 392–406 (1992)
20. The Whole Brain Atlas, http://www.med.harvard.edu/AANLIB/home.html

Real-Time Feedback and 3D Visualization of Unmanned Aerial Vehicle for Low-Cost Development

Mohammad Sibghotulloh Ikhmatiar[1], Rathiah Hashim[1], Prima Adhi Yudistira[1], and Tutut Herawan[2,*]

[1] Faculty of Information Technology and Multimedia
Universiti Tun Hussein Onn Malaysia
Parit Raja, Batu Pahat 86400, Johor, Malaysia
[2] Faculty of Computer System and Software Engineering
Universiti Malaysia Pahang
Lebuhraya Tun Razak, Gambang 26300, Kuantan, Pahang, Malaysia
{ikhmatiar,reddish.blue}@gmail.com, radhiah@uthm.edu.my,
tutut@ump.edu.my

Abstract. The implication of emergence of Unmanned Aerial Vehicle (UAV) is to avoid human victim risks and to gain lower costs from real-scale of aerial vehicles. Visual aid in UAV is one of the important elements that allow pilots to control them from the ground. Yet, some other experts are still using 2D graphics to visualize UAV movements which limits the pilot in a single expression. However, many experts are still doing research on UAV regarding its better visualization technique, autonomous system, GPS synchronization, precision on telemetry and image processing. In this paper, we present an alternative methodology the development of real-time feedback visualization from UAV and 3D Graphical User Interface (GUI) control. It is transmitting feedback of UAV movements through the surveillance camera by installing tilt sensor on UAV model and receiving real-time environment of First Person View (FPV) of aircraft's pilot. It is aimed in low-cost development and coming with 3D graphic environment and the interface uses DirectX SDK as graphics engine. With 3D view, pilot will be easier to obtain feedback of UAV which visualizes 3D mesh of UAV model.

Keywords: Feedback Visualization, Unmanned Aerial Vehicle, Real-time Visualization.

1 Introduction

The significance of appearance of UAV are avoiding human victim risks and lower cost of real-scale aerial vehicle and many applications that can be applied by UAV on nowadays. The aim on military, UAV will be used primarily for surveillance, reconnaissance and interdiction of surrounding areas, even United States Department of Defence (DoD) has developed a combat style UAV which is named as Predator

---

* Corresponding author.

V. Snasel, J. Platos, and E. El-Qawasmeh (Eds.): ICDIPC 2011, Part I, CCIS 188, pp. 475–485, 2011.
© Springer-Verlag Berlin Heidelberg 2011

RQ-1/MQ-1/MQ-9 Reaper. It has surveillance imagery from synthetic aperture radar, video cameras and a forward-looking infrared (FLIR) can be distributed in real-time both to the front line soldier and to the operational commander, or worldwide in real-time via satellite communication links. Basic methodology of main navigation view was utilized a camera that relays images back to its operators. The images not only provide reconnaissance information but are also used for controlling the aircraft remotely. In order to improve the control of the UAV and perform simulations and training, an interface is needed which displays the aircraft in a virtual three dimensional (3D) environment. Currently, many air forces are still using a roadmap-like 2D display to control the flight path of the UAV [1]. This is not satisfactory for mission critical deployments.

However, the prominent difficulty of UAV is visual control which could not be separated from navigation control of an aerial vehicle. The important of well recognizing of surrounding aerial vehicle in real time is extremely high. Further research about feedback visualization of UAV as visual control has been done in this paper. The paper aims to apply the experiments utilizing low-cost system. And so do with the simulation performance also will be utilizing low-cost Virtual Reality (VR) system.

The rest of the paper is organized as follows. Section 2 describes the related work. Section 3 explains the basic concepts of flight Simulators. Section 4 discusses the proposed method for 3D modeling UAV. This is followed by UAV feedback visualization system design and the result in section 5 and 6, respectively. Finally, conclusion and future direction are reported in section 7.

2   Related Works

The idea of using visual information for UAV attitude estimation is not new. The first experiments attempted to obtain the skyline from images taken by a single perspective camera looking forward on the aircraft, using this to estimate the roll angle with a horizontal reference [2, 3, 4, 5]. These works differ in the way that they segment the sky and ground and in how they estimate the horizon line. Recent works of UAV explained that most of previous UAV's control system which has been developed is still using 2D graphic representation [6] where visualized graphic makes the components of UAV's manual control which has many indication views such as attitude indicator, altimeter, turn coordinator, heading indicator, and vertical speed indicator. Specifically in turn coordinator, heading indicator and vertical speed indicator which is supposed to be monitored easily and obviously visible as original shape of aerial vehicle. Another work has been done by G. Cai et al. [7], which is related to systematic design methodology of UAV helicopters. And this paper is utilized to have more systematic design of UAV 3D model. The other adopted concepts which have Virtual Environment application with feedback, written by J. Dionisio et al. [8, 9]. Feedback visualization of UAV is simply designed following with 3D mesh and terrain become virtual environment. In this work is proposing graphic visual of UAV's feedback instruments on 3D views, where the user is able to obtain better perspective view on real-time visualization. It also allows the unit on the ground to monitor and remote relevantly the UAV with knowing the real condition thoroughly in an UAV's flight. The similar previous works of this paper is on real-time and 3D vision for autonomous small and micro air vehicle, which is done by T. Kanade, O. Amidi, Q. Ke [10]. Their work was introducing 3d vision of surrounding environment from video and laser scanning which has several distinct advantages. And another interesting work in last 4 years which is done on UAV visualization system are Omni directional Vision System for Control of UAV [11, 12], where this research is applying the optical flow based control principles observed in insects to an Omni directional vision system and was testing this system on small UAVs.

Virtual reality is applied in this work, and combined 3D mesh and terrain become a flight simulator [13, 14, 15], where it allows the user to virtually flies with complex environments and aircraft's attitudes. Flight simulator is a simulation system for large-scale. Due to the limitation by computer powers, only high specification computers ever were used to realize flight dynamics simulation and image generation in full flight simulator in the past [16]. With the development of computer powers, high-performance computation and simulation can be realized applying by PC. While the need to reduce costs in every aspects of flight simulator become significant. A PC-based prototype system was implemented according to the architecture of flight simulator featuring a generic double engine airplane. Commercial-off-the-shelf (COTS) software components were utilized on cost reducing and improve developing efficiency. Flight simulator SDK inspires the betterment of visualization system for a low-cost UAV's development.

3 Flight Simulators

The virtual environment of flight simulators was appropriate approach to design feedback visualization of UAV. The following constraints have to be met by the flight simulator: the UAV data needs to be plugged into the flight simulator so that the correct position and orientation of the aircraft can be displayed (including roll, pitch, yaw and altitude). It must be possible to convert real terrain data from the Joint Geospatial Facility (JGSF) and GISs from their original form (i.e. Digital Elevation Maps (DEM) and Vector Product Formats (VPF)) into the terrain format used by the flight simulator. It must be possible to augment the terrain with features including roads, rivers, lakes and cities to provide a realistic 3D environment. Initial research narrowed the possible choices for a flight simulator down to FlightGear and Microsoft Flight Simulator 2002 (MSFS) SDK. In making our choice we considered their usability, extendibility; graphics rendering quality, and tools available for scenery generation.

Microsoft Flight Simulator 2002 is a proprietary flight simulator developed by Microsoft Corporation. It is supported by commercial plug-ins that can be purchased online. The main interfaces that can be used for interaction use DirectX [17, 18]. FlightGear is an Open-Source flight simulator developed in C/C++ under Linux and distributed to most operating system platform, including Microsoft Windows [19]. FlightGear is chosen due to its usability, specifically in terms of network play. It allows the slaving of an instance of FlightGear from another instance by sending packets of information using an exposed C++ interface class (FGNetFDM). By altering the fields in this class and then sending it to an instance of FlightGear we can control the aircraft. A second advantage of FlightGear is that its graphics output is superior to MSFS and higher resolution terrains are available (3-arcsec scenery ≡ 100m resolution).

Finally several excellent tools are available for FlightGear, specifically for terrain generation. In particular the open source project Terra gear [20] was commenced for developing scenery for FlightGear. Scenery can be represented as Digital Elevation Maps (DEM) or by Vector Product Formats (VPF) which are supported by geographical associations around the world. In contrast the Boost Graph Library (BGL) terrain format used by the MSFS terrain engine is a proprietary format and no tools seem to be available for converting common terrain formats into BGL scenery files. Two other useful FlightGear tools for military simulations are Atlas, which provides a 2Dmap with moving map pointer for FlightGear; and the Flight Gear Scenery Designer project, which provides a way of generating terrain data from maps including placement of 3D objects and the use of photos for scenery.

4 3D Modeling UAV

Glider plane is an aerial vehicle model which is used in this work. The reasons of applying glider plane are reconnaissance purpose and energy saving. Glider does not have hard noise as other airplane model due to the airfoils (wings) and fuselage's design of glider which has boundary layer control could be used in a high performance and less sound created [21, 22]. And in this work will discuss the systematic movement design of glider before we represent it into 3D model.

4.1 Modeling a Pitch Controller

The equations governing the motion of an airplane are a very complicated set of six non-linear coupled differential equations. However, under certain assumptions, they can be decoupled and linearized into the longitudinal and lateral equations. Pitch control is a longitudinal problem, and in this work, we will design a model that controls the pitch of an airplane. The basic coordinate axes and forces acting on an airplane are shown in the figure 3 below.

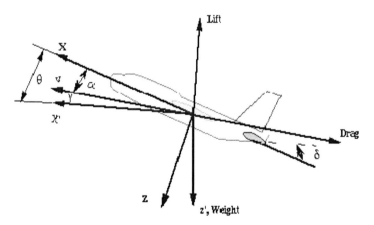

Fig. 1. Basic coordinate axes and forces acting on an airplane

Assume that the aircraft is in steady-cruise at constant altitude and velocity; thus, the thrust and drag cancel out and the lift and weight balance out each other. Also, assume that change in pitch angle does not change the speed of an aircraft under any circumstance (unrealistic but simplifies the problem a bit). Under these assumptions, the longitudinal equations of motion of an aircraft can be written as:

$$\dot{\alpha} = \mu\Omega\sigma[-(C_{L\alpha} + C_{D\alpha})\alpha + \left(\frac{1}{\mu} - C_{Lq}\right)q - (C_{w\alpha}\sin\gamma_e)\theta + C_{L\delta}]$$

$$\dot{q} = \mu\Omega/2i_{yq}\{[C_{M\alpha} - \eta(C_{L\alpha} + C_{D\alpha})]\alpha + [C_{Mq} + \sigma C_{M\alpha}(1 - \mu C_{L\alpha})]q + (\eta C_{w\alpha}\sin\gamma_e)\delta_e\}$$

$$\dot{\theta} = \Omega q \tag{1}$$

For this system, the input will be the elevator deflection angle, and the output will be the pitch angle.

4.1.1 Design Requirements

The next step is to set some design criteria. We want to design a feedback controller so that the output has an overshoot of less than 10%, rise time of less than 2 seconds, settling time of less than 10 seconds, and the steady-state error of less than 2%. For example, if the input is 0.2 rad (11 degress), then the pitch angle will not exceed 0.22 rad, reaches 0.2 rad within 2 seconds, settles 2% of the steady-state within 10 seconds, and stays within 0.196 to 0.204 rad at the steady-state.

- Overshoot: Less than 10%
- Rise time: Less than 2 seconds
- Settling time: Less than 10 seconds
- Steady-state error: Less than 2%

4.1.2 Transfer Function and the State-Space

Before finding transfer function and the state-space model, let's plug in some numerical values to simplify the modeling equations (1) shown above.

$$\dot{\alpha} = -0.313\alpha + 56.7q + 0.232\delta_e$$
$$\dot{q} = -0.0139\alpha - 0.426q + 0.0203\,\delta_e\}$$

$$\dot{\theta} = 56.7q \tag{2}$$

These values are taken from the data from one of the Boeing's commercial aircraft.

4.1.2.1 Transfer Function. To find the transfer function of the above system, we need to take the Laplace transform of the above modeling equations (2). Recall from your control textbook, when finding a transfer function, zero initial conditions must be assumed. The Laplace transform of the above equations are shown below.

$$s\alpha(s) = -0.313\alpha(s) + 56.7q(s) + 0.232\delta_e(s)$$
$$sq(s) = -0.0139\alpha(s) - 0.426q(s) + 0.0203\,\delta_e(s)$$
$$s\theta(s) = 56.7q(s)$$

After few steps of algebraic manipulation, we will obtain the following transfer function

$$\frac{\theta(s)}{\delta_e(s)} = \frac{1.151s + 0.1774}{s^3 + 0.739s^2 + 0.921s}$$

4.1.2.2 State-Space. Knowing the fact that the modeling equations (2) are already in the state-variable form, we can rewrite them into the state-space model.

$$\begin{bmatrix} \dot{\alpha} \\ \dot{q} \\ \dot{\theta} \end{bmatrix} = \begin{bmatrix} -0.313 & 56.7 & 0 \\ -0.0139 & -0.426 & 0 \\ 0 & 56.7 & 0 \end{bmatrix} \begin{bmatrix} \alpha \\ q \\ \theta \end{bmatrix} + \begin{bmatrix} 0.232 \\ 0.0203 \\ 0 \end{bmatrix} [\delta_e].$$

Since our output is the pitch angle, the output equation is such shown below.

$$y = \begin{bmatrix} 0 & 0 & 1 \end{bmatrix} \begin{bmatrix} \alpha \\ q \\ \theta \end{bmatrix} + [0][\delta_e].$$

4.2 Modeling a 3D Glider (RedGlide)

The first step for constructing the UAV glider is to choose a suitable virtual design environment. The design procedure in the construction of RedGlide (figure 2) was mainly based on two dimensional computer-aided-design (2D CAD) blueprints. The lack of a powerful 3D design environment caused great difficulty in layout design and the integration of hardware components. As a result the design and integration procedure was iterated for quite a number of times, which had prolonged the total constructing time for months. To avoid such a problem, in constructing RedGlide, we employ a powerful virtual design environment, Blender 3D software, which has the following main advantages:

- Easy to use: Blender 3D has the most user-friendly 3D environment and complete reference is available on the software documentation.

Fig. 2. 3D model of UAV RedGlide

- Open Source Software: The main concept for all low-cost developments is utilizing open source software and Blender 3D is one of the open source software most people used.
- Animation function: Blender 3D is like other 3D software that can animate the 3d model through rendered object. Besides, Blender is also cooperated with several open source render software (i.e. Yafray).
- DirectX and OpenGL compatibility: The important thing before programming phase, the 3D file extension should be concerned. Blender has most 3D compatible file extension of many graphic programming requirements and in this work is using .x file extension in order to be accessed by DirectX graphic engine.

5   UAV Feedback Visualization System Design

Figure 3 shows an overview of our system. Feedback of UAV movement will send feedback data to UAV interface receives flight data and images from the UAV via a wireless connection. Several instances of FlightGear can be connected to the interface showing different views of the data. For example, one instance shows the terrain from the camera position for use by military planners and strategists, whereas another instance can show a 3_{rd} person view of the UAV in order to facilitate its remote control.

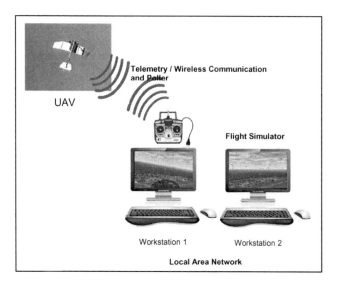

Fig. 3. Overview of Feedback 3D Visualization of UAV

The design of the UAV interface is illustrated in figure 4. The "UAV Poller" handles the polling of the UAV (using self-defined packet-based communication) and the processing of packets and then the delivery of formatted data to FlightGear. Communication with the UAV is handled via serial port, but the code is modular enough so that any future communication medium (e.g. USB, Fire wire) can be used. In our work, we had modified the radio frequency transmitter embedded with USB serial port. The self defined packets are small and contain a few ASCII characters that are used as values depending on the packet header. Packets also have checksum fields to test the integrity of the packet [23]. Faulty packets are detected and discarded.

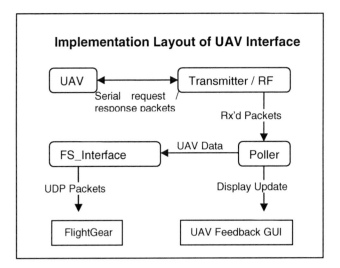

Fig. 4. Flow diagram design of UAV Feedback 3D visualization

6 Result

The initial test results for our simulation interface are promising and we were able to simulate UAV reconnaissance missions over local terrain. Figure 5 shows the UAV over the UTHM Ville with the palm forest of Batupahat, Johor, Malaysia in the background. Since the model of the UAV is classified we use instead a model of a Red Glide which is most similar to the UAV in terms of size and shape. In these test is also comparing the Hypermedia video capturing every20ms to obtain UAV data. The RVU-CAM updated itself every 20 ms (50 Hz) however there was still some lagging on the display. This could be due to the UAV simulator, giving approximate data. It could also be attributed to slow hardware and network connections. The purpose of this application of RVU Flightsim is to enable a broad dissemination of UAV information to personnel in the navy. The X-axis and Y-axis enumeration has been successfully recorded using MATLAB Version 2009b, so that it will allow us to replay and analyze captured UAV's movements.

Fig. 5. Testing of Red Glide with geo-mapping and visual 3D Feedback

7 Conclusion

This paper has provided evidence the complete part of real-time feedback and 3D visualization of UAV at low-cost development. Integrating the UAV into flight simulator was a success. The FlightGear instance flew according to the data that it received from the UAV and gave the correct position and orientation. The application is a small step towards a 3D environment to aid command and control. And low-cost development has been exhibited from the used development tool and development processes. Further work needs to be carried out before commencing large scale projects. However, current feedback indicates that this work worthwhile.

Acknowledgement

The authors would like to thank Universiti Tun Hussein Onn Malaysia for supporting this project.

References

1. Kim, Y., Gu, D.-W., Postlethwaite, I.: Real-time path planning with limited information for autonomous unmanned air vehicles. Automatica 44(3), 696–712 (2008), ISSN 0005-1098 doi:10.1016/j.automatica.2007.07.023
2. Dusha, D., Boles, W., Walker, R.: Fixed-wing attitude estimation using computer vision based horizon detection. In: Proceedings 12th Australian International Aerospace Congress, Melbourne, Australia, pp. 1–19 (2007)
3. Karimoddini, A., Lin, H., Chen, B.M., Lee, T.H.: Hybrid formation control of the Unmanned Aerial Vehicles, Mechatronics. In Press, Corrected Proof (December 15, 2010), ISSN 0957-4158 doi: 10.1016/j.mechatronics.2010.09.007
4. Kurdila, A., et al.: Vision-based control of micro-air-vehicles: progress and problems in estimation. In: 43rd IEEE Conference on Decision and Control, CDC 2004, vol. 2, pp. 1635–1642(December 14- 17, 2004)
5. Peng, K., Cai, G., Chen, B.M., Dong, M., Lum, K.Y., Lee, T.H.: Design and implementation of an autonomous flight control law for a UAV helicopter. Automatica 45(10), 2333–2338 (2009), ISSN 0005-1098 doi:10.1016/j.automatica.2009.06.016
6. Todorovic, S., Nechyba, M., Ifju, P.: Sky/ground modeling for autonomous MAV ight. In: IEEE International Conference on Proceedings of Robotics and Automation ICRA 2003, vol. 1, pp.1422–1427. doi:10.1109/ROBOT.2003.1241791
7. Cai, G., Feng, L., Chen, B.M., Lee, T.H.: Systematic design methodology and construction of UAV helicopters. Mechatronics 18(10), 545–558 (2008), ISSN 0957-4158 doi:10.1016/j.mechatronics.2008.05.011
8. Dionisio, J., Henrich, V., Jakob, U., Rettig, A., Ziegler, R.: The virtual touch: Haptic interfaces in virtual environments. Computers & Graphics 21(4), 459–468 (1997), ISSN 0097-8493 doi:10.1016/S0097-8493(97)00029-0
9. Fairen, M., Brunet, P., Techmann, T.: MiniVR: a portable virtual reality system. Computers & Graphics 28(2), 289–296 (2004), ISSN 0097-8493 doi:10.1016/j.cag.2003.12.013
10. Kanade, T., Amidi, O., Ke, Q.: Real-time and 3D vision for autonomous small and micro air vehicles. In: 43rd IEEE Conference on Decision and Control CDC 2004, vol. 2, pp. 1655–1662 (December 14-17, 2004) doi:10.1109/CDC.2004.1430282
11. Mondragon, I.F., Campoy, P., Martinez, C., Olivares, M.: Omnidirectional vision applied to Unmanned Aerial Vehicles (UAVs) attitude and heading estimation. Robotics and Autonomous Systems 58(6), 809–819 (2010), ISSN 0921-8890, doi:10.1016/j.robot.2010.02.012
12. Demonceaux, C., Vasseur, P., Regard, C.: Omnidirectional vision on UAV for attitude computation. In: IEEE International Conference on Proceedings of Robotics and Automation ICRA 2006, pp. 2842–2847 (May 15-19 2006), doi:10.1109/ROBOT.2006.1642132
13. Loguidice, B., Barton, M.: Flight Simulator (1980): Digital Reality, Vintage Games, pp. 93–104. Focal Press, Boston (2009), ISBN 978-0-24-081146-8 doi:10.1016/B978-0-240-81146-8.00018-X

14. Wen, C., Liu, Z.: Simulation study on the architecture optimization and task scheduling of a parallel flight training simulator. Mathematics and Computers in Simulation 34(3-4), 341–350 (1992), ISSN 0378-4754 doi:13.1016/0378-4754(92)90010-E

15. Schwid, H.A.: A flight simulator for general anesthesia training. Computers and Biomedical Research 20(1), 64–75 (1987), ISSN 0010-4809 doi:10.1016/0010-4809(87)

16. Rolfe, J.M., Caro, P.W.: Determining the training effectiveness of flight simulators: Some basic issues and practical developments. Applied Ergonomics 13(4), 243–250 (1982), ISSN 0003-6870 doi:10.1016/0003-6870(82)90063-1

17. Teulière, C., Eck, L., Marchand, E., Guénard, N.: 3D model-based tracking for UAV position control. In: IEEE/RSJ International Conference on Intelligent Robots and Systems (IROS) 2010, pp. 1084–1089 (October 18-22, 2010), doi:10.1109/IROS.2010.5649700

18. Sinopoli, B., Micheli, M., Donato, G., Koo, T.J.: Vision based navigation for an unmanned aerial vehicle. In: IEEE International Conference on Proceedings of Robotics and Automation ICRA 2001, vol. 2, pp. 1757–1764 (2001), doi:10.1109/ROBOT.2001.932864

19. Ettinger, S.M., Nechyba, M.C., Ifju, P.G., Waszak, M.: Vision-guided flight stability and control for micro air vehicles. In: IEEE International Conference on Intelligent Robots and Systems, IEEE, Los Alamitos (2002)

20. Shutao, Z., Jingfeng, H., Qitao, H., Junwei, H.: A low-cost PC-based flight simulator development. In: 2nd International Symposium on Systems and Control in Aerospace and Astronautics ISSCAA 2008, pp. 1–5 (December 10-12, 2008), doi:10.1109/ISSCAA.2008.4776379

21. Hart, W.B.: Glider fuselage design with the aid of computer graphics. Computer-Aided Design 3(2), 3–8 (1971), ISSN 0010-4485 doi:10.1016/0010-4485(71)90061-3

22. van Rijn, L.P.V.M.: Structural solution for a composite glider wing with suction boundary layer control for 100% laminar flow. Composites Part A: Applied Science and Manufacturing 28(12), 1013–1018 (1997), ISSN 1359-835X doi:10.1016/S1359-835X(97)00059-6

23. Taha, Z., Tang, Y.R., Yap, K.C.: Development of an onboard system for flight data collection of a small-scale UAV helicopter. Mechatronics, In Press, Corrected Proof (November 3, 2010), ISSN 0957-4158, doi:10.1016/j.mechatronics.2010.09.008

Symmetry Based 2D Singular Value Decomposition for Face Recognition

Falah E. Alsaqre and Saja Al-Rawi

Department of Computer Communications Engineering,
College of Computer Engineering and Sciences, Gulf University
Sanad, Kingdom of Bahrain
{dr.falah,dr.saja}@gulfuniversity.net

Abstract. Two-dimensional singular value decomposition (2DSVD) is latterly presented attempt to preserve the local nature of 2D face images, and at same time alleviate the computational complexity in standard singular value decomposition (1DSVD). Human face symmetry is also a profitable natural property of face images and allowed better feature extraction capability in face recognition. This paper introduces new method for face recognition coined as symmetry based two-dimensional singular value decomposition (S2DSVD), which relies on the strengths of both 2DSVD and human face symmetry. The proposed method offers two significant advantages over 2DSVD: improves the stability of feature extraction, and increases the valuable discriminative information, hence raising recognition accuracy. S2DSVD is compared to both 1DSVD and 2DSVD on two well-known databases. Experimental results show improvement in recognition accuracy over 2DSVD and superior to 1DSVD.

Keywords: face recognition, 1DSVD, 2DSVD, symmetrical face.

1 Introduction

Singular value decomposition (SVD) is one of the most important and useful tools for reducing high dimensional patterns such as images into lower dimensional ones. It is applied to pattern recognition problems including face recognition to produce an efficient features representation for face images [1, 2, 3]. From dimensional perspective, SVD is considered as 1D subspace method analogous to principal component analysis (PCA) and linear discriminant analysis (LDA) that are widely applied in face recognition [4, 5, 6].

In 1D subspace methods, the 2D image matrices must be previously converted to 1D image vectors. However, this conversion usually produces a high dimensional vector space, wherein it is very difficult to evaluate the covariance matrices. For instant, the computational process in 1DSVD involves constructing two covariance matrices corresponding to row-row and column-column directions for a set of image vectors. In fact, evaluating such matrices is very computationally expensive and may exceed the memory capacity of the system machine.

In recent years, several methods have been showed subspace features can be derived from 2D image matrices rather than 1D image vectors. The methods were

V. Snasel, J. Platos, and E. El-Qawasmeh (Eds.): ICDIPC 2011, Part I, CCIS 188, pp. 486–495, 2011.
© Springer-Verlag Berlin Heidelberg 2011

named 2DSVD [7], 2DPCA [8, 9], and 2DLDA [10]. In the context of face recognition, 2D methods having two common advantages over 1D methods. First, they remarkably alleviate the computational complexity in obtaining feature matrices. Second, they are more straightforward in features extraction, i.e., more accurate. In addition to the aforementioned advantages, 2DSVD preserves the local 2D structure of face images by evaluating the averaged row-row and column-column covariance matrices of training set, hence achieving further improvement in recognition rate.

Human face symmetry has acquired more interest in developing face recognition algorithms [11, 12, 13, 14]. The common underlying idea behind emergence of these algorithms is that even and odd symmetrical decomposition of face image provides more valuable discriminative information than traditional algorithms. In [11], an algorithm called symmetrical PCA (SPCA) is presented in which even and odd symmetrical principal components are extracted based on combining PCA with even-odd decomposition concept. A symmetry based 2DPCA (S2DPCA) is developed in [14] following same principles used in SPCA except that even and odd symmetrical eigenvectors are derived from image covariance matrices. Both SPCA and 2DPCA are shown improvement in face recognition rates comparing to their conventional versions.

In view of this, a method for face recognition based on combining the strengths of 2DSVD and symmetrical property of human face, which is called symmetry based 2DSVD (S2DSVD), is introduced in this paper. The method starts with the separation of training set into even and odd symmetrical sets. For each set, we evaluate row-row and column-column covariance matrices, followed by applying 2DSVD to compute even and odd principal eigenvectors. After that, left and right projection matrices are constructed by concatenating their corresponding even and odd principal eigenvectors. Moreover, the numbers of contributed principal eigenvectors are chosen according to their energy in face images. The resulted projection matrices map training set into reduced feature subspace in which the similarity between training and testing samples can be measured.

The remainder of this paper is organized as follows: Section 2 describes 1DSVD and 2DSVD in face recognition. The S2DSVD is presented in Section 3, where the experimental results are given in Section 4. Conclusions are drawn in Section 5.

2 Singular Value Decomposition (SVD) in Face Recognition

Singular value decomposition is usually applied to obtain low-rank approximation for high dimensional data such as a training set of images. Further, in image recognition, the main advantage of exploiting SVD is in its ability to preserve the meaningful features of the images in reduced subspace. Subsequently, deployment of SVD in face recognition will afford an efficient solution to image representation and classification.

2.1 One-Dimensional Singular Value Decomposition (1DSVD)

The process in face recognition based 1DSVD starts with transformation of 2D image matrices into 1D image vectors and combines these vectors together as a large matrix. Particularly, assume that there are n training face images in total, the ith training image is denoted by an $r \times c$ matrix A_i, $i = 1,\ldots,n$, i.e., $\{A_i\}_{i=1}^n$. Each image A_i is converted into a vector a_i of length rc. The image vectors are then packed to form an $rc \times n$ rectangular matrix $a = [a_1 a_2 \ldots a_n]$. Let $\bar{a}$ be the centroid vector of training set a. By subtracting $\bar{a}$ from each a_i such that $b_i = a_i - \bar{a}$, we obtain the following $rc \times n$ matrix,

$$A = [b_1 b_2 \ldots b_n] \tag{1}$$

Suppose the rank of A is k, where $k \leq n << rc$. It is proven that A has the following singular value decomposition [15],

$$A = USV^T \quad , \quad S = U^T AV \tag{2}$$

where $U = [u_1 u_2 \ldots u_k]$ contains k principal eigenvectors of AA^T, $V = [v_1 v_2 \ldots v_k]$ contains k principal eigenvectors of inner-product matrix $A^T A$, and $S = diag(\sigma_1, \sigma_2 \ldots, \sigma_k)$ are singular values of A. The eigenvalues of AA^T and $A^T A$ are identical, and U provides common subspace basis for image vectors to project to as follows [1],

$$X = [u_1 u_2 \ldots u_k]^T A \tag{3}$$

where X is a $k \times rc$ subspace feature vectors. For a given test image, classification is carried out by projecting the test image onto subspace feature vector. The distance of test image from training set is calculating in subspace vectors, and nearest neighbor classifier can be used to classify test image.

2.2 Two-Dimensional Singular Value Decomposition (2DSVD)

The computation of 2DSVD [7] for a set of 2D face matrices in same way as SVD computed for a set of 1D image vectors. That is, for a 2D face images training set $\{A_i\}_{i=1}^n$, 2DSVD defines the averaged row-row and column-column covariance matrices as follows,

$$F = 1/n \sum_{i=1}^n (A_i - \bar{A})(A_i - \bar{A})^T$$
$$G = 1/n \sum_{i=1}^n (A_i - \bar{A})^T (A_i - \bar{A}) \tag{4}$$

where $\bar{A}$ is the mean image of $\{A_i\}_{i=1}^n$. It is obvious that covariance matrices F and G of sizes $r \times r$ and $c \times c$, respectively. Applying SVD to F and G yields,

$$F = U_r S_r V_r^T \quad , \quad U_r \equiv [u_1 u_2 \ldots u_k]$$
$$G = U_c S_c V_c^T \quad , \quad U_c \equiv [v_1 v_2 \ldots v_s] \tag{5}$$

where U_r contains k principal eigenvectors of F and U_c contains s principal eigenvectors of G. The diagonal elements of S_r and S_c are the singular values of F and G, respectively. U_r and U_c provide two common subspace bases for 2D face images to (left and right) project to. Then, the training set $\{A_i\}_{i=1}^n$ can be projected onto a set of feature matrices such that

$$\{Y_i\}_{i=1}^n = U_r^T \{A_i\}_{i=1}^n U_c \tag{6}$$

where Y_i is a $k \times s$ feature matrix of A_i. In classification phase, the test image is also projected using U_r and U_c as a left and right projection matrices. The typical classification measure is Euclidean distance between test and training feature matrices; more details will be given in succeeding section.

3 Symmetry Based Two-Dimensional Singular Value Decomposition (S2DSVD)

3.1 Method Description

Symmetry based face recognition algorithms [11, 12, 13, 14] are extrapolated from a simple idea of even/odd decomposition to face images. They follow that, any function $f(t)$ can be expressed as $f(t) = f_e(t) + f_o(t)$ in which $f_e(t) = (f(t) + f_m(t))/2$ and $f_o(t) = (f(t) - f_m(t))/2$, where $f_m(t) = f(-t)$ is symmetry counterpart of $f(t)$. $f_e(t)$ and $f_o(t)$ are the even and odd symmetrical functions, respectively. Through further decomposition, both $f_e(t)$ and $f_o(t)$ can be described by a linear combination of a set of even/odd symmetrical basis functions. This concept has been extended to face images by defining symmetry to be the horizontal mirror symmetry with vertical midline of the image as its axis [11].

In previous section, 2DSVD is formulated based on row-row and column-column covariance matrices in order to preserve the local 2D structure of face images. Furthermore, as reported in [11, 14], exploiting symmetry property in face recognition provides a better features extraction. Consequently, the strengths of 2DSVD and symmetrical property of human face can be incorporated in one approach in order to add a positive contribution to face recognition accuracy.

According to symmetrical property of human faces, training set $\{A_i\}_{i=1}^n$ can be decomposed into even and odd training sets,

$$\{A_i\}_{i=1}^n = \{A_{ei}\}_{i=1}^n + \{A_{oi}\}_{i=1}^n \tag{7}$$

where $A_{ei} = (A_i + A_{mi})/2$, $A_{oi} = (A_i - A_{mi})/2$, and A_{mi} are sequentially even symmetrical image, odd symmetrical image, and mirror image of A_i. Next, we apply 2DSVD to each symmetrical set. Let $\overline{A}_e$ and $\overline{A}_o$ denote the mean images of $\{A_{ei}\}_{i=1}^n$ and $\{A_{oi}\}_{i=1}^n$, respectively. The row-row and column-column covariance matrices F and G can be evaluated as follows,

$$F = F_e + F_o \tag{8}$$

$$G = G_e + G_o \tag{9}$$

where

$$F_e = 1/n \sum_{i=1}^{n} (A_{ei} - \overline{A}_e)(A_{ei} - \overline{A}_e)^T$$

$$F_o = 1/n \sum_{i=1}^{n} (A_{oi} - \overline{A}_o)(A_{oi} - \overline{A}_o)^T$$

$$G_e = 1/n \sum_{i=1}^{n} (A_{ei} - \overline{A}_e)^T (A_{ei} - \overline{A}_e) \tag{10}$$

$$G_o = 1/n \sum_{i=1}^{n} (A_{oi} - \overline{A}_o)^T (A_{oi} - \overline{A}_o)$$

The singular value decompositions on F and G are equal to the singular value decompositions on right sides of Eq.8 and Eq.9. Based on Eq.5, we can then write,

$$F_e = U_{er} S_{er} V_{er}^T \;,\; U_{er} \equiv [u_{e1} u_{e2} ... u_{el}]$$

$$F_o = U_{or} S_{or} V_{or}^T \;,\; U_{or} \equiv [u_{o1} u_{o2} ... u_{ol}]$$

$$G_e = U_{ec} S_{ec} V_{ec}^T \;,\; U_{ec} \equiv [v_{e1} v_{e2} ... v_{eh}] \tag{11}$$

$$G_o = U_{oc} S_{oc} V_{oc}^T \;,\; U_{oc} \equiv [v_{e1} v_{e2} ... v_{oh}]$$

where each of U_{er} and U_{or} comprises l principal eigenvectors of F_e and F_o, while U_{ec} and U_{oc} comprises h principal eigenvectors of G_e and G_o. The diagonal elements of matrices S_{er}, S_{or}, S_{ec}, and S_{oc} are sequentially the singular values of F_e, F_o, G_e, and G_o. In order to facilitate and unify the solution in S2DSVD, we retain only k principal eigenvectors in U_{er} and U_{ec} as well as s principal eigenvectors in U_{or} and U_{oc}.

In standard 2DSVD, two unitary matrices have been used to both (left and right) sides of the training images to derive feature matrices. Herein, left projection matrix is constructed by concatenating U_{er} and U_{or}, whereas the concatenating of U_{ec} and U_{oc} will result right projection matrix. Thus, the feature matrices $\{Z_i\}_{i=1}^{n}$ of training set $\{A_i\}_{i=1}^{n}$ can be obtained by

$$\{Z_i\}_{i=1}^{n} = [U_{er} U_{or}]^T \{A_i\}_{i=1}^{n} [U_{ec} U_{oc}] . \tag{12}$$

Note that, each Z_i is a $(k+s) \times (k+s)$ matrix.

It is important to point out that, symmetrical feature matrices having different sensitivities to face image variations such as rotation, angles of view, and illumination changes [11], and these variations may cause asymmetry in face images. If so, the asymmetry is wholly contained in odd symmetrical feature matrices. This implies that odd symmetrical eigenvectors are more sensitive to image variations than even ones.

Another important aspect involves both even and odd symmetrical feature matrices keeping different energy of face images and even symmetrical features keep larger energy than odd ones. Although even symmetrical eigenvectors are more valuable, odd symmetrical eigenvectors cannot be completely discarded due to some of them may hold important discriminative information. In result, both even and odd symmetrical eigenvectors can be utilized to construct projection matrices with a restriction that the numbers of even symmetrical eigenvectors should be increased while of odd ones should be suppressed.

3.2 Classification in S2DSVD

After transformation in (12), a S2DSVD feature matrix is derived for each training image. Likewise, we can   derive the feature matrix for each test image. Let T be an $r \times c$ test image. T can be transformed into a feature matrix Z such that $Z = [U_{er}U_{or}]^T T [U_{ec}U_{oc}]$. Suppose the training set is partitioned into w_p classes. The nearest neighbor classifier based on Euclidean distance in S2DSVD subspace can be used for classification. The distance d is carried out by

$$d(T, A_i) = \| Z - Z_i \|_2. \tag{13}$$

The classification rules imply that, if $d(T, A_j) = \min_i d(T, A_i)$ and $A_j \in w_p$, then $T \in w_p$.

4   Experimental Results

Presented S2DSVD in this paper is devoted for face recognition. Experiments are conducted to evaluate the performance of S2DSVD and compare it to those of 1DSVD [1] and 2DSVD [7] on two well-known face image databases (ORL [16] and Yale [17]). The ORL database is used to examine the performance of S2DSVD under the conditions pose, face expressions, and face scale are varied. Yale dataset is exploited to test the performance when facial expressions and light conditions are changed.

4.1 Experiments on ORL Database

ORL dataset contains face images of 40 individuals, each owning 10 grayscale images of size 112×92. Five images of an individual are depicted in Fig.1. All experiments are conducted on ORL database by randomly splitting the entire database into training and testing sets without overlapping between them. Three scenarios are adopted to split the database and details are given in Table 1.

First experiment is performed by selecting the first 2 principal eigenvectors of U_{or} and U_{oc}, i.e., $s = 2$, and the retained even principal eigenvectors of U_{er} and U_{ec} are incrementally varied from 2 to 6, i.e., $k = 2,3,4,5,6$. For every k, we obtained the recognition rates in each scenario based on 1DSVD, 2DSVD, and S2DSVD. The results are summarized in Table 2. From results, it is evident that recognition rates achieved by S2DSVD in various scenarios are consistently higher than those of

1DSVD and 2DSVD. For instance, in scenario 2, highest recognition rate is 91.5% by S2DSVD, since by 1DSVD and 2DSVD are 76.5% and 85.5%, respectively. Results also showed that total average recognition rate in S2DSVD is improved by 26.38% and 6.85% in comparison to 1DSVD and 2DSVD, respectively.

Fig. 1. Images from ORL database

Table 1. ORL database splitting scenarios

Scenario	Training set		Testing set	
	Images/ individual	*Total*	*Images/ individual*	*Total*
1	2	80	8	320
2	5	200	5	200
3	8	320	2	80

Table 2. Recognition rates (%) in ORL database when $s=2$

Scenario	1			2			3		
k	1D	2D	S2D	1D	2D	S2D	1D	2D	S2D
2	36.25	53.12	63.13	37.55	60.5	80.5	41.25	71.25	93.75
3	50	69.37	70.62	54	77.5	86.5	60	86	97.25
4	54.68	73.75	75.31	62	83.5	88	70	91.25	97.25
5	55.68	76.56	77.8	67.5	85	90	78.75	96.25	97.25
6	62.2	79	80.22	76.5	85.5	91.5	85	95	97.25
Average	51.62	70.36	73.42	59.51	78.4	87.3	67	87.95	96.55

Note that, in all tables 1D, 2D, and S2D are sequentially referred to 1DSVD, 2DSVD, and S2DSVD. Also, in 1DSVD only the left principal eigenvectors (k's) are used for image projection.

Another experiment is carried out by fixing $s = 4$ and k values are set same as in previous experiment. The results from this experiment are given in Table 3. Obviously, performance of S2DSVD is better than that of 2DSVD in all scenarios. Specifically, the average recognition rate based S2DSVD is increased by 3.33%, 4.2%, and 3.15% in scenario 1, 2, and 3, respectively.

The results in two previous experiments indicated the recognition rate is rapidly increased when considering more even principal eigenvectors. This is due to most face images in ORL database are frontal viewed. On other words, faces are more likely symmetrical and few of them having asymmetrical components. To emphasize this aspect, we performed an experiment on scenario 2 with $s = 2$ and $k = 1,2,...30$. Fig.2 shows recognition rates in 1DSVD, 2DSVD, and S2DSVD. It also notable S2DSVD provides a better averaged recognition rate (92.93%) than 1DSVD (78.02%) and 2DSVD (88.36%).

Table 3. Recognition rates (%) in ORL database when $s=4$

Scenario	1		2		3	
k	2D	S2D	2D	S2D	2D	S2D
2	62.5	70.62	75	83	88.75	96.25
3	72.2	75	85	90.5	95	98.75
4	77.5	77.8	88.5	90.5	96.5	98.25
5	82.18	83.6	87.5	91	96.5	97.5
6	82.8	86.8	89.5	91.5	96.5	98.25
Average	75.43	78.77	85.1	89.3	94.65	97.8

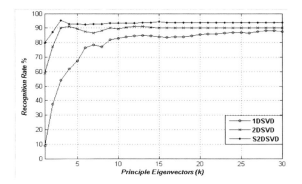

Fig. 2. Comparison of 1DSVD, 2DSVD, and S2DSVD on ORL dataset

4.2 Experiments on Yale Database

Yale database contains 165 frontal facial images, covering 15 persons taken under 11 different conditions. For efficiency, a preprocessing is applied to locate the faces by cropping each original image to 100×80. Fig.3 shows five images for one person from Yale database after preprocessing.

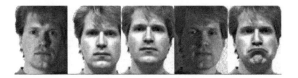

Fig. 3. Five Images from Yale database

The obtained recognition rates using 1DSVD, 2DSVD, and S2SVD when $s = 2$, and $k = 2,...,6$ are given in Table 5. It is clear that, recognition rates achieved by S2DSVD are outperformed those by 1DSVD and 2DSVD. Note that, in scenario 3 the average recognition rate of S2DSVD is 94.62% which around 20% and 10% higher than 1DSVD and 2DSVD, respectively. Also, an experiment is carried out based on scenario 2 with an increased numbers of even and odd principal eigenvectors. Herein, we set $s = 6$ and k is varied from 1 to 30. The corresponding recognition rates in

S2DSVD and 2DSVD are illustrated in Fig. 4. As can see, S2DSVD performed better than 2DSVD with an improvement of 6%. The experiment is repeated with $s = 7,8,9$ and we have noted no significant improvement is reported due to faces in Yale dataset are mostly symmetric.

Table 4. Splitting scenarios on Yale database

Scenario	Training set		Testing set	
	Images/ individual	*Total*	*Images/ individual*	*Total*
1	2	80	8	320
2	5	200	5	200
3	8	320	2	80

Table 5. Recognition rates (%) in Yale database when $s=2$

Scenario	1			2			3		
k	1D	2D	S2D	1D	2D	S2D	1D	2D	S2D
2	37.5	54.1	65	38.6	62.6	73.4	43.3	73.3	90.6
3	51.6	62.5	67.5	57.3	69.3	74.7	70	80	93.3
4	64.2	66.6	70	66.7	73.4	77.4	83	86.7	96.6
5	64.16	70	70.2	72	76	78.4	87.3	90	96.6
6	65.83	70.8	72.5	73.4	78.7	79.7	89	93.3	96.6
Average	56.65	64.8	69.04	61.6	72	76.72	74.52	84.66	94.74

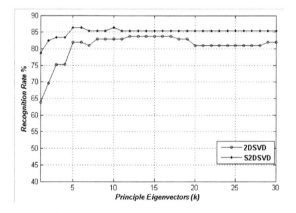

Fig. 4. S2DSVD versus 2DSVD on Yale dataset

5   Conclusions

In this paper, we introduced a new method named S2DSVD which successfully applied in face recognition. In this method, advantages of 2DSVD and symmetry property of human face are combined not only to improve recognition accuracy but also alleviate computational complexity in standard singular value decomposition. Unlike both 1DSVD and 2DSVD, S2DSVD utilizes even and odd symmetrical principal eigenvectors of training set to extract a stable feature matrices. At the same time, for an image, S2DSVD implicitly uses two images, the even symmetrical image and the odd symmetrical image, which means that the number of training samples is doubled. Hence, S2DSVD is very useful with a few image samples in training set. However, the process in S2DSVD requires evaluating covariance matrices of even symmetrical set and of odd symmetrical set. As a result, computational time will be slightly increased comparing to 2DSVD. Future work will consider the reducing of such time-consuming.

References

1. Zeng, G.: Facial Recognition with Singular Value Decomposition. Advances and Innovations in Systems, Computing Sciences and Software Engineering, 145–148 (2007)
2. Zhang, D., Chen, S., Zhou, Z.: A New Face Recognition Method Based on SVD Perturbation for Single Example Image per Person. Applied Mathematics and Computation 163(2), 895–907 (2005)
3. Xu, Y., Zhao, Y.: Comparison Study on SVD-Based Face Classification. In: International Conference on Intelligent Information Hiding and Multimedia Signal processing (IIH-MSP 2006), pp. 343–346. IEEE Press, California (2006)
4. Turk, M., Pentland, A.: Eigenfaces for Recognition. J. Cognitive Neuroscience 3(1), 71–86 (1991)
5. Belhumeur, P.N., Hespanha, J.P., Kriegman, D.J.: Eigenfaces vs. Fisherfaces: Recognition Using Class Specific Linear Projection. IEEE Trans. Pattern Recognition and Machine Intelligence 19(7), 711–720 (1997)
6. Martinez, A., Kak, A.: PCA versus LDA. IEEE Trans. Pattern Analysis and Machine Intelligence 23(2), 228–233 (2001)
7. Ding, C., Ye, J.: Two-Dimensional Singular Value Decomposition (2DSVD) for 2D Maps and Images. In: SIAM International Conference on Data Mining (SDM 2005), Newport Beach, CA, pp. 32–43 (2005)
8. Yang, J., Zhang, D., Frangi, A.: Two-dimensional PCA: A New Approach to Appearance-Based Face Representation and Recognition. IEEE Trans. Pattern Analysis and Machine Intelligence. 26(1), 131–137 (2004)
9. Shengliang, Z., Jingyu, Y.: A Survey of Two-dimensional PCA and 2DLDA. World Sci-Tech R&S 26(3), 286–289 (2008)
10. Li, M., Yuan, B.: 2D-LDA: A statistical Linear Discriminant Analysis for Image Matrix. Pattern Recognition Letter 26(5), 527–532 (2005)
11. Yang, Q., Ding, X.: Symmetrical PCA in Face Recognition. In: International Conference on Image Processing (ICIP 2002), pp. 97–100. IEEE Press, New York (2002)
12. Ming, J., Zhang, W.: S2DPCA with DM and FM in Face Recognition. In: International Conference on Apperceiving Computing and Intelligence Analysis (ICACIA 2008), pp. 365–368. IEEE Press, Chengdu (2008)
13. Zeng, Y., Feng, D., Xiong, L.: An Algorithm of Face Recognition Based on the Variation of 2DPCA. J. Computational Information Systems 7(1), 303–310 (2011)
14. Ding, M., Lu, C., Lin, Y., Tong, L.: Symmetry based two-dimensional principal component analysis for face recognition. In: Liu, D., Fei, S., Hou, Z., Zhang, H., Sun, C. (eds.) ISNN 2007. LNCS, vol. 4492, pp. 1048–1055. Springer, Heidelberg (2007)
15. Golub, G., Van Loan, C.: Matrix Computations, 3rd edn. Johns Hopkins, Baltimore (1996)
16. http://www.uk.research.att.com/facedatabase.html
17. http://cvc.yale.edu/projects/yalefacesB/yalefacesB.html

The Role of the Feature Extraction Methods in Improving the Textural Model of the Hepatocellular Carcinoma, Based on Ultrasound Images

Delia Mitrea[1], Sergiu Nedevschi[1], Mihai Socaciu[2], and Radu Badea[2]

[1] Computer Science Department, Technical University of Cluj-Napoca, Romania
delia.mitrea@cs.utcluj.ro, sergiu.nedevschi@cs.utcluj.ro
[2] Iuliu Hatieganu University of Medicine and Pharmacy, Cluj-Napoca, Romania
socacium@yahoo.com, rbadea2003@yahoo.com

Abstract. The non-invasive diagnosis of the malignant tumors is a very important issue in nowadays research. Our purpose is to elaborate computerized, texture-based methods for performing automatic recognition of the hepatocellular carcinoma, the most frequent malignant liver tumor, using only information from ultrasound images. We previously defined the textural model of HCC, consisting in the exhaustive set of the textural features, relevant for HCC characterization, and in their specific values for the HCC class. In this work, we improve the textural model and the classification process, through dimensionality reduction techniques. From the feature extraction methods, we implemented the most representative ones - Principal Component Analysis (PCA), Kernel PCA, Linear Discriminant Analysis (LDA), Generalized Discriminant Analysis (GDA) and combinations of these methods. We also assessed the combination of the feature extraction techniques with feature selection techniques. All these methods were evaluated for distinguishing HCC from the cirrhotic liver parenchyma on which it evolves.

Keywords: Hepatocellular carcinoma (HCC), textural model of HCC, dimensionality reduction methods, relevant textural features, classification performance.

1 Introduction

The hepatocellular carcinoma (HCC) is the most frequent malignant liver tumor (75% of liver cancer cases). The human observations are not enough in order to give a reliable diagnosis, and the biopsy is an invasive, dangerous method. Thus, a more subtle analysis is due, and we perform this by using computerized methods. The texture is very important in this context, as it provides a lot of information concerning the pathological state of the tissue; it describes the regular arrangement of the grey levels in the region of interest, and also multi-resolution parameters can be computed. The texture-based methods, in combination with classifiers, have been widely used for the automatic diagnosis of various kinds of tumors [1], [2], [3], [4]. However, a systematic study of the relevant features and of their specific values for the characterization of HCC, based only on information extracted from ultrasound images, of the possibilities of obtaining an optimal model of HCC, and best results for

V. Snasel, J. Platos, and E. El-Qawasmeh (Eds.): ICDIPC 2011, Part I, CCIS 188, pp. 496–509, 2011.

classification, is not done yet. We aim to do this in our research, which consists in modeling the HCC tumor and the visually similar tissues through textural features. In this work, we analyze the effect that the dimensionality reduction techniques and their combinations can have on the improvement of the classification process of HCC. Both the feature selection and the feature extraction methods are analyzed in this context. The feature extraction methods improve the speed and accuracy of the classification, by reducing the dimensionality of the data, while emphasizing the most important characteristics. The method of Principal Component Analysis (PCA) is the best known linear feature extractor [5], which represents the data into a new space, lower in dimensions, in order to emphasize the main directions of data variation. The Kernel PCA method is a generalization of PCA that maps the data from the initial space into a space that is appropriate for PCA representation [5]. The methods of Linear Discriminant Analysis (LDA) and Generalized Discriminant Analysis (GDA) [5] aim to find the best directions of data projection, in order to emphasize the class separation ability of the data. We applied these methods individually, and also in combination. We also combined the method of Principal Component Analysis (PCA) with a feature selection method based on the univariate density modeling of the textural features through Gaussian mixtures [6], elaborated in order to provide the ability of class separation to the data obtained after applying PCA. The effect of these methods will be assessed by applying powerful classifiers, as Support Vector Machines, Multilayer Perceptron and Decision Trees, as well as classifier combinations (bagging, boosting, stacking) [7] that provided the best results in our former experiments [8].

2   The Hepatocellular Carcinoma (HCC): Main Characteristics and Visual Aspect in Ultrasound Images

The most relevant oncogenic agent for HCC development is the chronic viral infection with the hepatitis B virus (HBV), or hepatitis C virus (HCV), the next evolution phase, preceding HCC, being cirrhosis [9]. HCC evolves from cirrhosis, after a restructuring phase at the end of which dysplastic nodules (future malignant tumors) result. In incipient phase, HCC appears like a small region having a different texture than the other parts of the tissue and a diameter of about 1.5 cm to 2 cm. In the case of an evolved HCC, the essential textural attribute is that of heterogeneity, due to the co-existence of regions with necrosis, fibrosis, and of regions with active growths. HCC is also characterized through a complex structure of vessels [10].

3   The State of the Art Concerning the Texture-Based Tumor Characterization and Classification and the Implementation of the Dimensionality Reduction Methods in Medical Domain

The most frequently used methods in the field of texture-based characterization of the malignant tumors are the Grey Levels Co-occurrence Matrix (GLCM) and the associated Haralick parameters, the Run-Length Matrix parameters[1], fractal-based methods [2], the Wavelet [3] and Gabor transforms [4], combined with the k-nn classifiers, Bayesian classifiers [2], Artificial Neural Networks, Fisher Linear Discriminants [1], Support Vector Machines [3]. In [1] the authors computed the first order statistics, the Grey Level Co-occurrence Matrix and the Run-Length Matrix parameters, which were used in combination with Artificial Neural Networks, as well as with Linear Discriminants, for the classification of the liver lesions. The fractal-based methods were used in [2], in order to distinguish the salivary gland tumors from ultrasound images. The Wavelet transform was also implemented in order to analyze the values of the textural parameters at multiple resolutions, for differentiating malignant and benign liver tumors from ultrasound images [3]. Concerning the implementation of the dimensionality reduction methods, the method of Decision Trees was applied successfully for feature selection, when detecting the malignant breast tumors from ultrasound images [11]. In [12] the authors combined the method of Principal Component Analysis with genetic algorithms for the selection of the gene expressions. The new method, resulted through the combination of these techniques, led to the improvement of the classification accuracy, in comparison with the case when only the PCA method was applied. It results that a systematic study of the most relevant textural features, obtained from ultrasound images, that characterize the HCC tumor, is not done. The effect of the dimensionality reduction methods, of the combination of these methods and the influence of the feature selection methods on their final efficiency is not systematically analyzed. We aim to perform this study and also to improve the textural model of HCC regarding both the most important textural features that characterize this tumor, and the accuracy of the automatic diagnosis.

4 The Proposed Solution: The Textural Model of HCC and the Improvements through Dimensionality Reduction Methods

4.1 The Definition of the Textural Model

The textural model of HCC consists in the exhaustive set of relevant, independent textural features, able to distinguish this tumor from the cirrhotic liver parenchyma and from the benign tumors; the specific, statistical values of the textural features - mean, standard deviation and probability distribution are part of the model.

We first consider the initial space of the potentially relevant textural features:

$$F = \{f_i\}_{i=1,...,n} \tag{1}$$

The textural model of HCC will consist in the most appropriate features, able to characterize the HCC tumor, obtained by applying dimensionality reduction methods (the best combination of feature selection and feature extraction methods):

$$
\begin{aligned}
&F = \{\text{potentially\_relevant\_textural\_features}\} \\
&F_R = Dimensionality\_Reduction(F)
\end{aligned}
\tag{2}
$$

Finally, the textural model of HCC (TM) will be defined by the collection of the vectors representing the specific values associated with each relevant textural feature (relevance, mean, standard deviation, probability distribution):

$$TM = \{V_{f_r} \mid V_{f_r} = [\text{Re}\,levance, Mean, S\tan dard\ Deviation, \text{Pr}\,obability\_Distribution]\,\} \quad (3)$$

In order to build a reliable textural model, first, the image selection for the training set building is necessary. For each considered type of tissue a corresponding class is built. Then, an image analysis phase is due: the textural feature computation using specific methods for texture analysis is involved in this process. The learning phase is important in order to perform dimensionality reduction through feature extraction and relevant feature selection, to eliminate the redundant features, to determine the specific, statistical values and the corresponding probability distributions. We aim to refine this phase, by assessing the efficiency of the feature extraction methods and of their combination with feature selection methods, in the given context. At the end, we perform the validation phase, involving the evaluation of the generated model by providing the selected features at classifiers inputs and estimating the accuracy of each classifier.

4.2 The Image Analysis Phase

During the image analysis phase, we computed the following textural features: first order statistics of the grey levels - the mean, the maximum and minimum value [13], the Grey Levels Cooccurrence Matrix (GLCM) and the Haralick parameters, edge-based statistics (edge contrast, edge frequency, average edge orientation) [14], the Laws texture energy measures that determined the textural microstructures [13], the Shannon entropy [15] computed after applying the Wavelet Transform at two levels of resolution [16]. The features were determined on regions of interest having 50x50 pixels in size, situated inside the analyzed tissue: HCC or cirrhotic parenchyma.

4.3 Improvement of the Learning Phase

The considered techniques for feature selection and feature extraction, as well as the way to implement them are described below:

- **Probability density modeling through Gaussian mixtures**
For selecting the textural features which are relevant for the class separation, we implemented the method of univariate density modeling through Gaussian mixtures, in order to separate the unimodal textural features from the bimodal ones. An Expectation-Maximization clustering method [7] is involved in the modeling process. The unimodal textural features, having the probability distribution expressed by a single Gaussian distribution, are considered non-relevant, while the bimodal textural features, having the probability distribution expressed by a mixture of two Gaussian distributions, are considered relevant, each Gaussian representing a certain class. The mathematical expression of the relevance measure is illustrated in (4):

$$\text{Re}\,levance = \frac{\min(p_1, p_2)}{\max(p_1, p_2)} \cdot \left(1 - \frac{(\mu_1 + 2\sigma_1) - (\mu_2 - 2\sigma_2)}{(\mu_2 + 2\sigma_2) - (\mu_1 - 2\sigma 1)}\right) \quad (4)$$

In (4), p_1 and p_2 are the probabilities of the data to belong to the first, and respectively to the second cluster, μ_1 and μ_2 are the mean values of the first, respectively of the second cluster, while σ_1 and σ_2 are the standard deviations of the first, respectively of the second cluster. The formula evaluates the difference between the cluster proportions, as well as the size of the cluster overlapping regions (Fig.1).

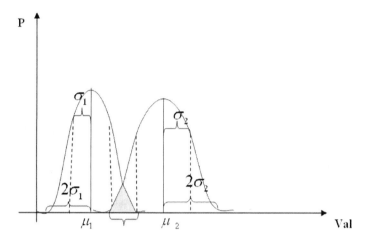

Fig. 1. Univariate density modeling through Gaussian mixtures

- **Principal Component Analysis (PCA) and Kernel PCA**

The method of Principal Component Analysis (PCA) is designed to reduce the dimensionality of the data by projecting it on a space of lower dimensions, putting in evidence the main variation modes. In mathematical terms, the purpose of PCA is to find a linear mapping matrix M, that maximizes the quantity $M_T \text{cov}(X)M$, where $\text{cov}(X)$ is the covariance matrix [17] of the dataset X. The transformation is a linear one, consisting in the computation of the covariance matrix of X, and of the eigenvectors and eigenvalues of this matrix. The mathematical expression of the transformation that must be applied to the original data is given below:

$$Y = (X - \bar{X})M \qquad (5)$$

In (5), X represents the original dataset, X is the mean subtracted data, M is the linear mapping matrix, and Y is the transformed dataset. The steps due for performing a reliable PCA are the following: 1. Subtract the mean of the original data, for each considered feature; 2. Compute $\text{cov}(X)$, the covariance matrix of the mean subtracted data; 3. Determine the eigenvalues and the eigenvectors of $\text{cov}(X)$; 4. Sort the eigenvalues ascending and choose the first eigenvectors X, corresponding to the highest eigenvalues, that cover a specified amount of variance in the data; 5. Transform the data according to the mathematical relation given by (1). PCA maximizes the variance of the extracted features, these features being also uncorrelated. The Kernel PCA method consists in the transposition of the initial data into a new space, built using a kernel method [5].

- **Linear discriminant analysis (LDA) and Generalized Discriminant Analysis (GDA)**

The method of Linear Discriminant Analysis (LDA) projects the data into a new space, lower in dimensions, emphasizing the class separation ability of the data. The purpose is that of finding the best directions of data projection, so that the new items resulted through the transformation are separated as well as possible with regard to their class labels. The mapping transformation is obtained by minimizing the Fisher criterion, [7], and then by solving a problem of generalized eigenvectors and eigenvalues [18].

The method of Linear Discriminant Analysis (LDA) is successful only in the case when the input data have linear properties, which not often happens in practice. In most cases, the input data must be transposed, through a non-linear transformation, into a new space, where the application of the LDA method provides the best results. The method of Generalized Discriminant Analysis (GDA) performs this task [19].

- **Combinations**

We studied the effect of combining the feature extraction methods in the best manner. The role of the above described feature selection method in improving the accuracy of the feature extraction methods is also analyzed. Thus, we combined the method of PCA with the feature selection method, in order to provide also class separation ability to the resulted data. The feature selection method was applied before the feature extraction method, as well as after it. All the combinations performed are compared and discussed.

4.4 The Validation Phase

We aimed for achieving the highest performance of the validation phase, by using individual classifiers, as well as classifier combination procedures. We compared the efficiency of the following classifier combination schemes: bagging, boosting and stacking, the purpose being to find the most appropriate one for accurately distinguishing HCC from the cirrhotic liver parenchyma. The basic classifiers were the Support Vector Machines (SVM), the Multilayer Perceptron (MLP) and the Decision Trees (DT) [7]. The classification accuracy was assessed through specific parameters, such as the rate of the correctly classified instances (recognition rate), the sensitivity (TP rate), the specificity (TN rate) and the area under the ROC curve [7].

5 Experiments and Discussions

5.1 Training Set Building

The experimental dataset contained the classes of HCC and cirrhotic parenchyma on which HCC had evolved. This dataset was formed from 130 cases; for each patient, three images were considered; the ultrasound images were acquired using various orientations of the transducer, under the same settings of the Logiq 7 ultrasound machine: the frequency was 5.5 MHz, the gain was 78 and the depth was 16 cm. Each class was formed by regions of interests selected on the desired type of tissue. The classes were combined in equal proportions.

5.2 Comparing the Efficiency of the Dimensionality Reduction Methods

The following classifiers were used in the Weka 3.5 environment [20], in order to assess the efficiency of the feature extraction methods: the Mutilayer Perceptron (MLP) classifier, with the learning rate of 0.1, the momentum of 0.9 and the number of nodes from the single hidden layer being the arithmetic mean between the number of the input features and the number of classes; the J48 method for decision trees, this being the Weka 3.5 equivalent of the C4.5 method [20]; the Support Vector Machines classifier with a polynomial kernel of third degree, which provided the best results in the case of HCC tumor classification. The classifier combination schemes of bagging, boosting and stacking were also experimented: the bagging combination scheme was used, with 100 bag size percent and 10 iterations; the Adaboost M1 combination procedure, with 10 iterations, was implemented as well; the StackingC method of Weka 3.5 was implemented, using the linear regression as a metaclassifier [7]. The stratified cross validation strategy with 5 folds was used for both the individual and combined classifiers. The values of the parameters corresponding to the best classifiers are illustrated in Table 1.

As Table 1 shows, the classifier of Decision Trees (DT), together with the bagging and boosting combination schemes in conjunction with Decision Trees provided the best results, from both time and accuracy points of view.

Table 1. The values of the accuracy parameters for the considered classifiers on the original data set

Classification method	Recognition Rate	TP Rate	TN Rate	AUC	Timee (model building)
MLP	67.42%	67.9%	67%	72.1%	32.17s
DT	68.66%	64.5%	72.9%	69.1%	0.86s
Bagging + DT	71.26%	68.6%	74%	78.9%	6.97s
AdaBoost + DT	71.38%	69.2%	73.5%	77.5%	7.86s
SVM	65.70%	62.5%	68.9%	65.7%	2.11s
Bagging + SVM	64.90%	65.4%	64.4%	70.4%	23.56s
AdaBoost + SVM	67.53%	63.6%	71.5%	72.7%	75.31s
Stacking (MLP + DT + SVM)	66.185%	64.4%	67.9%	70.4%	92.36s

Concerning the feature selection methods, the method of univariate density modeling through Gaussian mixtures, described in the paragraph 4.3, was applied. The Mixmod library [21] was used in Matlab 7.0 for applying the density modeling procedure, then the relevance coefficient was computed, as described in the paragraph 4.3. The following textural features resulted as being relevant (bimodal): GLCM homogeneity (relevance=0.3), GLCM correlation (relevance=0.45), the gradient magnitude (relevance=0.35), the entropies computed after applying the Wavelet transform (relevance> 0.47, in all cases), the frequency of the spot microstructures (relevance=0.31).

The classification accuracies obtained after performing feature selection using the method of probability density modeling through Gaussian mixtures are illustrated in Table 2.

Table 2. The values of the accuracy parameters after performing feature selection

Classification method	Recognition Rate	TP Rate	TN Rate	AUC	Time (model building)
MLP	65.158%	58.4%	71.9%	70%	10.25s
DT	68.43%	61.5%	75.3%	71.7%	0.3s
Bagging + DT	72.39%	68.8%	76%	80.4%	1.7s
AdaBoost + DT	68.66%	64.2%	72.6%	74.8%	1.55s
SVM	69.11%	61.3%	76.9%	69.1%	1.99s
Bagging + SVM	70.02%	63.3%	76.7%	73.2%	15.55s
AdaBoost + SVM	69.23%	62.9%	75.6%	71.9%	32.53s
Stacking (MLP + DT + SVM)	70.24%	65.8%	74.7%	78.1%	35.05s

The PCA and Kernel PCA methods were experimented, using the Gaussian, as well as the polynomial kernel. The Matlab Toolbox for Dimensionality Reduction [22] was used in Matlab 7.0. The PCA method of the Dimensionality Reduction Toolbox used the covariance matrix for determining the principal components. The feature extraction methods were applied on the normalized data. Initially, a number of 48 principal components were extracted, from 49 textural features. The number of the principal components was then reduced, searching for the smallest set of successive components that leaded to the highest recognition rate. The Weka feature selection method of PrincipalComponents, which used the correlation matrix in order to determine the principal components, was also tested in conjunction with the Ranker search method. The Ranker method selected the best combination of principal components, in order to cover 95% of the data variance [20]. The results obtained by assessing the data with the bagging combination scheme that used the Decision Trees as a basic classifier, are illustrated in Table 3. The PCA method implemented in the Dimensionality Reduction Toolbox of Matlab was denoted by PCA_1, while the second method, implemented in Weka, was denoted by PCA_2. The number of the principal components is specified in the second column of the table.

Table 3. The values of the accuracy parameters obtained after performing PCA and Kernel PCA

Feature extraction method	No. of PC	Recognition Rate	TP Rate	TN Rate	AUC	Time (model building)
Original dataset	49	71.26%	68.6%	74%	78.9%	6.45s
PCA_1	32	70.58%	68.3%	72.9%	76.1%	3.84s
Kernel PCA (Gaussian kernel)	13	70.24%	67.6%	72.9%	76.4%	1.78s
Kernel PCA polyn. kernel (2nd degree)	22	70.58%	67.9%	73.3%	77.2%	3.08s
PCA_2	19	70.54%	67.4%	74.7%	76.9%	3.05s

Table 3 shows that the PCA method didn't change the classification accuracy significantly, while it obviously reduced the time for model building. Among the two versions of the Kernel PCA methods, the one that used the polynomial kernel of 2_{nd} degree proved to be the best, giving classification results which were improved in comparison with the Kernel PCA method that used the Gaussian kernel.

The accuracy parameters obtained by applying the most powerful classifiers on the data resulted after performining PCA_1, are illustrated in Table 4. The PCA_1 method was also used in the next experiments.

Table 4. The values of the accuracy parameters obtained after performing PCA, assessed by multiple classifiers

Classification method	No. of PC	Recognition Rate	TP Rate	TN Rate	AUC	Time (model building)
MLP	9	67.72%	65.2%	70.2%	66.9%	3.08s
DT	30	66.89%	62.7%	71.1%	69.1%	0.33s
Bagging + DT	32	70.58%	67.9%	73.1%	76.4%	3.84s
AdaBoost + DT	32	69.38%	68.1%	70.6%	76.9%	2.38s
SVM	32	66.93%	63.4%	70.4%	66.9%	1.44s
Bagging + SVM	30	68.28%	67.9%	68.6%	72.6%	15.22s
AdaBoost + SVM	32	66.93%	63.4%	70.4%	68.8%	52.53s
Stacking (MLP + DT SVM)	32	67.72%	67.7%	67.7%	73.5%	61.63s

The results obtained by applying the methods of Linear Discriminant Analysis (LDA) and Generalized Discriminat Analysis (GDA) are illustrated below.

Both the polynomial kernel of 2nd degree and the Gaussian kernel were considered for the GDA method. The optimum number of components for which we obtained the maximum recognition accuracy, were selected. The LDA method provided better results than the GDA method, in both cases of Gaussian and polynomial kernel, emphasizing the linear nature of the considered data. Thus, in the case of the GDA method with Gaussian kernel, the recognition rate was 64.44%, in the case of LDA, the recognition rate was 68.71%. The results obtained by using the considered classifiers for assessment, after applying the LDA method are illustrated in Table 5.

Being interested in obtaining an increased accuracy for HCC tumor recognition, we combined the methods of PCA and LDA through successive application, in order to obtain the principal directions of data variation, and also to add the class sensitivity property to the final data set. The results of assessment through various classifiers and classifier combinations are illustrated in Table 6.

The values depicted in Table 6 demonstrate that the recognition accuracy usually increases in most of the cases, for all the parameters, while the model building time decreases.

Table 5. The values of the accuracy parameters after performing LDA

Classification method	No.of comp.	Recognition Rate	TP Rate	TN Rate	AUC	Time (model building)
MLP	48	67.49%	62.5%	72.5%	71.6%	28.97s
DT	48	65.46%	61.2%	68.6%	65.7%	0.49s
Bagging + DT	35	68.02%	64.3%	70%	73.4%	2.58s
AdaBoost + DT	48	67.15%	61.6%	70.4%	73.6%	4.28s
SVM	48	66.93%	62.3%	71.6%	66.9%	1.45s
Bagging + SVM	48	67.38%	65.2%	69.5%	71.3%	18.86s
AdaBoost + SVM	48	67.38%	65.9%	68.8%	72.8%	27.09
Stacking (MLP + DT + SVM)	48	68.171%	65.7%	70.7%	74.9%	30.73s

Table 6. The values of the accuracy parameters after performing PCA+LDA

Classification method	Recognition Rate	TP Rate	TN Rate	AUC	Time (model building)
MLP	74.54%	72%	76.7%	80.7%	5.22s
DT	80.12%	75.4%	84.4%	87.9%	0.25s
Bagging + DT	80. 92%	75.4%	86.5%	89%	1.08s
AdaBoost + DT	81.26%	79%	83.5%	88.5%	0.72s
SVM	79.99%	78.3%	81.7%	80%	0.83s
Bagging + SVM	80.10%	77.8%	82.4%	84.5%	6.94s
AdaBoost + SVM	80.07%	78.6%	81.5%	81.8%	17.8s
Stacking(MLP+DT+ SVM)	80.13%	75.4%	84.4%	88.6%	18.53s

Concerning the combination of PCA with the feature selection methods, the parameter values obtained after applying the feature selection method that consisted in the univariate density modeling of each feature through Gaussian mixtures, then the PCA method, are described in Table 7.

Table 7. The values of the accuracy parameters obtained after performing feature selection, then PCA

Classification method	Recognition Rate	TP Rate	TN Rate	AUC	Time(model building)
MLP	69.54%	67%	71.7%	75.7%	5.22s
DT	75.12%	70.4%	79.4%	82.9%	0.25s
Bagging + DT	75. 92%	70.4%	81.5%	84%	1.08s
AdaBoost + DT	76.26%	74%	78.5%	83.5%	0.72s
SVM	74.99%	73.3%	76.7%	75%	0.83s
Bagging + SVM	75.10%	72.8%	77.4%	79.5%	6.94s
AdaBoost + SVM	75.07%	73.6%	76.5%	76.8%	17.8s
Stacking (MLP+DT+ SVM)	75.13%	70.4%	79.4%	83.6%	18.53s

As Table 7 shows, the values of the accuracy parameters usually increase after successively applying the feature selection method based on the univariate density modeling of the textural features through Gaussian mixtures (first), and then the method of Principal Component Analysis (PCA).

Table 8. The values of the accuracy parameters obtained after performing PCA, then feature selection

Classification method	Recognition Rate	TP Rate	TN Rate	AUC	Time(model building)
MLP	67.98%	73.9%	62.1%	75.1%	5.99s
DT	74.91%	48%	61.8%	57.6%	0.2s
Bagging + DT	68.51%	65.9%	71.1%	76.1%	1.16s
AdaBoost + DT	65.83%	65.9%	69.8%	75.3%	1.33s
SVM	69.86%	65.7%	74.1%	69.9%	1.53s
Bagging + SVM	69.52%	65.7%	73.4%	74.9%	14.94s
AdaBoost + SVM	68.77 %	67.9%	73.6%	76.9%	33.08s
Stacking(MLP+DT+ SVM)	69%	70.2%	71.8%	76.8%	84.05%

As Table 8 shows, when applying the combination between the Principal Component Analysis (applied first) and the feature selection method based on the univariate density modeling of the principal components through Gaussian mixtures, the accuracy parameters are more increased than those corresponding to the original case. However, these parameters present lower values than those corresponding to the application of the PCA method alone, due to the fact that only a few principal components are used in this case, but not necessarily those corresponding to the highest eigenvalues.

5.3 The Relevant Textural Features Resulted after Applying the Feature Extraction Methods

The relevant features obtained after applying the dimensionality reduction methods which provided the best results are illustrated in Table 9. The features selected by the method of probability density modeling through Gaussian mixtures had a relevance factor above 0.3, while the features considered as being relevant after applying the method of Principal Component Analysis (PCA) had a weight value greater than 0.4 within the linear combination defining a certain principal component. Among the relevant textural features, the most important was the GLCM correlation, indicating differences in granularity between the HCC tumor and the cirrhotic parenchyma on which HCC had evolved. The GLCM entropy, the entropies computed at multiple resolutions after applying the Wavelet transform, as well as the variability in edge orientations, emphasize the chaotic character of the tumor tissue. We also notice the relevance of the Laws textural microstructures, especially concerning those of spot and ripple type, as illustrated in Fig. 2. These features, together with the edge frequency and gradient magnitude indicate the complexity of the tumor structure.

Table 9. The relevant textural features obtained after applying the dimensionality reduction methods

Dimensionality reduction method	Relevant textural features
Univariate density modeling	GLCM correlation, GLCM energy, Edge orientation variability, Gradient magnitude, Wavelet entropy at the 1st level, on the high-low low-high and high-high components, Wavelet entropy at the 2nd level, on the low-low and high-low components
PCA	GLCM correlation , Edge frequency, Laws levels frequency, Laws spot frequency, GLCM energy, GLCM entropy, Wavelet entropy at the 1st level, on the low-high component, Wavelet entropy at the second level, on the high-low and high-high component
Univariate density modeling + PCA	GLCM correlation, Laws wave frequency, Laws ripple frequency, Laws spot frequency, GLCM energy, Edge orientation variability
PCA + LDA	Edge orientation variability, gradient magnitude, GLCM Correlation, Laws level frequency, Laws spot frequency, Wavelet entropy on the low-high component, at the 1st level, Wavelet entropy on the high-high component, at the 2nd level, GLCM energy

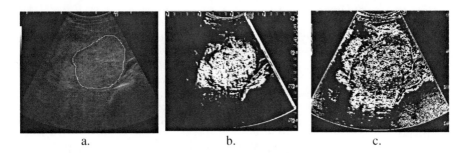

a.   b.   c.

Fig. 2. The detection of the spot and ripple microstructures inside the HCC tumor, by applying the corresponding Laws convolution filter: a. Original image; b. Detection of the spot microstructures; c. Detection of the ripple microstructures.

6 Conclusions and Future Work

As the experiments showed, the feature extraction methods brought a considerable improvement concerning the automatic diagnosis process, from both time and accuracy points of view. The method of Principal Component Analysis (PCA) proved to be efficient in most of the situations: the classic PCA method implemented in Matlab, as well as the Weka 3.5 version of this method didn't lter the recognition rate significantly, but they improved the execution time. the method of Linear Discriminant Analysis (LDA) provided an increase of the classification accuracy in most of the cases. Our feature selection method, based on univariate density modeling through Gaussian mixtures, demonstrated its qualities, providing an increase of the classification accuracy in the cases when it was applied alone, as well as when it was combined with the feature extraction methods. The application of the feature selection method before the feature extraction method resulted in a considerable increase of the classification accuracy. However, the application of the feature selection method after the feature extraction method proved to be less efficient, as it altered the order of the components, sometimes leading also to a small number of features. The combination between the feature extraction methods (PCA+LDA) provided an improvement of the classification accuracy in most situation, yielding a new feature extraction method able to emphasize both the principal directions of data variation, and also the class separation capacity of the data. The relevant textural features found by our dimensionality reduction methods indicate the complex and chaotic structure of the hepatocellular carcinoma, being able to distinguish this tumor from the cirrhotic liver parenchyma. Multiple classes will be taken into consideration as well, in our future research, resulted from the division of the HCC class into subclasses corresponding to the subtypes of HCC. The effect of the feature extraction methods will be also considered in this case. The comparison with the benign liver tumors will be taken into consideration, as well.

References

1. Sujana, H., Swarnamani, S.: Application of Artificial Neural Networks for the Classification of Liver Lesions by Texture Parameters. Ultrasound in Med. & Biol. 22(9), 1177–1181 (1996)
2. Chikui, T., Tokumori, K., Yoshiura, K.: Sonographic Texture Characterization of Salivary Gland Tumors by Fractal Analysis. Ultrasound in Med. & Biol. 31(10), 1297–1304 (2005)
3. Yoshida, H., Casalino, D., Keserci, B., Coskun, A., Ozturk, O., Savranlar, A.: Wavelet Packet based Texture Analysis for Diferentiation between Benign and Malignant Liver Tumours in Ultrasound Images. Phys. in Med. & Biol. 48, 3735–3753 (2003)
4. Madabhushi, A., Felman, M., Metaxas, D.: Automated Detection of Prostatic Adenocarcinoma from High-Resolution Ex Vivo MRI. IEEE Trans. on Medical Imaging, 1611–1626 (2005)
5. Van der Maaten, L., Postma, E., Van der Herick, H.: Dimensionality Reduction. A Comparative Review. Pattern Recognition Letters 42(9), 2054–2066 (2009)
6. Jain, A.K., Duin, R., Mao, J.: Statistical Pattern Recognition: A Review. IEEE Trans. On Pattern Analysis and Machine Intelligence 22(1), 4–37 (2000)
7. Duda, R.: Pattern Classification, 2nd edn. Wiley Interscience, Hoboken (2003)
8. Mitrea, D., Nedevschi, S., Lupsor, M., Socaciu, M., Badea, R.: Advanced Classification Methods for Improving the Automatic Diagnosis of the Hepatocellular Carcinoma, based on Ultrasound Images. In: Proceedings of the 2010 IEEE International Conference on Automation, Quality and Testing, Robotics, May 28-30, pp. 265–271. IEEE Press, Cluj-Napoca (2010)
9. Bruix, J.: Hepatitis B Virus and Hepatocellular Carcinoma. Journal of Hepatology 39(1), 59–63 (2003)
10. American Liver Foundation:
    http://www.liverfoundation.org/education/info/benigntumors/
11. Grabczewski, K., Jankowski, N.: Feature Selection with Decision Tree Criterion. In: Proceedings of the IEEE Fifth International Conference on Hybrid Intelligent Systems, pp. 212–217 (2005)

12. Pechenizkiy, M., Tsymbal, A., Puuronen, S.: PCA based Feature Transformation for Classification: Issues in Medical Diagnosis. In: Proceedings of the 17th IEEE Symposium on Computer-Based Medical Systems, pp. 535–540 (2004)
13. Jain, A.K.: Fundamentals of Digital Image Processing. Prentice Hall, Englewood Cliffs (1989)
14. Clausi, D.: An Analysis of Cooccurrence Texture Statistics as a Function of Grey Level Quantization. Canadian Journal of Remote Sensing 28(1), 45–62 (2002)
15. Stollnitz, E., DeRose, T.: Wavelets for Computer Graphics. IEEE Computer Graphics & Applications 15(3), 76–84 (1995)
16. Parker, J.R.: Algorithms of Image Processing and Computer Vision. Wiley Computer Publishing, Chichester (1996)
17. Smith, I.L.: A Tutorial on Principal Component Analysis (2002),
    http://www.cs.otago.ac.nz/cosc453/student_tutorials/principal_components.pdf
18. Balakrishnama, S., Ganapathiraju, A., Picone, J.: Linear Discriminant Analysis for Signal Processing Problems. In: Proceedings of IEEE Southeastcon, Lexington, Kentucky, pp. 78–81 (1999)
19. Baudat, G., Anouar, F.: Generalized Discriminant Analysis using a Kernel Approach. Pattern Recognition Letters 28(2), 254–259 (2007)
20. Weka 3, Data Mining Software in Java (2004),
    http://www.cs.waikato.ac.nz/ml/weka/
21. MixMod, V.: 2.0.1, (2007),
    http://www-math.univ-fcomte.fr/mixmod/index.php
22. Matlab Toolbox for Dimensionality Reduction, ver 7.0., (2008),
    http://ticc.uvt.nl/lvdrmaaten/Laurens_van_der_Maaten/Matlab_Toolbox_for_Dimensionality_Reduction.html

A New Approach Based on NμSMV Model to Query Semantic Graph

Mahdi Gueffaz, Sylvain Rampacek, and Christophe Nicolle

LE2I, UMR CNRS 5158
University of Bourgogne,
21000 Dijon, France
{Mahdi.Gueffaz,Sylvain.Rampacek,
Christophe.Nicolle}@u-bourgogne.fr

Abstract. The language most frequently used to represent the semantic graphs is the RDF (W3C standard for meta-modeling). The construction of semantic graphs is a source of numerous errors of interpretation. Processing of large semantic graphs can be a limit to use semantics in modern information systems. The work presented in this paper is part of a new research at the border between two areas: the semantic web and the model checking. For this, we developed a tool, RDF2NμSMV, which converts RDF graphs into NμSMV language. This conversion aims checking the semantic graphs with the model checker NμSMV in order to verify the consistency of the data. The data integration and sharing activities carried on the framework of the Semantic Web lead to large knowledge databases that must be queried, analyzed, and exploited efficiently. Many representation languages of the knowledge of the Semantic Web, starting with RDF, are based on directed, labeled graphs, which can be also manipulated using graph algorithms and tools coming from other domains. In this paper, we propose an analysis approach of RDF graphs by reusing the verification technology developed for concurrent systems. To this purpose, we define a translation from the SPARQL query language into temporal logic query, a general-purpose graph manipulation language implemented in the ScaleSem verification toolbox. This translation makes it possible to extend the expressive power of SPARQL naturally by adding temporal logic formulas characterizing sequences, trees, or general sub-graphs of the RDF graph. Our approach exhibits a performance comparable to dedicated SPARQL query evaluation engines, as illustrated by experiments on large RDF graphs.

Keywords: Semantic graph, RDF, Model Checking, Temporal logic, NμSMV, Query checking, SPARQL, temporal logic query.

1 Introduction

The increasing development of networks and especially the internet has greatly developed the heterogeneous gap between information systems. In glancing over the studies about interoperability of heterogeneous information systems we discover that all works tend to the resolution of semantic heterogeneity problems. The W3C[1]

---

[1] World Wide Web Consortium

V. Snasel, J. Platos, and E. El-Qawasmeh (Eds.): ICDIPC 2011, Part I, CCIS 188, pp. 510–524, 2011.
© Springer-Verlag Berlin Heidelberg 2011

suggest norms to represent the semantic by ontology. Ontology is becoming an inescapable support for information systems interoperability and particularly in the Semantic. Literature now generally agrees on the Gruber's terms to define an ontology: explicit specification of a shared conceptualization of a domain [1]. The physical structure of ontology is a combination of concepts, properties and relationships. This combination is also called a semantic graph.

Several languages have been developed in the context of Semantic Web and most of these languages use XML[2] as syntax [2]. The OWL[3] [3] and RDF[4] [4] are the most important languages of the semantic web, they are based on XML. OWL allows representing the ontology, and it offers large capacity machines performing web content. RDF enhances the ease of automatic processing of Web resources. The RDF (Resource Description Framework) is the first W3C standard for enriching resources on the web with detailed descriptions. The descriptions may be characteristics of resources, such as author or content of a website. These descriptions are metadata. Enriching the Web with metadata allows the development of so-called Semantic Web [5]. The RDF is also used to represent semantic graph corresponding to a specific knowledge modeling. In this paper, we propose a new way using formal verification, which consists in the transformation of semantic graphs into model and verifying them with a Model Checker [6].

We developed two tools, the first one called "RDF2NµSMV" that transforms semantic graphs into a model represented in NµSMV [7] language. After this transformation, NµSMV verifies the correctness of the model written in NµSMV language with temporal logic in order to verify the consistency of the data described in the model of the huge semantic graphs. The second tool, called "STL RESOLVOR", aims resolving the queries destined to the model of the semantic graph. This query was introduced the first time by William Chan in his innovative work [8].These requests are not used to verify the model representing the RDF graph, but rather to recognize it.

Our primary goal in this paper is to define a powerful and expressive query language for semantic graphs and to align with SPARQL [9], in order to improve the interoperability of applications on the Semantic Web. The other rather competing goal is to keep the query language simple enough that it can be easily built. To satisfy these requirements, we define a new query language that uses the operators of the temporal logic.

The rest of this paper is organized as follows. In Section 2 we present an overview of the semantic graphs, especially the structure of the RDF graphs and the model checking. Then, in section 3, we describe the SPARQL query. The Section 4 presents the temporal logic and the query checking. Section 5 refers to the mapping of the semantic graphs into models, section 6 to the transformation of SPARQL query to temporal logic query. Section 7 defines the functionalities of the STL Resolver tool and we present some benchmarks in section 9. Finally, we end with a conclusion.

---

[2] eXtensible Markup Language.
[3] Web Ontology Language.
[4] Resource Description Framework.

2   An overview of Semantic Graphs and Model Checking

Semantic graphs - The RDF is also used to represent semantic graphs corresponding to a specific knowledge modelling. It is a language developed by the W3C to bring a semantic layer to the Web [10]. It allows the connection of the Web resources using directed labelled edges. The structure of the RDF documents is a complex directed labelled graph. An RDF document is a set of triples <subject, predicate, object> as shown in the Figure1. In addition, the predicate (also called property) connects the subject (resource) to the object (value). Thus, the subject and the object are nodes of the graph connected by an edge directed from the subject towards the object. The nodes and the edges belong to the "resource" types. A resource is identified by an URI[5] [11, 12].

Fig. 1. RDF triplet

The declarations can also be represented as a graph, the nodes as resources and values, and the arcs as properties. The resources are represented in the graph by circles; the properties are represented by directed arcs and the values by a box (a rectangle). Values can be resources if they are described by additional properties. For example, when a value is a resource in another triplet, the value is represented by a circle.

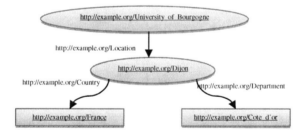

Fig. 2. Example of a partial RDF graph

The RDF graph in the Figure 2 defines a node "University of Bourgogne" located at "Dijon", having as country "France" and as department "Cote d'Or". RDF documents can be written in various syntaxes, e.g., N3 [13], N-Triple [14], and RDF/XML. Below, we present the RDF\XML document corresponding to Figure 2.

```
<rdf:Description rdf:about="http://example.org/university of
Bourgogne">
    <ex:Location>
```

---
[5] Uniform Resource Identifier.

```
    <rdf:Description rdf:about="http://example.org/Dijon">
    <ex:Country> France</ex:Country>
    <ex:Department>Cote d'or</ex:Department>
    </rdf:Description>
  </ex:Location>
</rdf:Description>
```

Model checking - The model checking [15] described in Figure 3 is a verification technique that explores all possible system states in a brute-force manner. Similar to a computer chess program that checks all possible moves, a model checker, the software tool that performs the model checking, examines all possible system scenarios in a systematic manner. In this way, it can be shown that a given system model truly satisfies a certain property. Even the subtle errors that remain undiscovered using emulation, testing and simulation can potentially be revealed using model checking.

To make a rigorous verification possible, properties should be described in a precise unambiguous way. It is the temporal logic that is used in order to express these properties. The temporal logic is a form of modal logic that is appropriate to specify relevant properties of the systems. It is basically an extension of traditional propositional logic with operators that refer to the behaviour of systems over time.

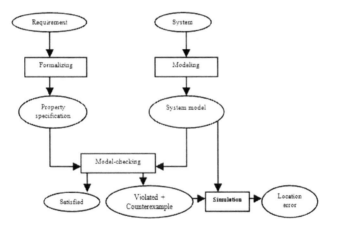

Fig. 3. Model checking approach

The following algorithm explains the way that the model checking works. First we put in the stack all the properties expressed in the temporal logic. All of them are verified one by one in the model and if a property does not satisfy the model, it is whether the model or the property that we must refine. In case of a memory overflow, the model must be reduced. Whereas formal verification techniques such as simulation and model checking are based on model description from which all possible system states can be generated, the test, that is a type of verification technique, is even applicable in cases where it is hard or even impossible to obtain a system model.

3 The SPARQL Query

SPARQL [9] is a query language for querying metadata and extraction data form an RDF graph or, more precisely a query language for RDF triples.

In SPARQL different query form are available:

- **Select:** return the value of variables which may be bound by a matching query pattern.
- **Ask:** return true if a given query matches and false if not.
- **Construct:** return an RDF graph by substituting the values in given templates.
- **Describe:** return an RDF graph which defines the matching resource.

The Select form is the most used. In this article we showed only the SPARQL query with the select form. A basic SPARQL query has the following form:

Select ?variable1, ?variable2,...
Where {pattern1.pattern2. ...}

Where each pattern consists of subject, predicate, object, and each of these is either a variable or a literal. The query model is query-by-example style: the query specifies the known literals and leaves the unknowns as variables. Variables can occur in multiple patterns and thus imply joins. The query processor needs to find all possible variable bindings that satisfy the given patterns and return the bindings from the projection clause to the application. Note that not all variables are necessarily bound (e.g., if a variable only occurs in the projection and not in a pattern), which results in NULL values.

Relational algebra [16] is introduced to facilitate the mapping of SPARQL query to the applications in temporal logic. We define the operators in RDF relations.

3.1 Selection

Selection (σ), sometimes also called restriction, is an unary operator that selects only those tuples of a relation for which a propositional formula holds. The propositions are assumed to have the expressivity of SPARQL Filter expressions.

3.2 Projection

The projection operator (π) restricts a relation to subset of its attributes.

3.3 Inner Join and Left Outer Join

The inner join ($\bowtie$) joins two relations on their shared attributes. A $\bowtie$ B contains all combinations of a tuple from A and a tuple from B, minus those where the shared attributes are not equal.

The left outer join ($\bowtie$) additionally contains all those tuples from the first relation that have no matching tuple in the second.

3.4 Union

The union $(\cup)$ of two relations A and B is the set of union of the tuples of A and B. unlike in regular relational algebra, the headings of A and B do not need to be identical.

4 Temporal Logic and the Query Checking

The concepts of temporal logic used for the first time by Pnueli [17] in the specification of formal properties are fairly easy to use. The operators are very close in terms of natural language. The formalization in temporal logic is simple enough although this apparent simplicity therefore requires significant expertise. Temporal logic allows representing and reasoning about certain properties of the system, so it is well-suited for the systems verification. There are two main temporal logics, that is linear time and branching time. In linear time temporal logic, each execution of the system is independently analyzed. In this case, a system satisfies a formula f, if f holds along every execution. The branching time combines all possible executions of the system into a single tree. Each path in the tree is a possible representation of the system execution [18].

- **Linear Temporal Logic** or LTL allow representing the behavior of reactive systems using properties that describe the system in which time proceeds linearly. Clearly, we specify the expected behavior of a system, by specifying the only possible future as a sequence of actions that follow, LTL uses for that temporal operators: X (Next), F (Finally), G (Always), U (Until).
- **Computation Tree Logic** or CTL suggest several possible futures from a system state rather than having a linear view of the system considered. The operators of CTL are obtained by adding A (for any execution) or E (there is an execution) before the operators of linear temporal logic that are: AX φ (all successor states immediately satisfy φ), EX φ (there is an execution whose next state satisfies φ), AF φ (for any execution, there is a state where φ is true), EF φ (there is an execution, leading to a true state φ), AG φ (for any execution, φ is always true), EG ϕ (there is an execution, where φ is always true), AφUψ (for any execution φ is true until ψ is true), EφUψ (there is an execution in which φ is true until ψ is true).

The Model-Checking was proposed as a verification technique, it is valuable for understanding the model: The user formulates a hypothesis of the system behavior, expressed as a formula in temporal logic, and tries to use the Model Checker to validate this hypothesis. This use of the model checking has not been sufficiently emphasized in the literature. So in order to help the user understand the system behavior, Chan [8] introduced the queries in temporal logic and used a technique similar to the Model-Checking to determine the temporal properties as opposed to simply verifying them.

The query checking is an extension of the Model checking who, instead of asking "does the system satisfy a temporal logic formula φ", allows us to ask "for what value of X does the system satisfy $\varphi(X)$?" Here, X is not a system parameter, but a property setting, that we seek to satisfy. These queries do not allow the verification of a specific property of the model but they allow the examination of the model by questioning it. The technique of query-checking can also be used to provide more information to the user in the Model Checking.

The query checking allows the writing of temporal logic formulas easily and can therefore verify any properties on both the data contained in the graph and the structure of the data.

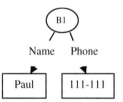

Fig. 4. The query execution time

In the graph of the Figure 4, we can see that there are two RDF triples (B1, name, Paul) and (B1, Phone, 111-111). The following SPARQL query:

> SELECT ?x
> WHERE {
>   ?x Name "Paul"}

whose representation in relational algebra is:

$$\pi_{?x} \rightarrow \sigma_{?\,predicate=Name \atop ?\,object=Paul} \rightarrow Triples$$

looks for a subject ?x which has the predicate "Name" and an object "Paul" (?x, name, Paul). The equivalent of the previous query in query using the temporal logic operators is:

$$\text{Finally (?x} \rightarrow \text{Next "Paul")} \tag{1}$$

This temporal logic query looks for the same subject ?x, as defined in the SPARQL query above.

5   The RDF Graph Transformation

This section speaks about our approach which consists in the transformation of semantic graphs into model in order to verify them with the model-checker. For this, we developed "RDF2NµSMV" tool that transform semantic graph into NµSMV [7] language for the Model-checker NµSMV.

NμSMV is the amelioration of SMV model checker; it works on the sample principles as SMV. NμSMV verify the properties in both linear time logic and computation tree logic.

The RDF graphs considered here are represented as XML verbose files, in which the information is not stored hierarchically (so-called graph point of view). On the one hand, these RDF graphs are not necessarily connected, meaning they may have no root vertex from which all the other vertices are reachable. On the other hand, the NμSMV language manipulated by the verification tools of NμSMV always have a root vertex, which corresponds to the initial state of the system whose behavior is represented by the NμSMV language. The RDF graph transformation into NμSMV language is articulated in three steps: exploring the RDF graph, determining a root vertex and, final step, generating the Model of the RDF graph. This final step is divided into three sub-steps. The first and the second steps consist in generating two tables (triples table and correspondence table). Firstly, the table of all triples is built by exploring the entire graph. The graph traversal algorithms go through the RDF graph and create a table consisting of resources, properties and values. In the source RDF graph, the resource is a vertex, the property represents the edge and the value is the successor vertex corresponding of the edge of the vertex. The table of triples of RDF graph is useful for the next sub-step.

Secondly, a correspondence table is generated. To build the table of correspondence, the algorithm associates an identifier for each resource, property and value.

The last step consists in producing from these tables the model writing in NμSMV language for the Model checker NμSMV. [19]

6   SPARQL Query to Temporal Logic Query

This section gives an overview of SPARQL query transformation into Temporal Logic query. We focus on the SELECT form. To illustrate this section, we use the RDF example shown in Figure 5.

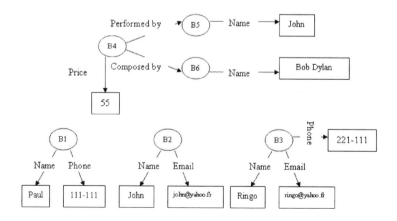

Fig. 5. RDF graph for SPARQL query

From the graph in Figure 5, we construct SPARQL queries and their query equivalent in temporal logic. The SPARQL query bellow selects the subject with the variable ?x which has Paul as object.

SPARQL	SELECT ?x WHERE { ?x nom "Paul"}
LT query	Finally (?x → Next "Paul")
Relational algebra	$\pi_{?x} \to \sigma_{?\,predicate=Name \land \atop ?\,object=Paul} \to Triples$

The SPARQL query bellow selects the subject ?x which has the variable ?y as object, who, at its turn, has "Bob Dylan" as object.

SPARQL	SELECT ?x WHERE { ?x composed_by ?y. ?y name "Bob Dylan"}
LT query	Finally (?x → Next Next "Bob Dylan")

The purpose of an optional pattern is to supplement the solution with additional information. If the pattern within an OPTIONAL clause matches, the variables defined within that pattern are bound to one or to many solutions. If the pattern does not match, the solution remains unchanged. The SPARQL query represented bellow selects the subject ?x that has "Paul" and/or "paul@yahoo.fr" as object.

SPARQL	SELECT ?x WHERE { ?x name "Paul" OPTIONAL {?x email paul@yahoo.com"}}
LT query	Finally (?x → Next "Paul" ∧ Finally ?x → "paul@yahoo.com")

A SPARQL **FILTER** function can be added to a basic graph pattern in order to restrict the result according to Boolean conditions. The SPARQL query bellow selects the subject ?x which has a word that contains at least the letter P as object.

SPARQL	SELECT ?x WHERE { ?x name ?y FILTER regex (?y, "P") }
LT query	Finally (?x → Next *P*)
Relational algebra	$\pi_{?x} \to \sigma_{?\,predicate=Name \land \atop ?\,object=?\,y \land regex(?\,y,P)} \to Triples$

The SPARQL query bellow selects the subjects ?x and ?y that have "John" and respectively "Paul" as objects.

SPARQL	SELECT ?x ?y WHERE { {?x name "John"} UNION { ?y name "Paul"}}
LT query	Finally (?x → Next "John" ∧ ?y → Next "Paul")

The SPARQL query bellow selects the objects ?x where "name" is the predicate.

SPARQL	SELECT ?x WHERE { ?y name ?x }
LT query	Finally (?y → Next ?x) where predicate=name/ ?x
Relational algebra	$\pi_{?x} \to \sigma_{?\,predicate=Name \land \atop ?\,subject=?\,y} \to Triples$

The SPARQL query bellow selects the object ?y. This query represents a SPARQL's join.

SPARQL	SELECT ?y WHERE { ?x name ?y. ?z performed_by ?x. ?z composed_by ?p. ?p name "Bob Dylan"}
LT query	Finally (?z → Next Next ?y ∧ ?z → Next Next "Bob Dylan") where predicate=nom/ ?y

The transformation of SPARQL queries into queries using operators of temporal logic was based on the representation of SPARQL queries in the relational algebra seen above.

The advantage of temporal logic queries is their simplicity to write. That means that the temporal logic is closer to the natural language and in addition, one of the great advantages of the temporal logic queries is that they are more expressive than the SPARQL queries using the temporal logic operators. [20]

We developed a tool called "SPARQL2LTQ" which aims to transform SPARQL queries into queries using operators of the temporal logic.

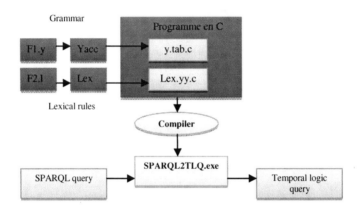

Fig. 6. The architecture of the transformation tool "SPARQL2RLT"

For the development of this tool, we use LEX & YACC to decompose the SPARQL query in order to facilitate the processing. LEX is used to recognize the lexical entities and replace them with keywords that will be recognized in the grammar of the language defined in YACC; then YACC will recognize and respect the expressions and will verify if they belong to the grammar. LEX & YACC are two very powerful tools, facilitating the lexical and respectively the syntactic analysis, which represent two stages of compilation difficult to program.

In order to demonstrate the usefulness of temporal logic queries we will illustrate an example. Here are two tables in a relational database, table 1 and table 2.

Table 1.			**Table 2.**	

Person	Name
id1	Alice
id3	Christophe
id2	Bob

Name	Age
Alice	33
Bob	42
Christophe	15

```
SELECT ?x
WHERE {
id1 ex :Name ?z
?z ex :HasAge ?x
}
```

The SPARQL query above seeks the age of the person identified by id1, corresponding to "Alice" in our case.

To answer this SPARQL query we must first make a join between the two previous relational database tables. A join is used for joining two multi sets with a constraint. In our example the constraint is the name, see table 3 below.

Table 3.

Person	Name	Age
1	Alice	33
2	Bob	42
3	Christophe	15

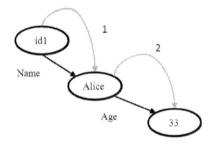

Fig. 7. The RDF graph model showing the movement to be done to achieve results

The equivalent of the previous SPARQL query in a query using operators of the temporal logic is as follows:

Finally (id → X X ?x)

In this query, in order to retrieve the age of the person identified by id1, one just moves two states (two "next" operators in our query represented by X) in the semantic graph model to find the result, as shown in Figure 7.

For results with temporal logic query one just moves around the graph with the operators of temporal logic. The new interrogation technique will allow us to avoid scanning the graph several times as with SPARQL queries.

7 The STL Resolver

The ScaleSem toolbox contains a tool used to resolve queries in temporal logic that we have previously seen. This tool is called STL RESOLVOR, it takes as input the temporal logic query and the NμSMV graph representing the semantic graph.

The query checking is an extension of the Model checking. A temporal logic query is a formula with a missing propositional formula, designated by a placeholder ("?"). A solution to a temporal logic query is the set of all propositional formulas that satisfy the query, in our case the formula are the states represented in the NμSMV graph.

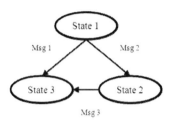

Fig. 8. An example of NμSMV graph

Table 4.

	Query	Result
1	Finally (?x → X State 3)	?x ={State 1, State 2}
2	Finally (?x → X X state 3)	?x={State 1}

The table above gives some example of temporal logic queries and their results.

8 Benchmark

We tested several RDF graphs on our tool "RDF2NμSMV", using a machine that runs on a processor with a capacity of 2.4 GHz and 4 GB of RAM, calculating the time of conversion as shown in Figure 9. Note that the RDF2NμSMV tool is faster in

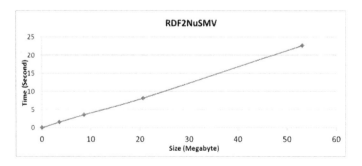

Fig. 9. Time conversion of semantic graphs

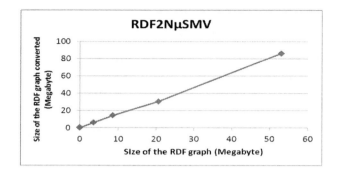

Fig. 10. Size of the models

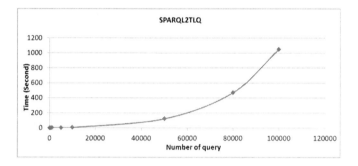

Fig. 11. Time conversion of SPARQL query

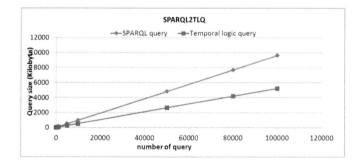

Fig. 12. Comparison of size in both SPARQL query and temporal logic query

converting semantic graphs. We have almost 22 seconds for a graph of 53 MB size. The transformation tool follows a polynomial curve. In Figure 10, we see the size of the converted semantic graphs from RDF to NµSMV language.

We calculate the time of transformation of the SPRAQL query into a query using the operators of the temporal logic with the SPARQL2TLQ tool. The graph of the Figure 11 shows that for 50 000 queries, we have over then 2 minutes and for 100 000 queries, we have 17 minutes. This transformation follows a polynomial curve. In Figure 12, we notice that the size of the queries in temporal logic is smaller than the size of the equivalent SPARQL queries.

9 Conclusion

This paper presents how to transform a semantic graph into a model for verification by using a powerful formal method, that is the "model checking". Knowing that the model checker does not understand the semantic graphs, we developed a tool called "RDF2NμSMV" to convert them into NμSMV graph in order to be verified with the temporal logics. This transformation is made for the purpose of classifying large semantic graphs in order to verify the consistency of the data from a different ontology. We notice the advantage of NμSMV, whose verification can be made with both linear time logic and computation tree logic formulas.

We also introduce a new tool called "STL RESOLVOR" that is used to find the solution of temporal logic queries to better know the model used by the model checker NμSMV.

We continue our research, understanding the SPARQL queries and trying to convert them into queries using the operators of the temporal logic. The goal of this transformation is to study a new way of expressing a new possibility to explore the semantic graphs.

References

1. Gruber, T.R.: Toward principles for the design of ontologies used for knowledge sharing. Presented at the Padua workshop on Formal Ontology, later published in International Journal of Human-Computer Studies 43(4-5), 907–928 (1995)
2. Bray, T., Paoli, J., Sperberg-McQueen, C.M., Maler, E., Yergeau, F., Cowan, J.: Extensible Markup Language (XML) 1.1, 2nd edn W3C recommendation (2006), http://www.w3.org/TR/2006/REC-xml11-20060816/.
3. Bechhofer, S., van Harmelen, F., Hendler, J., Horrocks, I., McGuinness, D., Patel-Schneijder, P., Andrea Stein, L.: OWL Web Ontology Language Reference, World Wide Web Consortium, W3C (2004), http://www.w3.org/TR/owl-ref/
4. Becket, D., McBride, B.: RDF/ XML Syntax Specification (Revised). W3C recommendation (2004), http://www.w3.org/TR/2004/REC-rdf-syntax-grammar-20040210/
5. Berners-Lee, T., Hendler, J., Lassila, O.: The Semantic Web. Scientific American. pp. 34–43 (2001)
6. Clarke, E.M.: The birth of model checking. In: Grumberg, O., Veith, H. (eds.) 25 Years of Model Checking. LNCS, vol. 5000, pp. 1–26. Springer, Heidelberg (2008)
7. Cimatti, A., Clarke, E.M., Giunchiglia, F., Roveri, M.: NuSMV: a new symbolic model checker, pp. 410–425 (2000)
8. Chan, W.: Temporal-logicqueries. In: Emerson, E.A., Sistla, A.P. (eds.) CAV 2000. LNCS, vol. 1855, Springer, Heidelberg (2000)
9. Chebotko, C., Lu, S., Fotouhi, F.: Semantics preserving SPARQL-to-SQL translation. Data & Knowledge Engineering (2009)

10. Klyne, J.J.C.G.: Resource Description Framework (rdf): Concepts and abstract syntax. Tech. rep., W3C (2004)
11. Bönström, V., Hinze, A., Schweppe, H.: Storing RDF as a graph. In: Latin American WWW conference, Santiago, Chile (2003)
12. Berners-Lee, T.: W3C recommendation. HTTP-URI (2007), http://www.w3.org/DesignIssues/
13. Berners-Lee, T., Connolly, D.: Notation3 (N3): A readable RDF syntax. W3C recommendation (2008), http://www.w3.org/TeamSubmission/n3/
14. Becket, D., McBride, B.: RDF test cases. W3C Working draft (2004), http://www.w3.org/TR/rdf-testcases/
15. Katoen, J.P.: The principal of Model Checking. University of Twente (2002)
16. Cyganiak, R.: A relational algebra for SPARQL.Digital Media Systems Laboratory, HP Laboratories Bristol (September 2005)
17. Pnueli, A.: The temporal logic of programs. In: Proc. 18th IEEE Symp. Foundations of Computer Science (FOCS 1977), Providence, RI, USA, pp. 46–57 (1977)
18. Mukund, M.: Model Checking, Automated Verification of Computational Systems, pp. 667-681 (2009)
19. Gueffaz, M., Rampacek, S., Nicolle, C.: ScaleSem: Evaluation of semantic graph based on Model Checking. In: Webist 2011- The 7th International Conference on Web Information Systems and Technologies, Noordwijkerhout, Hollande (May 2011)
20. Mateescu, R., Meriot, S., Rampacek, S.: Extending SPARQL with Temporal logic. Technical report (2009)

A Public Health Information System Design

Yasar Guneri Sahin and Ufuk Celikkan

Izmir University of Economics, Department of Software Engineering
Izmir-Turkey
{yasar.sahin,ufuk.celikkan}@ieu.edu.tr

Abstract. The integration of modern information technologies into health care resulted in development of public health care information systems for the purpose of aiding the medical community by providing for less error prone diagnoses and treatment of diseases. The architecture presented in this paper is an evidence-based health care information infrastructure which collects considerable amounts of reliable, evidence-based data over time from various sources, and that it classifies, interprets and makes the data readily available and accessible to the health care provider before patient consultations. Among many other goals, the proposed system's key objective and contribution is gathering Patients' Ancillary Data (PAD) and incorporating this information into the diagnosis and treatment workflow. The data from medical tests is enriched and complemented by patient ancillary data such as hereditary, residential, travel, custom, meteorological, biographical and demographical data. Automatic provisioning of PAD, another goal of the proposal, helps to diminish problems and misdiagnosis situations caused by language barriers-disorders that frequently prevent the acquisition of patient data. This attribute of the system assists physicians to shorten time for diagnosis and consultations, therefore dramatically improving quality and quantity of the physical examinations of patients.

Keywords: Medical information system, Public health care, Technology assisted health care.

1   Introduction

The quality of a diagnosis depends on the quality and quantity of patient data. A large data set of patient medical records enables the discovery of patterns in diseases and provides for the development of tools that can help doctors in the diagnosis and treatment of diseases. A Patient's Ancillary Data (PAD), including hereditary, residential, travel, custom, meteorological, biographical and demographical information should be considered an indispensible part of diagnosis and treatment of the patient. The impact of PAD on clinical decisions has been inadequately explored and is rarely incorporated into health care information systems.

In this paper we present a comprehensive, robust extensible architecture which collects, classifies, and interprets medical and non-medical data with a goal of aiding the medical community by providing less error-prone diagnoses and treatment of diseases. This architecture will be standards-compliant, and would therefore be complementary to the existing systems.

V. Snasel, J. Platos, and E. El-Qawasmeh (Eds.): ICDIPC 2011, Part I, CCIS 188, pp. 525–536, 2011.
© Springer-Verlag Berlin Heidelberg 2011

For many years, European countries have been expending great effort towards making progress on a common eHealth platform [1-3]. In spite of increased efforts to develop a seamless healthcare system, only a small number of countries have been able to achieve the construction of Patient Summaries Database, which was only a part of the original goal. Despite having the communication infrastructure, eHealth solutions in EU countries are either still at the planning stage, or not working efficiently and effectively due to a number of difficulties, such as political and economical problems. Some difficulties of integrating patient records into eHealth systems stem from interoperability, governmental policies, and privacy and security issues. In addition, there are some other difficulties such as cognitive errors, and faulty knowledge, data gathering and synthesis which can be possible reasons of a medical misdiagnosis [4-6]. An effective eHealth solution can be built by incorporating PAD.

Hereditary factors play a role in many diseases, for example, a family history of diabetes, gout, high blood pressure or high blood cholesterol increases the risk of heart disease. Although it is difficult to miss severe symptoms of heart attacks, other symptoms are identical to ones seen in other diseases [7, 8]. Symptoms can also vary from patient to patient. Thus knowing the medical history of first and second degree relatives improves the chances of a faster and more accurate diagnosis [9].

Several diseases originate or appear in greater proportions in certain locations in the world. A past visit by the patient to such a location is a strong indication of the likely cause of a disease. Knowing the past residential locations is very valuable in diagnosing diseases and determining subtypes (i.e. determining the subtype of influenza: swine or avian). Another factor to be careful about is that, when a patient visits multiple doctors or health institutions at multiple locations, it is seldom the case that the patient data is consolidated. The reason for this may be that information from previous visits to doctors was unavailable to subsequent doctors and, none of the doctors involved had the complete and full medical history of the patient.

Moreover, environmental data such as climate and geographic data can also significantly contribute to a more accurate and faster diagnosis of diseases. People who live in industrial areas have a higher risk of exposure to chemical compounds which can lead to cancer, lung and other diseases. Certain types of skin cancers tend to occur more often in locations which receive longer periods of sunlight all year long [10]. Crimean-Congo Hemorrhagic Fever Disease (CCHFD), a tick-borne disease caused by a virus, occurs more often in certain locations. It is evident that the past or present location of a patient provides important evidence for successful diagnosis.

Another benefit of ancillary data is to enable the medical practitioner to better utilize the time spent with the patient. Having already accumulated a substantial amount of medical and non-medical data, the doctor can concentrate on other fact-finding activities such as inquiring about a patient's psychological condition.

Our objective is to propose a flexible, robust, comprehensive and standards compliant Medical Information System's infrastructure that will facilitate collection of data from diverse sources, sharing of data with other health information systems and turning raw data into knowledge which can be used by a medical inference engine to aid physicians in their diagnosis and treatment of the diseases. In brief, our objective is to develop a comprehensive health information system that would be seamlessly integrated with other health information systems and government organizations working in harmony.

2   The Proposed System

In order to construct a well-designed healthcare system, as much information as possible about an individual should be stored and this data should be readily available in case of a request. Figure 1 shows several types of data source that may contribute to the successful monitoring of an individuals' lifelong healthcare. Many of the healthcare systems implementations cover information coming from group A, however any weaknesses of data originating from group B and C decreases the system accuracy and occasionally this situation leads to serious errors, which may be even fatal.

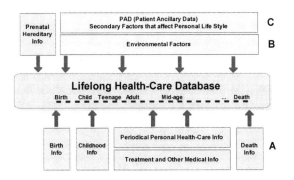

Fig. 1. Lifelong healthcare data of an individual

The infrastructure that we are proposing can easily be customized to different sub areas within the health domain. Likewise physicians, pharmacists and nursing professionals also make critical decisions, and thus are also the target users of the system. Obviously decision making processes are not unique to medical practice, and when the scope is widened, this infrastructure can be adapted to any domain which involves decision-making based on ·large quantities of data. One interesting application area would be the judicial system.

The system receives the data and knowledge from providers and converts data into knowledge represented in an appropriate form, and generates meaningful information and advising schema for use by stakeholders (patients, users, administrative, government entities). Since the proposed system presented in this paper is research in progress, it is considered appropriate to explain only the system level (high level) details and contextual descriptions of the system. In the following sections we shall describe the system's architecture, its interfaces and features.

2.1   The Proposed System Architecture

Figure 2 illustrates the proposed system's architecture. The system consists of three main layers: "Providers", "Security and Refinement Ring" and "Three Dimensional Inference Engine". The "Providers" layer is assigned the task of gathering information from data providers (i.e. governments, hospitals, doctors, pharmacies) which supply data and knowledge to the system either continuously or upon a request coming from the Inference Engine. The "Security and Refinement Ring (SRR)" is responsible for providing filtered and reliable data to the inference engine. The last and the innermost layer, the Inference Engine (IE) is based on a hybrid design which employs mechanisms and techniques from Expert Systems and Data-Mining, and provides information or advice to the stakeholders.

2.1.1 Information and Data Providers Layer

This layer is the interface layer of the system, enabling communication with data providers and stakeholders. In this layer, data providers supply the knowledge and raw data necessary for the inference engine to deliver meaningful information to and advise the stakeholders (physicians, nurses etc). Since the primary goal of the proposed system is to provide accurate and adequate information about patients, it has to communicate extensively with the environment. Most of the data and knowledge providers have already integrated with e-government solutions such as e-custom. This integration means the providers to be well structured and easily adaptable to other e-systems.

Communication with government organizations enables the proposed system to acquire many required and useful patient data items such as family or race, travel to other countries or regions, previously recorded accidents, residential information and weather parameters (average humidity, temperature, air pressure). In addition, the providers of the system supply the system with a number of additional patient data, such as new research and innovations in the field of bio-medical and medicine, pharmaceutical data required for treatment advice and alternative treatment strategies.

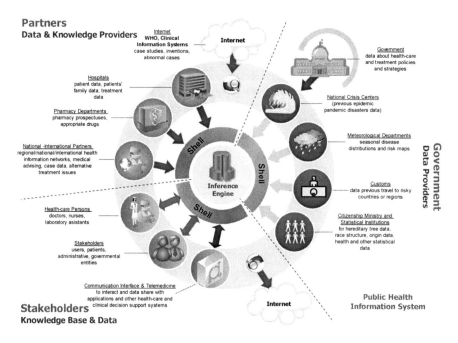

Fig. 2. The proposed system architecture [11]

2.1.2 SRR-Shell: Security and Refinement Ring

The collected medical data must be kept secure and private. In particular the proposed infrastructure will be very sensitive to privacy issues. This layer has crucial importance for the system, and is responsible for providing sanitized and reliable data to the next layer, the IE. Figure 3 illustrates the SRR-Shell structure. The system communicates and interacts with its environment via the web, making the proposed system dependent on the Internet, and consequently vulnerable to intruders. Thus, a security layer is used to protect the system against intruders or any other unauthorized access. The security layer incorporates many different security technologies, including but not limited to, IP control, trusted connections, intrusion detection and firewalls.

The safety and reliability check layer is responsible for protecting against the inclusion of unsafe and unreliable data into the system. Any data that reaches to this layer is known to be coming from trusted connections. However, these connections may sometimes provide corrupted or inaccurate data to the system. A reliability level filtering mechanism is, hence, used to promptly reject any incoming data deemed to be unreliable.

The data conversion layer is used to convert data obtained from many different institutions into a standard and commonly agreed format, since institutions which are the participants of the system provide different types of information and use different data format. Furthermore, this layer is also used for integration by other systems, and it supports the de facto medical information exchange protocol HL7 [12, 13].

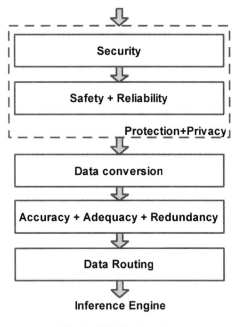

Fig. 3. SRR-Shell design

The next layer filters data, allowing only the relevant, accurate and adequate data to pass to subsequent layers. The accuracy filter is engaged in case the data is not properly measured, or given in incorrect units. If this is the case, it classifies the data as inaccurate, and rejects it.

The last layer is responsible for directing the data to proper channels in the Inference Engine. Since Inference Engine has three main input channels (Nursing, Medical and Pharmaceutical), the data coming from SRR-shell should, therefore, be directed to the proper channel.

2.1.3 The Inference Engine

The IE (Inference Engine) uses expert system technologies and data mining methods. The main purpose of the IE is to provide information and knowledge about a patient. In addition, it offers several recommendations to uncertainties that are normally one or more human experts would need to be consulted. It uses three methods of knowledge base creation: 1-uses a knowledge representation formalism to capture the SME (Subject Matter Expert) knowledge, 2- gathers knowledge from the SME and codifies it according to the formalism, 3- employs mining techniques on data stored by the IE's data-warehouse to provide knowledge and advise [14, 15]. Figure 4 shows the design of the IE.

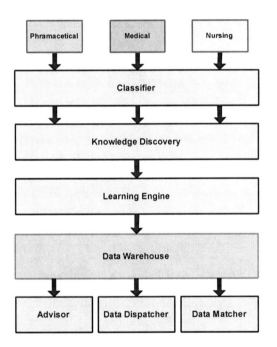

Fig. 4. S Design of the IE

The main differences between the IE and a Classical Inference Engines are that the former gathers data from three different domains separately (nursing, medical and pharmaceuticals). Moreover, it offers three distinct and one combined knowledge and advising work-flows, and it provides separate knowledge discoveries and learning methods for each domain. This schema ensures that the IE provides all possible advice alternatives for the cure and treatment of a particular disease, if there are alternative treatments inferred from knowledge directly gathered from physician and patient consultations, and indirectly from the learning engine.

The IE work flow is very straightforward: obtain and classify data and discover what kind of knowledge should be learned, then learn and store it. When advice is required by any stakeholder, the IE firstly receives and classifies the request, discovers the knowledge required, fetches the knowledge from data warehouse, integrates the knowledge with data, analyzes results, and finally dispatches results to the application layer. In addition, a Health Data Dictionary (HDD) capable of supporting technical words and expressions according to the field of medicine will be used in the system. A HDD improves the data understandability for medical practitioners.

2.2 The Proposed System's Interface and Features

The two main reasons that a physician shows a lack of willingness in using medical or clinical information systems are firstly, the fact that data entry that is viewed as a clerical task and a burden, and secondly poor data presentation. These two factors and a number of other expectations of physicians were the determinant and key factors in the design of the system interfaces. Besides, the Graphical User Interfaces (GUIs) of any system must be intuitive and easy to use, and information must be easily locatable and categorized correctly with relevant information grouped together. The proposed system has strong potential to offer very impressive user interfaces that present information which can be extremely useful for physicians to use for initial workups and diagnosis of any illness, especially for extraordinary problems caused by unknown origins.

In this section, several key interfaces will be illustrated using the case of Fever of Unknown Origin (FUO) as an example. This case demonstrates how the system can assist a physician in the decision process to determine the cause of fever. FUO is defined as follows: *"The definition in different studies is arbitrary, but basically [FUO] refers to at least 2 weeks of daily documented fever that is unexplained despite repeated physical examinations and initial laboratory investigation, in an immune-competent host"* [16]. When a patient reports to the health care professional with fever, a thorough medical examination is performed for diagnostic purposes. This includes physical examinations, test results and various kinds of information obtained from the patient about past medical history. Table 1 lists a number of workups and examinations which is used to identify the cause of fever. Reaching a conclusion that a patient has FUO would not be possible unless all workups listed here, and perhaps more should be performed.

The proposed system's goal is to automatically provide many of the items described in the table above with minimal patient consultation. Figure 5 depicts a screenshot of the design of possible the system's index page. As can easily be seen in the system's index interface, laboratory results and many of the previously digitized radiographic images of a patient can easily be reviewed by the physician. In addition, patient's data items 1, 2 and 4 can be provided by the system using IE (data warehouse of the proposed system) as well as visual records of patient.

Table 1. Workups and Diagnosis examinations and investigations samples for fever [16]

Item	Description
1	Daily documentation of fever, onset, duration
2	Weight loss, diet history, medications, sick contacts
3	Animal or tick exposure, travel, foreign contacts
4	Immune status, history of transfusion, surgery
5	Family history (FH) of autoimmune or neo-plastic diseases
6	Physical exams (Vital signs, growth parameters, Skin, Oral lesions, etc)
7	Labs (CBC, ESR, C-reactive protein, etc.)
8	Radiographic imaging with plain films, ultrasound, bone scan, etc

Fig. 5. Sample illustration of the system's user interface

Items 3 and 5 in Table 1 indicate that a patient's travel and hereditary data must be examined in addition to standard tests and imaging results for FUO. In the following sections we shall introduce how the proposed system presents a patient's hereditary, travel and residential information in such a way that it helps a physician to diagnose the cause of fever.

Family history is sometimes vital for many of the diseases especially for diabetes and cardio-vascular problems [17]. In the system, a hereditary map is generated automatically from Ministry of Citizenship database and the map is annotated by parental health data from the participant hospitals. This map can be used to understand the possible reasons for fever coming from genetic factors. Thus information supplied by this map can be useful for the 5th item of Table 1.

The proposed system illustrates a map which shows a particular patient's journeys over the past 6 months. This map is generated from the travel data provided by the customs control and statistical institute, and risk data from World Health Organization (WHO). This map is extremely important and it is used for tracing the patient's travel over the past six months. If the patient has visited a risky location and if the physician considers that the fever associated with a particular disease might be the result of any of the journeys, physician would prioritize the workups by first testing for diseases which can be caused by these journeys. Thus, travel, one of the factors in item 3 in Table 1 can be reviewed and a possible reason of fever might be found using this facility.

Ticks can be extremely dangerous for humans, especially for children, and a tick bite may cause pyrexia (fever) and may even lead to death [18]. Crimean-Congo Hemorrhagic Fever Disease is caused primarily by tick bites. If patient with a fever resides in a region with dense tick population and if the physical examination results indicates a tick bite, then a map showing dangerous tick habitat would be very useful in determining the kind of the tick and type of tests needed; thus, this information is also a part of 3rd item in Table 1.

Proposed system will have many different data representation styles such as graphical, related to patient history and other information. Figure 6 shows an example demonstration of HIV distribution of the countries [19]. These kinds of animated representations methods have very rich demonstration skills and they can present various data in single graphic. The proposed system will generate these graphical IE data sets for further uses.

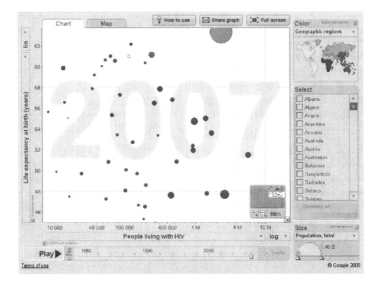

Fig. 6. A sample data representation schema [19]

3 Conclusion

Human life is precious and priceless. Medical errors can degrade the quality of life or even cost the life of a person, and are therefore intolerable. Even more intolerable are mistakes caused by data that is incomplete, delayed, or of insufficient quality. We propose a medical information infrastructure that addresses many issues that physicians frequently face in their diagnoses and treatment of patients.

The main contribution of the proposed system to the field of e-health solutions is that it provides data of such depth, breadth and reliability to enable physician to take a broader outlook in the assessment of patient conditions. The role of patient ancillary data in avoiding an incorrect diagnosis is irrefutable. Even more important is the accuracy of PAD. Patient ancillary data in the system is essentially derived from factual and evidential information rather than the patient's own statements or declarations. This is particularly important considering the fact that language barriers and disorders often prevent patients providing this data accurately and promptly. It is equally important that the data must be readily available to a health practitioner. The system's automatic provisioning of crucial patient data to the physicians helps to reduce time spent on paper-work and therefore increasing the number of patients examined and the time devoted to each patient. This eliminates the need to search other data sources by the physicians prior or during the consultations. The proposed system has a pluggable architecture that facilitates easy integration with other clinical support systems. Other health care institutions can be incorporated into a single platform under the auspices of the system which makes it possible to coherently manage security and reliability issues and dramatically reduce the number of security incidents. Its modular and flexible architecture allows institutions and even countries to make specific customizations where a feature or a combination of features can be activated, deactivated or changed. Therefore, if a country has regulative or political difficulties, the authority would only enable the applicable features. The breadth of data the system collects can be used to generate large scale data sets in specific areas for to be used by researchers and governmental entities engaged in drafting new policies or improving existing health care systems.

In spite of the advantages the system provides, there are some factors which may adversely affect the adaptation of it. However, it is worthwhile to note the fact that these factors are generic in nature, mainly non-technical and not unique to the system per se. The proposed system is a long term project, and it requires several years for gathering patients' data in order to realize full potential of the system. Regulative and political difficulties, compounded with the resistive attitudes of stakeholders, impose challenges when collecting patient data. Physicians often view data entry as a clerical task and a burden and may be reluctant to enter data, making data collection problematic [20]. Additionally, they may view the initial versions of the proposed system as less effective, and the evolution period of the system might cause strain. One other concern on behalf the physicians is the possibility of malpractice lawsuits that may result from the use of clinical decision support systems [21]. Finally, as in the case of any major software application, there may be doubts about the reliability of the system due to hardware, software and communication failures.

The proposed system in this paper is intended to assist physicians to reduce the workload and to shorten time for diagnosis and consultations; therefore both the quality and quantity of the physical examinations of patients will dramatically be increased.

Acknowledgment

Extended version of this paper can be found in Journal of Medical Systems with the following citation: SAHIN Y.G., CELIKKAN U. MedWise: An Innovative Public Health Information System Infrastructure, Journal of Medical Systems (In press: DOI: 10.1007/s10916-010-9632-7).

The authors would like to thank physicians and nurses of EGE and DOKUZ EYLUL Universities, especially Assoc. Prof. Dr. Fisun SENUZUN, Prof. Dr. Mehdi ZOGHI M.D., and Abide ÇAM for their generous helps.

References

1. Thiel, R.: eHealth Strategies of European Member States – Priorities, Experience, and Lessons Learned. In: First Southeast European eHealth Networking Conference, Bosnia, Herzegovina, September 3, pp. 8–9 (2009)
2. eHealth ERA Report. eHealth Priorities and Strategies in European Countries, http://ec.europa.eu/information_society/activities/health/do cs/policy/ehealth-era-full-report.pdf (accessed: 12-4-2010)
3. Grode, A.: The German e-Card Infrastructure Set-up. In: First Southeast European eHealth Networking Conference, Bosnia, Herzegovina, September 3, pp. 22–23 (2009)
4. Graber, M.L., Franklin, N., Gordon, R.: Diagnostic error in internal medicine. Archives of Internal Medicine 165(13), 1493–1499 (2005)
5. Hashem, A., Chi, M.T.H., Friedman, C.P.: Medical errors as a result of specialization. Journal of Biomedical Informatics 36(1-2), 61–69 (2003)
6. Singh, H., Thomas, E.J., Petersen, L.A., Studdert, D.M.: Medical errors involving trainees - A study of closed malpractice claims from 5 insurers. Archives of Internal Medicine 167(19), 2030–2036 (2007)
7. Pope, J.H., Aufderheide, T.P., Ruthazer, R., et al.: Missed Diagnoses of Acute Cardiac Ischemia in the Emergency Department. The New England Journal of Medicine 342, 1163–1170 (2000)
8. Schiff, G.D., Kim, S., Abrams, R., et al.: Diagnosing Diagnosis Errors: Lessons From A Multi-Institutional Collaborative Project. Agency For Healthcare Research And Quality Rockville Md, Report No.: ADA434037 (2005)
9. Yen, A.W., Fancher, T.L., Bowlus, C.L.: Revisiting Hereditary Hemochromatosis: Current Concepts and Progress. The American Journal of Medicine 119(5), 391–399 (2006)
10. Elwood, J.M., Jopson, J.: Melanoma and Sun Exposure: An Overview of Published Studies. International Journal of Cancer 73(2), 198–203 (1997)
11. Sahin, Y.G., Celikkan, U.: MEDWISE: An Innovative Public Health Information System Infrastructure. Journal of Medical Systems, doi:10.1007/s10916-010-9632-7 (in press)
12. HL7 Standards. Clinical Document Architecture (a V3-based standard), http://www.hl7.org/implement/standards/index.cfm?ref=nav (accessed: 5-5-2010)
13. HL7 Standards. HL7 Reference Information Model, http://www.hl7.org/implement/standards/rim.cfm (accessed: 5-5-2010)

14. Wikipedia. Expert Systems. Available from,
    http://en.wikipedia.org/wiki/Expert_systems (accessed: 1-3-2010)
15. Ignizio, J.P: An Introduction To Expert Systems Mcgraw-Hill College (1991)
16. Teitelbaum, J.E., Deantonis, K.O., Kahan, S.: In A Page: Pediatric Signs and Symptoms
    Lippincott Williams & Wilkins (2007)
17. Gilliam, L.K., Liese, A.D., Bloch, C.A., et al.: Family history of diabetes, autoimmunity,
    and risk factors for cardiovascular disease among children with diabetes in the SEARCH
    for Diabetes in Youth Study. Pediatric Diabetes 8(6), 354–361 (2007)
18. Tezer, H., Saylı, T.R., Bilir, O.A., Demirkapi, S.: Is A Tick Bite of Concern in Children?
    Our data for 2008. Journal of Pediatric Infection 3(2), 54–57 (2009)
19. Rosling, H.: People living with HIV: Graphical Demonstration,
    http://www.gapminder.org (accessed: 6-5-2010)
20. Ash, J.S., Berg, M., Coiera, E.: Some Unintended Consequences of Information
    Technology in Health Care: The Nature of Patient Care Information System-related Errors.
    Journal of the American Medical Informatics Association 11(2), 104–112 (2004)
21. Arkes, H.R., Shaffer, V.A., Medow, M.: The influence of a physician's use of a diagnostic
    decision aid on the malpractice verdicts of mock jurors. Medical Decision Making 28(2),
    201–208 (2008)

Comparison between Neural Networks against Decision Tree in Improving Prediction Accuracy for Diabetes Mellitus

Aliza Ahmad, Aida Mustapha, Eliza Dianna Zahadi, Norhayati Masah,
and Nur Yasmin Yahaya

Faculty of Computer Science and Information Technology, Universiti Putra Malaysia,
43400 UPM Serdang, Selangor, Malaysia
skdsn06@gmail.com, aida@fsktm.upm.edu.my,
eliza.dianna@gmail.com, yatimasah@gmail.com,
nuryasmin2009@gmail.com

Abstract. This study is to compare the prediction accuracy of multilayer perceptron in neural networks against tree-based algorithms, in particular the ID3 and J48 algorithms on Pima Indian diabetes mellitus data set. The classification experiment is performed using algorithms in WEKA to determine the class diabetes or non-diabetes with the data set of 768 patients. Results showed that a pruned J48 tree performed with higher accuracy, which is 89.3% as compared to 81.9% by the multilayer perceptrons. On further removal of the number of times pregnant attribute, the prediction accuracy for the pruned J48 tree improved to 89.7%.

Keywords: Classification, Decision tree, Multilayer perceptrons, Diabetes.

1 Introduction

Diabetes mellitus, often simply referred to as diabetes, is a major global health problem that affects millions of people worldwide. According to the World Health Organization, on a global scale, there are around 194 million people with diabetes in the adult population. In Malaysia alone, there are nearly 1.2 million people suffer from diabetes mellitus [1]. Diabetes is a general term for a number of separate but related, chronic disorders. Diabetes is a disease in which the body does not produce or properly use insulin, a hormone that is needed to convert sugar, starch, and other food into energy needed for daily life. The cause of diabetes is a mystery, although both genetics and environment appear to play roles.

There are two major types of diabetes, which are commonly referred to as Type 1 and Type 2. Type 1 diabetes is insulin-dependent, an autoimmune disease in which the body does not produce any insulin. Type 1 diabetes is most often occurring in children and young adults. People with Type 1 diabetes must take daily insulin injections to sustain life. The greater risks for Type 1 diabetes are siblings of people with Type 1 diabetes and children of parents with Type 1 diabetes. On the other hand, Type 2 diabetes is considered as non insulin-dependent. This is a metabolic disorder

V. Snasel, J. Platos, and E. El-Qawasmeh (Eds.): ICDIPC 2011, Part I, CCIS 188, pp. 537–545, 2011.
© Springer-Verlag Berlin Heidelberg 2011

resulting from the body's inability to make enough or properly use insulin and it is the most common form of the disease usually occurring after age 30. Type 2 diabetes is generally connected to with older age, a history of diabetes in the family, being overweight, lack of physical exercise and women who have had a baby that weighted more than nine pounds at birth.

The warning signs such as being extremely thirsty or hungry, having to urinate more often than usual, losing a lot of weight, irritability, and being extremely tired over a long period of time may all be symptoms of Type 1 diabetes. The symptoms for Type 2 diabetes are represented by any of the Type 1 symptoms, in addition to having blurry vision, numbness in the hands or feet, recurring skin, gum or bladder infections, and infections that take a long time to heal. Nonetheless, apart from the documented symptoms in the patients' personal medical records, 50% of patients with Type 1 and Type 2 symptoms remain under diagnosed. Due to the greatly increased amount of data gathered in medical databases, traditional manual analysis has become inadequate and methods for efficient computer-based analysis are indispensable.

The large growth of medical databases in advanced countries has motivated medical researchers to develop knowledge discovery methods from these databases. Knowledge discovery in database (KDD) attempts to identify patterns within the data that can be exploited to emphasize that knowledge is the end product of a data-driven discovery [2]. Nonetheless, as the volume of stored data increases, finding patterns and extracting knowledge in such large scale databases are indeed a great challenge. Data mining methods have been applied to a variety of medical domain in order to improve decision-making in both diagnostic and prognostic problems. Improved medical diagnosis and prognosis may be achieved through automatic analysis of patient data stored in their medical records, which is essentially learning from medical history.

In this research, we attempt to improve the prediction accuracy of multi-layer perceptrons with decision trees. The classification task is to categorize class labels: diabetes or non-diabetes sufferers based on the symptoms mined from the records of medical history. The remainder of this paper proceeds as follows. Section 2 presents the related work of classification experiments in the medical domain. Section 3 details up the material and methods to perform the experiment. Section 4 discusses the experimental results and finally Section 5 concludes the paper with some direction for future work.

2 Related Works

Classification is one particular data mining task that have been applied in the past [3, 4, 5] to predict patient profiles that are at greater risk of having diabetes, as well as to generate information that could be verified by clinicians, hence yielding new knowledge. In 2005, [3] propose Artificial Neural Network (ANN) to provide solutions to the medical staff in determining whether a patient is a diabetes sufferer or otherwise. The prediction is a proactive step rather than waiting for the diagnostic result from a blood test. In the research, a back-propagation algorithm is used to train and to test 768 data instances, whereby 268 of the patient instances are diagnosed with diabetes. Inputs to the network are the number of times pregnant, plasma glucose concentration, blood pressure, triceps skin fold thickness, serum insulin, body mass index, diabetes pedigree function, and finally the age factor. Nonetheless, known disadvantages of ANN are its black box experimental nature, a high computational burden, the proneness to over-fitting the data and the empirical nature of model development.

To gauge the performance of the back-propagation classifier, [6] compares the accuracy results and the length of training between a tree-based classifier, which is ID3 with the back-propagation classifier. The result for their study was back-propagation attained a slightly higher accuracy. Although [7, 8] find that the ID3 algorithm was faster than a back-propagation network, the back-propagation network is more adaptive to noisy data sets. Research in [8] actually compare between ID3 algorithm with neural network-based algorithms such as perceptron and back-propagation. The results show that the back-propagation algorithm requires more time to train but the accuracies varied slightly depending on the type of dataset. In the case of noise-free data, ID3 gives faster results and the accuracy is indeed comparable to the back-propagation algorithm [9]. But in the case of noisy data, neural networks will perform better than ID3, although the time taken will be longer.

In decision tree-based algorithms, there are several most popular algorithms such as the ID3, C4.5 and CART (classification and regression trees). Decision trees are a common, reliable, and effective decision-taking assistants. They provide higher classification accuracy and offer an easy way to understand graphic representation of gathered knowledge. In this paper, we have chosen two algorithms of decision tree techniques, which are J48 and ID3 [10] algorithm. C4.5 [11, 12] is an improved version of ID3 that prevents over-fitting of training data by pruning the decision tree when required, thus making it more noise resistant [9]. To implement C4.5, our experiment will utilize the J48 algorithm, which is the open source Java implementation of the C4.5 algorithm in the Waikato Environment for Knowledge Analysis (WEKA) data mining tool [13].

3   Materials and Methods

The main objective of this paper is to classify a patient's medical profile as diabetes or non-diabetes using data sourced from the Pima Indian database from the UCI Machine Learning Repository [14]. The Pima Indian Diabetes data set is to diagnose whether a patient would test positive or negative for diabetes. In preparing the data set, we performed pre-processing including data cleaning and data transformation before building the classifier using the multilayer perceptrons and decision tree algorithms. Their predictive performances were compared on the validation set.

3.1   Data Descriptions

The data set is sourced from the Pima Indian diabetes database, taken from the UCI Machine Learning Repository. The dataset consists of information on 768 female patients from a population near Phoenix, Arizona. This population has been under continuous study by the National Institute of Diabetes and Digestive and Kidney Diseases because of its high incidence rate of diabetes within the population. The diagnosis comprises of personal data such as age or the number of time pregnant and results from medical examination such as blood pressure or body mass index. The attributes collected by the UCI include the following. Table 1 shows an extract from the diabetes data set.

- Number of times pregnant (PREGNANT)
- Plasma glucose concentration in an oral glucose tolerance test (GTT)
- Diastolic blood pressure (mmHg) (BP)
- Triceps skin fold thickness (mm) (SKIN)
- Serum insulin (pU/ml) (INSULIN)
- Body mass index (weight in Kg/(Height in M)^2) (BMI)
- Diabetes pedigree function (DPF)
- Age (YEARS)
- Diabetes onset within five years (D = diabetes sufferer or ND = non-diabetes sufferer) (CLASS LABEL)

Table 1. Attributes from the Pima Indian Diabetes data set

Pregnant	GTT	BP	Skin	Insulin	BMI	DPF	Years	Class
8	197	74	0	0	25.9	1.191	39	ND
1	172	68	49	579	42.4	0.702	28	ND
2	128	78	37	182	43.3	1.224	31	ND
7	184	84	33	0	35.5	0.355	41	ND
9	152	78	34	171	34.2	0.893	33	ND
0	189	104	25	0	34.3	0.435	41	ND
1	122	64	32	156	35.1	0.692	30	ND
3	111	56	39	0	30.1	0.557	30	D
2	125	60	20	140	33.8	0.088	31	D
0	173	78	32	265	46.5	1.159	58	D

3.2 Data Preprocessing

As a real-world database, it is expected that the dataset will be incomplete and noisy with inconsistent values. One of the first and most important steps in any data processing task is to verify that the data values are correct. The accuracy during prediction will not be accurate because it does not reflect the actual representation of the data set.

The purpose of data pre-processing is to remove any noise or missing values from the data and/or to develop a method for accounting for noise in the data by looking at the strategies for handling missing data. The pre-processing work in this project involve data cleaning to handle the missing values and data transformation to consolidate the data into forms appropriate for mining.

Data Cleaning. The need for data cleaning is centered on improving the quality of data to make them "fit for use" by users through reducing errors in the data. Data cleaning routines attempt to fill in missing values, smooth out noise while identifying outliers, and correct inconsistencies in the data. The purpose of data cleaning is to help reduce confusion during mining procedure. In our dataset, there are five attributes with missing values, which are GTT, BP, SKIN, INSULIN, and BMI. In this data set, we also found that the PREGNANT attribute with the value '0' is presumed correct, meaning that the patient has never been pregnant.

In order to handle missing value for those attributes, the attribute mean for all samples belonging to the same class label applied. First, the data set is divided into two groups, which are diabetic and non-diabetic. Second, the attribute mean for each attribute in diabetic and non-diabetic group is calculated. Finally, the value '0' is replaced with the mean of each attribute.

Data Transformation. During data transformation, data is transformed or consolidated into forms appropriate for mining. Data transformations involve smoothing, aggregation, generalization of data, normalization and attribute construction. For the purpose of our experiment, we found two types of transformation involved, which are generalization and normalization.

Generalization of the data is where low-level or 'primitive' (raw) data are replaced by higher-level concept through the use of concept hierarchies. Referring to dataset, the attributes that are generalized are PREGNANT, BMI, and AGE, which are shown in Table 2(a), 2(b), and 2(c) respectively.

Table 2(a). Generalized Attribute for PREGNANT

PREGNANT	Pregnancy Status
0	No
	(Never been pregnant)
>=1	Yes
	(Has been pregnant)

Table 2(b). Generalized Attribute for BMI

Body Mass Index (BMI)	Weight Status
Below 18.5	Under weight
18.5 – 24.9	Normal
25 – 29.9	Over weight
30 & above	Obese

Table 2(c). Generalized Attribute for YEAR

YEAR	Age Category
20-39	Young
40-59	Middle-aged
60 & above	Senior

Normalizing the input values for attribute measured in the training samples help to speed up the learning phase. The attributes that are normalized include the GTT, BP, SKIN, INSULIN, and DPF. Next, the values for each attribute are scaled into a small specified range, which is between the range of 0.0 to 1.0. In preparing our data set, we employed min-max normalization by performing a linear transformation on the original data. The formula for min-max normalization is shown in Equation 1 below.

$$v' = \frac{(v - min_A)}{(max_A - min_A)} (new\_max_A - new\_min_A) + new\_min_A \qquad (1)$$

Table 3 shows the extract of attributes in the Pima Indian data set that has been generalized as italicized.

Table 3. Extract of data set before and after the generalization process

Pregnant	GTT	BP	Skin	Insulin	BMI	DPF	Years	Class
Yes	197	74	0	0	Over-weight	1.191	Young	ND
Yes	172	68	49	579	Obese	0.702	Young	ND
Yes	128	78	37	182	Obese	1.224	Young	ND
Yes	184	84	33	0	Obese	0.355	Middle-aged	ND
Yes	152	78	34	171	Obese	0.893	Young	ND
No	189	104	25	0	Obese	0.435	Middle-aged	ND
Yes	122	64	32	156	Obese	0.692	Young	ND
Yes	111	56	39	0	Obese	0.557	Young	D
Yes	125	60	20	140	Obese	0.088	Young	D
No	173	78	32	265	Obese	1.159	Middle-aged	D

3.3 Classification Task

For the experiment, we employed hold-out validation method with random partitioning of 70 percent training and 30 percent testing. The accuracy metric will be used to measure performance of all classifiers. Accuracy is the degree of closeness of the model predicts the class label, whereby it is represented as the ratio of the number of correctly classified instanced and the number of instances.

Previous work in [3] achieves the highest classification accuracy with the ANN having eight inputs and three hidden layers. We re-implement the experiment in [3] by using the Multilayer Perceptron (MLPs) in WEKA. In WEKA, the MLPs are feedforward neural networks trained with the standard back-propagation algorithm. The core experiment is to compare the baseline accuracy result from [3] against the Decision tree methodology, which are ID3 and J48 algorithms in WEKA.

MLP Algorithm. MLP is the implementation of the ANN algorithm in [3] that iss used as the baseline accuracy of the comparison against the decision tree algorithms, which are ID3 and J48. In this study, all eight attributes (Pregnant, GTT, BP, Skin, Insulin, BMI, DPF, Years) are used as input node for the MLP. The MLP also has three hidden layers and one output of diabetes. Figure 1 shows the ANN architecture as adapted from [3].

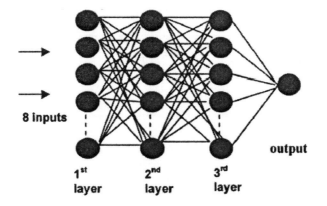

Fig. 1. The ANN architecture that consists eight inputs, three hidden layers, and single output. The output is a binary class with value 1 is interpreted as "tested positive for diabetes" and value 0 as "tested negative for diabetes".

ID3 Algorithm. Iterative Dichotomiser 3 or simply ID3 is an algorithm used to generate a decision tree. The disadvantage with ID3 is that it often overfits the training data. This gives rise to decision trees which are too specific and hence this approach is not noise-resistant when tested on novel examples. Another disadvantage is that it cannot deal with missing attributes and requires all attributes to have nominal values. ID3 do not have means to manage continuous attributes. To solve this, improvement of ID3 algorithm such as C4.5 promotes pruning when required to ensure the tree is resistant to noise.

J48 Algorithm. Based on the Information Gain Theory, J48 algorithm employs an automatic procedure capable to select relevant features from the training data. J48 is able to cut the poor or non-meaningful branches into an efficient pruning process as well as able to handle both continuous and discrete attributes. In handling continuous attributes, J48 creates a threshold and then splits the list into those whose attribute value is above the threshold and those that are less than or at least equal to the threshold value. Other improvements to the ID3 algorithm include the ability to handle training data with missing attribute values by employing gain and entropy calculations. This enables the J48 algorithm to handle attributes with differing cost and to cut the poor and non-meaningful branches into an efficient pruning process.

4   Results and Discussion

The highest accuracy achieved in this experiment is through pruned J48 decision tree with 89.3% accuracy. Pruned tree is used to avoid overfitting in classification. Many branches in the trees reflect anomalies in training data such as noise and outliers. Prunned tree also results in faster classification. The pruned tree yield number of times pregnant, plasma, skin, insulin, pressure, mass, pedigree, and age as significant attributes. Table 4 shows the comparison of results.

Table 4. Results for the classification experiment

Methods	Algorithm	Accuracy (%)
Neural networks [3]	MLP	81.9%
Decision trees	ID3	80.1%
	J48 (pruned)	89.3%
	J48 (unpruned)	86.6%

Recall that in Section 3.2, the attribute PREGNANT, which represents the number of times pregnant between 0 to x times has been generalized to binary values of 0 and 1. The value 0 indicates that the patient has never been pregnant and 1 indicates as otherwise. Due to the potential loss of information, following [15], SPSS is used to find the correlation between number of times pregnant and the possibility or chances of getting diabetes.

From the statistical analysis, at the 0.10 level, the significant correlation is 0.222. This shows a weak correlation between the number of times pregnant and the possibility of getting diabetes. To test the impact of such weak relationship on our classification accuracy, we repeated the classification experiment with only seven attributes, without the PREGNANT attribute. On further removal of this attribute, the prediction accuracy improved to 89.7%.

Table 5. Correlation between Number of Times Pregnant and the Chances of Getting Diabetes

		Number of times pregnant	Class Label
Number of times pregnant	Pearson Correlation	1	.222**
	Sig. (2-tailed)		.000
	N	768	768
Class Label	Pearson Correlation	.222**	1
	Sig. (2-tailed)	.000	
	N	768	768

**. Correlation is significant at the 0.01 level (2-tailed).

5 Conclusion and Future Works

In this paper, we have presented and compared the performance of two decision tree algorithms, which are ID3 and J48. The experiment showed that J48, a variant of C4.5 algorithm, resulted in higher classification accuracy in predicting patients of having diabetes or otherwise against the baseline result of ANN as reported in [3]. As for the future work, we will be looking at mining data from the Malaysian Diabetes Association [1] as well as databases from local medical institutions. We plan to prepare a bigger data set so that the classification results will be more accurate as well as useful to the medical institutions in Malaysia.

References

1. Malaysian Diabetes Association, (2010),
   `http://www.diabetes.org.my/article.php?aid=5` (retrieved from)
2. Piatetsky–Shapiro, G.: Knowledge Discovery in Real Databases: A Report on the IJCAI-89 Workshop. AI Magazine 11(5), 68–70 (1991)
3. Jaafar, S.F., Ali, D.M.: Diabetes Mellitus Forecast using Artificial Neural Network (2005)
4. Han, J., Rodriguez, J.C., Beheshti, M.: Discovering Decision Tree-based Diabetes Prediction Model. Department of Computer Science. California State University (2009)
5. Andrei, D., Viviana, A.: Overview on How Data Mining Tools may Support Cardiovascular Disease Prediction. Journal of Applied Computer Science & Mathematics 8(4), 57–62 (2010)
6. Fisher, D.H., McKusick, K.B.: An Empirical Comparison of ID3 and Backpropagation. In: Eleventh International Joint Conference on Artificial Intelligence, Detroit, MI, August 20-25, pp. 788–793 (1989)
7. Mooney, R., Shalvik, J., Towell, G.: Symbolic and Neural Learning Algorithms: An Experimental Comparison. Machine Learning 6, 11–143 (1991)
8. Mooney, R., Shavlik, J., Towell, G.,, G.: An Experimental Comparison of Symbolic and Connectionist Learning Algorithms. In: Eleventh International Joint Conference on Artificial Intelligence, Detroit, MI, August 20-25, pp. 77–780 (1989)
9. Konda, S.R.: A Comparative Evaluation of Symbolic Learning Methods and Neural Learning Methods
10. Chen, J., Luo, D.L., Mu, F.X.: An Improved ID3 Decision Tree Algorithm. In: Fourth International Conference on Computer Science and Education (2009)
11. C4.5 Algorithm (2010), `http://en.wikipedia.org/wiki/C4.5_algorithm` (retrieved from)
12. Xiaoliang, Z., Jian, W., Hongcan, Y., Shangzhuo, W.: Research and Application of the Improved Algorithm C4.5 on Decision Tree. In: International Conference on Test and Measurement (2009)
13. Hall, M., Frank, E., Holmes, G., Pfahringer, B., Reutemann, P., Witten, I.H.: The WEKA Data Mining Software: An Update; SIGKDD Explorations, vol. 11(1) (2009)
14. Asuncion, A., Newman, D.J.: UCI Machine Learning Repository. University of California, Department of Information and Computer Science, Irvine, (2010),
    `http://www.ics.uci.edu/~mlearn/MLRepository.html` (retrieved from)
15. Karegowda, A.G., Manjunath, A.S., Jayaram, M.A.: Comparative Study of Attribute Selection using Gain Ratio and Correlation-based Feature Selection. International Journal of Information Technology and Knowledge Management 2(2), 271–277 (2010)

Design and Development of Online Instructional Consultation for Higher Education in Malaysia

Ang Ling Weay and Abd Hadi Bin Abdul Razak

UUM College of Arts and Science
Universiti Utara Malaysia
06010 Sintok, Kedah
ling_weay@yahoo.com, ahadiar@uum.edu.my

Abstract. Nowadays, the use of communication technology in virtual discussion between students and lecturers become more easily and effectively. But there are some aspects that need attention, such as documentation, record log and the ability to see the records of these virtual relationships as most current virtual communications software component is focused on the communication and less on the process of before and after the communication. This paper focuses on design and development of Online Instructional Consultation (OICON) system for facilitating student-lecturer consultation for higher education mentor-mentee system in Malaysia. Researchers try to encounter with the typical consultation limitations such as distance constraints, time constraints and having no effective management of consultation-recorded document using the OICON. The general structure and modules of OICON system, multimedia communication components and communication server are illustrated and the potential benefits of OICON system are presented.

Keywords: Online Instructional Consultation (OICON), Mentor-mentee System, Real time communication technology, Flash Media Server, Computer-mediated Communication (CMC) tools.

1 Introduction

Over the last decade, technological advances have bring the dramatically change for the human communication at distance with the advancement of computer-mediated communication (CMC) tools. Online consultation or commonly known as e-consultation as one of the advancement of communication technology in various context [1], [2] and [3], offer great opportunity to enhance information delivery online across time and space. Indeed, shifting of purely asynchronous communication tools to hybrid mode of asynchronous and synchronous communication technology had catalyst the online conversation among the participants from all over the world on real time.

However, in education context, even though there are many suggestion regarding with provide consulting service online [4], [5], but yet the used of communication technology is not fully implemented as an essential support for instructional consultation in higher education. Communication tools involved in higher education are mostly one-way communication tools, rarely are making use of real-time

V. Snasel, J. Platos, and E. El-Qawasmeh (Eds.): ICDIPC 2011, Part I, CCIS 188, pp. 546–559, 2011.
© Springer-Verlag Berlin Heidelberg 2011

multimedia conferencing and study on the type of interactivity, communication and characteristics of instructional consultation. This may due to lack of investigation, analyzing and proper strategy planning on solving the problems encountered by students and lecturer for instructional consultation in education context. Due to [6], there is lack of quantitative research for study mentor-mentee system in education context. Face to face consultation would be increasing difficult when both students and lecturer are constraints by geographical distance, timing problem. Indeed, there should be an alternative way for consultation document management.

Thus, in this paper, we describe a method of conducting consultation among students and lecturer online through blending modes of communication tools, retrieving and playback of recorded consultation session as well as post-session online discussion. Hopefully, consultation among students and lecturer for mentor-mentee system would be offered with much more flexible information delivery ways through plethora of multimedia technologies, with the purpose to solving traditional consultation encountered by students and lecturer such as geographical constraints, ineffective time management and consultation document management for future review and follow-up.

1.1 Overview of Mentor-Mentee System for Higher Education

In most University in Malaysia, implementation of mentor-mentee system in which each lecturer is assigned particular responsibility to a numbers of students (mentees) in providing guidance and consults students in their academic and behavioural matters. For example in Faculty of Engineering, National University of Malaysia (UKM) [7] , mentor-mentee system is conducted with the purpose of identify the students' problem faced that lead to failure on academic result, motivate students on curriculum skills as well as enhance the good relationship and interaction among students and lecturer [8]. It can be seen that student's personal development as overall perspective career by not only care about their academic matter but also behavioural matter as well as mould the relationship among mentor, mentee and faculty. But in this research, the need for ongoing support for students' academic matter rather than their career and behavioural matter is recognized and highlighted.

Many research on the higher education in Malaysia had found that majority of students show their unsatisfactory on the mentor-mentee system on difficulties to meet with their supervisor for consultation [9]. Students having problem in meet their supervisor when both of them are at a distance sometimes, timing problem and having the problem in record consultation session or take note during consultation session [10]. This may due to sometimes, lecturer may have conduct emergency meeting, attend to the outstation seminar and may not meet their students for a period of time. Besides that, owning to the training and practical period for undergraduate students, both students and supervisor are constrained by distance. This indirectly leads to student frustration when the people they rely on solving urgent problem are probably at a distance.

Thus, in view of this situation faced by students and lecturers as the motivation to conduct this research, we design and develop an Online Instructional Consultation System (OICON) that will be able to facilitate the consultation between student and facilitators in higher education as well as overcome the distance and time barriers.

OICON system consists of communication server and multimedia components that provide the trustworthiness streaming video method in real-time and delayed-time for video on demand. Holistic approach in which designation of multimedia components provide support start from scheduling the consultation time until termination of consultation session as well as management of the recorded document online. Besides that, multimedia components are employed as strategic information tools within this well-planned online instructional consultation to solve the problem addressed that will be discussed at section below.

Hence, the questions addressed: what major consultation components could be integrated? To discover out the answer, it is necessary to review the existing consultation model, the consultation processes among students and lecturer. When planned the idea of implementing ICT tools for consultation in higher education, the first thing which map into mind was the recruitment of participants and adoption of technology based on correct consultation processes in higher education.

2   Review on Existing E-Consultation Model of Various Contexts

E-consultation for various contexts possesses their own objectives and consultation processes. However, their components and basic functions are easily being defined. Firstly, from operational perspective, the strength of online instructional consultation depends on its capability to provide web-based access to information and sophisticated the consultation processes with communication tools. Secondly, from functional perspective, online consultation aims at provide accessible at anytime and from anywhere people can access the Internet. Utilization of internet means that physically location does not matter, thus people can access the wide range of data resources when they need it besides access the online consulting service before the critical situation arise. Thirdly, from user perspective, online communication tools that familiar for certain focus group indirectly influence the successful of failure of online consultation.

The commonly model of online consultation shows some of the basic components, collaborative tools and their functionality, capability and consultation processes. Matching of alternative technology to consultation processes and more specifically the task involved is necessary. Since there is no specific online instructional consultation model for higher education and instructional consultation processes as revision, review on others online consultation for different contexts is conducted. It is expected that the features and communication components applied in these online consultation system would be complimented in OICON model. Two literatures of existing online consultation are review:

2.1   Financial Service Remote Consultation

Financial service consultation [11] is to provide assistant for customers in completing tele-consultation through touch screen interface at client side. It is designed as help desk or kiosk-like standalone system that serves one client at a particular time. The designation of this consultation takes into consideration remote conversation participants' different skills, roles and asymmetrical communication between customer and staff.   Thus, two additional functions that provide support for asymmetrical communication are proposed which is tele-monitoring and tele operating. Tele monitoring permits the staff to monitor the customers' terminal while tele-operating enable the staff guide the customer in completing the consultation procedure by remotely operating the customers' terminal. Customer's terminal side activities are captured and being observed at window for tele monitoring at staff's terminal. Both staff's and customer's terminal provided with window for tele-operating but with different function. Tele-operating window at staff terminal embedded with functional button that control activities such as the map or figure display at customer's terminal.

The customer may either obtain the financial information directly through the terminal or seek help from staff remotely on real time. With the advancement of videophone or videoconference and share-window function, consultant can provide instruction on remotely control the customer's terminal. Indeed, consultant can take over control of customer's operation in order to provide support for customer that lack of skills in using this remote consultation system. It is necessary to include this privileges grant feature in two-way communication to sophisticate the tele-consultation processes as illustrated in Figure 1 and stated below:

a)   Stage I: During problem-posing Phase: phase, client reveal his or her problem to consultant.

b)   Stage II: Consultant discusses with customer and find for solution.

c)   Stage III: Consultant explains solution to customer.

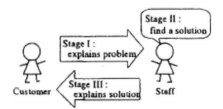

Fig. 1. Consultation Processes

2.2 Virtual Consultation for Telemedicine Education

Virtu@1 Consult@tion (Figure 2) is a Medical Simulation-based Training model by Ortega (2005) [12] and his partners with the purpose to provide support for students to simulate a medical consultation from distance, using the current pedagogical methods based on clinical cases and integrating electronic resources. According to Ortega (2005) [12], most of the computer support system available are not adapted for multi-users and asynchronously. Hence, they focus on synchronous consultation by adding some functionality in their model to compensate for the insufficient function in other model.

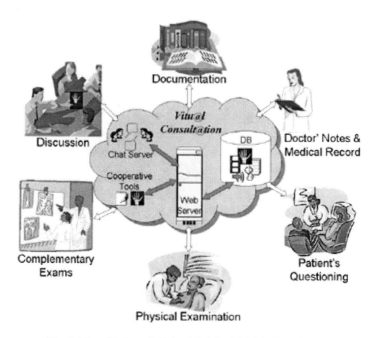

Fig. 2. Virtu@l Consult@tion Model with Main Functionality

The advantages of Virtu@l Consult@tion is it include multimedia data exchange that make simulation medicine consultation more realistic to face-to-face simulation, besides enable sharing of information among users. The main functionality of this model is it should enable the patient to be questioned as they are the person that encountered with one or more symptoms. The physicians try to guide them to present their problem by asking them question Indeed, idea of remotely display-change function as proposed in remote financial consultation and shared-window whiteboard function as proposed in medical tele-consultation system can be applied in this online instructional consultation model as document or application presentation function.

Ortega (2005) [12] emphasized that Virtu@l Consult@tion model provides an integrated medical education synchronous consultation which include the following functionality:

a) Virtu@l Consult@tion provides a medium for multi-users which include tutor, patient, secretary and physicians to collaborate and accelerates the access and delivery of information.

b) Through a friendly chat application interface, an individual is make informed other user's role with representative medical icons and different color per role was used during discussion and patient's questioning.

c) Multimedia data, principally medical imagery or photographs that use to complete the exams and medical records can be retrieved from graphic database and shares on cooperate electronic whiteboard. This electronic whiteboard component also implemented with modification tools that allow multi-users to zoom in, zoom out, write and draw annotation on the images.

d)   Sharing of physician's notes and comparison of their notes with other physician's notes. Tutor can evaluate their reasoning and send feedback immediately after review summary of the problem of patients.

e)   Images and sound player is implemented with the aim of human body images that simulate the patient's problem area. The multimedia information and learning material delivery during consultation session is stored in database.

f)   Accessing to external resources such as e-books, commented or interactive clinical cases, medical images and other can facilitate the learning process by provide extra knowledge. Simple website navigator is constructed to provide optional support for user to accessing these resources, besides use their own web browser.

As review from the financial service consultation and medical tele-consultation, the implementations of communication components videoconferencing and shared-window function are found to be effective in provide feedback immediately for assist user at remote location in solving problem. However, although videoconferencing provide the most demanding multimedia resource, it does not mean that only the use of video elements contributes entirely towards effectively two ways communication. A right combination of multimedia in online consultation prototype is efficiently to demonstrate users' thought and feelings. These multimedia elements include text, graphic, animation, audio and video elements should be integrate and linked to other computer resource and deployed with at least some understanding of user on how to react to these communication components.

2.3   Online Consultation Processes and Task Involved

In general, there are three core phases involved for instructional consultation in higher education: Pre-consultation, online consultation session and post-consultation in which 3 sub processes are included in online consultation session: problem-posing, discussion and decision making.

Pre-consultation included with introductory information of upcoming consultation, appointment making, announcement making, time and date scheduling and invitation mail sending. In this phase, students are the initiator that willing to seek help from their supervisor. They send online appointment form to request for the online consultation. Supervisor checks email and send the feedback either he or she reject or accept the appointment. If the supervisor accepts student's appointment, he or she need to create online consultation room. Meanwhile, a notification mail that contains the minutes and agenda meeting are sent to students' mailbox. For this respect, email or text-based CMC tools are integrated due to their ability in reduces ambiguity of communication. However, students and supervisor are free to choose which communication tools to use for various tasks for consultation, either asynchronous communication or synchronous communication.

Consultation Session or Presentation phase during which participants engage in consultation events such as online consultation, submits form, monitor the on-going consultation as well as provide guide for participants on how to take part. During consultation session, lecturer has autonomy to control the participant's activity during consultation session. Students explain the problem to lecturer. Lecturer may ask for clarification to understand briefly on student's problem and search for the solution. Several important tasks such as problem posing, online discussion, and decision-making session require multiplicity of cues and immediacy of feedback. Text-based CMC cannot communicate nonverbal information and communicate gesture cues as possess by videoconference component. Hence, for this purpose of communication, combination of rich medium and lean medium is necessary. Some communication components that aid in enhancing the virtual consultation environment provides user multiple choices of communication tools that enable them share ideas, obtain immediate feedback, feel a sense of community as if they are not inhibited with each other on virtual environment.

Post-consultation phase include post session discussion and follow-up delayed consultation session. During decision-making session, lecturer may suggest and explain for the solutions. This session may end up when they achieve on consensus or left the consultant to decide the solutions. Sometimes, the less rush consultation conclusion may delay to next time consultation. Not all the decision can be made on the short time and may delay to next time consultation. Thus, consultant may retrieve last time consultation session recorded document, agenda and list of participants involved by send again the invitation mail. For this respect, a combination of communication technologies with consultation document management feature can also create a spectrum of media richness, increase the effectiveness of information delivery and thereby leading to higher performance of satisfaction. This research is based on client-server architecture in which a web-based consultation platform that served as client-side is used to access the HTML page with the online consultation that built in Shockwave (SWF) file embedded. The server-side serves the HTML pages content; deliver the content stored in database to be display in web sites.

Figure 3 shows the client-server architecture of OICON system, which consisted of two main servers: Web Server and Flash Media Server. In Adobe Flash Media Server, the client and server connect through Real Time Messaging (RTMP) Protocol. A web server delivers the clients over HTTP (Hypertext Transfer Protocol). A PC that acts as server side has web server and Flash Media Server. Firstly, the client sends the request to view the website that contains flash application in web server. Then, web server streams the data to display the flash on web browser through the reliable protocol HTTP. After that, the SWF file connects to an application on Flash Media Server and the server will streams the data over a persistent connection using RTMP. This means that user work on both protocols simultaneously.

Synchronous communication tools such as instant messaging, videoconference and screen sharing that stream data in real time are supported by functionality provided in Flash Media Server. Real Time Messaging Protocol (RTMP) is a reliable TCP/IP protocol developed by Adobe system for delivers the high impact audio, video and data stream over the flash player and server. RTMP enable the multiple transmission of synchronous audio, video and data channel along the single communication channel. In this research prototype, seven modules had been constructed. The registration and authentication modules control accessibility and identity authentication of user into online consultation platform through web server. When a facilitator or student pass the authentication, the contact module and authentication module pass list of personal details information and online activities option corresponding to the identity and access level of user to sign in. There are two conditions in which consultation can be initiated:

a) Consultation session initiated by students for emergency consultation.
b) Consultation session conducted by following facilitator's consultation schedule

First condition is corresponding to informal mentoring in which the consultation time is not bounded to lecturer's working hour. It is frequently conducted at anytime especially when student deal with emergency thing [13]. Student makes appointment online with facilitator through online appointment form. They receive the feedback form from facilitator. If facilitator approves the appointment, student can schedule the meeting, send invitation mail to other peers and join the meeting room. All these agenda and setting will be stored in recorded information database.

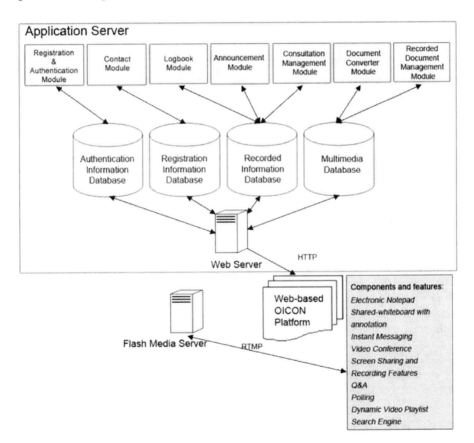

Fig. 3. Client-server Architecture of OICON System

The second condition, the consultation session is conducted by following the facilitator's consultation schedule, which is time-bounded and always conducted, by following mentoring procedure that had been planned. Formal consultation session is initiated by facilitator by uploading the online consultation schedule, create the new conference room, send invitation mail to students and join conference room. Students as the mentee can get informed the latest announcement of their lecturer through announcement module.

Once participants pass the authentication processes and enter the conference room, an instruction video will be displayed as the assistance for novice user on using the online consultation CMC tools. During online consultation session, students and lecturer's terminal are provided with a set of communication tools and features in which this data, video and audio are streaming through RTMP protocol as included in Flash Media Server.

As the consultation document increasing added, there is a need to organize them in systematic way so that to prevent daunting task for every time update. These consultation recorded document are categorized into 2 types:

a)   Audio-visual recorded document
b)   Consultation documents other than audio-visual document.

The ways to organize and playback of these 2 types recorded document are generally different. Video asset are organized in list of dynamic thumbnail view, provide user briefly dynamic preview of video segment before retrieve the video. There are two media player; Live Streaming Media Player is for stream the real-time video during audio or video conferencing. Whereas, Recorded Media Player are for playback recorded audio and video document that stored in multimedia database. Put in simple, by using video streaming mechanism, the media assets are not stored in clients Internet temporary cache files. This prevents the media asset to be saved and modified by unauthorized people. Besides that, streaming media method enables the live video and audio to be recorded and playback as video on demand (VOD) in recorded media player.

Whereas for other recorded document such as presentation slide, word document and spreadsheet, document are organized in thread and sequential model. This method is used to handle increasing added consultation document as well as simplified the daunting task on update every time turn taking of recorded document uploaded. Nonetheless, this model enable online playback document with the designation of multimedia document slide show. For retrieving recorded document from multimedia database, search engine system is developed. Retrieving of video asset by using calendar, chat room ID, agenda ID and name of participants are functional [14]. Thus, in this research model, keyword such as participants' name, selection of chat room, date by using calendar component, agenda and topic related are applied.

3 The Potential to Enhance the Value of the Utilization of Online Instructional Consultation Application for Higher Education

Typically, the interaction of consultation relationships among lecturers and students starting with phone consultation, email-based consultation until communication that entailed with technology such as instant messaging, audio and video conferencing as well as online discussion board. In time, blending modes of synchronous and asynchronous communication tools had make the consultation ways more easier, provide user various options to suit their online communication pattern and consultation environment. Now, with the advent of Web pages that in associate with application, which asked user to identify themselves as students or lecturers, these web pages will link to pertinent pages according to their roles identified which deliver contents relevant to their roles and preferences.

Obviously, new features and components will be the added advantages to online instructional consultation application. Literature review on the consultation model for instructional technology, characteristics and concepts of consultation and existing e-consultation model had found online instructional consultation model should be possible to:

a)   To facilitate one to many consultation
b)   To provide participants various options of communication tools
c)   To request data stored in database
d)   To request help from peers other than facilitator
e)   To increase problem solving skills with the help of shared-window components
f)   To obtain multi-participants through online polling for decision making stages

The major values of online instructional consultation application for education contexts are discussed at section below.

3.1 Shifting from Asynchronous Consultation to Blending Modes Consultation

A closer examination of the asynchronous and synchronous modes of e-consultation considered valuable and essential to educational context in term of advantages and benefits it brings to the effectiveness of online consultation. There are two types of consultation: Real time tele-consultation, store and forward tele-consultation.

Real time consultation conducted by using advance information communication technology such as audio conference or videoconference, instant messaging to enable live communication. Videoconference combines video and audio transmits the information on real time that mimic face to face interaction. This -real time communication usually need equipment such as webcam, built-in sound system and software installed in client side computer. Auditory and visual cues that included in videoconference are important in which the movement of facial gesture influence the delivery of information.

Asynchronous consultation involved collection of consultation documents and transmission of data through equipment such as computer. Asynchronous e-consultation refers to the online consultation that occurs independently of geographical location and time in which participants' communications are not happening simultaneously. It is same with asynchronous e learning in which information is commonly delivery through portal, forum discussion, email or well-developed learning management system such as virtual classroom. The advantage of asynchronous e-consultation is it provides a way user can access to the delayed materials as well as permanent record or archives that can be retrieved for future review. Early e-consultation was often entirely asynchronous. For example, email had been employed as the important communication tool due to its benefits in contemplated and answered for a period of time. However, the level of immediacy of asynchronous communication is not as high as synchronous communication. Participants who are curiously to get the feedback cannot get the answer immediately. Thus, existence of synchronous communication tools is necessary for those who need immediate reply.

In practice, e-consultation communication tool had been increasingly shifted from purely asynchronous communication tool to hybrid mode of asynchronous and synchronous communication technology. This asynchronous consultation always involves the exchanges of consultation document, for example, exchanges of clinical information, static images and radiographs over the networks. Online recordings or multimedia, online-recorded document and threaded discussion forum are the example of asynchronous collaboration. However, lack of immediate social interaction on asynchronous communication may cause online participants report that they have feelings of isolation and loneliness [15]. Hence, implementation of blending modes consultation would help to reduce this limitation while this hybrid communication, if properly planned, would sophisticate the consulting service online effectively.

3.2   Shifting to Virtual Consultation Environment

Typical consultation may constraints by distance and time that needed to schedule consultation session. However, existence of Internet has brought innumerous advantages for learners especially those regarding with the academic. A host of sophisticated internet-based applications makes online consultation possible with the aim of video or audio conferencing, email or online forum for instance- eliminating time and money spending on travel to far distance. Nowadays, internet technology jointly associated with asynchronous computer-mediated communication allows consultation sessions happen at any time convenient to both parties especially when the participants do not expect immediate response to the proffered comment. Computer communications are synchronous when the participants are aware of real time interaction with others online simultaneously.

3.3   The Need of Personalization for Online Instructional Consultation

The objective of personalization is to deliver pertinent contents to an individual or group of users according to their roles and preferences [16], [17]. Basically, a student will be assigned with an experienced lecturer that having expertise and knowledge that relevant in student's academic course. Each user usually has different level of access authorization and preferences to webpage contents. User are given authority to subscribe to a particular consultation newsletter, keep in touch with groups of people with common interest, and then informed by the updates of consultation events or particular topics currently under discussion.

Due to [18], the ability to recruit participant to online events as well as dissemination of consultation contents to participants after consultation session is crucial for an online consultation success. Personalization as the process of providing relevant content based on each person's profile. These profiles created by user themselves by submit online sign-up form or through user data details from existing database. Through user's profile, students can view consultation contents that they subscribe, latest consultation that posted by their mentor, send mail or make appointment online, create consultation room as well as involved in post-session discussion and leave comments on recorded consultation document. Indeed, with the aim of personalization functionality, facilitator can manage their mentee's information such as students' attendance list, send appointment feedback for mentee as well as send invitation mail to group of mentee.

Furthermore, user profiles as components that keeping in touch with groups of people. If an online consultation application can get people in sign up as mentee under their supervisor, then they can get notice updates of consultation sessions that they get involved before, or received consultation invitation mail from other mentee under same supervisor.

3.4 The Need of Recorded Consultation Document Management

Participants of an online consultation should be informed consultation contents such as consultation decision, result of survey, recorded consultation document. Sometimes, the consultation session may be terminated before the problem being solved. Thus, there is a necessity to store consultation information of particular consultation session include participants information, recorded consultation document to engaged participants, and send them feedback at the end of consultation session. Besides, students who subscribe as mentee under a supervisor but does not take part in online consultation session may feel digestion about the consultation lessons. Online-recorded consultation document retrieving and playback provide easy accesses for them to follow up the missing session.

The way the consultation information stored, retrieving and organized in a manner should be concerned by researcher as there is large portion of information available over network is stored in unstructured form, and current information retrieval tools are poor at finding heterogeneous information. The way the consultation document and information being organized that do not follow consistent pattern will cause people with poor understanding and difficult to search for it.

4 Conclusion

Enhancing instructional consultation for higher education through technology, in this research study, is conceptualized as an effective way on support typical consultation processes and more specifically task scenario by take into consideration both students and lecturer's requirement. OICON system provides alternative means of delivery of the contents and services as well as provides participants an extraordinary range of option. In this way, students and lecturer can involved actively at online consultation at remote place, not just between lecturer and students but also on post-session discussion among peers. Point of correspondence includes implementation of CMC tools to facilitate online consultation processes for academic advisory purpose. This prototype system consists of communication server and multimedia components that provide the trustworthiness streaming video method in real-time and delayed-time for video on demand. Holistic approach is considered in this system in which designation of multimedia components provide support start from scheduling the consultation time until termination of consultation session as well as management of the recorded document online. For maximum effectiveness, designation of OICON system based on preliminary study on students' requirement for mentor-mentee system in higher education, the functionality and features to be included [10] besides principles and guideline for online consultation as posited by [18]. It is hope that future development of communication technologies in assisting online consultation in higher education will be considered at relevant points in the future research.

References

1. Costanzo, G., Monari, P.: Experience with asynchronous medical teleconsultation in the Alliance of the Italian Hospitals Worldwide. J Telemed Telecare 2006 12, 382–386 (2006)
2. Medelez, E., Ortega, Y., Lessard, A., Burgun1, P., Beux1, L.: Virtu@l Consult@tion: an Interactive and Multimedia Environment for Remote Clinical Reasoning Learning in Cardiology (2005)
3. Honor Fagan, G., R Newman, D., Paul, M., Murray, M.: E-consultation: evaluating appropriate technologies and processes for citizens' participation in public Policy (2006)
4. Sabella, R.A., Booker, B.L.: Using technology to promote your guidance and counseling program among stake holders. Journal of Professional School Counseling 6, 206–214 (2003)
5. Van Horn, S.M., Myrick, R.D.: Computer technology and the 21st century school counselor. Professional School Counseling 5(2), 124–131 (2001)
6. Omar, H.B.D.: Persepsi Pelajar-pelajar terhadap Sistem Mentor-mentee di Universiti Utara Malaysia. Universiti Utara Malaysia, Sintok (2004)
7. Mohamed, R., Hussain, A., Samad, S.A., Sanusi, H., Mohamed, A., dan M.M. Mustafa.: Penilaian Keberkesanan Sistem Mentor-mentee di Jabatan Kejuruteraan Elektrik, Elektronik dan Sistem (2004),
   http://pkukmweb.ukm.my/~upak/pdffile/2005/4~JKEES%20Mentor_
   Mentee%20_Ramizi.pdf
8. Karim, O.A., Kamarudin, A.T., Suraya, S., Roszilah, A.H., Noraini, H., Nur, I.Z.Y., Azrul, A.M., Khairul, N.A.M., dan Shahrizan, B.: Pembudayaan Ilmu dan Pelaksanaan Sistem Mentor-mentee di Jabatan Kejuruteraan Awam dan Struktur- Suatu Analisis (2005)
9. Haslina, Khadijah.: Towards A Quality Support Service: The Academic Advising System: A Lesson from the FSS Mentor-Mentee System (2007),
   http://www.calm.unimas.my/calm_arc/insite_v10/article2.html
10. Hadi, Ang: Enhancing Multimedia Communication Components in Instructional Consulting Service Online: Students' Perspective and Perception. J.Advances in Multimedia 1, 26–48 (2010)
11. Tanaka, T., Koga, A., et al.: Design of User Interface for Tele-consultation system over the Web. In: SMC 1999 IEEE International Conference on Systems Man and Cybernetics (1999)
12. Medelez Ortega, E., Lessard, Y., Burgun1, A., Le Beux1, P.: Virtu@l Consult@tion: an Interactive and Multimedia Environment for Remote Clinical Reasoning Learning in Cardiology (2005)

13. Azman Ismail, K.H., Bakar, R.A., Ahmad, R., Junoh, A.M.: Pemindahan Pengetahuan, Kemahiran dan Kebolehan Mempengaruhi Kesan Amalan Komunikasi antara Mentor dan Mente: Satu Kajian di sebuah Institusi Pengajian Tinggi Awam di Malaysia Timur. J. Kemanusiaan 7, 33–55 (2006)

14. Jaimes, A., Omura, K., et al.: Memory cues for meeting video retrieval. In: International Multimedia Conference- Proceedings of the the 1st ACM Workshop on Continuous Archival and Retrieval of Personal Experiences, ACM, New York (2004)

15. Kurtz, G., Friedman, B.: A Holistic, Individual, Technologically-Mediated Learning Environment at the Open University of Israel. In: A paper presented at the ICDE Conference, Vienna (1999)

16. Aneja, A., Rowan, C., Brooksby, B.: Corporate Portal Framework for Transforming Content Chaos on Intranets. Intel Technology Journal (11), 21–28 (2000)

17. Strauss, H.: What is a portal Anyway. Interview in TechTalk, January Series (2000), http://www.cren.net/know/techtalk/trans/portals_1.html

18. Clift, S.: Online Consultations and Events - Top Ten Tips for Government and Civic Hosts (2002), http://www.publicus.net/articles/consult.html

On the Multi-Agent Modelling of Complex Knowledge Society for Business and Management System Using Distributed Agencies

Eduardo Ahumada-Tello[1], Manuel Castañón-Puga[1], Juan–Ramón Castro[1],
Eugenio D. Suarez[2], Bogart–Yail Márquez[1],
Carelia Gaxiola–Pacheco[1], and Dora–Luz Flores[1]

[1] Universidad Autonoma de Baja California
Calzada Universidad 14418, Tijuana, Baja California, México. 22390
{eahumada,puga,jrcastro,bmarquez,cgaxiola,dflores}@uabc.edu.mx
http://www.uabc.mx
[2] Trinity University
One Trinity Place, San Antonio, TX, USA. 78212
eugenio.suarez@trinity.edu
http://www.trinity.edu

Abstract. This work is motivated by need for a model that addresses the study of Knowledge Society for Business and Management in situations where conventional analysis is insufficient in describing the intricacies of realistic social phenomena and social actors. We use Distributed Agency methodology that requires the use of all available computational techniques and interdisciplinary theories. We use Data Mining and Neuro-Fuzzy System as an approach to discover and assign rules on agents that represent real-world companies. The case study is based on several companies in the region of Baja California, México and in the policies they implement to achieve greater competitiveness based on the development of knowledge.

1 Introduction

The public and private organizations that promote the generation of knowledge environments in dynamic productive sectors highlight the need to determine the axes of competitiveness and can be leveraged to encourage actions that result in it.

The information technology in industrial sector presents a number of distinctive features, since the staff working in this industry must have technical and scientific capabilities that require vision and training in the area of mathematical logic and in several cases also in computer science. In turn, businesses and government are partners in the generation of internal and public policies that support the strengthening of human capital and growth of business competitiveness.

This study examines the factors that promote increased competitiveness from the point of view of knowledge and business value. The study variables are:

V. Snasel, J. Platos, and E. El-Qawasmeh (Eds.): ICDIPC 2011, Part I, CCIS 188, pp. 560–569, 2011.
© Springer-Verlag Berlin Heidelberg 2011

intellectual capital, business intelligence (BI) and business clusters. It performs the analysis of these variables with the formation of knowledge environments for increased competitiveness.

In this paper, are presented advances and partial results of the research being conducted in several SMEs companies of Information Technology of Baja California. These companies have being used research tools for obtaining information and statistical tests were performed to identify the relationship between variables to determine and assess the level of influence of the factors analysed.

The proposal of this research is a conceptual model to describe the variables that determine the development of competitiveness of industries through the development of knowledge in Baja California, México.

1.1 Knowledge Society

Knowledge. Arises when an entity holds the perception that their own experience and ability has given it the capability to interpret information that is received at a particular time [1].

Knowledge derived from information and information is derived from the data. There is a direct relationship between data, information and knowledge. If the information becomes knowledge, then the intervention of a person has occurred. The knowledge generation activities occur in humans [2]. Information technologies cannot generate knowledge by itself, its mandatory the intervention of a person [3].

Knowledge is presented as an alternative to the social development of individuals, which arises from the empirical experiences, but that may later lead to their accumulation and also lead to new ways of understanding a phenomenon, and at some point this new knowledge can find a way to improve the quality of life of people who are part of a given society.

Knowledge Society. When a company achieves a majority of number of jobs that are based on the manipulation and management of information over those associated with some kind of physical exertion, it is said that an information society is formed. And when the company achieves to base its entire economical activities over the knowledge constantly generated and being managed, then, this entity has formed a knowledge society [4].

This particular model of business is being use in several companies and also is being implemented in countries all over the world. And in order for this model to be able to carried out successfully in the operation of the organization it assumes that the institution has entities to support this policy, examples of this entities could be the following: workers, offices, laboratories, computer equipment, practices, social responsibility, cultural activities and sports among others.

The main purpose of this type of company requires that the persons in the organization are able to acquire the following capacities:

1. Instrumental competences (the ability to obtain information and learn from it),

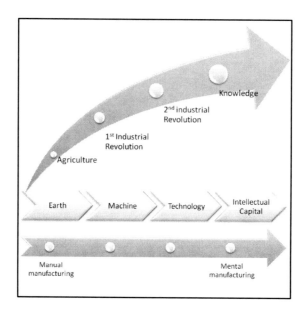

Fig. 1. Evolution of business toward Knowledge Society

2. Interpersonal competences (the ability to collaborate and generate knowledge together),
3. and Systemic competences (Ability to apply knowledge in real life environments)

The actions or plans that must be made in the model for achieving the objectives are divided into the following actions:

1. Instrumental: to manage the employee's ability to analyse and synthesize, organize and plan, develop knowledge, obtain oral and written proficiency among others;
2. Interpersonal: to develop conducts like the self-criticism, teamwork, interdisciplinary and ethically behavior;
3. Systemic: which allow to apply knowledge, learning ability, adaptability, creativity, leadership, multiculturalism, allowing him to be self-taught, to design and manage projects, and to have initiative.

1.2 Distributed Agency

The modelling of a realistic social system cannot be achieved by resorting to only one particular type of architecture or methodology. The growing methodology of Distributed Agency (DA) represents a promising research avenue with promising generalized attributes, with potentially ground-breaking applications in engineering and in the social sciences areas in which it minimizes the natural distances between physical and sociological systems. In this work we thus lay the foundations for a DA description of socio-economic realities, in a process that weaves different available computational techniques in the context of DA to represent social and individual behavior in a contextualized fashion, accommodating agents with limited rationality and complex interactions. We believe that this research avenue will improve our understanding of social complexity, as it moves the discussion in the field towards the capability of describing the vast array of linear and non-linear realities, interlocking levels and currently non-consilient theories in existence.

The methodology we are aiming to create represents a novel approach to simulation architectures, creating a language that links the social sciences to programmable terminology and that can thus be broadly applied. The methodology of DA represents a general theory of collective behavior and structure formation [5], which intends to redefine agency and reflect it in multiple layers of information and interaction, as opposed to the traditional approach in which agency is only reflected in individual, atomized and isolated agents.

1.3 Data Mining and Neuro–Fuzzy System

Using Interval Type–2 Fuzzy Neural Network (IT2FNN) for automatically generating the necessary rules, this phase of data mining with an Interval Type–2 Fuzzy Logic Systems (IT2FLS) [6][7] becomes complicated, as there are enough rules to determine which variables one should take into account. Using the search method of back–propagation and hybrid learning (BP+RLS); being more efficient on other methods such as genetic algorithms, shown in other studies [8][9]. Since the IT2FNN method seems to produce more accurate models with fewer rules. This optimization algorithm is widely used and is a numerical method to minimize an objective function in a multidimensional space, find the approximate global optimal solution to a problem with N variables, which minimize the function varies smoothly [10].

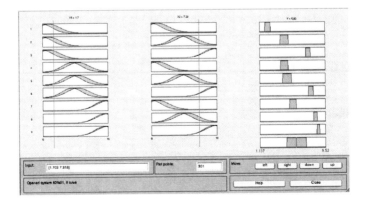

Fig. 2. Rule Evolution of business toward Knowledge Society

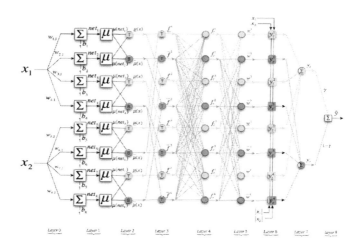

Fig. 3. Architecture IT2FNN of business toward Knowledge Society

Using this grouping algorithm we obtain the rules, the agent receives inputs from its environment and also must choose an action in an autonomous and flexible way to fulfill its function [11].

2   Previous and Related Work

Previously worked in proposing a methodology for modeling complex problems oriented simulation. First we proposed fuzzy agents to represent agencies that can not be modeled with specific actors [5]. Then proposed "distributed agency" as a simulation language for describing social phenomena [12].

In [13] we present an approach to decision-making system based on cognitive agents that use a type–2 fuzzy inference for implement fuzziness on agencies. This model was introduced subjectivity and uncertainty in modelling agents preferences levels were influenced by different agencies. Preferences for choosing one option competing with each other, but also were influenced by endogenous and exogenous variables that could affect the levels of uncertainty and, therefore, affect the way the agents interpret the messages.

An important work related to these approaches is presented in [14] where we find an example of the application of type-2 fuzzy logic to model a system of subjective decision making or perception. We are using Mendel's ideas for modelling Distributed Agencies. We are working in combine Neuro-Fuzzy techniques for configure Fuzzy Inference Systems [15].

3   Case of Study

The information technology sector in Baja California has great advantages over other states in Mexico largely because it has overlooked the economy with most number of consumers of technologies in the world: the United States of America. Who uses all sorts of technologies and software in addition to currently presents certain problems with Asian suppliers of services in technology due in part to geographic differences and schedules.

From general to particular, from global to regional exist data showing that Baja California count with and attractive elements of this industry for many economies worldwide. Mexico has the elements needed to sustain economic progress in exploiting opportunities in the IT market, according to studies conducted in the technology observatories [16].

In Mexico, the IT market is underdeveloped. In 2005, this market reached U.S. $ 8.254 million, of which the packaged software reached $ 817 million and services totaled U.S. $ 2.311 million, nearly three times moret. Companies are much smaller than the international average, which is 250 employees, and identifies clear gaps between them. Along with a handful of large companies, mostly foreign and some national, some hundreds of Small and Medium Enterprises (SMEs) mainly develop customized services. Furthermore, in the field of software developed by specialized firms have a much lower value than that made universities, public institutions and large companies do not specialize in software [17].

The current global environment in the IT sector has attracted public and private efforts to build the conditions for the formation of a critical mass of companies. These processes not only involve a clear definition of public policy, but the promotion of entrepreneurial behavior, especially aimed at young people who are the key driving force of competition. The development of an entrepreneur is influenced by a context that facilitates their performance, if present trends towards bureaucratization; it creates an atmosphere not conducive to the generation of new companies introducing creative and innovative products. To this must be added to regional weaknesses in innovation processes that can hinder the construction of a favorable environment [17].

Therefore, this paper bases its research in three aspects of the companies: intellectual capital, business intelligence and business cluster. The first approach consists in the analysis of the people of the organization, the forms and ways they generate knowledge and how the transmitted to one another. The second one, is the study of the business activities to take action to maintain the knowledge its employees generates on the core of the organizations for support to decision making strategies. Finally, the third approach is intended to understand the interaction between companies and how the share processes, knowledge and connections to achieve greater competitiveness [18].

3.1   Research Sample

This study is conducted on the premises of the various stakeholders that comprise the study group. The companies selected for the research, which as part of it were asked about their practices in terms of innovation and technological development, are highly competitive in their respective sectors, some of them at the regional level, others at many national and international ambits. The common denominator of these businesses is the recognition for scientific research,

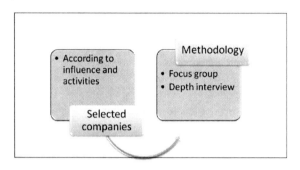

Fig. 4. Applied methodology

technological development and innovation so that demand highly qualified staff and its processes are of high value added that according to the theoretical framework, the approach applies plausibly knowledge management. Such companies are desirable for the state of Baja California regardless of place of origin.

Table 1. Selected companies to conduct this research

1	Gameloft
2	Honneywell Aerospace
3	Factory of ideas - CETYS
4	Grupo Red
5	Skyworks
6	Kenworth
7	Ajosía Prototype and manufacturing
8	Scantibodies
9	Baja Innova
10	Softek
11	Dr. Alexei Licea - CICESE
12	Technys
13	Siscor
14	Genetic Solutions and Labs (LSG)

The methodology proposed would subdivide observed behavior into many different levels of agency. At each one of these levels, the analysis took place to collect information in every level of the study: intellectual capital, business intelligence and business cluster[18] .

4   Modelling Distributed Complexity

To build the model of Knowledge Society for Business and Management will follow the Distributed Agency methodological steps [15]:

1. Determining the levels of agency and their implicit relationships
2. Data mining
3. Generating a rule-set
4. The modelling based on Distributed Agency
5. Implementation
6. Validating the model
7. A simulation and optimization experiment
8. Analysing the outputs

4.1   Case Study Distributed Agents

In this research, the analysis of the agency define three factors: 1. Intellectual capital: employees and people working in the organization, human, structural and relational capital 2. Business intelligence: business strategies, innovation tendencies and decision making process. 3. Business cluster: Society, regional environment, public policies.

Each company fundamentals it grows in the interaction of the three agencies mention above. As part of the strategies that every one of the studied companies used, they all considered that the concepts found in this research are part of the fundamental ways they use to achieve competitiveness; in fact, the three aspects studied are interrelated between each other[18] .

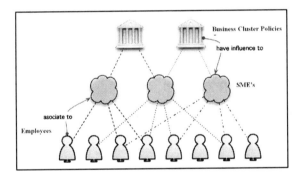

Fig. 5. Distributed agency applied to the companies part of this research

The development of intellectual capital is an important step to achieve business intelligence in order to standardize the decision making process and when this second step is completed, then the business clustering its the natural consequence for the information technology economical sector, trying to influence in the public policies made by the government.

5   Conclusion

In this paper the agencies (employee, SMEs, business clusters) consider knowledge as one of the most valuable assets that companies can give. The study indicates that key leaders and human elements of the organizations that were studied are an important reference to knowledge. Second, they consider business environment is essentially a joint effort between business and government, though the latter is the responsibility of providing the necessary conditions to facilitate companies realize more projects. Finally, Business clustering strengthens the image of the sector while providing the opportunity to do business and good performance is a joint responsibility of businesses, educational institutions and government.

This paper illustrates the first three steps mention in the Modelling Distributed Complexity section.

6   Future Work

In future works it's going to take part the implementation of the model using the data we collect in NetLogo simulation software. Also its necessary implement the other factors that we found as derived from the initial ones in its goal of increase the knowledge acquisition to develop competitiveness.

References

1. Zapata-Cantú, L.E.: Las determinantes de la generación y la transferencia del conocimiento en pequeñas y medianas empresas del sector de tecnologías de información en Barcelona. PhD thesis, Universitat Autónoma de Barcelona, Barcelona, Spain (2004)
2. Davenport, T., Prusak, L.: Conocimiento en acción. In: Cómo las organizaciones manejan lo que saben. Prentice Hall, Buenos Aires (2001)
3. Bueno, E.: Perspectivas sobre dirección del conocimiento y capital intelectual. Instituto Universitario Euroforum Escoria, Madrid, Spain (2000)
4. Rodríguez Rojas, P.: La sociedad del conocimiento y el fin de la escuela. Artículos Educere 5(13) (2001)
5. Suarez, E., Rodríguez-Díaz, A., Castañón-Puga, M.: Fuzzy Agents. In: Soft Computing for Hybrid Intelligent Systems. LNCS, vol. 154, pp. 269–293. Spinger, Heidelberg (2008)
6. Castillo, O., Melín, P., Castro, J.R.: Computational intelligence software for interval type2 fuzzy logic. Journal Computer Applications in Engineering Education (2010)
7. Castro, J.R., Castillo, O., Melín, P., Mendoza, O., Rodríguez-Díaz, A.: An interval type2 fuzzy neural network for chaotic time series prediction with crossvalidation and akaike test. Soft Computing for Intelligent Control and Mobile Robotics 318, 269–285 (2010)
8. Rantala, J., Koivisto, H.: Optimised subtractive clustering for neuro-fuzzy models. In: 3rd WSEAS International Conference on Fuzzy Sets and Fuzzy Systems, Interlaken, Switzerland (2002)
9. Castro, J.R., Castillo, O., Melín, P., Rodríguez-Díaz, A.: A hybrid learning algorithm for a class of interval type2 fuzzy neural networks. Journal of Information Sciences 179(13), 2175–2193 (2008)

10. Stefanescu, S.: Applying nelder meads optimization algorithm for multiple global minima. Romanian Journal of Economic Forecasting, 97–103 (2007)
11. Nigel, G.: Computational social science: Agent-based social simulation. Bardwell, Oxford (2007)
12. Suarez, E., Castañón-Puga, M.: Distributed agency, a simulation language for describing social phenomena. In: IV Edition of Epistemological Perspectives on Simulation, Hamburg, Germany (2010)
13. Suarez, E., Castañón-Puga, M., Flores, D.-L., Rodríguez-Díaz, A., Castro, J.R., Gaxiola-Pacheco, C., Gonzalez-Fuentes, M.: A multi-layered agency analysis of voting models. In: The 3rd World Congress on Social Simulation WCSS 2010, Kassel, Germany (2010)
14. Mendel, J.M., Wu, D.: Perceptual Computing, Aiding People in Making Subjective Judgments. IEEE Press, Los Alamitos (2010)
15. Márquez, B.Y., Castañón-Puga, M., Castro, J.R., Suarez, E.: Methodology for the modeling of complex social system using neuro-fuzzy and distributed agencies. Multidisciplinary Journals in Science and Technology. Journal of Selected Areas in Software Engineering, JSSE (2011)
16. Gartner, I.: Technology research & business leader insight, http://www.gartner.com
17. Casalet, M.: El impacto de las políticas e instituciones locales y sectoriales en el desarrollo de clusters en México: el caso del sector de software. Facultad Latinoamericana de Ciencias Sociales, México (2007)
18. Ahumada-Tello, E.: La Gestión del Conocimiento para la Generación de Competitividad Sistémica: El Sector de Tecnologías de la Información en Tijuana, Baja California, 2009-2010. PhD thesis, Universidad Autónoma de Baja California, México (2011)

Author Index